Greenhill Books

A HISTORY OF
THE PENINSULAR WAR

A HISTORY OF
THE PENINSULAR WAR

by Sir Charles Oman

VOLUME I: 1807–1809
From the Treaty of Fontainebleau to the Battle of Corunna
ISBN 1-85367-214-9

VOLUME II: January–September 1809
From the Battle of Corunna to the End of the Talavera Campaign
ISBN 1-85367-215-7

VOLUME III: September 1809–December 1810
Ocaña, Cadiz, Bussaco, Torres Vedras
ISBN 1-85367-223-8

VOLUME IV: December 1810–December 1811
Masséna's Retreat, Fuentes d'Oñoro, Albuera, Tarragona
ISBN 1-85367-224-6

VOLUME V: October 1811–August 1812
Valencia, Ciudad Rodrigo, Badajoz, Salamanca, Madrid
ISBN 1-85367-225-4

VOLUME VI: September 1, 1812–August 5, 1813
The Siege of Burgos, the Retreat from Burgos, the Campaign of
Vittoria, the Battles of the Pyrenees
ISBN 1-85367-226-2

VOLUME VII: August 1813–April 14, 1814
The Capture of St. Sebastian, Wellington's Invasion of France,
Battles of the Nivelle, the Nive, Orthez and Toulouse
ISBN 1-85367-227-0

**VOLUME VIII: The Biographical Dictionary of British Officers
Killed and Wounded, 1808–1814**
by Dr John A. Hall
ISBN 1-85367-315-3

**VOLUME IX: Modern Studies of the War in Spain and
Portugal, 1808–1814**
Edited by Paddy Griffith
ISBN 1-85367-348-X

A HISTORY OF
THE PENINSULAR WAR

Volume IX
Modern Studies of the War in
Spain and Portugal, 1808–1814

Edited by Paddy Griffith

Greenhill Books, London
Stackpole Books, Pennsylvania

Greenhill Books

A History of the Peninsular War, Volume IX: Modern Studies of the War in Spain and Portugal, 1808-1814 first published 1999 by Greenhill Books, Lionel Leventhal Limited, Park House, 1 Russell Gardens, London NW11 9NN
and
Stackpole Books, 5067 Ritter Road, Mechanicsburg, PA 17055, USA

British Library Cataloguing in Publication Data
A history of the Peninsular War
Vol. 9: Modern studies of the war in Spain and Portugal, 1808–1814
1. Peninsular War, 1807–1814
I. Griffith, Paddy
940.2'7

ISBN 1-85367-348-X

Library of Congress Cataloging-in-Publication Data available

Printed and bound in Great Britain by Creative Print and Design (Wales), Ebbw Vale

Contents

List of Illustrations

Pages 193–208

Illustrations 5, 6, 7, 8, 21, 24 and 25 were photographed by Andy Grainger.

Maps

Family Trees

Editor's Preface

Second only to *Battle Studies* by the spiritual Ardant du Picq, Sir Charles Oman's *History of the Peninsular War* has always been my favourite military book. Whereas Ardant explained the general psychology of combat, Oman provided a rich mine of specific examples. He demonstrated how a variety of personal memoirs could be woven together to make an impressively authoritative narrative of a battle, even at its lowest levels, at the same time as he linked the individual details into higher concerns of operations and strategy. Oman's work was also, of course, monumentally weighty and apparently complete. Throughout my professional life I have rarely been far away from a copy, and I have regarded it as the ultimate reference for what – rightly, wrongly, or just plain romantically – I have always subconsciously tended to regard as the ultimate war.

The Peninsular War has everything that a modern amateur visitor to any war could possibly desire. Its uniforms were as colourful as its personalities, and it was chock-full of exciting all-arms action on many fronts. The passions it raised were intense at the time; yet today they are safely tamed by a protective barrier of almost 200 years. For the patriotic Briton the main passion is, in any case, a profound national pride in victory, since this war provides the central prop to the claim that 'Britain defeated Napoleon'. It is also the source of some embedded national myths, such as the invincibility of the 'thin red line' of British infantry battalions; of British riflemen in small groups; and of the Duke of Wellington as an individual British military genius.

Even if he despises all such patriotic flag waving as 'the last refuge of the scoundrel', the military technician may still find a certain satisfying (or 'classical') purity, reminiscent of Frederick the Great, in many of the stately, regular manoeuvres of this war. Conversely its guerrilla campaign has often been seen as the first manifestation of a much more modern era, which would burst into full flower under the likes of Chairman Mao and General Giap. Then again, the quaint volumes of memoirs which have come down to us from the Peninsula may speak to the bedtime reader in the homely language of Jane Austen's Hampshire – but transposed to a landscape that is harshly and hauntingly alien. The very place-names listed in Oman's book speak of sun beating down on green cliffs, and of red roads winding through unending ochre plains.

Hence the suburban British escapist can easily be transported far,
far and away, merely by skimming through the page headings of the
History.

However respectable and valid such allurements of the
Peninsular War may or may not be, I still have to confess that
Oman's great book has always acted as a sort of sheet-anchor to my
own thinking about military history. Alongside Ardant, it was the
place where I first began to explore that field on a professional
basis. I am therefore especially proud to assemble the present
collection of essays, which are written by an international team of
acknowledged experts in various aspects of Peninsular War studies.
By taking a new look at Sir Charles' work, I hope that we will be
able to enhance our appreciation of it, and pay off at least a part of
the debt that we all owe to that illustrious author.

The contributors have been set the double aim of reassessing
Oman's contribution in the light of modern scholarship, while also
explaining something of their own new findings about these
subjects. Taken as a whole, our book seeks to direct the interested
reader (supported, it is hoped, by plentiful signposting) towards
features of the Peninsular War which may be new, or unfamiliar, or
which are simply 'not in Oman'. Hence we will be supplementing
him, rather than supplanting him. It would be a perilous task indeed
to write a history of this war which did aim to replace all seven of
his magisterial volumes, and so no attempt is made to do so here.

Against this, it would be equally unhelpful if we were merely to
re-assess Oman in a spirit of uncritical adulation, going no further
than applauding his achievement and recommending his wisdom to
our readers. Many of us – although perhaps not all – might
instinctively incline to adopt that approach; but in the event none
of us has followed it. Instead, we have tried to reinforce Oman's
message where it was accurate, but to correct it where it was not,
or elaborate it where it was incomplete. It transpires that many sins
of both commission and omission may be found within his pages,
which comes as something of a disappointment to those, such as
myself, who had always subliminally viewed his work as a definitive
masterpiece. It is nevertheless our duty to point out his mistakes as
much as his triumphs, and in this we hope we have been even-
handed and fair.

Unfortunately, however, this type of analysis still inevitably runs
a severe risk of damning Oman with unduly faint praise, or of
dwelling too long upon his faults. However fair we try to be, our
disagreements with him tend to need many more words of
explanation than do our agreements, and those words of
disagreement will themselves tend to appear more forceful simply
because they have an argument to win rather than an established
opinion to repeat. Thus our book as a whole, regrettably, will seem
to display a more critical tone towards Oman than we really intend.

The reader is warned to make all appropriate allowances for this distortion since, in common with newspaper journalists, we have often tended to assume that 'it's not news unless it's bad news'.

It is actually only too easy for a pedant to pick holes in Oman's text, since it is now almost a century old, and very much a document of its age. It uses phraseology that is often more rhetorical than scientific, and has a scholarly apparatus that is frustratingly sparse and uninformative. Much additional research has been conducted since it was written, into archives that Oman did not examine as closely, or into subject areas that he did not find as relevant, perhaps, as he might have done. It is also a very personal text, taking not only a partisan British perspective, but a particular historiographical approach which seeks to explain events mainly by the actions of 'great men'. Oman had no time for the 'continental' and 'socialist' influences which were already turning many of his contemporaries to look at deeper social or economic forces. As such, there was a sense in which his *History* was already out of date at the time when it was being written. It is true that Oman did represent a majestic advance upon the passionate Napier, who had written his own *History* a whole lifetime - some sixty or seventy years - earlier. But today we are yet another lifetime beyond Oman's final volume, and we can no longer ignore the great changes in historical outlook that have intervened during that time.

Although we can today see the distortions caused by Oman's Victorian prejudices with greater clarity than ever before, we should nevertheless always bear in mind that by far the greater part of his work still stands solid and reliable, and indeed admirable. It makes an excellent basic narrative which lays out a bewilderingly complex series of operations with wonderful clarity. The 'Peninsular War' continued at varying levels of intensity for over six long years, and involved four major powers (not to mention all the German, Dutch, Italian, and even Polish soldiers who found themselves mixed up in it). It was never really one war at all, but several different ones taking place concurrently in several overlapping theatres. None of them was individually as big as the various escapades of the *Grande Armée* in central Europe; but most of them lasted longer and were accompanied by no less military science and personal sacrifice, not to mention naked savagery and shocking inhumanity. It is one of Oman's great strengths that he succeeds in dissecting almost all of these sequences in considerable detail, if perhaps still showing rather less sympathy towards foreigners than towards the British.

At the moment of its appearance, Oman's work was as nearly 'definitive' as any history could reasonably hope to be, and we have always been right to accept it as such. Yet the very concept of a 'definitive' history is itself fraught with pitfalls since, however well informed it may be, all history is, by its nature, highly subjective and selective. This applies as much to our own writings today as it did to Oman's in the past, and so it must be understood that each expert author in the present volume is giving no more than his own personal sidelight on what is, overall, an incredibly big and complicated picture. What the reader will find here is no more than eleven different, and in some cases even conflicting, personal points of view. As the general editor I have not been able to resolve all the differences between contributors, and in some cases I have not even tried.

I am also conscious that there are very many other modern experts who could easily have added as much, and often a great deal more, to our story, who are not represented in these pages. It is, alas, too late for some of them to contribute – particularly regretted is the passing of the late, genial, Michael Glover – while for many others it was a matter of either tight writing schedules, or the convoluted protocols by which such collective publications are grown, which meant that they did not have the chance to join us. There is a particularly glaring gap insofar as we have no account of the war by a French national – only a French Canadian – and so we inadvertently find ourselves as much 'onside' with the allies as was Oman himself.

There is still, without a doubt, plenty of room for a 'Part Two' to be written to this 'ninth volume of Oman', and we can only hope that it will one day come to adorn our shelves. Something very close to it has, in fact, already been written, in the shape of Ian Fletcher's most interesting 1998 collection of essays, *The Peninsular War: Aspects of the Struggle for the Iberian Peninsula*. Equally, a rather different approach to much the same goal has been adopted by Michael Oliver and Richard Partridge, in their projected multi-volume reworking of many of the individual battles in the light of recent findings (*Battle Studies in the Peninsula*: Volume I was published in 1998). Professor Donald Horward's Consortium on Revolutionary Europe takes yet a third approach, with a long-standing annual conference to review many diverse aspects of the era, including much new light shed on Iberian problems. All of these authorities, who are not represented directly in our pages, are worthy of high acclaim, and I would like to thank them profoundly for the extensive hidden help that they have given to the present undertaking.

Of course, I particularly want to thank all the authors of the essays, which without exception I greatly enjoyed, although it would be otiose to single out individual pieces. It may nevertheless be in order to offer my special thanks for editorial help to Charles Esdaile, and to Jim Arnold and Arthur Harman for tactical or Wellingtonian insights over many years as well as, in Jim's case, my first visit to a game of baseball. Beyond this immediate circle, I owe an enormous debt to Ian Beer and my wife Geneviève for their help

with translations; to my son Robert for his help with computers; to
John Hussey for his extensive knowledge and invaluable insight; to
Lionel Leventhal and his team; to Matthew Bennett, Jean Lochet and
professors Clive Willis and Geoffrey Best for their specialist advice;
to Ned Zuparko for his 'tactical snippetting', and to Antony and
Nicky Bird for their massive assistance with the *Wellington -
Commander* project in 1983. I am also very grateful to the
librarians and staff of the Birmingham University, Bodleian,
Codrington, London, and Royal Military Academy libraries, and
notably to Sarah Newton of the Corpus Christi College library.

Paddy Griffith
Nuneaton 1999

Notes on Contributors

(See also the Bibliography, for further details of publications.)

James R. Arnold is a professional author, based in Virginia. He has written widely about Napoleon's army, including its tactics, its Austrian campaign of 1809 (in *Crisis on the Danube*, 1990, and *Napoleon Conquers Austria*, 1995), and its battles of *Marengo and Hohenlinden* (forthcoming, 1999). He has also written over a dozen other books, split between the American Civil War and Vietnam. His hobbies include wargaming, natural history, and farming.

René Chartrand is a French Canadian who lives, with his family, in Quebec. He was a senior curator with Canada's National Historic Sites for nearly three decades, and is now a freelance writer, and consultant for cinema and historic site restorations. He has authored many articles and books, including titles on Canadian, American, French, Spanish, and British military history and material culture. He is also a student of vintage wines.

Dr Charles Esdaile held the Wellington Papers Fellowship at Southampton University from 1985 to 1989, and is now a lecturer in history at Liverpool University. He is a leading authority on the Spanish in the Peninsular War, but has also written important general studies of *The Wars of Napoleon* (1995), and of *Spain in the Liberal Age, 1808–1939* (forthcoming). He is a re-enactor of long standing, and a founder-member of the Napoleonic Association.

Dr Paddy Griffith was a lecturer in War Studies at the Royal Military Academy, Sandhurst, before he became a freelance author and publisher in 1989. He was conceived one month before Oman's death, and began to study Peninsular tactics some nineteen years later. He went on to examine tactics in the American Civil War, in the British Army of 1916–18, in 'the near future' – and in the equally unknowable Viking age. His hobby is wargaming.

Arthur Harman read jurisprudence at Oxford in the 1970s, where he also became interested in collecting Napoleonic memoirs, and joined a re-enactment unit. He currently lives with his family in Wimbledon, and is Director of Studies and Head of History at the

Hampshire Schools. He has long been involved in historical wargaming, was a founder member of 'Wargame Developments', has edited two wargame journals, has written extensively for others, and has contributed the wargame sections to many titles in the Osprey Campaign series.

Philip Haythornthwaite has combined a business career with historical research and writing for many years, based in his native Lancashire. He has written a series of essential military reference works, concentrating on the Napoleonic Wars (including *The Napoleonic Source Book* and *The Armies of Wellington*) but also visiting later colonial wars, the Great War, and the English Civil War. Among his other interests he includes antiquities of all kinds, gardening, and cricket.

Professor Harold Livermore is the former head of the Department of Hispanic and Italian Studies at the University of British Columbia, and lecturer in Spanish and Portuguese at Cambridge. Author of numerous histories, including *A History of Portugal* (various editions from 1947), *Portugal and Brazil* (1953), *A History of Spain*, *Origins of Spain and Portugal*, and *Essays on Iberian History and Literature* (forthcoming), and (also forthcoming) a new biography of Beresford. He currently lives in Twickenham.

Dr Rory Muir is Visiting Research Fellow at the Department of History, University of Adelaide, in his native Australia, and is the author of *Britain and the Defeat of Napoleon, 1807-1815*, and *Tactics and the Experience of Battle in the Age of Napoleon*.

Brent Nosworthy was born in Canada and now lives in New York. He started his career in conflict simulations, and progressed to become president of Operational Studies Group. He has written two highly acclaimed books: *The Anatomy of Victory: Battle Tactics 1689-1763* (1990), and *Battle Tactics of Napoleon and his Enemies* (1995).

Colonel J.J. Sañudo, Knight's Cross of the Order of San Hermenegildo and Military Medal 1st Class, began his career in the infantry and later specialised in the armoured forces. He also served on the Staff in Madrid, where he still lives. Since his retirement he has devoted himself to many detailed studies of the Peninsular War, which he has presented in the journals *Revista de Historia Militar* and *Researching & Dragona*, in three books, and on television.

Ambassador D. Leopoldo Stampa is a career diplomat, born in

Valladolid in 1949. Among his postings he has served in Budapest, NATO, Brussels, and Houston, Texas, and as Ambassador of Spain to Indonesia, then Singapore (1992); and to the Organisation for Security and Co-operation in Europe (Vienna, 1994). He has written, with Julio Albi, two histories of Spanish cavalry, *Campañas de la Caballería española en el siglo XIX* (2 vols, 1985) and *Un eco de clarines* (1992); and an account of the Spanish presence in the Moluccan islands, *Galleons around the World* (1992). His extensive Peninsular War studies include many articles in journals such as *Researching & Dragona*, and *Revista de Historia Militar*, as well as collaboration with Colonel Sañudo in *La Crisis de una Alianza* (1996). He is a widower with two daughters.

Glossary of Terms and Abbreviations

Afrancesados: Spaniards favourable to the French.

Alcade: A Spanish local government official or town mayor.

Aquilifère: A French eagle-bearer.

Bandit: Peasant, artisan, or landless labourer, driven to robbery and extortion by poverty.

Blanquillos: Foot-soldiers dressed in white.

Caçadores: Portuguese light troops (lit. 'hunters').

Carabinier: French term for elite light troops or a type of elite cuirassier. Also, in English, an unarmoured heavy dragoon.

Cazadores: Spanish light troops (lit. 'hunters').

Chasseurs: French light troops (lit. 'hunters'); may be cavalry (*chasseurs à cheval*) or infantry.

Chef de bataillon: French battalion commander, often translated as 'major'.

Chevaux-Légers: One name among many for light cavalry.

Cortes: Spanish term for parliament.

CREP: *Consortion of Revolutionary Europe, Proceedings*.

Cuadrilla: Spanish term for a squad of Home Guards or guerrillas.

Demi Brigade: French term of the 1790s for an infantry regiment (normally three battalions).

Division (with capital 'D'): A formation of many battalions.

division (with small 'd'): A unit of two companies or platoons.

Cuirassiers: A type of heavy cavalry wearing armour.

DNB: *Dictionary of National Biography*.

EEL: *Empires, Eagles and Lions* journal.

en débandade: French for without formal order (either a skirmish line or a mob of fugitives).

Grande Armée: The 'Great Army', normally referring to Napoleon's main force, of many army corps, that was kept concentrated in central Europe.

Grenadiers: Supposedly the best company in a line infantry battalion, used as 'heavy' or assault troops.

Guerrilla: In English, a member of a force of regular or irregular soldiers operating inside, or on the fringes of, areas of enemy occupation (also 'Guerrillero'). In Spanish, irregular, low-level warfare which can be waged either by regular soldiers or armed civilians.

Intendance: French term for the supply services.

Jacquerie: French term for an agrarian rising or riot.

JRUSI: *Journal of the Royal United Services Institution.*

JSAHR: *Journal of the Society of Army Historical Research.*

Junta: Spanish term for a committee set up to act as a municipal, provincial, or national government in time of emergency.

KGL: King's German Legion.

KIA: Killed in action.

LD: Light Dragoons, a British term which covered several types of light cavalry (including Hussars, etc).

Légère: French term for light infantry. (It is an adjective which assumes the feminine noun *infanterie*.)

Liberales: A reformist political faction headed by, among others, Agustín Argüelles and the Conde de Toreno, which dominated the *cortes* of Cádiz and was responsible for the constitution of 1812. It is the origin of the modern word 'liberal'.

Ligne: French term for line infantry.

Miqueletes: Spanish term for irregular troops or home guards.

Mentalités: French term used by modern historians as shorthand for 'outlook' or 'world view'.

OTC: Officers' Training Corps.

OB: Order of Battle.

Ordenança: Portuguese Home Guards.

Ordre mixte: French for a tactical formation of 'mixed order', including both columns and lines.

Parallel: Term in siegecraft for a trench dug roughly parallel to a fortress wall, to shelter an attacker's troops and artillery.

Partida: Spanish for a guerrilla band or militia company (theoretically 100 strong).

Patriot: The term adopted by the Spanish opponents of French rule to describe themselves; hence 'Patriot Spain' means all those parts of Spain free of French occupation at any given time.

POW: Prisoner of war.

PRO WO: The Public Record Office, War Office series.

Règlement: French for a regulation or set of instructions, which may add up to a 'manual'.

Serviles: a largely clerical and aristocratic political faction that emerged in Cádiz in 1812–13 in opposition to the reforms of the *Liberales*. It was also determined to combat any further manifestation of enlightened absolutism on the part of the monarchy, by entrenching the privileges of the Church and the nobility.

SD: Wellington's Supplementary Despatches (see Bibliography for full reference).

Somatenes: A type of Spanish 'home guard'.

Tiradores: Spanish term for infantry skirmishers (lit. 'shooters').

Tirailleurs: French term for infantry skirmishers (lit. 'shooters').

Voltigeurs: French term for light infantry (lit. 'jumpers').

WD: Wellington's Despatches (see Bibliography for full reference).

Chapter 1

OMAN'S PENINSULAR WAR TODAY

by Paddy Griffith

The perspective of our contributors

The Peninsular War may be viewed in many different ways by many different people. Some will see it mainly as a vindication of idealised national heroines such as Britannia or Marianne, while others will prefer to remember Agustina de Aragón, 'the maid of Saragossa', who found glory (and a guaranteed career in the artillery!) when she fired her fallen lover's 12-pdr cannon into the faces of the attacking French. For some people the war will be interesting for the lives of common soldiers; for others, its interest lies in the clash of distinguished personalities – generals, politicians, and even a whole squad of kings or would-be kings. For others yet again, still higher forces will be pre-eminent, such as economic dislocations, social redistributions, or the onward march of ideological purities. For Sir Charles Oman, however, it was rather 'the military specificity' which seems to have counted for most, and it was as a specifically military study that he wrote his great *History*. Within that general framework he found more than enough material to keep himself busy for over a quarter of his long and very busy lifetime, especially since he remained free to ring the changes between the four classic military 'levels', *ie* strategy, operational art, minor tactics, and individual experience.

When we look back at his book today, we too will view it from many different perspectives, and it is the intention of the present volume to reflect as many of these as possible. Our contributors come from many different backgrounds – and, indeed, from five different countries – so it is natural that they will have much to say that goes beyond the purely military (and mainly British) starting point taken by Sir Charles. We do still try, nevertheless, to give a degree of precedence to the subjects that were of greatest interest to him.

Perhaps the phenomenon that has generated most public interest in the Peninsular War during the past few years has been a series of fictional romantic novels and television dramas portraying the exploits of some sharp-shooting, green-coated heroes from the British 95th Rifles. In the present book Arthur

Harman goes back to the original memoirs that were written by real members of that unit, as well as by other members of Wellington's light infantry, in an attempt to disentangle fact from fantasy. He takes an innovative look at their firefights and methods of skirmishing, and finds that their all-conquering domination of military literature was scarcely matched by anything like a decisive role in actual battle. Every shot did *not* find its mark, and it was often the French, rather than the British, who really dominated the skirmish line. Indeed, Oman himself had noted that the high mortality among French officers probably had as much to do with their inspirational obstinacy in standing too near to the enemy firing line, far ahead of their own less enthusiastic followers, as it did with keen-eyed British marksmanship.[1] In any case, no light troops had ever been seen as anything other than 'auxiliary' at the best of times; but it is now interesting to find that even the best of them sometimes verged on the 'completely marginal'. Some of their victories were even won in close order, where their celebrated skirmishing skills could be of no possible use to them at all.

In his analysis of the French Army, James Arnold corroborates Harman's view that there were often many more French troops skirmishing than Oman would have us believe, although he is more ready than Harman to concede that the British still enjoyed a great qualitative superiority in this type of service. He also explains how Oman held an over-simplified view of the many different phases by which the French army evolved, from 1792 to 1815. There was not just one French army in these years, but many. The *Grande Armée* at its peak used far more sophisticated tactics than the massed columnar battering-rams that British accounts so often portray. In fact the British are found to have used columns almost as much as the French themselves, and so it would seem that the two sides were both fundamentally singing from exactly the same tactical hymn sheet. Brent Nosworthy takes a very similar view in his treatment of the 'line versus column' debate, and in a number of respects he improves and expands on Sir Charles' simple stereotype of how such clashes tended to unfold. Both he and Arnold insist that from at least 1793 the French army had really believed in fighting in line rather than column, at least if their troops had been properly trained. Oman certainly should have seen this point, since we know that he had read Jean Colin's classic exposition of it in *La Tactique et la Discipline*, which appeared in 1902; and he had even, albeit belatedly, come to see that his own 'model firefight' at Maida (1806) had really been fought out between two opposing lines rather than between a British line and a French column.

While accepting the essential truth of this 'modern' view, however, the present editor rather tends to dissent from some of the slanting put upon it by Arnold and Nosworthy, or at least from the implication that Oman was quite as blind to the realities as they seem to suggest. Sir Charles does often say that the French attempted to deploy into line in many of their battles, but their troops were not sufficiently well trained to complete the manoeuvre in the face of superior British battalions. He also rightly says that column attacks worked well against poor troops, such as many of the Spanish field armies, and so it was by no means a tactic to be shunned on every occasion. It was nevertheless preferable for columns to be properly supported by artillery, which was often impractical in the hilly Peninsular terrain. Hence if we concede – and Arnold explains just why we must do so – that the quality of the French Peninsular army was distinctly inferior to that of the Emperor's own personal *Grande Armée*, then there seems to be little in modern research to undermine Oman's general picture of how French commanders set out to attack British positions. They first tried to attack in column, hoping that the opposition would be of lower quality than their own troops, but then, when they discovered this was not the case, they tried to convert their attack into a line, only to find that by then it was normally too late to be effective.

We may argue over the precise intentions of the French commanders; but at least there seems to be little dispute over those of the British. Contrary to Oman's opinion, the general culture of the British army was not to stand stationary, giving repeated volleys of musketry with a greater number of muskets than the French could bring to bear; but instead they tried to reserve fire until the French approached to very close range, then give a single devastating volley and a controlled cheer, as part of a still more devastating counter-attack with the bayonet. All contributors to this volume generally accept this stereotype as more accurate than Oman's 'musket-counting' version, and Brent Nosworthy tellingly traces its pedigree all the way back to the doctrines of a certain James Wolfe, some thirty years before the Duke of Wellington had even been born.

There is a curious anomaly between Oman's idealised theoretical model of a 'thin red line' winning all its combats by musketry, and the many examples that he himself gives of decisive British counter-charges. Vimeiro (1808) was the present editor's starting point for understanding this; but perhaps the battle of Bussaco (1810) stands out as a clearer example. It is certainly one that has attracted the attention of several of our contributors. In his narrative Oman explained exactly how at least three of the five French attacks were repulsed by the bayonet – and yet in his more doctrinaire formulae he continued to state that the musket-count was the only truly decisive element. Arnold, Nosworthy and others look into this in admirable detail, with the benefit of new documentation, to which the present editor would add only that the terrain contours alone could surely explain most of the result. Wellington's position was such a 'damned long [and high] ridge' that in many respects the tactics of the two sides were completely irrelevant. Whoever was on top of it could pour so much ordure (of whatever variety) over any assailant, that to all intents and purposes the position should never have been described as anything but 'impregnable'.[2]

Moving beyond the field of minor tactics, we find that a very high proportion of the ink spilled over the Peninsular War, from at least the time of Napier onwards, seems to have been devoted to the reputations of individual generals. Napier had preferred Moore to Wellington – and almost anyone to Beresford – but Oman was able to put all three of them back into a more balanced perspective. We can now refine that perspective further still, as Philip Hay-thornthwaite has done with Wellington and Moore, and as Harold Livermore has done with Beresford. Between them, they reveal a number of areas in which Oman's view may be amplified, although, as Juan José Sañudo darkly hints, even more might perhaps have been added about Wellington's manipulation of his Spanish allies. Today we have a number of searching studies, most notably Peter Hofschröer's account of Ligny and Quatre Bras (1815), which show Wellington's inner nature to have been closer to that of a 'diplomat'[3] than his admirers have normally been ready to concede. In the present book Rory Muir has at least filled in the essential British political background, which was missing from Oman. He explains how Wellesley, Moore, and Beresford each came to be appointed and then supported, with varying degrees of enthusiasm, even through the risky early years when Masséna might so easily have taken Lisbon, and when many in London thought that South America would have been an altogether safer and more profitable arena for British arms. Muir also describes the shockingly small circle of 'friends and relations' from which every government was drawn. Since this included at least three Wellesley brothers, there is a very real sense in which the whole war in the Peninsula should be seen as an entrepreneurial Wellesley family enterprise.

The French side of the war was also, of course, very aggressively a 'family business', as between Napoleon Bonaparte and his brother Joseph, not to mention a few other brothers who had declined the poisoned chalice of the Spanish throne. Leopoldo Stampa gives us a damning insight into this supremely dysfunctional family, as well as into some of its political implications for Spain (not least in the Americas) that Oman missed. He takes us far from Napier's near-worship of Napoleon; although perhaps not so far from Oman's military insight into the many self-imposed problems experienced by the restless Corsican when he chose to run a war in Spain from such remote sites as Paris, Vienna, or Moscow. Even in our own day it has not proved easy to run a war in Vietnam from as far away as Washington DC, despite all the wonders of modern telecom-munications; so the French chain of command in 1809–14 obviously faced a very deep difficulty as soon as it became stretched to continental distances. Even within the Iberian Peninsula – a 'near island', or even a 'sub-continent' – the distances remained very great, and the transmission of messages along all those 'red roads winding through unending ochre plains' became as wearisome as it was dangerous to the couriers. For all the high virtuosity displayed by many of the French commanders in tactics (*eg* Soult at Ocaña, 1809) or in operations (*eg* the same Soult in setting up Albuera, 1811), there always remained a black hole of disconnected strategic purpose, as between one army corps area in the Peninsula and another. These problems are elaborated in our present volume by both James Arnold and Leopoldo Stampa.

Of course, this fragmentation of the war was more than matched on the allied side, which surely suffered two or three conflicting authorities for every one that faced the French. 'Imperative' orders kept on coming in not only from such far-flung places as London and Rio de Janeiro, but from still more bitterly antagonistic local centres such as Seville versus León, Cádiz versus Lisbon, or Saragossa versus Tarragona. Oman's grasp of all this – and his use of archival material – was considerably less assured in the case of the Spanish and Portuguese than it was for the French, which in turn often led him into unfair prejudices against the Iberians.

In recent years Charles Esdaile has done much to correct such mistakes, while greatly enlarging our knowledge of what is, after all, a very fundamental aspect of the whole conflict. In his present chapter he offers a refreshing (partial) rehabilitation of Godoy, as well as a useful working analysis of the complex social forces which underlay the otherwise inexplicable workings of Spanish politics. In this he has the full support of Juan José Sañudo. Equally, Harold Livermore points out that the origins of this whole war go back at least as far as the execution of Louis XVI in Paris, which sparked a traumatic Franco-Spanish campaign in the Pyrenees from 1793 to 1795. Oman did not explain the history of the mutual hostilities between France, Spain, Portugal, and Britain (perm any combination!) during the fifteen years leading up to 1807 – so we are now particularly grateful to Professor Livermore for filling in this important gap.

The social and economic disruption of Spain in 1807–8 led not merely to political fragmentation, but also to widespread banditry, much of which was instantly renamed 'guerrilla warfare' and hailed as 'patriotic heroism'. Charles Esdaile describes its origins, but he also breaks the news – which somehow seems surprising, when surely it should not be – that some of the bandit raids were actually directed against the allies, and not always against the French. Elsewhere in our volume a fuller description of the 'guerrillas' is given by René Chartrand, who has discovered many telling documents on their numbers, organisation, and effectiveness, as well as on the doomed attempts by central government to regulate their action. This whole subject is today a much more vibrant area of research than it has ever been in the past, enabling us to add a great deal to Oman's sparse comments about it.

Of course, far from all the Spanish combatants were guerrillas or near-irregular 'home guards'. Hundreds of thousands more served as volunteers or regulars in the many field armies and standing garrisons. They were formed into a bewildering array of diverse units, many of which had no more than a fleeting existence, and many more of which irritatingly shared the same names and numbers with other, doubtless equally worthy, units. Few of the necessary archives survive, so disentangling even the order of battle (OB) for the Spanish constitutes a lifetime's work which Oman, alas, was able to complete only partially and imperfectly. In his present chapter Juan José Sañudo gives some valuable pointers in this task.[4] He also ranges widely over other aspects of the Spanish armies, especially their economic basis, that were overlooked by Oman – and subsequently by his (alas all too numerous) narrowly-nationalistic British followers.

For the latter, the Peninsular War will always represent a triumph of the British army over excitable and unreliable foreigners, regardless of whether they happened to be allies or enemies at the time. Yet that British army was itself riddled with some very glaring defects and weaknesses. There were problems with promotions, appointments, and administration, not to mention an apparently autonomous cavalry force, the highest exponent of which chose to elope with no less a personage than Wellington's own sister-in-law! All this aside, the most serious structural weaknesses really lay in the transport services and in combat engineering. In the former department Wellington was gradually able to improvise a workable local solution, but in the latter he always stood in relation to any French army (or fortress) pretty much as David did to Goliath. His sieges were usually highly painful, embarrassing, and bloody events, with Third Badajoz (1812) equalling the scale of casualties seen in each of his three bloodiest battles before Waterloo,[5] and with Burgos (later in 1812) standing as one of the darkest stains on his entire record. In common with David he did, admittedly, manage to score some lucky hits – but in general the odds were usually stacked heavily on the side of Goliath.

In his two essays in the present volume Philip Haythornthwaite analyses the whole structure of Wellington's army and its siegecraft, demonstrating that it would take the best part of a century to reform it properly. Although Wellington made some excellent reforms and achieved a very fine standard of efficiency within his own command, he fatally lacked the ability – or even the will – to transmit his expertise into the institutional practices of Whitehall and the Horseguards. Hence we must conclude that he was a life-long politician (rising even to become prime minister) who signally failed to reform the one political department in which he had originally been most centrally interested!

In my own essay, in chapter 8, I try to show that Oman was at heart more centrally concerned with what is today known as the 'operational art' than he was with any other subject. Hence he was a child of his time, not only because he wanted to re-interpret minor tactics (contrary to the evidence) to fit into a battlefield dominated by quick-firing smallarms; but especially because he was a keen student of the operational debates taking place in every European staff college at the time he was writing. It is not true to say that Oman was cut off from these debates, or ignored them, or that as a civilian he was incapable of understanding them. On the contrary, he understood them very well indeed, and was one of their absolutely most successful interpreters to the Anglo-Saxon world. His *History of the Peninsular War* must therefore be ranked alongside the works of Henderson, de Grandmaison, and von Bernhardi, as a major contribution to his generation's conception of just how the operational art had worked in the past and was expected to work in the future. We now know that the experiences of 1914–18 would bash a very rude and unexpected dent into all such speculations – but we should not thereby lose sight of the very clear vision of their own age, as well as of their collective past, that such writers actually displayed. We may, indeed, be entitled to pick up many of their themes once again in the operational art that was demonstrated in the new world war of 1939–45, which was, perhaps, a little closer to 'Napoleonic' conditions than its immediate predecessor had been.[6]

A book about another book

Outside the ethereal realms of literary criticism, it is perhaps somewhat unusual to find a book that is written mainly about another book. In the field of military history this can sometimes happen when practical battlefield events are claimed to have resulted from some brilliant intellectual text, such as the *Précis* of the renegade Baron Jomini, or that puzzling version of *On War* which was published by Countess Marie von Brühl soon after the death of her husband, Karl von Clausewitz. We sometimes also find discussions of particular tactical doctrines, manuals, or instructions for drill, although it is always difficult to establish precisely what influence, if any, such documents really exerted upon the way that wars were fought. To the present author, at least, it seems probable that 'military doctrine' is a distinctly chimerical phenomenon, which tends to have far less concrete existence than it is often fashionable to assert.[7]

Surely more important than writings about doctrine, to the true military historian, are the works of other military historians, whose concern is not to discover how the next war should be fought, but rather how the last one actually was fought. In order to find the truth of what happened, the military historian must constantly interrogate and criticise the work of his predecessors, so that new horizons and perspectives may be achieved through a process of Socratic dialogue. In its crudest form this activity may be observed when, as is far from unknown, one general criticises the war memoirs published by another general. In terms of the Peninsular War, for example, the classic case of this occurred when Marshal Beresford dissented (to say the least) from Major General Napier's widely-acclaimed interpretation of the battle of Albuera.[8] An exceptionally bitter exchange of pamphlets ensued, in which it was generally accepted that the outraged (Tory) critic of superior rank, who had actually commanded in the battle, was worsted by the (Liberal) historian of lesser rank, who had not even been present. That verdict certainly makes the point that a given individual's literary merit is eminently separable both from his hierarchical status and from the special credentials that an eyewitness may enjoy, although it may not necessarily be quite so separable from his politics. However, it also reminds us that even within the plodding field of military history it is still sometimes possible to find vividly electrifying writings that concern themselves more with the discussion of other writings than with giving a simple narrative account of battles and campaigns.

Admittedly the bare-knuckle bout of Beresford versus Napier finally generated rather more heat than light, and it would require a whole new generation of historians, who had not personally been involved in the Napoleonic Wars, to put the whole issue of Albuera – and, beyond that individual battle, of the whole Peninsular conflict – into a more sophisticated and comprehensible perspective. The two main standard-bearers of this new perspective turned out to be Sir John Fortescue (1859–1933) and Sir Charles Oman (1860–1946), who both came from privileged backgrounds, but who surely had some very different perspectives. Fortescue was the fifth son of an Earl, whereas Oman's father had owned an indigo factory in India until forced by ill health to abandon it. Fortescue was a robust huntsman with an even greater penchant for pithy judgements than Oman himself, but perhaps rather less depth of scholarship. From 1905 to 1926 he was the librarian at Windsor Castle, while Oman pursued a more varied life teaching in Oxford. Nevertheless, Fortescue and Oman each offered the public (among other things) a monumental multi-volume work about the Peninsular War.[9] They were good friends, collaborated closely, hesitated to express criticisms of each other's work, and often referred to each other's writings in their own. For example, in Fortescue's sixth, seventh, and eighth volumes, which appeared between 1910 and 1917, there are no less than 121 references to

Oman's book, whereas in the last two volumes of the latter, which appeared in 1922 and 1930, there are some 31 references to Fortescue's. To that extent both works were actually 'books about other books', just as both of them were also partly books about Napier's book.

In the event Fortescue's coverage of the Peninsula was less completely focused than Oman's. Because the title of his book was specifically *A History of the British Army*, it included operations in India, the West Indies, and the central Mediterranean as much as in Portugal and Spain, while at the same time excluding, by definition, much of the Portuguese and Spanish participation. Hence it is Oman who normally holds the palm for the 'definitive' late-Victorian view of the Peninsular War, and it is with his work, rather than Fortescue's, that we are here most centrally concerned.

When it first started to appear in 1902, the *History of the Peninsular War* seemed to be remarkable to contemporaries in Britain because it represented a far more 'scientific', 'systematic' (and therefore 'modern') approach to the subject than Napier's six volumes, which had held the field for over a generation. At first these qualities were rather held against it by Napier's faithful followers; but by the time of the second volume in 1903, most of them were ready to acknowledge that Oman's work was superior.[10] This must have come as a great relief to the author, who had expended so much personal capital in the project. It also seems to have resolved the development of his academic career, in that he was finally confirmed in the Chichele chair of modern history at Oxford in 1905, never to look back.

Taken as a whole, the *History* was not only monumental in scale and scope, but also displayed a clarity of exposition and a depth of documentation that went some way beyond Napier. Those few British scholars who had been following continental trends would perhaps have been slightly less impressed, since many other 'monumental' studies of the Revolutionary and Napoleonic Wars had recently been published in Paris, Berlin, and Vienna, and even in Lisbon and Madrid. Some remarkably 'modern' and 'scientific' analyses had been published in what was, after all, the golden age of General Staff History. It is, nevertheless, still fair to say that Oman's was the best account of the so-called 'Peninsular War'[11] to be published in any country. It has never yet been superseded, and seems unlikely to be in the future.

Having said that, our present perspective in 1999 allows us to find many defects in Oman's work which were not immediately apparent to his contemporaries. The first volume, for example, today sits rather oddly beside the subsequent six. It covers more subjects – and arguably more important ones – than they do, including the initial French invasion, Bailén, Saragossa, Vimeiro, and even Moore's final battle in January 1809. That makes a dauntingly wide sweep to be

compressed into a single volume, even though Oman himself
claimed they needed fewer pages than the events of later years, since
operations displayed a greater unity and simplicity as long as
Napoleon personally remained in Spain.[12] Yet he compounds the
difficulties of volume I by including a Section II (*The Land and the
Combatants*) in which he prematurely summarises his general
findings about the whole war. Oman obviously believed that the
reader needed a 'taster' of what was still to come – but it is
regrettable that he wrote it before he had even completed his
researches, let alone undergone the necessary discipline of writing
them up. In effect, he was guessing at what his eventual opinions
would be, some 28 years before he would be in a position to make
them! Yet because this section came so early in the book, and
purported to offer a sort of 'executive summary' or instant guide to
the whole, it has often been unduly influential. It is written with
vigour and authority, and at times it is even truly seminal. The
discussion of logistics and the rhythm they imposed upon
operations,[13] for example, cannot be bettered. Much of the rest is
unexceptionable. However, it is particularly unfortunate that Oman
chose to give us a series of ill-considered stereotypes of the British,
French, and Spanish armies, at this particular point in his work,
before he had been able to digest the full details of the story he was
about to write. These stereotypes were often disproved by the
contents of his own later volumes, and have not weathered well
since then. It would seem that a great deal of our modern difficulties
with Oman spring from this single section, and it is noticeable that
many of the contributors to the present book often return to it.

We may speculate that the pyrotechnics in Oman's first volume
sprang from the novelty of his undertaking and his own inner
uncertainty about the welcome it would receive from critics. He felt
he had to put as much into his shop window as he possibly could,
to establish his credentials as a worthy challenger to Napier. By
contrast all his later volumes display a markedly more assured,
careful, and exhaustive approach. They are no longer the advertise-
ment, but are the product itself. Doubtless some of the promised
excitement is lost in the process, and we are given rather fewer
glimpses of Oman's fiery inner temperament; but it is these
volumes, rather than the first, which should really stand as his true
achievement and monument.

Beyond the unevenness between the first volume and those
which followed, we may identify a number of areas in which the
modern reader might justifiably raise some complaints:

i)   Oman's scholarly apparatus;
ii)   The accuracy of his research;
iii) His prejudices;
iv)   His omissions.

Oman's lapses: (i) His scholarly apparatus

Oman composed the *History* at a time when the style of scholarly writing was changing rapidly. It was moving away from the somewhat slapdash journalistic conventions followed by Napier – who normally preferred pungent personal convictions to careful footnotes – and was moving towards the dry, detached, and hyper-documented tone that we see in modern university dissertations. Today we may lament the excesses to which 'foot and notes disease' can sometimes lead; but we are also justly irritated when slack middlebrow writers offer us no references by which to cross-check the crucial points in their argument. The general standard of scholarship has certainly improved dramatically since Napier's day – even though we do still seem to find only too many 'slack middlebrow writers' elevated to the highest pinnacles of praise by the unscholarly mass media.

It so happened that Oman himself arrived absolutely in the middle of this transition, at a time when many of the highest scholars were still perfectly happy to accept Napier's conventions, whereas others were already thinking in the more meticulous terms that would only become generally accepted fifty years later. Nor, in the event, did he really take sides between the two schools. The style that he adopted in his *History* actually split the difference between them with uncanny accuracy. For Napierist dinosaurs his work represented a thunderclap of modernity; while for the most advanced scholars it appeared to be distressingly old-fashioned, antiquarian, and over-personalised. This was especially important to them because it so happened that Oman held a highly prestigious chair of history in an Oxford University that was (and arguably still is) one of the most advanced centres of learning in the world, not least in the humanities. Therefore the particular style of scholarship that he chose to follow could never remain merely a private matter between him and the 'Peninsular buffs' who happened to read him for amusement. Instead, it affected the many historians throughout the world who were striving to set and maintain a new and forward-looking professional standard.

Alas, it would seem that Sir Charles was a great disappointment to them. Admittedly he was an exemplary researcher, looking into all sorts of unexpected corners for new material, and visiting all the relevant archives in Britain, France, Portugal, and Spain. But the problem was that he seemed unable to break free from his highly personal prejudices, just as he failed to present his scholarly references in a truly modern format. This affected both his footnotes and his bibliography.

Oman's footnotes are far more numerous than Napier's, and often quite discursive; but they still fall far short of completeness. We cannot always be sure that we will be able to trace his statements in the text back to the sources upon which he based them. Equally, there is little attempt to give precise reference numbers to individual manuscript documents, even when they are printed in full, in the appendices. We would not be able to go to archives and ask to see the originals, without enduring an unnecessarily laborious and frustrating process of trying to guess which carton they might be in. Nor does Oman even supply the consolidated list of published works that he promised in the preface to his first volume. The nearest he came to it is in appendix III of *Wellington's Army* (pp.375–83), where he lists the main British army memoirs by regiment. This is very useful within its own terms of reference; but it makes 'no pretensions to be exhaustive'[14] for the wider study even of the British, let alone of their allies and enemies.

In summary, therefore, we can award Oman high marks for his diligent researches, and his occasional published comments on sources can still be very helpful; but the fact remains that by the standards of the late 1990s he infuriatingly omitted to write down a great deal of what he knew. He apparently felt little urgency either for publishing all his findings, or for offering completeness in his footnotes. He assumed that if a student had a query, he could simply pop round to see the professor in his lodgings, and all would be explained. Clearly the scholarly world of 1902 was a much smaller and more intimate place than it is today. By the same token, Oman doubtless saw little need to make much of a bibliographical note of the books he used, simply because there were far fewer books in existence. For example *The Memoirs of Rifleman Harris* existed only in the original limited edition of 1848, and had yet to be reprinted even once, whereas today we must distinguish carefully between at least six different reprints or new editions.[15]

Oman's lapses: (ii) The accuracy of his research

When it comes to the accuracy of Oman's findings, we can confidently award him much higher marks than we can for his apparatus. By and large we can rely upon him to give the correct names, dates, and places for any particular event that he describes. One of his greatest strengths, in fact, is the limpid clarity of his narrative. It takes the reader forward with a deceptive ease, while at the same time including a complex mass of many diverse considerations. Of course, he inevitably did make various slips and errors of detail – how could he possibly hope to avoid it, in a work of more than 4000 pages? – but we should beware of making too much of them. It would be easy, but quite unfair, to damn his reputation merely on the grounds that he occasionally stumbled.

When E.M. Lloyd reviewed Oman's first volume in 1902 he found some 'trifling corrections' that needed to be made, such as (on Oman's p.214) relocating the starting point of Spencer's Division from Sicily to England; re-dating Duhesme's supercession by Gouvion St Cyr (p.333) from 17 August to 7 September; and re-interpreting Paget's exclusion from the Peninsula (p.537) on the grounds of military seniority rather than of marital infidelity. He also points out that Oman's own appendices show a total French strength on 15 November of 125,000 men, whereas on his p.526 the author had claimed they added up to 250,000. When it came to the topography of Vimeiro, Oman (p.250) should have said 'down the Maceira' when he actually said 'up the Maceira'... and so on.[16]

Then again, in his 1995 introduction to the Greenhill edition of the *History*, Colonel John R. Elting listed some more of Oman's errors. These included an undue faith in the memoirs of Gleig, Miot de Melito, and Thiébault; poor translations of Marbot and Pelet; the inclusion of non-existent 'marines' and an 'Irish brigade' in the French order of battle, and a basic misunderstanding of 'the column versus the line'. Admittedly, that does not amount to a very damaging catalogue, especially since it may itself be questioned in a number of places.[17] We can nevertheless add plenty of additional items of our own. Although Oman's prodigious statistical appendices undoubtedly added a great deal to our knowledge of the orders of battle, their arithmetic did not always quite add up to the totals he claimed.[18] Equally, his topographical studies were very advanced for his day and he had, for example, established that Napier's 'ravine' at Albuera was a figment of the imagination.[19] Yet he was not invariably trustworthy, and did not visit every battlefield, so that the hills and valleys shown in his maps did sometimes fail to correspond with the reality of the terrain.[20]

New research allows us to refine Oman's account of various battles at certain points. For example, Ian Fletcher's recent publication of William Keep's memoirs from the 28th Foot has allowed us to see what happened in 1813 on the British right at Maya and on Hill's left at St Pierre.[21] Neither passage was known to Oman, especially since those battlefields were among the ones that he did not personally visit. Equally, we now know that Wellington quickly repented of, and withdrew, his censure of the 13th Light Dragoons for their action at Campo Mayor (1811) – but Oman never found this out.[22] He also believed that at Salamanca the 88th Foot captured the eagle of the French 101st regiment, when we now know that it was actually nothing more than a musical instrument – a 'Jingling Johnny'! In fact the eagle in question was taken from the 62nd regiment by the 44th Foot, whose museum still has it.[23]

In the pages which follow, our contributors give other examples of their own. For example, Professor Livermore finds that Oman wilfully distorted the record of Soult's defeat in Portugal, 1809, to the unjustified benefit of Wellesley and the discredit of Brigadier Silveira. Dr Muir shows that Oman gave the wrong dates for the arrival of the Asturian ambassadors in London in June 1808, while

Colonel Sañudo finds many faults with Oman's knowledge of the Spanish order of battle, particularly in the middle years of the war. He also believes that the steep gully conventionally used to excuse the defeat of the 23rd Light Dragoons at Talavera was merely a convenient myth propagated by that unfortunate regiment, and had no reality on the ground. Of course, we have a duty to get such things right, and it is salutary to remember that even Oman could get them wrong – but overall they surely cannot be taken as very serious blemishes on the central integrity of his work as a whole.

Oman's lapses: (iii) His prejudices

When it comes to matters of opinion, rather than of fact, Oman's work is more open to criticism. It has often been said that he was far more balanced and impartial than Napier had been, and he did indeed try to steer a steady course through the many shoals and reefs associated with the reputations of the leading British generals. Those reputations had always fuelled a large proportion of the discussion about the Peninsular War, at least in Britain, and so a 'definitive' reassessment of them must naturally have featured high on Oman's agenda. He was particularly careful to be even-handed towards both Beresford and Moore, around whom Napier's polemics had raged so long and loud in the 1830s. Oman therefore gave full credit to Beresford for building the Portuguese army and for actually winning the battle of Albuera, despite the long post-traumatic depression that he suffered as a result of the heavy losses there. Conversely, Oman could point out Moore's many defects at the same time as he itemised the massive scale of the indirect advantages that were won by the Coruña campaign.

If anything it was the gigantic personality of Wellington which caused Oman most difficulty, as it has done for many other writers before and since. Because Wellington was a major actor in all seven volumes of the *History*, his art of generalship was particularly difficult to summarise in a few brief paragraphs. Ultimately, however, the Tory in Oman opted for only muted criticism of the cold, autocratic, and ruthlessly domineering characteristics of the iron generalissimo, while rallying in enthusiastic support for his recidivistic Euro-scepticism. As long as Wellington was beating the French or complaining about the Spanish, his ends were apparently good enough to justify his means. However, there did come a resounding condemnation of Wellington's later record as prime minister, as soon as he started to preside over the destruction of the Tory party itself.[24]

If Oman trod carefully when discussing the reputations of British personalities, it can scarcely be said that he extended the same courtesy to foreigners. We must always remember that the *History* was written during years of inflamed international tensions and ultra-nationalism, when it was still politically correct to spice up any argument with at least a hint of racial disdain. From Oman's point of view, therefore, there was little doubt that both the French and the Spanish were morally wrong to have started the war in the first place; that Napoleon made some disastrous miscalculations of the Spanish national character; and that the Spanish themselves – presumably as a direct result of that same national character – were constitutionally incapable of setting up a workable government or structure of military command. Hence a corruptly centralised monarchy, led by a weak King Joseph and bolstered by some rapaciously self-centred French marshals, came to confront a corruptly localised democracy led by a whole string of weak Spanish and Portuguese adventurers, while the corrupt Spanish court abdicated meekly at Bayonne, and the corrupt Portuguese court fled selfishly to Rio de Janeiro. The reader is left to draw his own conclusion that, obviously, it was only the British Army that could provide any sort of solidity, backbone, or salvation amid such a state of suppurating anarchy. However, it is noticeable that Oman did not care to look very far into the crippling commercial terms that Britain systematically exacted from her allies as the price for her support, nor at the catastrophic results that ensued for both Portugal and Spain. It is surely no accident that the preface to his final volume ends with a limp excuse that he did not pursue the story beyond 1814 because 'the chronicle of the succeeding period was not a cheerful one'.[25]

When we descend from high political prejudices to the consideration of individual foreign generals, we find Oman at his most boisterous and dismissive. He delights in affecting astonishment at the sheer scale of the incompetence which his actors somehow contrive to display with apparently mechanical regularity. Thus of General Areizaga at Ocaña he finds 'it is impossible to speak with patience of his generalship' (vol.III, p.96). At Almonacid 'no words are too strong to use in condemnation of Venegas's conduct ... [his] criminal slackness ... the extreme of culpable rashness ... He should have been court-martialled and shot' (vol.II, p.616). Of the Conde de Belvedere he wrote that 'his family influence had made him a general at an age when he might reasonably have expected to command a company ... hence came the astonishing series of blunders that led to the combat of Gamonal' (vol.I, p.420). The Conde de Caldagues at Molins de Rey at first seems to be held outside this catalogue of woe, as 'the one first rate officer in their [*ie* the Spanish] ranks', until we realise that in the same paragraph this officer distinguishes himself only by being captured during the French pursuit, 'many miles from the field, when his exhausted horse fell under him' (vol.II, p.71).

Perhaps Oman's favourite target was General Cuesta, who seems to keep cropping up throughout the narrative like a bad penny. Quite

apart from his notorious arguments with Wellesley in the Talavera
campaign, we are told that at Medellin his 'blind self confidence
could go no further!' (vol.II, p.160), while elsewhere we hear of 'the
old man's selfish pride' and 'the incapacity of Cuesta' (vol.I, p.169).
Oman does at least praise the troops of the Asturian *junta* for their
'well-justified disbelief in Cuesta's ability' (vol.I, p.165). It seems that
only General Blake was redeemed, doubtless by his Irish blood, from
'the slackness [and] the arrogance which were the besetting sins of
so many of the Peninsular generals' (vol.I, p.163). However, even he
does not remain unscathed for long. By the time we reach the second
volume of the *History* we find he made a 'gross tactical error' at Maria
(vol.II, p.431), and then (vol.II, p.428) that 'it can only be considered
... a piece of mad presumption on the part of the Spanish general that
he halted at Belchite'. Finally, in the third volume, 'even after making
all possible allowances ... he must yet be pronounced guilty of
feebleness and want of ingenuity' (vol.III, p.64).

Nor do the French commanders get off particularly lightly. As
invading conquerors – and, indeed, as the opponents to Oman's
favoured British – it is perhaps natural that the French should often
be condemned for their cruelties and for pillaging towns 'from
cellar to garret'. Their love of plunder is a recurrent theme, not to
mention the illicit designs upon the Portuguese crown that were
allegedly harboured by both Junot (vol.I, p.207) and Soult (vol.II,
pp.273–85 and pp.632–9). Oman is particularly good at explaining
the difficulties of centralised command occasioned by Napoleon's
personal absence from the Peninsula, and the resulting jealousies
and squabbles between his subordinates. They do not emerge from
it all as loveable personalities, nor, despite their routine victories, is
their military efficiency routinely admired. We read of 'the
carelessness of the Duke of Dantzig and the unaccountable timidity
of the Duke of Belluno' (vol.I, p.418), and 'the reckless manner in
which Villatte and Victor attacked: it was not consonant with true
military principles' (vol.I p.415), while 'being timid or
unenterprising ... [Chabran] let the flying enemy pass across his
front unmolested' (vol.II, p.71).

Oman is particularly boisterous when he describes the
resounding Spanish victory at Bailén (July 1808), since he somehow
manages to condemn both sides together, for almost equal
incompetence. We should not perhaps object that he condemns
the French generalship in ringing phrases such as 'inexplicable
carelessness' and 'this astonishing display of sloth and slackness'
(vol.I, p.193); or 'even if we grant that Vedel made every possible
mistake, it is nevertheless true that Dupont fought his battle most
unskilfully' (vol.I, p.203) and 'mismanaged all the details of his
attack ... he showed great incapacity to grasp the situation, lost his
head, and threw away all his chances' (vol.I, p.204). It is rather
more striking that Oman also excoriates several of the victorious

Spanish commanders, and particularly Castaños, the commander-in-chief. Their plan, 'though ultimately crowned with success, was perilous in the highest degree.' Castaños 'seriously underestimated' his opponent, 'as well as misconceived his exact position' (vol.I, p.179). On 17 July, General Reding adopted 'a strange way to employ the day after a victory' by resting his men and 'enjoying a well-earned siesta!' (vol.I, pp.183–4); he 'acted in the most strange and unskilful way' (vol.I, p.204). On 19 July 'the Spanish commander-in-chief had displayed most blame-worthy torpidity' (vol.I, p.192); and finally, in early August, Captain-General Morla issued 'a most shameless and cynical letter' which sealed the fate of the French captives (vol.I, p.201). Overall, Oman concluded that the Spanish at Bailén 'were extremely fortunate, and even their mistakes helped them' (vol.I, p.204). This surely amounts to a classic case of damnation by faint praise, in which racial disdain lurks close beneath the surface.

Alas, these examples of Oman's damning judgements form only the tip of a very big iceberg. We could cite many more from the *History*, to the point where we might be tempted to agree with Colonel Elting that Oman was personally unsympathetic towards military officers in general, because he was 'a life-long academic, "smelling" ... of lamp oil and not gunpowder.'[26] We can certainly wish that Oman had given rather more analysis to the great difficulties faced by his Peninsular commanders as they tried to make their decisions – and especially the Spanish ones, who surely laboured under the greatest difficulties of all. Simply dismissing their errors as 'mad', 'astonishing', 'criminal', 'unaccountable', or 'inexplicable' represents a serious abdication of the historian's duty to explain rather than to judge. It is a double abdication if – as we are now told[27] – his snap judgements often turn out to be misdirected.

We should not, however, fall into Elting's mistake of assuming that the sentiment betrayed by Oman's snap judgements was actually an anti-military one. On the contrary, Oman was personally deeply pro-military, of which there could surely be no finer testament than the *History* itself. Going one step further, we may even suggest that his habit of instant condemnation smacks much more of the decisive military man than of the hesitant academic. Admittedly, it stops short of the five-letter expletives that Napoleon hurled at Dupont after Bailén; but it does seem to owe much more to the powder-stained Napier than to the lamp-oil-fragrant Stubbs. As at least a 'would-be' military officer, Oman displays an urge to impose clarity, precision and black-and-white values upon his subjects. The readership at which he is aiming is also surely more populist (and military?) than strictly academic.

Nor is it correct to say that Oman failed to understand the inner nature of war, or to see that 'war is an incredibly complex, chancy and messy business that will not fit itself into neat academic concepts'.[28] For all its over-confident certainties and judgmental lack of ambiguity, his account of Bailén does actually give us a very clear picture of exactly this uncertainty, this 'fog of war'. The two befuddled armies manoeuvre around each other without the vaguest notion of the true situation. They are both starving and parched with thirst and heat-stroke. The French generals know that they must at all costs protect their gigantic train of booty, while the Spanish soldiers know no more than that they have arrived where they have arrived, and find it easier to hold their ground than to move away. Personalities naturally get frayed in the process, and some generals can with hindsight be seen to have made faulty decisions. There is thus no failure on Oman's part to see that war is 'complex, chancy and messy'. However, it could be said that his readiness to make quick, dismissive summaries of the personalities rather spoils the 'foggy' effect of his picture, and makes it all look more straightforward and explicable than perhaps it really was.

There may well be some weight behind the charge that Oman was more sensitive to the horrors of war, and less sensitive to its glories, than a militarist might wish. In the particular case of Bailén, he certainly seems to favour a version of the 'lions led by donkeys' theory, in that he does often refer to the stoicism, resilience, and bravery of the common soldiers, while reserving highly barbed comments for their commanders. Elsewhere, and often, he could be equally unsparing in his scorn for the rank and file itself, when he believes it fled from its duty for too little cause. On those occasions he seems to opt for a 'sheep led by donkeys' interpretation, which is the most dismissive view of military transactions that there could possibly be. Only very rarely does he give us a truly admiring 'lions led by Titans' view of these battles, and so to that extent he may be accused of a certain anti-militarism.

Much more to the point, though, is the distinctive 'Britishness' of his underlying prejudices. He does not condemn his generals as incompetent just because they are generals, but mainly because they are *foreign* generals. Admittedly, some of the British ones also occasionally fall from grace[29] – but then they could be condemned for letting the side down, as even the Duke of Wellington eventually did with the Tory party.

Oman's lapses: (iv) His omissions

More serious than all of this, perhaps, is the fact that Oman's prejudices made him systematically omit some very generous slices of the overall story of the war. He admittedly did a great deal better than Napier – and, indeed, than Fortescue – in widening the story to include the Spanish, Portuguese, and French sides of the hill. Nevertheless, his main narrative, and the bulk of his research effort, was still concentrated firmly on the British. The further we stray away from the expeditionary force of Wellington and Moore (and let us not forget poor Cradock, who commanded for a short time in 1809), the less we find Oman to be either sympathetic or diligent.

This perspective is widely lamented by several of the contributors to the present volume. Thus, for example, Dr Muir shows how much of the war must be explained in terms of the political scene in London, which is mentioned far too little by Oman; while James Arnold and others complain that the wider context of the wars, alliances, and dynastic marriages taking place in central Europe, which were of absolutely crucial importance to the whole of French strategy, are also normally overlooked. Professor Livermore finds that Oman failed to understand the essential background to Portuguese politics and diplomacy before 1808, just as Dr Esdaile and Colonel Sañudo both detect an unduly superficial comprehension of the serious difficulties facing Spain, which had to cope with not two rival governments, but perhaps as many as a dozen. Those last three authors also deplore the lightness with which Oman skips over the deep and multi-faceted economic catastrophes suffered by the two Iberian states, which led in turn to traumatic social dislocation and a heritage of political turmoil which continued for well over a century. If France fell into a long term cycle of revolution and counter-revolution as a result of the events of 1789, the same could be said to a tenfold degree of Portugal and Spain after 1808.

We may, however, follow Dr Muir[30] in thinking that none of this is necessarily a *criticism* of Oman's book, since it was always intended to be a specifically military history, and an Anglocentric one at that. Nevertheless, it is something that we should always remember when we look into his pages. Many of the gaps that he left may now be filled in by modern scholars, and so a complete and balanced history of this war would doubtless have a very different profile today from the particular shape that he chose to give it in 1902.

If Oman deliberately steered away from discussion of politics, economics, and social forces, he correspondingly prided himself on his understanding of military strategy, operations, and tactics. Yet within that gamut he is clearly much stronger in the first two areas than in the third. He made many confident assertions about minor tactics, and in doing so he undoubtedly made a very great impact upon military historiography in general. But from a modern perspective some of his ideas turn out to be either simplistic or wrong, as the present writer tried to demonstrate in his earlier work,[31] and as James Arnold, Brent Nosworthy, and Arthur Harman have also explained in the past, as well as in their contributions to the present volume.

Oman's essential strength, therefore, resides squarely and centrally in his analysis of strategy and operations, as well as in his presentation of the orders of battle which underlay both of those activities. His almost obsessional interest in the basic numbers of combatants present in each operation may today appear to be somewhat irrelevant and antiquarian. Colonel Sañudo would argue that it is even deeply misleading. However, we must remember that such a systematic analysis had never previously been attempted. Even though we may be able to refine and correct his precise figures in particular instances, we should never lose sight of the originality and skill with which Oman collected them. Besides, the simple numbers were themselves always of enormous importance to the generals at the time. The first thing they would ask about any enemy was the numerical strength of his force, with such qualitative factors as moral resilience, previous combat experience, cavalry training, artillery throw-weight, or even chain of command efficiency, normally coming in as only secondary considerations.

Yet even within this more specialist 'military' area, we may nevertheless still criticise Oman for a number of significant omissions. The guerrillas make a particularly important example, since according to some methods of calculation they actually provided about half of the effective warlike activity against the French. Doubtless this is greatly exaggerated, and somewhat comparable to the claims of the French Resistance to have 'defeated the Germans in Normandy in 1944'; but it is nevertheless an important subject for discussion which Oman appears, by and large, to have dismissed in far too few words.

We may also suggest that Oman failed to give full credit to the Spanish field armies for winning time and space by their campaigns, even though they might be defeated ignominiously in ranged battles. He waxed lyrical in his praise for the time and space won by Moore's shrewd manoeuvre towards Irun, which led to near-total ruin at Coruña (some 180 degrees in the opposite direction from Irun); and he even found many words of praise for Wellesley's equivalent hazard towards Madrid, which was decisively rebuffed at Talavera – but he never finds sufficient generosity to accord similar recognition to the comparable Spanish undertakings, which must have numbered more than a dozen. He documents, but apparently does not fully understand, that the Spanish field armies were 'losing all the battles, but still winning the war'; and exactly the same could be said of the many Spanish fortresses which held out for far longer than French apologists would have us believe was reasonable. This was not merely a matter of Saragossa being a sort of unique 'Stalingrad on the Ebro', nor even of Cádiz being a second Gibraltar (and, incidentally, being equally dependent on the grace and favour of the Royal Navy). Instead, it was a much wider phenomenon than either of those, as a close study of the French advance down the east coast of Spain, from Perpignan to Valencia, will reveal.

This theatre was composed mainly of a narrow strip of fertile land cramped between the mountains and the sea, and largely cut off from the primary operations in the centre and west. From the French perspective the problem was a matter of rolling up a long, single string of fortresses, from north to south, while maintaining the communications between them against attacks by montagnard guerrillas from the west, and naval raiders from the east. They started well enough, when Duhesme seized Barcelona in a *coup de main* as early as 29 February 1808; but he soon found himself isolated and embattled there, deep in hostile territory. The Spanish held Rosas, Gerona, and Hostalrich in his rear, and his efforts to dislodge them all failed. He was replaced by Gouvion St Cyr in August but, despite some brilliant French victories in the open field, Rosas would not fall until 5 December 1808, Gerona not until 11 December 1809, and Hostalrich as late as 12 May 1810. In other words, it took the French more than two years to open the road from the frontier to Barcelona – a distance of only about 165 kilometres. Surely no decent army of the *ancien régime* could have taken longer! Thereafter Suchet and Macdonald made only slightly better headway against Tortosa (captured 2 January 1811) and Tarragona (captured 28 June 1811), and it would be 10 January 1812 before the ultimate prize of Valencia finally fell to the French. It had first been attacked by Moncey in June 1808, but had remained in Spanish hands for no less than three and a half years thereafter. Since the Emperor was then already moving the bulk of his army in the direction of Moscow, this represented a hollow victory indeed.

Oman faithfully chronicled all these events, but scarcely gave them full credit in his summations. He must therefore be criticised for missing some important aspects of the purely military picture, just as he missed some rather more obvious features of the socio-economic scene. No less than in his nationalistic prejudices, his errors of detail, and his failure to provide full scholarly apparatus, we find that his sins of omission also have to be marked down on the slate against his reputation as a truly 'definitive' author. For all that, nevertheless, we may still hail Sir Charles Oman as a 'nearly' definitive author, and we are strongly reminded of J.B. Bury's introduction to the 1896 edition of Gibbon's *Decline and fall of the Roman Empire*, where he wrote 'that Gibbon is behind date in many details, and in some departments of importance, simply signifies that we and our fathers have not lived in an absolutely incompetent world. But in the main things he is our master, above and beyond date.'[32]

Notes

1. Oman, *Studies in the Napoleonic Wars* (London, 1929), p.107.
2. I am deeply indebted to Dr Lim Meng Hooi for this insight, when he and I shared our first view of the terrain in 1968. It may not be irrelevant that his training is in psychology.

3. That is, a 'diplomat' in the sense of 'one who is economical with the truth'. Peter Hofschröer's book is *1815, the Waterloo Campaign: Wellington, his German Allies and the Battles of Ligny and Quatre Bras* (London 1998); Oman himself noted (in *Wellington's Army*, p.9) that 'the Duke forbade the publication of a great number of his more confidential letters, and ordered portions of others to be omitted. He had a strong notion that a great deal of historical information could be, and ought to be, suppressed'. The best work on Wellington's relations with the Spanish is Charles Esdaile, *The Duke of Wellington and the Command of the Spanish Army, 1812–14* (London, 1990).

4. Some of the details of Sañudo's OB information are presented, in English translation, in Michael Oliver and Richard Partridge, *Battle Studies in the Peninsula* (vol.I, London, 1998). For Charles Esdaile's version, see the appendices to his *The Duke of Wellington*, and his *The Spanish Army in the Peninsular War* (Manchester, 1988).

5. Total allied losses were around 5000 at Third Badajoz, which is equivalent to the casualties at each of the battles of Talavera, Salamanca, and Vitoria (and only at Vitoria was the subsequent British pillaging as bad). At Waterloo Wellington's casualties were around 15,000, which puts it into an altogether bloodier league.

6. I am indebted to Piers Mackesy, who tutored me at university, for making a very specific link between his own father's experiences in the Norwegian campaign of 1940 and the very many, very similar, tentative British landing operations between 1793 and 1815.

7. The classic case in recent times was the great American military-doctrinal debate through the sixteen years following the fall of Saigon in 1975. Every contributor to the new doctrine solemnly swore that in the next war the enemy would never ever – repeat, never *ever* – again be allowed to seek sanctuary in some 'safe zone' as defined by a politically-imposed line on the map. The result was 'Desert Storm' in 1991, when this immutable new doctrine survived for no more than a paltry 100 hours – to the utter astonishment of all impartial observers!

8. W.F.P. Napier's book was *History of the War in the Peninsula and in the South of France, from the year 1807 to the year 1814* (6 vols, London, 1828–40). The first volume was published by John Murray, but its instant notoriety meant that the remaining five had to be paid for by the author himself. The flavour of the subsequent pamphleteering war may be judged from the title of one of its products: *Colonel Napier's justification of his third volume; forming a sequel to his reply to various opponents, and containing some new and curious facts relative to the battle of Albuera* (London, 1833). Napier's life and work is fully described in Jay Luvaas' *The Education of an Army* (London, 1965), pp.7–38. See also Livermore's chapter below.

9. Sir J.W. Fortescue, *History of the British Army* (13 vols, London, 1899–1930) covered his subject from the beginnings to 1870, although his coverage of the Peninsular War began only in his sixth volume, which appeared some eight years after Oman's first. In common with Oman, his military historical interests ranged far and wide, and he penned some twenty-five books apart from the *British Army*. I am very grateful to John Hussey for all my information on Fortescue.

10. I am grateful to Rory Muir for showing me, among others, E.M. Lloyd's

reviews that greeted Oman's successive volumes, from the *English Historical Review* XVII (1902), pp.302–5; XIX (1904), pp.178–80; XXIII (1908), pp.595–6; XXVII (1912), pp.382–4; and XXX (1915), pp.355–7. In IXL (1924), pp.472–3, the reviewer of Oman's sixth volume was identified as 'W.B.W.' (actually W.B. Wood, brother-in-law to the official historian of the Great War, J.E. Edmonds); while apparently the seventh volume received no review from that journal. It is clear from these and other reviews that Oman's first volume was met with considerable hostility, which gradually fell away with the appearance of the second and later volumes – but perhaps the last volume fell victim to Oman's fading reputation during the pacifistic lack of interest in the 1930s.

11. The very phrase 'The Peninsular War' is now called into question by some authors, who see it as a patronisingly British concept. It was, after all, no more than the fourth or fifth war in or around the Peninsula within twenty years, and the battle of Trafalgar (1805) could in some ways be seen as a more decisive turning point in Spanish fortunes. However, it is equally difficult to sustain either the French 'Guerre d'Espagne', which excludes Portugal, or the Spanish 'Guerra de Independencia', which also begs quite a lot of the key questions.

12. Oman, *History*, vol.II, p.ix.

13. *Ibid*, vol.I, p.85.

14. *Wellington's Army*, p.375.

15. Oman was fully aware of the many defects in the memoirs of Rifleman Harris, whom he rather quaintly took to be typical of 'the ordinary private of the better sort'; but he still called for a reprint (*Wellington's Army*, pp.3, 23, 31). Compare Harman's complaint that there are now all too many such reprints, p.265 below.

16. *English Historical Review* XVII (1902), p.305; although Lloyd appears to have been wrong about the numbers.

17. Greenhill reprint of Oman's *History*, vol.I, pp.x–xi. Oman himself issued warnings about both Marbot and Thiébault in the preface to his first volume (p.xix): conversely, there does seem to be widespread support in the sources for the existence of at least a battalion each of Irish infantry and Guard sailors in the first invasion force of 1808 – eg Foy, *Histoire de la guerre de la Péninsule* (4 vols, Paris, 1827), vol.IV, table opposite p.376. See also A. Martinien, *Tableaux par corps et par batailles des officiers tués et blessés pendant les guerres de l'Empire* (Paris, 1899, reprinted by Editions Militaires Européennes, n.d.), pp.109, 499. As for the French preference for attacking in column, it remains controversial and is extensively discussed by Arnold and Nosworthy below.

18. Oman himself noticed these discrepancies in his prefaces to vols IV and V, but they continue in vol.VI: on p.741 he makes British losses at Burgos total 2064, when the figures he gives actually total 1990: on pp.742–5 he wrongly adds up the totals for each of six French armies, and continues with equal inexactitude (admittedly never erring by more than a few dozen out of tens of thousands in each case) on pp.746, 749, 752 and 773. I am particularly grateful to John Hussey for pointing this out to me.

19. *History*, vol.IV, p.374.

20. For example, he shows no ridge covering the Spanish centre at Uclés (vol.II, map opposite p.54), and he puts the French cavalry at Garcia Hernandez on to a non-existent ridge (vol.V, map backing p.482). By

contrast Fortescue's maps are far superior, while the best modern photographs are in Ian Fletcher, *Fields of Fire: Battlefields of the Peninsular War* (Staplehurst, 1994).

21. William T. Keep, *In the Service of the King* (Staplehurst, 1997).

22. I am very grateful to Ian Fletcher for this information.

23. Ian Fletcher, *Wellington's Regiments: The Men and their Battles from Roliça to Waterloo* (Staplehurst, 1994), pp.180, 159.

24. *Studies in the Napoleonic Wars*, pp.261–75. Compare Oman's treatment of Wellington as a general in the *History*, vol.II, pp.286–311 (*The general and the man*), and in *Wellington's Army*, pp.39–60 (*The man and the strategist*). Note that Oman was considerably less generous towards Wellington than was Fortescue, in the latter's ninth volume.

25. *History*, vol.VII, p.xi.

26. Greenhill edition, *History*, vol.I, p.xiii. A similar complaint was made in the review of Oman's first volume in *JRUSI* XLVI (1902), p.1647.

27. For example, Charles Esdaile on Oman's assessment of Palafox and La Romana, p.313 below.

28. *History*, vol.I, p.x.

29. Oman corrected Napier's prejudice against Craufurd and Picton, but was himself too casually dismissive of others such as Long, Slade, and Erskine. For Murray at Tarragona, however, there was absolutely no redemption possible (see the comments by René Chartrand in chapter 7).

30. See Muir, below.

31. Paddy Griffith, *Forward Into Battle* (Chichester, 1981; 2nd edn, Swindon, 1990), chapter on 'The Alleged Firepower of Wellington's Infantry'; and Paddy Griffith, ed., *Wellington – Commander* (Chichester, 1985), Chapter 7, 'The Myth of the Thin Red Line – Wellington's Tactics'.

32. J.B. Bury's introduction to a new edition of Gibbon's *Decline and fall of the Roman Empire* (7 vols, London, 1896), vol.I, p.lxvii.

Chapter 2

The Life of Sir Charles Oman

by Paddy Griffith

Sir Charles William Chadwick Oman (1860–1946, six feet tall and an only child) has always suffered from a double reputation. On the one hand, he must be considered one of the leading historians of his age, writing influential books on many diverse subjects – especially the great *History of the Peninsular War* – and holding the prestigious Chichele chair of Modern History at All Souls College, Oxford, from 1905 until the end of his life. With a double first in classics (especially ancient history) and modern history, his expertise spanned the whole of recorded 'Western Civilisation'. He was competent in at least five modern languages, and 'he delighted his friends by his ready omniscience on all manner of concrete and recondite fact.'[1] He was energetic in fields as far apart as numismatics, porcelain, the paranormal, and the listing of medieval castles. He helped to found a welter of learned societies – and one political journal – and he left his mark upon the Oxford Union, where he was Librarian for a time as an undergraduate; upon the Codrington and Imperial War Museum libraries; upon the Oxford university OTC; upon the debate over casualties in the Great War, and, indeed, upon the House of Commons itself, where he sat as burgess for the University of Oxford from 1919 to 1935.[2] He was also doubtless highly influential in establishing the Chichele chair of Military History in All Souls College in 1909, which would continue until 1968.

Yet on the other hand Sir Charles had a reputation among scholars as a somewhat less than serious scholar, and among politicians as a somewhat less than serious politician. As a schoolboy at Winchester College he had quickly encountered great difficulties in mastering the more grammatical, syntactical, and philosophical aspects of the classical Greek and Latin curricula;[3] while in the Oxford of the 1920s, A.L. Rowse reports that his fellow academics 'thought that Oman was out of date, with his Right-wing views and his interest in war'.[4] In parliament he was 'out of place' and he was nicknamed 'Stone Age Man'.[5] We must remember that outspoken Tory MPs with a liking for military history have always been particularly open to caricature,[6] as have been the last-ditch defenders of Latin and Greek as non-negotiable requirements for matriculation into the University of Oxford. Yet even as early as 1883 Charles Oman had already been forced to accept that some of his opinions were widely seen as antediluvian (and to an embarrassing degree), even by the standards of his own day. At the tender age of 23 he was at the end of five years as an undergraduate, when he suffered what was probably the most hurtful and traumatic of all the setbacks he ever experienced in his otherwise enviably smooth and successful rise to academic glory. What happened was that the 'Liberal and modernist' senior common room of his own Oxford college (New College) conspired – apparently consciously and deliberately – to exclude him from a Wykehamical fellowship in the humanities that he had believed would be his almost by right,[7] and gifted it instead onto some mathematician from Cambridge. This represented a deep and highly personal rejection to Oman,[8] who had previously known nothing but academic success (albeit always diluted by sporting and social failures, as well as some bullying at school). He believed that New College had acted only out of a political dislike for his outspoken reactionary opinions – his 'strong Conservatism and old-fashioned churchmanship'[9] – at a time when each of the Oxford colleges tended to rally round its own particular well-defined (and self-perpetuating) corporate position on the political spectrum.

Oman had certainly hoped to complete a 'Wykehamist hat-trick' by graduating from Winchester to the New College junior common room, and thence to its senior common room; but when that last path was barred to him, he very quickly found an attractive alternative in All Souls College, in October 1883, where he won a still more prestigious fellowship than even New College could offer. In so doing he also subconsciously transferred his personal allegiance from Bishop Wykeham (1324–1404), to Archbishop Henry Chichele (1364–1443), the co-founder of All Souls – who had also been educated at Winchester and New College, thereby making the young Oman's personal transition all the easier. Although he maintained strong teaching links with New College, there can be no doubt that the remainder of Oman's life would be spent in the service of Chichele. He became the deputy Chichele professor of modern history in 1900, and the following year he named his only son Charles Chichele Oman – presumably to the great embarrassment of the latter. He was blocked from the full chair until 1905 only by the irritating longevity of the deaf and debilitated incumbent, Montagu Burrows;[10] but he did, meanwhile, loyally refuse an offer of the more senior Regius chair of modern history. Thereafter he remained very solidly based – or rather 'entrenched' – in All Souls until his dying day.

It is worth remembering that the original Archbishop Chichele had been active in fighting against both the French and the Lollards

– the external and the internal enemy – which is an association that must have appealed to Oman's deep English conservatism. It is doubtless no accident that in 1906 he wrote what he called a 'research' book (as opposed to a 'manual', or digest of other people's research) on *The Great Revolt of 1381*.[11] More directly to the point, however, were the many allurements of All Souls as a college that was entirely free from undergraduates or even, after a fellow's first year in residence, any actual requirement to hang around the place at all. Oman tells us that when he was first appointed there were no more than half a dozen fellows in residence on weekdays, but that some two dozen more would come in from their professional careers 'in the outside world' (normally London) at weekends.[12] This was clearly an ideal environment for a hard-working academic who would not find his wife until 1892,[13] but who still wished to keep in touch with a world that was rather wider than Oxford.

The plain fact is that Oman was the purest and inkiest type of 'inky swot'. He was socially awkward: 'no good at games',[14] no good at parties or dances,[15] and not even any good at facing up to the general public. When in 1883 he was thinking about his options for a career, he reports with admirable candour that he was not attracted to the Law because he might have to deal with dishonest clients. He felt no calling to the Church because his parishioners might prove to be beyond spiritual redemption; and he had no desire to go into politics because of the 'nauseous preliminary work of propitiating the great, and canvassing a constituency'.[16] When he did finally enter parliament, he did so only because election to his specialised university seat required no such distasteful exposure to people from other walks of life. He does not tell us precisely why he declined a perfectly good offer of a job in the civil service; but we may infer from his repeated pleas for freedom to speak his own mind[17] that he simply did not want to become a member of any closed hierarchy that might try to impose restrictions upon his opinions. He had already run foul of the fellows of New College over this issue, so he was more than delighted to find the full liberty he craved – a liberty without responsibility – in the bosom of Chichele's foundation.

Oman felt he could use this new unfettered liberty in two different ways. The first was to preach reactionary doctrines that were unfashionable at the time, in the fields of national politics, church politics, and, especially, Oxford academic politics. He believed his beloved university was going to the dogs before his eyes, what with the abolition of the 'Rudiments of Religion' entrance test; the increase in female members (whom he saw as 'Greekless school mistresses', good for filling seats in lectures, but not for putting anything back into the university); the 'Balliol' tendency to attract students from far flung corners of the globe (in this

Oman was certainly exhibiting racism); Dr Jowett's encouragement of student theatricals (worse than athletics for wasting time and producing 'self sufficiency' – presumably he meant 'for destroying team spirit'); and the multiplication of new pseudo-subjects that did not require a background in the classics (*eg* Modern Languages; English Language and Literature, and 'Politics, Philosophy and Economics'). Oman believed all this was pandering to those who lacked culture, or the money to buy a good private education, and so it was watering down the old purity of the institution.[18] Of particular interest to the present author, he was scandalised by the introduction of the D.Phil. degree, since it allowed 'degree-hunting persons' who were complete outsiders to the university, to present doctoral dissertations, based on research conducted in distant places such as 'Paris or Quebec', on subjects so arcane that no-one in Oxford would be qualified to examine them. They could thereby win impressive letters to put after their names, while effectively by-passing the degree-giving university itself, almost totally.[19]

Oman was constitutionally incapable of sympathising with 'Progressists', 'Academic Liberals', 'Modernists', and proponents of 'the Wider Oneness' (whatever that may have been), and he pursued a campaign against them throughout his entire life in Oxford. As librarian of the Union in 1883 he was criticised for 'not buying left wing books in sufficient numbers',[20] and he went on to help found, and then to edit, a humorous right wing journal, the *Oxford Review*. He inevitably became involved in the so-called 'Non Placet' Society, which opposed all changes in the university, but which seems to have accepted final defeat around 1900. However, after 1919 Oman revived his campaigning through his parliamentary seat. He gloated that by winning it and being re-elected four times over, he had demonstrated that a majority of university members still supported his views, even though the majority of its decision-makers had left them behind many decades earlier.

The freedom that Oman found at All Souls also enabled him to strike out in a second direction, which was to write the books that he wanted to write, rather than simply the 'manuals' (or school text-books) that publishers asked him for. He subscribed to the admirable principle that 'accumulating merit',[21] rather than making money, was the true reason for working as an historian – although, of course, he could afford to adopt this stance since he enjoyed an adequate salary for teaching just twenty-seven hours per week. He had found that a higher workload became too stressful to allow him to write, and on medical advice he also helped to calm his stress by smoking cigarettes between tutorials.[22] From 1907 he also enjoyed the happy benefits of an independent income, from his parents' legacy, so he was always able to find sufficient leisure time to exercise his energetic pen.

Oman produced a long series of 'manuals' on ancient history and more modern English history, some of which were extremely successful, including *A History of Greece from the Earliest Times to the Macedonian Conquest* (1890), *The Byzantine Empire* (1892), *Europe 476-918* (1893), *A History of England* (1895), *England in the Nineteenth Century* (1899), and *Seven Roman Statesmen of the Later Republic* (1902). He was perhaps lucky to be a member of what was only the second generation of professional British historians, the subject having been founded by the likes of Stubbs at Oxford, Seeley at Cambridge, and Gardiner at London, who had all been born around thirty or forty years before Oman. His own generation, born in the 1850s and 1860s, included such figures as Firth, Armstrong, Lodge, and Tout. Each of these two generations had found it was both easy and necessary to write books which explained wide areas of the past that had never been covered systematically before. They were operating in what was essentially virgin territory, and filling in vast swathes of historical knowledge that no one had previously bothered to turn into 'manuals'. They felt it was their professional duty to write such works, which might today be considered elementary or even mercenary, simply because nothing of the sort had existed before.

Nevertheless, Oman was also able to indulge his own personal interests in many and varied directions. *Warwick the Kingmaker* (1891) was his first work specifically designed as a 'research' book, while the *History of the Peninsular War* would be a later and much greater example of a similar initiative. He was drawn to the latter subject mainly because he had long been a wargamer, an admirer of military tattoos, and a student of Napier – and upon his arrival in All Souls he had been delighted to find that the Warden was not only a Unionist in politics, but also the grandson of no less than two of Wellington's brigadiers.[23] It was particularly stimulating to discover that the All Souls' college library, the Codrington – of which Oman was destined to be the devoted librarian for some thirty years – contained extensive manuscript material from the Peninsula, notably in the despatches of the diplomat Sir Charles Vaughan.

Before he settled on the Peninsula, however, Oman's long-standing interest in military things had already led him into competing for – and winning – an Oxford university essay prize, with an account of *The Art of War in the Middle Ages*. This broke new ground in a number of ways, especially after it had been published as a book in 1885,[24] and it firmly established its author as a leading military historian. It was dazzlingly encyclopaedic, an apparently authoritative – and, indeed, 'monumental'[25] – overview, and it preceded its main competitor, Hans Delbrück's *History of the Art of War in the Framework of Political History*,[26] by some fifteen years. In the English-speaking world Oman's work held centre stage for the best part of a century, particularly after a significant (if excessively hurried) updating and expansion to two volumes in 1924. In its field it was even more influential than his

History of the Peninsular War, and although it was always questioned by some, it has been fully superseded only in the past generation. Its main message seemed to be, firstly, that set-piece battles were more important than sieges; secondly, that almost all of medieval warfare could be explained by the supremacy of knightly heavy cavalry; and thirdly, that these knights operated only as anarchic individualists, unbroken to corporate discipline or to any higher science of tactics. We know today that none of those three theories is correct – but they were all accepted enthusiastically by the late-Victorians, and right up to the global intellectual revolution of the 1960s. The bubble finally burst around 1966 when, among others, John Beeler attacked the proponents of such ideas for 'misinterpretation, distortion of evidence, ignorance, or any combination of the three.' He noted that 'such a synthesis as Oman's is especially vulnerable because its vastness of scope has served to discourage any attempt to supplant the only comprehensive work in English on medieval warfare'.[27] Indeed, something similar could probably be said today of the great Peninsular *History* itself.

The idea that medieval warfare depended on great battles in the open field was particularly attractive to those who had been reared on Napoleonic doctrines of decisive manoeuvre and the annihilating 'victory without a morrow'. It was the mindset with which Europe rushed into combat in 1914 and, even despite its deep disappointments on that occasion, again in 1938–41. It would need later 'cold' wars, proxy wars, guerrilla wars, and stand-off nuclear deterrence to reveal the true value of the indecisive strategies that had underpinned so much of medieval military thinking, and it was only then that Oman's cheerful anachronisms would be revealed. Even though Delbrück had argued in an opposite sense – and Oman's own *Peninsular War* showed plentiful examples of armies avoiding battles, or losing battles but nevertheless winning wars – the 'management' and 'limitation' of violence were not yet concepts with which his generation was either familiar or comfortable. It is only by long and painful experience that we have once again come to understand the advantages that may flow from such approaches.

As for the chivalric ideal of 'the man on horseback', that too was surely a Victorian aspiration which continued to resonate universally until it was finally relegated to the backwaters of the hunting field or the children's gymkhana by the onset of mechanisation. Oman believed it was born in the battle of Adrianople in 378 AD and ended at Crécy in 1346,[28] although he appears to have paid but scant attention to the many important achievements of soldiers on foot during the intervening years – many of which he himself documented in his *Art of War*.[29] Doubtless he was right that 'pure' infantry normally lacked cohesion in the open field, at least until the

Swiss re-invented drill in the fourteenth century; but that did not prevent him from wilfully over-emphasising the alleged power of the mounted knight. Even the Normans had often dismounted to fight, as had the Anglo-Saxons and many others besides.[30] They had also mixed archers with well-armoured men, light troops with heavy, and field fortifications with both. For all medieval soldiers, true tactical efficiency surely sprang from 'the intelligent combination of all arms', rather than simply from the unsubtle head-down mounted charge.

By the same token Oman again fell into over-simplified stereotypes when he assumed that medieval commanders acted without discipline, method, or science. They did not simply charge forward and bash at everything in sight, but actually displayed some perfectly sophisticated military thinking, with an understanding not only of all-arms co-operation but also of such things as feints, deceptions, and the proper use of reserves.[31] Equally, their building of castles was not random, anarchic, and local, as Oman seemed to believe, but systematic and strategic at the highest level of planning for national defence.[32] Medieval commanders studied warfare very carefully indeed, even if they did not have the benefit of 'classical' strategic texts by the likes of Clausewitz or Jomini. Hence we can say that they did in fact have an 'art of war' even if, paradoxically, Oman's book with that title generally tends to deny such a concept.

Overall, it is fair to say that Oman's *Art of War in the Middle Ages* was almost as great an achievement as his Peninsular *History*: but it has, alas, withstood the acid test of time rather less well – and, in fact, less well than his solid 1930s work on the 'art of war' of the fifteenth and sixteenth centuries.[33] We should, nevertheless, remember that when the *Art of War in the Middle Ages* first appeared it was a glorious product indeed – and it certainly still has some value today. Even its fiercest modern critics concede that the scope of Oman's research and opinions was prodigious,[34] and that he was indeed absolutely right about some of the subjects that he tackled.[35] Hence it is clear that his work in this field can never be ignored, and for all its defects it must still stand as one of the greatest legacies that he has left us.

Oman could not, of course, keep his political orientation out of his historical writing, and so we find a series of denunciations of Whig, Liberal, and Progressive historians scattered throughout his works. He was particularly bitter against J.R. Green, a prominent senior historian of England, who had made the unforgivable mistake of opposing 'drum and trumpet' history, on the grounds that 'war plays a small part in the real story of European nations, and in that of England its part is smaller than any.'[36] Oman waxed totally incandescent at this barefaced falsehood, although his perfectly justifiable demonstration that wars are in fact extremely important did not really say much about just why the 'drum and trumpet' school should know the best way to study them. The defence he put forward was merely that events were moulded by 'great men' (*ie* Carlyle's 'Heroes'), rather than by more democratic 'forces'; and that important events were themselves cataclysmic rather than evolutionary; unpredictable rather than inevitable. He did not stop to consider that the truth probably lay somewhere between those two extremes, nor that the best military history should analyse the muskets and bayonets rather than the drums and trumpets, and the middle-management decision-makers rather than merely the 'great men'.

Perhaps Oman's problem may be traced to his life-long suspicion of 'Philosophy', which in pre-Freudian days he sometimes confused with 'psychology'.[37] He had apparently suffered some unfortunate brushes with the Greek philosophers during his cramming for classical examinations at school and university, and had never properly appreciated their musings as a solid academic subject, let alone as a sound basis for historical or political analysis. He liked to think that he approached the classics from a more concrete historical and archaeological (especially numismatic) direction, just as in modern history he insisted that any high-faluting theory should be solidly underpinned by facts rather than by pretentious waffle about 'tendencies'.

Yet while deriding the theoretical constructs and prejudices of others, Oman was very happy to admit to plenty of 'philosophies' of his own. This went far beyond his habitual unsubstantiated mockery of Spanish generals, but extended to the very heart of his writing style, and, indeed, the style he recommended to his students. In essence he told them to deal in 'ideas not facts', while he himself made sure that he put some sort of 'message' or 'moral' into each of his books.[38] In the case of the *Peninsular War* he said his central purpose was to tone down Napier's worship of Napoleon, while also emphasising the support given to Wellington by his home government.[39] He even confessed to a particular type of vanity that must surely motivate many other writers – 'the pleasure of seeing that I could put such views as I pleased into print, and be certain of their being widely circulated'.[40] It is at this point that we are reminded of the essential irresponsibility, or at least subjectivity, of all historical writing.

If we probe Oman's own subjectivity a little more deeply, we may suggest that his politico-philosophical extremism was perhaps explained by his distaste for – and even fear of – the rough and tumble of the outside world. Possibly by way of compensation, he also indulged in some distinctly other-worldly pastimes. His almost obsessional churchgoing and sermon-tasting may surely be counted as one of them, although his role in founding the Oxford Phantasmagorical Society ('The Phas') in 1879 doubtless appeared somewhat less conventional at the time. He was its president for five years and took part in many earnest overnight investigations of haunted houses, as well as interrogations of those who purported to have seen ghosts. Fortunately for his reputation, he and most of his fellow-researchers eventually concluded that they were personally immune to psychic experiences, even though many of the people they met were apparently receptive to them. Oman did not, however, offer any explanation for the violent gymnastics conducted by an ouija board one night in Hertford college, which he witnessed with his own eyes.[41]

Yet another interest which transported Oman into 'another world' was his military history. This may be traced back to his earliest years, when he heard his father's vivid stories of a terrifying year under blockade in his bungalow during the Indian mutiny of 1857. Oman also had an abiding memory of Paris in 1868, where he saw Napoleon III and the Prince Imperial at the head of their soldiers; just as in 1870 he saw the *Chasseurs à Pied* at Boulogne, on their way to the battle of Sedan. By the end of 1876 he had read Creasy's *Decisive Battles* and had visited the field of Waterloo. His military interests were already well launched, and at seventeen years of age he was ready to take an active day-by day interest in the news from the Balkans during the Russo-Turkish conflict of 1877, which he regarded as his own 'first war'.[42]

The 'serious' side of Oman's military interest is well known through his writings; but his three hobbies associated with it are less familiar. The first of these was wargaming, which 'remained one of my favourite amusements for many a year'.[43] The Oxford Kriegsspiel club had been founded by Spenser Wilkinson in 1873 as part of the volunteer corps (later Officers' Training Corps, or OTC),[44] and it continued to flourish until the Great War. By that time Oman had graduated through the ranks of company, battalion, and Division commander, to the lofty status of umpire and problem-setter. He could imagine a Fuzzy-Wuzzy rising on the Ridgeway near Wantage as easily as he could conjure up a British Expeditionary Force refighting the battle of Sadowa; and he could refight Chesney's imagined 'Battle of Dorking' as readily as he could update the real 1644 scenario around Salisbury and Devizes, or realign the Salamanca campaign of 1812 to fit into the terrain between the Severn and Oxford. The February 1909 game against the Inns of Court was particularly elaborate and prestigious, although regrettably the Oxford team contrived to snatch defeat from the jaws of victory.[45] Oman was also involved in the 'Martians' military discussion group about the present and future state of warfare, and he participated in the OTC's staff rides and other tactical exercises.

Secondly, he became involved in the organisation of pageants, which were surely the Victorian predecessors of what we would today call 're-enactments'. He had always had an admiration for military bands, tattoos, drill parades, and historical pageantry in

The Oman Family

(Orkney origins as, variously, 'Omand', 'Omond', and finally 'Oman')

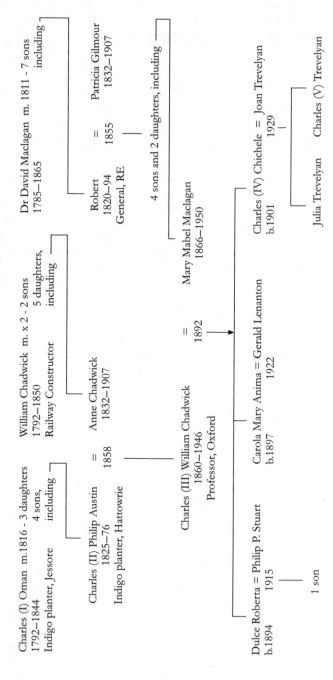

Charles (I) Oman m.1816 - 3 daughters
1792–1844   4 sons,
Indigo planter, Jessore   including

William Chadwick m. x 2 - 2 sons
1792–1850   5 daughters,
Railway Constructor   including

Dr David Maclagan m. 1811 - 7 sons
1785–1865   including

Robert   =   Patricia Gilmour
1820–94   1855   1832–1907
General, RE

4 sons and 2 daughters, including

Charles (II) Philip Austin   =   Anne Chadwick
1825–76   1858   1832–1907
Indigo planter, Hattowrie

Mary Mabel Maclagan
1866–1950

Charles (III) William Chadwick
1860–1946
Professor, Oxford

Carola Mary Anima = Gerald Lenanton
b.1897   1922
=
1892

Charles (IV) Chichele = Joan Trevelyan
b.1901   1929

Dulce Roberta = Philip P. Stuart
b.1894   1915

Julia Trevelyan   Charles (V) Trevelyan

1 son

general, which was equal and opposite to his dislike of plays and the theatre, apart from 'properly produced Shakespearean plays ... and some opera'.[46] What he hated was the individuality, conceit, and implied personal intimacy of starred actors, so his preference was always for a grand spectacle in which the individual was submerged in the mass. He wanted the 'triumph of colour, melody, and rhythmical action',[47] rather than the fancy 'psychology' that might be encountered in Dr Jowett's New Theatre. In fact he himself only once took a role as an actor in a pageant – as Edward the Confessor, in Winchester in 1884 – and thereafter he confined himself to writing scenes for pageants and advising on them, especially as an assistant to his distant relative, the gifted director Frank Lascelles. These events especially proliferated between 1901 and 1911, although Oman was always conscious that they were not universally admired: 'This sort of activity may seem rather unacademic – at least my high-brow contemporaries somewhat contemned it ... [they] were inclined to think the venture frivolous.'[48]

Oman is indeed still being condemned for his military 'frivolity', or at least for his lack of service in any army, by those who believe that only old soldiers can be competent to write about military affairs. To this the clear riposte must be that although military historians may be amateurs in living the military life, they are nevertheless professionals in studying and analysing it. One does not have to be an insect in order to be an entomologist or, as Oman himself put it rather more diplomatically, 'it is no more right to hand over the study of military history to professional soldiers alone than it would be to permit no-one but lawyers to touch constitutional history ... It is not the soldier alone who should know the outlines of the past history of his art.'[49] The truth of this assertion was proved in the debate about the German casualties suffered in the battle of the Somme (1916), when Oman was able to demonstrate convincingly that Lieutenant-Colonel Winston Churchill, sometime First Lord of the Admiralty, had set the figure far too low, while the army's Official Historian, the eccentric Brigadier Sir James Edmonds, had set it far too high. Unlike them, Oman made a careful study of the losses reported by each German regiment at the time, rather than of the lesser totals admitted by higher formations – which Churchill had merely accepted, whereas Edmonds had routinely multiplied them by 130 per cent. Hence Oman was able to show that the Germans had lost at least as many men as the British.[50] This finding has never been accepted by believers in allied incompetence on the Somme, but neither has it ever been seriously tested or scrutinised by anyone. It is probably the closest to the truth. To help him in this work Oman had, of course, the benefit of twenty years' experience studying the Peninsular OBs and casualties, as well as the Waterloo casualties which he had analysed in the *English Historical Review* in 1904 and 1906.

Thirdly, Oman travelled regularly to Paris, Italy, and Scotland, and occasionally also to Germany, Switzerland, and the Netherlands. Eventually he came to base an important part of his holiday travel and tourism upon his Peninsular interests, although it is relevant to note that he first went to Spain only in the summer of 1903,[51] which was *after* the first volume of the *History* had been published, and perilously close to the second going to press. This means that he took to archival research in Madrid, and to battlefield touring, only rather late in the day. Admittedly, in 1903 he did visit his fellow 'definitive' historian Arteche y Moro, and he did write some of his account of Talavera on the field itself; but we must remember that he was able to visit by no means all of the battlefields he described in his book, and his exposure to the Iberian archives was necessarily very limited. Of course, it was not easy to travel in those days, especially for one who, although in theory he had liberty to depart from Oxford at any time, made it a strict lifetime rule to remain in residence during all the university terms, apart from his war work in London – at the Press Bureau and the Foreign Office – in 1914–18.[52]

Oman had very many other interests, not least his wife Mary, the youngest daughter of General Robert Maclagan RE – who was himself the son of a distinguished surgeon from the Peninsular War, and brother of an archbishop of York. They married in 1892, and she must have been as patient, tactful, and self-effacing as she was fragile-looking.[53] She suffered a miscarriage in 1893, followed by the successful birth of three children between 1894 and 1901: Dulce, Carola, and Charles. Of the three, Dulce turned out to be relatively normal, while Carola comes across as assertively hyper-active and Charles, who had a stammer, seems to have been somewhat repressed – not only by his father's imperative expectations, but also by serious bullying at Winchester.[54] Both Carola and Charles became noteworthy historians; but it was the former who would be more widely known, not least for her very substantial biography of Sir John Moore.

The Oman dynasty eventually came to inhabit Frewin Hall, a very grand city-centre house that had once been the Oxford lodgings of the young Edward VII, and which dated as far back as Norman times. They lived in a world of privilege, if not of excessive wealth, and were fully accepted among the highest society that Oxford had to offer. Carola's memoirs of her childhood are packed with family visits to or from all the most famous scholars of the day, many of whose names were still legendary in the Oxford of the 1960s, even if they may be fading over the horizon today. The military historian C.T. Atkinson was a particularly close associate (and wargaming companion) of 'The Prof', as his children nicknamed him after he won his chair; but such figures as Dr Spooner, Rudyard Kipling, and the great Sir George Curzon, Viceroy of India, also play a part in the story.

Sir Charles' life must therefore be counted a resounding success, despite his early fears that incompetence in games and a somewhat questionable command of Greek grammar would prove to be insuperable obstacles to his progress. His life was sheltered and in many ways very narrowly academic; but at least he made the most of it, spreading his energy, inspiration and sense of fun - not to mention his startling prejudices and blind spots - into many different historical periods and history-related activities. He made a major mark upon his own age, and is still a figure of importance today. It is only a pity that he never did succeed in finding a way to stop the railway company misdirecting his luggage to Oban...[55]

Notes

1. *Dictionary of National Biography* (*DNB*), 1941-50, p.643, article by A.T.P. Williams, Bishop of Winchester, published 1950.

2. Only graduates of the university were entitled to a vote in the elections to this seat. Apart from that, Oman was also 'elected F.B.A. [Fellow of the British Academy] in 1905, served as president of the Royal Historical and Numismatic societies and of the Royal Archaeological Institute; he became an honorary fellow of New College in 1936 and received the honorary degrees of D.C.L. (Oxford, 1926) and LL.D. (Edinburgh, 1911, and Cambridge, 1927).' *DNB*, pp.643-4.

3. C.W.C. Oman, *Memories of Victorian Oxford and of some Early Years* (London, 1941), pp.54-7.

4. A.L. Rowse, *Historians I Have Known* (London, 1995), p.47.

5. *Ibid* p.52.

6. In our own day one thinks of such figures as Alan Clark; but *cf* Oman's own (actually misplaced) remarks about the Duke of Wellington's eventual soldierly impatience with democracy in the 1830s, and his desire to become a military dictator, in *Studies in the Napoleonic Wars* (London, 1929), pp.272-4.

7. 'Wykehamical' from William of Wykeham or Wickham, who was a spectacular politician and Bishop of Winchester in the fourteenth century. He founded (and linked together) New College, Oxford, and the college in Winchester which later became a leading public school. Hence the alumni of the Winchester school, and the endowed scholars of New College (or like Oman, both), were called 'Wykehamists'.

8. Oman, *Memories of Victorian Oxford*, pp.109-10.

9. *DNB*, p.643.

10. Oman, *Memories of Victorian Oxford*, pp.258-9. Oman's daughter Carola betrays a little more of the family's impatience at Burrows' continuance in post than 'The Prof' himself does, in her *An Oxford Childhood* (Hodder & Stoughton, London, 1976), p.89. Yet it must also be admitted that when his own time came, 'The Prof' proved to be no less stubbornly anxious to remain in his chair than had his immediate predecessor.

11. Oman, *Memories of Victorian Oxford*, p.163. See also pp.154-8 for Oman's distinction between 'manuals' (or 'textbooks') and originally researched books.

12. *Ibid* p.116.

13. The word 'celibate' is scattered liberally around Oman's descriptions of his peers, and indeed a statutory requirement for celibacy had been lifted from many Oxford fellowships only a comparatively short time before he joined the university. He sometimes makes a slight distinction with 'unmarried'. However, when he uses the word 'gay' it is in the only sense for it that was known at the time, and he himself does appear to have been heterosexual, albeit somewhat uncomfortable in the society of most women.

14. Oman, *Memories of Victorian Oxford*, p.52; *cf* Carola Oman, *An Oxford Childhood*, p.174.

15. Oman, *Memories of Victorian Oxford*, p.137.

16. *Ibid* pp.131-5.

17. He wanted to 'vote in a minority of one'; *ibid* p.134.

18. *Ibid* pp.232-44. His own family money derived not only from his father's indigo factory, but from his maternal grandfather, William Chadwick, who built many railway lines both in Britain and overseas.

19. *Ibid* pp.241-2. Fortunately the present author, although admittedly conducting his D.Phil. researches in Paris, was not a 'carpet-bagger' in the way Oman described - but he knows a few who were.

20. *Ibid* pp.107-8.

21. *Ibid* p.160.

22. *Ibid* p.136.

23. They were Anson and Pack; *ibid* pp.119-20. See p.14 for Oman's toy gunnery of peas against tin soldiers at the age of eight, and pp.108-9 for his later love of the Oxford University Kriegsspiel Club. This may also be pursued in Professor John Cook Wilson, *Statement and Inference, and other philosophical papers*; edited by A.S.L. Farquharson (Oxford, 1926), pp.xiv, xlvlii and lxiv.

24. Lothian Prize essay awarded March 1884; first published by Blackwells, Oxford, 1885; new and greatly expanded Methuen edition 1898; further expanded and revised Methuen edition, 2 vols, 1924 (reprinted Greenhill, London, 1991); new revision edited by John H. Beeler (Ithaca, 1953).

25. Stephen Morillo, *Warfare under the Anglo-Norman kings* (Woodbridge, 1994), p.151. I am very grateful to Matthew Bennett for drawing my attention to this and other modern reassessments of Oman as a medieval military historian.

26. *Geschichte der Kriegskunst im rahmen der politischen geschichte* (Berlin, 1900). See discussion in Gordon A. Craig, 'Delbrück: the Military Historian' in Peter Paret, ed., *Makers of Modern Strategy from Machiavelli to the Nuclear Age* (Princeton, 1986), pp.326-53.

27. John H. Beeler, *Warfare in England 1066-1189* (New York, 1966), p.1.

28. During the centuries after Crécy the 'knightly flame' presumably burned more brightly among the less disciplined cavalry forces - *eg* Prince Rupert's in the Civil War, or Wellington's in the Peninsular War - than among more carefully regulated and ordered ones, such as the Ironsides or the KGL cavalry, respectively.

29. Beeler, *Warfare in England*, p.1. We are reminded that Oman also documented very many examples of Wellington's men defeating the French by shock action rather than firepower, and yet he persisted in seeing the

latter as the norm and the former as only the exception.

30. Morillo, *op cit.* pp.151–62.

31. J.F. Verbruggen, *The Art of Warfare in Western Europe during the Middle Ages* (Brussels, 1954; English translation Woodbridge, 1997), p.2. On p.256 he castigates Oman for describing Bouvines (1214) as just 'a vast tourney' of individual knights, rather than the result of tactical manoeuvres that it actually was.

32. Beeler, *op.cit.* pp.50–5.

33. 'The Art of War in the Fifteenth Century' in *Cambridge Medieval History*, vol.VIII (Cambridge, 1936); and, particularly fresh, interesting, and still useful, *A History of the Art of War in the Sixteenth Century* (Oxford, 1937).

34. Oman was deeply familiar with the medieval chronicles and comparable texts, but was perhaps less diligent in his search of archival sources than he would be for his Peninsular studies.

35. For example, Beeler, *op.cit.* pp.91, 113, for Oman's accuracy on, respectively, the Scottish formation at the battle of the Standard (1138), and the location of the first battle of Lincoln (1141).

36. Oman, *Memories of Victorian Oxford*, p.161; compare his 'Historical Perspective - Man's Outlook on History', and 'A Defence of Military History' in *Studies in the Napoleonic Wars*, pp.1–36 (see especially around p.29); and 'A Plea for Military History' in his *On the Writing of History* (Methuen, London, 1939).

37. Oman was indiscriminate in his condemnation of any word or phrase in which he suspected the dreaded 'P' word was lurking, as in 'D.Phil.', 'P.P.E.', 'the philosophy of history' etc. One is reminded of Baroness Thatcher's apparently similar animus against any word she thought might trace its lineage, however remotely, from 'Society' or 'Social'.

38. Oman, *Memories of Victorian Oxford*, pp.150, 165.

39. *Ibid* pp.162–4. We can say he was rather more successful in debunking Napoleon than in rehabilitating Lord Liverpool; *cf* René Chartrand's point below that however many supplies the British government may have sent to Wellington, it seems to have sent remarkably few to the Spanish guerrillas.

40. Oman, *Memories of Victorian Oxford*, p.165.

41. *Ibid* p.231. See also pp.ix, 220–30. Various forms of spiritualism or interest in the occult were clandestinely quite common, and even respectable, during Oman's times; *cf* the career of that other noted military opinion-former, J.F.C. Fuller.

42. *Ibid* p.159; and see p.129 for his resulting party-piece singing about the exploits of 'Abdullah Bulbul Ameer'. For his early exposure to high military affairs, see pp.17–18, 56, 71.

43. *Ibid* p.109.

44. Luvaas, *Education of an Army*, pp.254–5. Wilkinson would progress from Oxford to found the Manchester Tactical Society in 1881, returning to Oxford in 1909 as the first Chichele professor of military history.

45. I gained sight of the minutes of the Oxford University Wargame Club for 1908–14 through Don Featherstone's *Wargamer's Newsletter* in 1970. See also Oman, *Memories of Victorian Oxford*; and Professor John Cook Wilson, *op.cit.*

46. Oman, *Memories of Victorian Oxford*, p.253, and see pp.254–7 for his

main thoughts on pageants; *cf* Carola Oman, *Oxford Childhood*, pp.179–81.

47. Oman, *Memories of Victorian Oxford*, p.255.

48. *Ibid* pp.ix, 254. A similar reaction, in relation to both wargaming and re-enactment, persists to the present day among the stupider type of pompous military history snob.

49. Oman, *Studies in the Napoleonic Wars*, pp.33–4. See also p.29 for his view that it is 'unphilosophic and unworthy of the self-respecting [general] historian' to abdicate coverage of military affairs to the (mere) military specialist.

50. Oman, 'The German Losses on the Somme, July–December 1916' in Lord Sydenham of Combe, ed., *'The World Crisis' by Winston Churchill, a Criticism* (London, 1927). I am very grateful to John Hussey for this information, who adds that the Somme volumes of the German Official History, *Der Weltkrieg 1914-18,* published in the 1930s, do not seem to undermine Oman's view.

51. Oman, *Memories of Victorian Oxford*, pp.189–92; and Carola Oman, *op.cit.* p.75. Oman gave a fuller account of his travels – including three risings or revolutions – in his book *Things I Have Seen* (London, 1933).

52. Such is the nature of Whitehall and the Palace that it was his wartime propaganda-writing and intelligence analyses which won him his knighthood (KBE), not his historical work.

53. Apart from her many other labours, poor Mary was recruited for the indexing of all seven volumes of the *History*. She was indirectly thanked in every preface – but never actually named!

54. Carola Oman, *op.cit. passim.*

55. *Ibid* p.49.

Chapter 3

The French Army in the Peninsula

by James R. Arnold

The quality of the Peninsular Army

In *A History of the Peninsular War*, Sir Charles Oman introduces us
to the French army in the second section of his first volume. In less
than five pages he briskly details the character and organisation of
the 1808 army that entered Spain. This was indeed a woeful array of
second-rate units; conscript 'legions of reserve', ad hoc 'provisional
regiments', *'regiments de marche'* who were the off-scourings of
the dépôts in southern France. Along with 14,000 foreign infantry,
an overconfident Napoleon expected that they would be sufficient
to conquer the Peninsula. Marshal Moncey's retreat from Valencia
and General Dupont's disaster at Bailén proved him wrong. So
Napoleon personally conducted a second army into the Peninsula in
the autumn of 1808. They were, Oman writes, 'composed of his
finest old regiments from the Rhine and Elbe, the flower of the
victors of Jena and Friedland.'[1]

Excluding the Imperial Guard, Oman lists some 284 infantry
battalions among the eight corps present in Spain in November
1808. Ninety-seven of these belonged to regiments that had fought
at either Jena, or Friedland, or both. Twenty-eight more battalions
belonged to regiments that earned battle honours during the Ulm-
Austerlitz campaign of 1805. However, at least eleven of these were
fourth battalions which had been raised the previous year and had
never seen combat. In other words, out of the entire army only forty
per cent of the infantry had any association with the *Grande
Armée*. Oman's comment about 'finest old regiments' is misleading.
While Napoleon did bring experienced veterans into the field in
1808, the majority of the infantry remained second rate.

The difference between the *Grande Armée* veterans and the
others is described by General (soon to be Marshal) Suchet. Suchet's
Division was a veteran formation that had trained at the camp at
Boulogne and fought in the campaigns of 1805–7. In the Peninsula it
served in Marshal Mortier's V Corps and comprised the 17th *Légère*
and 34th, 40th, 64th, and 88th *Ligne*. Suchet wrote of them that they
'resembled in all respects a Roman legion; animated by one spirit,

united under a chief to whom it was strongly attached, it had grown to be a well disciplined, a skilful, and an indefatigable body of men.' In contrast, when Suchet transferred to the III Corps he found it 'wholly a stranger' to discipline and military spirit. The III Corps contained two veteran regiments, but the balance of its men were conscripts, 'young soldiers ... in need of fresh lessons of discipline and experience', hastily organised into new regiments.[2] In addition most of the experienced artillerymen had been recalled to Germany to confront the Austrians, which left the corps' field artillery crewed by foot-soldiers.

Suchet joined the III Corps while it was manoeuvring to cover the French base of Saragossa in May 1809. The corps fell into near panic at the approach of a Spanish army, and Suchet resolved to make an example. A drummer had spread the alarm by claiming that Spanish cavalry had ridden down the 2nd Regiment of the Vistula, and when Suchet realised this he ordered the drummer tried and executed in front of the entire army. He then set the corps to drill intensively over the next three weeks. There were frequent reviews, much target practice, and large-scale manoeuvres. In other words the corps had an abbreviated camp of instruction like that of the *Grande Armée*. The reward came on 15 June at the battle of Maria. Suchet describes how a battalion of the 114th *Ligne*, a newly-raised unit full of young soldiers, formed column and charged to gain time for the balance of the corps to prepare. Later the 114th and the 115th, which were deployed in line, formed columns and climbed the heights with shouldered muskets to charge the Spanish centre. Next an entire battalion of the 5th *Légère* dispersed into skirmish order to lead a charge of the 14th *Ligne*. The French cavalry then rapidly switched fronts to perform a passage of the lines through the infantry and deliver a decisive charge. The battle is another illustration of French tactical flexibility. In passing, it is worth noting that Oman provides a good description of the campaign. He cites Suchet's *Memoirs* and even mentions the execution of the drummer, and offers a nice map, but omits any mention of French tactical formations.

Suchet was a conscientious officer who worked hard to improve his corps' efficiency. Indeed, he was the only general elevated to the rank of marshal for service in the Peninsula. Less diligent officers did not attend so carefully to their soldiers' discipline and training. This was particularly harmful when one considers the decline in French troop quality during the Peninsular conflict. In the decisive years 1808 to 1812, annual conscription ranged from 181,000 to 217,000,[3] and when France was at peace outside of the Peninsula in 1810 and 1811 the majority of these conscripts served in Spain and Portugal. Their level of training was much inferior to that of the first *Grande Armée*.

Consider the experience of Phillipe Gille.[4] Mobilised in France in 1808, Gille apparently did not even receive his musket until he arrived at the Spanish border. There he joined a provisional conscript unit, crossed into Spain, and soon engaged in combat with guerrillas. Eventually his ad hoc formation merged with other similar units to join Dupont's ill-fated army. Near the Spanish town of Jaén they faced their first opposition from Spanish regulars. In spite of their inexperience, the conscripts formed line, advanced upon the Spanish with trailed arms, received a close-range volley, charged at the bayonet, and routed their foes. Three points deserve emphasis from Gille's account: the conscripts entered combat virtually untrained; they formed line for combat; and they did not attempt a musketry duel but relied upon shock action.

In addition to the influx of poorly-trained conscripts, troop quality further declined as veterans suffered some of the nearly 100,000 casualties sustained in the Peninsula in 1810–11. The consequences could be foreseen as early as 1809. Reporting on the battle of Essling, General Savary wrote about how the dense French formations suffered from Austrian fire. He contrasted their inability to manoeuvre with *Grande Armée* veterans and mused how things would have been better 'if, instead of troops consisting of war levies, we had opposed to them such soldiers as those of the camp of Boulogne, which we might easily have moved in any direction, and made to deploy under the enemy's fire without any danger of their being thrown into disorder'.[5]

French replacement policy was ill-calculated to maximise the soldiers' potential. Depleted units sent cadres to reorganise at the regimental dépôts in France. Because there were not enough veteran officers – consider that while officer schools turned out about 4000 graduates from 1802 to 1815, this number was insufficient to meet the officer losses suffered in two such major battles as Essling and Wagram – mutilated veterans or inexperienced National Guard officers led replacement units back into Spain. The situation deteriorated as the Peninsula became a secondary theatre. To provide manpower for Napoleon's campaigns, a typical 2500-man regiment would send 120 to 200 men back to France as a dépôt unit, fifty to the artillery, ten to the gendarmes, and twelve of the best men to the Imperial Guard. These losses seriously eroded the infantry's combat capability.

The opening encounters between rival military forces are critical. Officers and men evaluate their foes and one side establishes a moral superiority. The first forces Wellesley confronted in Portugal belonged to General Junot's VIII Corps. Most were second-line troops. Defeat at Roliça and Vimeiro discouraged them. Veteran reinforcements joined for the pursuit of Moore, but most of the French at Coruña had no connection with the *Grande Armée*. Consequently, inexperienced British forces were able to gain confidence by defeating inexperienced French soldiers. Talavera was different. Here, for the first time, the French fought with a truly veteran force. Their failure in this battle had a great deal to do with lack of leadership. However capable the troops, neither Joseph Bonaparte nor Marshal Jourdan were the men to devise battle-winning grand tactics or to control opinionated, stubborn subordinates. Because of these defeats, by as early as 1810 the British Army had achieved morale superiority. While assessing the forces that Marshal Masséna assembled for his invasion of Portugal in 1810, staff officer Jean Jacques Pelet observed that most of the II Corps were veterans. But it had taken part in Soult's failed expedition on Oporto 'with disastrous results which it had not yet forgotten.'[6]

The quality of the troops aside, there was little opportunity for either the soldiers or their leaders to learn by experience. The VIII Corps under Junot fought at Vimeiro; Soult led elements of this corps at Coruña; Joseph Bonaparte, advised by Jourdan, commanded the I and IV corps at Talavera; Masséna the II, VI, and VIII at Bussaco; Masséna again commanded these corps, plus a Division from the IX, at Fuentes de Oñoro; and the V and attached units were under Soult at Albuera. Within this list, only Masséna's soldiers had an opportunity to profit from experience. Whereas at Bussaco they climbed the rugged slope in battalion column to deliver a frontal charge (and some attempted to deploy into line once they sighted their foes), at Fuentes they performed an elegant flanking manoeuvre. Soult led different units at Coruña and Albuera, and he also changed his tactical approach. At Coruña, eight battalion columns struggled up a slope and over stone walls to encounter a spirited British counter-attack. At Albuera, Soult employed a mixed order formation featuring battalions in line flanked by battalions in column to deliver the day's climactic charge. It required the gallant self-sacrifice of the British infantry – here the West Middlesex earned their name the 'Die Hards' – to defeat this charge. One new and one familiar French leader entered the lists for the next two major battles: Marmont at Salamanca and Joseph at Vitoria. Soult would later return to command during the campaigns in the Pyrenees and southern France.

The point in this recitation is that there was little command continuity. A succession of commanders had to confront Welling-ton's novel reverse slope tactics. Of these, only Masséna and Soult had the chance to try again. But Masséna was no longer the man of Zurich and Genoa. Strenuous years sat heavily upon both his body and his soul. General Foy encountered him in 1810 and wrote: 'He is no longer the Masséna with the sparkling eye, the changeable face, the intensive figure whom I saw in 1799.'[7] Thiébault agreed. Bluntly referring to Masséna's time in the Peninsula, he wrote that 'his tenacity alone was left, but not a single inspiration.'[8]

Soult, on the other hand, was closer to his prime. He had displayed an adroit tactical touch at Genoa in 1800 and again while storming the Pratzen Heights in 1805. He was the best French commander Wellington confronted. Wellington knew he had to manoeuvre carefully when in Soult's presence. It was with a sense of delight and relief that when the two met at the coronation of Queen Victoria in 1838, Wellington stealthily approached his old foe and said, 'Ah, got you after all these years!'[9]

Operational considerations

The French army displayed an astonishing strategic mobility. One of the keys to its ability to advance rapidly was its habit of living off the land. While this was hardly a novel concept, no other European army relied so extensively upon local requisitions and marched with such a small logistical tail. The system worked as long as the army passed through relatively prosperous territory and as long as it did not linger. It collapsed in Spain and Portugal for three major reasons. Firstly, both countries were poorer and less fertile than the lands where the *Grande Armée* gained its great victories. Even so, as long as the army moved quickly it could endure. During the 1810 invasion of Portugal, Masséna's army did not really suffer until it ground to a halt before the lines of the Torres Vedras. A month of near starvation then compelled it to withdraw.

Secondly, a less extensive road net and mountainous topography compelled the army to march repeatedly through the same country. The two invasion corridors that linked Spain and Portugal – Ciudad Rodrigo and Badajoz – were so frequented that they became stripped bare. Then even a simple route march strained French logistics. Marmont wrote in 1812: 'His Majesty does not understand that in these parts even the smallest movement causes an enormous loss of means. It costs us as much as a major battle. If the army marches against Rodrigo now we should not be able to stay there for three days for lack of food. We should achieve nothing as the enemy knows we cannot stay there. It would cost us 500 horses and immobilise us for six weeks.'[10] When the army became tied down the situation worsened. At the siege of Almeida in 1810, General Jean-Baptiste Eblé complained to Marshal Berthier that lack of subsistence was killing the horses. So weakened were the draft animals that even with double teams, movements required twice as long as normal. Pelet confirms the exhausted, poorly-nourished state of the equines, noting that they were 'dying like flies.'[11]

Thirdly, an implacable guerrilla force severely curtailed foraging. Armed soldiers confronting complacent German burghers or sympathetic Polish peasants could easily obtain food and forage. In the Peninsula, casual foraging brought torture and death. The Spanish government and the Catholic Church officially fanned the flames of Spanish resistance. The Church disseminated the 'Citizen's Catechism' which in part read:

Question: Is it a sin to kill a Frenchman?

Answer: Yes, excepting those who are fighting under Napoleon's standards.[12]

So omnipresent were the guerrillas that the normally loosely-militarised staff of the Intendance gradually had to learn to work in close co-operation with combat troops in order to procure sustenance. But struggle as they might, they were seldom able to accumulate supplies to support prolonged operations. No French commander could ignore attrition's crippling impact if he was forced to linger long in any one spot.

Any nation's service zone is rife with inefficiency and corruption. It was worse in Spain. The guerrillas effectively isolated regional French commanders from one another. More than a few fell prey to the temptation to establish minor fiefdoms outside of control from higher authority. 'After all,' General François Kellermann is reputed to have said when charged with excessive looting, 'do they think I crossed the Pyrenees for my health?' Indeed, several Peninsular commanders believed that Soult's reluctance to co-operate with them stemmed from his overarching goal of lining his pockets with Andalucia's wealth. Finally, there was a certain French bureaucratic attitude that worked against establishing a rational logistic basis. When French prisoners escaped from a Spanish prison hulk they found themselves thrust into a quarantine hospital and, in spite of their extreme malnourishment, still remained unfed: 'In order to give food to Frenchmen escaped from shipwreck, it was necessary that the commandant wrote to the governor, the governor to the general of Division, the general of the Division to [Marshal Victor]. The marshal gave orders to the *ordonnateur en chef*, who transmitted them to the *ordonnateur* responsible, who had to communicate them to the *commissaire des guerres*, who turned them over to the *inspecteur des vivres*. That inspector passed the orders to the *garde-magasin*, who gave them to his assistants, who then – and only then – killed the cattle and prepared the bread ... to distribute to us.'[13]

Throughout his career, Napoleon worked hard to wed the army to his person. Particularly during the glory days of the *Grande Armée*, he convinced the soldiers that their conduct, his own conduct, and France's destiny were one. The stories of the Emperor identifying an old comrade during a review or on the eve of battle are legion. He gave the army's rank and file muskets, swords, trumpets and drums of honour; monetary grants, promotions, and nomination to the Imperial Guard. Deserving officers received these awards and more, including the coveted entrance into the imperial nobility. The *Grande Armée* returned an esteem that surpassed the popularity typically associated with a successful general. In its adoration it approached idolatry, revering Napoleon as a sort of father figure and demigod. This made his absence all the more acute. Not only was he not there to care for and to inspire them; the Peninsular soldiers toiled with the knowledge that their exploits were largely outside the Emperor's gaze. This greatly reduced opportunities for distinction and advancement. Particularly after the first set of defeats, the French Army in the Peninsula did not exhibit the same effort it displayed when working with Napoleon.

For different reasons, as long as the marshals operated under Napoleon's direct control major command problems either did not occur or were ameliorated by the Emperor's genius. Yet he neither granted his subordinates much command latitude nor, with the exception of his step-son Eugène, rigorously instructed them in his art of war. When geography and scale expanded after 1808, he reaped the consequences of his unwillingness to nurture generals in the art of independent command. He blamed his subordinates for many of the disasters in the Peninsula and Russia and railed against their follies of 1813 and 1814. But the fault was his. Not only did he decline to teach his subordinates, he violated one of his own tenets of man management. Early in his career he wrote that it was vitally important for successful government not to let men grow old in their jobs. However, in 1809 – arguably the apex of his empire – the average age of his eighteen active marshals was just under forty-five years. These men had been fighting since they were teenagers. Masséna's trials in Spain and Portugal demonstrated the peril of entrusting a prematurely aged officer with a challenging, independent command. On the whole, the Peninsular marshals lacked the energy and ambition to perform to the standard the situation demanded.

When evaluating the performance of the French Army in the Peninsula, Oman correctly identified the destructive influence of the lack of co-operation among the marshals. The blame must begin with Napoleon. He encouraged rivalry in the belief that it produced the best efforts. In Spain and Portugal, rivalry among senior officers produced disaster. Staff officer Pelet relates how Ney constantly quarrelled with Masséna. With one breath Ney would snap: 'Give your orders since you command.'[14] With the next he complained that Masséna should never have accepted a command over a comrade, by which he meant one marshal should not presume to issue orders to another. The lack of co-operation surfaced on the eve of the battle of Bussaco. Ney encountered Wellington's ridge-top position and after examining it wrote to Reynier that the British were in motion and if he had been in command he would have attacked without a moment's hesitation. Ney's attitude goaded Masséna into ordering an ill-advised frontal attack. He preferred to see Masséna discredited even if it meant the death of his own troops.

Another component of French failure was misguided strategic directives from Paris and Madrid. When he was not quarrelling with his fellow marshals, Ney explained the problem in a letter to Berthier on 18 April 1810. He asked for the Emperor to come to Bayonne in southern France 'to regulate the principal operations and give each army corps positive instructions ... This seems to be the only way to avoid all the orders and counter-orders that constantly arrive from the King's headquarters'. Napoleon understood the problem. Pelet relates his long series of conversations with the Emperor in 1811 in which Napoleon repeatedly observed: 'We can decide nothing here since events have long passed by the time we receive the first news ... I cannot wage war five hundred leagues away'.[15]

During the interlude between the successful conclusion of the 1809 war against Austria and the 1812 invasion of Russia, Napoleon had the opportunity to return to Spain. Instead he became a family man, preferring the ardent embrace of young Marie-Louise and related domestic comforts to the rigours of another campaign across the Pyrenees. On Saint Helena he at last comprehended what he had lost in Spain: 'The roots of my disasters were attached to this fatal knob; it destroyed my moral standing in Europe, complicated my every position, opened a school for the English soldier.'[16]

Infantry tactics

On 16 March 1910, Oman delivered a lecture entitled 'Column and Line in the Peninsular War'. This lecture presented his views on the salient tactical factors that determined battlefield outcomes when the British and French fought during the Napoleonic Wars. Although the lecture's primary intent was to explicate Wellington's tactical system, it also dealt in great detail with French tactical methods. Presented after completing the bulk of his seven-volume *History of the Peninsular War*, the lecture represents Oman's formative thinking about the French army. The lecture, coupled with his other writings and the works of his great contemporary, John W. Fortescue, provides the foundation for English language readers' understanding of the tactical details of Napoleonic warfare. Among many, Oman's works profoundly influenced Jac Weller's 1969 *Wellington in the Peninsula*, and they are cited in virtually all popular references.

Yet his writings about the French army are a remarkable combination of solid research and ignorance. He diligently mined the army archives at Vincennes for order of battle data, and the results splendidly adorn the appendices to his *History of the Peninsular War*. Likewise, Oman ably explores the rivalries and feuding among senior French generals and rightfully emphasises their pernicious influence upon military operations. But Sir Charles apparently possessed the sketchiest of notions about how the French army conducted its battles outside the Peninsula. Moreover, he based his combat analysis of Peninsular encounters upon an erroneous understanding of French tactical methods.

In his 'Column and Line' lecture, Oman states that the massive column had 'become the regular formation for a French army acting on the offensive during the later years' of the Napoleonic wars. He asserts that it originated in the early Revolutionary days when the French discarded the linear tactics of Frederick the Great and improvised a new system in which a very thick skirmish line was thrown forward followed by a 'row of columns of the heaviest sort.' Oman explains that when Napoleon delivered 'his decisive blows, he often used pure columnar formations, covering the front of the mass ... by a skirmish line, and if possible supporting it by a heavy artillery fire.'

To counter these tactics, Wellington would choose a covered position with secure flanks, generally the reverse slope of a convenient ridge, in order to negate opposing artillery fire. He engaged the French skirmishers with a heavier skirmish line to screen his own men until the decisive moment. According to Oman, at the point of decision 'the decisive fact ... was that the two deep line enabled a force to use every musket with effect, while the column put seven-ninths of the men forming it in a position where they could not shoot at all, and even the *ordre mixte* praised by Napoleon placed from seven-twelfths to two-thirds of the rank and file in the same unhappy condition.'[17] This 'musket-counting' formula has often been repeated by subsequent historians to describe French tactical orthodoxy and consequent failure against the British.

The theoretical foundation of French infantry tactics throughout the wars of the Republic and Empire was the drill set forth in the *Règlement* of 1791. According to a critic, Marshal Gouvion St Cyr, its authors were learned men who possessed no practical experience in war. The manual defined small unit manoeuvres appropriate for the battlefield but, while covering such details as spacing between individual soldiers, alternative fire disciplines, and methods for changing formations, it did not prescribe any particular attack formation. Indeed, one of the strengths of the *Règlement* of 1791 was precisely its flexibility, permitting a combat commander a variety of choices for executing a manoeuvre. Because he had erroneously concluded that French preferences virtually dictated an attack in column, Oman did not see this flexibility even when it occurred in the Peninsula.

Contrary to Oman's impression, attacks featuring clouds of skirmishers and heavy columns were far from routine even during the Revolution. It is true that the untrained soldiers herded to the front to defend France's frontiers in 1792 and 1793 lacked the ability to manoeuvre on the battlefield, but the practice of amalgamating two battalions of volunteers with one battalion of regular infantry, which was ordered on 21 January 1793, led to an enormous improvement. By 1794, officers could select whichever formation was best suited to the tactical situation. Historian John Lynn studied the tactical formations utilised in 108 engagements fought by the *Armée du Nord* between April 1792 and July 1794. He found fifty-five recorded instances of the line in battle and cites seven examples of the line in the attack and thirty-five cases of assaults in column. A French officer describes a typical charge at Jemappes: 'We marched in ... column up to one-quarter of cannon range. Then, since we were losing men, Generals Dumouriez and Beurnonville ordered me to deploy the columns ... The movement was made like a peacetime manoeuvre ... As soon as the eight battalions had finished deploying, I commanded them to march forward and to beat the charge.' Lynn concludes that 'commanders placed their soldiers, primarily their infantry, in ways which exploited the terrain and met the tactical challenge. Battalions stood in a full close order repertoire of line, column, and square or dispersed in open order, either as large bands of *tirailleurs* or as thin skirmish lines.'[18] It is a conclusion that applies to the French infantry throughout the Napoleonic Wars.

Consider the battle of Montebello, fought on 9 June 1800. General Watrin opens the fight by deploying two battalions of the 6th *Légère* into line and charging the Casteggio heights. Later, when General Victor arrives on the field, he orders the 43rd *Demi Brigade* to attack. That unit's brigadier places his two flank battalions in open order and keeps his centre battalion in column. The next unit onto the field, the 96th *Demi Brigade*, charges toward Casteggio in battalion column. Throughout the battle, the French infantry exhibited a fine variety of tactical formations, effortlessly ploying from one formation to another while under artillery fire. Depending on the tactical dictates, they charged in column, line, or open order.[19] Three days later, at Marengo's climactic encounter, division general Boudet saw advancing enemy infantry with masses of Austrian cavalry securing their flanks. Confronting the twin threats of hostile infantry and cavalry, he chose the *ordre mixte*, deploying the 9th *Légère* with two battalions in column on either flank to oppose the Hapsburg cavalry and the centre battalion in line to confront the Austrian infantry.

In sum, the Revolutionary and Consular armies did not adhere to any tactical orthodoxy. Instead, they availed themselves of the *Règlement* of 1791's flexibility to choose formations appropriate to the tactical situation. Their choices were most frequently a far cry from Oman's 'row of columns of the heaviest sort.'

Let us consider Oman's assertion that heavy columns became 'the regular formation for a French army acting on the offensive during the later years.' To evaluate this claim, indeed to understand the French triumphs of 1805–9, requires an understanding of what occurred along the French northern coast from 1803 to 1805. This was the time of the formation of the *Grande Armée*. Here the

French army and its commanders had an unequalled opportunity to drill in all aspects of tactics.

The experience of each regiment in General Marmont's Corps was typical. It spent its first month relearning individual and platoon manoeuvres; then two days a week occupied with battalion drill and three with divisional manoeuvres. On Sunday the entire corps drilled together, while twice a month a large-scale manoeuvre was staged complete with live musket and cannon fire at targets. The soldiers were honed to a fine edge of discipline that persisted as long as the veterans of the *Grande Armée* survived. Marmont wrote that the residual beneficial effects could still be seen even after many years of subsequent warfare.[20] Never again would the French have such an extended period to prepare for combat. The *Grande Armée* became a team by training and campaigning together. Likewise, Wellington's army served together for six years, giving it ample opportunity to forge team bonds. As we shall see, this was far from the case for the French in the Peninsula.

Before the camps of instruction broke up in 1805, the future Peninsular marshal Michel Ney codified his tactical notions in a set of 'Instructions for the Troops Comprising the Left Corps'. The first section describes marches and evolutions in column. It is very clear that the column's purpose is to provide a rapid and flexible formation for approaching the combat zone. The majority of the text explores techniques for ploying from column to line in order to engage the enemy. Only in the second section is there mention of infantry charges. All the discussion specifies a charge in line with the bayonet. Concerning the principles of a charge in line, Ney writes: 'a French commander ought never to hesitate in marching against the enemy with the bayonet, if the ground is at all adapted to a charge in line with one or more battalions.'[21]

With the *Règlement* of 1791 drill imposed upon it by months of training, how did the *Grande Armée*'s infantry perform in battle? Oman restates his immutable conviction in his *Studies in the Napoleonic Wars* (1929), writing that the Emperor's 'most celebrated battle strokes seem frequently to have been made by very gross and heavy columns.'[22] He cites Austerlitz as an example. The tactical details of the decisive attack by Marshal Soult's 1st Division are clearly described by a French participant, General Thiébault. Nearing the village of Pratzen, the 1st Battalion of the 14th Regiment deploys into line and is rebuffed in its attack upon the village. Thiébault leads a counter-attack with the regiment's 2nd Battalion, which 'deployed as it ran.' Gaining the heights, he is confronted with a Russian counter-attack, much in the manner that the British infantry charged the French when they neared the crest line in the Peninsula. Thiébault responds by ordering 'the 36th to deploy with all speed.'[23] Lest there be any doubt about these manoeuvres, the deployment into line is observed and recorded by an Austrian eyewitness.[24] Thus, contrary to Oman, the spearhead of Napoleon's 'battle stroke', at the Emperor's most celebrated battle, fights the decisive action in line.

Turning to the 1806 campaign, we can follow the evolutions of Suchet's Division as it manoeuvres on the Jena battlefield:

> At the break of day I formed the brigade Claparède in line with two pieces of artillery attached, in order to seize the little village of Closewitz ... I put the brigade Reille in two lines, the artillery in their intervals and the 40e in column with orders to deploy as soon as there was enough space. Finally, the brigade Vedel was in close column placed in reserve.

During the ensuing engagement, the 17th *Légère* runs short of ammunition so Suchet orders Reille to replace it with the 34th: 'The passage of the lines was executed by battalions, perfectly.' Two battalions of the 34th then advance against three opposing battalions while firing, and then perform a change of front to engage a Prussian grenadier unit and several artillery pieces. Supporting battalions advance in close column but remain in reserve.[25]

At the parallel battle of Auerstadt, General Grandeau describes the evolutions of his regiment: 'I received orders to form the 111th Regiment in square by battalion, they marched for a few minutes, they formed in column of attack, continued their march ... The ball and canister ravaged their ranks, they were compelled to deploy'.[26] The regiment completes its deployment and continues the fight.

As these accounts clearly show, like the veterans of the wars of the Republic, the *Grande Armée* displayed a fine ability to manoeuvre on the battlefield and its commanders employed a variety of tactical formations. In fact, there was more similarity between French and British infantry tactics than Oman would have the reader believe.

A British lieutenant describes Wellington shifting his reserves behind the Bussaco ridge. When within a quarter-mile of the combat 'I cast my eye back to see if I could discover the rear of our division: eleven thousand men were following; all in sight, all in open column, all rapidly advancing in double quick time.'[27] In Wellington's first great offensive battle at Salamanca, the 3rd Division – assigned to make the critical first thrust – forms column to make its approach march. It deploys into line when about 250 yards from the French. Similarly, during the approach march of the Connaught Rangers at Vitoria, the Rangers were seen 'marching in close column of companies to attack a French regiment which was drawn up in line on the verge of a small hill.'[28] As they came within musket range of the French, the Rangers did exactly what the French would have done: they deployed into line. The British upon occasion manoeuvred in what the French called *ordre mixte*. Describing a combat in 1811, a British fusilier wrote that 'our

Regiment advanced in line with the 23rd and 48th in close column on each flank'.[29]

Returning to French infantry tactics, upon occasion during the wars of the Empire, French generals dissolved entire battalions into skirmish order. These were not the untrained hordes of the early Revolution. Rather, they were all-purpose infantry equally capable of fighting in open (or skirmish) order or shoulder to shoulder in standard formations. Oman is mistaken about this capacity. He writes: 'I do not remember any case in the Peninsula battles where whole battalions were broken into skirmishers ... nor do I think that it occurred often, if ever, in any of the imperial battles.'[30]

However, Masséna's aide, Major Pelet, relates that at Bussaco an entire brigade in Ney's Corps dispersed into skirmish order as they fought along the ridge slopes. He adds that 'our system permitted the French regiments to be dispersed during a battle'.[31] Following the battle of Salamanca, General Joseph Souham's men engaged in heavy skirmishing with the British. At the forefront of the fight was a Colonel Béchaud, who provides a detailed account: 'the two left flank companies fired upon the advancing enemy columns ... the remainder of the 15th dispersed into skirmish order ... after twenty-five minutes ... the enemy turned our left ... and our cloud of skirmishers was forced to retreat.'[32] The 15th then reformed into a two-deep line and opened fire. Later in the day eight companies of the 15th and 66th again broke into skirmish order.

Similarly, many French units fought in imperial battles while in skirmish order. In 1806 the report of the 16th *Légère* at Jena describes how 'the third battalion advanced into the woods in skirmish order.'[33] During the struggle along the Teugen-Hausen ridge in 1809, the 10th *Légère* advanced to support the 57th *Ligne* (which had climbed the ridge in battalion column, encountered the Austrians, and deployed into line), charged a battery, and then opened into skirmish order to continue up the slope.[34]

All during the wars of the Republic and Empire, the French enjoyed an advantage in open order tactics when fighting continental powers. The ability of formed units to disperse into open order, and the skirmish ability of the *voltigeur* and *carabinier* companies allowed the French to dominate combat in broken ground or in villages. They could not do this when facing the British in the Peninsula and their inability shocked them. British skirmisher dominance began at the first Peninsular battles. A French captain described his experience upon skirmishing with the British rifles at Vimeiro: 'They were behind every bush and stone, and soon made sad havoc among my men, killing all the officers of my company, and wounding myself without being able to do them any injury.'[35]

The inability of the French skirmish line to contend effectively with the thick British skirmish line had two important tactical consequences. The first of these was that advancing French formations suffered significant losses, particularly among officers, before they even reached the main British battle line. An astounding statistic suggests the impact of British skirmisher dominance: of the twenty French generals killed fighting the British between 1809 and 1814 one died from a cannon shot, while the other nineteen were killed by small arms fire, typically while well forward either with the skirmish line or at the head of the column.[36] Perhaps more importantly, the British skirmishers prevented French officers from scouting the British position. Because Wellington customarily hid his troops on a reverse slope, this meant that the French advanced in ignorance of what they faced. They reached the crest, encountered an unnerving volley or two, tried to deploy, and recoiled before the British bayonet charge.

According to French accounts, only at Coruña did their skirmish line manage to screen the advancing ranks effectively. Here the celebrated veteran, General Jardon, assembled nine *voltigeur* companies, numbering perhaps 500 men, and spearheaded the advance of the 31st *Légère* and 47th *Ligne*. Jardon's men drove the British skirmishers up a slope, cleared out the village of Elvira, and opened fire on the British formed units. A British counter-attack drove back the 31st *Légère* and recaptured the village, but Jardon reformed his *voltigeurs* behind nearby rocks and walls to deliver a punishing fire that caused the British to waver. The *Légère*'s third battalion then counter-attacked and reclaimed the village from the disordered British.

More typical contests pitted French skirmishers against a reinforced British skirmish line against which they could not advance. Such was the case at the battle of Bussaco. Here it is instructive to consider the battle from the perspective of the French infantry climbing the ridge. General Louis Loison's division spearheads the advance, moving up the slope under 'a rain of ball and canister.' The lead brigade is checked by the first British line along the lower slope. They do not realise that this is, in fact, merely the British skirmish line. But it is a skirmish line unlike anything these veterans have previously encountered, comprising 550 men of the 4th *Caçadores*, 656 of the 3rd *Caçadores*, and 766 riflemen of the 95th Foot. The French *voltigeurs* are outnumbered by this force. The battalion columns must advance to support them. Finally, 'after a vigorous resistance', Loison drives the line back. Fatigued and disordered, the lead brigade encounters the British main line of resistance and is repulsed. Brigadier General Simon brings up a second brigade, places himself among his skirmishers, and the columns continue to climb. The brigade orients on Ross' horse artillery battery. It advances into canister range, Simon falls with a crippling wound, and the brigade endures enfilade fire from Cleeves' KGL battery. It now encounters what it perceives to be a second line, which is, in fact, once again the British main line of resistance. Several Portuguese units (in fact, British supported by Portuguese *Caçadores*) appear on the flank. A fierce combat ensues, 'but overwhelmed by numbers, riddled with impunity by canister, ruined by the disadvantages of the ground, our soldiers, after the handsomest of efforts, retire'.[37]

It seems apparent that Oman had important misapprehensions about the infantry tactics the French employed on continental battlefields and they influenced his descriptions of French versus British encounters. His basic misunderstanding undoubtedly stems from his initial study of the battle of Maida. He was proud of his findings about this little-known affair fought in Italy in 1806 between a small British army commanded by Sir John Stuart and a slightly larger force led by General Jean Reynier; proud, but indisputably wrong.

Oman first dealt with Maida in a lecture given in 1907 to the Royal Artillery Institution. In this talk he attributed the French defeat to the inherent difficulty of a column formation assaulting a linear one. Speaking of the decisive clash between the 1st *Légère* and the British Light Battalion, he said: 'It was the fairest fight between column and line that had been seen since the Napoleonic wars began, on the one side two heavy columns of 800 men each, drawn up in column of companies ... The front of each was not more than sixty yards. Kempt, on the other hand, had his battalion in line ... every one of them could use his musket against either the front or flank of one of the two columns.'[38] He repeated this description three years later in his 'Column and Line' lecture, while labouring on volume IV of his *History of the Peninsular War*: '5000 infantry in line received the shock of 6000 in column, and inflicted on them one of the most crushing defeats on a small scale that took place during the whole war.'[39] So, here was Oman's immutable conviction, his scientific 'musket-counting' explanation complete with details about the width of the French attacking columns, showing why the French infantry failed so repeatedly against the British. It was neat, logical, and unfortunately based upon a false understanding of what took place at Maida.

In fact, the French infantry contested the battle's critical first encounter while deployed in line. There is ironclad evidence to support this description. Oman apparently was unaware of Ensign Joseph Anderson's account (perhaps because it was not formally published until 1913), which describes the French deploying into line to exchange volleys.[40] But there were other sources available to a diligent researcher: a British staff officer named Ryves, whose account, written in 1807, describes the 1st *Légère* rising 'suddenly to our view from behind a thick brushwood, in a well formed line'; brigade commander General Lowry Cole's letter written on 18 August 1806; a letter by Lieutenant-Colonel Lemoine (present with the artillery) published in the *History of the Royal Regiment of*

Artillery; another letter, by Second Lieutenant Thomas Dyneley (also present with the artillery), written in August 1806; the account of John T. Jones (present with the Royal Engineers) published in his famous *Journals of Sieges Carried on by the Army under The Duke of Wellington in Spain*; and that of David Stewart (present with the 78th Foot) published in 1825. All of these place Reynier's attacking wing in line. Moreover, and contrary to Oman's revised claim about lack of French documentation, there is the account written by a Lieutenant Griois, who commanded a battery at the battle: 'General Reynier gave the order to advance to engage the enemy, and to accomplish this to form on the left in line.'[41]

It is, perhaps, unreasonable to expect Oman to have been aware of all these accounts when he first explored the battle. However, given the key role Maida played in forming his convictions about Franco-British infantry encounters, Oman really should not have overlooked a letter, dated the day after the battle, that Reynier sent to Joseph Bonaparte. In part, Reynier wrote: 'The 1st and 42nd Regiments, 2400 strong, under the orders of General Compère, passed the Lamato, and formed into line.' Reynier's report is at Vincennes and is reproduced in the English translation of Joseph Bonaparte's correspondence.[42]

By 1912 Oman had partially recognised his error. In a footnote to his *Wellington's Army*, he wrote: 'Till lately I had supposed that Reynier had at least his left wing ... in columns of battalions, but evidence put before me seems to prove that despite of the fact the French narratives do not show it, the majority at least of Reynier's men were deployed.'[43] The evidence Oman refers to are two British eyewitness accounts of Maida, one of which, written by Henry Bunbury, explicitly describes the French infantry as it 'advanced in line upon the brigade of British Light Infantry'.[44] In addition, Oman had now read the writings of his French contemporary, Commandant Colin. In his lengthy preface to *La Tactique et la Discipline dans les Armées de la Révolution*, published in 1902, Colin offers example after example of the Imperial French infantry attacking in line or in *ordre mixte*, in battles from Austerlitz to Bautzen. Colin, along with Bunbury's and Boothby's narratives, prompted Oman to revise his account of Maida. Now, instead of demonstrating the superiority of line over column, the battle was 'conclusive proof of the efficacy of the double when opposed to the triple rank'.[45] Curiously, following Oman's *mea culpa* of 1912, he repeated his erroneous 1907 version in his 1929 *Studies in the Napoleonic Wars*.

The true history of Maida aside, the important point is that Oman (and Fortescue) wrote their influential histories while operating under false premises generated by their misapprehensions of Maida. The consequences are immediately apparent in Oman's description of the first important Franco-British encounter in the Peninsula, the battle of Vimeiro. He writes: 'The French came on in their usual style, a thick line of *tirailleurs*, supported by battalion columns close in their rear.'[46] He depicts the collision of Solignac's brigade with four British battalions as a classic line versus column affair. He writes that only after being shattered by fire do the French return fire irregularly and endeavour to deploy. In contrast is William Vane's account: 'Their line was likewise formed in a moment; and several terrible discharges of musketry were exchanged at a distance which hardly allowed of a single bullet passing wide of its mark.'[47] General Maximilien Foy also mentions how on another part of the field the French responded to British fire by trying to deploy. A British account provides the details: 'the enemy having very quickly approached the guns to within sixty or seventy yards, they halted, and endeavoured to deploy and form their line, under cover of the *Voltigeurs*.'[48] But such nuances do not interest Oman. He had previously reached his immutable convictions and they would colour his entire seven-volume history.

At most Peninsular battles, a set of plausible excuses – second-rate troops, command rivalries, poor logistics, Wellington's novel tactics – can account for French defeats. Indeed, French writers and historians must be read with some scepticism because they understandably focus on these excuses to explain their embarrassing run of defeats. If the explanation for French failure against the British goes far beyond Oman's 'musket-counting' calculus, there still remains at the end of the day a niggling question of whether the British infantry was simply superior to the French. To reach a conclusion one must evaluate the battle of Barrossa, fought on 5 March 1811.

At Barrossa the French enjoyed nearly every possible advantage. The commander, Marshal Victor, was a gifted tactical commander who had experience fighting the British. He had displayed his battle skills on many fields including Marengo, where he recovered from a surprise Austrian counter-offensive to conduct a stubborn defence until reinforcements arrived. He had devised a Cannae-like plan for the 1809 battle of Medellin and executed it almost to perfection. His troops were as good as any French soldiers in Spain. They were first and second battalions of regiments that had marched with the *Grande Armée*. Among them was 96th *Ligne*, whom Victor had commanded at Marengo, and the 'Incomparable' 9th *Légère*, a unit that had gained its glorious name on that same field. Victor commanded about 7000 men at Barrossa; his opponent, General Thomas Graham, had about 5000.

The battle began with Graham in a most unfavourable situation, caused when his Spanish allies unexpectedly abandoned the key height overlooking the field. Graham was compelled to launch a hasty uphill assault against Ruffin's waiting Division. With surprise on the side of the French, and in spite of the presence of veteran troops led by able officers, French numerical superiority, and

French terrain advantage, Graham's men soundly defeated Victor's. It was on this field that Sergeant Masterson ran a French *aquilifère* through with his pike to obtain the first eagle captured by the British during the Peninsular War.

The French had contested Barrossa manfully. At the decisive encounter atop the Cerro del Puerco, ten men in every thirty-five became casualties. As in every battle, there were unique circumstances that influenced the result. On the Cerro Del Puerco, Victor's counter-attack contacted two Guards battalions, the élite units in the British Army. In the fight against Leval's Division, the British enjoyed close-range fire support from Duncan's ten guns. Duncan's artillery battered Leval's men before the infantry fight began. Nonetheless, one must seriously consider the modern conclusion reached by General Jean Regnault after he pondered Barrossa: 'the basic cause of these checks is the qualitative superiority of the British infantry.'[49] Such a conclusion is not too surprising. Compared to the French army, the British army was smaller by an order of magnitude. Unlike the detested Napoleonic conscription, a well conceived, limited conscription fed Wellington's war machine. Oman points out that in 1808, British conscription 'gave 41,786 men to the line, and these not raw recruits, but already more or less trained to arms by their service in the militia. All through the war this system continued: the Peninsular army ... drew more than half its reinforcing drafts' from the trained militia.[50]

Peninsular battles hinged on the combat between rival infantries. But the *Grande Armée* generally achieved its tactical triumphs through a fine interplay of the three arms. It is time to turn to the supporting arms.

The cavalry

Service in the Peninsula was hard on Napoleon's cavalry. Local forage was usually in short supply and less sustaining to horses accustomed to northern European fodder. Locally procured remounts were often inferior nags of the worst sort. Because Napoleon considered the Peninsula a secondary theatre, he sent many newly-raised or ad hoc units to Spain. Oman identified only three veteran French regiments among the 12,000 horsemen who formed the cavalry element of the first 'Army of Spain'. Indeed, Lord Paget's celebrated success at the cavalry battle of Sahagun initially came when his hussars charged the 1st Provisional *Chasseurs*. Napoleon also employed many troopers from his vassal states. The Polish lancers of the Vistula Legion and the Westphalian *Chevaux-Légèrs* were present at Talavera; the Hanoverian *Chasseurs* accompanied Masséna into Portugal; several more allied formations of indifferent quality including Italians, Neapolitans, and the somewhat better Lancers of Berg served throughout Spain.

In spite of all of these, there were never enough mounted men to perform all the necessary duties, so Napoleon turned to improvised expedient. He detached squadrons from regiments stationed elsewhere in his empire for temporary duty in Spain. It proved impossible to keep them up to strength. Next he tried assembling squadrons – usually by selecting the fourth squadrons from assorted regiments – into provisional units. These lacked adequate administrative and logistical support, but the worst problem was that they never developed the essential *ésprit de corps* to evolve into reliable regiments. Although some provisional regiments experienced a long life, most converted back into regular units or dissolved, victims of an unwise experiment. Throughout it all the French cavalry was, nevertheless, a professional arm whose discipline in battle attracted the admiration of Wellington himself.

Oman erroneously believed that Napoleon often used his mounted arm as a great battering ram to bludgeon a hole in his opponent's line and thus contribute to eventual victory. In fact, the cavalry needed to, and frequently did, co-operate with the other two arms in a seamless tactical whole. In the Peninsula, against the poorly-mounted, weakly-led Spanish, they achieved great victories on their own. At Ocaña, Soult massed more than 3500 sabres, and while his infantry and artillery fixed the Spanish left and centre, his concentrated cavalry charged the right and drove the Spanish horse from the field. After detailing three or four regiments to pursue, the rest turned inward against the Spanish infantry and successively overran brigade after brigade. But such events were exceptional.

Most of the cavalry's combat in the Peninsula came in hundreds of small actions before and after a pitched battle. Here individual training, equipment, and most importantly the quality of the horses, had a surpassing influence. Because they were less well mounted than their British and German opponents, the French troopers encountered difficulties when engaged in skirmish and outpost combats with Wellington's cavalry. Their skills became apparent when manoeuvring in regiment-sized formations on the battlefield. Wellington trembled when he saw contests between full British and French regiments. He did not doubt his troopers' courage, but feared his officers' judgement. In contrast, French cavalry officers usually maintained control over their troopers and even managed to rally them quickly after a successful charge.

Nowhere did morale play a larger role than in cavalry versus cavalry fights. Whereas some men will sacrifice their lives in a death or glory charge, horses instinctively shy away from collisions. When awe-struck foot-soldiers watched opposing mounted forces charge at one another, they expected to witness a tremendous collision. Instead, one of three things occurred: one contestant would falter and turn about due to a failure of nerve; the rival lines would pass through each other (the least common occurrence); or the contestants would check on contact to begin a hack-and-thrust mêlée. The physical and psychological factors influencing a cavalry charge account for General Lasalle's comment 'there are lost men' whenever he saw a rival force charging at a gallop. A galloping line could not maintain order. It was full of gaps that encouraged the horses to shy away before contact, while simultaneously encouraging the foe to advance confidently – because rider and horse alike could see that they could avoid the shock by entering intervals between enemy riders. Consequently, French officers often charged at the trot or at a controlled canter whereas too many British officers equated a cavalry charge with fox hunting, and leadership with being stretched out at full gallop at the front of their men.

The most common cavalry type to serve in the Peninsula were the dragoons. Napoleon believed that a dragoon's cross-training in mounted and dismounted tactics was ideal for the assorted demands that arose in Spain and Portugal. Twenty-four of his thirty available dragoon regiments served in the Peninsula, although their high riding boots made dismounted service difficult. Seldom did they actually manoeuvre on foot as opposed to merely stand dismounted while on outpost duty. Yet at Coruña the 27th Dragoons did dismount alongside the 47th *Ligne* in order to prolong the battle line at a critical moment, and dismounted dragoons occupied villages or defiles at Calcalbellos and Usagre.

Whereas the dragoon's ability to manoeuvre rapidly on the battlefield caused distress to the somewhat inflexible Spanish, they seemed to have enjoyed no particular successes against the British or the King's German Legion. In part this may be because of the cross-training they received. As one cavalry veteran observed, 'it is hard to know what to think when we are first taught that nothing can resist an all out mounted charge and then are taught to dismount and wield our firearms since nothing can break a stout line of infantry!' The difficulty of being 'neither fish nor fowl' is seen at the combat of Pombal, fought on 11 March 1811. Here General Montbrun's dragoons received Arentschildt's light horse at a standstill, their sword tips pointed toward the charging enemy. Most cavalry recognised that to receive a charge at the standstill was to invite disaster.

In response to the Austrian war of 1809, Napoleon ordered the dragoons to send back to France the cadres of their third and fourth squadrons. Similarly, when he decided to raise six lancer regiments the burden fell upon units serving in Spain. Five of the six dragoon regiments to be converted were in Spain. Rather than recall the entire unit, he took the regimental headquarters and cadres composed of officers, non-commissioned officers, trumpeters, and ten picked troopers from two squadrons per regiment. He distributed the balance of the troopers and horses among the other

Peninsular dragoon regiments. This, too, proved corrosive to *ésprit de corps*. Years of hard service toughened the dragoons, but they seldom performed the outstanding exploits associated with the cuirassiers or hussars. Much of their fame comes from their effectiveness after being recalled to France in 1814. On several memorable fields the 'dragoons of Spain' cleaved their way through the allied ranks. But their success in 1814 must be put in perspective. After the Russian disaster, most of Napoleon's cavalry were a pitiful lot, comprising untrained riders aboard third-rate mounts. The dragoons, who were capable equestrians and combat veterans, towered above them.

Three 'Provisional Regiments of Heavy Cavalry' served in the Peninsula. They were formed from the fifth squadrons of existing cuirassier and *carabinier* regiments. Those who escaped Dupont's capitulation at Bailén merged to form the 13th Cuirassiers, named 'The Intrepid', which served with Suchet on Spain's east coast. No other heavy cavalry fought in the Peninsula. Napoleon rightly appreciated that the large, heavy horses of the cuirassiers and *carabiniers* could not survive on arid Spanish browse, and that when they perished they could not be replaced locally.

In addition to the dragoons were the regiments of light horse. Aside from their uniforms, there was no essential difference between the *chasseurs à cheval* and the hussars. The hussars' great day came at Albuera, where the 2nd Hussars, alongside the 1st Lancers of the Vistula, charged and slaughtered Colborne's brigade. In less than five minutes, some 800 French troopers killed, wounded, or captured fifty-eight officers out of eighty and 1190 men out of 1568. But from a French standpoint, such exploits were few and far between. Against the Spanish, French troopers delivered powerful strokes: Wellington, by virtue of his careful tactical dispositions, largely negated the cavalry's prowess.

The artillery

Wellington's gunners felt themselves disadvantaged by the heavier weight of French 8-pdrs and 12-pdrs, so they welcomed the introduction of the 9-pdr to replace their light 6-pdrs. Whereas in May 1809 the British artillery comprised light 6-pdr and 3-pdr batteries, by the time of the battle of Vitoria in 1813 there were seven 9-pdr batteries, two heavy 6-pdr batteries, and only four remaining light 6-pdr batteries. Meanwhile, the French went in the opposite direction. Artillery reforms of 1803 involved the substitution of lighter-weight, more mobile 6-pdr guns for the older 4 and 8-pdrs. Because of technical advances, these 6-pdrs almost matched the 8-pdrs' range and punch while having nearly the same mobility as 4-pdrs. Similarly, improved howitzers replaced the older Gribeauval model weapons. It took until the end of 1809 to complete the

modernisation programme within the forces stationed in Germany.
The programme lagged in secondary fronts, including the Peninsula,
where the British captured numerous older types at the battle of
Salamanca in 1812, including three 8-pdrs and nine 4-pdrs.

A French battery consisted of six guns and two howitzers.
Ideally, each infantry Division had one foot and one horse battery
for direct support, while each Corps retained a reserve built around
the hard-hitting 12-pdr. But logistical constraints – primarily a lack
of forage to sustain the horses – prevented the French in the
Peninsula from enjoying their customary artillery support. In their
Peninsular battles against the British, the proportion of guns to men
never rose above two per thousand, and occasionally barely
exceeded one per thousand.

The gunners' accuracy depended upon being able to see the
target. Continental commanders made little effort to conceal their
forces, arraying them on the front slopes of convenient heights.
This practice made them vulnerable to artillery fire. Only natural
obstacles such as hillsides and minor undulations or stoutly-built
stone structures slowed or deflected a cannon-ball's path.
Otherwise it continued bounding along the ground until it ran
out of kinetic energy. If a cannon-ball encountered human flesh
during its passage, it tore off limbs and crushed internal organs. The
more densely-packed the target, the more damage the cannon-ball
inflicted by striking multiple ranks. Even after the target became
hidden by battle smoke, gunners could continue to cause significant
losses by merely firing into the roiling, surging smoke cloud that
identified the enemy position. By 1809, all of these factors
combined to make massed artillery the dominant weapon in
Napoleon's battles.

This was not the case in the Peninsula. Wellington's reverse
slope tactics sheltered his army from French artillery. At Bussaco,
the French artillery could not contribute usefully since its firing
positions at the foot of the ridge were well below any possible
targets. Only at Talavera was Wellesley unable to shelter his men,
and not surprisingly this battle is the only one where massed French
artillery punished the exposed British infantry. At ranges of 600 to
800 yards, Victor's twenty-four guns opened fire from the Cascajal
heights and some thirty more joined in from the adjacent lower
ground. Wellesley immediately ordered two brigades in Hill's line to
withdraw behind the skyline. But Sherbrooke's division, stationed
on level ground behind the Portiña Brook, had no such recourse
and suffered accordingly. This seems to be the only instance where
massed artillery, acting offensively, made a useful contribution.
Defensively, Soult managed to assemble some forty artillery pieces
to cover the withdrawal of his infantry following Myers' counter-
attack at Albuera. Otherwise, in the fights against the British, French
artillery played a minor role in determining tactical outcomes.

This wasn't for lack of capable officers. Like Napoleon, Marshal Marmont was a trained artillerist, although it helped him not at all at Salamanca, where he contrived to lose the battle and twenty artillery pieces to boot. Count Charles Ruty rose from a second lieutenant in the artillery in 1793 to lieutenant general in 1813. He commanded the siege artillery of the Army of Spain, and performed so ably that Napoleon recalled him in 1813 to become commander-in-chief of the *Grande Armée*'s artillery. General Alexandre Senarmont was one of the Empire's most renowned artillerists. His aggressive handling of his guns at Friedland had brought victory and earned him a special commendation. He commanded the guns of Victor's I Corps in the Army of Spain. At Ocaña in 1809, he massed thirty guns on a low knoll from where they partially enfiladed the Spanish line and contributed to Soult's victory. A howitzer shell killed him at the siege of Cádiz the following year. But as was the case with the infantry, artillery officers had never previously encountered Wellington's tactics. At Vimeiro and Talavera, officers advanced their batteries to support the infantry and lost their guns to British counter-attacks before some of the pieces had managed to fire a single round.

Addressing the tactical mosaic, Napoleon said: 'Of the three arms – cavalry, infantry, and artillery – none must be despised. All three are equally important.'[51] On the Napoleonic battlefield, the interplay of the three arms was crucial for both attacker and defender. An attacking commander employing a combined-arms assault featuring infantry, artillery, and cavalry put enormous stress on the defender. The tactical problem this sort of assault posed to a defending infantry battalion commander reduced to a conundrum: to remain in line would allow the opposing cavalry to overrun him, while to form square permitted the attacker's infantry and cannon to shoot his unit into red ruin. Hence a general using a properly-managed combined-arms assault possessed a tactical trump to any defensive manoeuvre, but orchestrating a combined-arms assault amid the chaos of battle was extremely difficult. No French commander managed it against Wellington in the Peninsula. Marshal Ney did conduct a combined arms attack at the encounter battle of Quatre Bras in 1815 and here, for the first time, Wellington's losses were higher than his opponent's.

Conclusion

When reading Oman's account of the French army and the war in general, one must remember that he was a Briton writing about the French. He was proud of what the British Army had accomplished – and why not? Under Wellington it enjoyed an unsullied string of victories. When one reads a French account of a Peninsular battle, regardless of whether written by a veteran or by a more modern historian, it often seems that they are not describing the same events at all. Yet the French accounts – as biased, or perhaps even more biased, than Oman's (after all, the loser always has a great deal more explaining to do) – still provide an important perspective that differs from Oman's. Consider General Jean Regnault's 1951 essay about the tactical lessons of Peninsular combat. Regnault comments with astonishment how the British command, after the army has been driven into the sea at Coruña, authorised the twenty-eight regiments present to inscribe the battle honour 'Coruña' on their flags, regardless of whether they had even been engaged. His perspective is that of Napoleon, who allowed units to inscribe their standards only if they had truly distinguished themselves at clear-cut victories. For Regnault, Bussaco reduces to 14,000 English, solidly established atop a formidable ridge, defeating 7000 or 8000 French at the points of decision. His observation has merit. Only four of seven infantry Divisions, and none of the cavalry, actually engaged. Of the engaged troops, the attack involved two mutually insupportable advances, and the advancing columns fought piecemeal. Only in summary do French and British accounts congrue. Referring to Talavera, Regnault writes: 'each [French] Division shared a common experience: courageous advance in spite of hostile skirmish fire, impossibility of deploying while under fire from the main line of resistance, enormous losses and impotence to resist the enemy's reserves.'[52]

A complex interplay of strategic factors determined the morale, manpower and logistical characteristics affecting French battlefield efficiency. A summary of salient factors includes outdated central strategic direction from Napoleon in Paris and Joseph in Madrid; rivalry among the Peninsula marshals; lack of command continuity so that seldom were officers and men able to learn from the experience of fighting the British; inadequate replacement policies coupled with a general decline in manpower quality; and the impact of guerrilla warfare. Recognition of these factors does not overshadow Wellington's marvellous tactical direction or the performance of his staunch infantry, and Oman vividly celebrates these attributes.

As far as they illuminate the workings of the French Army, Oman's works must be read sceptically. But they do retain value, not least in his attention to topographical detail. He visited the fields to gain an appreciation of the ground before committing himself to paper. Indeed, he delayed his volume IV for three years in order first to visit the battlefields of 1811. He wrote his account of the topography of Albuera while present on the field on 'a blazing April day'. By tramping the ground he gained an unsurpassed appreciation of the terrain. Given the modern despoiling of most of these battlefields – a recent highway heedlessly constructed through Talavera uncovered heaps of bones from a British burial ground, and only strident objections caused them to be decently reinterred - Oman's description will be the last, best view we have of much of this ground.

Notes

1. Oman, *History*, vol.I, p.107.
2. Marshal Louis Suchet, *Memoirs of the War in Spain* (2 vols, London, 1829), vol.I, pp.8-9.
3. Albert Meynier, 'Levées et Pertes d'Hommes sous le Consulat et l'Empire', *Revue des Etudes* XXX (1930).
4. Philippe Gille, *Mémoires d'un Conscript de 1808* (Paris, 1893); see particularly pp.15-95.
5. Anne Savary, *Memoirs of the Duke of Rovigo* (vol.II, London, 1828), p.84.
6. Jean Jacques Pelet, *The French Campaign in Portugal, 1810-1811* (Minneapolis, 1973), p.23.
7. Foy's writing is reproduced in Pelet, *op.cit.* p.88 n.1.
8. Baron Thiébault, *The Memoirs of Baron Thiébault* (New York, 1896), vol.II, p.84.
9. Richard Humble, *Napoleon's Peninsular Marshals* (New York, 1974), p.219.
10. 'Marmont to Berthier', 26 February 1812, cited in Michael Glover, *The Peninsular War* (London, 1974), p.31.
11. Pelet, *op.cit.* p.98.
12. Cited in Walter Langsam, *The Napoleonic Wars and German Nationalism in Austria* (New York, 1930), p.72.
13. Sebastien Blaze's *Mémoires*, cited in John R. Elting, *Swords Around A Throne* (New York, 1988), pp.556-7.
14. Pelet, *op.cit.* p.69.
15. *Ibid* p.39 n.43 and p.505.
16. Ernest Picard, ed., *Préceptes et Jugements de Napoléon* (Paris, 1913), p.295.
17. Oman, 'Column and Line in the Peninsular War', read to the British Academy 16 March 1910; published in *Studies in the Napoleonic Wars* (Oxford, 1929). The quotes are from *Studies in the Napoleonic Wars*, pp.325, 329, 339.
18. John A. Lynn, *The Bayonets of the Republic: Motivation and Tactics in the Army of Revolutionary France 1791-94* (Chicago, 1984), pp.250-1, 281.
19. For a detailed description of the battles of 1800, see James R. Arnold, *Marengo and Hohenlinden: Napoleon's Rise to Power* (Lexington, VA, 1999).
20. Marshal A. Marmont, *Mémoires* (9 vols, Paris, 1857 *et.seq.*); see vol.VII, p.251.
21. Marshal M. Ney, 'Instructions for the Troops Comprising the Left Corps', reprinted in *The Memoirs of Marshal Ney* (Boston, 1834), p.190.
22. Oman, *Studies in the Napoleonic Wars*, pp.330-1.
23. Thiébault, *op.cit.* p.160.
24. Major General Karl Stutterheim, *A Detailed Account of the Battle of Austerlitz* (London, 1807), p.101.

25. Suchet's report is cited by Jean Colin, *La tactique et la discipline dans les armées de la Révolution* (Paris, 1902), pp.lxxxv-lxxxvii.

26. Marshal Davout, *Opérations du 3e corps 1806-1807: Raport du Maréchal Davout Duc d'Auerstadt* (Paris, 1896), p.365.

27. Moyle Sherer, *Recollections of the Peninsula* (Kent, 1996), p.109.

28. Antony Brett-James, ed., *Edward Costello: The Peninsular and Waterloo Campaigns* (London, 1967), p.168.

29. Robert Knowles, *The War in the Peninsula* (Bolton, 1913), p.27.

30. Oman, *Studies in the Napoleonic Wars*, p.330.

31. Pelet, *op.cit.* p.181.

32. Colonel Béchaud, 'La campagne de trente cinq jours, par un officier superieur de l'avant garde, l'armée de Portugal', reprinted in *Revue des Etudes Napoleon* (July-November 1912), pp.408-9.

33. Colin, *op.cit.* pp.lxxxvi-lxxxvii.

34. For details of how Davout's *Grande Armée* veterans dealt with a Peninsular-type defended ridge, see James R. Arnold, *Crisis on the Danube* (New York, 1990), p.87.

35. George Simmons, *A British Rifle Man* (London, 1899), p.102.

36. General Jean Regnault, 'Une Leçon du Feu et de la Manoeuvre', *Revue Historique de l'Armée* 3 (1951), p.46.

37. André Delagrave, *Campagne de l'armée Francaise en Portugal, 1810-1811* (Paris, 1815), pp.59-61.

38. Sir Charles Oman, 'An Historical Sketch of the battle of Maida', read to the Royal Artillery Institution 28 November 1907; published in the *Journal of the Royal Artillery Institution* XXXIV, p.53.

39. Oman, *Studies in the Napoleonic Wars*, p.333.

40. Joseph Anderson, *Recollections of a Peninsular Veteran* (London, 1913), pp.12-13.

41. Lieutenant Griois, 'Combat de Maida', in *Spectateur Militaire* IV (1928). There are also Griois' memoirs, published in Paris in 1909. See pp.308-13.

42. *Correspondence du Général Reynier ... du 11 fevrier 1806 au 29 décembre 1807*, Archives de l'Armée (Vincennes), Registre No.C5/31; and Joseph Bonaparte, *Confidential Correspondence of Napoleon Bonaparte* (London, 1855), p.161.

43. Oman, *Wellington's Army* (London, 1912), p.78.

44. Sir Henry Bunbury, *Narratives of Some Passages in the Great War with France* (London, 1854), p.244.

45. Oman, *Wellington's Army*, p.77.

46. Oman, *History*, vol.I, p.254.

47. Charles William Vane, *Narrative of the Peninsular War* (London, 1829), p.144.

48. Landmann's eyewitness relation is provided at length in Paddy Griffith, *Forward Into Battle* (2nd edn, Swindon, 1990), p.18.

49. Regnault, *op.cit.* p.48.

50. Oman, *History*, vol.I, p.224.

51. J. Christopher Herold, *The Mind of Napoleon* (New York, 1955), p.219.

52. Regnault, *op.cit.* p. 47.

Chapter 4

The British Army, Wellington, and Moore
Some Aspects of Service in the Peninsular War

by Philip Haythornthwaite

The actions of the British Army were of crucial significance to the outcome of the Peninsular War. Britain's role in the war and its influence upon the fate of Napoleon were equally dependent upon the will of the government to support and sustain the war, and upon the Royal Navy which protected its communications; but the British Army and its leaders feature importantly in every history, notably in Sir Charles Oman's magisterial study and in his associated work *Wellington's Army* (1912).

The first great history of the war to be written in English was violently partisan, its author (William Napier) being determined to vindicate his hero, Sir John Moore. Oman's history, conversely, was written (as its author commented) more than ninety years after the beginning of the Peninsular War,[1] which could thus be viewed with 'impartial eyes', and avoiding the colouring given to the 'accepted view' by the widespread influence of Napier. Even so, there are some areas concerning the British Army which were not fully explored by Oman, including subjects relating to the structures of the army; or which might be interpreted differently in the light of subsequent publications (including a considerable number of contemporary accounts not available to him).

Misleading though it may be to treat the subject in terms of personalities, the campaigns of the principal field armies are associated with their commanders, and it is perhaps inevitable that the contributions and effect upon the British Army of Sir John Moore and the Duke of Wellington be compared and contrasted. But if the Peninsular War established their fame, it also established the reputation of the British Army itself, which became very different from that of a few years earlier. Wellington's comment upon the performance of the army in the Netherlands (1793-5) was that there 'I learnt what one ought not to do, and that is always something';[2] yet by the conclusion of the Peninsular War he could justifiably claim that the army he commanded was the most complete force, for its numbers, then existing in Europe. Dominant though the personalities of Wellington and Moore might be, the process which had brought about this radical change in the nature and efficiency of the army was of longer duration and more complex than their personal contributions.[3]

A crucial factor was an improvement in the officer corps, some aspects of which were discussed by Oman in chapter XI of *Wellington's Army*. Professionalism was certainly evident in the 18th century; but the calibre of officer in the Peninsular War was much superior to that evident in the early Revolutionary Wars. The case can be over-stated, but there was some justification to J.F. Neville's complaint that in the earlier campaign 'commissions were thrown away on persons unworthy of bearing them, or incapable of performing the duties which the letter and spirit of them religiously enjoined ... the son of a low, but opulent mechanic, by means of a bribe, saw himself at the head of a troop of horse, which he had neither the courage nor the abilities to lead',[4] which led to the adjutant-general to the army in the Netherlands reporting that of forty-one regiments, twenty-one were commanded by boys or idiots. Although the system of obtaining commissions by purchase (not abolished until 1871; the last 'purchase' officer served until January 1910) did produce such absurdities, it also enable some gifted individuals to rise more rapidly than if promotion by seniority had been the sole criterion. The worst excesses were ended by reforms introduced by the Duke of York, who, as commander-in-chief, was an interested and conscientious administrator and was responsible for much improvement in the army. He abolished the practice of buying commissions for children by introducing a regulation that no-one under sixteen years of age could be eligible (though this continued to be contravened in a minor way), and prevented promotion to captain without two years' service as a subaltern, and to major without six years' service. In 1809 this was revised so that no officer could become a captain until he had served three years as a subaltern; no promotion to major was allowed without seven years' service, at least two as a captain; and none to lieutenant-colonel without nine years' service. No officer was to occupy a staff position (ADC excepted) without four years' service. These beneficial regulations were enforced and a General Order re-stated the rules in December 1809, perhaps in response to the case of Lord Burghersh, whose promotion to lieutenant-colonel after only eight years' service was revoked after an outcry in Parliament. In fact, promotion by purchase has been over-emphasised, including in Oman's *Wellington's Army*; an analysis of promotions during 1810–13 shows that only twenty per cent were purchased, ten per cent granted by what might be described as patronage, and seventy per cent by seniority; and this does not include the Ordnance services (Royal Artillery and Royal Engineers), where promotion was dependent entirely upon seniority.[5]

A similar change occurred in the recruiting of rank and file, some aspects of which appear in chapter XII of Oman's *Wellington's Army*. Despite the pressing need for recruits, military service remained entirely voluntary, and was thus still largely the preserve of the lowest strata of society, a system which led Wellington to make perhaps his most misquoted remark when comparing his troops with the French system of conscription:

> The conscription calls out a share of every class – no matter whether your son or my son – all must march; but our friends [the British soldiers] are the very scum of the earth. People talk of their enlisting from their fine military feeling – all stuff – no such thing. Some of our men enlist from having got bastard children – some for minor offences – many more for drink; but you can hardly conceive such a set brought together, and it really is wonderful that we should have made them the fine fellows they are.[6]

Nevertheless, two measures changed the nature of recruiting, at least one of which helped raise the overall standard. 'To bring [military service] into fair competition with a sufficient portion of the habits and calling of the lower orders'[7] and to increase its appeal, Grenville's administration introduced limited service as an alternative to the previous enlistment for life. William Windham's scheme permitted recruits to engage for three periods of service: for infantry, an enrolment of seven years, followed by two optional periods of the same length; for cavalry, ten years in the first period followed by two of seven years; and for artillery, twelve years with two extensions of five years each. When proposed earlier, Moore feared that limited service would make soldiers discontented and reduce enthusiasm, knowing that they were not engaged upon a career for life; though in the event, although the scheme did not have the effect envisaged in that most soldiers still chose to enlist for life, limited service must have brought into the ranks numbers who would not otherwise have wanted to sign away the whole of their remaining active life.

A more fundamental change in recruitment practice came with successive Acts of Parliament which authorised militiamen to volunteer for regular service. The first experiment with the scheme (1798-9) was not an unqualified success, but in successive years (regular volunteering was permitted from 1809) the recruits thus forthcoming were of a superior quality to those obtained by ordinary means. The prevalent use of substitutes for men balloted (conscripted) for militia service (a balloted man could pay for another to perform his period of duty) prevented what might otherwise have been an intake of recruits from a wider social spectrum. Nevertheless, the recruits from the militia joined the regular army already inured to military discipline and trained in the handling of arms, and, until the numbers of volunteers declined late in the war, more recruits than required were forthcoming, so only the best were selected, a great advantage over men taken directly from civilian life. The system was not immune from criticism, though most was directed towards the system of militia substitution, which must have taken up many men who would have joined the regular army directly. Again, although the allocation of county titles to most infantry regiments in 1782 had been a deliberate attempt to foster *esprit de corps* and an affiliation (by recruiting) with a particular area, no attempt was made by regiments to recruit specifically from their own county militias. This does not, however, seem to have damaged regimental pride or identity, and any disadvantages were more than redressed by the beneficial effects. Criticism has been made of Oman's comment on the number of ex-militiamen in Wellesley's army in 1809,[8] to the extent that even at Talavera many still carried their old militia knapsacks, implying that such troops were of less value than seasoned campaigners; yet Oman was certainly correct in indicating the lack of campaign experience of such troops, although elsewhere he highlighted the great advantage of recruits obtained in this manner.[9] Even so, Oman did not stress the large numbers of militiamen who became regular soldiers: from 1805 until the end of the war some 100,000 men were recruited in this way, a fact inevitably related to the marked improvement in standards which led to the excellence of the Peninsular army.

It was with its two principal commanders that this army was most associated. By virtue of his successes, Wellington has claims to be known as the greatest of all British soldiers; conversely, Moore was killed at the conclusion of his one campaign, the merits of which can still be debated, and has attracted less attention from biographers (a notable exception being Carola Oman's *Sir John Moore*, London, 1953). Both generals aroused sentiments among their adherents which could prejudice an objective view of their achievements, and political considerations were of significance in both cases. It is interesting to compare Sir Charles Oman's balanced assessment of the character and achievements of Moore and Wellington.[10] Modern opinions can be as diverse as those of the early 19th century; but Oman's reasoned comments avoid both the tendency towards uncritical adulation and the undue censure from which both commanders suffered at various times.

Wellington's demeanour and natural reserve were never calculated to win the adoration of his army; what he achieved instead was admiration and trust. Perhaps the best expression of the regard in which he was held was that recorded by John Kincaid:

He was not only head of the army but obliged to descend to the responsibility of every department in it ... whenever he went at its head, glory followed its steps – wherever he was not – I will not say disgrace, but something akin to it ensued ... Lord Wellington appeared to us never to leave anything to chance. However desperate the undertaking ... we ever felt confident that a redeeming power was at hand, nor were we ever deceived. Those only, too, who have served under such a master-mind and one of inferior calibre can appreciate the difference in a physical as well as a moral point of view – for when in the presence of the enemy, under him, we were never deprived of our personal comforts until prudence rendered it necessary, and they were always restored to us at the earliest possible moment.[11]

Such trust extended throughout the army, as articulated by Fusilier Horsefall of the 7th Foot when advancing into a cauldron of fire at Albuera: 'Whore's ar Arthur? Aw wish he wor here'.[12] Eventually the entire army would have agreed with Kincaid that 'we would rather see his long nose in the fight than a reinforcement of ten thousand men any day'.[13]

This had not been the case in previous years, however, when there had been considerable criticism from subordinates, some of which appeared in the British press. For example, one officer who had participated in the Talavera campaign wrote of Wellington's mistakes, as problems 'in military science, which it requires a clearer head than mine to solve!', and wondered if Wellington were distracted: 'To account for these things, in a man of Sir Arthur's reputation, is impossible. Some have asked, Who lost Mark Anthony the world? – A female (once, I believe, the mistress of Soult, and captured at Oporto), accompanies the head-quarter establishment. She has not a handsome face, but a good figure, and sits astride on horseback as knowingly and neatly as Mister Buckle himself'.[14]

Most of the criticism Wellington received at home was politically inspired. His Tory politics and friendships were of obvious assistance in his appointment and subsequent conduct of the Peninsular War, but these associations and family connections provoked a more vehement response among the political opposition than would otherwise have been the case. Typical were comments made after his return from Portugal and before the Sintra enquiry, to the effect that even if he were absolved of responsibility, 'who that witnessed the sinister efforts of his friends, will not suspect that he has owed his acquittal less to the eviction of that innocence than to the influence of those efforts?', especially when compared with the lack of support for the other generals, 'unbefriended individuals'.[15] At the same time, in a speech at

Winchester in November 1808, William Cobbett linked Wellesley's return from Portugal with the fact that the Wellesley family received some £23,766 annually from the public finances; equivalent, he said, to the poor rate on sixty parishes.

Such comments continued to he made even after Wellington began to achieve success in the Peninsula; for example, when, in the House of Lords, Liverpool moved a vote of thanks to Wellington and his army for the victory of Talavera, Lords Grosvenor, Grey, and Grenville opposed it, the last stating that he would vote for any motion which congratulated the army, but not one which included Wellington. Family connections continued to blight his reputation. When, in May 1811, the Court of Common Council in London voted to present him with a 200-guinea sword, several members objected, and one claimed that 'the Wellesley family had been sufficiently paid'[16] and alluded to Sintra; however, the objection was defeated after another member declared that Sintra had been a wise measure after all! Criticism diminished as Wellington's successes multiplied. When it was proposed in parliament in 1812 that an annuity of £2000 should be granted to him, Sir Francis Burdett objected, saying that although he was uninformed in military affairs, it seemed that insufficient had been achieved for the resources expended; but after a fierce rebuttal by Canning, Burdett's was the only vote against. By May 1814, when the government proposed to award Wellington £300,000 to purchase an estate, and that an annuity of £13,000 should be paid until that estate began to produce an income, Samuel Whitbread duly objected – but only because he considered such a reward insufficient!

Moore's position was influenced by politics in a somewhat different way, in that 'he is always treated as the Whig general par excellence'.[17] This has affected the perception both of Moore as a soldier, and the conduct of his Peninsular campaign. Although much criticism was silenced by the manner of his death, strong remarks were made about Moore, or the ministers who had sent him to the Peninsula, by those of conflicting political opinions.

Unlike Wellington, Moore's personality produced something akin to reverence among those who knew him well. Even in old age, that tough and experienced old warrior Thomas Graham became choked with emotion when he spoke of Moore, and fifty years after Moore's death the same thing was observed of John Colborne. The latter was among those captivated by Moore's personality, writing in 1809 that he was:

> a most extraordinary man. The nearer you saw him, the more he was admired. He was superior by many degrees to everyone I have seen: he had a magnificent mind. A most perfect gentleman. a determined enemy to the corrupt, corruption, and jobs, he never spared where he thought it

his duty to inflict. A man of this cast must create a host of enemies, and he certainly had his share of them.[18]

Moore also made an indelible mark upon the Napier brothers, Charles James, George (who served as Moore's ADC), and William; their strength of feeling may be gauged by the fact that both George and William named their sons John Moore Napier, and by their expressions of regard. George Napier recalled that Moore

> treated me like a son. I never was from under his command ... till that dreadful night when I saw him to whom I looked up as the first of men, a bloody corpse, without the melancholy satisfaction of hearing his last heroic words, 'I hope the people of England will be satisfied', addressed to that country which he loved with an ardour equal to the Roman patriot's, and had served to the hour of his death with a zeal and gallantry equalled by a few, surpassed by none.[19]

And, he added, 'was there ever an act of his during his life that was not perfect?'[20]

Sir Charles Oman describes Moore as 'perhaps the most distinguished officer in the British service' when recording his appointment to command in the Peninsula, but it is perhaps worth noting in addition that the choice of Moore illustrates that political favouritism was not a dominant factor in the determination of such appointments, if Whig generals like Moore were employed. Officers of talent were too rare to ignore, irrespective of their politics, if only because of a dearth of capable commanders. This recalls an early comment by John Colborne, writing from Messina in 1807, that 'Sir John Moore is one of the best generals we have (that, you will say, is not much to his credit)'; but, he continued more sympathetically, 'he is one of those determined and independent characters who act and speak what they think just and proper, without paying the least regard to the opinion of persons of interest or in power'.[21]

Moore's talents must have been recognised despite aspects of his career which had not been blameless. He seems to have harboured a low opinion, even distrust, of ministers, diplomats, and other generals, which had led him into stormy waters in Corsica and Sicily, which led to his removal from the latter place, where he had recently taken over from General Henry Fox, of whom he had no high opinion. Nevertheless, Moore was selected for the Swedish expedition and for the Peninsula, and although Sir Charles Oman records that the ministry did support Moore and left all possible matters in his hands, it might be remarked that the government was probably no happier about the situation than was Moore with the ministry. While not criticising him in public, much disquiet was felt in private, to the extent that Canning tried to persuade Portland in mid-campaign that Moore should be replaced by Lord Moira; but nothing came of the suggestion, either because of its impracticality, or because the question was overtaken by events.[22] Had the Spanish campaign ended in disaster – despite the evacuation, the battle of Coruña was heralded as a victory, quite apart from the strategic effects of Moore's campaign having perhaps saved the Peninsula from French domination – Moore would probably have taken most of the blame and been used as a shield to deflect attacks from the ministry. In the event, Moore became a hero by the manner of his death, and by acknowledging him as such the ministry helped prevent the opposition from using his cause as a means of attack.[23]

Early published comments on Moore were adulatory; for example, the Duke of York's General Order of 1 February 1809 stated that:

> Regardless of personal considerations, he esteemed that to which his Country called him the post of honour, and by his undaunted spirit, and unconquerable perseverance, he pointed the way to victory. His Country, the object of his latest solicitude, will rear a monument to his lamented memory; and the Commander in Chief feels he is paying the best tribute to his fame by thus holding him forth as an example to the Army.

Robert Ker Porter exemplified the perception of Moore which had arisen from the circumstances of his death: 'Gallant Moore, low art thou laid! In blood has [sic] the rays of thy fame been sunk, but not extinguished; they shoot the brighter from thine ashes, and settle on thy grave'; and stated that his last words 'seemed to wing his soul to regions where his glories will shine for ever without a cloud'.[24] Eight years before the publication of Charles Wolfe's immortal poem *The Burial of Sir John Moore*, other poetic offerings which appeared in the immediate aftermath of the event praised Moore unreservedly:

> *England's tried soldier from his dawn of youth,*
> *His deeds were godlike, and his words were truth;*
> *His life was perfect – glorious was his fall;*
> *Gallia's torn banners form'd his funeral pall!*[25]

At the same time, Moore's conduct of the Coruña campaign was being questioned; even the author of his obituary in *The Gentleman's Magazine* thought it necessary to note that 'when the plan and motives upon which General Moore acted shall be fully laid before the Publick, we have no doubt that his character will be rescued from those insinuations of tardiness which some persons seem disposed to attach to it'.[26] Some criticism was directed upon Moore by participants in the Coruña campaign, like Alexander Gordon of the 15th Light Dragoons, who wrote that

I have frequently heard it asserted by the advocates of Sir John Moore that the plan traced out for him was so ill-conceived ... that success was altogether unattainable ... But even if this be admitted, I am fully persuaded that the distresses the army encountered are chiefly to be attributed to the misconduct of its leader. It may appear invidious to reflect upon the character of an amiable and gallant officer, whose death in the moment of victory has cast a veil of glory over the errors of his judgement; but it is only an act of justice towards the brave men he commanded to point out the causes of the misbehaviour which, unhappily, tarnished their fame ... the ill-judged precipitancy of the retreat, and the undecided measures of the commander, by which he forfeited the confidence of his troops.[27]

The legitimacy of Gordon's opinion is not, perhaps, much reinforced by his view that the whole attempt to assist Spain was entirely without benefit to the cause which they were supporting.

Conversely, George Napier (one of Moore's most ardent supporters) believed that the blame lay elsewhere, that

the officers of that army were more engaged in looking after themselves and their own comforts, and openly murmuring against the commander-in-chief, than in looking after the soldiers and keeping up proper discipline ... the great cause of the disorganised state of the troops was mainly owing to the supineness of the general officers ... and to the imprudent language they used themselves, and permitted their staff to make use of, when speaking of the retreat and the conduct of it by the commander-in-chief.[28]

Certainly, some of the army's misbehaviour seems to have arisen from the disappointment of having to retreat; Robert Ker Porter recalled of this decision that 'a thunderbolt falling at the feet of each man could not have transfixed them more ... every countenance was changed; the proud glow on their cheeks was lost in a fearful paleness; the strongly-braced arm sunk listlessly to the side; a few murmurs were heard, and the army of England was no more.'[29] Basil Hall saw something similar when he toured the army immediately before the battle of Coruña, and asked an officer if anything could rouse the silent and evidently dispirited men. 'You'll see by-and-by, sir, if the French there choose to come over', was the reply; and when, moments later, the firing commenced and the troops formed up, Hall admitted that

I really could scarcely believe my eyes when I beheld these men spring from the ground, full of life and vigour, though but one minute before they had all been stretched out listlessly in the sun. I have already noticed the silence which reigned over the field; now, however, there could be heard a loud hum, and occasionally a jolly shout, and many a peal of laughter ... All had become animation and cheerfulness in minds from which, but a short time before, it seemed as if every particle of spirit had fled.[30]

Some of the questions surrounding Moore's conduct might have been resolved had the MP George Ponsonby carried his motion, proposed in the House of Commons on 24 February 1809, for an enquiry into the whole conduct of the campaign in Spain. His own lengthy speech was seconded by others critical of the government for, in effect, handing Moore an unattainable task; the debate (interrupted by concerns of the fire which was at that moment destroying the Drury Lane Theatre) involved the government's entire policy and the influence of John Hookham Frere; but Canning made a spirited defence and Ponsonby's motion was defeated by 220 votes to 127.

Ponsonby had stated that with Moore unable to speak for himself, he might become the subject of unfair blame; which, at least in the view of Moore's supporters, is exactly what occurred. In response to Southey's *History of the Peninsular War* published in 1827, John Colborne claimed that

the reputation of Sir John Moore was basely sacrificed to party spirit, and ... the attacks with which his character has been continually assailed, are as inconsiderate as they are unmerited ... The depreciation of the services of Sir John Moore and the defence of Mr Frere seems the grand object of Mr Southey's work ... Mr Frere ... certainly deserves many of the eulogiums passed upon him, but if Mr Southey has attempted to wind him up at the expense of a man whose whole life and energies [were devoted] to his country and profession, whose ability and decision did materially aid the Spanish people, he has for ever forfeited any claim he might have had to the character of a just and diligent historian.[31]

These attacks on Moore had a more profound effect, by inspiring what Oman called 'the immortal six volumes of that grand old soldier'[32] Sir William Napier, and thus influencing the popular perception of the Peninsular War for generations, until the publication of Oman's own history. Napier at first doubted his ability to write a history of the war,

and his scruples were finally overcome only by his burning desire to vindicate the memory of his beloved chieftain from the unjust aspersions with which it had been assailed ... when he, at length, determined to attempt the task, he limited his intentions to the narration of those operations which terminated at Corunna, and was only induced to proceed by the encouragement he derived from the success of the first volume.[33]

For all its imperfections, Napier's history (which elicited criticism over his prejudices at the time of publication, perhaps most notably in his conflict with Beresford) was a major landmark in the foundation of the study of military history, and is still distinguished for the style of its prose. The adulation of Moore which appears in Napier's history may be gauged from the extract quoted by Oman (*History*, vol.I, p.602), which continued:

Confiding in the strength of his genius, he disregarded the clamours of presumptuous ignorance, and opposing sound military views to the foolish projects so insolently thrust upon him by the ambassador, he conducted a long and arduous retreat with sagacity, intelligence, and fortitude; no insult disturbed, no falsehood deceived him, no remonstrance shook his determination; fortune frowned without subsiding his constancy, death struck but the spirit of the man remained unbroken when his shattered body scarcely afforded it a habitation.[34]

Unsurprisingly, Napier was equally vehement in his attitude to those who sought to criticise Moore, who 'have nothing but opinions, unsupported by facts, to offer to the world',[35] 'interested men, who were eager to cast a shade over one of the brightest characters that ever adorned the country. Those calumnies triumphed for a moment; but ... posterity ... will visit such of his odious calumniators as are not too contemptible to be remembered with a just and severe retribution'.[36]

If the foregoing explains how the earlier perception of the Peninsular War was influenced by partisan factors, it is perhaps worth remarking that Wellington's command was affected by political considerations in a somewhat different manner. Sir Charles Oman describes Wellington's relationship with the government (for example, *History*, vol.VI, chapter III of section XXV), which was altogether more cordial than that experienced by Moore, as might have been expected for a general who was a 'friend' of the ministry and who had himself been involved in it as Chief Secretary for Ireland. While Wellington's task was defined by the government, he was allowed considerable discretion in the conduct of operations, given the restriction of resources which were, of course, determined by the ministry. On this subject, it is perhaps worth remarking that both Moore and Wellington were burdened by the knowledge that, as Napier commented about the former, 'the best blood of England was committed to his charge, and that not an English army, but the very heart, the pith of the military power of his country was in his keeping'.[37] Wellington emphasised the same point when commenting upon the cautious nature of his operations: 'we have but one army, and ... the same men who fought at Vimeiro and Talavera fought the other day at Sorauren ... if I am to preserve that army, I must proceed with caution'.[38]

In his relations with the military establishment Wellington had less discretion, and notable difficulties were posed by the commander-in-chief, the Duke of York (see, for example, Oman's comments in *History*, vol.VI, p.223*ff*). The selection of subordinate commanders gave him many worries and was the subject of much correspondence. In January 1810 he asked Liverpool: 'I only beg you do not send me any violent party men. We must keep the spirit of party out of the army, or we shall be in a bad way indeed'.[39] The wisdom of this comment was perhaps proven by the affair of James Willoughby Gordon some years later (*History*, vol.IV, pp.224-6). Wellington's authority to select subordinates was limited; he recalled that he remembered 'what Miranda had said to me, and I wrote to the Government to ask them to send me Picton ... I found him a rough foul-mouthed devil as ever lived, but he always behaved extremely well.'[40] Many others came without his recommendation or approval, some entirely incompetent; perhaps the most surprising appointment was that of poor William Erskine, who was generally acknowledged to be mentally disturbed. Wellington did query this appointment, to be told by Torrens that Erskine 'in his lucid intervals ... is an uncommonly clever fellow; and I trust he may have no fit during the campaign, though he looked a little wild before he embarked.'[41] Wellington's attempts to dispense with the incompetents were complicated by his wish not to cause offence; as he told Torrens in December 1811, concerning one general who had been ill and another who wished to return home to be married, 'neither of them very fit to take charge of a large body ... I shall try if I can to get them away in this manner, as I would not on any account hurt the feelings of either.'[42]

As mentioned by Oman (*History*, vol.VI, pp.228-9), the etiquette of seniority was another complication to the employment of general officers, as it was not possible to expect any officer to be subordinate to one of lesser seniority, no matter how deserving the latter might be. The problem was complicated by the large number of generals in the service (in July 1815, for example, there were five field-marshals, 113 generals, 217 lieutenant-generals and 313 major-generals, far more than could ever be employed), and the situation was exemplified by Wellington's reply to Robert Craufurd's request for leave in December 1810: 'Adverting to the number of General Officers senior to you in the army, it has not been an easy task to keep you in your command; and if you should go, I fear that I should not be able to appoint you to it again, or to one that would be so agreeable to you, or in which you would be so useful.'[43]

The rigours of campaigning cost Wellington the services of some valued subordinates, either killed (Craufurd and Le Marchant, for example) or wounded (like Edward Paget, who was singularly unfortunate to be captured almost immediately after rejoining the army in 1812, having earlier lost an arm); but not all shared Wellington's relentless good health or determination to subordinate personal concerns to the demands of the service. Some genuinely fell ill and had to return home to recuperate, but Wellington was scathing about those who requested leave for other reasons. An example of his anger appears in a letter to Craufurd, subsequent to that quoted above:

> I see no reason why I should depart from the rule which I have laid down for myself in these cases ... my opinion is that there is no private concern that cannot be settled by instruction and power of attorney ... It is certainly the greatest inconvenience to the service that officers should absent themselves as they do, each of them requiring, at the same time, that when it shall be convenient to return, he shall find himself in the same situation as when he left the army. In the mean time, who is to do the duty? How am I to be responsible for the army? ... I may be obliged to consent to the absence of an officer, but I cannot approve of it.[44]

He complained to Torrens on the same day:

> They come to me to ask leave of absence, under pretence of business, which they say it is important to them to transact; and indeed I go so far as to make them declare that it is paramount to every other consideration in life. At the same time, I know that many of them have no business ... The inconvenience of their going is terrible, and the detail it throws upon me greater than I can well manage; for I am first to instruct one, then a second, and afterwards, upon his return, the first again, upon every duty.[45]

The prevalence of such practices makes all the more creditable decisions like that of Le Marchant, to decline a leave of absence even after receipt of the news of the death of his wife, which left their eight young children without a parent in England.

Despite the presence of excellent subordinates in some of the key positions – Hill, Beresford, George Murray, Dickson, etc – it was presumably the calibre of the rest which led to Wellington's comments of 15 May 1811, concerning the errors which led to the escape of the French garrison of Almeida:

> Possibly I have to reproach myself for not having been on the spot; but really ... having employed two divisions and a brigade, to prevent the escape of 1400 men, who I did not

think it likely would attempt to escape, the necessity of my attending personally ... did not occur to me ... I certainly feel, every day, more and more the difficulty of the situation in which I am placed. I am obliged to be every where, and if absent from any operation, something goes wrong.[46]

Nevertheless, a likely consequence of Wellington's attitude towards his subordinates was a tendency to stifle initiative and experience in independent command, even with those officers capable of exercising it usefully, like Hill or (to a lesser extent) Graham. It is perhaps a measure of Wellington's level of control that there was rarely an official 'second-in-command' (see, for example, *History*, vol.VI, pp.227–30) – hence the discussion in which Wellington nominated Beresford as 'the ablest man I have yet seen with the army', albeit only because 'what we want now is some one to feed our troops, and I know of no one fitter for the purpose than Beresford.'[47] Perhaps Wellington's attitude to delegation of authority is exemplified by his conversation with Uxbridge on the eve of the battle of Waterloo. Knowing that he would succeed to command if Wellington were killed, yet without 'the slightest idea what are the projects of the Duke', with much trepidation Uxbridge raised the matter.

The Duke listened to him quietly to the end without saying a single word; and when he replied, it was without impatience, without surprise, and without emotion. He said calmly, 'Who will attack the first to-morrow – I or Bonaparte?' 'Bonaparte' ... 'Well,' continued the Duke in the same tone, 'Bonaparte has not given me any idea of his projects; and as my plans will depend upon his, how can you expect me to tell you what mine are?' ... The Duke then said, rising and at the same time touching him in a friendly way on the shoulder, 'There is one thing certain, Uxbridge; that is, that whatever happens, you and I will do our duty.'[48]

An example of the interference with which Wellington had to contend, in what might be considered as operational matters, were attempts by the Duke of York to withdraw from the Peninsula units whose strength had fallen below what might be considered an effective level. In 1812 Wellington was ordered to send home second battalions, which by their very nature did not have a pool of reserves upon which to draw, unlike first battalions which could take men from the second. He complied but commented to Liverpool, somewhat ironically, that 'Your Lordship and His Royal Highness [the Duke of York] are the best judges of what description of troops it is expedient that this army should be composed', but then continued,

some of the best and most experienced soldiers in this army, the most healthy and capable of bearing fatigue, are in the 2nd battalions. The 2nd batts. 53rd, 31st, and 66th, for instance, are much more efficient, and have always more men for duty in proportion to their gross numbers, and fewer sick than any of the 1st battalions recently arrived which had been in Walcheren; and it is certain that this army will not be so strong by the exchange of new for old soldiers.[49]

Nevertheless, the same thing occurred in early 1813 (*History*, vol.VI, pp.231–5) when the Duke of York tried to recall under-strength units home to recruit. Wellington continued to protest:

It is better for the service here to have one soldier or officer, whether of cavalry or infantry, who has served one or two campaigns, than it is to have two or even three who have not. Not only the new soldiers can perform no service, but by filling the hospital they are a burthen to us. For this reason, I am so unwilling to part with the men whom I have formed into the provisional battalions; and I never will part with them as long as it is left to my discretion.

He then went on to state that the Duke of York 'must excuse me if I take my own view of the case, however limited, and act according to my judgement of what will be the best for the particular service entrusted to my charge.'[50]

As noted above, his solution to the problem of under-strength units was to amalgamate two into one 'provisional battalion', sending home only those officers and NCOs surplus to requirements. Not only was this a sensible expedient to retain experienced men, but it was merely an extension of the established practice of forming composite 'flank battalions' from the flank companies of several units. Although not an unqualified success – the Duke of York's objections probably had some merit – such composite units were perfectly workable tactical entities, despite having their personnel drawn from different corps (although the most extreme case, the two 'battalions of detachments' which served at Talavera appear to have drawn their rank and file from as many as nine and ten different battalions).[51] The system was even operated at home: in 1798 the flank battalions formed in the Yorkshire District, for example, combined companies from one line, two militia, and three supplementary militia regiments. Wellington was even more concerned over similar orders to withdraw weak but experienced cavalry regiments; but in the event had to bow to the Duke of York's wishes, though he managed to retain his three existing provisional battalions.

It is surprising to reflect that even after all his achievements, Wellington continued to be troubled by such interference. Even for the 1815 campaign he had to complain to Bathurst that:

To tell the truth, I am not very well pleased with the manner in which the Horse Guards have conducted themselves towards me ... I might have expected that the Generals and Staff formed by me in the last war would have been allowed to come to me again; but instead of that, I am overloaded with people I have never seen before; and it appears to be purposely intended to keep those out of my way whom I wished to have. However I'll do the best I can with the instruments which have been sent to assist me.[52]

Such factors lend support to Wellington's claim that 'the real reason why I succeeded in my own campaigns is because I was always on the spot – I saw everything, and did everything for myself.'[53]

If the consequences of the presence of Moore and Wellington upon the campaigns in the Peninsula are largely self-evident, their effect upon the British Army is worthy of consideration, and is a subject upon which Sir Charles Oman did not concentrate. Oman notes of Moore that 'he had reorganised the light infantry tactics of the British army, and had won the enthusiastic admiration of all who had ever served under him for his zeal and intelligent activity',[54] but it could be argued that his influence was much greater, and somewhat removed, from his command in the Coruña campaign. Despite his reputation as the architect of light infantry tactics, primarily during his tenure as commander at Shorncliffe, the extent to which Moore was responsible for the resulting system in a purely tactical sense is debatable, and to some extent it was less a new system that a development of existing practice.

From an early period Moore accepted the premise that the most effective light troops were not those employed exclusively as skirmishers, but those equally able to act in line, in a more conventional manner; as he had noted when instructing his composite battalion of militia light companies in Ireland in 1798-9: 'Our Light Infantry ... are in fact a mixture of the Yager, and the Grenadier'.[55] This was not a new concept, however, but had been stated by Francis de Rottenburg, author of an influential manual (*Regulations for the Exercise of Riflemen and Light Infantry*, London, 1798), which had been given official sanction by the Duke of York. As commander of the 5/60th, de Rottenburg had come under Moore's command in Ireland, and much of Moore's 1798-9 instructions were taken from his book almost verbatim.

However, it is with the light infantry at Shorncliffe that Moore is most popularly associated, for which service he was (unsurprisingly) praised by William Napier, who remarked that Moore would have been known as the modern-day Iphicrates (after the Athenian general of the 4th century BC, known for his improvements in the equipment of the peltasts, the light troops of the day), had he not won greater renown by dying like the Spartan general Brasidas (killed in battle in 422 BC).[56] In the techniques of light infantry service, however, Moore was much indebted to the officer he selected as lieutenant-colonel of his 52nd Foot (of which Moore had been appointed colonel in May 1801), and which he converted into a corps of light infantry, with the encouragement of the Duke of York, who was himself interested in the development of light troops. The officer selected by Moore was Lieutenant-Colonel Kenneth Mackenzie of the 44th, whom he had encountered performing light infantry drill at Minorca, and who was a specialist in light infantry service: he had been given responsibility for drilling Thomas Graham's 90th Perthshire Volunteers (effectively a light regiment from its formation in 1794, though not officially titled as such until May 1815), and had trained as light infantry a flank battalion in Sir Charles Stuart's expedition to Portugal.

It was Mackenzie, rather than Moore, who devised and carried out the light infantry drill used by the 52nd, and extended to the other light infantry regiment at Shorncliffe, the 43rd; as his obituary recorded, 'he commenced with the 52d, a system of movements and exercise, in which Sir John Moore, at first, acquiesced with reluctance, the style of drill, march, and platoon exercise, being entirely new; but when he saw the effect of the whole, he was not only highly gratified, but became its warmest supporter.'[57] Mackenzie's contribution was confirmed by others, for example Jonathan Leach, who was present at Shorncliffe with the 70th, and was later a distinguished Rifles officer: 'The new system of drill which Lieutenant Colonel M'Kenzie introduced at this period, and which has been adopted by other light infantry regiments, it will scarcely be denied by the most prejudiced persons, has been attended with the most complete success. I allude to the ease and correctness with which the regiments drilled according to that system, marched and manoeuvred ever after.'[58] Mackenzie's contribution might have been better-known had his active career not been curtailed by the recurring effects of a severe concussion caused by a fall from his horse at Shorncliffe, though he served subsequently under Graham at Cádiz and in Holland and rose to the rank of lieutenant-general. (He is also known as Sir Kenneth Douglas of Glenbirvie, the name he adopted upon his elevation in 1830 to a baronetcy dormant since the death of his maternal uncle in 1812.)

The three regiments trained as light infantry at Shorncliffe, and which later formed the nucleus of the Peninsular Light Division, included the 95th Rifles, which under Coote Manningham and William Stewart had already begun the development of 'rifle tactics'; the other regiments at the camp (the 4th, 59th, and 70th) were not light infantry. How far Mackenzie's system extended to the 95th is uncertain, and other light infantry corps may not have been influenced directly; in 1808 it was de Rottenburg himself who supervised the training of the 68th, 71st, and 85th at Brabourn Lees, near Ashford.[59]

Probably more significant than light infantry tactics, however, was Moore's concept of discipline. Although especially relevant to the greater degree of initiative and independence required of a light infantry soldier, Moore's ideas on the most effective and humane approach towards the leadership and treatment of soldiers were applicable to all parts of the army, and involved what he termed the discipline of the mind as much as that of the body. It was based upon a premise that a soldier should be contented with his lot and determined in all ways to do his best, sentiments best derived from personal and regimental pride and comradeship, and encouraged by officers using emulation and explanation rather than punishment to obtain obedience. Moore put these theories into practice with his own 52nd, of which George Napier recalled he 'was proud to the greatest degree, and loved and treated us all as if we were his children. It was impossible for any father to devote himself more to the welfare of his sons than did Sir John Moore to that of his officers, and no parent could be more revered and beloved than he was by us all – officers, non-commissioned officers, and privates'.[60]

In this regard also, it appears that Mackenzie was an important factor, as George Napier recorded:

Colonel MacKenzie began by assembling the officers and telling them that the only way of having a regiment in good order was by every individual thoroughly knowing and performing his duty; and that if the officers did not fully understand their duty, it would be quite impossible to expect that the men either could or would perform them as they ought; therefore the best and surest method was to commence drilling the whole of the officers, and when they became perfectly acquainted with the system, they could teach the men, and by their zeal, knowledge, and, above all, good temper and kind treatment of the soldier, make the regiment the best in the service; and, as he predicted, it did become the finest and best behaved corps, both as regard officers and men, that ever was seen; and ... was considered a model for the rest of the army ... The great thing that Sir John Moore and Colonel Mackenzie used to impress upon the minds of the officers was that our duty was to do everything in our power to prevent crime, and then there would be no occasion for punishment.[61]

It is perhaps worth remarking that Moore and Mackenzie did have a superior grade of personnel to begin with; when the 52nd was converted to light infantry in January 1803, its 2nd Battalion was made into an independent regiment (the 96th Foot) and Moore was authorised to transfer from it any men he might judge 'best adapted for the Light Infantry' and replace them with less-suitable men from the 52nd, so that the latter was very much a regiment of selected personnel.

Under Moore's authority, the same system was extended at least to the 43rd, but it is possible that something similar already existed within the 95th; Coote Manningham published a series of lectures delivered to the officers of the 95th in spring 1803 which recognised that light infantry should be skilled in more than 'the old and practised stratagems of a partisan only' and hinted at the revised role of the officer, discipline being maintained 'without harassing the soldier, and the officers should set the example'.[62] Perhaps the effectiveness of Moore's system is demonstrated by the fact that the *esprit de corps* which came with light infantry status, and training by other hands, was not sufficient alone to produce the excellence of Moore's regiments; the 85th, for example, was converted to light infantry in September 1808 and served in the early part of the Peninsular War, but after its withdrawal from the campaign was so riven by dissension among the officer corps that the entire body was transferred out and replaced by selected officers from other regiments, including two from the 43rd and two captains from the 52nd, whereupon the improvement in the unit was marked.

Evidence of the spread of Moore's doctrine is provided by the case of another light infantry regiment, the 71st, which after the death of Lieutenant-Colonel Hon. Henry Cadogan at Vitoria was led by the lamentable Sir Nathaniel Peacock, until he was dismissed for cowardice. His successor, George Napier of the 52nd, noted that so pernicious had been Peacock's influence – 'weak, overbearing and insolent beyond everything' – that the officers were demoralised and 'discipline so relaxed that neither officers nor men were very well inclined to submit cheerfully to my orders';[63] but having returned the officers to their duty, the other ranks followed their example. The extent to which Moore's ideas influenced his followers may be gauged from George Napier's remarks to the effect that:

> the first and greatest duty an officer has to perform is that of preventing crime in the soldier, and the surest and most honourable means of doing so is to look upon the soldier as a fellow-citizen, who, by the admitted laws of society and for the general good of the State placed under you in rank and station, is nevertheless as good a man and as good a Christian as yourself, born in the same country, amenable to the same laws, and above all possessing the same feelings as the proudest peer in the land.[64]

In this there was perhaps a slight echo of Dr Samuel Johnson's essay 'On the Bravery of the English Common Soldiers', which was reprinted as late as 1801 in *The British Military Library or Journal*, and which commented on the unservile nature of a society in which it was accepted that a man 'is no less necessary to his employer, than his employer is to him'.[65]

It might be said that Wellington was more representative of the older form of discipline, enforced by corporal punishment, exemplified by such statements as his complaint to Bathurst in July 1813:

> It is quite impossible for me or any other man to command a British army under the existing system. We have in the service the scum of the earth as common soldiers; and of late years we have been doing every thing in our power, both by law and by publications, to relax the discipline by which alone such men can be kept in order ... It really is a disgrace to have any thing to say to such men as some of our soldiers are.[66]

He remained convinced of the need for an ultimate, extreme form of punishment (*ie* the lash), remarking of the system of 'billing up' (confining to barracks with extra drill) that 'who would bear to be billed up, but for the fear of a stronger punishment? he would knock down the sentry and walk out!',[67] and that attempts to reform malefactors should be secondary to 'the prevention of crime and the impression made by the punishment upon the public mind'.[68] Nevertheless, when presenting Colours to the 93rd at Canterbury in 1834, he expressed views reminiscent of the more 'enlightened' system which might be attributed to Moore and his followers:

> The rules of discipline, subordination, and good order teach the Officers their duties towards the soldiers ... they teach the soldiers to respect their superiors the non-commissioned Officers and the Officers; and to consider them as their best friends and protectors. The enforcement of these rules will enable the Officers to conduct with kindness towards the soldier those duties with which he is charged; and to preserve him in a state ... to perform the services required from him, without undue severity, or unnecessary restraint or interference with his habits. It will enable the soldier to enjoy in comfort and happiness the moments of leisure and relaxation from duty which the nature of the service may afford him ... enforce the observance of the rules of discipline, subordination, and good order, if you mean to be efficient, to render service to the public, to be respectable in the eyes of the military world as a military body; to be respected by the community; to be comfortable and happy among yourselves.[69]

In the British Army of the post-Waterloo era, it was the philosophy of command associated with Moore which came to predominate, even though the change was initiated more at battalion level than from above, developing what might almost be termed a form of paternalism in relations between the most forward-thinking officers and their subordinates. The effect was not immediate and progress may not have been rapid, but it was probably in this respect that Moore's influence was most significant and lasting.

The influence of the Peninsular War, and of the generals who commanded there, extended to the various branches of the army in different ways. Sir Charles Oman summarised the various branches of the staff in chapter VIII of *Wellington's Army*, though it is perhaps worth remarking that despite the existence of a form of staff college in the Senior Department of the Royal Military College, compared with the large staff organisations of some armies that of the British remained very small. Excluding general officers and the commandants of garrisons, the only full-time staff officers were the ten Permanent Assistants of the Quartermaster-General's Department; all other posts were filled by officers detached from regimental duty. Although the staff organisation perfected by Wellington in general ran efficiently, untrained officers did cause problems. For example, although concerning only a minor position, Wellington's exasperation is evident in his letter to Colville in February 1814 regarding the telegraph at Arcangues being put in charge of an officer known 'to be so stupid as to be unfit to be trusted in any way ... when I call upon a General Officer to recommend an officer to fill a station in the public service, I mean that he should recommend one fit to perform some duty, and not one so stupid as to be unable to comprehend that which he is to perform; who is recommended only because he is a favorite with such General Officer.'[70]

An expansion and refining of the staff system was certainly necessary during the Peninsular War, if only to accommodate the increasing size of the force to be administered; for example, Wellington's field army in the Vitoria campaign (not including other forces under his jurisdiction) was between two and three times as great as that commanded by Moore in the Coruña campaign. An important step was the establishment of a divisional system, instead of the previous reliance upon brigades as the principal unit, as covered by Sir Charles Oman in chapter IX of *Wellington's Army*. Wellington's organisation of his forces into Divisions dated only from 18 June 1809, though such a disposition had been used in the expedition to Denmark, and by Moore in his Spanish campaign. Wellington's numbers were never sufficient, or perhaps the circumstances never appropriate, officially to form separate *corps d'armée* in the Napoleonic sense, even though latterly there was some use of a similar expedient.[71]

Considerable improvements were made within the Ordnance services during the French Wars, but not many were attributable

directly to Peninsular War experience; and Oman's coverage of
Wellington's field artillery is restricted to pp.113–14 of his
Wellington's Army, with the various appendices in the *History*
(vol.II, pp.654–5; vol.III, pp.558–61; vol.IV, pp.650–2; and vol.V,
pp.619–22) being limited to the disposition of units. A number of
important developments pre-dated the Peninsular War, notably the
creation of horse artillery (1793), the militarisation of the artillery
transport personnel by the creation of the Corps of Drivers (1794),
the abandoning of the concept of 'battalion guns' (light field-pieces
attached to individual battalions), and the development of spherical
case-shot, better-known by the name of its inventor, Shrapnel (first
used 1804). With the other new development, the Congreve rocket,
Wellington was unimpressed, remarking that he had no wish to set
light to any town and knew of no other use for them (perhaps
remembering their deployment at Copenhagen). Trials with rockets
had been made in the Peninsula as early as October 1808, when
Lieutenant-Colonel William Robe supervised a demonstration for
Moore and Burrard, in which seven rockets were launched, six of
them from a bombarding frame of which two were roughly on
target, one seventy yards wide, and the other three so far off-target
that they were never found. The one launched from a field carriage
veered off course and exploded against a house, but did no more
damage than dent a wall and break some windows, whereupon the
trial was abandoned.[72] Despite some successful use of rockets late
in the Peninsular War, it. was presumably such erratic behaviour
which aroused Wellington's dislike, his most famous comment on
the subject being that made in reply to a plea not to take the rockets
from Edward Whinyates' troop at the start of the Waterloo
campaign, lest it break that officer's heart: 'Damn his heart, sir;
let my order be obeyed.'[73] (In the event Whinyates was allowed to
keep – and use – his rockets, in addition to the field-pieces with
which his troop was equipped at Wellington's direction.)

In employment in the field, artillery remained largely a
supporting arm, with batteries attached to particular formations.
No attempt was made to assemble a strong reserve as an offensive
weapon in its own right, to concentrate fire upon a particular part
of the enemy's line prior to an attack, as was Napoleon's practice.
Initially Wellington had insufficient artillery to make such a tactic
possible, but the style of employment continued even after guns
became more plentiful. Although he endeavoured to assemble an
artillery reserve at Waterloo, it was of necessity committed to
bolstering the line relatively early in the battle.

The other service controlled by the Master-General of Ordnance,
the engineers, was more affected by the Peninsular War. At the
outset there were two bodies, the Corps of Royal Engineers,
consisting exclusively of officers, and the rank and file of the Royal
Military Artificers. The latter comprised twelve companies of

artisans stationed in fortresses, from which small detachments were seconded for campaign service; their numbers were so few that in November 1809 there were just twenty-five with the army in the Peninsula, only nineteen of whom were effective. Even when supplemented by the members of the Royal Staff Corps (formed in 1798 as part of the army rather than under Ordnance control) and officers detached from other units as 'assistant engineers', the number of trained personnel was woefully insufficient to undertake any major engineering task. At the siege of Badajoz in 1812, for example, there were only nineteen engineer officers, of whom four were killed and nine wounded. William Napier wrote with the anger of one who had seen the consequences at first hand:

> To the discredit of the English government, no army was ever so ill provided with the means of prosecuting such enterprises. The engineer officers were exceedingly zealous ... but the ablest trembled when reflecting upon their utter destitution of all that belonged to real service ... the best officers and the finest soldiers were obliged to sacrifice themselves in a lamentable manner ... The sieges carried on in Spain were a succession of butcheries, because the commonest resources of their art were denied to the engineers.[74]

Even given Napier's tendency for a partisan view, as noted by Oman in chapter XVII of *Wellington's Army*, such were the imperfections in the engineer service that a fundamental change had to be made, at Wellington's behest, by the creation of the Royal Military Artificers or Sappers and Miners (titled Royal Sappers and Miners from 1813), a corps of other ranks trained in field engineering and officered by Royal Engineers. This led to a marked improvement in the engineer capability of the Peninsular army from 1813, when 300 were deployed in the field.

Wellington's concern for the supplying of his troops was well-known, and, as detailed in chapter XIX of Oman's *Wellington's Army*, the commissariat system generally worked adequately; but government parsimony was one factor which prevented the entire reconstruction and militarisation of the transport service. Although the Royal Waggon Train had been formed in 1799, it remained too small to make much impression upon the problem of fulfilling the army's transport needs, so the existing system of hiring local civilian transport remained in use, leading to complaints like that made by Wellington to Liverpool, on the reason for delays in beginning the siege of Ciudad Rodrigo: 'we must expect disappointments where we have to deal with Portuguese and Spanish carters and muleteers, and therefore I cannot invest the place till to-morrow. What do you think of empty carts taking two days to go ten miles on a good road? After all, I am obliged to appear satisfied, or they would all desert!'[75]

Although it was recognised that a permanent and militarised transport service was a vital necessity to avoid the ills of creating such a corps at the beginning of every campaign, the Royal Waggon Train was disbanded in 1833 in spite of the experiences of the Peninsular War, and only after the first Crimean winter was something similar re-established, in the Land Transport Corps, created in January 1855.

Perhaps due to the nature of the terrain in some parts of the Iberian Peninsula, the cavalry did not attain the same level of importance as the infantry, by whom they were regarded, according to George Gleig of the 85th, as 'more ornamental than useful'.[76] This is certainly an unfair judgement, and, as Sir Charles Oman remarked in chapter V of *Wellington's Army*, the cavalry probably received more criticism (including from Wellington himself) than was really justified, despite a number of unfortunate and well-publicised incidents.

Such as they were, the cavalry's failings were the consequence of imperfect leadership and training, emphasising again the great value of units inured to campaign service when compared with the newly-arrived. The difference was probably most evident in 'outpost' or reconnaissance duty; as William Tomkinson of the 16th Light Dragoons commented: 'To attempt giving men or officers any idea in England of outpost duty was considered absurd, and when they came abroad, they had all this to learn. In fact, there was no one to teach them'.[77] In time, and led by the cavalry of the King's German Legion, who were acknowledged as experts in the field, the cavalry became proficient, with the heavier regiments of dragoons becoming as adept as the light regiments, the distinction between the two declining in significance.

Although the cavalry achieved a number of marked successes in action, their reputation suffered from a number of unfortunate occurrences arising from bad leadership and want of discipline, what Wellington described as 'the trick our officers of cavalry have acquired of galloping at every thing, and their galloping back as fast as they gallop on the enemy. They never consider the situation, and never think of manoeuvering before an enemy ... [and] never keep nor provide for a reserve'.[78] Another comment on the same subject was recorded by Oman (*Wellington's Army*, p.104): 'I considered our cavalry so inferior from want of order, although I consider one squadron a match for two French squadrons, that I should not have liked to see four British squadrons opposed to four French'.[79] The dearth of capable cavalry commanders is demonstrated by the continued employment of Sir John ('Jack') Slade – 'that damned stupid fellow' according to Paget[80] – who in 1811 even briefly commanded the entire cavalry during the absence of Stapleton Cotton. Both Cotton (later Viscount Combermere) and Henry Paget (later Earl of Uxbridge and Marquess of Anglesey) were competent cavalry leaders, but the former was sometimes absent from the Peninsula and Paget's services were denied to Wellington until the Waterloo campaign by a matter of etiquette, Paget having eloped with the wife of Wellington's brother Henry. Otherwise, the reputation of the cavalry command was such that Charles Boutflower of the 40th could write in 1812 of 'the incapacity, not to add, want of courage, of many of the Generals ... has become so notorious, that there is scarcely a Dinner party, or assemblage ... where the conduct of our Cavalry Generals is not spoken of with disgust & contempt.'[81]

The problem of cavalry charges sometimes getting out of hand persisted until the end of the period, the best-known of all, perhaps, being that of the Union Brigade at Waterloo, which was mauled severely by failing to rally, or to keep a covering reserve, after a successful beginning. Perhaps confirming the great value of experienced regiments, it is worth noting that two of the three regiments involved in this last example of over-zealous indiscipline had seen no campaign service for twenty years before Waterloo. It was presumably this which finally led Wellington to issue his memorandum for cavalry charges, as quoted by Oman in *Wellington's Army*, pp.111–12.

The principal development concerning the infantry which arose from the era of the Peninsular War was probably that already mentioned – the spread of what might be termed a light infantry doctrine to the line. The essence of Wellington's infantry tactics is well-known, although the value of the bayonet within them was a topic which aroused much discussion and some controversy in the post-Peninsular War era. Contrary to the pride felt by several nations on their traditional abilities with the bayonet, one of the most prolific writers on tactics, Colonel John Mitchell, described it as a 'rickety zigzag' of no use in modern war, and despite the protestations of the pro-bayonet faction, very few instances of its use in open warfare could be recalled (to the extent that the bayonet-fight near Roncesvalles between Captain George Tovey's company of the 20th Foot and the 6me *Légère*, which occurred by accident when the French ascended a ridge unseen, was discussed in greater detail than its significance would otherwise have warranted). In reality, it was the effect on the morale of a unit already shaken by musketry that constituted the value of the bayonet, one or other side almost always giving way before steel could be crossed. As one writer commented, 'no shock or contact takes place, or can take place, with modern infantry arms',[82] while another claimed that 'the Swedes, the Americans, the Turks, if un-Italianised, and our own mutinous population, are the only enemies now who will wait a bayonet shock'.[83] William Napier, a champion of the bayonet, commented upon its great 'moral influence':

Men know psychologically and physiologically, that whether it be called a 'rickety zigzag', or any other name, it will prick their flesh and let out life, and, therefore, they eschew it. Many persons will stand fire, who will not stand a charge, and for this plain psychological reason, that there is great hope of escape in the first case, very little in the second, and hope is the great sustainer of courage.[84]

In fact, both sides of the argument had some validity, in that the psychological aspect of the bayonet only really came into play after the enemy had been disorganised by musketry, though this seems not always to have been appreciated. Graham is reported to have declared at Barrossa (March 1811), upon the approach of the enemy: 'Now, my lads, there they are – spare your powder, but give them steel enough';[85] and the same attitude was applied by Gough (a veteran of the same battle) in his campaigns against the Sikhs, most memorably at Sobraon (1846), when, being told that his artillery had expended its ammunition, he supposedly thanked God that 'we'll be at them with the bayonet'. (Even if apocryphal, this seems typical of Gough's 'ill-judged valour' which led one participant in the battle of Chillianwalla in 1849 to remark that 'His Lordship fancied himself at Donnybrook Fair, and was in the thick of it, in the mêlée, and lost to sight.')[86]

It is a not uncommon belief that military developments entirely stagnated in the years after the Peninsular War, leading to the great administrative and other problems of the Crimean War; but the question is by no means so clearly defined.[87] The British Army of the Peninsular and Waterloo campaigns had achieved success with a system more rooted in the 18th century than in the system employed by Napoleon; and having achieved success by those methods, it is perhaps not too surprising that Wellington (who even when not himself commander-in-chief retained much influence) should be unwilling to support change.

Change, however, there was, even if it originated more from middle-ranking and regimental officers than from the highest level, including officers who had been influenced in their early careers as much by Moore as by Wellington. While the events of the Peninsular War continued to be quoted as tactical examples, in the period after Waterloo there was much debate on the methods of taking forward progress in the military system, notably in such 'professional' publications as the *United Service Journal* (founded in 1827 and subsequently appearing under various names), of which the 'bayonet question' mentioned above was typical. Experiences in numerous colonial campaigns, where the 'traditional' style of warfare was hardly appropriate, was also beneficial towards the process of development. Much post-Waterloo publication concerned developments in light infantry service, and in this way

- coupled with the revised ideas of discipline and the relationship between officers and other ranks – it might be said that it was the legacy of Moore, rather than that of Wellington, which prevailed in the long term. In addition to the tactical and technological changes which occurred after the Peninsular War (the technological drawing less upon the experiences of that war than the tactical), the Peninsula exerted another important effect upon the army, in the development of enhanced pride and self-esteem in addition to the increasing professionalism of its members. The public perception of soldiers as individuals might still hearken back to Lord Erskine's remark about 'a brutal and insolent soldiery', but set against that was the influence of such commentators as the ubiquitous William Napier, for all that he was hardly an unbiased judge. When writing of the British soldier, he informed his readers that:

> The whole world cannot produce a nobler specimen of military bearing, nor is the mind unworthy of the outward man. He does not, indeed, possess that presumptuous vivacity which would lead him to dictate to his commanders, or even censure real errors, although he may perceive them; but he is observant, and quick to comprehend his orders, full of resources under difficulties, calm and resolute in danger, and more than usually obedient and careful of his officers in moments of imminent peril. It has been asserted that his undeniable firmness in battle, is the result of a phlegmatic constitution uninspired by moral feeling. Never was a more stupid calumny uttered! Napoleon's troops fought in bright fields, where every helmet caught some beams of glory, but the British soldier conquered under the cold shade of aristocracy; no honours awaited his daring, no despatch gave him name to the applause of his countrymen; his life of danger and hardship was uncheered by hope, his death unnoticed. Did his heart sink therefore? Did he not endure with surpassing fortitude the sorest of ills, sustain the most terrible assaults in battle unmoved, and, with incredible energy overthrow every opponent, at all times proving that, while no physical military qualification was wanting, the fount of honour was also full and fresh within him![88]

The successes of the Peninsular and Waterloo campaigns, reinforced by such eulogies as the above, helped develop the priceless fund of regimental tradition which became so important to the British Army, as a source of inspiration for future generations. This was exemplified by the accumulation of battle-honours, as emblazoned on the regimental Colours. Prior to the Peninsular War, only a few regiments possessed these distinctions, beyond the 'Egypt' badge authorised in 1802 for those regiments which had served there. The others were very few: Gibraltar, Minden, Maida, and a handful of restricted honours such as the 15th Light Dragoons' 'Emsdorf', the 73rd's 'Mangalore', and the 78th's 'Assaye' (honours for earlier actions were awarded retrospectively, like the 39th's 'Plassey' in 1835, or the 5th's 'Wilhelmstahl' in 1836). After the Peninsular War, however, regimental pride and tradition was reinforced by the granting of a host of honours, and with them a number of commemorations of Peninsular War events, as diverse as the Sherwood Foresters' hoisting of a red jacket on the flagstaff on the anniversary of the storming of Badajoz; the use by the Border Regiment of the drums captured from the French 34th on the anniversary of Arroyo dos Molinos; and regimental toasts like that to 'The Corunna Majors' drunk by the Queen's Own Royal West Kent Regiment on the anniversary of that battle (and commemorating Charles Napier and Charles Stanhope). The extent to which the influence of the Peninsular War was felt would seem to be exemplified by a poignant incident at Ypres in April 1914, when the mortally-wounded Lieutenant-Colonel Eric Stephenson of the 3rd Battalion, Middlesex Regiment, exhorted his men to 'Die hard, boys, die hard!', using a phrase which would have been known, via regimental tradition, to every one of his men, and which originated with his predecessor William Inglis on another sanguinary field almost 104 years earlier, at Albuera. As far as the British Army is concerned, it is probably in such ways that the legacy of the Peninsular War has been of the longest duration.

Notes

1. Oman, *History*, vol.I, p.597.
2. Earl Stanhope, *Notes on Conversations with the Duke of Wellington* (London, 1888), p.182.
3. R. Glover, *Peninsular Preparation: The Reform of the British Army 1795-1804* (Cambridge,1963).
4. 'A Veteran British Officer' (J.F. Neville), *Leisure Moments in the Camp and Guard-Room* (York, 1812), p.98.
5. See M. Glover, 'The Purchase of Commissions: A Reappraisal', *JSAHR* LVIII (1980), pp.223-35.
6. Stanhope, *Conversations*, p.18.
7. 'Notes Respecting the Recruiting of the Army during the Last and Present Century', *United Service Journal* 1839, vol.I, p.528.
8. Oman, *History*, vol.II, p.313; *cf* Jac Weller, *Wellington in the Peninsula 1808-1814* (London, 1962), pp.104-5.
9. *Wellington's Army*, pp.209-11.
10. Oman, *History*, vol.I, pp.597-602; vol.II, pp.294-311; vol.VII, p.524; and chapter III of *Wellington's Army* respectively.
11. Sir John Kincaid, *Adventures in the Rifle Brigade and Random Shots from a Rifleman* (combined edn., London, 1908), pp.245-6.
12. J.S. Cooper, *Rough Notes of Seven Campaigns in Portugal, Spain,*

France and America (Carlisle, 1869, reprinted 1914), pp.67–8.

13. Kincaid, *op.cit.* p.36.

14. *The Monthly Magazine* XXVIII, no.191 (1 November 1809), p.353.

15. *The News*, 6 November 1808.

16. *Gentleman's Magazine*, May 1811, p.487.

17. J.H. Anderson, *The Spanish Campaign of Sir John Moore* (London, 1905), p.55.

18. G.C. Moore Smith, *The Life of John Colborne, Field-Marshal Lord Seaton* (London, 1903), p.109.

19. W.C.E. Napier, ed., *Passages in the Early Military Life of General Sir George T. Napier* (London, 1884), p.84.

20. *Ibid* p.55.

21. Moore Smith, *Life of John Colborne*, p.61.

22. Quotations from Canning and Portland on the subject may be found in Rory Muir, *Britain and the Defeat of Napoleon, 1807–1815* (New Haven and London, 1996), pp.76–7.

23. A significant essay on the role of government, with Moore as a case study, is Rory Muir and Charles Esdaile, 'Strategic Planning in a Time of Small Government: the Wars against Revolutionary and Napoleonic France, 1793–1815', in *Wellington Studies* I (ed. C.M. Woolgar, Southampton, 1996).

24. R. Ker Porter, *Letters from Portugal and Spain written during the March of the British Troops under Sir John Moore* ('by An Officer', London, 1809), pp.310–11.

25. 'Tributary Lines to the Memory of Lieut. Gen. Sir John Moore' by 'Mr Roberdeau of Bath', spoken by Miss Fisher at the Bath Theatre; *Gentleman's Magazine*, March 1809, p.253.

26. *Ibid* February 1809, p.177.

27. Captain A. Gordon, *A Cavalry Officer in the Corunna Campaign* (ed. Colonel H.C. Wylly, London, 1913), pp.208–10.

28. Sir George Napier, *Passages*, pp.60–1.

29. Porter, *op.cit.* pp.234–5.

30. B. Hall, *Voyages and Travels of Captain Basil Hall RN* (London, 1895), pp.227–8.

31. Moore Smith, *op.cit.* p.101.

32. Oman, *History*, vol.I, pp.viii–ix.

33. H.A. Bruce, *Life of General Sir William Napier* (London, 1864), vol.I, p.23.

34. Sir William Napier, *History of the War in the Peninsula* (London, 1832–40), vol.I, pp.493–4.

35. Sir William Napier, 'A Reply to Various Opponents, together with Observations illustrating Sir John Moore's Campaign', published with the 2nd edn of *War in the Peninsula*, vol.I, p.lx.

36. *Ibid* vol.I, p.523.

37. *Ibid* vol.I, p.427.

38. Duke of Wellington, *Dispatches of Field Marshal the Duke of Wellington* (ed. J. Gurwood, London, 1834–8), vol.XI, pp.34–5.

39. *Ibid* vol.V, p.404.

40. Stanhope, *op.cit.* pp.68–9.

41. Sir John Fortescue, *History of the British Army* (London, 1899–1920), vol.VII, p.419.

42. *WD*, vol.VIII, p.417.

43. *Ibid* vol.VII, p.35.

44. *Ibid* vol.VII, p.191.

45. *Ibid* vol.VII, pp.196-7.

46. *Ibid* vol.VII, p.552.

47. A.J. Griffiths, *The Wellington Memorial* (London, 1897), p.308.

48. Sir William Fraser, *Words on Wellington* (London, 1889), pp.1-3.

49. *WD*, vol.IX, pp.52-3.

50. *Ibid* vol.X, pp.76-7.

51. See C.T. Atkinson, 'The "Battalions of Detachments" at Talavera', *JSAHR* XV (1936), pp.32-8.

52. Duke of Wellington, *Supplementary Despatches and Memoranda of Field Marshal the Duke of Wellington* (ed. 2nd Duke of Wellington, London, 1858-72), vol.X, p.219.

53. Stanhope, *op.cit.* p.182.

54. Oman, *History*, vol.I, p 226.

55. See Major-General J.F.C. Fuller, 'Sir John Moore's Light Infantry Instructions of 1798-99', *JSAHR* XXX (1952), pp.68-75.

56. Sir William Napier, *The Life and Opinions of Sir Charles James Napier* (London, 1857), vol.I, p.58.

57. *United Service Journal* 1834, vol.I, p.235.

58. Lieutenant-Colonel J. Leach, *Rough Sketches of the Life of an Old Soldier* (London, 1831), p.4.

59. For a modern account of all aspects of light infantry service, which tends to downplay Moore's personal contribution, see David Gates, *The British Light Infantry Arm c.1790-1815: Its Creation, Training and Operational Role* (London, 1987).

60. Sir George Napier, *Passages*, p.13.

61. *Ibid* pp.13-14.

62. Coote Manningham, *Military Lectures delivered to the Officers of the 95th (Rifle) Regiment at Shorn-Cliff Barracks, Kent, during the Spring of 1803* (London, 1803, reprinted 1897).

63. Sir George Napier, *Passages*, pp.265-6.

64. *Ibid* p.270.

65. *British Military Library or Journal*, vol.II, p.379.

66. *WD*, vol.X, pp.495-6.

67. Stanhope, *op.cit.* p.18.

68. *Ibid* p.264.

69. *United Service Journal* 1834, vol.II, pp.413-14.

70. *WD*, vol.XI, pp.499-500.

71. For an excellent study of Wellington's staff system, see S.G.P. Ward, *Wellington's Headquarters* (London, 1957).

72. J.O. Robson, 'Rockets in the Napoleonic Wars: The Diary of William Laycock', in *JSAHR* XXVI (1948), p.148.

73. A.C. Mercer, *Journal of the Waterloo Campaign* (Edinburgh and London, 1870), vol.I, p.166.

74. Sir William Napier, *War in the Peninsula*, vol.III, pp.525-6.

75. *WD*, vol.VIII, p.514.

76. Reverend G.R. Gleig, *The Subaltern* (Edinburgh, 1872), p.163.

77. W. Tomkinson, *The Diary of a Cavalry Officer in the Peninsula and Waterloo Campaign* (ed. J. Tomkinson, London, 1895), p.135.

78. *WD*, vol.IX, p.240.

79. Sir Herbert Maxwell, *The Life of Wellington* (London, 1899), vol.II, p.138.

80. Gordon, *A Cavalry Officer in the Corunna Campaign*, p.66.

81. C. Boutflower, *The Journal of an Army Surgeon during the Peninsular War* (privately published, 1912), p.173.

82. 'The Campaign of Waterloo Strategically Examined', in *Colburn's United Service Magazine* 1843, vol.II, p.477.

83. 'The Lance and the Bayonet', by 'Fluellyn', in *United Service Journal* 1839, vol.I, pp.391-2. The 'mutinous population' refers to the fight at Bossenden Wood in Kent in 1838, between the 45th Foot and the gang of 'Mad Tom' Courteney.

84. 'Colonel Mitchell in Conclusion of the Bayonet Discussion', quoting William Napier, in *United Service Journal* 1840, vol.I, p.263.

85. *Gentleman's Magazine*, April 1811, p.383.

86. Letter quoted in *Illustrated London News*, 10 March 1849.

87. See Hew Strachan, *Wellington's Legacy: the Reform of the British Army 1830-54* (Manchester, 1984), and *From Waterloo to Balaclava: Tactics, Technology, and the British Army, 1815-54* (Cambridge, 1985). See also the same author's essay, 'The British Army's Legacy from the Revolutionary and Napoleonic Wars', in *The Road to Waterloo: The British Army and the Struggle Against Revolutionary and Napoleonic France, 1793-1815*, ed. A.J. Guy, Stroud, 1990.

88. Sir William Napier, *War in the Peninsula*, vol.III, pp.271-2.

Chapter 5

Beresford and the Reform of the Portuguese Army

by Professor Harold Livermore

Oman's development

When Sir Charles Oman embarked on his massive task Britain had still not emerged from a century of righteous imperialism. The Boer War was the news of the day when his first volume appeared. In his introduction to volume V, which bears the date 5 August 1914, Oman noted that Britain was 'most unexpectedly involved in a war to which there can be no parallel named save the struggle that ended just a hundred years ago.' His volume VII was published in 1930, when Britain was in the throes of the great slump. These two events changed Britain, and it is inevitable that he himself also changed: 'times change, and we change with them'.

By 1902 Napier's *History of the War in the Peninsula* had swept the board, driving Southey off the field, and it had held sway for two generations.[1] The book was belligerent and its author a radical, heavily prejudiced against Tories of all shades. Napier did not venture to question the opinions of Wellington, but he had no hesitation in waging a running battle with Marshal Beresford (1768–1854), getting the better of his victim in a war of words. Although Oman began as a corrective to the trenchant opinions of Napier, at the outset he was inclined to accept the judgements of his predecessor. It was only as his work gathered momentum and he himself gained in self-confidence that he established his independence. In his summing up in volume VII he records that Beresford

> returned to spend a long old age in England. Many years of it were occupied in a fierce pamphleteering battle with William Napier, whose history of the Peninsular War had, as one of its minor purposes, the consistent depreciation of everything that Beresford had ever done. The old Marshal was lured into controversy, and his pen was less skilful, if not less vitriolic, than that of the colonel. The result has been that his reputation has been unfairly lessened: Wellington regarded

him as not only a good organizer but as a competent second in
command, and such a verdict must outweigh much criticism.[2]

He adds Wellington's comment to Bathurst: 'All that I can tell you is
that the ablest man I have yet seen with the army, and the one having
the largest views is Beresford. He wants decision when I am not
present, but he is the only person capable of conducting a large
concern.'[3] Oman comments further that Wellington 'was himself in
no small degree to blame since he was averse to the delegation of
responsibility' and was 'jealous of initiatives in his subordinates.'[4]
While Wellington lies in some state beside J.M.W. Turner and other
great men in St Paul's, Beresford's tomb, scandalously neglected, is
outside the village church of Kilndown in Kent. He alone of the
Peninsular generals has had no formal biography, and it was partly in
awareness of injustice that I undertook the task, by no means facili-
tated by the dispersal of his documents, while those of Wellington
were neatly preserved for the attention of the diligent Gurwood.[5]
  Oman's first volume plunges into his subject without
preparation. It reveals a propensity for dramatic adjectives and
snap judgements, perhaps acquired from Napier. This is in contrast
with the close analysis of situations and the balanced assessment of
military possibilities and decisions that mark his more mature and
better later work. A tendency to overlook the shortcomings of his
own government and to misconceive those of others is nowhere
more evident than in the references to Spain and Portugal. Having
noted Nelson's destruction of the Spanish fleet at Trafalgar (was this
not part of the war, and was there no struggle at sea?), he expects
Spain to have marched 100,000 men against Bordeaux while
Napoleon was at Jena, and finds Charles IV's impassioned plea to
the people of Spain to take up arms *en masse* simply 'strange'.[6] He
has decided that the king of Spain was 'under the imbecile
guidance' of Godoy, the young guards officer promoted favourite by
Queen Maria Luisa. Yet his own idea of what should have been done
is little more than puerile. When he gets to describing the state of
the Spanish army in 1808, he rejects the censorious attitude of
Napier, saying: 'It is only fair to examine the state and character of
the Spanish army when the war broke out. Only when we know the
difficulties can we judge with fairness of its conduct or decide upon
its merits and shortcomings'.[7] But the hypothetical army that ought
to have marched on Bordeaux under the guidance of General Oman
would certainly have been imbecile.
  The Portuguese fare no better: 'There is certainly no example in
history of a kingdom conquered in a few days with such small
trouble as was Portugal in 1807.' Oman found it 'astonishing' that
the 'nation should yield without firing a single shot'.[8] He falls short
of repeating the popular fallacy that the British envoy, Lord
Strangford, improvised the policy of withdrawing to Brazil, but

notes that Strangford 'continued to exchange notes with the miserable Portuguese government from Sir S. Smith's flagship.' The Prince-Regent John, 'abandoning his wonted indecision, hurried on ship-board with his treasure, his state papers, his insane mother and his young family and all the hangers-on of his court'.[9] What would Oman have said if the Prince-Regent had let himself be captured, and what would the Portuguese have said if he had left his post before the very last moment? In Spain, Charles IV and his son Fernando let themselves be ensnared and then abdicated, vacating the legitimate throne for the comic-opera reign of Napoleon's brother; but it was too late for Prince Fernando to go to Mexico since Nelson had seen to it that he had no fleet to take him. Queen Maria I of Portugal certainly suffered from a melancholy madness that made her unfit to reign in such troublous times; but would George III's reason have withstood the excitement of a similarly enforced voyage to America? Prince John, called upon to succeed when his elder brother Joseph died of smallpox in 1778, was perhaps the most decent monarch of his day, though no great hero. But would the British Prince-Regent have done any better than Godoy, whom he faintly resembled?

British intervention and the war in northern Portugal, 1808–9

In Britain the sudden reverse of French fortunes, coupled with the sudden self-confidence of the Spanish *juntas*, aroused a surge of enthusiasm. Wellesley, freshly promoted lieutenant-general from Copenhagen on 25 April, was almost the most junior of his rank. When the Spanish emissaries arrived, he had been working with the Venezuelan Miranda for a South American expedition to avenge the humiliating defeat of Whitelocke at Buenos Aires in July 1807. A force of some 9000 men was assembled at Cork. The news altered all this. On 8 June the Spaniards applied to Canning; ten days later *The Times* had heard that the expedition would go to Gibraltar, not South America, and Wellesley had to appease the wrathful Miranda: 'I think I never had a more difficult business'.[10] He was 'to command a detachment to be employed on a particular service.' The vagueness of the wording owed less to confidentiality than to uncertainty. When the evacuation of the Portuguese royal family was first bruited, Sir John Moore was ordered to bring troops from the Mediterranean to Gibraltar to reinforce Lisbon in case of need. Events had outpaced the order, but Sir Hew Dalrymple had several thousand men at Gibraltar. In June 1808 the barbaric sack of Cordoba (which, according to Napier, did not happen) and the Spanish victory at Bailén, seemed to beckon towards Andalucia.[11] But it was the Asturian delegation that arrived in England and the 'spirit of exertion' was thought to be strongest in the north.

Wellesley left Cork on 12 July, ahead of his army; found Coruña freed; learned that the Portuguese *junta* at Oporto lacked trained men, and that he could safely disembark his army at the mouth of the Mondego.

Oman's account of the Portuguese response to Junot is self-contradictory. The French arrived with 25,000 troops[12] and were also 'lent' (Oman's word) two Spanish Divisions of 13,000. 'There were no signs of a general rising: the means indeed were almost entirely wanting. The regular army had been disbanded or sent off to France. The organisation of the militia had been dissolved'.[13] Portugal was without an army, an arsenal, a defensible fortress, or legal organisation, 'otherwise it would have seemed strange that a nation of over 2 million souls could not anywhere produce forces sufficient to resist for a single day a column of 3000 or 4000 French soldiers.'[14] But things were not otherwise. The French army was not 3000 but 30,000, and it was not a question of resisting for a single day, but of ejecting the whole lot. In Oporto, Bishop Castro was enthusiastic, but knew well that he could not liberate Lisbon without assistance. The leading general was Bernardim Freire de Andrade, a veteran of the Roussillon war, whose brother Nuno commanded at Coimbra, which had also been liberated. The troops were recently recalled and insufficiently armed, and the *ordenanças* lacked training. Their pressing need was for muskets, which Wellesley could only partially satisfy. His plan was to move south without straying far from the coast and his sources of supply. In Oporto, the chief threat was seen as Loison, who left his weakest men to hold the fortress of Almeida and moved south towards Abrantes, harassed by infuriated countrymen, whom he plundered. When Wellesley landed on 1 August, Junot had placed his Hanoverians in Santarém, and had sent Loison to open the south-easterly route to Evora, where the local forces were outnumbered and could not save the city from a brutal sack before the French were recalled to Lisbon.

Oman follows Napier in making much of the disagreement between Wellesley and Freire at Leiria, which arose simply from Portuguese anxiety about the centre, exposed to the enemy at Santarém. General Bernardim adhered as closely as possible to the plans of Bishop Castro's *junta*.[15]

The victories of Roliça and Vimeiro paved the way for Junot's surrender and the Convention of Sintra, which bears comparison with Dupont's submission at Bailén. Wellesley had been superseded by Sir Hew Dalrymple and Sir Harry Burrard, and for good measure Sir John Moore was also in the offing. Beresford arrived from Madeira only in time to be commandant of Lisbon and to implement the Convention which, without consultation with General Bernardim or any other Portuguese, provided British ships for Junot to retire with his booty. The famous Court of Enquiry into the

Convention, under Dundas, was held in November and the sittings lasted until 22 December. Wellesley coolly expounded his own plans, and 'practically impeached Burrard and Dalrymple for unwarrantable slackness and indecision'. Other witnesses supported Wellesley, who cross-examined his superiors, and reduced them to justifying caution by lack of information. The report was that no further proceeding was necessary. Only Lord Moira dissented in a lengthy opinion, pointing out that the liberation of Lisbon was one object, which had been achieved, but that the other object was the destruction of the French army, which had failed. Beresford, called upon to allow the robbers to retire with their spoils, observed in a letter that it was a bad agreement: 'a clever fellow would not have made it'. Dalrymple escaped with a grave censure of which Oman approves, adding – quite unnecessarily – that Dalrymple's delay gave time 'for the unreasoning popular agitation against the whole agreement made with Junot.' This ignores the grotesque acceptance of open robbery, even after the precedent of Bailén was known. Neither Burrard nor Dalrymple was employed again. Nor were the sixty-eight generals and 124 lieutenant-generals who were senior to Wellesley.

Oman says little about Sir Robert Wilson and the formation of the Loyal Lusitanian Legion. Wilson, a cavalryman, had composed an account of the Egyptian campaign, derogatory to Napoleon but read with pleasure by King George. He had joined Baird in the expedition to the Cape, but refused to take part with Popham and Beresford in the Buenos Aires adventure, though he composed a pamphlet defending it. He was, as Beresford perceived, anxious for an 'independent command', the gateway to promotion. In London, Dom Domingos António was enlisting and arming Portuguese subjects, and readily fell in with Wilson's plan for the Legion, which was supported by Canning, who persuaded Castlereagh. In Oporto, Wilson organised a battalion, and set Baron Eben – a German who had served in Dillon's Irish – to start another. Wilson found plenty of radical enthusiasm to his taste. He was well received by Bishop Castro, who installed him grandly. He then persuaded the bishop to give the 'legionaries' higher pay than the Portuguese regulars, thus completing his first battalion at the expense of the extant army.

Dalrymple's errors had been compounded by his restoration of the Council of Regency as appointed in 1807 (with the exception of those members who had served the French), ignoring the *junta* at Oporto, which had popular support and vaunted the style of 'Supreme'. Bishop Castro had therefore sent to inform the Prince-Regent, and refused to go to Lisbon until a reply came. Wilson went to Sintra and saw Dalrymple, who gave him no instructions, and on his return he ran into the anger of General Bernardim and the bishop over the deplorable Convention, while the Lisbon Regency Council annulled his extra pay. (This circumstance encouraged him to exploit his cherished ambition of an independent command, under neither Portuguese nor British orders). In October 1808 the French garrison at Almeida was repatriated through Oporto, amidst popular demands that their baggage should be searched. According to Oman 'the baggage of the French was seized and plundered.'[16] Order was restored only by calling on some Spanish troops, and a panicking Wilson told Canning that 3000 British soldiers must be sent or Oporto abandoned.[17] Oman's high opinion of Wilson's abilities[18] is totally at variance with those reached by Wellesley and Beresford, who gave him every latitude until, having sought to use his vaunted latitude to liberate Madrid, they found him quite uncontrollable. When Beresford decided that the Legion should no longer have its own artillery, Wilson went to Lisbon to sort out its finances and was, rather appropriately, stung on the tongue by a wasp, and suffered convulsions and fainting fits. The forbearance he had hitherto enjoyed was due to the failure of Dalrymple to recognise the Oporto *junta*; to the anomalous situation Wilson himself had created; and to his habit of using his acquaintance with the Duke of York and Canning, which ended when Castlereagh's pistol put Canning out of the government.

Oman's account of Napoleon's visit to Spain, his attempt to place Joseph on an improvised throne in Madrid, and Moore's excursion and death at Coruña, do not concern us here. Beresford accompanied the retreat, oversaw the embarkation at Coruña, and landed in England with the tattered regiments in January 1809, while Napoleon left Soult to open the second invasion of Portugal. Moore's retreat had drawn a large French force into Galicia, and on leaving for France Napoleon had set Soult the task of taking Lisbon by 10 February. Canning had the idea of sending a British force to hold Cádiz rather than Lisbon, where Cradock held a rather nervous outpost. (Napier was highly critical of Canning, whom Oman thought himself called upon to defend.) There was a muddle: Canning sounded the Spanish *junta*, and it was they who stressed the importance of holding Lisbon; but Cradock sent part of his troops to Cádiz while himself remaining west of Lisbon as if preparing to embark rather than to defend the city.[19]

In February 1809, a month after his return from Coruña, Beresford was appointed to command the Portuguese army. He was a close associate of Wellesley and a fellow Irishman, an illegitimate son of the Marquis of Waterford. He was unquestionably suited to the task in hand, although others doubtless wished they had been appointed. Napier exaggerates their claims, and Oman retreats behind an ambiguous 'into the secrets of ministerial privilege it is useless to pry'.[20] Oman's account of the history of the Portuguese army is superficial. Since 1640, when it had to be created, its purpose had been defensive, each province being called upon to raise and supply its own contingent. What Oman fails to notice is that the reforming generals, Gomes Freire and Alorna, had antagonised the Prince-Regent and joined Junot's Portuguese Legion, taking with them such officers as would go. In Oporto the two local regiments, lately disbanded, were recalled, but lacked officers. There was no lack of enthusiastic volunteers, but a serious want of muskets and equipment, of horses, and of system. Oman notes a deficiency of 19,000 muskets and 1400 horses. Above all, there was no capacity to deal with light and fast-moving forces, such as Napoleon used with great effect. Oman totally under-estimates the effectiveness of a patriotic countryside in dealing with isolated detachments of trained Frenchmen sent to hold them down. Beresford had barely arrived in Portugal when Soult, obeying Napoleon's orders to get to Oporto by 5 February, reached the Minho at Tuy, was prevented from crossing by the cannon at Valença (which Oman dismisses as dilapidated), and was obliged to follow the north bank to Orense in order to cross. He left Orense on 4 March. By then Galician countrymen had scared Ney. The Spaniard La Romana, who might have contributed to the defence of Portugal, had withdrawn to Sanabria, abandoning his Portuguese allies in a 'sudden move which bore the appearance of a mean desertion in their day of peril: but it was in other respects wise and prudent.'[21]

According to Oman, the Portuguese regency council displayed 'a considerable amount of energy' in the first two months of 1809, but it was 'in great part misdirected', since they diverted their zeal to a *levée en masse* instead of completing the regular army. But, as Oman says, Junot had confiscated and destroyed almost all the store of arms belonging to the old army. Every regiment was mobilised at its own headquarters, the only concentration being at Lisbon. It is hard to see how else it should be.

On his arrival Beresford borrowed officers from Cradock and began his training programme. In six weeks he collected ten of the sixteen Portuguese regiments at Tomar and Abrantes, and raised three battalions of *Caçadores* (light infantry). There was still a shortage of horses, but the infantry were drilled twice a day, and Beresford replaced officers he found wanting. Londonderry reported that 'they had applied of late so much ardour in their military education some were already fit to take the field, and it only required a little experience to put them on a level with the best troops of Europe'.

Wilson, whose Lusitanian Legion should have defended Oporto, had 'fallen foul of Bishop Castro, and set himself up at and near Almeida'. He informed Cradock that if he had to retreat he would not go to Oporto, as it was the government of a mob, of which he had too much experience. Later, some claimed that by staying at Ciudad Rodrigo he had 'saved Portugal from invasion.'[22] Oman notes that the other Portuguese commanders were also at variance, but without attempting to show why. The Bishop's *junta* in Oporto had been the first to assert Portuguese independence, but Dalrymple had recognised the depleted Council of Regency without reference to him. The senior general was Bernardim Freire de Andrade, whom Oman sets down as 'a timid rather than a cautious general. The indiscipline and mutinous spirit of the motley levies which he commanded had reduced him to despair.' Yet General Oman would have him 'march forward and fortify the frontier passes'.[23] Bernardim was commander-in-chief when Beresford arrived, though for only a few days, since he was murdered at his headquarters in Braga on 17 March by the unruly and impassioned citizens. Bernardim had followed the Oporto *junta*'s instructions in his dealings with Wellesley, but it is unlikely that the excited defenders of Braga distinguished him clearly from his brother Gomes, who had defected to the French. The *junta* had sent forward the incomplete second battalion of the Loyal Lusitanian Legion under Baron Eben, whose attempt to shield the general had led to his being handed over to the mob.[24]

None of the weapons sent by the British is said to have gone to Silveira, the defender of Trás-os-Montes.[25] Silveira, promoted brigadier on 15 February, was a native of Vila Real and was placed in command of the Second Division, which was left to face Soult as La Romana withdrew. He had little choice but to fall back on Chaves, then to retire from it with the bulk of his troops. A captain of engineers sided with the excited populace in wanting to defend it, and distributed arms to volunteers. The two forts, unrepaired since 1762, had some fifty pieces of artillery, but insufficient ammunition. When Soult sent in a fruitless summons to the town, 'all night the garrison kept up a haphazard cannonade and shouted defiance to the French.' When Soult again summoned them 'the garrison seem to have tired themselves out with hours of patriotic shouting and to have used up a great part of their munitions in their silly nocturnal fireworks.' They then 'displayed more cowardice on the 11th than indiscipline on the 10th.' Soult was 'much embarrassed by the multitude of captives he had taken' and 'offered them the choice between captivity and enlisting in a Franco-Portuguese Legion, which he proposed to raise. To their great discredit, the majority of both officers and men took the latter alternative – though it was with the sole idea of deserting as soon as possible.' Soult made the same offer to the Spanish captives: 'they behaved no better than the Portuguese.'[26] It seems not to have occurred to Oman that a promise made under duress or intimidation has no validity.

Chaves fell in a day, but the whole countryside resisted, village by village and cottage by cottage. Oman commends Silveira's 'laudable prudence in refusing to let himself be caught', but overall his judgement is still typically contorted. Silveira had already recovered Chaves before the fall of Oporto, and had intended to mount a surprise attack on Braga, but instead occupied Vila Real and Amarante, in order to hold the line of the River Támega. Oman tells us that he 'boldly but unwisely offered battle ... in front of Amarante ... his conduct can only be described as rash in the extreme'; and when he had recovered Chaves and confronted Loison at Penafiel, 'his fault was not a want of initiative'.[27] Yet it was Silveira's entry into Amarante which closed Soult's line of retreat, and his advance to Penafiel forced Loison to call for reinforcements, and so brought matters to a head.

Soult had certainly been glad to take Oporto, but the appearance of Wellesley at Lisbon destroyed any possibility of realising Napoleon's hare-brained scheme for a convergence and rapid conquest there. The inability of other forces to converge owed more to the resistance of the enraged countryside than to the interested caperings of Wilson, who imagined that the French would simply withdraw and leave him to take Madrid single-handed. As Warre observed, Wilson 'would never lack a trumpeter while he lived'. Soult, Duke of Dalmatia, relatively safe in Oporto, meanwhile toyed with the idea of proclaiming himself king of Northern Lusitania. This arose from the example of Junot in Lisbon, and a perception of the conservative monarchism of the patriotic and traditionalist Minho. Soult wanted to disarm the hostility of the countryside by winning over Catholics and monarchists.[28] He had not the sanction of Napoleon, with whom he was out of touch, and some of his officers would doubtless have preferred to surrender at once, if they could have got the same advantageous terms as those of Sintra. That was the origin of the conspiracy of Captain d'Argenton, who was clearly acting for more senior officers. His approach underlined for Wellesley and Beresford the weakness of Soult's hold, and increased their confidence. It was further strengthened by an intercepted message from Victor to Soult which revealed the difficulties of the French in Spain.

The recovery of Oporto on 12 May was considered by Napier 'nowise to have diminished' Wellesley's reputation: Oman thought it 'one of his strongest titles to fame'.[29] But it needs to be added that Soult already knew the game was up, that he abandoned his sick, destroyed his guns, and retreated in a *sauve qui peut* so ignominious as to reverse the tide of war. His invasion of Portugal (the last for the north) ended as his rearguard scrambled up the valley of the Cávado, which they littered with stolen Portuguese coin in an attempt to delay pursuit, to Montealegre and Galicia. The dire straits to which the French were reduced is seen from their own records. They had been in Oporto from 29 March to 12 May, and had lost over a quarter of their men. This result was achieved in no small part by the exertions of unnamed villagers intent on defending their homes from pillage and conquest. Of the Portuguese commanders it is Silveira who rightly receives the commendation of Brigadier Azeredo: 'overshadowed by generals more politicians than soldiers, whose statues and plaques adorn our cities, but they are of less national significance than Silveira, unquestionably the most notable officer in the Portuguese army.'[30] It is a pity that Oman closes his chapter with an attempt to apportion blame for the escape of the French main body, which he places on Silveira, adding an erratum that a despatch of Beresford's 'clears up my doubts as to Silveira's culpability. Beresford complains that the latter lost a whole day by marching from Amarante without orders ... The time lost could never be made up.' As Brigadier Azeredo points out, Wellesley *lost* 12-15 May at Oporto, and Beresford *lost* 8-12 May at Lamego, and 13-15 May at Amarante. When Soult chose the route by the valley of the Cavádo, he already knew that his men could not fight. Oman makes no reference to Silveira's appeal for reinforcements on 2 May, which went unheeded. But the true cause of defeat was with Napoleon himself who, secure in his self-esteem and surrounded by his comic-opera cronies and sycophants, set his Dalmatian a task no sensible person would have dreamed of.

If the defeat of Soult was the consequence of Napoleon's own directions, his armies in Galicia fared no better. Ney was obliged to invent his own actions, ignoring the measures imposed by his master, who tendered irrelevant advice when reinforcements and supplies alone could have altered the situation. Oman's chapter on Galicia contains much tactical speculation, and its eventual loss, albeit without the loss of Ney's entire command, inspires the comment that 'it was not the Emperor's fault that this disaster failed to occur.'[31] One wonders what General Oman's staff would have made of this type of tautology.

There was no question of pursuing Soult into Spain. Napoleon in all his glory might ignore the existence of national frontiers; but his enemies could not. In Portugal, land wars were by definition defensive and Portuguese troops did not enter Spain, at least without the explicit orders of the monarch, now safely installed in Brazil. But in Madrid King Joseph gave directions to Victor ('Duke of Belluno'), based on insufficient information and forwarded ingenuously to his brother in Paris. Home games are different from away games, and the visible differences of supply and equipment rest on a whole system of invisibles, not seen in imperial Paris. Oman prints an intercept from Victor to King Joseph of 25 June 1809 so abject that it might have been composed by Wilson himself.[32]

Beresford and the defence of Portugal 1809–11

During the marchings, counter-marchings and confrontations around Talavera, Beresford assembled most of the Portuguese army on the eastern frontier. Soult had in mind that his master's main object was to take Lisbon and force Wellesley to evacuate like Sir John Moore. If the opportunity had offered, he would have occupied Lisbon, whether or not Joseph and Victor had succeeded in retaining Madrid. However, it happened that King Joseph wanted to use Soult to take over Andalucia, thus giving time for Napoleon to provide the 100,000 men thought necessary to crush the Iberian Peninsula without much depleting the armies that held down central Europe. To Joseph it seemed more important to impose himself in Spain than to proceed to the conquest of Portugal. He had his way, although Napoleon's previous orders implied the opposite. Soult commanded the Army of Andalucia, and it was not until April 1810 that Masséna (whose *noms de guerre* were Duke of Rivoli and Prince of Essling) was appointed to the Army of Portugal.

Wellington knew very well that his own priority was to defend Portugal. The cardinal difference was that he commanded the Portuguese army, under the Prince-Regent in Brazil; while the king of Spain was in comfortable security under French control at Talleyrand's house in Valençay. Legitimacy was an important factor in the Peninsula, and Oman's references to the Spanish governing bodies as illegal overlooks the fact that nobody in Spain enjoyed undisputed authority. Wellesley was not commander-in-chief of the Spanish armies, and his course in withdrawing from Spanish soil after Talavera was the correct one: any other would have embroiled him in a civil war. Napoleon himself was well aware of the importance of legitimism, and it was with this in mind that he dismissed his leading lady to take a Habsburg consort: Spaniards not reconciled to the Bourbons might respect an heiress of Charles V. In Portugal no such problem existed. Queen Maria and her son were indisputably the legitimate rulers and they were secure in Brazil. They and Dom Rodrigo de Sousa Coutinho had accepted that Bishop Castro, promoted Patriarch-elect, should preside over the Council of Regency. Dom Rodrigo's brother, the Principal (*ie* 'Dean') Sousa, joined the body, and the third brother, Dom Domingos António, remained ambassador in London. The long delay in consulting Rio de Janeiro was remedied by including Charles Stuart as a regent in order to expedite communications between the two nations. These were complicated by the fact that Portugal contributed a number of men far greater than Britain in proportion to the two populations; but the Portuguese army could be paid, fed, and clothed only with the aid of the British subsidy. The inability of the Portuguese commissariat, now styled the *Junta de Víveres*, to provide supplies, or to compete with the British in buying horses, is condemned by Oman, who blames the traditional Portuguese system for corruption. In fact, graver problems were to be caused by the few contractors who manipulated the new centralised demand and were able to make vast fortunes for themselves.

The chief issue between the Regency and the commander-in-chief was Wellington's insistence on allowing Masséna to advance into central Portugal. The two churchmen on the Council were anxious to avoid the general distress caused by a burnt-earth policy and the threat to public order as masses of refugees flocked to the capital. There is little justification for Oman's Panglossian belief that the Portuguese country people were used to this sort of thing.[33] It is one thing to deprive invaders of facilities, and another deliberately to destroy these in advance of their appearance. If the chief fear of some English was that the Portuguese would run away when faced by Masséna, the chief fear of the Portuguese was no different, that Wellington would follow the example of Moore and seek salvation in a glorious embarkation. The Patriarch-elect and the Principal knew that a small group of Portuguese was with Masséna, but they could not know the extent of their masonic affiliations, which they perhaps exaggerated in the light of the papal condemnation. The sudden arrest of some fifty prominent Portuguese and their deportation to Britain, despite the appeals of their families to Stuart, may have been summary, but the Portuguese had as much reason to play for safety as Wellesley. For this period Oman relies on the papers of Benjamin d'Urban, which he describes as 'invaluable'. D'Urban's papers, published in 1930, show him to have been a Jeremiah, tolerated by Beresford (whose letters to his sister reveal a much more decided and hopeful character) because he was an efficient quartermaster-general. His observations should be matched by those of Warre, who, if inclined to be his master's trumpeter, had a more balanced view of the situation.[34]

It is not easy to assess Beresford's contribution to the recreation of the Portuguese army. His energy and efforts were immense, occasioned less by lack of manpower than by lack of almost everything else. In February the Regency Council had issued a general call-up for men under thirty, which met with an enthusiastic response, though conditioned by the belief that the service would be brief. But the British had on various occasions thought that the Portuguese could not or would not be able to fight, and the French, having nursed the idea of a legion under their command, pretended that the Portuguese army did not exist, whence Napoleon's under-estimate of the numbers that would be required to drive the English into the sea. Beresford was promoted lieutenant-general on 15 February 1809, and appointed to command the Portuguese army at Wellesley's behest to meet Portuguese wishes. He arrived in Lisbon on 2 March, where it emerged that he would have to be made Marshal in order to command the senior Portuguese generals. He claimed to be a reluctant marshal, though he clearly liked the attendant pomp and pay. He issued his first order on 15 March, as Soult was approaching Braga, where General Bernardim was murdered two days later. The

Portuguese would have liked to go to the relief of Oporto, but Cradock, left in command of the British at Lisbon, was unwilling to join without express orders, and nothing could be done until Wellesley had arrived on 22 April. Castlereagh had authorised the supply of 10,000 muskets, but Beresford soon asked for as many again, and 20,000 uniforms. Little could be done for the cavalry owing to the shortage of horses: Beresford's immediate exertions were for the infantry. The idea of integrating the two armies to respond to the same orders was already conceived. Cradock provided twenty-six officers, who received a step of one rank: Beresford at first asked for six British officers to every Portuguese regiment, but Wellesley could not find so many. The core of the Portuguese army was concentrated at Tomar, and by May Beresford reported that 19,000 were ready to march. He personally inspected the work of training, riding long distances in all weathers. The results were seen in the pursuit of Soult northward to the Spanish border, and especially at Bussaco, where the number of Portuguese and British participants was about equal, and the number of reported casualties the same.

Portuguese nobles regarded it almost as a right to become officers, and some performed their duties negligently. As commander-in-chief Beresford exerted his right to dismiss all who could not or would not accept their responsibilities. He made some enemies. Punishments were rigorously enforced, without much regard to Portuguese law, which provided numerous recourses for appeal. For Wellesley, the unpleasant tasks of discipline were performed by Colonel Peacock, but Beresford, as a foreigner, had to bear the brunt of his own decisions, which were generally accepted.[35] While Beresford never lost the confidence of the Prince-Regent, he had constant brushes with the Portuguese treasury and with the *Junta de Víveres*. By tradition there had been no central deposit for supply, each regiment contracting suppliers in its own province. This practice was replaced by the *Junta de Víveres*, while Beresford insisted on a daily ration comparable with that of the British allies, requiring unprecedented quantities of meat. Once the war was carried into Spain local supplies could no longer be obtained, and the only solution was for a single system to provide for both armies. The successful moulding together of the two forces was an important innovation. It was precisely the refusal of the Spaniards to accept a unified command and all that this entailed which caused Wellesley to despair of them.[36]

Wellesley regarded Beresford as the most loyal and consistent of his colleagues, and 'the only one capable of conducting a large concern'. If at times the former seemed glacial, the latter was hot-blooded and always prepared to risk his own life. In May 1809 Wellesley had advised him: 'You are commander-in-chief [*ie* of the Portuguese army], and you must not be beaten'. The circumstances were altered some months later when Wellesley himself was formally given that title.[37] He later found Beresford 'wanting in decision when I am not present', probably referring to the battle of Albuera – a victory so costly that it shook confidence in his leadership. It was the second time Beresford had the better of Soult, who abandoned the field and departed, though his report claimed a victory. But Beresford, inferior in cavalry, had suffered such terrible losses that he could not offer pursuit. Wellington, arriving the next day, destroyed Beresford's dejected report with the celebrated phrase: 'This will not do. Write me down a victory.' The appalling loss of life was so at variance with Wellington's careful husbandry of his forces that the occasion could not be ignored. Beresford had never before held so large and independent a command, and did not again. He was so overcome that he relinquished his command ten days after the battle and spent three months in or near Lisbon, suffering from some uncertainly identified disorder which responded only slowly to rest and sea-baths. Napier blamed Beresford for inadequate generalship in a sustained personal attack.[38] Oman noted this, and observed that Napier did not know the field and invented a ravine where there was not one.[39] In fact he had been engaged in burying the dead at Fuentes de Oñoro at the time.[40]

Napier's observations on the French at Albuera does not stand examination: 'being of one nation, obedient to one discipline and animated by one spirit, their excellent composition amply compensated for their inferiority of numbers and their general's talent was immeasurably greater than his adversary's.'[41] Soult used his superiority of cavalry, which included a large number of Poles, to pass through the British lines. It was Wellington who had negotiated the participation of the Spaniards, despite his reservations as reported by Napier, and they defended their position bravely until pushed off it. Wellington had originally taken the command in the Alentejo from Sir William Stewart, thinking him too adventurous, and had given it to Beresford, whose deliberate precautions accorded more with his own desires. Hence Beresford's care in securing the crossing of the Guadiana in the manoeuvres before Albuera, and his wrath when his cavalry commander, Long, disappeared in a headlong pursuit of the enemy, which led to his removal from command. It was also Wellington who had chosen the site for the battle, probably underestimating Soult's vigour and pace, which brought the French very near to a victory which would have relieved Badajoz and compensated for the wearisome retreat of Masséna from Torres Vedras.

Oman is at his best in his tireless quest for details of military operations, and his assessment of the number of combatants and the value of their positions. He applies the same qualities in following subordinate campaigns which occurred in various parts of the Peninsula, though this must inevitably obscure his central argument. In Spain the guerrilla leaders acquired local and even international fame since they each exercised independent authority, when it was not always clear what were the objects of the regular armies, or how far their operations were concerted. In Portugal this scarcely applied, since the heroic defenders of villages and towns were all in touch with their own militia and regular units who were under the centralised command of Beresford. Some Spanish *guerrilleros* such as Espoz y Mina achieved political careers in the ensuing convulsions. But in Portugal Beresford's meritocracy ensured that the demand to change the old order emerged from the army itself, coupled with the influence of local magistrates who had served in the commissariat or had similar functions.

The problems of victory, 1812–14

For some, the war ended with the expulsion of the French from the national territory, followed by the defeat of the Army of Portugal at Salamanca in July 1812. Beresford was twice wounded, the second time seriously (though not gravely) by a bullet which pierced his left breast and lodged near the ribs. It was extracted and he was sent to Oporto, where he was warmly received. His enforced absence raised the question of the command of the Portuguese army, which was now, in effect, so much integrated with the British as to form a single machine. Oman himself is inclined to use the term 'British army' when what he means is the 'allied army'. The Portuguese contingent was now more compact and less numerous. The *ordenanças* had returned to their homes. The militia were also discharged. The Portuguese nation could no longer afford to keep so large a proportion of its men under arms. Central Portugal was full of starving and ragged people. The inability of the Regency to feed and clothe the forces was real enough. The British parliament voted £100,000 to relieve distress, and £84,000 more was collected in donations; but this would have been insufficient even if the administrative system had not been destroyed, so that it could not be fairly distributed. The main source of revenue was the Lisbon custom house. A report made in January 1811 showed that it was active enough, though entirely in imports. Vast quantities of wheat and other staples were brought in; but the opening of the Brazilian ports had crippled Lisbon's role as an entrepôt, since goods were no longer required to land before onward shipment. Military expenditure was more than four times non-military, and was more than half deficitary. The difference had to be covered by the export of coin and by promissory notes, which were heavily discounted. Wellington thought that the budget could be balanced, but he was perhaps influenced by the presence in Lisbon of the wealthier refugees and by a small handful of contractors serving the British army; moreover, those who had gone to Brazil wanted to export their Portuguese incomes. The Regents had little power to raise revenue in the absence of the Prince-Regent, and the death of Dom Rodrigo in Brazil in January 1812 opened the way to his rivals. The Lisbon Regency thought rather of reducing the cost of expensive arms such as the cavalry. These problems exercised Beresford and Dom Miguel Forjaz Pereira. The Prince-Regent made Beresford Count of Trancoso, but in the prolonged absence of Wellington from Lisbon he also had to bear the complaints. He held the power of promotion and exercised it freely. Saldanha, a captain at sixteen, was a lieutenant-colonel at twenty-one – passing over twenty-one majors – and colonel at twenty-two. Grudges were inevitable, and they were contagious.

If Beresford's costly victory at Albuera was thought to render him unsuitable as commander-in-chief, his wound at Salamanca and enforced absence raised the question of Wellington's second-in-command. Liverpool proved reluctant to name Beresford for the post, while Sir T. Graham was threatened with blindness and had to go on leave. Wellington affected to believe a second a useless and meaningless post, and pointed out that Beresford, as Marshal, must succeed unless another candidate was acceptable to the Prince-Regent's government. Beresford was on the point of resigning, and said as much in his letters to his family. In fact Paget, sent by the British government, was almost immediately captured by the French in November 1812, but Graham turned out to be less blind than was feared.

In this context it is worth citing a letter from Beresford to Torrens of 8 April 1812, answering a suggested appointment:

Tho' a British officer commands this Army, yet it is the Army of an Independent Sovereign, & officers lent to him (supposed to be so at least during the war) by his Ally, cannot be called for in that manner [*ie* the officers cannot be put into specific posts by Beresford and/or Torrens without reference to the Portuguese]. We certainly, as is right, contrive to meet as well as we can all their discordances, but however we must take care of the vital principle, as that being overset all goes. I can no longer, as formerly, be placing British officers where I please, & in the principal commands: the Portuguese officers have now too just pretentions to be so treated, & yet the mixture is quite necessary, & if the officers who are in command of corps are taken away I cannot replace them for two reasons: the first, that I do not now get many officers of that rank, & the second that I cannot with any justice to the Portuguese officers, supersede them. And indeed not only the feelings of the officers, but those of the Nation are much agitated on this subject: it is a Cord that cannot be overstretched, it is one of the most difficult things I have had to effect, that of reconciling and keeping temperate the minds of this nation on that head. I am sure of all assistance, as I have in all things and cases experienced it from His Royal Highness, and the great import of this makes me anxious about it.[42]

Ten days later, he voiced his own dissatisfaction in writing to his brother, Sir John Poo:

I think I shall not long hold or remain in my present situation ... I see no further chance of any consideration for me whatever because I do not see any possibility of doing more than I have done. The Portuguese army is at its height of perfection ... It is now I believe confessed by all to be in all points equal with the British, & in the storm of Badajoz its fame had perhaps reached its height. No troops could behave more nobly. It is not probable that an opportunity such as occurred at the battle of Albuhera will again fall to my lot ... from these considerations I am of the opinion that I cannot long remain here where I am.

Whether he was as discontented as he said is doubtful: his object was to curb his brother's expensive mode of life by pointing out that the 'few hundred a year' he lent to Poo were contingent, and that Poo ought to settle his own debts, which were numerous. But Poo thought Beresford slighted, and on 15 June, before Salamanca, the Marshal wrote: 'about what you consider neglect of me. That is a thing that ought to be taken up when it occurs, or actively given up ... I think the thing ought to drop till at least some further act of injustice or unpleasantness is committed against us, and the only manly way is to resign my situation.'[43]

The intense activity at Salamanca, and his wound and convalescence, put these considerations aside. But the problem of the succession towards the end of the year led Beresford to regret having 'had a rank conferred on me that now may put difficulty to the service in general,' though 'to command the senior Portuguese generals I must admit that it was necessary.' Wellington sent this statement to Bathurst adding that there was no doubt that Beresford ranked next to himself in the allied army: 'in the event of an accident to Wellington either the second in command of the British army must be Marshal-General and Beresford must quit the army at a moment when his departure might be attributed to his disadvantage, or he must assume the command of the allied army, and not the officer appointed by the British government.' Thus Wellington defended Beresford by placing the onus on Bathurst. To Beresford he wrote: 'what I have always felt was that you had too many duties of a general nature to perform, and it was necessary to refer to you too often to charge you with the details of a command.'

Bathurst then persuaded Graham to return with only one good eye, and the understanding that if Wellington were disabled he should take over only *pro tem*. Beresford's difficulty came from the Duke of York, whose sense of hierarchy was such that if Beresford became second-in-command, it would be necessary to recall lieutenant-generals senior to him who were serving in the Peninsula. Merit, not seniority, might be a good enough principle for the Portuguese army, but the British must be protected from its subversive implications.

After Salamanca and Beresford's wound, the Anglo-Portuguese army advanced to, and then retreated from, Burgos. Beresford convalesced at Sintra then remained in Lisbon, where he worked with Forjaz on matters of administration. The Spaniards were at last inclined to recognise Wellington as *generalissimo*, and he visited Cádiz accordingly. He also visited Lisbon, at last, in January 1813. He was given a rapturous reception. His ostensible purpose was to decorate Beresford with the Order of the Bath, but both marshals met the regents and urged them to find resources for the continuation of the war. On 12 April, when the new campaign opened, there were arrears of pay dating to the previous June. Lord Liverpool moved the renewal of the subsidy, assuring Parliament that the money had been well spent. It had, but there was not enough of it. Suppliers and carriers were still paid with notes that they were obliged to sell at a fraction of their face value. In Spain they were not received at all, and the procurement system ceased to function. The solution lay in merging the supply systems of the two armies. In Portugal such devices as the sale of royal property and of church possessions were discussed, but general application of these drastic steps required the presence of the Prince-Regent, who showed no signs of leaving Brazil.

In 1813, at the time of Vitoria and the invasion of France, more than a third of Wellington's army was Portuguese. Beresford now had twenty-one regiments and eleven battalions of *caçadores,* and Wellington wrote that 'the good conduct of the Portuguese officers and troops in all the operations of the present campaign and the spirit which they show on every occasion are not less honourable to that nation than they are to the military character of the officer who by his judicious measures has re-established discipline and revived a military spirit in the army.' Other writers confirmed this. In distant Rio de Janeiro the fall of the pretender-king of Spain was celebrated. Carlota Joaquina was a Spanish Bourbon, and the fall of Joseph was particularly significant for her. The Prince-Regent made Wellington Duke of Victory, his first dukedom, and the first Portuguese dukedom to be awarded outside the royal house. But the regency in Lisbon was no better able to pay the troops, despite the nagging of Stuart and Beresford. The war in the Pyrenees began to seem remote, and the cost of reconstruction more pressing. Beresford returned to Lisbon in August 1813 and recruitment improved, but only by lowering the minimum age to seventeen.

Although the successes of the Portuguese troops were celebrated in the Portuguese press, the regency began to notice that in the British parliament thanks were extended to the British army without reference to its allies. This was a consequence of the increasing integration of the forces and to the fact that they were no longer in Portugal. Forjaz suggested that the two armies should be considered as separate. The very idea alarmed Wellington, who knew that integration was the secret of his success, and lack of it the clue to the slow development of collaboration with the Spaniards. He pointed out that the Portuguese 'were part of ourselves', the unified commissariat having become essential. The Portuguese had to be content with separate references to promotions and awards in the British parliament. Beresford himself began to look to his own future. In March 1814 he was sent to receive the surrender of Bordeaux, where the appearance of the Duke of Angoulême, the future Louis XVIII, assured the Bourbon restoration. Although Wellington himself claimed to be neutral, Beresford's presence was proof that the allies would not oppose the solution. The last battle of the war was at Toulouse, which Soult attempted to defend, not knowing that Napoleon had fled from Paris. With characteristic ardour Beresford led the assault on the heights of La Rive, and reported 'the battle of Toulouse' to his brother: but the feat was drowned by the universal noise of victory. Beresford hastened home to see his family after an absence of five years. At Bordeaux there was no shipping to spare to repatriate the Portuguese, except the sick and wounded, and after a series of farewells between comrades in arms the Portuguese army, led by Lecor, marched back across northern Spain. It lost only one man, by drowning while swimming in the Douro.[44]

Notes

In general I have attempted to avoid overburdening this article with footnotes, and have relied heavily upon my own, as yet unpublished, biography of Marshal Beresford. The quotations from his family letters are from copies which I have.

1. Robert Southey, *History of the Peninsular War* (3 vols, London, 1823–32); Lieutenant-Colonel W.P. Napier, *History of the War in the Peninsula and the South of France* (6 vols, London, 1828–40). Napier's habit of telling generals what they should have done in the light of hindsight, coupled with his apparently realistic maps, explains his popularity twenty years after the events.
2. Oman, *History*, vol.VII, p.525.
3. *Ibid*.
4. *Ibid* p.527. Oman observes that Beresford 'stayed too long in Portugal

after the war had ended, clinging on to his post as commander-in-chief (p.525). Perhaps so, but Beresford was loyal to the Prince-Regent in Brazil and to his fellow British officers in Portuguese service, just as he was impeccably loyal to Wellington. His last mission to Brazil was to attempt to persuade John VI to return to Portugal, or to send money to save the army. He failed, and Wellington condemned the mission as foolish. But Beresford was better aware of the gravity of the situation.

5. Acknowledgement is due to S.E. Vichness' Ph.D. thesis, *Marshal of Portugal: The Military Career of William Carr Beresford, 1785-1814* (Florida State University, 1976), which assembles much information for the Peninsular War period.

6. See *History*, vol.I, pp.3-9.

7. *Ibid* p.89.

8. *Ibid* p.26.

9. *Ibid* p.30.

10. P.H. Stanhope, *Notes of Conversations with the Duke of Wellington* (London, 1888), p.69; W.S. Robertson, *Francisco de Miranda* (1929), vol.II, p.23.

11. After Bailén the Spanish accepted that the French troops should be allowed to go home by sea; but the convention made no reference to the British. When Admiral Collingwood flatly refused to grant them passage the French accused the Spanish of ill-faith, which was hotly denied (Oman, *History*, vol.I, pp.201, 624). The French had also obtained permission to take away their 'baggage' and to make search for stolen church silver (*ibid* vol.I, p.198), which made an interesting, if highly contentious, precedent for a similar clause in the Convention of Sintra. But Oman is at fault both for accusing the Spanish of 'shameless cynicism' over the supposed British dimension to the capitulation, and for accusing the French negotiators of 'scandalous' behaviour in implicitly confessing to pillage.

12. *History*, vol.I, p.206.

13. *Ibid*.

14. *Ibid* p.210.

15. António Pedro Vicente, *Um soldado da guerra peninsular, o General Bernardim Freire de Andrade,* (including documents; Lisbon, 1970). The adjectives applied by Oman might better have been applied to Sir Robert Wilson, 'a self-willed and shifty man'.

16. *History*, vol.I, p.280.

17. Michael Glover, *A Very Slippery Fellow* (Oxford, 1978). The phrase used in Glover's title came from Wellesley, when he was finally convinced that Wilson was 'not able to tell the truth on any subject' (p.77).

18. *History*, vol.II, p.253*ff.*

19. Oman refers to Sir George Smith's 'hasty and unauthorised scheme' to reinforce Cádiz. The appearance of the British set off a popular clamour for them to land, which the Spanish authorities resisted. Smith died of a fever, and Oman (vol.II, p.27) calls him 'hasty and presumptuous'. Freire's part in the incident is given in a footnote.

20. *History*, vol.II, p.217.

21. *Ibid* p.194.

22. Glover, *op.cit.* p.58, who adds 'this opinion has been adopted by many subsequent historians' – but Wilson himself did not subscribe to this view. In March, Cradock reported him as saying that the whole French army

would retire altogether from Spain. His motive in staying away was to remain isolated from both the Portuguese and British, to preserve his cherished 'independent command'. He sent exaggerated accounts of his minor successes (or 'buccaneering', in Glover's expression). When Cradock informed him of Beresford's arrival on 3 March, Wilson decided to join Cuesta. Beresford ordered him to Lisbon and they met at Tomar on 20 April, when Beresford offered him the rank of brigadier. Wilson considered resigning, having too many commanders – or powerful rivals – to present opportunities for distinction. On 23 May he did resign, and when Beresford asked him to think again, attempted to claim his right 'under the laws and usages of Portugal' to command. Beresford knew of no such laws. But on 14 May the Legion was attacked and lost almost half its strength. It was only after Talavera that, having exaggerated his own resistance to Ney, he was at length rumbled, leaving Portugal in October. He importuned various parties for redress and became chief military adviser to the opposition, his prognostications on the course of the war being 'wrong with a magnificent consistency'.

23. *History*, vol.II, p.228.

24. Oman accepts the version of the Loyal Lusitanian Legion given in the book by Lieutenant-Colonel Mayne, who had been made governor of Almeida by Wilson. According to Glover, Mayne 'seems to have had no military experience of any kind' (p.51).

Oman condemns the practice of selling commissions which had existed in the Portuguese army: Wilson had sold his captaincy of dragoons (regulated price £3150) to acquire a majority from Major Bylandt in Hompesch's German Hussars, for which the regulation price was £4250 (Glover, p.16).

25. Brigadeiro Carlos de Azeredo, *As populações do norte ... em 1808 e 1809* (Porto, 1984), p.79.

26. *History*, vol.II, p.226.

27. *Ibid* p.267.

28. Soult's attempt to make himself king is denied in Peter Hayman, *Soult: Napoleon's Maligned Marshal* (London, 1990), pp.107–14.

29. *History*, vol.II, p.363.

30. Azeredo, *op cit.* p.233.

31. *History*, vol.II, p.389.

32. *Ibid* p.459. Could it have been concocted to lure Wellesley to Talavera? On 12 June Napoleon at Schönbrunn had ordered Soult to command a single force, with the armies of Ney and Mortier, to drive Wellesley out. (He was then unaware of Soult's defeat and of the general rising in Galicia.) Oman says this order reached Joseph on 1 July, and Soult at Zamora on 2 July. It is likely that the intercept was predated in an attempt to draw Wellesley into a trap. But Oman misinterprets Soult's attempt to make himself king of Northern Lusitania; and so, of the emotions he supposes Napoleon's new plan to have aroused in Soult's breast (vol.II, p.461), Oman observes that 'Wellesley and Cuesta had no conception that any force save that of Soult was likely to menace their northern front' (vol.II, p.475). 'It is clear that they did not expect to have to fight Victor, the king and Sebastiani combined, as they were ultimately forced to do on July 28'. When Soult learned of the battle of Talavera, he 'discovered that his adversary, only two days before, was grossly underrating the numbers of the army that was marching against his rear. He was led on to hope that

Wellesley would presently advance against him with inferior numbers, and court destruction by attacking the united 2nd and 5th corps.' In the event Wellesley was saved by an intercept handed on by Cuesta.

33. *History*, vol.III, p.184.

34. Oman states that Silveira was sent to Trás-os-Montes 'where it was unlikely that any serious irruption of the French would take place ... to curb his eccentricities as far as possible.' This is gratuitous and unjust. Silveira was a successful commander and a native of Trás-os-Montes, and the most natural appointment for the job. Masséna did consider making for Oporto rather than Lisbon after his defeat at Bussaco, but was deterred partly because it was not what Napoleon had ordered, and partly because he would have met with resistance. He also relied too much on his few Portuguese adherents, who would carry no weight in Oporto.

35. The best-known case of conflict was that of Colonel Costa e Almeida, *tenente-rei*, or governor, of the fortress of Almeida, who was outranked by William Cox, whose 'step' made him brigadier. After the famous explosion which blew up the magazine Cox hoped, in vain, for Wellesley to come to the relief, while Colonel Almeida recognised that further resistance was impossible. He was shot for insubordination. After a lengthy delay, the case was revived when Beresford exerted his right to promote Cox. The question was submitted to a joint court, which disagreed, dividing on national lines.

36. Napier concludes his vol.II (pp.465–7) with a diatribe against Spain in his most offensive style, citing Wellesley: 'I have fished in many troubled waters, but Spanish troubled waters will I never try again.' He adds that Spain was 'ripe for destruction', clearly a reference to the state of affairs in 1829, when the Spanish traditionalists were hounding Napier's radical friends. (Wellesley did not lose his reservations even when he became Captain-General and commander-in-chief in Spain.).

37. In Portugal, Wellesley was accorded the style of Marshal-General, last held by Lafões as a member of the royal house. If Beresford was ruffled by this, it was not because of what was done but the manner in which it was done, without previous consultation. There was probably no ill-intent: the Prince-Regent had hoped to get Wellesley as his commander-in-chief not only because of his victories, but because of his stand over the Convention of Sintra. He had accepted Beresford, but got his own way by conferring the higher title on Wellesley. Beresford's letter of 4 October 1809 to Lady Anne, his half-sister, shows that, if the thought of resignation crossed his mind, it was soon brushed aside. He had rejected Wellesley's advice to give up his British rank and pay, and enjoyed having two salaries, part of which he used to pay the debts of his naval brother, Sir John Poo. Wellesley professed to be ignorant of Portuguese politics, did not return to Lisbon for nearly three years after advancing from Torres Vedras, and was content to leave contacts to Beresford and Charles Stuart.

38. Beresford was not the only victim of Napier's criticisms. When his first volume was published in 1828 by John Murray (who also published Southey), it accused Strangford of falsifying his account of the departure of the Portuguese royal family in 1807. Strangford published a reply and Napier retorted with his *Reply to Lord Strangford's Observations*. His method was to accept the criticism but to repeat the charge in a different

form. When finally Strangford went to law against the editor of the *Sun*, the judge ruled that he had no case and Napier triumphed. Beresford also attempted to refute his aspersions, with no better result. Wellington, by contrast, had been the subject of Napier's dedication in volume I; but by 1830 his Tory policy had alienated the author (not least over the Portuguese succession crisis, in which Napier's brother Charles commanded the navy of Dom Pedro).

39. Oman's reconstruction of the battle was based on a careful examination of the site: S.E. Vichness also describes it from a visit made in 1971, while Michael Glover's inspection at about the same time confirmed that Napier's 'ravine' had never existed.

40. Napier, *op.cit.* vol.III, p.517, where he says that the French were erroneously estimated to have lost 5000, from the supposition that 400 dead were found lying about Fuentes, whereas he found not more than 130, of whom a third were British. He remarks that 'all armies make rash statements on such occasions'. His account of Fuentes is brief: 'Both sides claimed the victory: the French because they forced Lord Wellington to relinquish three miles of ground, the English because the village was successfully defended.' Masséna had exposed 'all the errors of the English general's position, and Napoleon would have made them fatal.' But Ney had left in dudgeon, in 'actual insubordination' against Masséna, who had been replaced by Marmont.

41. Napier, *op.cit.* vol.III (1833), p.532.

42. Beresford to Torrens, 8 April 1812 (PRO).

43. Beresford to Sir John Poo.

44. Beresford's post-war experiences while still Marshal of the Portuguese army form a separate story. His attempt to hold Portugal on behalf of the still-absent John VI ended with the revolution of 1820. Later he was briefly Master General of Ordnance in Wellington's government, was the last life governor of Jersey, and died at his home at Bedgebury in Kent in 1854.

Chapter 6

Oman's View of the Spanish Army in the Peninsular War Reassessed

by Colonel Juan José Sañudo

Oman's approach

All history is necessarily a simplified resumé of events, quite apart from the subjectivity inseparable from the human condition. Logically Oman's history cannot be any different, so the present chapter tries to assess his assertions about the Spanish army; to complete and modernise them in the light of today's knowledge. In particular we will consider the judgement on 'The Spanish Army in 1808' in the first volume of his great work (section II, chapter II, pp.89–102), which was his first look at the subject and would determine his perspective throughout the remaining volumes.

From the start Oman displayed a great understanding of the Spanish situation, which was very advanced for his time, and represents a very significant achievement. This line has, fortunately, been followed by later British authors such as David Gates and Charles Esdaile. However, Oman too unreservedly accepted the opinions of writers who had been eyewitnesses to the historical events – such as the Duke of Wellington, Napier,[1] Lord Londonderry, etc – simply because of their personal involvement. This method, typical of Oman's age, would not be acceptable today. It lacks both systematic scepticism and the indispensable contrasting of his own prejudices against other, non-British, opinions. There is also another basic problem, in his lack of knowledge of how Spain and her army evolved during the following six years of war. This constitutes, perhaps, his main deficiency; although it was completely unavoidable. Neither Oman nor any other historian has been able to utilise post-war Spanish work on the subject, for the simple reason that none exists. After the end of the war Spain experienced an interminable series of civil wars which, continuing through the whole of the nineteenth century and part of the twentieth, totally absorbed historical attention. Entire archives were lost – along with public interest. Popular Spanish ideas about the Peninsular War today rise no higher than cliché.

The Spanish Army

We can very quickly establish, from official data, that at the start of the war there were 7222 field and subaltern officers and 131,019 other ranks, with the following important qualifications:

– The availability of horses was restricted to a little under 6000, which reduced the twenty-four cavalry regiments to little more than one operational squadron each.

– In addition to the Division of the North, detached to Denmark with some 10,000 men, a further two Divisions with about 26,000 men (neither mentioned by Oman) were initially in Portugal, at Oporto and Lisbon. Although the first of these was able to return to Galicia without difficulty, the men of the second were for the most part detained as prisoners.

Even though it was so limited in effectives, the Spanish army could still have conducted a defensive action – assisted by the natural fortress of the Pyrenees and the poor lines of communication imposed on an enemy by the terrain – at least long enough to buy time for a general mobilisation. It could not, however, hope to resist an attack coming from Madrid, Lisbon, Pamplona, or Barcelona, etc, which not only lacked a single unified direction, but which had plenty of Spanish leaders to support it, from the very top downward. The obvious importance of this point is very often forgotten: Spain was entering a revolution rather more than an international war. We must also remember that from 1810 until 1814 there were further risings in the American colonies, from Argentina to California, which forced Spain to despatch troops to Vera Cruz, Maracaibo, and Montevideo. Some 14,000 men eventually had to be sent, given the absolute lack of Spanish units in the New World. Mexico and Venezuela were initially recovered, but this was not the case with Argentina and Uruguay; the garrison in Montevideo was starved out in 1814, and the war would continue until 1825.

In France and Great Britain, safe from invasions, the documentation of this war has been preserved in a more or less orderly way. In Spain, which – apart from the cities of Cádiz, Tarifa, and Alicante – was eventually occupied in its entirety, the equivalent archives were lost, so that it has become not only very difficult to trace the evolution of units, especially for the later years of the war, but actually impossible in only too many cases. For example, it is quite normal to find several units operating at the same time and place with the same number, since the Supreme *Junta* was unable to prevent a flood of new units in every region, authorised by local *juntas* which preferred to create fresh regiments with the name of their own city or area, and officered according to their own arbitrary whims. In general terms the number of small units (both infantry and cavalry) which fell between the size of a regiment and an independent company, was as follows:

	Units in the Spanish Army				Units in Wellington's Army			
	Veteran	New	Total	British	German	Portuguese	Other	Total
1808	139	305	444	46	7	13	1	67
1809	340	63	403	61	8	41	–	110
1810	290	72	362	53	7	32	–	92
1811	300	71	371	69	10	46	1	126
1812	276	21	297	69	14	41	7	131
1813	240	14	254	82	16	40	11	149
1814	202	1	203	75	9	39	2	125

This list does not include artillery units, since they did not operate as regiments but only as tactically independent batteries. However, it does show a steady reduction in the abusive creation of new units, in order to provide subsistence with greater regularity. The number of units decreased, but not the number of combatants (which was limited only by the availability of economic resources).

In 1808 the Spanish army still had an antiquated organisation, even though it had confronted the armies of the French Republic during the preceding decade, and had experienced to its cost the power of their simple but extremely effective tactics (being pushed back as far as the banks of the Ebro in 1793-5). Yet the secrets of French efficiency were not, apparently, reported or studied, and still less adopted. We cannot say that this neglect was born of distance or lack of knowledge, since the Northern Division in Denmark, and those of generals Carrafa and Solano in Portugal, were acting as allies integrated into the French army; as observers in the front line itself. The Spanish had no lack of knowledge of their profession, nor did they lack means – but did they understand the basis of French success? Indeed, did the French really understand it themselves?

Operationally, the limited possibilities open to the French in the tortured terrain of the Peninsula cannot be compared with their fluid manoeuvres in the central European theatre – but in the tactical field they were just as decisive, notably through the flexible organisation of their army corps. By contrast there were no Spanish army corps, the nearest equivalent being the 'Army Grand Units' (*ie* independent field armies). Not only were these normally limited to operating on exterior lines to the centre of the Peninsula (which was dominated by the French), but they were organised with every one of their effectives assigned to and integrated within Divisions: that is to say, there were no 'Corps troops', so the cohesion of the higher unit was easily lost during a battle. Its commander had no major unit in reserve, and the Grand Unit's movements were tied to the speed of its slowest arm, the artillery, which was normally short of horses and had to rely on oxen or mules. Hence in practice the manoeuvrability of a Grand Unit was negligible – a decisive factor which normally led to its being surrounded or outflanked by the enemy's cavalry, which could always be concentrated for a decisive attack. Each Spanish Division also lacked articulation into brigades, restricting its own manoeuvrability in turn. The few Cavalry Divisions were reduced to a handful of precious squadrons, without any organisational link between regiments. Badly mounted, they were even less well trained, and consequently they lacked morale. As a result they were completely ineffective in the face of French cavalry, which was united and superior in every respect.

In a country of very few artillery roads, arranged like the spokes of a wheel, strategic superiority came from manoeuvres on interior lines from the centre, *ie* Madrid. Apart from brief interludes resulting from the battles of Bailén and Salamanca, the French held on to Madrid as their key centre throughout the conflict. Hence the imperial side immediately enjoyed the upper hand in strategic terms, as against a Spanish strategy of repeated convergent efforts against the centre, which were naturally prone to collapse because of the difficulties of co-ordination. The campaigns of Talavera and Ocaña are clear examples of this, with scarce resources being wasted in the vain pursuit of a political objective that was made all the more urgent by the very weakness of the Supreme *Junta*'s position.

By way of contrast, Wellington's strategic method was initially to wear down the enemy with delaying actions in depth (*eg* the combat of the Coa), and only to accept battle when in a strong position, especially if it had been pre-prepared (*eg* Bussaco, and the impregnable triple lines of Torres Vedras), not to mention the abandonment of almost all Portuguese territory to scorched earth. Avoidance was the only strategy that was possible until, following Marmont's mistake at Salamanca in 1812, Wellington improvised a plan for the offensive. However, this proved to be faulty, since it split his effort between Burgos and Madrid. He threatened to cut the imperials' umbilical cord in Burgos, but the operation failed because of the chronic British deficiency in siege-work. Yet the British commander did possess a vital ability to learn from his mistakes, so for 1813 he knew how to exploit the predictable French strategy of controlling the centre. They wanted to lure Wellington towards Madrid, and confront him with retrograde delaying actions in depth, astride the main Madrid–Burgos–Vitoria highway; so his solution was to make a wide detour round their right flank, avoiding any confrontation until he had passed the Ebro, by which time the imperials were threatened with general encirclement before they had understood what was happening. This demonstrates the personal importance of a good commander, which unfortunately the Spanish army lacked during the first four years of the war. It was a lack accentuated by political failures in overcoming the chronic tendency to regionalisation, linked to an equally disgraceful insistence on the principle of seniority, as well as a demand for submissive loyalty to the Supreme *Junta* and the *Cortes,* and by intrigues among the generals themselves. The destitutions of Castaños and Ballasteros, and other generals of tested aptitude, are clear examples of this, compared to the elevations of such commanders as Blake, Venegas, and Ariezaga.

In the tactical field, where everything must come together, the indispensable cavalry screen was often absent from Spanish armies. These were therefore prone to being surprised at dawn by the French, whose rapid nocturnal marches often enabled them to fall on the Spanish bivouacs and encampments. The battles of Rio Seco, Santa Engracia (Gebora), Almonacid, and Ocaña demonstrate this. Only a fortuitous reveille at 3:00 am at Bailén prevented a similar disaster. Even where it was present, the inevitable defeat of the Spanish cavalry once a battle had started, as a result of its numerical inferiority, notified the infantry that it was surrounded and cut off, leading directly to a collapse in morale. Add to that the clear numerical superiority of the French *voltigeurs* over the Spanish light infantry, which inevitably led to the loss of a Spanish army's commanders. Espinosa de los Monteros offers a clear example: there were five dead or mortally wounded generals in the Asturian, Tercera, and Northern Divisions. Thus the Spanish started their battles already surrounded, and with a fair number of commanders lost. However, in some cases - Bailén is one example, as are Tamanes, Alcañiz, Albuera, and San Marcial - the strength of the terrain and/or properly efficient artillery were able to shore up the morale of the infantry sufficiently for them to beat the imperial forces by the superiority of the line over the column. Nevertheless, on most occasions the latter managed to overcome their own morale disadvantage and so precipitate a Spanish flight. The French cavalry, however, though absolute queen of the battlefield, rarely exploited its success to the full with a pursuit. Sometimes the cause was fatigue after the battle; at other times it was the lure of plunder.

Just as Oman related, training and drill manoeuvres were specific to individual regiments, with different words of command for each one. In general they tried to follow contemporary French tactics as far as the smallest units were concerned, but it was an impossible aspiration in view of the deep structural differences between the two armies. As a result every unit adopted whatever system seemed to be most appropriate. Thus in the 1808 exercises at Getafe, near Madrid, General Blake failed to persuade the army to follow the practice of his own regiment in loading the musket on the right hand side of the man, instead of the left. Elsewhere the frequency of exercises was so low that when the Swiss Colonel Traxler marched out of Cartagena to fight for the first time, he found his troops deplorably unfit because they had not left their garrison for *eight years*.

In the period immediately preceding the war the kingdom was convulsed by the extreme political stresses which would lead to the coup of Aranjuez on 17–19 March 1808. The highest members of the military command favoured Godoy and were turning towards the Francophile faction, in a reaction against the revolutionary attitude of Fernando VII's party, which was supported by the rank and file of the army, and particularly the Royal Guard. After the events of 2 May in Madrid the high command would try to maintain that attitude, although it found itself leaning towards the dominant faction in each particular location, with a few tragic (and fairly well-known) exceptions. The generals and officers observed obedience towards their superiors in principle, but naturally felt more closely tied to their NCOs and troops, and, identifying with the army's indignation at grass roots level, followed the path of insurrection.

The soldiers and NCOs had fewer privileges to protect than their officers, so it was among them that the real riots took place. However, these were never directed against their immediate officers, but rather against the Francophile policies of the higher leadership. The absence of fratricidal violence was striking: tensions were resolved instead by desertion, both from units which were reluctant to riot and from others which had already done so. Reduced to officers without troops, even previously reluctant regiments eventually joined in. Not a single unit of the Spanish army remained in the service of King Joseph, who was left to create – without success – a new royal Spanish army from scratch.

The biggest mistake the French made lay in their misunder-standing of the historical sensitivities of the Spanish people, which quickly led to a generalised uprising against both the foreign occupation and the Spanish ruling class, whose privileges and standard of living had aroused bitter envy. Yet because so much of the resistance was directed against the existing authorities, it pro-duced new local chiefs who imposed their own control over the regular military commanders, with the consequent loss – if not impossibility – of efficiency. It was not long before shortages of clothing and food, the fatigue of marches, and the harshness of the climate, led to widespread desertion. This factor, which was to have decisive importance, has often been ignored by historians – and even modern-day Spaniards would be surprised to learn that as early as 2 August 1808 it was necessary to resort to selective amnesties in order to allow deserters to reconsider their actions and return to the colours. Even before they saw the enemy, the first volunteers were so obviously demoralised that they were often given permission to return to their homes. It is paradoxical that throughout the war, conjointly with abundant demonstrations of heroism in certain circumstances, the population, local authorities and citizens alike, generally refused to fulfil their basic duty of service in the army.

The infantry

Oman's opinions about the initial order of battle in 1808 were largely correct, even in details such as his assessment of the composition of the Walloon Guard regiment (*ie* the soldiers were foreigners, but not Walloons, although he did miss the fact that its commanders *were* Walloons, at least in theory). The only major mistake he made was with the territorially-named regiments. Their denomination as 'from' the Asturias, Toledo, etc, was and is merely honorary, and did not indicate either where they originated, where they served, or where their soldiers came from.

Over half of the Spanish line infantry was customarily intended to be recruited at the last moment, for immediate incorporation after a war had actually started.[2] However, exemptions in recruiting, the scarcity of men and matériel, and the general lack of fighting spirit in the civil population after the first few months, made it impossible to reach anything like the theoretical total strength. Regimental organisation into three battalions was normally reduced to two, with the third remaining in the dépôt to instruct recruits. Sometimes, out of necessity, the regiment went out on campaign with all three battalions, thereby renouncing methodical instruction in favour of 'training on the march'. The traditional and antiquated practice of gathering together the two companies of grenadiers (both of which were in the first battalion) with those of other regiments, to form supposedly élite columns of grenadiers, normally meant that the parent regiment was in effect reduced to just one-and-a-half battalions.[3] In the field these would turn themselves into a single reinforced battalion, or two very reduced ones, which made regulation manoeuvres all but impossible, and at best 'monolithic'.

Against good cavalry the morale of the infantry was *a priori* very low, but the truly decisive factor in Spanish infantry morale still lay in the very low number of *tiradores*, of whom there were only eight per fusilier company, or thirty-two per battalion in the most favourable case. Nor were these organised together under any united command. Their fundamental mission in combat was to advance some 100–200 metres ahead of the battalion as skirmishers, to prevent their opposite numbers from working forward under cover to within close musket range of the main formation, from where they could inflict casualties on the battalion, and especially among its officers. Against these thirty-two *tiradores*, however, a French battalion could put forward a company of about 140 *voltigeurs*, who, as well as being numerically superior, were commanded by their own officers and NCOs – a feature which did not exist in Spanish *tirador* organisation. The inevitable outcome of such a confrontation is obvious.

The 1790s campaign in the Pyrenees had underlined the need for Spain to increase her light infantry, the majority of whom at that time were Catalans. At the start of hostilities in 1808 there were twelve light battalions,[4] although the relative scarcity of these units led to their employment as half-battalions, which was considered normal in the early campaigns. In tactics they suffered from the same defect as the French, in that they were often used merely as line units integrated in bigger formations. They normally formed part of the so-called vanguard of an army and, due to the sparsity of proper cavalry, were expected to perform many of its security duties. Certainly the need for this type of unit – and the suitability of the average Spaniard, agile and of small stature, for such service – meant that light infantry numbers gradually increased. By January 1810 there were thirty-two battalions, although most were under half their established strength and their fifth and sixth companies generally considered themselves to be in 'reserve' or in the dépôt. However, on 8 May 1812 all light infantry units were suppressed and fully integrated into the line infantry.

At the start of the war the Provincial Militia numbered forty-three battalions which had already served for five years, as the first reserve to be mobilised (in the war against Great Britain). Consequently its units could be considered at a level of efficiency similar to that of the line infantry. The Militia was organised in regiments of five companies, one of grenadiers and four of fusiliers, with theoretical strengths of seventy and 168 men respectively. The grenadier companies operated separately from their parent battalions, in four 'divisions' of two battalions each, named for Old Castile, New Castile, Andalucia, and Galicia. On 4 January 1810 the provincial regiments were reorganised into two battalions, including one in reserve (with *chasseurs* and fusiliers equal to those in line units). Then on 1 July 1810 they were confusingly named 'line' and 'second' (and even 'third') regiments, in the vain hope of avoiding coincidences in nomenclature with already existing line units. The surviving militia grenadier divisions were also reshaped from two battalions to one, organised like the line with six companies including one of grenadiers, to a total of 781 men. In all this the successive creations, suppressions, and transfers of troops from one unit to another make the OB very difficult to follow.

The Urban Militia Infantry, considered as a second reserve in the army of Carlos IV, had 114 companies; but it was inoperative in the tactical field. Even in its primary role as a force of public order it generally failed in its mission. The urban militias, or *Guardias Civicas*, were unable to prevent tragic consequences following from the popular uprising throughout Spain.

Oman was right to consider the cavalry as the weakest part of the Spanish army. It had at its disposal less than 6000 horses rather than the 9000 it was supposed to have. There was no heavy cavalry in 1808, nor even any helmets. Nor was there any differentiation according to the size of the horses, hence one could not distinguish between hussars, dragoons, or line cavalry – they all used whatever horses they could get. In the Army of the Left (Galicia), General Mahy even built some wooden horses to make up for the lack of real ones, at least for training. Without doubt this was the arm which suffered most from economic penury, and its chronic numerical inferiority was in turn the direct cause of the majority of Spanish defeats. Oman said 'it is still impossible to explain the consistent misbehaviour of these evasive squadrons', but in reality their low strength in battle constitutes a blindingly obvious factor. At Medina de Rio Seco there were just 710 Spanish cavalry, compared to 1732 French; at Bailén 997 compared to 2676; at Gamonal (Burgos) 958 compared to as many as 5181; and at Zornoza none at all, compared to 1340 French. During May 1808 the Spanish cavalry as a whole had 5500 horses of generally low quality, which had to equip twelve line regiments, eight of dragoons, two of *chasseurs*, and two of hussars.[5]

In tactics the line cavalry formed the main combat force, to neutralise the actions of the enemy's cavalry and act upon the flanks. For combat it formed two close-order lines which advanced towards the enemy at a trot. They would charge the last 100 metres at the gallop, knee to knee, with the arms of the first line extended forwards, their sabre points level with the riders' line of sight. Meanwhile the second line advanced with the sabre shouldered, ready to strike any horseman or foot-soldier missed by the first line. Dragoons had originally been mounted infantry; but they had since become almost identical with line cavalry, except that their mounts were, if anything, of an even worse quality. *Chasseur* and hussar regiments theoretically provided an army's security and scouts, and supposedly had faster horses. In reality, however, shortages of men and horses did not allow them to field more than one or two squadrons each, poorly mounted and worse instructed. On many occasions it would be necessary to collect together several regiments in order to deploy just one squadron. This was, for example, the maximum total ever achieved by the entire Army of the Left, responsible for the defence of Galicia, a good part of Asturias, and Zamora, as well as el Bierzo.

In the first excitement of 1808 three new line, four dragoon, five *chasseur*, and four hussar regiments were created. During 1809 the number of line regiments increased to twenty-one, while the dragoons were reduced to six. The *chasseurs* increased to fourteen, and the hussars to sixteen – almost all irregulars. On 30 January 1809 two regiments of lancers were also created (following some mythical success with that arm at Bailén), initially with four squadrons of three companies, totalling 852 horses. (Strangely the French army would not create lancer units until 1812; and the British would create none throughout the war). The crushing defeats of 1810 make it very difficult to give the precise number of line units – there were perhaps twenty-three – but on 18 July it was laid down that there should be a total of sixteen *chasseur* regiments, nineteen of hussars, and four of lancers. There was also to be one regiment of cuirassiers and one of mounted grenadiers, in imitation of the French. In April 1811 there were thirty regiments with three squadrons, although there were also additional independent squadrons: twelve of line cavalry, ten of dragoons, four of *chasseurs*, and four of hussars. A few lancer companies were also retained.

In general terms Oman has sound views on the artillery, although we may disagree with him over a few specifics. For example, although sufficient reserves of guns and ammunition did normally exist, some 16-pdr guns still had to be improvised out of wood strengthened with metal hoops made by a blacksmith. In addition, the handling of cannons was practised by all soldiers. Infantry companies were frequently encountered attached to the artillery, and grenadiers were particularly instructed in that service. Even peasants and women were familiar with handling guns, not least the famous Agustina de Aragón at the first siege of Saragossa. Yet Spanish tactical manoeuvres with artillery were nevertheless generally ineffective, and did not extend further than establishing the guns in their firing positions. As soon as they left the roads they easily broke their axles, because of their great weight and weak carriages. They tended to remain bogged down in the mud, and could not be manhandled into negotiating slopes, hedges or fences.

As for the engineers, at the beginning of the war there was only one regiment, as Oman hints.[6] Later, in Calatayud, some engineer deserters were formed into the Fernando VII Regiment, called the 'Sappers of Aragón'; and in Valencia, with its base in the Plana Mayor, the 1st Engineer Battalion formed the Regiment of Sappers and Miners of Valencia. Both units participated in the defence of Saragossa until its fall in February 1809. Tarragona also provided a company of volunteer sappers who helped defend Gerona until its surrender in December 1809.

The administration of Godoy and his successors

Oman knew all about the difficulties of supplying the army; but his prejudices made him blame it systematically on defects of administration, on corruption, and on other vices. Yet in reality it was the result of a deeper and more obvious cause: the endemic weakness of the economy. Oman blames the state of the army mainly on Godoy, even though the *juntas* which succeeded him failed to improve the situation; nor did either the *cortes* of Cádiz or the Duke of Wellington himself, when he took command. Ideas and experience were in plentiful supply; but there was simply a shortage of money. Oman's final statement on Godoy (*History*, vol.I, p.98) suggests that in any other country he would have been dismissed much earlier; but this cannot be sustained in the light of the historical record. It was widely understood that Spain had faced far more difficulties than was normal, and Godoy had done his best. During the coup of Aranjuez he could even find an ally in Murat.[7] There was certainly great resentment against him in the army; but the military had a duty to adapt to political developments, just as today civil servants must work under very different ideologies which ensue from electoral changes. Then again, Oman was perfectly correct to say that the level of skill, patriotism, and integrity among the highest ranks of the army was very low. Yet such defects were unique neither to Spain nor to that period. In essence promotions were arbitrary; but this too was far from uncommon, as may be illustrated by the British system of purchasing commissions.

With a population of 10.5 million according to the latest census, Spain theoretically enjoyed a capability to mobilise more than enough men to provide for the needs of the army, at least for a frontier war such as had been fought fifteen years earlier against Revolutionary France. However, it is axiomatic that the experience of the last war will be of little use for the next one – and in the first moments of the 1808 crisis some absurd local mobilisations were attempted. All single men and widowers between the ages of sixteen and forty were called up, only to find it was impossible to give them arms, clothes, officers, or even food. This demonstrated the true limits of possible mobilisation. The extreme generosity of individuals – nobles, plebeians, and clergy – who during the early part of the conflict donated money, arms, and horses, also declined as time passed. Then the revolt of the American provinces in 1810 cut the flow of resources, and this event can be pinpointed as plunging the Spanish army into the most absolute poverty. It became normal for soldiers, and even officers, to lack shoes, and the army's daily diet was reduced to little more than bread. We must remember the reaction of General Castaños of the Fifth Army, when disturbed by the behaviour of his men: he gave them a good *gazpacho* as the best possible luxury; and we must remember his letter to another Spanish general, commenting how worried he was by Wellesley's insistent invitation to dinner, since he would then have to reciprocate, and 'as you know, on my table there is never anything more than bread.' We can also find reports such as 'in this regiment there are so many officers who are excused service for not having any shoes or having only boiled bread to eat.'

In demographic terms Spain could have tripled her forces, if only she had disposed of sufficient economic resources to support and equip them. This meant that destroyed armies could be, and regularly were, rebuilt. They might disappear, but they would reappear within three months provided some general could reanimate their spirit. However, the morale of the civil population was another matter. It was always weaker, and its chronic lack of productivity was well known, whereas the government was running an annual deficit of 219 million *reales*. The result was that, at a rough estimate, the total manpower of the French Imperial army could be maintained at a level some ten times greater than that of the Spanish, although the forces it put into Spain were only a little more than double.

If we take the start of 1809 in León as an example, we find that La Romana had 23,000 men facing Soult's 13,000, but only 9000 of the Spanish had arms and almost all were recently recruited from their homes. They also lacked cavalry, whereas the French had some 2000. Similarly, on 13 August 1808 the army of Aragón totalled 13,375 men but lacked any cavalry and was armed with only 8927 muskets of many different calibres, many of which were useless. The men were all recruits without training, and their officers were reserves or, even worse, arbitrarily chosen. Hence we cannot make sensible numerical comparisons between Spanish troops and the French, who were veterans of many campaigns, and well equipped and commanded. Admittedly they, too, experienced many logistical problems, but they could solve these by devastating the countryside – a solution obviously impracticable for Spanish troops.

In the second session of the *Cortes* on 22 January 1814, four months before the end of the war, and hence with the administrative experience of almost six years of conflict, the state of poverty of the troops was blamed not on the administration, but on the low national income of 300 million *reales*. This must be contrasted with figures published in 1991 by the University of Granada,[8] showing that in 1807 the national income had been 699.5 million *reales,* including revenues of 150 million coming annually from America – which were no longer available in 1814. Even excluding these, the difference of revenue in Spain itself between 1807 and 1814 was still 249.5 million. In other words, the occupation of Spanish territory by the French produced a fall in income of approximately fifty per cent, which is truly catastrophic. By contrast the French budget for 1807 had been the equivalent of 3,313 million *reales*, or more than quadruple that of Spain for the same year.

The British critique

After Wellington took command of the Spanish armies in September 1812 he would systematically excuse himself for its deficiencies and blame his subordinates, regardless of whether they were Spanish or British. In reality he would make value judgements on the spur of the moment, although on the whole they were obviously contradictory. The fact that one is an eyewitness of an event is never a guarantee that one's account of it is correct; for example on 20 June and 4 July 1810 Ensign John Aitchison seemed to believe that Don Julian Sanchez commanded a band of guerrillas,[9] which was not strictly true. The fearsome and heterogeneous aspect of his men, and their lack of uniforms, made many of the British, such as Aitchison, believe that most Spanish troops were indeed *guerrilleros*, when they were actually from regular units. The lack of relevant publications has long helped to perpetuate errors of this sort, including among the majority of the Spanish population today, for whom it seems more romantic to think that their ancestors were all *guerrilleros*, when they were not...

Oman laments the lack of discipline of the Spanish troops, and their disobedience towards their officers, while tending to gloss over the villages burned and hundreds of Spanish people murdered by insubordinate British soldiers during Moore's retreat; not to mention the sackings of Ciudad Rodrigo, San Sebastian, or Badajoz. Oman also gives a simplified view of the abilities and promotion system of Spanish officers, not understanding that when the revolution took place in 1808 whole armies were created from almost nothing. The ranks, from sergeant to marshal, were assigned according to an officer's loyalties to his local *junta* or *caudillo* - although some also came from the reserve or from civilian life. The Asturian and Aragón armies and the Miño Division are clear examples. Hence the most widespread British error in regard to the Spanish army lies in praising the disposition of the Spanish soldiers, while expecting their officers to be something they could not be. In the light of the surviving documentation a very different perspective would surely be appropriate.

Inter-Allied friction

By accepting eyewitness opinions, such as those of the Count of Munster or Sergeant Surtees, as 'indubitable truth', Oman fails to notice that, in reality, during the first three years of the war the knowledge that such men could have had of the Spanish was very limited indeed. In Moore's campaign of 1808–9 the British had only the briefest contact with La Romana's army, which it crossed paths with in Astorga when both were in retreat. There was no collaboration between them, and they continued separately on their respective ways. Then in Wellesley's campaign of 1809 the British were in contact with the Spanish only between 21 July and 4 August - just fifteen days. Then, strongly conditioned by the British government, Wellesley abandoned the operation, which was in reality only part of a strategic diversion in favour of Austria – at the same time and in the same shape as that of Stuart in Italy, and the disembarkation at Walcheren. Once Austria was defeated, the government ordered them all to withdraw. Conversely, in Graham's battle of Barrossa on 5 March 1811, La Peña certainly did not come to the rescue of the British rearguard with his Spanish vanguard, as can be verified in the account by Schepeler, who was present. The red feathers of the French grenadiers at the head of their columns threw everybody into confusion until the last moment, since they were mistaken for British troops from Cádiz. To come to the help of Graham it would have been necessary to abandon the bridge over the canal Sancti Petri, thereby losing the only possible road to Cádiz. The brevity of the action and the distances would have made it impossible for La Peña to arrive in time, although the truth remains that he never intended to move. Graham nevertheless withdrew his co-operation immediately after the battle and retired to Cádiz.

Although each of the actions quoted would need more than 500 pages for a study in depth,[10] it is easy to see that the duration of Spanish–British contact was minimal, and in each case there was a unilateral abandonment of the action by the British general – who was different on each occasion. This looks less like a series of coincidences than a predetermined plan. It is surely impossible that the commanding generals of an expeditionary force should have enjoyed sufficient freedom of action to endanger – not to say rupture – the alliance between Britain and Spain without previous instructions from their home government. Obviously such instructions would be kept safe, secure from the examination of subsequent historians. But the pattern of behaviour is only too clear: 'We are leaving because our allies don't deserve us' would become the systematic excuse to justify every withdrawal before the court of British public opinion.

The fatal influence of Napier's picture of the Spanish panic at Talavera is strong in Oman, and in other British historians of the present day. Allegedly 10,000 Spanish fled without cause – or were 'only frightened by the noise of their own fire'[11] – yet the memoirs of a British officer, Captain Whittingham, who was present and who was wounded by a shot in the mouth, confirm that they were, in fact, attacked during the night. Certainly the four battalions of the first line did flee – about 3000 'soldiers', if one could give such a name to men with only three months' service since the massacre of Medellín, which had been their first baptism of fire, and in which many had been killed. Yet at the same place and time some British troops also fled, although we cannot give numbers. Throughout the war there were many other occasions of collective panic, and they were not confined to the Spanish. After its defeat at Alcañiz the French army corps of Marshal Suchet disbanded during the night-time withdrawal, when a drummer shouted that the enemy was approaching. The drummer was executed and the incident was hushed up; but because of such episodes one is permitted to doubt the valour of the Imperial troops.

Oman does explain that from about May 1811, after three years of continuous fighting, against Napoleon's war machine, and outnumbered two to one, the Spanish army had been reduced to a terrible condition, and inevitably produced a bad impression when compared with the small but professional British force. Most of the professional Spanish generals, officers, NCOs, and soldiers had already been killed, mutilated, or captured; but they had in turn irreparably worn down the French invaders' forces, which, when added to Napoleon's redeployment of his armies towards Russia in 1812, had resulted in better units having to be replaced by others of less experience. The enemy confronting the Duke of Wellington would never thereafter be of the same high standard as the one which had destroyed the Spanish armies in the winter campaign of 1808.

Conclusion

On the whole, Oman's opinions are fair. Given his restricted knowledge, through the sources he used, one must admire his ability to understand the difficulties of the Spanish army in unfalteringly confronting a war without hope against an enemy of overwhelming superiority. It is certainly an illusion to believe that, either alone or together with the British, the Spanish could have managed to be victorious against the whole strength of the Napoleonic Empire. If the 450,000 men of the *Grande Armée* had come back to the Peninsula, instead of attacking Russia in 1812, and had united with the 300,000 already there, nothing and nobody could have held out against them.

In conclusion the present author would like to express his personal admiration for the Spanish army, which in the midst of so many problems and traumas, knew how to oppose, unfalteringly for six years, the best war machine of its day. It had successes and it made mistakes, but we can say with justification that it was the only European army capable of opposing Napoleon continuously during that time, and thereby ensure that his 'Spanish ulcer' would not stop bleeding until his final defeat had been accomplished.

Notes

1. It is unfortunate that Oman followed too many of Napier's errors, such as the non-existent ditch at Talavera into which the 23rd Light Dragoons supposedly crashed!

2. In peacetime a regiment had seventy commissioned and non-commissioned officers, and 1008 men, intended to expand in time of war to thirty-six officers, sixty sergeants, and 2160 men.

3. The first battalions included two grenadier companies each with seventy-seven men, and two of fusiliers (*blanquillos*, or foot-soldiers dressed in white) at theoretically between 191 and 125 men, but in reality much less, *eg* the company of Lieutenant Ruiz on 2 May 1808 had only thirty-five *blanquillos*. The second and third battalions each had four companies of fusiliers.

4. Light battalions had six companies each, with a total rank and file strength of thirty-six sergeants, 1146 soldiers, a drum major, and eighteen musicians.

5. Oman confuses the line with 'heavy' cavalry and the Dragoons with 'light'. The law of 13 January 1803 had organised regiments into five squadrons of two companies each, with three officers and fifty-nine other ranks per company. On 1 October 1808 the regiment was reorganised into four squadrons, each of three companies of fifty men and horses, totalling about 600 men in all. This organisation prevailed until 15 July of the following year, when the regiments were theoretically reduced to three squadrons. In December 1814, as the war was ending, another law re-established regimental strength as five squadrons of two companies, each of sixty men, which was a return to the situation at the start of the war. Sixteen line regiments were maintained, with between one and five of dragoons, three of *chasseurs*, and three of hussars, once again marking a return to almost the same strength as existed at the start of the conflict.

6. Two battalions of five companies, one of miners and four of sappers, in total about 800 men, commanded by specialist engineer officers. On 23 July 1808 the number of battalions was increased to six.

7. Compare the analysis by Charles Esdaile in chapter 12.

8. Various authors, *Entre la guerra y la paz, Jaén 1808–14* (Granada, 1991).

9. W.F.K. Thompson, ed., *An Ensign in the Peninsular War: The Letters of John Aitchison* (London, 1981; reprinted 1994).

10. For example, the present author's book on Talavera, *La Crisis de una Alianza*, written with Leopoldo Stampa (Madrid, 1996).

11. Wellesley, quoted in Oman, *History*, vol.II, p.514.

Chapter 7

The Guerrillas
How Oman Underestimated the Role of Irregular Forces

by René Chartrand

In his monumental *History of the Peninsular War*, Sir Charles Oman had many good words to say about the contribution of the guerrillas. He certainly agreed that they were a nuisance to the French. Most of the comments about them that are found scattered through his various volumes are about their successful raids on French units, and their occasional capture of a convoy. The value of guerrillas as providers of captured French dispatches to Wellington, and their fine intelligence as to the movements of French troops, were much appreciated. The benefits to Wellington's army were quite obvious. But Oman's passages on guerrillas were not very long and are generally about particular cases, with occasional passing remarks – not always savoury – on the uncouth practices of some of their individual leaders.

Clearly the guerrillas were an important element in the war, but they did not quite fit into the category of 'armies'. At the time Oman was writing, it was well-trained and well-equipped national armies which were thought to be the overriding and final key to all military success. He did not, however, fail to make a comparison between the Iberians of Napoleon's day and the Boers of South Africa during 1900 and 1901. Boer commandos were, indeed, a foretaste of things to come, although it would be much later in the 20th century – especially after the Second World War – that guerrilla warfare really came into its own in many parts of the globe. It was then realised that covert guerrilla armies could seriously affect the balance of power by beating regular armies and toppling governments. Not even the might of the American and Soviet military machines could overcome guerrillas in the jungles of Indochina or the mountains of Afghanistan.

Naturally, Sir Charles could not have foreseen the development of guerrilla warfare to such a high level of threat against regular national armies. His *History* was centred around the Duke of Wellington and his British regular army, as the essential catalyst without which the expulsion of the French from Spain and Portugal would have been impossible. Everything else, be it the restructured Portuguese army, the constantly defeated and reconstituted Spanish armies, or the lacklustre British operations in eastern Spain, all hovered around this central theme and were overshadowed by it. As a result, Oman has been accused of being somewhat unsympathetic to the Spanish military. There may be grains of truth in this view but, in fairness, he could also be very hard indeed on any British general whose leadership was questionable – and correspondingly favourable to the Spanish – *eg* his account of operations in eastern Spain in 1812–13, which was the second most important British effort in the Peninsula. Spanish regulars and guerrillas in southern Catalonia and Valencia did all they could to help the British, as when in June 1812 General Copóns' 1st Spanish Army marched to meet Sir John Murray's Anglo-Sicilian corps at Tarragona, only to be disgracefully abandoned by Murray, who re-embarked his troops without letting Copóns know and left the 1st Army to its fate. Murray was never even censured for his action until Sir Charles strongly denounced 'his worse offence – the callous betrayal of the Spanish colleague who had done his best to serve him.'[1] Viewed in this light, it seems obvious that Oman was not necessarily unsympathetic to the Spaniards. He was unsympathetic to anyone, from any nationality, that did not come up to the superlatively high standard set by Wellington.

In this context, Oman is hard to pin down when it comes to guerrillas. They represented a new phenomenon, carrying on a passionate, brutal, and often cruel war, not only against soldiers but also against civilians and property. Indeed, reprisal attacks could be, and often were, blurred with 'military' objectives; banditry with patriotism. However, in his third volume Oman moved beyond reporting the actions of individual guerrillas and devoted some very interesting pages to reflections on the effects of guerrilla warfare, with some telling remarks revealing that he sensed the geostrategic importance that such a mode of warfare could have (and indeed would have). In his assessment he especially noted the tremendous numbers of men that it took the French to hold positions, to escort convoys, and to chase guerrillas. He had access to the memoir of Espoz y Mina, a primary document in the study of the Spanish guerrillas which established Mina's claims to have pinned down tens of thousands of troops which would have otherwise been deployed against Wellington; and Oman added that 'there was no exaggeration in this' by Mina. However, he remained silent on the casualties reported inflicted on the French by Mina, feeling that they must have been too inflated. For all their exploits, he concluded there

were probably never more than 20,000 *guerrilleros* in arms at once, in the whole region between the Sierra de Guadarrama and the shore of the Bay of Biscay. They never succeeded in beating any French force more than two or three battalions strong, and were being continually hunted from corner to corner. Yet, despite their weakness in the open field, their internecine quarrels, their frequent oppression of the countryside, and their ferocity, they rendered good service to Spain, and incidentally to Great Britain and to all Europe, by pinning down to the soil twice their own numbers of good French troops.[2]

The Spanish view of the guerrillas and guerrilla warfare has been basically at odds with that of British historians before, during, and after the publication of Oman's *History*. To the Spanish, the guerrillas made life impossible for the French in Spain, inflicted huge casualties, and saved the national honour. The high casualty figures given by Mina and other guerrilla leaders only seemed to corroborate this. However, they have generally been dismissed as fanciful in British and French studies. Works since published dealing with the Peninsular War, when dealing with guerrillas, have mostly concentrated on their impact from the French or British points of view, rather than from the Spanish.

Without pretending to ever even begin to fill such a vast area of study, this essay aims to trace, albeit briefly, a) the evolution of the guerrillas from a violently spontaneous rejection movement to an organised force under local and national government regulations; b) the failed attempts of the French to control the situation; c) the impact on British opinion of the guerrillas and the importance of British supplies; and d) the numbers involved and the latest interpretations of the guerrilla movement.

One of the most valuable aspects of Oman's *History* is its lengthy and extraordinarily fine appendices at the end of each volume. We may now add to these from modern research at the Public Record Office, which reveals an amazing number of reports to the British forces from guerrilla groups in the interior – sometimes translated into English, but mostly not. Equally, the British on their side were trying to get information on who the guerrillas were, where they were operating, and how many men they mustered. Some of these key documents are reproduced in appendix 4 below.

The rise of the guerrilla movement

Even before the successes of the French against the Spanish and British forces towards the end of 1808, there were incidents between Spanish citizens and French soldiers in remote areas, which gave a foretaste of the guerrilla warfare to come. One of the first engagements of this kind occurred on 6 June 1808 in the mountainous and wooded area near the Catalan village of El Bruch de Arriba. A column of Neapolitan troops, part of the French army, were ambushed at a bend of the road by several hundred local irregular volunteers aided by a few Swiss in Spanish service. In what would become one of the classic guerrilla tactics, the Spaniards withdrew after firing. The Neapolitans/French soon regrouped and pursued them, only to be met by another ambush from which they retreated in disorder. The column's retreat to Barcelona was then harassed all the way by snipers, rocks and boiling water hurled from rooftops, and a mined bridge where it lost two field-guns. For the French it was an inauspicious start.

There were violent outbursts in many cities as popular uprisings took over in an explosion of patriotic feelings against the French and anyone seemingly favourable to them. Scores of officials were killed by patriots, including the captains-general at Cartagena and Cádiz, as well as several governors and intendants. The nobility, which had shown some sympathy for the French, was called to rally or to die. Collaboration with the enemy was totally unacceptable in this context, and anyone who dabbled in it could suffer the worst possible consequences. Terrorising civilians was soon found to be a necessary tool of guerrilla warfare, and it was found to work extremely well. French troops could never be posted everywhere to protect the *Afrancesados* (as the Spaniards favourable to the French were called). During 1808 all central government broke down while local assemblies (called *juntas*) emerged everywhere, and started raising their own forces with the weapons seized in the national arsenals of various cities. To co-ordinate things after a fashion, a Supreme *Junta* was appointed to act in the name of Fernando VII, but its executive powers were limited to its immediate area – the city of Seville – and it could do little or nothing to help patriots elsewhere in Spain. It did, nevertheless, exert a certain moral power over isolated groups, and could influence their actions by giving them an official existence as servants of the cause of national independence. It thus recognised scores of volunteer regiments which were raised from 1808, and it issued many commissions.[3]

Regulations for the Guerrillas

By the end of 1808, with various defeats and catastrophes befalling the Spanish and British armies at the hands of Napoleon's *Grande Armée*, the Supreme *Junta* saw the value of the nascent irregular bands roaming the countryside and looking to harass isolated French forces. In an inspired piece of legislation, it legitimised the existing groups and encouraged the formation of new units of *Partidas* for partisan warfare, soon to be universally known as guerrillas. The decree, issued at Seville on 28 December 1808,[4] consisted of a 'Regulation by the Supreme *Junta*' designed to create 'a new species of militia, named *Partidas* and *Cuadrillas*' which was to operate under the provisions of its twenty-four articles. Naturally, this was not followed to the letter, or even broadly; but it did at least provide guidelines to all aspiring guerrillas.

The main articles concerning organisation were Article 1, which specified that 'each *Partida* will consist of 50 mounted men, more or less, and as many on foot'; and Article 5, which stated that 'each *Partida* will have a chief with the title of commandant, a second [in command], two mounted subalterns and three on foot.' Article 13 declared the members of the *Partidas* were to be subject to the same royal regulations as other troops. This, in effect, put them on the same military footing as other Spanish troops in the realm. Article 14 quite logically stated that arms and clothing were to be at the discretion of the commandant according to what was available. Other articles concerned pay, booty, and subsistence.

The principal articles concerning the duties and objectives to be pursued were towards the end of the document. They proved to be excellent guidelines. Article 22 directed that the *Partidas* would intercept enemy parties, capture their couriers, impede their entry into villages for collecting money and food, and disturb their marches by shooting at the enemy from suitable positions. Article 23 went further and asked commanders that, when convenient, two, three, or more *Partidas* would assemble to defend difficult and narrow passes, intercept convoys, and keep the enemy constantly on alert by false attacks, especially at night, so that enemy troops would find it difficult to rest. Here, in these two articles, were laid out the main objectives and the scourges to the French soldiers for the next five years. The guerrilla bands would unite and attack a weaker French force, then scatter into the mountains in dozens of small groups as large French forces chased them. And, as French soldiers were to learn, there was to be no safety for stragglers, sentries, or lone parties separated from a respectable force, by either night or day.

Article 24 was the one that was just about totally ignored by all leaders. It stated that, in order to prevent disorders and operate with advantage against the enemy, the *Partidas* would be attached to Divisions of the army under the orders of its generals. This was not actually done until fairly late in the war, when the nature of the conflict waged in Spain was changing to a more regular style, calling again for the tactics of regular armies.

A second ordinance from the Supreme *Junta* was issued on 17 April 1809, which further attempted to somewhat regulate the *Corsa Terrestre* (or 'Land Corsairs'), as the guerrilla bands were termed. The legislators probably knew that the regulations would be largely ignored, so the duties were moved up to Article 1. It stated that all inhabitants 'of the provinces occupied by French troops, who are capable of bearing arms, are authorised to arm themselves, even with prohibited weapons, to attack and loot, on all favourable occasions, the French soldiers, either individually or in groups, to take the food and the supplies intended for their use: in a word, to cause them as much harm and damage as possible.' This was the very definition of guerrilla warfare: total war with little quarter asked or given. The population was called upon to feed and support the patriot guerrilla irregulars who, in turn, were reminded to collaborate with the regular Spanish armies.

With the disasters which beset the Spanish regular armies in 1809, especially at Ocaña, the local *juntas* echoed the Supreme *Junta*'s regulations for guerrilla warfare by fostering, as in Badajoz, the raising of 'the greatest possible number of detached corps', and specified also the weapons to be used, namely, 'the musket for attacking the enemy's convoys and detachments by ambush and surprise; and the *cuchillo* [or side knife] for attacks by night and in the streets.' Such edicts were also issued by the *juntas* of Galicia and of Asturias, and passed on quickly to areas occupied by the French, where

> parties were formed to fall suddenly on the French and their partisans, to arrest their convoys, carry off their advanced guards, watch and harass their patrols, surprise stragglers, make an attack when they had the advantage of numbers, and lie in ambush when their safety depended on flight. They were again to re-organise themselves, to re-appear, to stand, and to multiply themselves by the rapidity of their marches, and their acquaintance with all the roads and defiles. Among the most renowned chiefs or leaders of the Guerrillas, as the parties of armed Spaniards were called, were Longa in Galicia and Asturias; Mina in the north of Castile; Santochildes in Leon; Don Juan Sanchez near Salamanca; Baron d'Eroles in Aragon; and l'Empecinado in the vicinity of Madrid.

The effect was that the French, in spite of superior numbers, were 'unable to invade all at once all parts of the country. Harassed on every side by an hostile population, they were ignorant of the numbers of enemies they had to contend with. The Guerrillas, dispersed by superior forces in one place, appeared re-organised in another. New bodies of armed men appeared to spring up from the earth after they were supposed to be destroyed.'[5]

The French Reaction

Faced with such warfare, the French, unfortunately, decided that the guerrillas were bandits and brigands rather than legitimate troops. They would deal with them as with criminals rather than as soldiers. Indeed, the French armies in Spain soon decided that the only useful response could be near-systematic pillage by columns of soldiers. They were given a free rein to deal with property and inhabitants in the most arbitrary and shocking manner. Thus armed bands, left almost free to run wild, would rob anything from peasant huts to churches, and woe betide any fair woman who fell into their hands. The French marshals and other senior officers were no better and, throughout the Peninsular War, they all seem to have been involved in the large-scale pillage of state revenues and art treasures. Instead of the more liberal régime promised by Napoleon, what was actually being set up and maintained by force of arms was a brutal feudal society.

By a reign of physical and economic terror, it was hoped to subdue the resistance of the population which, fearful of the French, would then turn in the guerrillas. Far from discouraging the Spaniards, however, summary executions and punishments only made them more resolved than ever to be rid of the usurpers. Even in quiet zones where the populace seemed to tolerate their presence, French soldiers were detested even by the prostitutes whose fortune they made. Thus, gradually, the French soldiers' morale descended to a low ebb indeed, and Spain was increasingly seen as the death of soldiers, and the ruin of officers and generals.

In this, the incredible resistance of Spaniards to very determined French forces gave a tremendous example to all in Spain who loved their country. They proved to be far more willing to lay down their lives for their independence than had normally been the case in previous French conquests. An heroic example was the defence of the city of Saragossa. Although this was not strictly a 'guerrilla' action, it exerted profound influences on the movement. First besieged unsuccessfully between June and August 1808, Saragossa underwent a second siege from 20 December by French forces led by, successively, marshals Moncey, Mortier, Junot, and Lannes. The Spanish defenders, galvanised by General José Palafox, put up an incredible, even fanatical resistance, against all odds. The whole populace joined the regular soldiers and militiamen, with even women and monks fighting with an unparalleled fierceness. Eventually, epidemic fevers broke out and tens of thousands died of sickness; but the survivors fought on. Finally, Palafox too fell ill and became delirious. On 21 February 1809, the half-destroyed city of Saragossa at last surrendered. The church square was covered with coffins and dead bodies. The casualties were horrendous. An estimated 48,000 Spanish men, women, and children had died of pestilence, with another 6000 killed in action. The French had lost about 10,000 soldiers. The city's population of 55,000 was now reduced to about 15,000 souls.

How could the rest of the nation fail to be inspired by such an heroic example – guerrilla bands in particular? Indeed, the part of the city's garrison which escaped capture included Francisco Espoz y Mina, soon to become Spain's greatest guerrilla leader. As Oman was to observe so correctly, the 'example of Saragossa was invaluable to the nation and to Europe. The knowledge of it did much to sicken the French soldiery of the whole war, and to make every officer and man who entered Spain march, not with the light heart that he felt in Germany or Italy, but with gloom and disgust and want of confidence.'[6]

But Napoleon's France was not a nation to be intimidated easily, even by resistance to the death. A few months later the French besieged Gerona in Catalonia. Again, an incredible and heroic resistance was displayed by the Spanish soldiers and citizens, in a siege which lasted from 24 May to 11 December 1809. By the time of the surrender, there were 14,000 Spanish dead, half of them civilians, and 13,000 French. New Spanish armies had meanwhile been raised, often without proper ammunition, supplies, and logistics. The men were mostly new to the soldier's trade, with little training and with officers who usually lacked experience and military schooling. They had their successes until the main Spanish army of 53,000 men was ordered by the Supreme *Junta* to free Madrid. Unfortunately, it walked into a strong French army and consequently was crushed by Marshal Soult at Ocaña on 17 November. This disaster yet again largely wiped out the organised regular army. With about 30,000 regulars left to fight more than 60,000 French troops, the way to Andalucia was open and the French immediately invaded it. Resistance soon collapsed. The Supreme *Junta* handed over power to an elected *cortes* (or legislative assembly), which assembled in Cádiz. On 5 February 1810 the advancing French forces invested that city. Reinforced by British and Portuguese troops, Cádiz was to remain under siege for two-and-a-half years from the landward side. Its port, however, remained open, and became an important supply centre for patriot forces in southern Spain..

The French now controlled nearly all of Spain except for parts of Galicia, Valencia, and Catalonia. By October 1810 they had gone as far as the outskirts of Lisbon, and stayed in central Portugal until 1811. It basically took the rest of that year for Wellington and Beresford's Anglo-Portuguese, assisted by Spanish troops, to establish solid positions in the Spanish provinces of Extremadura and León. However, the French 'control' of their areas in Spain was always very tenuous, thanks to the guerrillas. To protect convoys from France over the mountain passes of northern Spain, Napoleon ordered thousands of mounted Gendarmes to assist the regular troops, a few squadrons eventually being converted into lancers to better accomplish their protective tasks.

Curiously, and fortunately for the patriots, the French were not too swift nor interested in organising real counter-guerrilla forces. Wellington, who appreciated and saw the tactical value of guerrillas early on, reported to Lord Liverpool with some concern that 'a detachment consisting of 2000 men raised in Andalucia, called Juramentados from their having taken the oath of allegiance to King Joseph, are employed against the guerrillas in La Mancha.'[7] However, nothing much came of this effort, which sounds more like a punitive column than a true counter-insurgency grouping, and the local Somatenes guerrillas continued to raise havoc.

Another counter-guerrilla group, raised at Tudela (southern Navarre), was much smaller, consisting of fifty French volunteers who slipped out of the city in December 1809, roamed the countryside, and only came back in July 1810. They claimed over seventy skirmishes with the Spanish guerrillas and said they had caused many casualties. However, they don't seem to have caused as much trouble as they claimed, since they were not noted by the Spaniards. Wandering in the hills must have been exciting for the French volunteers, but it sounds more like a hide-and-seek affair rather than the serious pursuing and elimination of guerrilla bands. Nor could they transmit useful intelligence if absent for so long.

Yet another counter-guerrilla group was that of Juan Pujol, nicknamed Boquica, a former guerrilla leader who went over to the French. He raised several companies of renegades recruited with condemned men, mostly from Catalonia, Andalucia, and Mallorca. His force may have peaked at about 600 men, but their exploits were mostly limited to murdering, looting, and burning houses.

There were undoubtedly other volunteer groups formed temporarily but, obviously, the French high command saw no great use for such irregular counter-guerrilla forces. It instead put its faith in 'big battalions' (or columns) of thousands of its normal soldiers, for escorting convoys and for going into guerrilla country. In Navarre, for instance, some 10–20,000 men pursued the guerrillas into the mountains in strong columns of several thousand men each. But such forays could last only a few weeks and, as a frustrated General Reille wrote in 1810, the 'great difficulty [was] not fighting them but finding them.'[8] And it took a substantial force to march into guerrilla country: in July 1810 a French column of over 2500 men was driven back into Pamplona.

Following Mina's signal victory at Arlaban (27 May 1811), the French were outraged and poured 20,000 men into upper Navarre in a major effort to crush the guerrillas. They nearly succeeded when General Reille's column of some 5500 men came dangerously close to Mina's main force and defeated some of it with loss. But Mina vanished and his units simply dispersed. They would soon reunite to raid weaker columns numbering 2000 men or less. By the autumn of 1811 the French, who could not remain in the field without subsistence, withdrew without having achieved any of their main objectives of capturing Mina or destroying his units. By December the French had only 6400 men left in Navarre, hardly daring to come out of their forts. On the contrary, the Navarre guerrillas were on the prowl again, even making sweeps into Aragón. So, in spite of the devastation a strong French column might cause to isolated mountain villages, the Spanish knew that it would be gone in a few weeks, having accomplished essentially nothing. On the other hand, if the column was too weak, the guerrillas would surround it, harass it, and perhaps even destroy it.

Amongst favourite guerrilla targets were convoys of supplies. Those moving in the rugged mountains of Navarre between Madrid and France were especially sought-after, as they could be quite vulnerable. Many were taken, even when escorted by 2000 men. As a result, more and more troops had to be devoted to escorting the convoys, and the trip would consequently take longer. An extravagant case was the convoy of some sixty vehicles which left Irun for Madrid on 4 February 1812. Escorted by 3000 troops with two cannons, it finally reached its destination on 11 March after much harassment. The seven carriages of the French ambassador to King Joseph in Madrid were not so well escorted; they were captured by Bartholomeo Munos' guerrillas in August, and he sent back a polite message to 'The Ambassador of the Wandering King' about this feat.[9] With such constraints, French communications would be constantly delayed and the latest information could rarely travel quickly.

As for French dispatch riders, they had a near-suicidal occupation. They would often be captured, their dispatches sometimes being sent to Wellington. The guerrillas of Don Julian Sanchez and Porlier were especially good at this, and Wellington came to appreciate them well. He was even seen in November 1812 at Guinaldo by Rifleman Costello, walking around 'linked in arms' with 'Don Julian Sanchez, the noted Guerrilla leader ... an instance peculiar to the time of obscure merit rising of its own impulse to an equality with the greatest man of the age.'[10] That Wellington should do this gives a clear measure of his appreciation of the value of guerrillas to the British cause. The French, too, saw the importance of guerrillas in no uncertain terms. One of their officers wrote that:

> the bands of Spanish insurgents and the English army supported each other. Without the English the Spanish would have been quickly dispersed or crushed. In the absence of the guerrillas, the French armies would have acquired a unity and strength that they were never able to achieve in this country, and the Anglo-Portuguese army, unwarned of our operations and projects, would have been unable to withstand concentrated operations.[11]

The British and the Guerrillas

There can be little doubt that, at the outset of the movement in the latter part of 1808, British observers and liaison officers were probably just as dumbfounded as the French at the emergence of the guerrillas. It was obviously yet another one of those strange manifestations of the Spanish character. Here it must be understood that 'selling' Spain as an ally to the British public in 1808 was no small challenge. In ancient British propaganda, which had become popular opinion since the time of Queen Elizabeth, Drake, and the 1588 Great Spanish Armada, the Spaniards were the ancestral enemy. They were dark, cruel individuals who dressed in black and enjoyed torturing Indians and Protestants with the blessing of the Inquisition, while filling their pockets with seized gold and silver 'doubloons'. Since the 16th century, it was fair game for any red-blooded seafaring Englishman to go out and liberate some of the ill-gotten gold 'of the Indies' by seizing Spanish galleons and colonial cities whenever possible. As late as 1806–7, a year before the start of the Peninsular War, the British press was cheering the (unexpected and unplanned) capture of Montevideo and Buenos Aires in Spanish South America. Shares were soon being sold on the London market for the anticipated booty, although, as had so often been the case in the past, the Spaniards turned out to be much more resilient than expected, and the whole semi-piratical scheme was abandoned with loss...

Certainly there was a culture shock for the British. When they landed as allies in the Spain of 1808, they were totally taken aback by a way of life which seemed to them primitive. Throughout the Peninsular War, British officers and officials in Spain were often unsparing in their sweeping and unfairly scathing comments as to the quality of Spanish troops and the character of the Spanish people. This spread widely to the British army's lower ranks, as many journals and letters testify. It also spread to the British press. In an 1812 compilation, one could read that 'the manners, customs, mode of living in Spain, are so widely different than those of England, that every candid and liberal-minded person should make great allowances for these circumstances'. The circumstances, for Englishmen 'so accustomed to the enjoyment of every comfort', were the poorly kept inns, the flea-ridden beds, and the 'cookery' of which 'nothing could be more disgusting to an English palate, most of their favourite dishes being seasoned with articles, amongst which garlic and rancid oil generally compose the principal ingredients.' This account concluded, however, that the 'interesting and sublime scenes' in the Peninsula easily recompensed an open-minded person.[12] And these are very mild comments compared to some much less polite. An explanation, perhaps, was that these men came from a Britain which was experiencing the world's first Industrial Revolution; a country they believed to be at the world's very height of scientific, economic, technical, and democratic progress. Obviously, when thrown into what they perceived as a poor, semi-feudal, agrarian, and narrow-minded society, their prejudiced opinions came quickly to the fore at the first negative impressions or incidents.

It must be admitted that the lack of success of the Spanish regular armies did not help their 'public relations' effort in Britain. Privately, many officers in the field even despaired that there was such a thing as a Spanish army by 1810. There might have been, in their eyes, a force of sorts claiming to be one; but not at all effective against the French.[13] There was, naturally, also some political bias in the coverage of the war by the press, the most extreme negative views being expressed in Cobbett's newspaper, which flatly stated many times over that there was simply no hope of winning in Spain. As the Spanish were not always victorious, its reasoning went, they could not really be serious about expelling the French from their country! Such extreme views were tempered by the many balanced or openly sympathetic articles carried in most of the British press. However, 'the Spanish' were generally regarded as a homogenous fighting force, with little or no clues to differentiate between regulars, guerrillas, or whatever. Except for a few particularly colourful figures such as Agustina, the heroic maid of Saragossa; General Romana, or Espoz y Mina, the British popular press gave little attention to Spanish personalities.[14]

But, increasingly, accounts of a covert 'brigand' force causing havoc to French convoys were reaching Britain. In this respect, the narrative of a German drafted into the French army and captured by the guerrillas, published in the November 1810 *Bath Herald*, was quite revealing.[15] The *Annual Register* also published various articles on the Spanish which had appeared in other newspapers or magazines. Perhaps in an attempt to moderate British prejudices towards Spanish ways and customs, and inform the Britons that Spain was really a very complex country with strong regional roots, the 1809 edition devoted many pages to the 'Characters, Manners, Customs, Habits, Dress, and Languages' of Catalonia, Andalucia, etc, and the 'Spaniards in general'. In its 1810 edition were accounts of the 'Nature of Warfare carried on by the Guerrillas'.[16] In the *Gentleman's Magazine* supplement for 1811 was an extensive 'Short Account' of Espoz y Mina, translated from the report of a Spanish colonel by a British officer at Cádiz. This account apparently received wide coverage in Britain. (See extracts in appendix 4, document 2.)

All these accounts proved to British opinion that, in spite of pessimistic views such as Cobbett's, there was real fighting going on deep in Spain itself, and that some colourful patriots called 'guerrillas' and '*guerrilleros*' were really giving the French occupation forces a difficult time. An important feature is that this was corroborated in the private correspondence of officers in the field, as many published letters have since shown. Warre, for instance, often wrote to his father of the exploits of the guerrillas.[17]

This favourable opinion of the British public towards guerrillas obviously had a positive effect in the assistance that Britain gave Spain from 1808 onwards; but especially from 1812, when it practically took over the armament and supply of most of the Spanish army. The cost of this was great to the British taxpayer and added a major burden to an already spiralling national debt. But there was relatively little grumbling in England, since serious fighting was seen to be taking place in Spain, even outside the actions of Wellington's army. Indeed, a British Member of Parliament could exclaim in July 1812 that 'I tremble, when I think of Spain. Surely, something more might be done by us'.[18]

One might well ask what was done by the British for the guerrillas – not for the Spanish regular army, which benefited from large supplies, but, specifically, for the guerrillas? General opinion, even today, is that they were armed, supplied, sometimes fed, sometimes clothed, and sometimes even given the benefit of British advisers. Certainly the French believed this, from Napoleon down; and it was featured in many of their memoirs and letters. On the other hand our own recent research into British supplies sent to the Peninsula between 1808 and 1814 reveal that although large shipments were sent to the Spanish army there was, by comparison, surprisingly very little for the guerrillas.

One of the early records specific to a guerrilla group is a shipment of 500 muskets and bayonets, 400 jackets, pantaloons, shakos and cockades to Coruña, for General Porlier's men, in December 1810. In January 1811, Wellington ordered 'nine pieces of ordnance and their stores, to be delivered to the guerrillas in Castile.' In May 1811 a shipment 'for the use of the Spanish Patriots [assumed to be guerrillas] of Guadalajara, viz.., 2000 muskets, pouches & sets of accoutrements; medicines and surgical instruments &c for 5000 men, 2000 blankets.' At that time the British government wished to have direct contact with the guerrillas. An officer was accordingly sent to the coast of northern Spain to meet the leaders, distribute a few arms and enquire as to needs. This occurred at possibly the worst time during the entire war in that area. The French had then invaded Navarre with 20,000 men in an all-out bid to destroy the guerrillas and capture Espoz y Mina. It of course failed; but the report makes great reading, giving the electric feeling of guerrilla leaders being just a jump ahead of the pursuing French. (See appendix 4, document 5.) Rather surprisingly, the guerrilla chiefs stated that they were properly armed, but lacked ammunition and clothing.

Curiously, on the British side Sir Howard Douglas, who looked after issues at Coruña, was a bit tight-fisted with the supplies destined to Spanish troops and guerrillas, going so far as to state, in one of his March 1812 reports, that if 'Mina had arms, he could raise 10,000 men tomorrow – but it would not be advantageous. The corps would ... loose its impetus, and I do not afford him means to increase it.' (See appendix 4, document 7) Fortunately, Mina did not really need British arms badly – he obtained and made his own. Still, Sir Howard's action was not indicative of any great hurry on his part to help the guerrillas. In the event, Mina eventually obtained British weapons through drops from British ships in the Gulf of Biscay from the latter part of 1812, and they did indeed substantially help to increase his force. Meanwhile the British government felt that ornate presentation arms would make a nice gesture to Spanish leaders (appendix 4, document 8). Clearly, it wanted to establish direct links with the senior guerrillas, but it does not seem to have sustained such contacts. It was impractical due to the distance and the uncertain political benefits, whereas the only Englishman who was really trusted by Espoz y Mina and Don Julian Sanchez was Wellington, who could and did deliver military support when needed.[19]

As guerrilla Divisions came alongside the Spanish regular armies from late-1812 onwards, they were supplied with some of the arms, uniforms, and equipment for 100,000 men that had been sent earlier in 1812. Porlier obtained supplies for 5000 men in November 1812. In March 1813 some of Mina's Navarre Division finally obtained British clothing, consisting of blue coatees and pantaloons with red collar, cuffs and piping; shoes, shakos, and British knapsacks. In March 1814 General Mina's Division was again issued clothing from Britain: 2000 suits with red facings, 2000 suits with green facings.[20] These appear to have been the groups which received the largest issues. Other guerrilla groups no doubt also received various British arms and supplies, but obviously in smaller numbers, if at all. And it must be especially noted that it was when the various guerrilla Divisions became part of the Spanish armies that British supplies began to arrive in quantity. Before 1812, although they arguably bore the brunt of fighting the French, the supplies reaching them from Britain were a mere trickle.

One of the most important contributions of Spanish guerrillas to the British forces in the Peninsula was their pinning down of troops which would otherwise have borne down upon Wellington's Anglo-Portuguese, particularly during the French assaults on Portugal in 1809–11. This was acknowledged by Oman, although not developed much further. However, it is the incidents surrounding the battle of Vitoria on 21 June 1813 which are, perhaps, most revealing. When one writes in detail about that event, the operations of obscure guerrillas – occupying a French army corps which would otherwise have been on the battlefield – seem secondary. Nevertheless, in that case, as Mina tells us, Wellington had asked him to divert French troops in Navarre and Aragón so as to prevent them from joining the main French army. Mina therefore ordered his battalions to operate separately, harassing the French, with the result that the latter sent 14,000 men to penetrate Navarre and completely sacked Roncal. But they suffered 2500 casualties in April and May 1813 during this venture, which finally pinned down 19,000 men in Navarre. Meanwhile, in Aragón other battalions of Mina's Division, along with the bands of other guerrilla commanders, succeeded in keeping up to 35,000 French troops running after them and maintaining garrisons.[21] Could Wellington really have won the battle of Vitoria if Generals Clausel and Foy had been left free to bear down on his rear with some 25,000 troops?

Indeed, in a more general context, the English traveller William Jacobs was already asking in 1811: 'Could British arms, deprived of that powerful aid [by the guerrillas] which operates without éclat, which in the obscurity of local patriotism acquires no fame beyond its own district, but which creates distrust and terror in the enemy have made that firm stand which has lately been displayed?'[22]

Numbers of guerrillas and interpretations of the movement

One of the hardest, and still unresolved, great questions of the Peninsular War is: just how many guerrillas were there? By the very nature of the guerrilla movement, keeping accurate statistics was all but impossible. Indeed, it could be very dangerous, if such documents should ever have fallen into French hands. So, when numbers were given, they tended to be quite inflated, regardless of whether they were intended for friends or foes. For instance, in 1811 General Hugo thought he was chasing some 10,000 guerrillas led by El Empecinado, when in fact it was less than half that number. British Rifleman Costello thought Don Julian Sanchez had some 20,000 guerrillas in 1812 – or as many as all the guerrilla groups in northern Spain, according to Sir Charles Oman!

No single precise document exists for the whole of Spain, either as to numbers or listing all groups. The closest thing to such a list found in our research is a report compiled early in 1811 for the benefit of the British high command (see appendix 4, document 4). For all the names given, some guerrillas familiar to the French are not mentioned: for instance Cura de la Palma, Villamil, Perena, Villacampa, Carabajal, Gayan, Pedrosa, Baget, Sarraza, Theobaldo, and Paniza, who were active partisans in Aragón. As for numbers, about 28,000 guerrillas are computed in the list from the figures given next to the name of the group ... but about half of the names have no numbers. Assuming the bigger groups would have supplied what seem to be reasonably accurate figures, while the lesser groups might not, an estimate of 35,000 in all of Spain at that time might be entertained.

Other figures have been put forward. E. Rodriguez Solis worked on the numbers of *Partidas* active in Spain, finding fifty-eight in 1808, rising to 156 in 1810, and declining to only thirty-five in 1813. But total numbers of men remain opaque. Juan Priego Lopez advanced some 25,000 men between the Gulf of Biscay and the Castilian mountain range; but British intelligence reports (see appendix 4, documents 6 and 10) give much lower estimates – about 11,000 in late-1811, and over 20,000 listed but less than 15,000 effective in December 1812. Perhaps the most exact estimates are those dealing with Espoz y Mina's guerrillas in Navarre. These were 650 strong in 1809; 2900 in September 1810; 5000 in May 1811; 7000 in January 1812, and 8000 in June 1812.[23]

Until recently, very few authors raised the question of just who the guerrillas were. Successive works have mentioned that they were often former soldiers or former officers, or hardy mountaineers, or rural types displeased with the French. But the reasons why they became guerrillas and their sociological backgrounds remained in a haze until the publication in 1994 of John Lawrence Tone's *The Fatal Knot: The Guerrilla War in Navarre and the Defeat of Napoleon in Spain*. In this outstanding study, Professor Tone went into the land records, the history, the economics, and the customs of the Navarrese to find answers as to who Espoz y Mina's men were, and why they waged such a war on the French. It turns out that the economy of Navarre, especially in the mountains which cover the northerly two-thirds of the province, was deeply affected by Napoleon's invasion and tax decrees. This mountain country was a region of moderately prosperous land and mountain herd owners, fiercely independent and attached to various exemptions granted by the Spanish Crown over the centuries. In the Montana, nearly all owned their land and their livelihoods, a situation much different from the southern plain country around Tudela, where there were great landowners. In the Montana, far more owned and knew how to use guns than in the plain – and they knew every mountain pass and trail.

With all these findings, and many more for which Tone's work is highly recommended, certain patterns become clearer. Geography and society go hand in hand in some cases. A comparison can be attempted – and should be the subject of future scholarly work – with Andalucia, where the French had a relatively easy time in the plains (dominated by large landowners), with problems increasing where steep hills appeared, culminating in impossible forays against guerrillas in the snow-capped mountains of the Sierra Nevada, east of Granada.

The tactics used by the guerrillas are also worth looking at further. Did they come from 'warrior instinct', or was there an unwritten tactical doctrine? The present author favours the second option. Mina's tactics were certainly effective and can be reconstructed from the various accounts. The main type of action was the ambush, although, since there was a constant lack of ammunition, only one round was issued per man. In the ambush, half of the men, their muskets with bayonets fixed, would spring out of hiding, fire a volley on the French, and immediately charge. The other half would be in reserve ready to fire another volley to cover any retreat, should enemy reinforcements show up. It was simple and it worked well, with the guerrilla casualties being kept to a minimum by the surprise of a bayonet attack. The massed French soldiers could hardly react before the guerrillas were upon them, and their casualties were consequently higher. Coupled with the rapidity of movement, especially if the second half came into the fray once it was assured that no other troops were nearby, these tactics may explain why the French officers always reported more guerrillas than there really were. Such tactics were used mainly in the mountains, but were somewhat copied in the Castilan plains by El Empecinado, whose force consisted mostly of cavalry.

When we turn to the guerrillas' battle effectiveness, and French casualties, Oman stated that guerrillas could never beat a French force of more than two or three battalions - say a force of 2–3000 men. Certainly Mina did defeat such numbers, several times over. At Rocaforte (11 January 1812), Mina defeated General Abbé's 2000 French, inflicting some 600 casualties. At Sanguesa (5 February 1812), Mina attacked the 2000-strong crack 'Infernals' Division, which fled after losing over 600 men by General Soulier's account. And on the Tafalla Road near Tiebas came General Abbé's 'day of humiliation' (19 August 1812), when his 3200 men were smashed by four of Mina's battalions. Eventually, in 1813, the Navarra Division blockaded Pamplona, repulsing all sorties, until it surrendered. Seemingly, then, some guerrilla groups could smash as well as harass.

Total casualty figures are a subject that is as shrouded in mystery as total guerrilla numbers. No overall figures are known with precision. Mina claimed that in 'killed, wounded and prisoners ... my losses amounted to 5000 men, and those of the enemy, including the prisoners, were no less than 40,000 men.' This statement, made nearly two centuries, ago seemed unrealistic at the time. Today, however, after studying French and Spanish archives, Tone, in his *Fatal Knot*, states that Mina underestimated the French losses in killed and wounded during the six years of fighting. They 'could not have been less than 50,000.'[24]

So it now appears that, far from being overstated, the guerrillas' claims for French casualties might well be realistic, and even - at least in the case of Navarre - on the conservative side. This is a reversal from the theory of 'inflated figures from excitable Spaniards' long held by French and British historians. It certainly invites more research - long and painstaking as it may be - into more Spanish and French archives. If Mina did as well as he claimed, what of El Empecinado, Don Julian Sanchez, and other sizeable groups? The answers certainly could be most revealing for our view of the Peninsular War. Mina's 50,000 French casualties are three-quarters of the 65,000 casualties inflicted on the French by Wellington's army in all the battles of the Peninsular War ... perhaps further studies will reveal that guerrillas equalled that figure.

Certainly, if battle effectiveness can be counted by the numbers of casualties inflicted, the guerrillas may be said to have played a larger part in the Peninsular War than they have previously been credited with.

Conclusion

In all this, the quality of Oman's work was such that he would surely have been pleased and grateful to see the type of data on the guerrillas that has recently been produced. He had already sensed the general importance of the guerrillas, and could have written many more pages if he had had access to a larger body of information about them.

As to the guerrillas themselves, they disappeared almost as quickly as they had appeared, once the war was over and the French gone.[25] Independence had been preserved; but the effects of Napoleon's invasion were considerable. Spain and the Spanish people could never be the same again after such a trauma. 'Guerrilla' was not the only Spanish word to enter the international dictionary as a result of this war; soon there would be a vicious series of civil wars with *Pronunciamientos* and *Caudillos* becoming equally familiar and meaningful to the world's press.[26]

For many Spaniards, violent and autocratic habits that had initially been learned as guerrillas were now being put to use in politics. Mid-nineteenth century author B. Perez Galdos perhaps put it best in his historical novel *Juan Martin, El Empecinado*, a classic of Spanish literature: 'the War of Independence was the grand school of the *caudillaje*, because it was at that school that Spaniards learned the art, incomprehensible to others, of improvising armies and dominating a country for a more or less lengthy period of time. They learned the science of insurrection, and the marvels of those times, we have since wept over with tears of blood.'

Notes

1. Oman, *History*, vol.VI, p.522.
2. *Ibid* vol.III, pp.489, 491–2.
3. Conde de Clonard, *Historia Organica de la Infanteria y Caballeria*

Espanola (16 vols, Madrid, 1847–56), vol. 6, pp.284–96 and 310–12, lists a great number of these units, including some that were raised by guerrillas. See also the comments on the Spanish order of battle in Colonel Sañudo's chapter 6, above.

4. Fernando Diaz-Plaja, *Historia de Espana en sus documentos: siglo XIX* (Madrid, 1983), pp.61–3.

5. *Annual Register*, 1810, pp.210–11.

6. Oman, *History*, vol.II, p.142.

7. Wellington to Liverpool, Colesico, 23 May 1810, PRO WO 1/244.

8. Reille to Neuchatel, 4 September 1810, quoted in John Lawrence Tone, *The Fatal Knot: The Guerrilla War in Navarre and the Defeat of Napoleon in Spain* (Chapel Hill, 1994), p.105.

9. Michael Glover, *Legacy of Glory: The Bonaparte Kingdom of Spain* (London, 1971), p. 248.

10. Costello also went on to describe Sanchez's 'square well-set figure, dark scowl and flashing eyes of the Guerrilla ... he first began his career as a pig-boy, but owing to some cruelties exercised on a branch of his family by the French, he took an inveterate hatred to them ... increased his sanguinary feats, and gradually collected a small band, then a body, and eventually commanded upwards of twenty thousand Guerrillas, well armed, and equipped with British arms and accoutrements, and who rendered more assistance to the cause of the British than all the Spanish troops besides.' Antony Brett-James ed., *Edward Costello: Military Memoirs, Adventures of a Soldier* (London, 1967), p.117. The '20,000 guerrillas' are certainly an exaggeration, but interesting in that it was the opinion of an enlisted man. Something closer to the much lower true figure was known by senior British officers (see appendix 4). Benjamin D'Urban, *The Penisnsular Journal, 1808-1817* (1930 edition, reprinted Greenhill, London, 1988), makes remarks on the guerrillas' interception of letters and transmission of information, as does William Warre, *Letters from the Peninsula 1808–1812* (London, 1909). Both had important posts in the Portuguese army, D'Urban being its Quartermaster-General and Warre the aide-de-camp to Marshal William Beresford.

11. J.J. Pelet, *The French Campaign in Portugal 1810-1811* (Minneapolis, 1973), pp.31–2.

12. *A History of the Campaigns of the British Forces in Spain and Portugal* (London, 1812), vol.III, pp.475–7.

13. Such opinions are expressed by Warre in 1810, *op.cit.* p.105; and D'Urban in 1811, *op.cit.* p.232.

14. I am much indebted to Philip Haythornthwaite for sharing the results of his extensive readings of British newspapers and magazines of this period and his observations regarding the press coverage of the Spanish.

15. Filed in PRO WO 1/847.

16. *Annual Register*, 1809, pp.765–88; 1810, pp.209–12.

17. Warre, *op.cit.* pp.138, 159–61, 163, 283–4. Word of this must have been transmitted in London society, as James Warre, his father, was a man of some influence, both in Portugal and in England, and a partner in the famous Port house of Warre & Co.

18. *Memoirs and Correspondence of Francis Horner, MP* (2 vols, Boston, 1852), vol.II, p.102.

19. Coruña, 15 December 1810, PRO WO 1/261; Wellington to H.

Wellesley, Cartaxo, 28 January 1811; Lieutenant-Colonel Gurwood, ed., *The Dispatches of Field Marshal the Duke of Wellington* (London, 1838), vol.VII, p.204; G. Harrison to Storekeeper General, 4 May 1811, PRO T 28/8; James Johnston, ADC, to Major General Walker, Coruña, 6 September 1811, PRO WO 1/261; Sir Howard Douglas to Colonel Torrens, Villagarcia, 22 March 1812, PRO WO 1/262; S.W. Fullum, *The Life of General Sir Howard Douglas* (London, 1853), is an admiring biography which naturally paints a somewhat different picture of Sir Howard's time at Coruña; Tone, *op.cit.* p.130.

20. Wellington to General Castaños, Freneda, 13 February 1813; Gurwood, *op.cit.* vol.X, p.113; Tone, *op.cit.* p.130; *Relacion de las prendas de vestuario y equipo que devon recibir de los almacenes del puerto de Passages, los 3e, 4e, Reserva de Andalucia y Division del General Mina [March 1814]*, University of Southampton, Wellington Papers, 1/358.

21. Mina's memoir, and Tone *op.cit.* pp.144-5.

22. William Jacobs, *Travels in the South of Spain*, quoted in Gabriel H. Lovett, *Napoleon and the Birth of Modern Spain* (2 vols, New York, 1965), vol.II, p.807. Chapter XVII, 'Albion in Spain' (pp.753-808) is a recommended account of Anglo-Spanish relations and issues.

23. The figures from Rodriguez Solis and Priego Perez are given in Jean-René Aymes, 'Comment la guérrilla espagnole a chassée Napoléon', *L'Histoire* 75 (February 1985), pp.31-2; Tone, *op.cit.* pp.79, 103, 119, 130, 137.

24. *Ibid* p.177.

25. But compare Charles Esdaile's perception in chapter 11 that many, out of economic desperation, reverted to banditry against the Anglo-Portuguese and Spanish forces in areas that had been cleared of the French.

26. *Pronunciamientos* were formal 'pronouncements' announcing a military insurrection and coup. A *Caudillo* was a military dictator, the last and best-known being Francisco Franco, who was *Caudillo* of Spain from 1939 to his death in 1975. This ended *caudillaje* - military dictatorships - in contemporary Spain.

Chapter 8

Oman and the Operational Art

by Paddy Griffith

Although Oman made a famous and ground-breaking (albeit misleading) summary of the structure of minor tactics, as between the line and the column, he left us no comparable analytical summary of 'grand tactics', or what is today called 'the operational art'. This makes a significant omission in his general coverage, especially since so much of the *History* is concerned in describing a long series of operations and the making of many individual operational decisions. The operational art must be regarded as a very central concern to Oman, and it would not even be excessive to describe his great work as essentially a study of that level of war, rather than of any other. He did, indeed, often make indirect references to it; but the fact remains that he explained it in only a fragmentary fashion, and *en passant*. This chapter will therefore try to fill in some of the gap, by offering a few guesses at what he might have said, if only he had brought all his thoughts on operational generalship together into one place.

As he set about his researches and writing, Oman must surely have thought long and hard about the level of military action that is classified as higher than 'minor tactical' but lower than 'strategic'. It is at this 'operational' level that Divisions or Army Corps are detached to manoeuvre for some specific goal, as a subordinate part of a wider effort, possibly resulting in a series of battles or 'non-battles', and only then bringing into play the somewhat different type of calculus associated with minor tactics and low-level leadership. Yet when we ask just how he would have summed up all his Peninsular operations as a 'system', we find that Oman offers us only a series of frustratingly short passages, which are often buried deep in sections which deal with apparently tangential subjects. Thus one of his most pregnant pages is hidden in the chapter on 'military geography',[1] where he is explaining the great difficulty of transporting supplies across the grain of the mountain ranges. He demonstrates that this imposed a rhythm on operations whereby a lengthy period stockpiling foodstuffs would be followed by a relatively short period of strenuous movement until those supplies were exhausted.[2] He was implying that each new operational impulse would be limited to a certain 'maximum range', which would be a much lesser distance than the full extent of the whole Peninsula. Hence the war could not be won in a single operation unless exceptional circumstances applied.[3] The full proof of this may be found in the multiplicity of different theatres within Iberia which continued to be active for so many years. Oman seemed to be suggesting that the main key to success in this type of warfare was for the side taking the offensive to make only limited 'bite and hold' attacks at each stage, and especially to keep its preparations hidden from the enemy, in order to win a clear start of a couple of weeks and so keep ahead of the enemy's counter-manoeuvres. If he did but know it, this was precisely the lesson that would be learned during the Great War of 1914–18, albeit on very different scales of time and distance. Hence it is doubly frustrating that he failed to lay out his operational insight in any extended exposition that was comparable to his influential formula for the line versus the column in minor tactics.

Perhaps Oman's nearest approach to a formal analysis of the operational art came in his essay 'The Army on the March' in *Wellington's Army*,[4] which begins with an unconsciously self-revealing admission that 'it is rare in Peninsula literature to find any general descriptions of the normal working of the military machine.'[5] Yes indeed! This is exactly the area in which we need more understanding and more studies of staff practice, together with an analysis of the assumptions behind operational generalship – and from Oman as much as anyone. Yet his essay then goes on, rather disappointingly, to quote long passages from a contemporary text (first published in Gurwood's *Selected General Orders, 1837*), which itemises the routine arrangements for setting a Division on the road at dawn, and then taking it through a day's marching to new billets selected in advance by specialist officers. Dozens of little administrative details are explained *en route*, but overall they remain minor points that illuminate how the thing was supposed to be done rather than why it was done or how it normally turned out in practice. All Oman himself can add at the end is a dire warning that in any case it is only an ideal blueprint for a mechanism which might work pretty well in good conditions – such as the sun-soaked advance to Madrid in 1812 – but which would immediately fall apart in conditions of rain and defeat, such as the retreat from Burgos which followed soon afterwards.[6] Unfortunately he does not here tell us very much more about the type of higher operational calculations that a general had to make before he set this 'mechanism' into motion in the first place; and if he does not give us this perspective for British generals, he certainly does not offer many suggestions about how it might have differed for Spanish or French ones.

Beyond the somewhat slight essay on 'The Army on the March', there are other sections of *Wellington's Army* which discuss such matters as the organisation of the staff or of the commissariat; but these are still relatively short and fragmentary treatments by comparison with the importance of their subjects. In the end we had to wait for more than thirty years after the completion of the *History* before these matters began to be tackled seriously on the scale they deserved; most notably in S.G.P. Ward's excellent book, *Wellington's Headquarters*.[7] Ward showed us how Wellington might set up his headquarters; how the various staff branches would be clustered around his office, and how they would first receive incoming mail and then generate new orders. He gave us an essential insight into the way a Napoleonic army was articulated. Yet not even the admirable Ward quite managed to write the analysis of generalship at the operational level which Oman was always, albeit perhaps tacitly and unconsciously, trying to put across.

Let us therefore attempt to construct our own model from first principles. The general begins with a document, usually deliberately phrased in ambiguously unhelpful terms, which gives him some idea of what his immediate superior - his local *junta*, his home government, or his military hierarchical chief - wants him to do. At this stage he will probably know only too well about how he personally stands in relation to this immediate superior; but he may still have only a rather vague idea of the terrain, the enemy, and his own troops, which will be the tools of his trade. He must do some hard thinking about all four of these factors, and he must do it pretty fast, since his superior will expect an early report. It is best for correspondence to be turned round as quickly as possible at each end, especially if it takes two or three weeks for a message to pass from the general to his immediate superior.

The general's diagnosis of the situation requires him to be master of 'an infinite number of notions',[8] and it is precisely the complexity of this task which makes good generalship such a rare, precious, and highly-paid commodity. By no means everyone is capable of understanding it and, to judge by Oman's scathing comments about so many of them, the Peninsular generals often failed to discharge this duty efficiently. They had to know what was politically possible within their theatre of operations, as well as what their men would accept as reasonable orders. They had to understand the personal character of each of their own colleagues and subordinates, and make at least guesses at those of their adversaries.[9] They had to work hard at a diversity of incoming intelligence statistics and intercepted dispatches to form a view of the enemy's numbers - an activity that was apparently no more foolproof at Goose Green in 1982 than it had been at Vimeiro in 1808.[10] More immediately, they had to know just which troops they

could themselves command, where they were, and to what extent
they were fit for service. And beyond all that they had to understand
not only the climate, but 'the resources of the country' in terms of
water, wood, foodstuffs, and shelter, as well as the state of the
roads, the fortifications, and the defiles.

In Iberia it was rather more difficult to obtain good information
on many of these points than it would have been in Germany or
France, since the towns were further apart and the intervening
spaces were neither as fertile nor as densely populated. Oman tells
us of the wretched state of the town of Almeida even in the early
1900s,[11] so it can surely have been no better in wartime a century
earlier. With fewer well-fed (and therefore active) citizens at hand
to observe the enemy and intercept his messages, the total volume
of intelligence must surely have been reduced, although,
admittedly, a population which generally sympathised with the
allied side could be expected to service the Spanish and British
generals better than the French. Nevertheless, collecting
intelligence always required hard work and a complex network of
contacts and couriers. It was never provided 'free' to either side.

Against all this, on the other hand, the very starkness of the
theatre, and its lack of communications, were themselves a great aid
to the collecting of intelligence. Since good roads were very few
and far between, a general enjoyed correspondingly few options for
his main axis of operations, and so his enemy had an equivalently
simplified task in guessing just what that axis might be. This was
especially true in the desolate uplands of eastern Portugal, which in
military terms offered protection to the coastal settlements further
west that may be compared, to some degree, with the protection
afforded to southern England by the Channel. Armies attempting to
manoeuvre across these hills were forced to use highly predictable
routes which could be blocked, slighted, or otherwise harassed
with comparative ease – as Masséna discovered during his advance
on Lisbon in 1810. Alternatively they might prefer to use more
unobtrusive back roads: but they could do so only if they discarded
their guns and baggage, as Soult had to do in his evacuation of
Oporto in 1809. Something very similar could be said of the
Pyrenees, the imposing strategic barrier which protects France
from Spain, where in July 1813 Soult again found himself marching
an entire army in single file along mule tracks, for fear of attracting
attention by using the obvious main roads. Under such conditions
the whole concept of 'an army' would suddenly take on a radically
new meaning, since without guns and baggage it would have to be
considered as a force composed almost entirely of 'light infantry'.[12]

Elsewhere in Iberia there were many other features – either
mountain ranges with long and narrow passes, or strong fortresses –
behind which a defeated army might hope to regroup in
comparative safety. Provided they enjoyed space into which to

retreat, even defeated armies could still retain a considerable fighting strength, which might be destroyed only by a major, and expensive, new offensive effort on the part of their opponents. If, as often happened, those opponents found some more pressing object to distract them from immediate pursuit, then the original fugitive could rebuild his strength and once again sally forth in an offensive, perhaps causing his opponent to retire in turn behind yet another range of mountains. Hence there would be an inconclusive cycle of advance and retreat, which might be repeated several times over within the same region of the Peninsula, before any 'final' decision was reached.

The process could often be extended over a number of years. For example, the Anglo-Portuguese forces disputed the Portuguese borderlands from the Sintra convention in 1808 all the way through to the Vitoria campaign in 1813. Sometimes they were forced back – South of Oporto in 1809 and as far as Torres Vedras in 1810 – while at other times they attempted to break loose and capture Madrid – twice unsuccessfully in 1808-9, and then with a short-lived success in 1812. Equally, the Spanish Supreme *Junta* based in Seville was able to dispute the no man's land between that city and Madrid for a considerable time, first destroying the French offensive at Bailén in 1808, then suffering defeats when it pushed its pursuits too far on three separate occasions in 1809 – at Uclés and Medellin in the spring, at Almonacid in August, and again at Ocaña in November. Only the last of these sequences was 'decisive' for the fate of Andalucia, which was finally overrun by the French in the winter of 1809-10, although it continued to be ringed by allied fortresses – Gibraltar, Tarifa, Cádiz, and Elvas (and sometimes also Badajoz) – from which new offensives might be launched when circumstances permitted.

There were many 'non-battles' in these operations, in the course of which two opposing armies approached each other to almost tactical range, eyed each other carefully, assessed the essential balance of numbers and victuals, and maybe even skirmished a little; but finally failed to take the initiative of launching a major attack.[13] There were also many real battles in which that final initiative was indeed taken, although few of them may be counted as truly 'decisive'. Not even the shock of Bailén itself was sufficient to settle the question of who should control southern Spain. It set the French invasion back by as much as a year, but it could not ultimately prevent it. Nor could the French operational victories at Talavera, Coruña, and Bussaco[14] secure a second occupation of Lisbon. Instead, they led to the prolonged 'non-battle' of Torres Vedras, which was accompanied by a cruel British policy of scorched earth.

Salamanca in 1812 may perhaps be accounted a 'decisive' battle, but less for allowing Wellington to make a fleeting visit to Madrid than for definitively forcing the French out of Andalucia. As far as Wellington's own theatre of operations was concerned, he had to wait a year for Vitoria before he could honestly claim that a final decision had been reached. Such decisions were really very few and far between in this war, and it was much more normal for confrontations to end either in bloodless 'non-battles', or in 'ordinary victories' which had many local and temporary results but which brought about no global change.

Nor could the scale of casualties normally be considered 'decisive'. The relatively small scale of the armies taking the field was often more than matched by the comparatively small number of casualties suffered, even on some occasions of total defeat and humiliation. Thus, for example, the ghastly rout of Medina del Rio Seco (14 July 1808) – which inflicted instant and profound damage upon overall Spanish strategy – cost only some 3000 Spanish casualties out of a total force of around 22,000 (*ie* fourteen per cent), of which less than 500 (2.3 per cent) were killed.[15] This is really very small beer when compared with the great slaughter-pens of the high Empire in central Europe. Then again, Napoleon's miraculous passage of the pass of Somosierra (30 November 1808), which opened the road to Madrid and brought him such a glittering prize, cost the defeated Spaniards a total of only some 200 casualties out of 12,000 men engaged, or about 1.7 per cent. Admittedly there were a few days on which the Spanish losses mounted to genuinely catastrophic levels – over fifty per cent at each of Uclés (13 January 1809) and Ocaña (19 November 1809)[16] – but by and large the true measure of defeat lay far more in the neutralisation of Spanish plans and aspirations than in the physical destruction of Spanish soldiers.

All this leads us to question the glib popular slogan that 'in Spain large armies starve, and small armies get beaten.'[17] The large armies might starve, right enough, although even then the French often showed they had means of eking out their subsistence for longer than expected.[18] However, small armies could starve almost equally easily, so there is probably little value in making a distinction based on army size. In both cases the hungry armies often found that they had to keep on moving, to find fresh fields for foraging. Thus Victor in June 1809 had to abandon Estremadura with his 25,000 men since 'we are menaced with absolute famine, which we can only avoid by moving off'.[19] It is also very important to note that small armies could often continue to lead an operationally very useful existence, almost regardless of whether or not they happened to be either starving or beaten at the time. The ability of such forces to survive, and to pose a significant problem to the enemy, was potentially very great. The guerrillas knew this; the Spanish field armies sometimes knew it; and Sir John Moore had suspected it, even though his own disaster at Coruña left a rather smaller percentage of his army as a viable force-in-being than was normal under the conditions of the day. Even the temperamentally decisive and aggressive Wellington knew it during his long and cautious defensive phase between Talavera and Salamanca, when he had resolved to cling on to the Portuguese mountains – and behind them the lines of Torres Vedras – despite the deep pessimism of both London and the 'croakers' in his own army.

The Peninsular War – and particularly the guerrilla war – has often been identified as a war of attrition, in the sense of 'grinding down' (*Zermurbung*) and causing maximum casualties, as practised by the likes of von Falkenhayn at Verdun in 1916. What has been noticed rather less often, however, is that it was actually rather more a war of attrition in the less murderous eighteenth-century sense of 'wearing out' (*Ermattung*) by interminable harassing or delaying movements from one strong position to another.[20] Circumstances had forced both Frederick the Great and Maria Theresa to become experts in this style of warfare, which nineteenth-century German scholars had liked to compare with that of the ancient Roman general, Fabius Cunctator. That officer had eventually won a decisive result against Hannibal by systematically avoiding all decisive confrontations – and in later years it was a somewhat similar technique that would be practised by the likes of Blake, Venegas, and Wellington.

It is paradoxical to find that the same Peninsular conflict that would be remembered mainly as a deadly 'war to the knife' was also often a war of elegant and sometimes even bloodless manoeuvre. The individual armies were usually relatively small (the equivalent of no more than one or two Army Corps each), and so they were forced to use the duellist's rapier rather than the massive sledgehammer that was available to a *Grande Armée* of many closely-concentrated Army Corps. Neither side in the Peninsula found it easy to keep an overwhelmingly large force concentrated for long enough to finish off its opponent, and so the duel (or 'minuet') dragged on for a very long time. The smallness of the armies has often been attributed to the endemic shortage of food supplies, but it may also be explained by more 'political' factors, such as the inability of the Spanish *juntas* to agree a co-ordinated strategy; the inability of the British government to recruit truly large numbers of men; and the inability of the Emperor to control his bickering marshals when they were operating a thousand miles away from Paris. Apart from anything else, the French could never concentrate the enormous army they kept in the Peninsula, simply because they had to leave some sort of cover in each of about six widely-dispersed regions. The picture was further complicated by the wars in central Europe, which led Napoleon to 'play the accordion with the manpower totals'[21] available for Spain – flooding it with troops at one moment, and then denuding it the next. The Peninsula must often have contained as many troops marching in or out as it had actually fulfilling local tasks. As a general summation, therefore, we might perhaps suggest that large armies quickly had to split up for a diversity of more pressing strategic tasks, while small armies could usually live to fight another day.

The French army started off in 1808 as numerically equivalent to a 'Grand' army, with some 165,000 men deployed in the Peninsula by August.[22] It was all co-ordinated by a centralised Imperial HQ, and was split into higher formations, designated as 'Army Corps', intended to operate as integral parts of the wider whole. In organisational terms, this arrangement was modelled precisely on the Army Corps structure that had been used by the 'real' *Grande Armée* for its concentrated victories at Austerlitz, Jena, and Friedland. The Corps was the primary formation, so each of its constituent Divisions was in practice incomplete within itself, and to some extent dependent upon the Corps HQ for essential assistance in such areas as logistics or specialist combat services (*eg* cavalry or engineers).

However, when these forces entered Spain in 1808 they quickly disintegrated into what were in effect half-a-dozen small armies, each fighting its own separate war under very little central control. The deeper the mass penetrated into the Peninsula, the less 'massed' it could remain, and the more fragmented its constituent parts inevitably became. Each Corps found it had to fend for itself over long periods of time, with each of its constituent Divisions dispersed widely across the ground and having to face a highly varied type of threat. Under those conditions each Army Corps gradually turned into an independent 'Army' in its own right, so that by July 1811 they had been re-designated into the 'Armies' of the Centre, of Portugal, of Aragón, of the North, and of Catalonia.[23] Only Soult's Army of the South (with some 90,000 men) was still subdivided into several Army Corps, although by the time of Vitoria in 1813 even these had each shrunk to a Division.[24] Under these circumstances it was normal from at least 1811 for a French Division in the Peninsula to take on a more self-sufficient all-arms role, equivalent to what had previously been done by a Corps. Thus each Division began to act out the same role in relation to its Corps HQ that the Corps had previously acted in relation to the Imperial HQ of the *Grande Armée*. This represented a reversion to an earlier concept of the roles of both the Division and the Corps, which dated from an era when truly 'Grand' armies were still unknown.[25]

By the same token the allied armies normally remained too small and scattered to necessitate the use of Army Corps. Indeed, at Vimeiro in 1808 the British had still not even adopted Divisions, but kept to the brigade as the highest formation, as they had done in the 1790s and in Egypt.[26] Thereafter, and in the Spanish service, the allies stuck to armies which had constituent Divisions, but no

Corps. Certain Divisions might be allocated to specialist tasks, such as a vanguard (or 'Light') Division, or a Heavy Reserve, while others might be split up to provide garrisons or independent brigades. Yet all of this was traditional eighteenth-century practice. It is true that Wellington did adopt three shadowy Army Corps in 1813–14, but they remained personal and ad hoc. They were more like the 'wings' or 'columns' of the Old Régime than the permanent Army Corps of the *Grande Armée*.

Apart from organisational matters, one vital statistic that all Napoleonic generals had to keep firmly fixed in their minds was the actual speed at which they could expect their troops to move, assuming that they had first solved such intractable problems as subsistence and political purpose. As a record best figure, an infantry Division might make forty-three miles in twenty-two hours, as Craufurd's did in its (actually belated) march to Talavera.[27] However, the realistic average figure would be but a third of that, and on many occasions still less. Much would depend on the freshness of the troops (and of their shoes!), the determination of their commander, and the state of the roads, the weather, and the overall situation. There would inevitably have to be frequent rest-days, especially whenever a force arrived at a town that could offer more varied facilities than the average rural hamlet. Movements would therefore display a creaky stop-start rhythm, such as might baffle statisticians. Nevertheless, the theoretically sustainable pace might still work out at around 100 miles per week, or fourteen miles per day. This looks surprisingly high, if we consider that the total length of the Peninsula from Gibraltar to Irun is little more than 500 miles – a paltry month's marching. In reality, however, such speeds were rarely sustained for long, since extraneous forces would normally intervene. For example, it took Wellesley some seventy days to march his army the 300 miles from Montalegre, north of Oporto, to the battlefield at Talavera, averaging merely 4.3 miles per day. The discrepancy may be explained by a variety of long halts that were imposed upon him: to wait for supplies to arrive from Lisbon, to wait for the Spanish to concert their action with his, or to reconnoitre and probe the French.

Yet even at this somewhat leisurely rate of progress, it is worth considering that most of the Peninsular campaigns were still very mobile by comparison with some of their predecessors in the 1790s, when in most theatres the front lines had moved backwards and forwards only by an average of some thirty miles per year.[28] In the Eastern Pyrenees, for example, the main Spanish force had first advanced twenty miles, then retreated sixty, making eighty miles in all, during two years of war between 1793 and 1795. By contrast, the three months of the Talavera campaign alone saw sweeping movements by Wellesley through three different regions, and an equally sweeping conforming manoeuvre by the forces of Soult and

Ney. Meanwhile Cuesta, Venegas, Victor, Joseph, and Sebastiani each moved significant forces more than 100 miles as they sought to threaten or defend Madrid. This surely shows that the manoeuvrability and operational confidence of all armies, but especially the French, had increased greatly since the early days of the Revolutionary Wars, when they had been struggling to re-learn some half-forgotten skills.

In proportion as they opted for manoeuvre, they correspondingly reduced their reliance on fieldworks. The Talavera campaign may have been 'positional warfare', in the sense that each army tried to anchor itself on some strong natural feature at the end of each day's march, while control of the specific spots at which the Tagus was bridged took on a very high operational importance; but it was not 'positional' in the sense of protracted siege-work or the occupation of static fortified lines. It must be seen as fluid 'manoeuvre warfare', fully worthy of Frederick the Great, in which the kaleidoscope of forces in play was constantly changing.

There were, of course, many big and bloody sieges in the Peninsula, as the following chapter will demonstrate. Fortified lines were also an occasional recourse, notably for the Anglo-Portuguese at Torres Vedras; but also sometimes along mountain chains, such as the Spanish defence of the Guadarrama in November 1808, or the French redoubts in the Western Pyrenees in late-1813. The French were also great builders of block-houses or other types of fortified barracks which might protect their lines of communication from guerrilla attack. This was not a British invention of the Boer War, as is sometimes alleged, but a time-honoured practice which was well known throughout the eighteenth century, and indeed every other century before that.[29] It may even be stated that a well-fortified line of communication is actually a *sine qua non* of efficient manoeuvre warfare. Napoleon certainly thought so as he laid out his *route de l'armée* through Austria, Germany, and Poland in 1805-7;[30] and the Peninsular generals do not appear to have dissented from the habit. The point is that although such a line cannot prevent the enemy from making deep, speculative incursions against your own territory, it does at least provide a solid guarantee that your forces will be able to keep moving forward in a regular and sustained manner into his.

What we see in the Peninsular War is in many ways a classic demonstration of the operational art as it had come to be perfected during the eighteenth century, but without the mass and gigantism which Bonaparte had added to it in his campaigns in central Europe. With very few exceptions – such as the second French march on Madrid, or Masséna's invasion of Portugal – the many theatres of war within the Peninsula normally contained relatively few troops by comparison with the highest standards of the time. They were not massively swamped with soldiers, as the area around

Vienna was in 1809, or as Saxony would be in 1813. Instead, there was still plenty of space for operational manoeuvre. A good general could therefore hope to double or triple the power of his small army simply by getting it to the right place at the right time, or by concentrating at a decisive point more rapidly than his enemy. This factor surely lay at the root of many of the Spanish defeats, since the French were often badly outnumbered within any given theatre. At Tudela, for example, Lannes had 32,000 as against the 48,000 of Castaños – yet the latter contrived to leave at least 20,000 of his men out of the battle. This was perhaps 'sporting', but it was scarcely taken from any operational textbook.[31]

We are entitled to ask just which 'operational textbooks' were actually being used. The answer must be that although a few had recently been written by such authors as von Bülow or the Archduke Charles, or by teachers in various military academies, none would rise to generalised international acceptance until Jomini began his bulk output in the years following Waterloo.[32] During the Napoleonic Wars themselves, generals had to rely partly upon a collection of eighteenth-century texts of dubious relevance, but mainly upon a very powerful oral tradition that was handed down from generation to generation through the closed guild of staff officers. That tradition had been crystallised during the wars of Frederick and Maria Theresa, but had received a very rich new layer of experience, example, and precept in the years between 1792 and 1808. Every young general entering the Peninsular War must have heard very many stories about the manoeuvres and stratagems used in the recent French wars, while most of the older generals must have personally exercised command in them. In this respect Moore was clearly more experienced than the 'sepoy general' Wellesley, while Cuesta was rather more experienced than either of them. However, it was the French themselves who naturally enjoyed the most concentrated and continuous insight into the operational art, in some cases stretching back to personal triumphs as early as the War of the First Coalition. Victor had first become a general in 1793, and Gouvion St Cyr in 1794, while Jourdan's decisive victory at Fleurus (also 1794) was won only fourteen years before he became chief of staff to the *Armée d'Espagne* – but what cataclysmic events had occurred during those intervening years!

We do not and cannot know very much about just how the Peninsular generals absorbed and utilised the operational lessons of their immediate past, although it would probably be fair to suggest that in this department the French had a much better and more consistent record than the Spanish. For their part the British were always dependent upon a perilously small reservoir of particularly talented individuals, and we must remember that there was a Murray at Tarragona for every Wellington at Vitoria. The French could doubtless field the most professional staff officers and middle-ranking generals, quite apart from their many highly acclaimed army (or Corps) commanders. They were ultimately betrayed by an almost totally untenable strategic and political position; but in matters of operational art they generally seemed to know what they were doing.

The fact nevertheless remains that every army in the Peninsula was forced to use a relatively old-fashioned operational art of small armies moving around large theatres of war. This actually presented Oman with something of a dilemma, since the war he was describing was not at all the same as the supposedly 'highest state of the art' type of warfare that was concurrently being demonstrated at Wagram, Borodino, and Leipzig. It perhaps seemed to him to be less conclusive, less simple, and longer protracted than the supposedly more 'modern' wars of Napoleon. It could not even show the same type of decisive and clear-cut victories as could 'line versus column' in minor tactics, or indeed the heavy charge of mounted knights in *The Art of War in the Middle Ages*. We may conjecture that it was therefore somewhat harder for Oman to turn the Peninsular art of operations into another magisterial essay comparable to those searing prototypes. The subject may also have appeared to be somewhat less than relevant to the concerns of the 1890s and 1900s, which was an era that Oman at his peak happened to share with such expert operationalists as von Schlieffen and de Grandmaison, who were then themselves at their own personal peaks.

We know that Oman was well abreast of the many theories of operational manoeuvre (or grand 'march manoeuvres') that were being discussed internationally in the decades just before the World War of 1914-18;[33] and yet he seems to have shown a certain reluctance to mention them in his own personal masterpiece about the Peninsula. We can speculate that he may have adopted this attitude because each Army Corps was too widely dispersed and unsupported in the Peninsula, so that it made little sense to talk, for example, of a whole Corps as a screening or holding force which would pin the enemy while all the other Corps manoeuvred behind it for their best positions in the eventual battle. Alternatively, the British scholars of Oman's time tended to shun the continental habit of formulating a legalistic 'military doctrine',[34] so he may have been content to leave it as (at best) a 'science-in-waiting', or (at worst) as perhaps just one of those airy-fairy 'conceptual' things that Marxists and other radical historians liked to rant about. Conversely, it is possible that Oman simply felt that the fundamentals of operational art were already sufficiently well understood by his readers, in a way that those of minor tactics were not. Whatever the reason for his reticence may have been, we must nevertheless accept that it conceals an important – if little-noticed – omission in his work. We can say that although he was actually a

Left: The newly married
Charles and Mary Oman.
They married in 1892.
(Courtesy of Julia Trevelyan
Oman)

Below: The Omans
photographed about 1910.
From left to right: 'The Prof.',
Dulce, Charles, Carola, Patch
and Mary. (Courtesy of Julia
Trevelyan Oman)

The mature Professor Oman. (Courtesy of Julia Trevelyan Oman)

Above: Sir John Moore is hit by a roundshot at Coruña as the young Henry Hardinge (later commander in chief of the British Army) announces the arrival of the Brigade of Guards. From J. Jenkins' *Martial Achievements of Great Britain &c.* (Courtesy of Arthur Harman)

Below: Marshal Beresford disarming a Polish lancer at Albuera. From J. Jenkins' *Martial Achievements of Great Britain &c.* (Courtesy of Arthur Harman)

Right: The brief and minuscule 'battle' of Maida, 1806. Oman at first thought the French had attacked in column, but later realised their whole intention had been to use the line. From J. Jenkins' *Martial Achievements of Great Britain &c.* (Courtesy of Arthur Harman)

Above: General Sir Thomas Picton storming the Moorish castle at Badajoz. From J. Jenkins' *Martial Achievements of Great Britain &c.* (Courtesy of Arthur Harman)

Below: A British Tower Musket bayonet – an implement that exerted a greater tactical influence than Oman believed. (Courtesy of Arthur Harman)

Above: The Duke of Wellington. From an engraving by W. Say after Thomas Philips. (Courtesy of Philip Haythornthwaite)

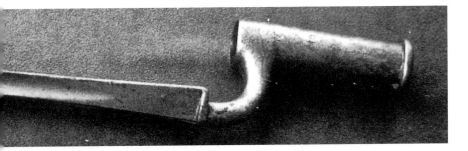

Right: Sir John Moore. From an engraving by Turner after Sir Thomas Lawrence. (Courtesy of Philip Haythornthwaite)

Right: William Napier as an officer in the 43rd Light Infantry, including a rare depiction of the regimental pelisse. From an engraving by Miss Jones. (Courtesy of Philip Haythornthwaite)

Left: William Napier
as an historian aged
68. From an engraving
by G. F. Watts.
(Courtesy of Philip
Haythornthwaite)

Left: King Joseph I.
From an engraving
by L. Rados after
J. B. Bosio.
(Courtesy of Philip
Haythornthwaite)

Above: An artist's impression of the escalade at Badajoz. (Courtesy of Philip Haythornthwaite)

Below: Grenadiers of the Imperial Guard in Spain. Note the drill procedure of the rear ranks loading for the front ranks, some descriptions of which do exist. From an engraving by H. Bellangé. (Courtesy of Philip Haythornthwaite)

Left: Francisco Espoz
y Mina. Nicknamed
the king of Navarre,
he led the largest
guerrilla force which
eventually became a
division of the
Spanish regular army.
(Courtesy of René
Chartrand)

Left: Don Juan
Martin Diez, El
Empecinado (The
Obstinate). A former
private regular soldier
and farm labourer, he
eventually led
thousands of
guerrillas in central
Spain and became
brigadier-general.
(Courtesy of the
Museo de Ejercito,
Madrid, via René
Chartrand)

Right: A contemporary sketch of Spanish guerrillas. (Courtesy of René Chartrand)

Above: A guerrilla attack on a French convoy on a remote road in an exceptionally craggy Sierra Morena. (Courtesy of René Chartrand)

Left: The Gentleman's Magazine supplement of 1811 reported 'Killed by a guerrilla mistaking him for a Frenchman, whilst escorting a French captain exchanged for an English one, Lt. King, 13th Light Drag. son of Mrs K. wine-merchant, Ipswich. His remains were conveyed to Badajoz, and interred by the French General Philipon, with all the honours of war.' A century later, the incident was portrayed in this print by Henry Payne. (Courtesy of René Chartrand)

Above: An artist's impression of the defeat of a French attack at Bussaco. Note the closeness of the opposing lines and the British riflemen hovering on the flanks. From J. Jenkins' *Martial Achievements of Great Britain &c.* (Courtesy of Arthur Harman)

Above: The view from Wellington's HQ at Bussaco, looking southeast over the scene of Reynier's assault. (Courtesy of Paddy Griffith)

Below: The view from the main road crossing Bussaco ridge, looking down towards Moura and the steep ground up which Ney attacked. (Courtesy of Paddy Griffith)

Above: British rifles give support from the edges of a combat of formed infantry at Vitoria. From J. Jenkins' *Martial Achievements of Great Britain &c.* (Courtesy of Arthur Harman)

Below: Linear tactics in use by both sides in the battle of the Nivelle. From J. Jenkins' *Martial Achievements of Great Britain &c.* (Courtesy of Arthur Harman)

Above: The stream-bed on the eastern side of the village of Fuentes d'Oñoro which marked 'no man's land' during part of the battle. (Courtesy of Paddy Griffith)

Below: The bridge over the Coa near Almeida, where Craufurd's rash deployment almost led to a defeat on 24 July 1810. His men were chased across the bridge (rebuilt 1823) and had to scramble up the rocky slope shown in the background. (Courtesy of Paddy Griffith)

Above: The Medellin hill at Talavera, as seen from the French hill, the Cascajal. It was not as steep as some of Wellington's defensive positions and was twice almost captured during the bloody fighting. (Courtesy of Paddy Griffith)

Below: The bridge at Sorauren, where Wellington coolly dashed off his orders for the battle just as the enemy were entering the village at the other end. (Courtesy of Paddy Griffith)

Above: A view from the summit of the British right flank at Sorauren, showing the height and steepness of the hill. (Courtesy of Paddy Griffith)

Below: The fort of Fuentarrabia, covering the Spanish side of the main frontier crossing at the mouth of the Bidassoa. (Courtesy of Paddy Griffith)

highly skilled analyst of the operational art, he dared not breathe its name.

Notes

1. Oman, *History*, vol.I, p.85.

2. This rhythm is comparable to the North Vietnamese system of the 1960s, known as 'one slow, four quick': See my *Forward Into Battle* (2nd edn, Swindon, 1990), p.161, based partly on the works of S.L.A. Marshall.

3. When Wellington *did* finally 'win the war in a single operation', at Vitoria (1813), not only did he himself enjoy an exceptionally thorough logistic and intelligence advantage, which extended the range of his thrust beyond normal expectations; but also the French found themselves in an unusually vulnerable, localised position. They were not able to utilise the whole area and depth of the Peninsula, which had often been their refuge in the past; but were tied to a monster baggage train that was crawling along a highly predictable line of retreat, and very close to the extreme northern edge of the theatre.

4. Oman, *Wellington's Army*, pp.255–67.

5. *Ibid* p.255.

6. *Ibid* p.265.

7. S.G.P. Ward, *Wellington's Headquarters* (London, 1957). Some related aspects are also discussed in A. Brett-James, *Life in Wellington's Army* (London, 1972); Michael Glover, *Wellington's Army in the Peninsula, 1808-14* (Newton Abbot, 1977); J. Guy, ed., *The Road to Waterloo: The British Army and the Struggle Against Revolutionary and Napoleonic France, 1793-1815* (London, 1990); Philip Haythornthwaite, *The Armies of Wellington* (London, 1994); *Wellington's Military Machine* (Tunbridge Wells, 1989); and T.M.O. Redgrave, *Wellington's Logistical Arrangements in the Peninsular War, 1809-14* (unpublished Ph.D. thesis, University of London, n.d.).

8. P.N. Chantreau, *Elements d'Histoire Militaire* (Paris, 1808), p.30.

9. One often gets the impression that, throughout history, something like ninety per cent of every general's time has been spent in gossiping about other generals.

10. On both occasions enemy numbers had originally been badly – and dangerously – underestimated, eventually leading to an embarrassing superabundance of POWs.

11. Oman, *Memories of Victorian Oxford and of Some Early Years* (London, 1941), p.189. The present author's mother reported finding something similar at Coruña in about 1930.

12. Little wonder, then, that at the end of its advance – and also at the end of its rations – Soult's force seemed to deploy a reinforced screen of *tirailleurs* in the battle of Sorauren; *cf* Harman's comments in chapter 11 below. For another 'all light infantry' mainforce operation by the French, see Gouvion St Cyr's relief of Barcelona in December 1808, which skirted around all the main roads that were blocked by Spanish fortresses: Oman, *History,* vol.II, p.59*ff.*

13. Among Wellington's 'non-battles' may be counted Almaraz 1809; Santarem/Sobral 1810; the Caia 1811; Fuenteguinaldo/El Bodon 1811; First San Christoval 1812; and Second San Christoval 1812. The actual battle of

Salamanca had been shaping up well as the 'Second non-battle of San
Christoval' until Wellington took his unexpected decision to attack –
thereby relegating that title to what was really his third encounter with the
French on the same ground, later in the year. See my 'The Peninsular
Generals and the Art of the Non Battle' in *Empires, Eagles and Lions* 74
(September 1983), pp.8–11; and the appendix to my *Wellington –
Commander* (Chichester, 1985), pp.188–9, and discussions in the text.

14. Each of these three battles was immodestly written up as a 'triumph' by
the British, even though their troops had to retreat immediately from the
field in every case!

15. Oman, *History*, vol.I, p.171, with corrections in Richard Partridge and
Michael Oliver, *Battle Studies in the Peninsula* (London, 1998), vol.I, p.60.

16. Specifically, a total of some 7000 casualties were suffered at Uclés and
as many as 27,000 at Ocaña. These figures are far higher than those suffered
by the Anglo-Portuguese in any of their Peninsular battles or sieges,
although at Waterloo Wellington would suffer some 15,000, which falls
between the two.

17. Oman, *History*, vol.I, p.85; see also his explanation in *Wellington's
Army*, pp.308–9.

18. In late-1810 Masséna maintained some 50,000 men for over two months
in a central Portugal that had already been systematically denuded of
foodstuffs. He cannot have done this by conventional commissariat
methods, but only through a mixture of living off systematic pillage (as in
Oman's phrase 'from cellar to garret') and by living literally 'off the land' (as
in gathering berries, hunting, fishing and, of course, catching frogs).

19. Oman, *History*, vol.II, p.444.

20. For the terminology, see discussion in *eg* Peter Paret, ed., *Makers of
Modern Strategy* (Princeton, 1986), pp.342–3 (for Delbrück's view of
Frederick) and p.535 (for Falkenhayn).

21. The phrase is Robert McNamara's, discussing the 'two and a half war
standard' for manpower planning, as US Defense Secretary in 1965.

22. Or 222,000 by October – see appendices to Oman, *History*, vol.I,
pp.615, 645.

23. *Ibid* vol.IV, pp.638–42.

24. *Ibid* vol.VI, p.754.

25. I am very grateful to Jean Lochet for pointing me towards all these
organisational features. For French practice in the 1790s see my *The Art of
War of Revolutionary France, 1789–1802* (London, 1998), pp.156–65.

26. Oman, *Wellington's Army*, p.163.

27. Oman corrected Napier's figure of sixty-two miles to the more credible
forty-three miles (*History*, vol.II, pp.560–1).

28. See my *Art of War of Revolutionary France*, p.174.

29. For example, the English had built fortified barracks at Ruthven, Cock
Bridge, etc, in their pacification of the Highlands during the 1740s. By
contrast their other claimed counter-guerrilla 'invention of the Boer War' –
the concentration camp for entire populations deemed to be potentially
hostile – was, indeed, a true innovation. Yet it must surely be accounted a
relatively humane one, when set beside the purely genocidal practices that
had preceded it, *eg* some of the French counter-insurgency policies in
Algeria during the 1830s.

30. See G. Lechartier, *Les Services de l'Arrière à la Grande Armée, 1806–7*

(Paris, 1910).

31. Excellent modern analysis and OB (correcting Oman) in Oliver and Partridge, *op.cit.* pp.184–223.

32. See Paret, *op.cit.* pp.91–185; *cf* my *Military Thought in the French Army* (Manchester, 1989), *passim.*

33. One of Oman's most specific references to the continental debate arises in his discussion of 'Napoleon and his Cavalry', in *Studies in the Napoleonic Wars* (London, 1929), pp.231–60, which draws on Camon and several other French authorities. He shows how the cuirassiers had a highly specialised role in central Europe, whereas they were scarcely deployed to the Peninsula at all. The Peninsula was left to the dragoons and light cavalry, since it was not seen as the domain of truly 'great' battles. For some of the background to the French debate before 1914 see my *Forward Into Battle*, pp.84–94.

34. There were exceptions, such as Spenser Wilkinson, whose *The Brain of an Army: A Popular Account of the German General Staff* (London, 1890) advocated that the British should adopt German staff methods.

Chapter 9

Sieges in the Peninsular War

by Philip Haythornthwaite

Siege warfare in the Napoleonic era did not attain the level of importance which it had enjoyed in some earlier conflicts, certainly not after the advent of Napoleon's system of war, which was usually directed towards the destruction of the enemy's field army, rather than upon the occupation of territory, thus tending to reduce the significance of fortified places. The situation was rather different in the Peninsula, where siege warfare assumed an importance greater than in some other Napoleonic campaigns. Although the events of the Peninsular sieges are recorded by Sir Charles Oman in his *History of the Peninsular War*, some aspects of the mechanics of siegecraft were not explored in that work; and his chapter XVII ('A Note on Sieges') of *Wellington's Army* (1912) concentrates, by virtue of the very nature of that work, upon the sieges undertaken by the British, whereas (as shown by the list of sieges in appendix 5 of the present volume), well over half the sieges which occurred during the war had no Anglo-Portuguese participation.

The reasons for the importance of fortified places in the Peninsula was partly geographical, and partly the result of the nature of the war. As centres of population and administration, and by controlling vital routes of communication, some fortified places were of obvious strategic significance. French endeavours to pacify 'occupied' areas gave incentive to neutralise potential centres of resistance, and from the Allied viewpoint, the French occupation of key fortifications could not be ignored. Wellington's strategy was more cautious than that preferred by Napoleon; whereas the latter might have been content to ignore fortifications occupied by the enemy, merely using a blockade or containment in the interest of a rapid advance against the enemy's field army, Wellington was unable to pursue such an objective. The necessity of securing his routes of supply required the elimination of French garrisons along those routes, most notably in the two 'corridors' between Portugal and Spain, guarded by the great fortresses of Almeida and Ciudad Rodrigo in the north, and Elvas and Badajoz in the south. It was against such fortified centres that some of the most significant actions of the Peninsular War occurred, involving some of the heaviest casualties. A similar series of fortifications, notably San Sebastian and Pamplona, played an equivalent role in the frontier between France and Spain.

The circumstances of every siege were different, the various considerations being listed thus in a contemporary manual:

> The force, situation, and condition of the place to be besieged; whether it be susceptible of more than one attack; whether lines of circumvallation or countervallation will be necessary; whether it be situated upon a height, upon a rocky soil, upon good ground, or in a marsh; whether divided by a river, or in the neighbourhood of one; whether the river will admit of forming inundations; its size and depth; whether the place be near a wood, and whether that wood can supply stuff for fascines, gabions, &c.; whether it be situated near any other place where a depot can be formed to supply stores for the siege.[1]

The term 'siege' might be accorded various grades of meaning, from a full investment leading to the breaching of the enemy's enceinte in preparation for an assault, to something looser – a blockade, or, looser still, a 'containment', inhibiting the garrison of the fortified place from making effective sallies much beyond its immediate environs, and denying it reinforcement and logistic supplies in any appreciable quantities. Not even the strongest fortresses were designed or intended to be impregnable; rather, they had to be sufficiently robust to defy the enemy for a reasonable period of time, until the besiegers could be driven away by a relief force, or until their resources became so stretched as to prevent them continuing the siege.

If the maintenance of a fortified place required considerable efforts on the part of the garrison, then a full siege demanded many times that effort on the part of the besiegers. Although each siege involved factors peculiar to that one operation, engineers could make rough estimates of the resources required to mount a regular investment. Lieutenant-Colonel John T. Jones, one of the senior British engineers in the Peninsular War, and historian of the British sieges, based a calculation upon a suggested front of 180 toises (roughly 350 metres) and against defences which included a ravelin. For the first and second nights' work in beginning the siege-trenches, he estimated that a working-party of 3000 men was necessary, but that the number of workmen could be reduced on subsequent days of the siege, so that it was possible to average the working-parties at 2000 men each. So hard was the manual labour that Jones stated that four 'reliefs' were essential, *ie* four shifts per day, thus evidently of six hours each, giving a total of 8000 workmen for such a project. To protect the working-parties, a trench-guard was required of three-quarters of the numerical strength of the garrison; thus, taking as an example a garrison 5000-strong, 3750 men were needed to protect the trenches. These could manage with three 'reliefs' per day, giving a total of 11,250 men. For camp and escort duties, Jones recommended a force numbering one-tenth of the whole army, in four reliefs, thus, in the above instance, 1925 men multiplied by four, equalling 7700. Adding to these the 8000 workers and 11,250 trench-guards, the requisite number of men was 26,950, plus whatever surplus was necessary to offset casualties and those who fell sick during the siege. (Presumably, if circumstances permitted a siege of longer duration to be contemplated, the same results could be obtained with a smaller number of workmen, though this point was not made in Jones' calculations.) In addition, he noted that the trench-guard should include cavalry to the amount of one-and-a-half times the number possessed by the garrison, to meet any sally by the enemy's horse. One-third of the besiegers' cavalry, he wrote, should be positioned at each flank of the siege-works, with the remaining third in reserve, behind the trenches, prepared to support either wing; with the cavalry on either flank reinforced by the reserve, the besiegers could be certain of meeting the enemy's cavalry on terms of parity, instead of being outnumbered.[2]

Calculations to determine the requisite number of guns were less precise, the important criterion being the nature of the defences rather than the number of guns deployed by the garrison, as only a limited number of these could be directed against the attackers, given that the siege-works would not normally encompass the entire circuit of the defences. As a rough guide, Jones estimated that to attack a section of the defences (including a ravelin), about sixty guns, twenty-two howitzers, twenty-two mortars, and sixteen perriers (mortars firing small balls) would be sufficient to take into account the likelihood of a few guns being disabled by the enemy's counter-fire.[3]

Such statistics represented the ideal, rather than a guide to what actually occurred; it was not uncommon for a besieging force to have insufficient artillery to achieve its objective, as demonstrated, for example, at Badajoz in 1811, when the Anglo-Portuguese army had to rely upon a collection of veritable museum-pieces for use as a siege-train, as recorded by Oman (*History*, vol.IV, pp.275–6, 419). The rate of fire of these ancient guns was somewhat reduced, to avoid destroying them (they were prone to muzzle-droop and to the blowing-out of touch-holes), and indeed, the siege of May–June 1811 was delayed by the need to repair the artillery carriages, which had been shaken half to pieces by the effort of transporting the guns.

Having determined the number of troops required for the operation, the besiegers would normally follow a fairly standard course of action. At first a blockade would be enforced by establishing posts at some distance from the fortification, intended to prevent the enemy from communicating with, and re-supplying, the besieged garrison. Blockades were sometimes difficult to enforce, as proven perhaps most famously by the escape of Brennier's garrison from Almeida in May 1811. Having established a cordon around the fortified place, the commander and engineers would survey the works and decide upon their main points of attack. (Reconnaissance was often hazardous, and called for some nerve, at all stages of a siege; before the storm of the breaches at Badajoz in 1812, for example, Major William Nicholas of the Royal Engineers personally swam across the inundation from the river Rivillas to inspect the ground.) At the commencement of operations it might be decided to neutralise any 'outworks' or fortifications detached from the main defences; these might themselves be positions of some strength, protecting salient features of the fortification, for example forts Picurina, San Christobal, and Pardaleras at Badajoz. Such positions might be carried by an immediate assault, or require siege-works conducted in the same manner as those directed against the main defences. Sometimes more than one system of siege-works was opened, either to confuse the garrison about the exact intentions of the besiegers, or to allow a choice of options once the siege commenced.

The first stage of a regular siege was 'breaking ground', *ie* opening the first line of siege-trenches. It was usually commenced at night, and ideally completed during the hours of darkness, so as to provide some protection for the workmen when the light of dawn revealed their presence to the defenders; thus it represented the most intense period of labour in the entire siege, involving (according to Jones' calculations) one-third more men than would be employed for an ordinary day's work in the later stages of the siege (or at least the equivalent of one-third extra labour). By dawn of the day following the night of 'breaking ground', the first trench-line (known as the 'first parallel') should have been completed, the spoil from the excavation being thrown up to form a parapet, with approach-trenches leading from the besiegers' camp to the parallel, if that approach were within cannon-range of the defences. (The 'first parallel' was usually established at some considerable distance from the defences, near to the maximum effective range of the defenders' guns.) If the ground proved especially rocky in any place, preventing an effective trench and parapet, cover for the working-parties could be provided by gabions (wicker baskets filled with earth), although it was noted that these tended to attract the defenders' fire. An example of this occurred at Burgos, when a line of gabions was used to protect a communication-trench; but the French defenders, evidently believing that gabions indicated the position of a battery, so bombarded the 'gabionade' as to render the communication-trench unsafe for use. The gabions were then removed, showing to the French that they did not conceal a battery, whereupon the bombardment ceased, following which a simple earth rampart, erected the next night, provided all the protection necessary for the communication-trench.

Following the establishment of the 'first parallel', work commenced on the construction of successive lines of trenches nearer to the fortification, the second and third parallels. To reach the site of these trenches, communication- or approach-trenches, or saps, would be pushed forward from the first parallel, a most hazardous undertaking as the sappers would be visible to the defenders, and protected initially only by moveable screens. The approach-trenches could not be dug directly towards the fortification, lest the enemy's shot sweep right along the trench, killing everyone therein; instead they were dug in zigzag fashion, with construction becoming ever more dangerous as it neared the defences. Simultaneously with these trenches, the first batteries would be commenced, artillery-positions for the bombardment guns, the location of which it was advised should be concealed until they were actually ready to open fire. The first batteries were not usually built for the guns intended to breach the enemy's wall, but rather to subdue the fire directed against the advancing lines of trenches:

> It is useless to attempt to sap near to the place till the enemy's fire is subdued ... only five or six guns ... would effectually impede that operation: a steady fire of artillery at the distance of even 150 yards will always knock down the gabions as fast as sappers can place them: from these causes the silencing the fire of the place is the principal aim of all the operations of a regular siege.[4]

As the siege progressed, batteries would be constructed nearer to the fortification, including breaching-batteries for the heavy guns which would bombard the section of defences against which the final assault was planned.

The amount of physical effort involved in digging the trenches and battery-positions, using spades and picks, was prodigious. Other work included the construction of gabions, fascines (brushwood bundles), and other woodwork (gun-positions might have wooden flooring to prevent the guns sinking into the earth). The labour required obviously varied with the circumstances of the particular siege, but it was expected that when 'breaking ground' each man would, in that part of the night which remained after the engineer officers had marked out the location of the excavations, dig a section of trench four feet long, three feet six inches wide, and three feet deep, using the spoil to form a parapet to give the trench an effective depth of about six feet. The nature of the task may be gauged from the available statistics for the siege of Badajoz, between the nights of 17–18 March and 5–6 April 1812: from the number of workmen involved, and presuming that shifts were of six hours' duration, an estimate of some 180,000 man-hours was involved for the siege-works. Some 80,000 sand-bags were filled, and 1200 gabions and 700 fascines were constructed.

The amount of ammunition expended was similarly enormous, the statistics of which exemplify the huge logistic task involved in transporting powder and shot to the siege-works. At Badajoz in 1812, for example, the besiegers expended 19,941 rounds for 24-pdrs (18,832 roundshot, 839 grape, 112 case, and 158 rounds of grape fabricated from 1268 rounds of 3-pdr shot); 13,029 rounds of 18-pdr shot; and 507 rounds of 'common shell' and 1,319 of 'spherical case' (shrapnel) for 5½-inch howitzers. When the weight of powder is added (presuming powder to be one-third the weight of solid shot, one-quarter for case-shot, and presuming a 12 oz charge for howitzer shells (the quantity of charge might vary according to degree of elevation), the total weight of munitions expended amounted to over 437 tons.[5] Such statistics were not unusual; at San Sebastian in 1813, for example, some 47,391 rounds of 24-pdr ammunition were expended (including 43,367 roundshot), 9,453 rounds of 18-pdr shot (including 9303 roundshot), 3755 ten-inch shells, and 9964 eight-inch shells. This represented considerably more than 900 tons of shot, and the expenditure of 5579 barrels of powder at 90 lbs each added another 224 tons.[6] Some of the problems of transporting such quantities may be imagined from Kincaid's recollection of columns of Portuguese militia supplying the batteries at Badajoz in 1812 with ammunition from Elvas, each man carrying a 24-pound shot for some twelve miles, and, he added, each cursing all the way and back again! The above statistics also emphasise the insufficiency of the siege artillery deployed against Burgos in 1812: three 18-pdrs, five 24-pdr howitzers of little value, only 300 rounds of ammunition per piece (*ie* 2400 rounds in total), and but fifteen barrels of powder (little more than half a ton).

The direction of the bombardment of a fortified place involved one of the moral considerations of siege warfare, though these were far from being of universal concern. Jones expressed what might be termed the 'civilised' view that:

> To bombard a town, is merely to shower down upon it shells, carcasses, rockets, hot-shot, and other incendiary missiles to destroy the houses, and kill the inhabitants; leaving the fortifications entire. In a well built place, the military under a bombardment suffer little or nothing ... it is therefore apparent such mode of attack can never succeed but against

a very small place, where bomb-proof cover cannot be obtained; or where the Governor is a weak man whose sense of duty yields to his feelings of humanity.[7]

He held that such measures were only applied when the besiegers had insufficient engineers to conduct a regular attack against the fortifications, and condemned the bombardment of Copenhagen, in which the besiegers in three days expended 6412 shells, 4966 shot, and a proportionate number of carcasses (incendiaries):

> On the score of humanity such a method of attack should be for ever relinquished. The cruelty of it is inconceivable to those who have not witnessed it: its effects fall dreadfully heavy upon the unoffending inhabitants; the aged, the infirm, and the helpless are those that suffer from it. The heart revolts at the idea that the earnings of industry should be devoted to destruction, and women and innocent children be mutilated, for an object which might far more readily be attained without it.[8]

Moral considerations apart, indiscriminate bombardment could have practical difficulties; as Wellington commented on San Sebastian, 'if the general bombardment should set fire to the town, as it probably will, then the attack of the enemy's entrenchment will become impracticable ... the conflagration which it may occasion may be materially injurious to the attack, and will be very inconvenient to our friends the inhabitants, and eventually to ourselves'.[9]

Sadly, 'the unoffending inhabitants' paid a heavy price in more than one Peninsular siege. If the civilian population aided the defence, as at Saragossa, they might have expected to he treated like the garrison; but to use civilians as did Suchet at Lerida, for example, was 'scarcely to be admitted within the pale of civilised warfare'. This had involved driving the civilians in front of the attackers and upon the garrison, so that they would perish if hostilities continued:

> Suchet justifies it, on the ground, that he thus spared a great effusion of blood which must necessarily have attended a protracted siege, and the fact is true. But this is to spare soldiers' blood at the expense of women's and children's, and, had Garcia Conde's [commander of the garrison] nature been stern, he, too, might have pleaded expediency, and the victory would have fallen to him who could longest have sustained the sight of mangled infants and despairing mothers.[10]

William Napier's view, thus expressed, would have been shared by many of his contemporaries.

It was advocated that a regular rate of fire be maintained by the besiegers, both day and night. Jones recommended that each gun should be allocated sixty rounds per day – though this could be exceeded – even if a practical expenditure was less than 100 rounds per day, rather than in excess of that number. It was emphasised that great attention should be paid to re-laying the gun after each shot, for maximum effect, and although the breaching batteries should fire as quickly as possible over a shorter time, their expenditure should not exceed 120 rounds in twenty-four hours. Taking Badajoz in 1812 as an example, the roundshot expended by the sixteen 24-pdrs averaged almost sixty-two per day, the roundshot fired by the twenty 18-pdrs averaging more than thirty-four per day, per gun. Batteries could be directed to enfilade the enemy defences, and high-angle fire directed against the areas in the immediate rear of the main wall; and in breaching, the fire was ideally aimed at the base of the wall, to cause it to collapse from the bottom, rather than bring down the upper part which would fall into the ditch and leave the lower section of the wall impervious to further damage by virtue of the rubble piled against it.

Throughout the siege operations, and especially as the besiegers' trenches approached nearer the defences, the garrison would make every attempt to frustrate the enemy's work. Great quantities of artillery fire might be directed against the trenches; during the siege of Ciudad Rodrigo in 1812, for example, the French garrison ranged some forty-eight pieces of ordnance against the siege-works opposite the point to be attacked, firing almost 10,000 roundshot and 11,000 shells in the course of the siege. This made duties in the siege-trenches both dangerous and unpopular. Moyle Sherer, who seems to have looked for the best in every situation, remarked that a siege was 'highly interesting ... the fire of the batteries; the beautiful appearance of the shells and fire-balls by night; the challenge of the enemy's sentries; the sound of their drums and trumpets; all give a continued charm and animation to this service', but added that 'the duties of a besieging force are both harassing and severe; and, I know not how it is, death in the trenches never carries with it that stamp of glory, which seals the memory of those who perish in a well-fought field'.[11] Jones noted how the infantry (which performed most of the manual labour) found trench-duty thoroughly distasteful, 'tedious and irksome, and, added to its severity and danger, has given a disgust for the employment', so that 'there are few officers who would not prefer to risk every thing on the doubtful success of storming a place entire, to the small delay and the additional fatigue of surely gaining it without loss by art and labour'.[12] William Grattan recorded how the infantry were happy to engage in a 'stand-up fight', but regarded a life lost in the trenches as one thrown away ingloriously, while John Kincaid remarked that 'one day's trench-work is as like another as the days themselves; and like nothing better than serving an apprenticeship to the double calling of grave-digger and gamekeeper, for we found ample employment both for the spade and the rifle'.[13] The latter alludes to the sharpshooting which occurred as the siege-works pushed near to the defences. At Badajoz in 1812, for example, Lieutenant George Simmons of the 95th Rifles and a detachment of ten men silenced a troublesome French cannon by rifle-fire alone. Conversely, Jones recorded that the ordinary infantry who formed the trench-guards, not possessed of the skill of the riflemen, usually fired with little effect and often suffered heavier casualties than necessary by failing to provide sufficient cover by the use of sandbags. He contrasted this with the proficiency of the French sharpshooters, including one remarkable sniper at Burgos who killed a large number of besiegers by firing from cover, while his companions tricked those in the trenches into showing themselves, by making a noise, throwing stones, or waving a hat.

Some accounts suggest a degree of fatalism among the trench-workers, who became resigned to their arduous duty. Grattan recalled a member of the 88th who sat in view of the enemy at Badajoz in 1811, weaving a fascine and ignoring the flying shot. Sir Richard Fletcher urged him to take cover, but he replied that he was almost finished, 'and it isn't worth while to move now; those fellows can't hit me, for they've been trying these fifteen minutes';[14] whereupon a roundshot cut him in two. Altogether more careful was the Portuguese battery observed by Kincaid at Badajoz in 1812, which posted a sentry to watch for the approach of French shot (which could be seen with the naked eye). If a roundshot, he shouted 'balla', if a shell, 'bomba', 'and they ducked their heads until the missile passed; but, sometimes he would see a general discharge from all arms, when he threw himself down, screaming out, "Jesus, todos, todos!", meaning "everything".'[15]

Besiegers also needed to post trench-guards against the possibility of sallies by the garrison. These were sometimes made in daylight, and in considerable strength, such as that from Badajoz on 19 March 1812, on only the second full day of the siege, when some 1500 infantry issued from the city and fell upon the parallel, driving out the workmen and trench-guard; they filled in a small section of the trench and (more importantly) carried off some 200 entrenching-tools before the besiegers rallied and drove them back; among the casualties was the commanding engineer, Lieutenant-Colonel Richard Fletcher, who was wounded when a shot struck his purse and drove a dollar into his thigh. At the same time some forty cavalry outflanked the parallel and rode into the besiegers' camp about 1000 yards to the rear, causing some consternation but little damage before retiring upon the appearance of an armed force.

Depending upon the availability of trained personnel, mining was an effective tactic, which involved tunnelling beneath defences or siege-works and exploding a subterranean powder-charge to demolish what stood above. Combat might even occur below ground if one side broke into the other's galleries, as occurred at Saragossa, when the French used mining to destroy Spanish strongpoints in the city. The results of successful mining could be quite spectacular. When the French exploded two mines as the British attacked San Sebastian, the detonation

> drowned every other noise, and apparently confounded, for an instant, the combatants on both sides ... It was a spectacle as appalling and grand as the imagination can conceive, the sight of that explosion. The noise was more awful than any thing which I have ever heard before or since; while a bright flash, instantly succeeded by a smoke so dense as to obscure all vision, produced an effect upon those who witnessed it which no powers of language are adequate to describe. Such, indeed, was the effect of the whole occurrence, that for perhaps half a minute after not a shot was fired on either side. Both parties stood still to gaze upon the havoc which had been produced, insomuch that a whisper might have caught your ear for a distance of several yards.[16]

Some hours previously, the besiegers had blown up three shafts of their own, sunk eight feet below the surface and each filled with 540 lbs of powder, to demolish part of the city's sea wall.

A further danger to both sides was sickness. Trenches were often insanitary places, filled with stagnant, standing water or in flood after violent storms, the former leading to 'trench fever'. The longer a siege progressed, the more likely the outbreak of illness; thus at Saragossa both the besiegers and the inhabitants of that unfortunate city suffered terribly from sickness.

For a siege to be conducted effectively, a sufficient quantity of engineers was essential. In this matter the armies of the two principal protagonists were very different, for each French *corps d'armée* had a full complement of engineers, sappers and miners, whereas Wellington's army had but few engineer officers and other ranks. The comparison is exemplified by the resources deployed at two major sieges. For the second siege of Saragossa, the French engineer staff comprised forty-one officers (eight of whom were killed, including the commander, Lacoste, and ten wounded), three companies of miners (ten officers, 228 other ranks), and eight companies of sappers (thirty officers, 987 other ranks), supplemented by the engineers of the 5th Corps (eight officers – one killed, one wounded – and a sapper company of three officers and sixty-two other ranks). This produced a grand total of trained engineer personnel of ninety-two officers and 1277 other ranks; and this does not include the 5th Corps' companies of artillery *ouvriers* and *pontonniers*, who might have been expected to help with the engineering tasks.[17] These troops were equipped with 17,527 entrenching tools, 30,000 spare helves, and 370,000 sandbags. In contrast, when Wellington's army besieged Badajoz in 1812 it included nineteen engineer officers (four killed, nine wounded), 115 members of the Royal Military Artificers, and 120 men seconded from the 3rd Division (presumably because they had some digging or mining skills learned in their civilian occupation), and no other trained personnel whatsoever. All other labour had to be performed by untrained soldiers, for whom 3000 entrenching tools were provided (of inferior quality), with a few 'assistant engineers' from the infantry. Not all of the latter were necessarily largely unskilled in engineer duties, however; for example, Captain John Blakiston of the 17th Portuguese Regiment, a volunteer 'assistant' at San Sebastian, had trained with the Madras Engineers (he was the man who had blown in the gates of Vellore, allowing the remnant of the garrison to be saved and the mutiny suppressed). The composition of the engineer service at Burgos later the same year was even more feeble: five officers (one killed, one wounded), eight 'other ranks' of the Royal Military Artificers, eighty-one pioneers from Line regiments, 600 entrenching tools, 100 axes, and 200 bill-hooks, supplemented by some captured French tools.

The comparative dearth of trained engineers in the Anglo-Portuguese army was held to be a contributory factor in the heavy casualties sustained in such operations, and was duly condemned by Napier:

> It is most strange and culpable that a government, which had been so long engaged in war as the British, should have left the engineer department, with respect to organisation and equipment, in such a state as to make it, in despite of the officers' experience, bravery, and zeal, a very inefficient arm of war ... the very tools with which they worked ... were so shamefully bad that the work required could scarcely be performed; the captured French cutting-tools were eagerly sought for by the engineers as being infinitely better than the British.[18]

With a more professional eye, Jones concurred: 'at the first of these sieges it was difficult to find an individual who had ever worked under a fire of musketry; the undertaking was therefore new to all'; and not only were the infantry labourers untrained, but 'the few R.M. Artificers who were present, were equally uninstructed; so that an officer of Engineers often found himself appointed to direct a large body of men, all alike ignorant of what was ordered to be done, [thus] delay invariably took place, and that delay was frequently productive of great loss of life'. So dispirited did the men become as a consequence of these factors, he continued, that 'as soon as the troops had covered themselves from the enemy's fire, they ceased to do any thing further with cheerfulness or alacrity, and the work executed by any working party, seldom averaged one half the quantity which ought to have been performed, and which would have been executed by the troops of any other nation'.[19] The effect on morale was confirmed by an officer writing of the siege of Badajoz in 1811: 'our little corps bore the brunt of the enemy's exertions ... Both officers and men were exhausted, mind and body; they felt and saw that they were absurdly sacrificed'.[20]

Another factor with a bearing upon the course of sieges conducted with insufficient resources, and commented upon by Oman (*Wellington's Army*, pp.282–5), was the pressure of time under which the engineers laboured, to complete their operations before the arrival of an enemy relief-force. Thus they proceeded in a manner calculated more to bring about a speedy conclusion than to progress more regularly and with less hazard, although abilities to follow the latter course were restricted severely by inadequate means. Appalled by the losses incurred in the storming of Badajoz in 1812, Wellington urged Lord Liverpool to create a corps of trained sappers and miners (see the letter quoted by Oman in *Wellington's Army*, pp.284–5, and my own comments in chapter 4, above). Only after the formation of the resulting Royal Military Artificers or Sappers and Miners (Royal Sappers and Miners after 1813) did the situation begin to improve.

The primary objective of the bombardment of a fortified place was to create a 'practicable' breach in the outer wall, *ie* one that would admit a storming-party. It was at this stage of the operation that what might be described as the etiquette of siegecraft was perhaps most marked, it being accepted that the generosity of treatment which might be received by the governor and garrison was dependent upon the amount of trouble which they had caused the besiegers. An example of how this might work was the brief attack (it can hardly be called a siege) on Olivenza in April 1811. This place was largely indefensible, having a garrison of only 370, with five serviceable field-pieces and twelve bad old iron guns, without carriages but mounted upon carts. On 9 April Beresford demanded its surrender, offering handsome terms, but these were rejected. Between 11 and 14 April a battery was constructed by Major-General Galbraith Lowry Cole, who had been given the task of capturing the place, to contain four heavy guns, with field-howitzers sited to shell the areas in the immediate rear of the section of the wall to be breached. On the morning of 15 April, Cole offered terms to the governor before a shot was fired, provided he would surrender in half an hour; when no reply was received the bombardment opened, and at 11 am a white flag was hoisted by the garrison. The governor declared himself ready to accept Cole's terms, but as his earlier failure to reply had led to the commencement of the bombardment, Cole replied that he would now only accept unconditional surrender, and resumed firing. By 1 pm a breach was almost practicable, and the governor surrendered unconditionally rather than face an assault.

The accepted (but unwritten) 'laws of war' held that the governor of a fortified place could surrender legitimately once his position became untenable, without in any way impugning his honour or that of his troops. In some cases, it was thought that once a breach was 'practicable', a governor might surrender; but it was accepted that if defences had been constructed behind a breach, it was not unreasonable for the garrison to continue to resist. Otherwise, it was held that to incur bloodshed without a specific aim was mere barbarism. In an attempt to prevent useless resistance and unnecessary loss of life, a convention had evolved that if a garrison refused to surrender when the outcome was inevitable, forcing the besieger to suffer casualties in an assault, the garrison might forfeit the normal courtesies of war, could be put to the sword, and the place ransacked (see, for example, Oman's comments, *History*, vol.V, pp.260-2). This terrible practice was accepted, even if criticised; William Napier, for example, noted that 'though a town, taken by assault, be considered the lawful prey of a licentious soldiery', it was still a 'remnant of barbarism, disgracing the military profession'.[21] Nevertheless, even the most honourable of commanders accepted its necessity. As Ney wrote to Herrasti at Ciudad Rodrigo on 28 June 1810, a continued defence 'would force His Highness the Prince of Essling [Masséna] to treat you with all the rigour authorised by the laws of war ... you have to choose between an honourable capitulation and the terrible vengeance of a victorious army'.[22] Given the circumstances, Herrasti was quite justified in surrendering, saving the lives of his garrison and the attackers, and receiving in return all the 'honours of war'.

Criticism was levelled against French commanders who, following remarks on the subject by Napoleon, determined to hold out longer than justified by the old convention, which Jones condemned as 'of a nature to introduce barbarity into war, and to throw nations two thousand years backward in civilisation'.[23] Jones declared that only by adopting inhuman means could such inhuman practices be stopped, advocating that when a governor

> insists on the ceremony of storming the last entrenchment, as he thereby unnecessarily, and without an object, spills the blood of many brave men, his life and the lives of the garrison should be made the forfeit. A system enforced by terror, must be counteracted by yet greater terror; humanity towards the enemy in such a case, is cruelty to our own troops ... the principle to be combated is not the obligation to resist behind the breach; for where there is a good retrenchment the

bastion should be disputed ... but the abominable doctrine that surrender is not to take place when resistance can no longer be made – a doctrine too inhuman for a Turk, and not to be tolerated in a Christian.[24]

An example of the use of the undefined 'rules of war' occurred in the negotiations for the capitulation of Pamplona. To deter Cassan from carrying out his threat of blowing up the fortress, Wellington declared it 'contre toutes les lois de la guerre' ('against all the laws of war')[25] and directed Carlos de España to execute Cassan, his officers and NCOs, and a tenth of his troops should this take place. Napier's comment was that Cassan's action, if coupled with a realistic attempt to break out, would have been quite in accordance with the 'laws of war', but if the break-out were impossible (which was the case, given the state of Cassan's troops), and just a device to excuse destroying the place, then the besiegers 'might have justly exercised that severe but undoubted right of war, refusing quarter to an enemy'. Yet Wellington's suggestion, being 'quite contrary to the usages of civilised nations', was as much a bluff as was Cassan's threat to break out, 'and the threat must undoubtedly be considered only as a device to save the works of Pamplona and to avoid the odium of refusing quarter'.[26]

It was against this background that assaults were made, and the consequences assessed. Few experiences can have been more awful, and potentially more deadly, than the storm of a defended breach; yet there was usually great competition to achieve a place in the front rank of the attackers, the so-called 'forlorn hope' (an Anglicisation of the Dutch *verloren hoop*, 'lost party'), or its French equivalent, *les enfants perdus* ('the lost children'). Officers might volunteer in the hope of gaining advancement – 'a gold chain or a wooden leg' was a common British expression – but the motivation of the rank and file is more difficult to appreciate, evidently based upon personal pride and the concept that it was particularly honourable to be in the forefront. Kincaid recalled how at Badajoz in 1812 and at San Sebastian, when as adjutant he had to select the 'stormers' from his battalion, 'there was as much anxiety expressed, and as much interest made by all ranks to be appointed to the post of honour, as if it had been sinecure situations, in place of death-warrants, which I had at my disposal'.[27] Even bribery was used to obtain a place in the front rank, and as there were often more volunteers than were required, to avoid charges of favouritism measures had to be used like that by the 51st at Badajoz in 1811, when the adjutant was blindfolded and selected those men he touched at random when passing down the ranks of the volunteers. Perhaps the desire to be in the van of the assault was influenced by the belief expressed by Kincaid, that it made little difference whether one went first or last, as even those at the rear were just as likely to be killed!

Jones held that daylight was the best time for storming a position, to avoid the 'imaginary terrors' which might occur at night, when the darkness made the flash of the explosion of mines and shells seem more terrible, although an assault in daylight required more extensive siege-works to allow the attackers to approach their target under cover, the alternative, as shown by the French attack on Tarifa in January 1812, was to be shot to pieces in the advance; and where such covering works had not been constructed, a nocturnal attack was the only alternative.

In storming a breach, the attackers might encounter a variety of armaments not normally found on the battlefield. An energetic defender might re-fortify the breach, an example of what could be achieved being provided by the defences put in place at Badajoz in 1812. At the summit of the breaches *chevaux-de-frise* (beams into which sword-blades had been set) were chained into place, and all manner of obstacles had been thrown into the ditch to make climbing the rubble more difficult – carts, rope entanglements, broken gabions, doors and beams studded with nails, and caltrops to impale the feet. The garrison was provided with improvised grenades and armed with musket-ammunition consisting of both the usual ball and a wooden cylinder filled with lead slugs, to scatter like a shotgun. So expertly were the breaches defended that Jones stated that:

> Probably never since the discovery of gunpowder, were men more seriously exposed to the effects of it than those assembled in the ditch this night; many thousand shells and hand grenades, numerous bags filled with powder, every kind of burning composition, and destructive missile had been prepared, and placed behind the parapets of the whole front; these, under an incessant roll of musketry, were hurled into the ditch without intermission for upwards of two hours, giving it its whole surface an appearance of vomiting fire, and creating occasional flashes of light more vivid than the day, followed by a momentary utter darkness – in fact it is quite beyond the powers of description to convey an adequate idea of the awful grandeur of the scene.[28]

As Kincaid recalled, the result was 'as respectable a representation of hell itself as fire, and sword, and human sacrifice could make it; for, in one instant, every engine of destruction was in full operation'.[29]

Even the horrors of such an assault might not necessarily be the extent of the ordeal; another was recounted by Harry Jones of the Royal Engineers, who was wounded in the unsuccessful attack on San Sebastian on 25 July 1813. While lying helpless,

> my attention ... was aroused by an exclamation from the soldier lying next to me – 'Oh, they are murdering us all!'

Upon looking up, I perceived a number of French grenadiers, under a heavy fire of grape, sword in hand, stepping over the dead, and stabbing the wounded; my companion was treated in the same manner: the sword withdrawn from his body, and reeking with his blood, was raised to give me the *coup de grace*, when fortunately the uplifted arm was arrested by a smart little man, a serjeant, who cried out, '*Oh mon Colonel, êtes-vous blessé!*' (the serjeant must have mistaken my rank, from seeing a large gold bullion epaulette on my right shoulder, and the blue uniform, rendering it more conspicuous) and immediately ordered some of his men to remove me into the town.[30]

Having been rescued, he was treated with every consideration.

After enduring the tribulations of an assault, coupled with the unwritten tradition which gave license to the victorious attackers, it is perhaps not altogether surprising that discipline should break down in the afterrnath, although the orgies of violence and destruction which sometimes followed were such as to revolt even the most hardened campaigners. Some distinction was made at the time between the plundering propensities of British and French; William Surtees, for example, claimed that the latter 'keep themselves more sober, and look more to the solid and substantial benefit to be derived from it, while the former sacrifice everything to drink; and once in a state of intoxication, with all the bad passions set loose at the same time, I know not what they will hesitate to perpetrate.'[31] One witness of the sack of Badajoz offered a partial excuse that the desire for liquor arose in the first instance from the thirst caused by the great exertions of combat; but after the soldier had drunk 'every trace of human nature vanishes, and no brutal outrage can be named which he does not commit.'[32] The appalling experiences which might be endured by besiegers, defenders, and civilian population fully justified Blakiston's comment on San Sebastian, echoed by other witnesses: 'Such is war, even among the most civilized people! O, my countrymen! may its horrors never be brought home to you! and, while you sit snugly by your fire-sides, grumble not, I beseech you, at your taxes, so long as they keep the enemy from your gates!'[33]

Notes

1. R.W. Adye, *The Bombardier and Pocket Gunner* (London, 1802), p.29.
2. Colonel J.T. Jones, *Journals of the Sieges undertaken by the Allies in Spain* (London, 1814), pp.335-7.
3. *Ibid* p.340.
4. *Ibid* p.343.
5. *Ibid* p.144.
6. *Ibid* p.244.
7. *Ibid* pp.345-6.

8. *Ibid* pp.347-8.

9. Duke of Wellington, *Dispatches of Field Marshal the Duke of Wellington* (ed. J. Gurwood, London, 1834-8) vol.XI, pp.32-3.

10. Sir William Napier, *History of the War in the Peninsula* (6 vols, London, 1832-40), vol. III, p.157.

11. M. Sherer, *Recollections of the Peninsula* (London, 1823), p.208.

12. Jones, *op.cit.* p.275.

13. Sir John Kincaid, *Adventures in the Rifle Brigade and Random Shots from a Rifleman* (combined edn, London, 1908), p.63.

14. *United Service Journal* 1831, vol.II, p.329.

15. Kincaid, *op.cit.* p.64.

16. Reverend G.R. Gleig, *The Subaltern* (Edinburgh, 1872), pp.51-2.

17. J. Belmas, *Journaux des Sièges faits ou soutenus par les français dans la Peninsule, de 1807 à 1814* (Paris, 1836), vol.II, pp.337-9.

18. Napier, *op.cit.* vol.IV, p.193.

19. Jones, *op.cit.* pp.259-60.

20. Captain John Squire RE, in Napier, *op.cit.* vol.III, pp.638-9.

21. Napier, *op.cit.* vol.III, p.157.

22. Belmas, *op.cit.* vol.III, p. 287.

23. Jones, *op.cit.* p.332.

24. *Ibid* p.334.

25. *WD* vol.XI, p.211 (written in French to Carlos de España).

26. Napier, *op.cit.* vol.IV, p.293.

27. Kincaid, *op.cit.* p.273.

28. Jones, *op.cit.* p.150.

29. Kincaid, *op.cit.* p.66.

30. Lieutenant-Colonel H. Jones, 'Narrative of Seven Weeks' Captivity in St Sebastian', in *United Service Journal* 1841, vol.I, p.193.

31. W. Surtees, *Twenty-Five Years in the Rifle Brigade* (London, 1833), p.149.

32. C. von Hodenberg, 'A Dragoon of the Legion', ed. Sir Charles Oman, in *Blackwood's Magazine*, March 1913, pp.303-4.

33. J. Blakiston, *Twelve Years' Military Adventures in Three Quarters of the Globe* (2 vols, London, 1829), vol.II, p.271.

Chapter 10

Sir Charles Oman on Line versus Column

by Brent Nosworthy

While piecing together his epic history of the Peninsular campaigns, Oman had to assemble what at the time were considered detailed descriptions of the various battles that punctuated the campaigning. Not surprisingly, Oman soon felt he was able to isolate the basic principles that underlay both the British and French systems of fighting, and an entire chapter in the first volume of the *History of the Peninsular War* was devoted to this subject. Although Oman quickly established the foundations of his theories of British versus French tactical capabilities, at least in the details, his analysis continued to evolve throughout his career, and he revisited the subject in the chapter entitled 'Wellington's Infantry Tactics: Line Versus Column' in *Wellington's Army, 1809–1814* (1912), and again in a chapter of the same name in *Studies in the Napoleonic Wars* (1929). Since Oman's analyses and the data he used to support his theories are distributed among a number of works, it is probably not out of place to provide a summary of his views on these matters.

When considering all of his writings on Napoleonic tactics, it is evident that the great historian felt French tactics were the more straightforward and, once established by the mid-1790s, displayed relatively little variation and underwent little subsequent development. Oman minimised the difference, for example, between the way the French generals handled their troops in Spain and Portugal and the methods used by the Emperor several years previously.[1] The French generally preferred to assume an offensive role. The preponderance of the attacking force would be directed at one or more key points along the defending line, while the remainder of the troops would be spread out along the position to preoccupy or hold down those defenders not directly attacked. After penetrating the selected points, the attacking force was to roll up the rest of the defending line. Though the attacking forces might sustain heavy casualties, such losses were well worth it if their objectives were achieved, since a penetration and rolling up of adjoining lines could spell the destruction of the entire defending army.[2]

Usually, the French attack consisted of two waves. In the forefront came a thick cloud of skirmishers which had been sent to draw the enemy's attention and fire. Scattered in a loose formation, they would hide behind whatever cover they could find and, firing individually, pick off men along the defending line. The main body of French troops advancing behind the skirmisher screen was drawn up in 'lines of columns'. Here, a 'line of columns' referred to a series of battalions in column placed laterally along the line of battle. The battalions along this 'line' were positioned so that the space between each battalion and its neighbour was equivalent to the width of the battalion in line. This permitted the battalion to deploy, if forced to do so by circumstances. Sometimes, especially when they had to advance through rough terrain – as through a narrow defile or up a mountain road or pass – the attacking battalions would be placed one behind another. In any case, the skirmishers in front were to draw the fire of the enemy line, so that hopefully the battalions in column would advance without suffering significant casualties.[3] According to Oman, this was the system that had won the French countless victories over the Austrians, Prussians, and Russians, and is that which Wellington in 1808 had referred to as the 'French old style'.[4]

Impressed with the long and near-continuous string of British successes over their Gallic adversaries, Oman next sought to isolate the principles underlying Wellington's tactics. At the heart of his tactical system was the recognition that when called upon to defend, the British infantry had to be sheltered from the inevitable French preliminary effort to harass, disrupt, and injure the defending line which, in the Peninsula, usually meant an attack by a company or so of skirmishers. To neutralise these initial French efforts, Wellington generally employed three separate precautions. To prevent the enemy from working his way around and attacking the weakest part of the line, *ie* its flanks, both ends of the line were – to use the military parlance of the time – to be properly 'appuyed' (anchored). This was usually accomplished by extending the line to some natural obstacle or strong point, such as a river or marsh in the former case and a village or town in the latter. Of course, sometimes it was necessary to fight when such convenient boundaries were not to be had. Then it became necessary to anchor the end of the line with artillery or cavalry. This was a standard precaution, prescribed by almost every treatise on the military art at least as far back as the late-sixteenth century.

Wellington also took steps to ensure that the men along the line were never needlessly exposed to either small arms or artillery fire before it was time for them to enter the action. Wherever possible, the line was masked behind available cover until, at the critical moment, the commander was finally ready to order the infantry to stand up and advance. Hedges, walls, or a convenient undulation of the ground were to be exploited. Most frequently, however, Wellington exploited the rough Spanish and Portuguese terrain and hid his infantry behind a crest running parallel to the line of battle.[5] Thus safe from the fire of enemy skirmishers and artillery, the British troops stood, lay down, or crouched, until they received the order to advance.

However, it was not enough to anchor the line and initially hide most of the defenders behind protective or covering terrain. Adequate countermeasures had to be taken to neutralise the French skirmishers. Wellington's solution was to send out skirmishers of his own, who would not only contest their opponent's advance but force the opposing commander to send out ever-increasing numbers of skirmishers or, even better, force the men in the French columns to fight the defending screen of skirmishers.[6]

Although Oman recognised the value in Wellington's methods, he also believed that the long continuum of British successes in the Peninsula, and later at Waterloo, was attributable to more basic underlying tactical phenomena – the intrinsic differences between the basic formations employed by the two armies. Specifically, this was what Oman considered to be the intrinsic advantage of the British two-rank line as against the 'heavy and inefficient' columns so frequently relied upon by their French adversaries. This by itself certainly wasn't an original observation, and Oman began his discussion of tactical issues in both his *Wellington's Army* and *Studies in the Napoleonic Wars* with the same assertion: 'Every student who takes a serious interest in military history is aware that, in a general way, the victories of Wellington over his French adversaries were due to skilful use of the two-deep British line against the massive column, which had become the usual formation for a French army acting on the offensive.'[7]

Since the introduction of firearms, all tactical doctrine could be divided into two general approaches, according to the role of firepower during the assault. One school favoured the use of firepower and advocated attacking only after the defender was sufficiently weakened by the resulting casualties. The Dutch, the Prussians under Frederick William, and some English tacticians such as Colonel Humphrey Bland belonged squarely in this camp. The opposing school continued to rely upon cold steel and the threat of hand-to-hand fighting, *ie* quick determined charges with lowered bayonet. The French and Bavarians, as well as the Swedes under Charles XII and the Prussians during the first part of Frederick the Great's reign, were all proponents of this tactical approach.

Based on his writings, it is fair to say that Oman appears to have been a more ardent advocate of firepower than most of those in the British army he spent his adult life describing. Oman reasoned that

BATTLE OF BUSSACO Sep.27th 1810

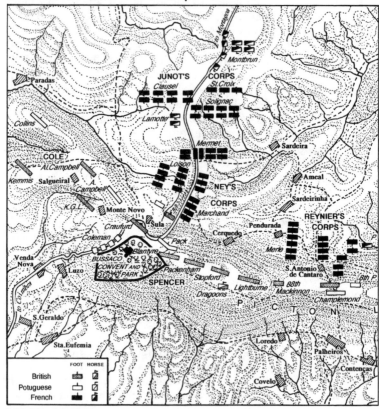

B.V.Darbishire, Oxford, 1907

the effectiveness of the infantrymen's firearms demanded the use of long thin lines where every soldier's musket could be brought to bear. According to him, it was the French failure to adhere to this most fundamental principle of warfare during the age of ranged weapons that was the cause of the repeated French misfortunes. Unlike their continental allies, who chose to await the oncoming rush of French masses in the open, and were weakened by French skirmishers, the British infantry – safely ensconced behind a reverse slope and possessing greater determination – remained undaunted, and invariably stood up to the dense French masses. When the French columns had advanced to close quarters the British line stood up and delivered a murderous fire. In this mutual exchange, the long line of British defenders invariably enjoyed a tremendous advantage over attackers in their relatively narrow columns. Subjected to a numerically superior fire delivered at close range, the entire front of each column was annihilated. With its first ranks literally knocked down, the column and the attack ground to a sudden halt. In such cases, the French regimental commander and his subordinates would order their men to deploy quickly into line to try to increase the volume of fire that could be hurled at their tormentors. However, the close range ensured that most shots found their mark and many of the men were shot down as they tried to run out of the column and into the line to be formed. Those that survived returned to the momentary safety at the back of the column and the formation degenerated into a quivering, confused mass; and within moments the inevitable happened, and those of its men still standing fled precipitately to the rear, ending any hope of victory.[8]

Oman was convinced that this outcome was the only one possible whenever French columns encountered a thin British line; the inevitable result of an enormous discrepancy between the firepower delivered by the British two-rank line and that which could be generated by the deep, narrow French columns. Pointing out that everyone in the first two ranks of any formation could get off an unobstructed fire, Oman reasoned that the two-rank line was the only formation then in use which was 100 per cent effective when delivering fire. A column was a very much less efficient vehicle in this regard. Though the rear ranks provided the front ranks with 'moral support', and impressed the enemy with a 'sense of the solidity and inexorable strength of the approaching mass', none of the infantry in the rear ranks meaningfully contributed to the firefight. Not able to see the enemy, the men in the third and fourth ranks, etc, were unable to properly level their muskets and thus represented 'lost weapons'.[9]

Following this line of reasoning meticulously and literally, Oman argued that the effectiveness of any formation was proportional to the number of men in its ranks who could fire conveniently at a given moment. He defined this latter as the men in the first two ranks of any formation. Typically, French columns of attack were either drawn up by company, where one company was placed immediately behind the one in front, or by division. In the latter case, before 1808 the column was made up of four tiers, each two companies wide; but after the reorganisation of 1808 the same column consisted of three tiers. This meant that during the Peninsular War, only 132 men in a French battalion drawn up in column by companies would be able to fire, while the other 468 men behind them could not. In a British battalion of the same size, drawn up in a two-rank line, all 600 men could fire, and thus from a firepower point of view were 100 per cent effective. Convinced that British firepower was five times more effective than its French counterpart, Oman asked rhetorically: 'How could it be expected that the column would prevail? Effective against an enemy who allowed himself to be cowed and beaten by the sight of the formidable mass, it was helpless against steady troops, who stood their ground and emptied their muskets, as fast as they could load, into a mark which it was impossible to miss.'[10]

If one accepts the legitimacy of this type of 'mathematical' analysis of firepower, even the *ordre mixte* ('mixed order') was discernibly inferior to line in this regard. Three French battalions, each of 900 men, allowed no more than 720 infantrymen to fire when drawn up in *ordre mixte*. Although this was certainly a great improvement over the paltry 180 men able to use their weapons if the three battalions remained in column, it was still dramatically less than the 2700 muskets that could be brought to bear by an equivalent number of British infantrymen.[11]

Oman's belief in the superiority of the thin British line over dense attack columns and the inevitable success of British infantry, if properly led and positioned, was based, in turn, upon his conviction that firepower played the dominant role during the critical crisis of battle, *ie* when the attackers had approached to within 100 yards of the defenders. Although recognising that morale did come into play during the heat of the battle, in Sir Charles' view it was subservient to, and stemmed from, more fundamental issues such as the nature of the formation that was adopted and its firepower capabilities. The confidence of the British soldier arose from his awareness that he was well led and, given the superiority of British tactical practices over those of the French, that he could expect to be victorious. Oman felt that morale considerations at the critical moment would work against the French. Sensing the disparity between the fire received and that returned, the attackers would quickly despair. Then, panic and its companion, rout, were just a few moments away, and defeat was thus certain.

Analysis applied to battle-studies

Combining lucid analysis with compelling narrative, Oman's works enjoyed both popular and critical acclaim at the time, and interest in the *History of the Peninsular War* has undergone a recent revival as a result of two reprints. Even today, almost a hundred years after Oman began his writing career, his works are still widely consulted by those interested in the British Army during the Napoleonic Wars and the Peninsular campaigns. The measure of Oman's true impact on military historiography, however, is not measured by the number of works he authored, or even by the size of his readership. Rather, his lasting influence is more accurately demonstrated by the extent to which he has influenced succeeding generations of English-speaking military historians, both in Great Britain and abroad. The majority of British and a great many American military historians writing about either the Peninsular Wars or the British Army have used Oman's analysis as a convenient starting point for their own work. This is as true for generalised works that deal with large time-frames as it is for specialised works focusing on the 1808-14 campaigns in Spain. R.E. Dupuy and T.N. Dupuy's *The Encyclopedia of Military History* provides an excellent example of the former. Thus when called upon to summarise the difference between British and French fighting methods during the Napoleonic period, the synopsis of the 'French Infantry Column' and 'The English Line' by the Dupuys regurgitates Oman's views on the superiority of the line's fire.[12] Michael Glover, a popular historian who wrote several books on the British effort in the Peninsula, was also clearly influenced by Sir Charles' tactical analyses. In his *Wellington's Army in the Peninsula 1808-1814*, a work with almost the same title as Oman's work on the same subject, Glover devoted a chapter to the British infantryman. Called upon to explain their repeated success over their French counterparts, Glover essentially repeated the same mathematical analysis proffered by Oman sixty years earlier, *ie* the firepower from a long British two-rank line would necessarily overpower that fired from the first two ranks of the one or two companies at the head of an advancing French column.[13]

This trend continued unabated well into the 1980s, and it could be argued that the 1960s and 1970s represented the high point of Oman's impact on British military historiography. The author's attribution of near continual British success to the 'intrinsic' qualities of the formations they employed, and the attempt to quantify these capabilities in precise mathematical terms, captured the imagination of an entire new generation of historians and enthusiasts. One such writer was Jac Weller, whose own works on the British army and the Peninsular War appeared during this time. Seeking to explain the preponderance of British victories, like so many before him, Weller evoked Oman's concept of the superior fire capabilities of the British two-rank line, the comparative frontages of each formation, and the number of muskets that could be brought to bear in each case.

Weller's analysis, however, added a new parameter to the analysis – rate of fire. Oman had sought only to quantify the number of muskets that could fire effectively on each side. Though he did suggest that, when afforded the opportunity, the British infantry fired quickly and continuously, his description of this aspect of the firefight was couched in loose, ambiguous language. In his *Wellington's Army*, for example, he opined that the British infantry 'stood their grounds and emptied their muskets, as fast as they could load, into a mark which it was impossible to miss.'[14] Weller quantified the amount of shots that the British hurled at their French opponents. Explaining the reasons for the destruction of Thomières' column at Vimeiro, Weller explained that after opening fire when the French columns were still 100 yards distant, they maintained this volley fire 'regularly at 15 second intervals as the range gradually shortened.' Continuing on, very much in Oman's style, Weller theorised that the British victory was inevitable, their 1200 muskets completely overpowering the 200 that could be used by the large French column.[15]

The implications of Weller's seemingly minor addition to Oman's analysis of line versus column capabilities would be far-reaching, and probably exceeded that author's expectations. The rate of fire when combined with the number of men involved in a firefight yields the total number of shots fired. Of course, historians have long recognised that most of the musket balls harmlessly overshot their intended targets or if fired too low were buried in the ground in front. It wouldn't require much of an intellectual leap for someone interested in the microdynamics of a Napoleonic firefight to try to establish the effectiveness of musket fire, at various ranges and at different key stages of an exchange of musketry.

This was exactly the contribution of the next author to enter the arena. B.P. Hughes, who ended his military career as a major-general in the Royal Artillery, was perfectly suited to the rigorous analysis of the effectiveness of Napoleonic period weaponry. Displaying a penchant for statistical analysis, in his now classic *Firepower: Weapons Effectiveness on the Battlefield, 1630–1850* (London, 1974), Hughes eagerly waded through battle accounts, not merely to chronicle the unfolding events but to determine the performance of each type of weapon at critical points during the battle. By estimating ranges for each engagement within a chosen battle, applying a rate of fire, and consulting known casualty returns, Hughes sought to establish the percentage of shots that hit their mark in each situation. In this way, Hughes sought not only to establish what weapons had been at work at each stage of the battle but, on a step by step basis, how each was used and the degree to which it contributed to the outcome at each stage.

Around the time Hughes' work was being published, another, unrelated, event would ultimately have a profound impact on the way in which military history would henceforth be studied. This was the advent of sophisticated and frequently complex military historical simulations, which often took the form of table-top miniatures and wargames. The ability to quantify troops' ability to move was, by definition, an important consideration to anyone designing such vehicles, and within a few years a number of writers began to look at the various drill regulations, and applied the prescribed military paces – *eg* seventy-five paces for normal marching speed, 108 when British infantry at the double quick, etc – in an attempt to establish how far each type of fighting force (a British line infantrymen and his French counterpart) could move per time unit.

Although these last efforts might, at first glance, appear to have little to do with Sir Charles' military historical efforts, they are, in fact, a direct descendant of the intellectual tradition founded by the great historian, and are no more than an extension of the same type of conceptual apparatus. Oman, Weller, Hughes, and a sea of wargame designers, including the present author, have all utilised the same basic technique: measure some objectively identifiable parameter, such as the number of available men or the rate at which they were supposed to march; construct an algorithm; and then mathematically apply the value of the selected parameter in an attempt to determine performance.

The example of Bussaco

Oman, Weller, and Hughes did not see their efforts as being purely abstract or theoretical. Rather, they believed they were attempting to reconstruct what had actually occurred on the field of battle. Since Oman's analysis of the differences between French and British tactics and intrinsic capabilities was embedded in his epic *History of the Peninsular War*, the author understandably felt that his theories were substantiated by his descriptions of what had transpired during the major battles. The battle of Bussaco and its five component engagements – each taking place more or less separately from one another – were regarded as particularly illuminating. During the first French assault, for example, the 31st *Légère* regiment, after doggedly continuing its advance in the face of gruelling punishment being dealt out by Arentschildt's artillery, was finally stymied by a withering close-range fire delivered by the British 74th and the Portuguese 21st regiments, positioned on either side of the artillery. Unable to deploy, the attackers were immediately disordered and soon driven back down the hill.

Oman paints a similar picture of the events during the next French attack, by Merle, further to the British left, against the 88th Regiment and the left wing of the 45th Regiment (both in line), and the newly-arrived Portuguese 8th Regiment.[16] Oman then suggests that Foy's third and last stroke, delivered by Reynier's II Corps, fell victim to the same set of forces,[17] as did Loison's attack upon Craufurd,[18] and Marchand's upon Pack.[19] In the course of these examples Oman tends to downplay the importance of artillery fire – against the 31st *Légère* – and of the bayonet charge – by the 88th against Merle, by Leith against Foy, by Craufurd against Loison, and by Pack against Marchand. However, in the weeks and years following the battle, controversy gradually developed, particularly regarding the exact role played by the Portuguese 8th Regiment, and by Generals Picton and Leith, during the repulse of Foy. These debates generated a number of testimonials, letters, and memoirs that might otherwise have gone unrecorded. As a result, it is now possible to draw upon these first-hand accounts and assemble a much more detailed picture of the critical points of the battle than that produced by historians at the turn of the century.

The defeat of the first and last French attacks during the battle – that is, those made by the 31st *Légère* regiment and, much later, Marchand's Division – most accurately conform to Oman's model of British versus French tactical capabilities. And, though one can turn up the degree of magnification, Oman's account of these two actions is shown to be fairly accurate. However, when one assembles a more detailed account of the other actions during the battle, his accounts of the attacks conducted by Merle, Foy, and Loison become subject to question:

Merle's attack

Just as the remnants of the 31st *Légère* were struggling to extricate themselves from the destruction caused by Arentschildt's guns and their infantry pursuers, Merle advanced his Division – apparently formed in two close columns – up the hillside between the main body of Picton's and Lightbourne's Divisions, occupied by just the 88th Regiment (as an afterthought the night before). Merle's force worked its way unopposed to within about seventy yards of two artillery pieces on a knoll. The French columns, some of Surrat's 36th *Ligne*, managed to come within ten to twenty paces of the guns, but were repelled by a few hastily delivered rounds: they swerved to their left and started to march parallel to the crest. The few companies of British skirmishers were soon driven back by sheer weight of numbers, and the French skirmishers quickly gained possession of two or three rocky areas on the plateau. However, additional Anglo-Portuguese forces came down from the main crest to oppose them. The light companies from the 74th and 88th

Regiments were rallied and brought back to within sixty yards of the French in the right-hand group of rocks. A few moments later they charged the French skirmishers and, after some desperate hand-to-hand fighting, regained control of this area. Three other companies from the 88th performed a similar feat and repelled the French skirmishers from the left-hand collection of rocks. Exhausted after their long climb up the hillside, the main body of the attackers were momentarily forced to stop in order to regroup. The Portuguese 8th Regiment, meanwhile, came up a little further along the ridge, managed to deploy, and started to deliver a 'rolling fire' against the front of Graindorge's 4th Légère. Wallace's 88th first retired a short way upon a pre-arranged order, then advanced at the double quick from the left while a wing of the 45th quickly moved in from the British right. Together they formed a single line. Just as the 36th *Ligne* readied itself to attack, Wallace led his small command diagonally across the plateau towards the disordered French flank, now suffering from effective musket and artillery fire from both front and flank.[20] Immediately upon closing, Wallace ordered a bayonet charge. The result was no longer in question, and the leading French battalion was repulsed and forced back down the hill. The 4th and then the 2nd *Légère* regiments were overrun, after which the whole mass crumbled, signifying the complete defeat of Merle's attack. Rather than giving the usual hurrah, the British troops had remained silent in their attack and a general sobriety was noticeable, which according to one historian was indicative of 'much earnestness of purpose.'[21] Not only, in this case, was the French defeat inflicted by a determined British bayonet charge, but the British officer leading the charge had purposely caused his men to initially retreat to a specific point. Once there, they suddenly turned about and the French, having thought themselves victorious, were caught completely off guard and easily overthrown.

Foy's attack

Reynier now ordered Foy's brigade to begin its offensive immediately. Foy led his seven battalions towards the first and lowest hilltop on the right of the San Antonio pass on their way up the imposing hillside, working their way as fast as possible over the heather and patches of stones. Initially, the hilltop was defended by the right wing of the 45th Regiment led by Colonel Meade and the Portuguese 8th Regiment, which had already played a role in Merle's discomfiture. These were soon reinforced by a battalion from the Portuguese 9th Regiment sent from Champlemond's brigade, and the Thomar militia. Wellington had also ordered Leith, if he perceived no threat to his immediate front, to shift some of his 5th Division towards Picton's position by means of a country road running along the crest, while Hill was to occupy part of the vacated ground. Leith arrived with Spry's Portuguese brigade at the head of his column, followed by the two battalions of the Lusitanian legion, one of Dickson's Portuguese batteries, and Barnes' British brigade in the rear. The Portuguese battery was rushed up to Arentschildt's, which, running out of ammunition, had begun to slacken its fire. Meanwhile Spry and the Lusitanian legion were positioned to their rear near the country road, while Barnes continued to move towards the right. Picton asked Leith to assist in the defence against Foy's assault on his left, which every moment was becoming more dangerous. The French columns were overpowering the right wing of the 45th and the three Portuguese battalions by a 'destructive fire'. The Thomar militia fled towards the rear, while the 8th Portuguese fell back in disorder.

Fortunately, just as the leading French battalions gained the ridge, Barnes reached the threatened point. The smoke from the continuous firing initially hindered the British commanders from discerning the enemy's position on the ridge. As the smoke cleared, the French were found to have gained the high rocky ground and their officers were desperately trying to redress the dense formations, which had become disordered by the climb and the firing. The successive French columns were in echelon, thus their fire was directed diagonally against the left battalion of the Portuguese 8th and 9th British Foot regiments. Severely hard-pressed, both of these started to retire in increasing disorder, leaving Foy's leading elements in possession of the rocky eminence.[22] It was at this moment that Leith and his forces came up, but there are conflicting accounts of what happened next. In his 10 November report to Wellington, Leith claimed that after quickly deploying into line, the 9th British Foot charged forward without firing a shot. Intimidated by the bold show of force, Foy's men were precipitately thrown back down the hill. According to Leith's official account, only after the French attackers turned their backs to flee did the 9th open an extremely destructive fire.[23] Captain Carr Gomm would provide a slightly different account in a letter of the same day to his brother, Major Henry Gomm, which explained that the impassable rocky terrain had prevented the 9th from moving directly towards the French column. Instead, it had to march along the latter's flank until a passage could be found. Finding an opening, a mere ten paces from the enemy, it quickly wheeled into line. Both sides then delivered a single volley simultaneously. The 9th, however, was immediately ordered to charge, and it was this action that crushed French resistance.[24] In his *A Narrative of the Peninsular War*, Andrew Leith-Hay insists that the musket fire from the 9th began while both sides were still separated by 100 yards.[25]

It is one of the testimonials provoked by controversy over this action, written in Portsmouth on 6 July 1848, that best corroborates Leith's account. Lieutenant White was adjutant of the 74th Regiment, which at the time of the 9th's advance was positioned slightly in

front and to the right of the latter's position. Stationed on the left of
the rear rank, White wondered if any of the defenders would be
brought up to the crest in time to prevent Foy's column from rolling
up the 74th. Anxiously turning around, he noticed Barnes' brigade
advancing at the double quick along the communications road
almost at the last moment. The first regiment in the column of route
'wheeled round in close column on our left meeting the head of a
mass of the French in close contact, who were advancing up the hill
and likely to turn our left. This contact was immediate, and the hill so
steep, that the brigade of the 5th Division had not the time to deploy,
but literally ran down the enemy in close column, or nearly so'.[26]
White is surely incorrect to state that the 9th attacked in close
column, although his error is natural in view of the chaos then
erupting around him. His regiment at this point was still firing at
some of the French to its front, so his attention must have been
divided and his ears deafened by the rattle of musketry that
surrounded him. Not having seen the 9th form line (almost instantly
by a series of simultaneous quarter-wheels by section, which took
only a few seconds), he naturally assumed they attacked in column.
Two other eyewitnesses assure us that the 9th did indeed wheel into
line and delivered a volley before charging – the then Major-General
Sir John Cameron, writing to Napier in August 1834,[27] and Taylor, an
officer with the 9th, in other letters to Napier.[28]

The next battalion in the column, the 38th, was directed to work
its way between the French battalions and the reverse slope to their
rear. This proved impossible, however, as the ground in this area was
very steep and covered with huge boulders. Returning, it fell into
line on the right of the 9th Regiment. As it turned out, this proved to
be a needless precaution. Following Leith's lead, the 9th marched
diagonally across the plateau and gained the flank of the leading
French column. Delivering a volley at 100 yards, it continued its
forward motion, periodically firing a few volleys as it advanced. The
French were noticeably chagrined and failed to give back as much as
they received. When twenty yards from the French, Leith waved his
plumed hat, and the 9th lowered its bayonets and charged. The head
of the French column, threatened in several directions, now started
to fall back to its right. Foy desperately made every effort to rally his
men and get them to deploy into line, but it was useless. The 17th
and 70th *Ligne* regiments ran back down the hill in total confusion,
with the British pursuers close on their heels. The pursuit only let up
half-way down the hill when French artillery fire discouraged the
British from following any further.

Loison's attack

On the French right, Masséna had ordered Ney's VI Corps to attack
as soon as Reynier's leading elements had gained the crest on the

side of the San Antonio de Cantaro pass. Mist had obscured Merle's and then Foy's progress to those left in the valley below. When this finally dissipated, Ney could see Merle's large column established on the crest, and, conforming to the letter of Masséna's instructions, he immediately ordered two of his Divisions forward on either side of the Coimbra road. Loison's Division on the right of the road started off a few minutes before Marchand's Division on the left. Simon's and Ferrey's brigades, each of six battalions in closed columns, advanced side by side up the gentle slope towards Sulla village. Simon's brigade on the right was led by the 26th *Ligne*; Ferrey's on the left by the 66th *Ligne*, the whole preceded by a large 'chain of *tirailleurs*'. On the British side, Pack had dispersed all of the 4th *Caçadores* as skirmishers along the hillside below his portion of the defending line, while Craufurd had similarly thrown many of the 95th Rifles and over 600 more from the 3rd *Caçadores* into the woods around Sulla. The main Anglo-Portuguese line, however, lay hidden a few feet on the other side of the crest. It consisted of the 43rd and 52nd regiments, reinforced by the remainder of 95th Rifles on the southern flank, and one or more Portuguese regiments.[29]

The British skirmishers outnumbered their French counterparts before they reached Sulla, so Loison had to use entire battalions to push back the British screen. After a struggle, the *Caçadores* and Rifles were finally driven back from the village; but as the French columns entered it they were immediately subjected to a heavy artillery fire from Ross' and Cleeve's batteries above, which caused great carnage.[30] Loison ordered his brigadiers to hasten the assault, and directed them towards Ross' guns and a nearby windmill. But the slope had now become much steeper and the French found it increasingly difficult to advance. They also ran into the next wave of British skirmishers. Despite these difficulties the attackers pressed on, and, pushing back the British skirmishers, made their way to the crest of the hill. The 26th *Ligne* at the front appears to have stuck to the rough country road, while Ferrey's brigade behind moved slightly to the left at the northern edge of the ravine.[31] The British skirmishers, meanwhile, fell back before them, running up the hill and through the still hidden main line of defence. When the advancing French column arrived at a point about thirty yards from the defending line, it stopped for a few moments. It is disputed whether this was simply to regain their order and breath, or because they had unexpectedly encountered a steep rock incline almost immediately below the defending line. Whichever it was, just as the French column was about to run over the last twenty yards and take the guns Craufurd waved his hat and, as tradition has it, called out 'now 52nd, revenge the death of Sir John Moore.' There has always been a considerable difference of opinion about Craufurd's subsequent orders and what happened next.

In a letter to the Earl of Liverpool written shortly after the battle, Wellington explained simply that as the French reached the top of the hill they were repulsed by bayonet charges delivered by the 43rd, 52nd and 95th regiments and the Portuguese 3rd *Caçadores*.[32] A number of other accounts refer to the 1800 men along the defending line standing up and pouring a single, extremely short-ranged, and hence deadly, volley into the faces of the French before the charge. Both Oman and Chambers, however, felt that British firepower played a greater role in this engagement than has been implied by the above descriptions. According to these authors, Craufurd ordered the British line to stand up and advance a few yards to the crest of the hill, wheeling inwards to envelope the head of the advancing French column. In Chambers' account of the battle, Craufurd's Division was able to let off three destructive volleys before the French could close.[33] Oman, on the other hand, fails to mention a bayonet charge, and claims the first fire was delivered at ten paces, and completely flattened the front third of the battalion. The remainder, stunned by the sudden destruction of their comrades, remained motionless as Major Arbuthnot wheeled in the left-hand three companies of the 52nd while Lloyd wheeled an equivalent portion of the 43rd in the same way upon the right of the line, repelling the French by a 'semicircle of fire'.[34]

Just as in the final moment of Merle's assault, the picture was doubtless more complicated than these accounts suggest. The defenders were not locked into a single, uniform activity, but variations existed from battalion to battalion, or group to group. George Napier, brother to the famous historian, would later recollect in his autobiography the experience of one of the flank companies of the 52nd Regiment, which counter-attacked in column but was shot down by the French.[35] Such an account is incompatible with Oman's narrative that is partly based upon it, for Napier's charge was delivered against the 'head of the French column', which according to Oman had been totally wiped out by the first volley. Moreover, Napier and his men would not have even considered moving forward if everyone else was busy firing as fast as possible at the French column, since that would have put them in the killing zone of musket fire delivered by their own side. George Napier's recollections, incidentally, are confirmed by the regimental history of the 52nd, which tells of the bold attack made by a Captain William Jones, a 'fiery Welshman', who killed a French *chef de bataillon* with a single stroke of his sword.[36] This account also tells how during the final moments a French column tried vainly to deploy into line.

Oman's model versus historical examples

Of the five separate engagements that together make up the battle of Bussaco, the first and last – *ie* the attack by the 31st *Légère* and that by Marchand's forces – are the ones that most closely fit Oman's model. British successes elsewhere on the battlefield, however, were the result of a much more intricate set of forces than that suggested by Oman's analysis. Merle's columns, for example, were so pestered by allied artillery as they made their way up the hillside that they had to turn sharply to their left to avoid further punishment. True, they were eventually surrounded by Anglo-Portuguese forces as they neared the crest. However, it wasn't so much a case of a lengthy line overpowering a narrower formation unable to return the fire, as it was of defenders positioned on higher and more favourable ground being able to exploit the contours of the ravine, while the attacking formations, confined by the terrain, were thus caught in a trap or 'box canyon'. Moreover the defenders' fire, rather than coming simply from a linear formation, was the product of skirmishers on the flank and artillery firing upon the new rear of the attacking columns, as well as two distinct lines to the front and side of the attackers. It was a highly chaotic affair that saw the French skirmishers physically thrown back off both groups of rocks after a hand-to-hand struggle. The *coup de grâce*, at least for Sarrut's column, was delivered at the critical moment by Wallace's forceful bayonet charge, before much physical damage had been caused by allied musketry fire.

British firepower played even less of a role in the discomfiture of Foy, and it was the French, rather than the British, who impressed observers with their firepower at this point. Some of Foy's columns appear to have deployed and driven back the first defenders they encountered with several well-placed volleys. Once again, the issue was decided by a vigorous bayonet charge, well before the French columns had suffered significant casualties, the most trustworthy witnesses claiming that only a single volley was delivered before the charge. Contrary to Oman's suggestion that the French began to retire before the charge commenced, and that the bayonet charge was therefore superfluous, witnesses assure us that their precipitate backward motion only started after the charge began. Loison's defeat is clearly attributable to a similar set of dynamics. Firstly, we know that once again Anglo-Portuguese artillery, and not just the large numbers of skirmishers, played an important role in undermining the attacker's equilibrium. The main body of evidence suggests that the bayonet charge once again served as the final *coup de grâce*, and not merely as some sort of straw to push over an already teetering opponent. Thus, after a more detailed look at the five separate actions that occurred during the battle of Bussaco, defensive artillery is seen to have played a crucial role in three cases, while the attack was finally repelled by an adroitly delivered bayonet charge in another three. Clearly, Oman's model both of how the two contending armies fought, and the forces working to ensure British success, is mono-dimensional. Not only does it fail to account for the great variations that occurred from attack to attack, but it ignores the effectiveness of several key tactical elements, such as the use of artillery and the bayonet charge.

At the beginning of his own work on Bussaco, Lieutenant-Colonel George Chambers provided his own model of the complex interplay of British infantry tactics, one that, though obviously building upon Oman's, takes into account more of the tactical forces that were at work. Chambers agreed with Oman that, for the first time, the British began to throw out a large number of skirmishers, which were generally sufficient to counteract their French counterparts, and occasionally were numerous enough to even impede the main assault, such as during Loison's assault of Craufurd's position. Well-placed artillery was also trained on critical points through which the enemy would have to pass in order to attack that position. If possible, once the enemy had committed himself to the attack the artillery was re-positioned, or reinforcements moved in, to enfilade the attacking columns with canister or roundshot or both. Meanwhile, the main body of defending infantry was held in reserve behind available blocking terrain. This not only drastically reduced casualties while waiting for the enemy to close, but, since the enemy was usually unaware of these troops, introduced a valuable element of surprise. Once the enemy had closed to effective musketry range, the defenders would appear and – extended along a broader line – deliver a more effective fire. It was this combination of surprise and a brief, though highly effective, fire which almost invariably prevented the French columns from employing the appropriate response, *ie* themselves deploying into line. Lastly, as soon as the attackers showed the first sign of disorder, the defenders would immediately rush in with a determined bayonet charge. At first glance Chambers' model appears to be simply the addition of two new elements: the use of artillery during the early phases of the French assault, and the reliance upon a bayonet charge at the climax of the fighting. However, it also implies a more synergistic interplay of forces between the constituent tactical elements, which were not individually strong. For example, defensive artillery by itself was rarely capable of stopping a French attack, while a bayonet charge delivered before the attacking formations had been sufficiently disordered would have been doomed to failure.

Although Chambers' tactical model of 1910 is more comprehensive than that suggested eight years earlier by Oman, both analysts failed to identify one other tactical or grand tactical element that characterises almost all of Wellington's military efforts. This was his careful use of terrain to channel the attacking forces so that they had no recourse but to limit their assault to several easily identifiable, and hence more readily defensible, positions. Once again, Bussaco provides a perfect example of this technique. The rough terrain over which the French had to slowly make their way not only afforded the defenders ample time to reinforce a threatened position, but also made it impossible for any type of meaningful co-ordination of the attacking forces. The French assault, which otherwise might have been a massive affair that more thoroughly strained the defenders' capabilities, was reduced to a series of less threatening piecemeal attacks.

Oman's views on bayonet fighting

Of the various tactical elements utilised by Wellington, one in particular – the use of the bayonet – warrants further consideration. Since the introduction in modern times of rapid-fire weaponry, there has been a marked tendency not only to view this weapon as 'primitive', but to forget that it ever played a vital role on the European battlefield. Moreover, contrary to modern-day expectations, the effective use of this weapon was, in turn, dependent upon a highly sophisticated orchestration of micro-tactical elements that, unfortunately, have rarely been adequately considered. Such a tendency is particularly noticeable in Oman's works, where the bayonet is portrayed as playing only a minor role on the Napoleonic battlefield. His only mention of the weapon occurs in the tactical analysis provided in his *History of the Peninsular War*. His later writings make no mention of how the bayonet was used. Forced to acknowledge that contemporary observers often mentioned 'bayonet charges', Oman felt that the term was misleading. Although acknowledging that there had been notable occasions where bayonet fighting did occur in villages and other enclosed terrain, he pointed out that in open terrain it was extremely rare for opposing troops to come into physical contact and engage in hand-to-hand combat. In order to account for the references to bayonet charges, especially in French narratives, Oman argued that in the case of French infantry the term simply referred to the French advance up to the defending line 'without firing'. When applied to the British he believed it described a methodical advance with 'frequent volleys or independent file-firing.'[37]

This view of the bayonet and its efficacy during combat was typical of most military historians at the turn of the twentieth century. Impressed with the rapid-fire weapons then being introduced, most exhibited a noticeable preoccupation with such relatively new notions as 'firepower' and 'rate of fire'. Not surprisingly, edged weapons of any sort struck a discordant note with these newly emerging sensibilities and were dismissed out-of-hand as ineffective and hopelessly archaic. After examining casualty lists and finding how few wounds were inflicted by cold steel, historians chronicling the American Civil War echoed these sentiments. Throughout the writings on both sides of the Atlantic, however, there is an obvious confusion between the idea of 'bayonet fighting' and 'bayonet charges'. A bayonet *fight* involves both sides advancing to contact and, confronting one another face-to-face, the action then devolves into a confused mêlée in which individuals attempt to stab their opponents by lunging with their bayonets, or crack their skulls with the butts of their muskets or rifles. A bayonet *charge*, on the other hand, is a formal, pre-defined tactic whereby the men of one side or the other 'charge bayonets', that is to say, extend their muskets in front of them and rush in upon the enemy threatening to 'run in' whoever contemplates standing up to them.

Many historians, especially those writing after the 1880s, use the two terms indiscriminately and interchangeably, and Oman was also guilty of this error. He dismissed the bayonet's effectiveness, arguing that bayonet-fighting rarely occurred on open ground. In this he was quite correct. After the Napoleonic Wars, French veterans would often claim that the battle of Amstetten was the only instance where both sides actually fought with the bayonet in open terrain.[38] Military historians studying eighteenth-century warfare tell us that the battle of Moys provides the single example during the preceding period.[39] By contrast, bayonet charges, even by British infantry, were commonplace, even in clear, unobstructed terrain. A well-timed bayonet charge, delivered at close range and immediately after a devastating volley, repeatedly proved to be one of the most effective defensive tactics at Bussaco. This reliance upon the bayonet during the critical moment was certainly nothing new to British infantry. The same tactics had been used with equal effect several years previously during the battle of Vimeiro (21 August 1808), where the 50th Regiment delivered a volley and then charged successfully against a French force that had already been softened up by artillery and skirmishers,[40] and we know that several other regiments defeated attacking French columns with similar tactics elsewhere on the same battlefield. Dr Neale, a physician, tells us that the French columns which assaulted the right centre of the British line 'were checked by the bayonets' of the 92nd Regiment and 2nd battalion of the 52nd.[41] Meanwhile, the French attacking the British left (led by generals Ferguson and Nightingale) were discomfited by several determined bayonet charges. Posterity is indebted to an anonymous soldier in the 71st Regiment for a detailed description of the latter:

> [We] formed line and lay under cover of a hill for an hour, until they came to us. We gave them one volley and three cheers – three distinct cheers. Then all was silent as death. They came upon us, crying and shouting, to the very point of our bayonets. Our awful silence and determined advance they could not stand. They put about and fled without much resistance.[42]

All of the above accounts explicitly state that the decisive action took the form of a determined bayonet charge rather than a prolonged fusillade, and there is little in what we are able to learn from the battle of Vimeiro that supports Oman's view of how the British infantry defended itself against the French columns.

Bayonet charges were also frequently used in an offensive capacity. There are numerous accounts of the British infantry running in with lowered bayonets during the last moments of an advance. We learn from Kincaid, for example, that during the action at Vera (1813) his regiment advanced 'quietly and steadily' almost right up to the enemy position without firing a shot. Intimidated, the French fled and it was only then that the British regiment delivered a 'destructive discharge.'[43] At San Christoval (1812), Private Wheeler tells us that the 51st performed an identical accomplishment, albeit at a much faster gait.[44] During the battle of Vitoria (1813), the 88th performed yet another variant of a bayonet charge. After delivering a 'running fire' while still 300 or 400 yards distant, the regiment resumed the advance. After moving fifty yards closer to the enemy, it halted and delivered a second running fire. Then, without a pause, the men cheered and charged up the hill. Caught while reloading, the French panicked and fled.[45] These are but a few of the instances of where British infantry utilised bayonet charges in an attack. Many additional examples can be found by looking through the memoirs of other Peninsular War veterans.

Forced to speculate on the reason for consistent British success during the Peninsular War, General Mitchell, in the 1830s, would conclude that 'a charge of bayonets – a thing that hurt nobody, but was out of the conventional rules of European warfare – invariably put the whole to flight, though generally with what might be deemed a trifling loss. This was the constant tale from Vimeiro to Waterloo, whenever the British were the attacking party.'[46]

Throughout these campaigns, the British infantry would employ the same basic tactics for the defensive: awaiting the enemy's advance until almost the last possible moment, then delivering an overpowering volley or two and rushing in with lowered bayonets before the enemy could recover.

When one thinks of a bayonet charge, it is usual to conjure up images of the participants in the charge yelling and gesticulating wildly. In the case of French infantry charges, this is an accurate description of what generally occurred. The officers would lead the attack and do everything to encourage their troops, such as raising their swords and hats and calling upon their men to follow their example. Every effort was made to work the men up and heighten the ferocity of the first assault. This was done as much to frighten the enemy as it was to innervate those called upon to deliver the charge. James Anton, who served with the 42nd Royal Highlanders, remembers the effect of a charge on its participants:

No movement in the field is made with greater confidence of success than that of the charge; it affords little time for thinking, while it creates a fearless excitement, and tends to give a fresh impulse to the blood of the advancing soldier, rouses his courage, strengthens every nerve, and drowns every feat of danger or of death; thus emboldened amidst shouts that anticipate victory, he rushes on and mingles with the fleeing foe.[47]

There was, however, an unavoidable downside to the French version of the bayonet charge. By unleashing all of the men's emotional energy at the start of the charge, it was impossible to retain an emotional reserve, thus increasing the attackers' vulnerability to a counter-attack. The more fervent the soldier became at the beginning of the attack, the more likely he was to falter if his efforts should prove unsuccessful and a serious check was experienced.

By 1808, the bayonet charge delivered by British infantry relied upon a very different set of psychological microdynamics. Every element in the British bayonet charge was designed to control the men's emotions, in order to maintain an emotional reserve. Rather than trying to work up a frenzy, a strict silence was enforced. In his memoirs, an anonymous Scot described the impact of this silence on the men at the critical moment: 'In our first charge I felt my mind waiver; a breathless sensation came over me. The silence was appalling. I looked alongst the line. It was enough to assure me. The steady, determined scowl of my companions assured my heart and gave me determination. How unlike the noisy advance of the French.'[48]

The British advance, at least in its first stages, was conducted at a slower pace than its French counterpart. In contrast to French practice, most British officers were placed slightly behind the line, both to reduce officer casualties and to prevent stragglers from escaping to the rear. However, occasionally it became necessary to slow down the advance to maintain cohesion, and then the officers would move in front of the line. Of course, it was impossible to maintain such control indefinitely, and the 'British cheer', delivered either at a critical point during the advance or just before the actual charge, was an effective means of dissipating their emotions and anxieties in carefully controlled quantum amounts. The British hurrah or cheer was more controlled than that of their adversaries. Frequently it was a single, short 'huzzah', although it could consist of up to three cheers. An excellent example of the difference between the British cheer and that generally employed by continental armies occurred during an engagement between British and Dutch forces at Blueberg Hill (11 January 1806), in what is today South Africa: 'Sir David Baird ordered the Scotch brigade to charge. They gave three huzzas; the Dutch answered with nine.

Colonel Grant was wounded. As the highlanders moved on he got off his horse but mounted again, and a general burst of applause broke from the Scotch line at his determined gallantry. When they advanced within a hundred yards they fired a volley and rushed on' (successfully).[49]

The success of the British bayonet charge originated at a micro-tactical level. By carefully orchestrating when to cheer and when to keep silent, British officers had – albeit unconsciously – devised a more effective means of managing their men's emotions and fears. The retention of an emotional reservoir which could be unleashed during the final moments of a charge, long after their enemies' emotions had peaked, guaranteed the success of a British attack or defence. The charge, when it finally came, completely transformed the men from faceless, indistinguishable parts of a large formation, into a body of furious, single-minded individuals, determined to kill everyone who stood in their way.

Oman and the background to British tactics

In both *Wellington's Army* and *Studies in the Napoleonic Wars*, Oman suggests – if only by implication – that Wellesley had already devised a means of countering French fighting methods prior to his departure for Portugal, and that the tactical elements involved were his own creation. However, with a single possible exception virtually every tactic utilised by the British in the Peninsula had already been written about and discussed in knowledgeable British military circles. A portion of the tactical doctrine that would be used by Wellington and his officers had, in fact, been laid down many years previously by James Wolfe, while still a lieutenant-colonel. As a result of the apparent success of Prussian infantry with their reliance upon the cadenced manual of arms, the use of 'quick firing' had become popular in most European armies during the late-1740s. However, in his *Instructions for the 20th Regiment* issued at Canterbury on 15 December 1755, Wolfe enjoined his officers to reject the temptation to fire as quickly as possible and explained that 'a cool and well levelled fire, with the pieces carefully loaded, is much more destructive and formidable than the quickest fire in confusion.' Before the action began the officers were to advise their men to aim well to 'destroy their adversaries.' In most cases, Wolfe opined that the battalion would be ordered to deliver a bayonet charge after a few rounds. His regiment, however, was to avoid performing a bayonet charge in the way it was usually conducted at that date. Instead of yelling or crying out, they were to remain completely silent, even if every other regiment along the line was yelling at the top of their voices. Only when ordered to charge were they to give a 'war-like shout', and then immediately rush in with lowered bayonet.[50]

Wolfe was also adamant that his officers should make every effort to secure an advantage in firepower in those instances where the regiment was required to fire. When firing at a smaller enemy battalion, the platoons on each wing were to fire obliquely to bring the greatest number of muskets to bear. If the two battalions were roughly the same frontage, so that oblique fire was not possible, the same effect could be achieved by detaching the grenadiers and the picquet who would work their ways onto the enemy's flanks and rear while the remainder of the battalion charged in front. Wolfe recommended an even more effective means of achieving an advantage in firepower whenever the regiment was attacked by an enemy column. The portion of the regiment directly in front of the advancing enemy column was to reserve its fire, and, if possible, load two or three balls into the musket. As soon as the enemy had closed to twenty yards, these men were to take good aim and then fire. At the same time the platoons to the left and right were to wheel inwards and then, if they had not already fired, discharge their weapons and charge in with the bayonet.[51]

A second possible source of doctrinal inspiration appeared in a periodical entitled the *British Military Library* just a few years before the Peninsular campaigns commenced. First published in October 1798, this journal attempted to provide a forum for serious military scientific analysis and debate. Many of the articles were translations of key excerpts from seminal works such as De Saxe's *Mes Reveries*, Folard's various writings, Warnery's *Remarques sur le militaire des turcs et sur la façon de les combattre*, and so on. Contemporary British and foreign military experts also contributed a number of original articles, including one entitled *On the Defence of Heights by Light Infantry* by an author whose name, unfortunately, has been lost to posterity.

In many respects this article and its theories create a conundrum for those interested in the evolution of British military doctrine and practices. Examining the various measures light infantry should use to defend high ground, the article also briefly discussed the steps regular infantry should take in the same situation. The tactics suggested for the latter were the standard methods used to defend heights by fire, and were essentially those that Wellington would consciously reject. Every effort was to be made to stop the enemy's advance before it reached the summit. To this end, the defending line of troops was to be positioned on the crest of the hill or even the top of the initial slope, rather than the summit. Although the officers were to prevent their men from firing too soon, once the enemy had approached within effective range, they were to order the front rank to kneel, and then fire by either ranks or subdivisions, rather than by battalion (which would have temporarily denuded the entire battalion of fire). It was common knowledge that it was difficult to fire accurately at an enemy on a lower level, since all too often the defenders fired harmlessly over the enemy's heads. To prevent this, the men were instructed to fire at their opponent's feet.[52]

Wellington, of course, refrained from placing his infantry along a hill crest whenever possible, so the above recommendations do not appear to have made any impact on British infantry tactics in practice. However, continuing on with a more detailed discussion of how light infantry were to defend elevated positions, the anonymous author made a number of suggestions that are identical to some of those actually employed during the Peninsular War. The writer again stressed the importance of preventing the enemy from gaining the summit, since once the enemy had gained it, light troops would find it extremely difficult to push them back down the hill. To this end, they were to be placed on the forward slopes and along the crest further up. It was particularly important that the extended line of skirmishers should guard all defiles, ravines, and any other terrain features that might facilitate the enemy's movement up the hillside. A reserve, maintained in a close-order formation (*ie* line or column), was to be kept back on the 'crown of the hill'. The troops on the side of the hill, as well as those along the ridge defending the ravines etc, must from the very beginning of the action:

> dispute every inch of ground with the utmost intrepidity and valour. As their fire constitutes their principal defence, it should not only be kept up with spirit, but also not be thrown away at random, but peculiar attention be paid to its doing due effect. As to the enemy's fire which proceeds from a lower ground, it can hardly for this reason prove very hurtful to your troops, yet they should not neglect to avail themselves of every means which may offer to cover themselves from it, by throwing themselves into hollow ways, and firing out of them, or by taking shelter behind mounds, stone-walls, trees, palings, etc.

Should the enemy still manage to reach the top of the hillside despite all these efforts, the reserves were to be immediately thrown against them. Advancing in formation, these were to withhold their fire and charge with lowered bayonets. Only once the invaders were forcibly driven back were the reserves to deliver a 'well directed' fire. Officers were enjoined, however, not to allow their men to pursue the fleeing enemy.

Like Wolfe, the anonymous author felt that any enemy attack in column offered the defenders an opportunity to exploit a firepower advantage. The troops directly in front of the attacking columns were to keep up a 'brisk fire' while making a 'slow retrograde movement.' Those portions of the line not directly attacked, however, were to 'fall on the flanks of the enemy's column, and endeavour to throw it into confusion.' The reserve, meanwhile, would advance and assault the attacking columns in turn. Unlike regular infantry, which were enjoined not to follow the fleeing attackers, all light infantry except the reserve and those protecting important positions such as ravines, bridges, etc, should be encouraged to pursue them.[53]

Wolfe and the anonymous author suggested a number of tactics that would be practised repeatedly in the Peninsula. As we have seen, the British infantry in a great majority of cases adhered to Wolfe's fire and bayonet doctrine, *ie* they attempted to avoid needless or indecisive firefights that would result in a lengthy exchange where both sides would suffer an equal number of casualties. Firing was carried out with deliberation, and a bayonet charge was almost always ordered after a few volleys. In the Peninsula, seemingly following Wolfe's advice, officers generally controlled their men and prevented them from reaching emotional fever-pitch prematurely; the men's yells were postponed until the critical moment. When attacked by enemy columns the British defenders sometimes wheeled their flank companies inward, as suggested by Wolfe, and at other times ringed the crest line to outflank the French columns, as suggested in *On the Defence of Heights*. In both cases they would fire and then charge. The British were also known to throw in reserves against the French attackers, a tactic that had also been advocated in this article.

The one tactical element - admittedly one of the most fundamental - that neither of these authors discussed was Wellington's practice of hiding or protecting his defending line behind a reverse slope or hill crest. Strictly speaking, this cannot be claimed as Wellington's invention either, since other commanders had periodically followed this practice. French infantry during the battle of Friedland, for example, lay down in the tall grass to escape the effects of Russian artillery, while their adversaries stood erect and absorbed the full punishment of the French artillery.[54] What was distinctive about Wellington's use of the reverse slope tactic, however, was the frequency with which he employed it, and how it was combined with several other compatible practices to produce a set of highly effective defensive tactics.

It may be argued that any similarity between Wellington's defensive tactics and those described by Wolfe and *On the Defence of Heights* is purely coincidental. There is, however, one consideration which renders this unlikely: both works had been widely read. Although Wolfe's instructions had initially been penned solely for the benefit of his own regiment, the fame generated by his heroic death and epic success in the battle of Quebec (1757) led to his orders and papers being collected and published as *Instructions to Young Officers*. This went through several editions in the closing years of the eighteenth century. The

British Military Library, although enjoying a very brief lifespan from October 1798 to March 1801, was also widely distributed. Even if Wellesley had never picked up a copy, it is improbable that an officer rising to prominence among British military circles could remain oblivious to the debates of his peers, some at least of whom would have been sufficiently interested in contemporary military science to read these and other contemporary works.

Oman and the background to French tactics

If Oman had overlooked the full story of the evolution of tactics and fighting methods in the British army, when he attributed all of those employed by British troops to Wellington himself, he held an even more simplistic view of the development of French tactics. Near the beginning of his *History*, in the chapter devoted to a quick study of the tactics used by the combatant armies, Oman described the methods employed by the French as being the same as had been developed in Flanders during the opening campaigns of the French Revolutionary Wars. In order to distract the enemy, thick clouds of *tirailleurs* would precede the main French attack, which typically consisted of one or two lines of battalions in closed column. Screened by the skirmishers, the heavy columns, exposed to fire for only a few moments, would approach the enemy line without taking appreciable losses, and once close, they would be carried through the enemy by a physical and psychological momentum.[55] The more competent among the French officer class would eventually develop a professional finesse which enabled them to modify the 'brutal and unscientific methods of the Jacobin armies.' Henceforth the French would increasingly win by 'intelligent strategy' and 'brilliant manoeuvres', rather than by brute force and reliance upon sheer weight of numbers; but they would still cling to the use of skirmishers followed by close columns.

According to Oman, these were the same methods that would be employed by Napoleon and his armies even during his most successful campaigns. Oman believed that Napoleon had a penchant for the *ordre mixte* – a hybrid formation composed of some battalions in line and others in column – and cited Davout's 'refused' wing at Austerlitz, Masséna's at Wagram, and VI Corps at Waterloo. Realising that a column by itself lacked sufficient firepower to weaken a defending line that was properly positioned and well led, Napoleon once confided to Foy that for an attack in columns to be successful it had to be supported by artillery which would 'prepare the attack', *ie* sufficiently weaken the defending line.[56] Unlike the early campaigns, when entire battalions were thrown out to skirmish *en débandade*, he liked to rely more upon artillery, employing only a company or so of skirmishers in front of each column. This, wrote Oman, led to the practices observed in the Peninsula, where skirmishers were supplied by each battalion's *voltigeur* company.

This highly simplistic view of French tactics during the Revolutionary and Napoleonic period fails to account for either the tactical diversity that had characterised almost all of the campaigns since 1792, or the French army's conscious efforts to respond effectively to the tactics utilised by their various adversaries. Contrary to accepted wisdom, even early Revolutionary armies did not always fight in column. After examining 108 different engagements which took place between 1791 and 1794, Professor John A. Lynn (in his *Bayonets of the Republic*) found that French forces had adopted some variant of line formation on forty-four occasions. In most of these, line was used as a defensive formation, as at Bossu (26 April 1794);[57] but the battle of Fleurus (26 June 1794) provides an example of French infantry fighting in line on a much grander scale, and sometimes for an attack.[58] General Dumouriez, who generally advocated shock tactics, also initially positioned his troops in line; and General Dampierre beat the charge while using this formation.[59] Indeed, primary sources and archival records can reveal very many other examples of the French relying upon a wide range of tactical methods.

Although Oman recognised that from 1794 onward growing professionalism among the French military led to a refinement of tactical and grand tactical methods, his analysis of these is essentially a gross oversimplification which accounts neither for the tactical variety evinced by the French army between 1796 and 1807, nor for certain distinct 'phases' which can be identified during this development. When one takes a closer look at the tactical methods employed by French troops during each of the campaigns of 1796 to 1807, a number of trends or distinguishing characteristics begin to emerge. One sees, for example, an early large-scale use of what today would be called 'combined arms' tactics during Gouvion St Cyr's battle of Biberach (October 1796), where each arm was assigned a specific function and entered the fray at a pre-ordained stage.[60]

Although in many respects this is the beginning of the type of sophisticated grand tactical 'synchronicity' that would later be employed in even more elaborate forms at Austerlitz, Jena, and Auerstädt, French military thinkers resisted the natural inclination to complacency and continued to search for new methods. Given the vagaries of the ever-shifting political landscape, the French would be forced to face a series of opponents between 1796 and 1807. One of the least commented upon, but most remarkable, achievements of the French army during this entire period was its ability to proactively analyse the methods and capabilities of each of these adversaries, and then devise appropriate tactical and grand tactical countermeasures. Thus for the Egyptian campaign of 1798

French military authorities adopted the checkerbord of large, Division-sized squares, with six ranks of infantry on each side and smaller squares protecting the angles, similar to those which the Austrians and Russians had used against Turkish or Mameluke cavalry in similar circumstances.

These lessons were not lost, and French authorities realised that they could devise even more powerful formations to protect infantry against large masses of enemy cavalry. In 1801, the 33rd *Demi Brigade de Ligne*, generally regarded as the most proficient regiment when performing manoeuvres, experimented with a new type of square, the *carré oblique à la ligne de bataille* (square oblique to the line of battle).[61] Marshal Ney also wrote his *Military Instructions for the Troops Composing the Left Corps* at the Camp de Montreuil-sur-Mer in 1804, to address deficiencies of the 1791 infantry regulations, as well as to counterbalance a frequent over-reliance on columnar methods of movement and attack. When the French went to war against the Russians and Austrians late in 1805, one of their concerns was the need once again to protect French infantry against irregular but expert light horsemen, this time in the form of Cossacks. On the one hand the enemy's abundant supply of field-artillery discouraged the use of large static squares, while on the other hand these irregular cavalry were neither considered as much a threat as Turkish horsemen, nor were they available in the same massive numbers. On 26 November (a week before the battle of Austerlitz) Napoleon issued an order to Marshal Soult prescribing the adoption of a new, larger form of *ordre mixte*. The next year (1806) Napoleon declared war on Prussia. French military authorities, still intimidated by the lofty reputation of the Prussian cavalry steeped in the tradition of Seidlitz, Ziethen, and Warnery, etc, felt the need for greater countermeasures. The experiments of the 33rd *Demi Brigade* and its *carré oblique* were resurrected, and it was this very formation that allowed Morand to endure a massive Prussian cavalry assault at Auerstädt.[62]

Conclusion

The preceding discussion has attempted, albeit in a rather circuitous manner, to provide a brief distillation of Oman's views about how the British and French infantry fought during the Peninsular War and the relative merits of line versus column. The result of these and similar analyses forces one to regard Oman's work as a type of 'curate's egg'. In an effort to create a single, simple model that would explain not only the practices employed on each side but also why the British enjoyed such an overwhelming series of successes, Oman produced what must be regarded today as too simplistic a model. Recent studies not only reveal great variation from case to case - eg the artillery might play a prominent role in one instance while a bayonet charge was the decisive factor in another – but there were also many more tactical forces at work than those admitted to in Oman's analysis. Heavily influenced by the then-emerging notions of rapid fire and the physical destruction of an opponent's forces, Oman paid scant attention to the psychological dimensions of conflict and fighting methods. Observing that bayonet fights rarely, if ever, occurred on open ground, he refused to acknowledge that the bayonet's true purpose was to destroy the opponent's will to stand and fight, since, by definition, the more successful this tactic was, the fewer casualties there would be.

When attempting to understand Wellington's tactics, a rather different model must be developed from those already suggested by Oman and Chambers:

- Wellington sought to fight over the most advantageous terrain which would limit the scope of French attacks and channel their direction.
- Wherever possible, preliminary defensive artillery fire would hinder the assault during the early stages.
- Large numbers of skirmishers were thrown out to similarly disorder the advancing formations.
- The main line of defenders was ensconced behind available terrain, frequently a hill crest or reverse slope, not only to confuse the enemy about their whereabouts, but also to minimise casualties.
- By 1808 the British had developed a more effective method of managing their men's emotions during the moments immediately preceding a bayonet charge: the men were kept quiet until allowed one to three well-timed hurrahs.
- As soon as the attackers had advanced to close range, the defending line would stand up and deliver one or several volleys.
- Taking advantage of the resulting confusion, a bayonet charge would deliver the *coup de grâce*.

The debate as to which possessed superior capabilities, line or column, is largely spurious, created by the naïveté of turn-of-the-century historians who were either ignorant of, or eschewed, a more detailed understanding of Napoleonic era fighting methods. From the early eighteenth century onwards every competent officer, on both sides of the English Channel, had known that a line possessed much greater firepower than a column. Looking closely at the individual actions at battles like Bussaco it is incontrovertible that in most cases the French brigade or regimental commanders attempted to form line at the last moment when suddenly confronted by the defenders. Rather than being the product solely of greater infantry firepower, the repeated discomfiture of their assaults was instead the result of a sophisticated orchestration of many tactical elements, where artillery fire, a few effective volleys of musketry, or a well-timed bayonet charge might all play the lead role.

Oman's inability to accurately compare British and French practices during the Peninsular War with those used in earlier campaigns represented a much more serious inadequacy. By today's standards Oman, like most of his contemporaries, possessed but a sketchy understanding of not only how the French had fought during the 1805-7 campaigns – the zenith of French accomplishments during this period – but even of the early Revolutionary campaigns. Recent studies have shown convincingly that French tactical practices during even the earliest of these campaigns were much more variegated than had been previously thought. And, as we have seen, during the period separating the early fighting in Flanders and the commencement of hostilities in the Iberian Peninsula, there were a number of mini-eras, each of which emphasised a slightly different tactical approach. Other recent studies show that by 1809 the allies had gradually started to devise effective tactical countermeasures, increasing their ability to effectively compete against French armies. At the same time, the increasing loss of experienced officers and NCOs due to incessant campaigning gradually caused a corresponding decline in French tactical capabilities. All of these considerations thus undermine the feasibility of comparing French versus British methods during 1809-14 in order to generalise about their capabilities throughout the entire period 1792-1815. In other words, each campaign was much more distinctive than has previously been thought, and correspondingly less can be extrapolated that can automatically be applied to other campaigns without extensive research to verify any suspected commonalties.

It must not be thought, however, that Oman's tactical studies were completely invalid, or that his works no longer have relevance to modern historians and enthusiasts. Oman and his peers, such as Jean Colin, George Chambers, Frank Taylor and others, were writing in a period when their interest in the micro-tactical details of fighting methods during the Napoleonic period had long ceased to be relevant to military scientists and hence to a majority of military historians. Works that had dealt with purely technical areas, such as how to fire artillery, employ skirmishers, or perform all the manoeuvres of the period, had been consigned to dusty shelves labelled 'no longer useful'. Oman and his contemporaries were therefore obliged to begin the long and arduous process of analysing military practices, at least on a tactical level, almost 'from scratch'.

Even if Oman did possess a simplistic view of French and British fighting methods, he still succeeded in making a very important and lasting contribution to military history, that will continue undiminished into the twenty-first century. He and his French rival, Colin, resurrected interest in the detailed examination of how troops actually fought during the Napoleonic period. Hence in the long run the validity of his detailed conclusions about the relative merits of each tactical formation, or the completeness of his model of Wellington's methods, may even be seen as irrelevant. Merely by raising these issues, and stirring the emotion and imagination of his readers (positively or negatively), both he and Colin restored tactical military science to its rightful place within the rigorous study of military history.

Notes

1. Oman, *Studies in the Napoleonic Wars* (London, 1929), p.93. Compare James R. Arnold's commentary on these subjects in chapter 3 above.
2. Oman, *op.cit.* p.89, and *Wellington's Army, 1809-1814* (completed 1912, published London, 1913), p.67.
3. Oman, *History*, vol.I, pp.114-15.
4. *Ibid* pp.114-15.
5. *Ibid* pp.116-17.
6. Oman, *Studies in the Napoleonic Wars*, pp.99, 101. Arthur Harman also discusses the skirmish battle at length in chapter 11 below.
7. Oman, *Wellington's Army*, p.61. The only difference by 1929 is that Oman used 'regular' instead of 'usual' in *Studies in the Napoleonic Wars*, p.82.
8. Oman, *History*, vol.I, pp.114-15.
9. Oman, *Studies in the Napoleonic Wars*, p.82.
10. Oman, *Wellington's Army*, p.89.
11. Oman, *Studies in the Napoleonic Wars*, pp.91-2.
12. R. Ernest Dupuy and Trevor N. Dupuy, *The Encyclopedia of Military History* (2nd edn, New York, 1986), pp.734-5.
13. Michael Glover, *Wellington's Army in the Peninsula 1808-1814* (Newton Abbott, 1977), p.55.
14. Oman, *Wellington's Army*, p.89.
15. Jac Weller, *Wellington in the Peninsula, 1808-1814* (London, 1962), pp.47-8; at Salamanca he laments (p.219) that the 'brave French soldiers were stupidly betrayed by their formation.'
16. Oman, *History*, vol.III, pp.371-2.
17. *Ibid* pp.375-7.
18. *Ibid* pp.380-1.
19. *Ibid* pp.382-3.
20. Lieutenant-Colonel George L. Chambers, *Wellington's Battles Illustrated: Bussaco* (London, 1910), pp.56-61.
21. Lieutenant-Colonel H.F.N. Jourdain and Edward Fraser, *The Connaught Rangers 1st Battalion (formerly 88th Foot)* (London, 1924), p.48, citing the *Record of the 88th*; Cannon, p. 26.
22. Oman, *History*, vol.III, p.374.
23. Donald D. Horward, *The Battle of Bussaco: Masséna versus Wellington* (Tallahassee, 1965), p.110, citing Wellington on 10 November 1810 (from

Supplementary Dispatches of the Duke of Wellington, vol.VI, pp.635–9). See also Chambers, *op.cit.* pp.227–8, *Report of the Position and Movements of Major General Leith's Corps, particularly the British Brigade, during the battle of Bussaco on the 27th of September 1810*, Major-General Leith to Lieutenant-General Viscount Wellington at Camp of Sobral, 10 November 1810.

24. Horward, *op.cit.* p.110, citing Sir William Maynard Gomm, *Letters and Journals of Field Marshal William Maynard Gomm from 1799 to Waterloo 1815* (ed. Frances C. Carr Gomm, London, 1881), p.180; Chambers, *op cit.* pp.220–1, citing Captain Carr Gomm to Major Henry Gomm, 1 November 1810.

25. Horward, *op.cit.* p.110, citing Andrew Leith-Hay, *A Narrative of the Peninsular War* (London, 1850), p.164.

26. Statement of Town-Major White, Portsmouth, 6 July 1848, provided in appendix to Chambers, *op.cit.* pp.219–20.

27. Extracts from Major-General Sir John Cameron's Letters to Colonel Napier, Government House, Devonport, 9 August, 1834, provided in appendix to Chambers, *op cit.* p.235.

28. Extract from Colonel Taylor, 9th Regiment, to Colonel Napier, provided in appendix to Chambers, *op cit.* p.239.

29. Oman just mentions two British regiments (*History*, vol.I, p.380); Chambers (*op.cit.* p.99) says the line was reinforced by the 3rd *Caçadores*; Horward (*op.cit.* p.117), includes both the 1st and 3rd *Caçadores* in the defensive line.

30. Chambers, *op.cit.* p.200, citing testimonial of Captain William Jones in the *History of the 52nd Regiment*.

31. Oman, *History*, vol.III, p.380.

32. Chambers, *op.cit.* p.188.

33. *Ibid* p.97.

34. Oman, *History*, vol.III, p.381.

35. *Ibid* pp.381–2, citing p.143 of the autobiography of George Napier.

36. Chambers, *op cit.* p.200, citing Captain William Jones in the *History of the 52nd Regiment*.

37. Oman, *History*, vol.I, p.117.

38. Ardant du Picq, *Battle Studies* (Harrisburg, 1947), p.127.

39. Christopher Duffy, *The Army of Maria Theresa* (Newton Abbott, 1977), p.79.

40. The whole battle of the 50th Regiment at Vimeiro is explained in detail in Paddy Griffith, *Forward Into Battle* (1st edn, Chichester, 1981), pp.17–22.

41. Dr Adam Neale, *Letters from Spain and Portugal* (London, 1809), p.13.

42. Christopher Hibbert, ed, *A Soldier of the Seventy First* (Warren, Michigan, 1976), pp.17–18.

43. Ned Zuparko, 'Charges, Firefights and Morale, part 3', *EEL* 72, p.6, citing Kincaid at Vera.

44. Cited in Zuparko, 'Charges, Firefights and Morale, part 2' *EEL* 71, p.37.

45. *Ibid* p.39.

46. Lieutenant-Colonel John Mitchell, *Thoughts on Tactics and Military Organisation* (London, 1838), pp.64–5.

47. James Anton, *Retrospect of a Military Life during the Most Eventful Periods of the Last War* (Edinburgh, 1841), pp.107–8.

48. Hibbert, *op.cit.* p.18.

49. Sir Robert Wilson, *The Life of General Robert Wilson* (2 vols, London, 1861), vol.1, pp.340-1, letter to Lord Hutchison, Cape Town, 11 January 1806.

50. General Wolfe's *Instructions to Young Officers* (2nd edn, London, 1780), pp.47, 49, 52.

51. *Ibid* pp.49, 52.

52. *British Military Library* II (1801), p.348.

53. *Ibid* p.346.

54. Wilson, *op.cit.* vol.2, p.426, letter to Honourable George Canning, Memel, 22 June 1807, describing the battle of Friedland.

55. Oman, *History*, vol.I, pp.114-15.

56. Oman, *Studies in the Napoleonic Wars*, pp.87-90.

57. John A. Lynn, *Bayonets of the Republic: Motivation and Tactics in the Army of Revolutionary France, 1791-94* (Chicago, 1984), p.247.

58. Steven Ross, *From Flintlock to Rifle: Infantry Tactics 1740-1866* (London, 1789), p.71.

59. Lynn, *op.cit.* pp.250-1, citing Dampierre in La Jonquière, *Jemappes* (Paris, 1902), p.165.

60. Lieutenant-General Duhesme, *Essai sur l'infanterie légère: traité des petites opérations de guerre* (Paris, 1814), pp.134-5.

61. S.M. Le Directeur, *Spectateur Militaire* V (1828), pp.53-7. It should not be forgotten that large and small French squares had often proved to be disastrously weak in the Flanders campaign of 1793-4.

62. General Count Gneisenau, *The Life and Campaigns of Field Marshal Blücher* (trans. J.E. Marston, London, 1815), pp.37-8.

Chapter 11

'They decide not, nor are they chiefly relied upon in battle'[1]
British Rifles and Light Infantry in the Peninsular War

by Arthur Harman

The riflemen and light infantrymen of the Peninsular Army certainly considered themselves to be an élite: 'We Light Division, while ever conspicuous for undaunted bravery, prided ourselves upon destroying the enemy and preserving ourselves; for good light troops, like deer-stalkers, may effect feats of heroism by stratagem, ability, and cool daring.'[2] They were also respected by their comrades in the line regiments: 'I was appointed to the 8th Veteran Battalion and sent to Fort Cumberland ... I was again the only green jacket of the lot, and as we had a great reputation in the army at that time [1814], the officers assembled round me during the first muster and asked numerous questions about my service in the Rifles.'[3] Their memoirs comprise a highly significant proportion, albeit not a majority, of those listed by Oman in *Wellington's Army*[4] and by more recent historians of the war in Portugal and Spain.

It is notable that in many subsequent English novels set during the Peninsular War, their fictional heroes – from humble Matthew Dodd[5] to dashing Richard Sharpe[6] – have been riflemen or light infantrymen,[7] doubtless in part at least because of the ready availability of the original memoirs, one of which in particular seems destined to appear in more reprint editions than its author experienced battles![8] Another reason for the 'Light Bobs' dominance in fictitious adventures may be that the role of the rifleman or light infantryman seems to offer more scope for individual acts of daring – the very stuff of adventure stories – than that of his comrade in the line, standing stolidly, shoulder to shoulder with his fellows in relative anonymity, only able to await the random musket ball or cannon shot that will bring the brief chapter of his existence to a swift conclusion. That a realistic portrayal of the line infantryman's perspective would make dull fiction would appear to borne out by a British soldier's pithy comment on Waterloo: 'I'll be hanged if I know anything about the matter, for I was all day trodden in the mud and ridden over by every scoundrel who had a horse!'[9] Nevertheless, there are some more detailed descriptions by line infantrymen of that engagement[10] which might inspire pastiche memoirs in the manner of George MacDonald Fraser's 'Flashman Papers' series.[11] The writer of best-selling adventure stories has, of course, a different agenda to that of the historian, and must contrive to place his hero in situations where his decisions and skill can influence events – impossible for a hero condemned to look to his front, keep his dressing, and close up as subordinate characters fall.

Every age interprets history according to its own lights, and it is hardly surprising that the most recent fictional Peninsular hero, accompanied by his squad of 'Chosen Men', has undertaken a variety of missions and clandestine operations behind enemy lines reminiscent of today's 'Special Forces', such as the SAS or US Navy SEALs. But the reader of such fictions will search in vain for similar adventures in the original letters, diaries, or memoirs of real officers such as Kincaid, Leach, or Simmons.[12] Instead, he will discover – perhaps to his surprise – that riflemen and light infantrymen participated in several sieges, not only by giving covering fire, but also by joining forlorn hopes and storming parties, where their marksmanship would be irrelevant. Perhaps it is now time to dispel the growing 'myth of the rifleman' that has sprung up since the publication of Oman's *History*, largely perpetrated by fictions, and to re-examine the sources.

This essay does not deny the courage, skill, and *esprit de corps* exhibited by either the Light Division or British riflemen and light infantrymen in general during the Peninsular War, and deservedly celebrated by Sir Charles Oman in both his *History of The Peninsular War* and *Wellington's Army*. Nor will it examine the origins or training of the original 'Shorncliffe Regiments' that subsequently formed the Light Division, or Sir John Moore's role therein, which have been described in detail by David Gates in the definitive work upon those aspects of the subject.[13] Instead, it will concentrate upon 'the fundamental trait of light infantry that distinguished them from line infantry ... their ... general usage as skirmishers.'[14] It will consider whether Oman's analysis of the reasons for the success of the Anglo-Portuguese skirmishers in the Peninsular War needs revision, whilst endeavouring to provide a more detailed picture of life on the skirmish line.

Recent scholarship has been largely devoted to Oman's analysis of 'the Queen's Move of black-powder warfare, the head-on clash of heavy infantry, at close-range, in close-order, over levelled musket barrels.'[15] His belief that 'the essential fact which lay behind the oft-observed conclusion [the defeat of French attacks in column in the Peninsula] was simply that the two-deep line enabled a force to use every musket with effect, while the "column of divisions" put seven-ninths of the men forming it in a position where they could not shoot at all'[16] – and hence that 'fire was everything' – has been challenged and, by careful analysis of contemporary accounts, shown to be mistaken.[17] So much attention has been focused upon the 'Line versus Column' issue – there are, indeed, treatments of it by both Arnold and Nosworthy elsewhere in this volume – that Oman's analysis of British skirmishing has often been neglected or overlooked altogether.

In analysing Wellington's infantry tactics[18] Oman stated that the line 'must be screened by a line of skirmishers impenetrable to the enemy's *tirailleurs*',[19] and attributed Wellington's success against French attacks to the fact that this 'powerful screen of skirmishers' was 'so strong that the French *tirailleurs* should never be able to force it in and to get close to the main line.'[20] Therefore just as Oman regarded the number of muskets that could be brought to bear by the opposing troops as crucial to the defeat of an attack,[21] so he apparently saw numerical superiority in light troops as the key to success on the skirmish line: 'a French Division would send out 1000 to 1200 skirmishers, a force appreciably less than the light troops of a British Division of approximately equal force. Hence Wellington never seems to have been seriously incommoded by the French skirmishers.'[22]

Numerical superiority in light troops was certainly considered significant by contemporary theorists. General John Money, a British officer who had proposed a legion of *chasseurs à cheval* and riflemen for duty in the American War (but had his proposal rejected by the government), wrote in 1799: 'it is to this new system of bringing more Irregulars into the field than their opponents, that the French owe chiefly their success'.[23] He believed that 'whichever army has the best *Chasseurs* (supposing numbers equal) will prevail of course; those who have the most, will not fail of succeeding, judiciously disposed of.'[24]

A recent description of Wellesley's victory at Vimeiro follows Oman closely: 'So, what had happened? First, the French *voltigeurs*, whose task it was to drive back the British security line before setting about the main British line, came up against an unusually heavy line of skirmishers ... In fact, the French *voltigeurs* had their work cut out in driving back even the British skirmishers'.[25] Gates' more detailed analysis of Peninsular War skirmishing adopted the same view:

> The very high proportion of light infantry in his [Wellington's] forces enabled him to deploy screens of extraordinary strength as a matter of regular practice. Out of the eight Divisions he ultimately had at his disposal in the Peninsula, two – the Light and Seventh – usually consisted entirely of light troops. In addition to these forces there were regimental

light companies, detachments of riflemen, and several other battalions of Portuguese and British light infantry spread throughout the army.[26]

Such a screen was 'so considerable ... that the French not unfrequently mistook it for a front line, and speak of their column as piercing or thrusting back the first line of their opponents, when all that they had done was to drive in a powerful and obstinate body of skirmishers bickering in front of the real fighting formation.'[27] Gates concludes that 'whatever they may have lacked in skill, the British light infantry made up for it by their weight of numbers.'[28]

Yet one can find instances where eyewitnesses believed that, far from outnumbering the French *tirailleurs*, the British skirmishers were themselves outnumbered. For example, at Vimeiro 'the whole line seemed annoyed and angered at seeing the Rifles outnumbered by the Invincibles.'[29] At Coruña 'our bugles sounded the advance; away went the kettles; the word was given "Rifles in front extended by files in chain order!" The enemy's sharpshooters were double and triple our numbers.'[30] Again, in the Pyrenees:

> The French dashed at the hill gallantly – throwing out clouds of skirmishers, who forced ours back on the main body at the top. At one point near the centre of the position, they pushed so hard that the Light Companies came running in, close to where the General and his staff stood; and it required their utmost efforts to turn them back. On this occasion I distinctly saw Sir Rowland himself, turn right about face, three or four of the 50th Light Company, who, panting with heat, and with faces blackened with powder, had been forced up by superior numbers. Additional skirmishers were sent down at this point, and the enemy was repelled.[31]

Can the apparent contradiction between these eyewitnesses and Oman be resolved? A French account of Bussaco may offer a possible explanation: 'the enemy successively reinforced their line of skirmishers but these Allied troops were not allowed to stay there very long. They were recalled by horns and replaced by fresh troops – an excellent method neglected by us for too long.'[32] The British rotated companies of riflemen or light infantrymen on the skirmish line, so that, at any one moment, the French *tirailleurs* may have enjoyed a local, but not a total potential, numerical superiority over their opponents.

The numerical superiority claimed for Wellington's forces by Oman supposedly resulted from the French limiting their skirmish line to:

> no more than the *voltigeur* company of each battalion, no more than one-tenth of the whole unit when the battalion was at its original strength of ten companies, though somewhat

greater in proportion after the number of companies was cut down from ten to six after 1808. I do not remember any case in the Peninsular battles where whole battalions were broken up into skirmishers, and thrown forward ahead of the striking mass, as had been common in 1793 or 1794.[33]

It was on this basis that Oman produced the numbers quoted above, and justified his calculations of the relative strengths of the skirmishers deployed by French and British brigades, or by French and Anglo-Portuguese Divisions, in his reply to a query on this point. He noted that 'space forbids me to quote strings of original French authorities or official papers to prove that the normal skirmishing line of a Napoleonic regiment was simply composed of its *voltigeur* companies.'[34] Some contemporary accounts support this view. For example, at Maya:

> The light companies were, indeed, ordered up ... as a measure of precaution; how very weak and insufficient a one, will be seen. In less than two hours, my picquet and the light companies were heavily engaged with the enemies advance, which was composed entirely of *voltigeur* companies, unincumbered by knapsacks, and led by a chosen officer. These fellows fought with ardour, but we disputed our ground with them handsomely, and caused them severe loss; nor had we lost the position itself, though driven from the advances of it.[35]

There appears to be no reasonable explanation why the French should not have deployed more skirmishers themselves, rather than simply accepting the consequences of the 'unnecessary numerical weakness of their skirmisher screens'.[36] Why did French generals in Spain and Portugal not adapt the standard practice to suit the circumstances, as was done in 'some central European battles' where 'entire divisions of infantry were broken down to skirmish'?[37] They may indeed have done so on occasion, as Oman himself admits in his description of Sorauren, where 'Lecamus's brigade, starting from a short distance south of Sorauren, made for the north-west corner of the heights, – its four battalion columns screened by their eight *compagnies d'elite* in a dense swarm, much thicker than the usual French skirmishing line.'[38] In a footnote he states: 'This exceptional use of grenadiers in the skirmishing line, I get from an observation of Bainbrigge of the 20th, who expresses his surprise that the troops with whom he was engaged, though acting as *tirailleurs*, were not light infantry, but men in tall bearskin caps like the Guard'. However, having described this deployment of grenadiers as skirmishers as 'exceptional', only three pages later Oman comments that the 'very strong screen of skirmishers' preceding the attack by the 120th *Ligne* of Gauthier's Brigade was 'no doubt all the six *compagnies d'elite*',[39] which is presumably an assumption, since he quotes no eyewitness testimony in support.

Oman's description of Sorauren concludes that 'the French generals had learnt one thing at least from previous experience – they tried to sheathe and screen the column by exceptionally heavy skirmishing lines, but even so they could not achieve their purpose.'[40] This leaves the reader with the impression – perhaps unintentionally – that it had taken until July 1813 for any French general to decide to experiment by deploying a greater number of troops as skirmishers when attacking Anglo-Portuguese forces in a defensive position. Yet Rifleman Benjamin Harris recalled that, at Vimeiro in 1808:

> I particularly remarked the French lights and grenadiers who were, I think, the 70th. Our men seemed to know the grenadiers well. They were fine-looking young men with tremendous moustaches, and were wearing red shoulder-knots. As they came swarming up, they rained upon us a perfect shower of balls, which we returned quite as sharply. Whenever one of them was knocked over, our men called out: 'There goes another of Boney's Invincibles!'[41]

Harris' reference to the grenadiers 'swarming up' and firing upon the skirmishing Riflemen suggests that they may have been acting as skirmishers themselves, rather than advancing as members of an attack column. It is thus possible (even probable?), but not proven, that French grenadiers were deployed as skirmishers on other occasions.

Marshal Masséna's *Orders for Bussaco* (1810), quoted by Oman, may be revealing.[42] The Prince of Essling specifically mentions that the attack columns of both II Corps and VI Corps should be screened by skirmishers.[43] Why should he feel it necessary to order two experienced officers – Reynier commanding II Corps and Ney in VI Corps[44] – to take such an elementary precaution, if by this he meant no more than that they were to follow standard practice and deploy only the *voltigeurs* of each regiment? Does this document simply confirm Oman's view, since repeated in many modern works, that 'in the Peninsula, French commanders rarely used more than the *voltigeur* companies of line regiments for skirmishing. Indeed, even the light infantry battalions were invariably deployed in close order formation'?[45] Or are these two simple sentences referring to the deployment of additional skirmishers, agreed orally between the Prince and his corps commanders?

Sometimes additional troops were deployed as skirmishers in response to events, as at Bussaco where 'a brigade of Marchand's division was pushed forward ... After fighting for some time, it found itself almost entirely dispersed into groups of skirmishers, and in the end it was necessary to support this unit with the second brigade.'[46] The most obvious reason for such a deployment would be to match or outnumber the screen of British and Portuguese light troops, to enable the French attack columns to continue their advance.

Finally, troops were often forced by the terrain to adopt looser formations, or to abandon them altogether, as illustrated, again, in the description of Bussaco by Masséna's aide-de-camp, which refers to 'our soldiers, unable to keep their ranks on the steep slopes'.[47] The same writer comments that 'our system permitted the French regiments to be dispersed during a battle and in the end only the officers and the bravest soldiers were left, and they were completely disgusted, even with having to fight for an entire day'.[48] This would suggest that, although the usual practice in the Peninsula may have been to deploy only the *voltigeur* companies when commencing an attack, as stated by Oman, more troops would frequently join the skirmish line as the attack developed.

At this point it is appropriate to consider Oman's view of the provision of skirmishers in the Anglo-Portuguese army. Referring to contemporary British practice immediately before the Peninsular War, he wrote: 'Generals wanting more light troops habitually purloined the light companies of regiments to make "light battalions"; but not only did they do this, but they sometimes even stole the "flankers"[49] also from the centre companies', which were thus 'deprived of every marksman that they possessed – an execrable device ... Wellington never skimmed the centre companies of their good shots, though he did occasionally create a light battalion of light companies – even this was exceptional.'[50] Elsewhere, however, Oman appeared to contradict himself when he wrote:

> That the brigade light companies were used together as a single first-line fighting unit, is sufficiently proved from many of Wellington's despatches. See, for example, the Fuentes de Oñoro report (Despatches vii, 529), where he speaks of 'the light infantry battalion' of Nightingale's brigade, of Howard's brigade, of the K.G.L. brigade – these 'battalions' being the four or five light companies united.[51]

When British troops first campaigned in Portugal in 1808, Wellesley followed the existing practice of combining light companies from different regiments. At Roliça 'part of our army advanced to the attack, the light company only of our regiment [71st Foot] accompanied the attacking party.'[52] There is some other evidence that the practice of combining light companies did continue in the Peninsular War. Thus a letter from Major-General Thomas Picton to Lieutenant-Colonel Williams, dated 30 October 1810, quoted by Lieutenant-Colonel G.L. Chambers,[53] addresses him as 'Comdg. Light Corps, 3rd Division'. In a footnote to that letter the author states that 'Picton formed a light corps for divisional purposes of the head-quarters, and three companies of the 5th Battalion, 60th, and the light companies of the other regiments[54] under him.' Since the 5/60th was a Rifle regiment, this presumably gave Lieutenant-Colonel Williams a force of eleven companies, of which three were riflemen. May not other divisional commanders have done the same?

The Light Division, of course, as befitted its name, was composed entirely of light troops, and so was the Seventh Division. However, contemporary accounts demonstrate that the burden of skirmishing in such formations fell mainly upon the riflemen: 'Certainly I never saw such skirmishers as the 95th ... As our regiment [43rd Light Infantry] was often employed in supporting them, I think I am fairly well qualified to speak of their merits.'[55] This was the case when defending a position, such as Bussaco:

> We were retired a few yards from the brow of the hill, so that our line was concealed from the view of the enemy as they advanced up the heights, and our skirmishers retired, keeping up a constant and well directed running fire upon them; ... General Craufurd himself stood on the brow of the hill watching every movement of the attacking column, and when all our skirmishers had passed by and joined their respective corps, and the head of the enemy's column was within a very few yards of him, he ordered the 52nd to charge.[56]

It was equally the case when attacking, as at Sabugal:

> Our four companies had led up in skirmishing order, driving in the enemy's light troops; but the summit was defended by a strong compact body, against which we could make no head; but opening out, and allowing the 43rd to advance, with a tearing volley and a charge, sent the enemy rolling into the valley below, when the rifles again went to work in front, sticking to them like leeches.[57]

British Light Infantry battalions would also often support foreign riflemen, rather than skirmish themselves: 'our skirmishers (3rd *Caçadores*) opened upon them upon the brow of a hill and the French immediately returned it which passed mostly over our heads. We had express orders not to fire until ordered. Our regiment was well prepared to give them an excellent charge'.[58] The French certainly seem to have regarded the *Caçadores* as being as adept at skirmishing at Bussaco as British riflemen: 'The Portuguese were interspersed among the British; they acted perfectly'.[59]

Why were riflemen preferred for skirmishing above the light infantry battalions of the Light Division?

I beg to be understood as identifying our old and gallant associates, the forty-third and fifty-second, as a part of ourselves, for they bore their share in everything ... wherever we were, they were; and although the nature of our arm generally gave us more employment in the way of skirmishing, yet, whenever it came to a pinch ... we had only to look behind to see a line, in which we might place a degree of confidence, almost equal to our hopes in heaven; nor were we ever disappointed. There never was a corps of riflemen in the hands of such supporters![60]

Kincaid identified the Baker rifle as the reason why, in the Light Division, it was most often the 95th Rifles and the 3rd *Caçadores* who skirmished, while the 43rd and 52nd Light Infantry remained in line in support. What view did Oman, who had a firm belief in the tactical significance of infantry fire, have of these weapons? He stated that:

The weapon that mainly won the Peninsular victories was the 'Tower musket' of the line battalions, the famous 'Brown Bess'. Its effective range was about 300 yards, but no accurate shooting could be relied upon at any range over 100. Indeed, the man who could hit an individual at that distance must not only have been a good shot, but have possessed a firelock of over average quality. Compared with the rifle, already a weapon of precision, it was but a haphazard sort of arm.[61]

But Oman also asserted, more than once,[62] that the light infantry regiments 'were armed with a special musket of light weight' and, one presumes, may have believed that this difference between the weaponry carried by light infantrymen and that of the line was of some tactical significance, in view of his interpretation that infantry close combat was decided by the number of muskets that could be brought to bear upon the enemy.[63] On closer examination, however, this sweeping statement, implying that all light infantrymen were so armed, must be severely qualified.

There is no dispute that the weapon carried by the majority of British infantrymen throughout the Peninsular War, and at Waterloo, was the 'India' Pattern version of the Brown Bess (rather than the 'Tower' version): a smoothbore, 0.75-inch calibre, muzzle-loading flintlock musket with a thirty-nine-inch barrel.[64] In the latter part of the eighteenth century a 'New Land' musket had been designed to replace both the 'India' Pattern and the 'Short Land' musket, which was then being used by most regiments[65] of the British Army, but which was neither available in sufficient quantity, nor capable of being manufactured quickly enough, to meet wartime demands for weapons.[66] The 'New Land' musket was based upon two types of musket ordered in

1790 after a series of trials, and named 'The Duke of Richmond's two patterns',[67] after the Master-General of the Board of Ordnance. In its standard form it had a forty-two-inch barrel[68] but 'a version of this pattern was also approved for issue to light infantry. This had a thirty-nine-inch barrel equipped with a simple backsight, and a scroll grip on the trigger guard; features to assist the light infantry in the higher degree of marksmanship expected of them.'[69]

When he spoke of a special musket for the skirmish line, Oman was presumably referring to this 'New Land' Pattern 'Light Infantry' musket,[70] the design for which was 'approved in mid-1803 for use by the 52nd and other light infantry regiments.'[71] However, none would appear to have been manufactured before 1810 or 1811[72] and probably no more than 20,000 had been produced before Waterloo.[73] There is some evidence that the 52nd and 71st Light Infantry[74] had 'New Land' Pattern muskets on issue when they fought in that battle, but it has also been suggested that 'its issue seems generally to have been restricted to sergeants of light infantry regiments and of light companies within line regiments.'[75]

Nor is it at all clear that this 'special musket' was, indeed 'of light weight'! Common sense suggests that the respective weights quoted by Fosten for the 'New Land' and 'Light Infantry' Pattern muskets, with bayonets fitted,[76] cannot be correct – unless a brass scroll trigger guard outweighs a three-inch reduction in barrel length! Yet the 'Comparison of Ordnance Muskets of the Line Infantry'[77] would seem to demonstrate that the 'New Land' Pattern 'Light Infantry' musket, although it may have been a few ounces lighter than the 'Short Land' Pattern of the previous century, could not have been any lighter than the 'India' Pattern carried by most British infantrymen. Oman's assertion is therefore false in this respect.

Could this 'light infantry' pattern musket – if it was carried by many British light infantrymen – have had any significant effect upon their performance as skirmishers? Contemporary officers did not appear to think so, to judge from the observation of one that the French 'fine, long, light firelocks, with a small bore, are more efficient for skirmishing than our abominably clumsy machine'.[78] It is interesting that this comment specifies length as a virtue of the French musket, for even if – as seems most likely – he is comparing it to the 'India' Pattern, the 'New Land' Pattern 'Light Infantry' musket had the same barrel length, thirty-nine inches, whereas that of the French musket was forty-four inches. He may, of course, simply have shared the then common misapprehension that a longer barrel gave better accuracy.[79] Also noteworthy is his preference for a smaller calibre. Both the 'India' and 'New Land' Pattern muskets had a 0.75-inch bore, whilst the French 'Model 1777' and the slightly modified version of 'Year IX' – which remained the standard French musket throughout the Revolutionary and Napoleonic Wars – had only a 0.69-inch bore. In both cases the balls would have been cast between 0.07 and 0.10 inch smaller than the bore, this difference being known as 'windage', which reduced the weapons' accuracy. Loose-fitting balls were easier to insert into the muzzles and to ram down the barrels[80] in the heat of action, especially after the heavy fouling caused by the first few shots. Reducing windage would also result in greater recoil, causing the troops to complain about bruised shoulders and rendering them more liable to flinch at the moment of firing, so accuracy was unlikely to be much improved.[81]

The military has always demanded firearms that will knock a man down and render him, if not dead, *hors de combat* and no further threat. In the days of black-powder weapons and low muzzle velocities a large calibre was considered essential. Why, then, does this officer apparently recommend a lighter ball? The only obvious advantage would seem to be that a light infantryman could carry more of such ammunition about his person, without increasing his overall burden, and thus be capable of firing more shots at an approaching enemy or of remaining longer on the skirmish line before having to retire to refill his cartridge pouch. The Baker rifle had a calibre of 0.625 inch,[82] giving twenty balls to the pound. The memoirists agree that riflemen could carry up to eighty rounds:

'But we then had enough to carry: fifty round of ball cartridge; thirty loose balls in our waist belt; and a flask, and a horn of powder; and rifle, and sword; the two weighing 14 pounds.'[83]

'I also carried my canteen filled with water, my hatchet and rifle, and a pouch containing eighty rounds of ball cartridge.'[84]

'A powder-flask filled, a ball bag containing thirty loose balls, a small wooden mallet used to hammer the ball into the muzzle of our rifles; belt and pouch, the latter containing fifty rounds of ammunition, sword-belt and rifle.'[85]

Both Rifle and Light Infantry memoirists refer to skirmishers running short of, or exhausting, their ammunition:

'One of our men fixed himself behind a large stone, under cover from the enemy, and fired fourteen balls; he killed or wounded at every shot. He bid us bring him more ammunition, as he had fired off every round that he had. He was so near the enemy that no one dared to take him any, so he ran to us. Several shots were fired at him, but all missed!'[86]

'Whilst lying in this spot, I fired away every round I had in my pouch.'[87]

'At one period in the course of this eventful day, our ammunition ran so short, that three men in each company only could keep up a constant fire, they being supplied from their comrades' boxes: this plan was adopted to amuse the enemy for a while.'[88]

Oman presumably believed that it was the ability of Wellington's light infantrymen to kill or wound French *tirailleurs* by fire that enabled them to screen their own lines in defence and to drive in opposing skirmishers in attack, though he seems to have attributed this largely to their numerical superiority, rather than any differences in weaponry which would result in inflicting more casualties upon the enemy than they would suffer themselves. One French officer certainly experienced many casualties amongst his own men, but also commented upon their inability to return the fire effectively: 'I was sent out to skirmish against some of those in green - grasshoppers I call them; you call them Rifle Men. They were behind every bush and stone, and soon made sad havoc amongst my men, killing all the officers of my company, and wounding myself without being able to do them any injury. This drove me nearly to distraction.'[89]

Anecdotes in British memoirs reinforce the idea that riflemen could pick off individual French officers: 'A French officer on a grey horse was most gallant. Old Beckwith, in a voice like thunder, roared out to the Riflemen, "Shoot that fellow, will you?" In a moment he and his horse were knocked over, and Sydney exclaimed, "Alas! you were a noble fellow."'[90] Another story, although believed by Blakiston to be 'half of it a lie', again suggests that a rifleman could hit an individual French officer at whom he aimed:

> An officer of the rifles, who was known to one of our officers, came on a visit to our lines. He had on a new pair of boots, not exactly of the London cut, towards which he seemed desirous of drawing our attention. When he had succeeded in this, he said, 'Where do you think I got these boots?' 'We can't guess,' was the answer. 'Well, I'll tell you how it was. You must know that I have been in want of a pair of boots for some time; so, in the course of the skirmish, seeing a French officer rather actively employed, who I thought might supply the deficiency in my wardrobe, I said to Corporal Murphy, "Corporal Murphy," says I, "see if you can't pick me off that French officer who's so forward among the skirmishers." After some manoeuvring the corporal succeeded in bringing down his man, when I immediately ran up, put my foot on his body, pulled off the boots, and here they are; a nice pair, ar'n't they?'[91]

The oft-cited shooting of General Colbert by Rifleman Thomas Plunkett at Cacabellos, during the retreat to Coruña, is reported by Kincaid,[92] Costello,[93] and Surtees,[94] none of whom was with Sir Edward Paget's rearguard and so presumably heard the tale - which doubtless became part of regimental folklore - from their comrades at a later date. Oman remarks in a footnote that 'He [Colbert] was shot by Tom Plunkett, a noted character in the 95th, from a range that seemed extraordinary to the riflemen of that day'[95] – but he cites no authority.

Another recurring notion is that riflemen could score hits upon their opponents at greater ranges than those at which French *tirailleurs*, armed with smoothbore muskets, could reply effectively. George Gleig of the 85th was an eyewitness to an incident tending to show that a Rifleman could pick off musket-armed *tirailleurs* with impunity:

> The Portuguese ... consisted of three battalions of *caçadores*, and two of heavy infantry; of which the *caçadores* alone could, in strict propriety, be said to be engaged. Covering the front of the others, and communicating with our skirmishers, they spread themselves in extended order over the fields, and kept up a steady, cool, and well-directed fire, upon the cloud of *tirailleurs* which vainly endeavoured to drive them back upon the reserve ... I recollect that one Portuguese soldier, in particular, attracted my notice that day ... he looked neither to his right nor his left – paid no attention either to the momentary retrogression or advance of his comrades; but steadily kept his ground, or varied it only for the purpose of obtaining a better aim at his opponents. He had posted himself considerably in advance of his own line, behind a large furze-bush, or rather in the middle of a furze-bower, from which I saw him deliberately pick off three Frenchmen, one after another. At length he was noticed by the enemy, and six or seven of them turned towards his place of ambuscade. Nothing daunted, the Portuguese remained perfectly steady; he crouched down, indeed, to load, but the moment his rifle was charged, he leant over the bush, and fired. One of his assailants fell; while the rest, pointing their pieces to the spot from whence the smoke issued, gave him a volley; but it was harmless; he had darted to the other side of the bush, and every shot missed him. He knelt down and loaded again; the enemy were now within twenty yards of him; he fired, and an officer who accompanied them, walked off the field grasping his left arm in his right hand. The rest of his adversaries, as if panic-struck, retreated; and there he staid, till the close of the affair; after which, he returned to his ranks, apparently unhurt. That man killed and wounded not fewer than eight French soldiers during the day.[96]

Rifle officers, *pace* the fictitious Richard Sharpe, did not officially, or usually, carry rifles, though one rifleman thought they should:

> It is surprising that, in general, our officers do not carry a rifle into action. Superior to the sword and pistol, which are mere toys in the field, the defence it would afford them should carry its own argument. It would give additional efficiency and

strength to the regiments generally, from the number (50 to a regiment) that it would add to each volley. [Interesting that a Rifleman should think in terms of volleys!] It would inspire confidence in the officer, without preventing him from keeping his eye on his riflemen who, while in action, use their own judgement by getting under cover, and are consequently out of sight.[97]

The same writer mentions one 95th officer who did: 'Lieutenant Strode ... always carried a rifle, for the skilful use of which he was celebrated.'[98] This weapon passed to a fellow officer at Caza Noval: 'Strode when he fell called to me to take his rifle, exclaiming, "This, Simmons, may be of service." I had no time to stand on ceremony, but moved on.'[99] It proved of use - though not in the manner its original owner had intended - at Foz de Aronce, where 'a musket ball ... shattered the butt to pieces, which luckily saved my right thigh.'[100]

Light and line infantry memoirs contain several anecdotes which suggest that a good shot could hit his man even with a musket. For example:

> Joining the regiment in the midst of a severe skirmish, I was surprised to see one of our men with a long red feather stuck in his cap: on asking him the cause, I was informed that the unfortunate R——h had fallen a victim to the first shot in the engagement, and that he (the informant) had succeeded in shooting the French grenadier who had done the deed: the seizure of this man's feather was, therefore, intended as a sort of proof of revenge'.[101]

As in the Rifle regiments, officers did not normally snipe at the enemy:

> The conduct of Lieutenant Charles Brown of the light company was conspicuous; seeing the Frenchmen pressing closely in, he was determined to lend a hand in giving them a check, in a manner which he could not accomplish with the feeble weapon which he wielded; he therefore seized a musket, (plenty of which were scattered about), and extending himself upon a bank of earth, let fly with such deliberate aim, that many of the Frenchmen were effectually stopped in their career. Brown was an excellent shot, and enjoyed the thing amazingly, appearing quite in his element, going about his work as methodically as if he were shooting partridges or wild ducks, shewing a degree of skill worthy of the most practised amateur.
>
> This was the only instance of the kind that ever came within my observation, and can be justified only by the strong desire a sportsman ... had to indulge his ruling passion; for officers, in general, have too much to attend to, while in

action, and therefore could not, were they so inclined, indulge their fancy that way.[102]

Some accounts credit French musket-armed *tirailleurs* with accuracy worthy of rifles:

Early in the action [the battle of Maya], a fine young man, Ensign Dalmar, of the 28th, while carrying the colours, was shot through the heart by a French sharpshooter. Ensign Hill, seeing the colours fall, instantly ran and took them up, exclaiming at the same time that 'the colours of the "slashers" should never want a person to display them to the enemy.' – He had scarcely spoke, when the same Frenchman, having reloaded, hit him in the same place as poor Dalmar. Fortunately for Hill, he had a handkerchief in his breast, which saved him: the ball passed through his coat, waistcoat, thirteen folds of the handkerchief, and his shirt, giving him a severe contusion on the breast ... Two or three of our marksmen, having detected the Frenchman picking off our officers, he was soon tumbled down the rocks.[103]

Other memoirs actually refer to the French skirmishers as 'riflemen':

Their riflemen, with unparalleled boldness ferreting their way within less than pistol shot of where we stood, by a rambling fire did very great execution throughout our already diminished ranks. With such precision did those experienced artists do their duty that very many of our companions were killed or wounded on this height. A party of the officers of the 50th, who were collected in a knot, discussing the affairs of the eventful day, were quickly seen by those marksmen, who, from behind the rocks, dispatched with deadly aim a few rifle missiles, each with its billet.[104]

We soon got within range of their rifles, and began to pick them off.[105]

In two or three days the French cavalry, forming their advanced guard, were close up to our rear, and teasing us from morning till night. Their cavalry had a rifleman mounted behind each dragoon; and when any good position or bushes by the road side, gave them any advantage to give our men a few shots, those riflemen would dismount, and get under cover of the bushes: so that we were obliged to do the same; their dragoons at the same time dismounting, and laying their carbines on their saddles, with their horse standing in front of them for a sort of defence, would give us a few shots as well. In this way we were often obliged to make a stand and drive them back.[106]

Why this confusion? One can understand Patterson, a line officer, assuming that French *tirailleurs* had rifles when they appeared to be picking off his comrades so successfully; but Green, a rifleman, should have known better! Are both writers using the term 'riflemen' as a synonym for 'skirmishers', since they are familiar with rifle-armed troops – of whatever nationality – in that role? Or does this indiscriminate use of the word 'rifleman' imply that there was often little or no appreciable difference between the effectiveness of the fire of British and foreign riflemen and French *tirailleurs*?

Common sense suggests that such anecdotal evidence should be treated with caution. In many, if not all, of the incidents quoted above, so many musket and rifle balls must have been whistling through the air that it would have been impossible for anyone to be sure it was his own shot that had brought down a conspicuous enemy officer or skirmisher. Rifleman Thomas Plunkett received the credit for killing General Colbert, perhaps because he had already made a reputation for himself as a marksman at Buenos Aires;[107] how certain could he, or anyone then or since, be that it was his ball that hit the French general? It is clear that Riflemen themselves were not always certain of their shots; at Pombal, for example:

> During our approach to the bridge, Palmer and Treacy, two men of known daring, saw a French sergeant fall and ran up to claim the meed of conquest by relieving him of any valuable he might possess. They quarrelled as to the appropriation of the spoil. Palmer, who was an excellent shot, claimed to have shot the sergeant and told Treacy to go and 'kill a Frenchman for himself'.[108]

Rifleman Harris describes the limitations of the skirmisher's field of vision in the black-powder era:

> I myself was very soon hotly engaged. Loading and firing away I became enveloped in the smoke I created. Such was the cloud which hung about me from the continual fire of my comrades – the white vapour clinging to my very clothes – that for a few minutes I could see nothing but the red flash of my own piece. It is a great drawback of our present system of fighting that whilst in such a state, and unless some friendly breeze clears the space around, a soldier can know no more of his position, what is about to happen in his front, or what has happened – even amongst his own companions – than the dead lying around ... We were generally enveloped in smoke ... sometimes unable to distinguish what was going on around whilst we blazed away at our opponents.[109]

Pairs of riflemen, or light infantrymen, skirmishing in cover, must therefore have had to rely largely upon bugle-calls, whistles, and shouted orders by their officers in order to follow the course of an engagement. The latter must have had to expose themselves to enemy fire to communicate with men in extended order: one light company officer opined that 'it is really hard work to make them preserve their proper extended order, cover themselves, and not throw away their fire; and in the performance of this duty, an officer is, I think, far more exposed than in line fighting.'[110] Under such circumstances, casualties from 'friendly fire' were also possible: 'The next morning we resumed the offensive, attacking the enemy, who had retired under the covert of a brushwood jungle: some smart skirmishing ensued; but this Indian sort of warfare had its disadvantages, several of our men shooting each other, as the intense thickness of the wood deceived their eyes'.[111]

The same light infantryman, despite accepting a comrade's description of a revenge shooting[112] without question, pours scorn on the very idea that skirmishers can be certain of their shots:

> A severe skirmishing then took place. This system of fighting is of course already well known; but I may say, that although the combatants are in a scattered state, and take aim at each other, yet they very seldom know when they drop their men, – to speak in sportsmen's slang. The reason is obvious: so many firing at the same time, and that often obliquely.[113]

Perhaps the examples of marksmanship quoted in memoirs, even if literally true, were recorded because they were exceptional, rather than commonplace – although riflemen of the 95th, and modern novelists, might wish their readers to think otherwise! Contemporaries certainly seem to have believed that skirmish fire was deadly, but this may have been an impression resulting from operating in pairs in extended order, where the death or wounds of individual light infantrymen would affect their partners' morale more than when in close order. Casualties inflicted by skirmish fire might well result in two or three other men retiring to assist their wounded comrade to the rear; although this practice was discouraged, it must have been hard to prevent when troops were deployed in extended order and taking cover.[114]

The ardour of troops in close order could perhaps be restrained by their officers:

> The whole line seemed annoyed and angered at seeing the Rifles outnumbered by the Invincibles. As we fell back 'firing and retiring' – galling them handsomely as we did so – our men cried out, as if with one voice, to charge. 'Damn them!' they roared. 'Charge! Charge!' But General Fane restrained their impetuosity. He desired them to stand fast, and keep their ground.[115]

However, such tight control could not be enforced on the skirmish line, so that sometimes one man could encourage his comrades to take spontaneous action, without orders:

> There were two small buildings in our front. The French managed to get into them and therefore annoyed us much from that quarter. A small rise in the ground close before these houses also favoured them; and our men were handled very severely in consequence. So angry did they become that they would not stand it any longer. One skirmisher jumped up and rushed forward crying: 'Over Boys! Over! Over!' Instantly the whole line responded with 'Over, over, over!' They ran along the grass like wildfire and dashed at the rise, fixing their sword-bayonets as they did so. The French light bobs, unable to stand the sight, turned about and fled.[116]

One rifle officer admits that inexperience forced him to allow the men under his command to take the initiative: 'In one of the first smart actions that I ever was in, I was a young officer in command of experienced soldiers, and, therefore, found myself compelled to be an observer rather than an active leader in the scene.'[117] He describes how, in that same action, an individual rifleman's impetuosity galvanised men who had gone to ground under fire:

> We were engaged in a very hot skirmish, and had driven the enemy's light troops for a considerable distance with great rapidity, when we were at length stopped by some of their regiments in line, which opened such a terrific fire within a few yards that it obliged every one to shelter himself as he best could among the inequalities of the ground and the sprinkling of trees which the place afforded. We remained inactive for about ten minutes amidst a shower of balls that seemed to be almost like a hail-storm, and when at the very worst, when it appeared to me to be certain death to quit the cover, a young scampish fellow of the name of Priestly, at the adjoining tree, started out from behind it, saying, 'Well! I'll be d— —d if I'll be bothered any longer behind a tree, so here's at you,' and with that he banged off his rifle in the face of his foes, reloading very deliberately, while every one right and left followed his example, and the enemy, panic struck, took to their heels without firing another shot.[118]

Such initiative must have come more easily to troops who had not been trained primarily to fight in close order; those who had would tend, instinctively, to seek the psychological comfort of close proximity to their comrades and orders from an officer.

Another distinction between the riflemen and other light infantrymen of Wellington's Peninsular army was uniform. The former wore green, brown, or black, with black crossbelts; the latter had a red coatee, identical to that of the line infantrymen except for decorative shoulder-wings. French *voltigeurs'* uniforms only differed in details from those of fusiliers or grenadiers.[119] One rifleman identified three factors - uniform, experience, and weaponry - as significant in skirmishing at Fuentes de Oñoro:

> Just after this, a smart action commenced in the wood, and our company was ordered to take ground to the front, where the 85th Regiment, in their conspicuous red dresses, were being very roughly handled by the enemy in this their first engagement since arriving in the country. They were opposed to the well-trained and veteran French *tirailleurs*, so it is no wonder that this gallant regiment should suffer so severely. When we came up, our practised fellows in their dark clothing, soon turned back the advancing French with the murderous nature of our arms.[120]

The present writer's experience in a Napoleonic re-enactment society, however, has been that a British line infantryman or French fusilier or *voltigeur* who remains motionless in dense undergrowth, or behind a bush, is extremely difficult to spot from a distance of only a few yards, let alone effective musket range. Skirmishers in action, of course, could aim at the smoke generated by their opponents' fire, as is clear from Gleig's description,[121] even if they could not see their enemies clearly. The 85th at Fuentes probably suffered because, being inexperienced, they were not so adept at concealing themselves, so their red coats did provide highly visible targets.

Riflemen, by contrast, were very proficient at using cover: 'They [the 95th] could do the work much better and with infinitely less loss than any of our best Light troops. They possessed an individual boldness, a mutual understanding and a quickness of the eye in taking advantage of the ground'. Riflemen took cover in defence,[122] when obeying the order to 'Fire and Retire': 'The French, in great numbers, came steadily down on us, and we pelted upon them a shower of leaden hail. Under any cover we could find we lay, firing one moment, and jumping up and running for it the next.'[123] Even the bodies of dead comrades could afford protection: 'The Frenchmen's balls were flying very wickedly at that moment so I crept up to Ponton and took shelter by lying behind him. Of his dead body I made a rest for my rifle. Revenging his death by the assistance of his carcass, I tried my best to hit his enemies hard.'[124]

Walls also made obvious cover, and could be improved to afford greater protection if time permitted: 'There were many enclosures of stone walls, and these walls gave our sharpshooters a good cover. We made what are called loop-holes to fire through.'[125] When advancing, riflemen also used cover: 'Moving on in extended order, under whatever cover the nature of the ground afforded, we ...

began a sharp fire ... I took advantage of whatever cover I could find, throwing myself down behind a small bank where I lay so secure that, although the Frenchmen's bullets fell pretty thickly around, I was able to knock several over without being dislodged.'[126]

When there was no readily available cover, riflemen still made themselves small targets: 'it rested our weary limbs to lie down, and give them a few rifle balls; as lying down, or kneeling to fire was our general mode in action.'[127] The memoirists describe the French *tirailleurs* behaving in a similar manner:

'I observed a Frenchman amongst the bushes, not more than sixty to eighty yards distant, shifting about from one concealing place to another'.[128]

'The enemy ... lying down in the heath, [keeping] up a hot and constant fire ... the French ... retreated to the next hill when they again lay concealed'.[129]

'A sharp discharge of small arms was kept up by a cloud of French riflemen, who, gathering round under cover of the vines and cornfields, gave their fire with a degree of activity that certainly did them credit.'[130]

Several authors suggest that most Light Infantry battalions, and the light companies of other regiments, were simply not such good skirmishers as their French counterparts: 'their [the Guards Brigade's] light companies received a dreadful mauling from the French *voltigeurs*. The great John Bulls had no notion of screening themselves from the fire of their more cautious adversaries, and suffered accordingly.'[131] Even the two Shorncliffe Light Infantry regiments were, on occasions early in the Peninsular War, no match for French *tirailleurs*. At Vimeiro, 'the 43rd regiment was very much cut up, being, while employed in skirmishing, considerably exposed',[132] while a Rifleman recalled that 'on the 15th [January 1809] the 52nd regiment was on outlaying picquet. The French had sent out, in front of their army, a number of sharpshooters to attack our position. The 52nd were driven in. The bugle sounded the advance, and double-quick for the rifles, to attack their sharpshooters.'[133]

Battalion companies were sometimes sent to reinforce the skirmish line, but this description of the experience of the 4th battalion company of the 50th at Vimeiro suggests that they were ineffective:

A brisk firing of musquetry, among the troops in advance, announced that it was high time to reinforce the piquets, which were commanded by Captain Thomas Snowe, of the 50th regiment. They were immediately strengthened by the 4th battalion company of that regiment, under Captain Coote. Our men were at this time exposed in the open field, and scarcely knew from what direction the enemy were coming ... the enemy, still pressing in, galled us with a peppering that was rapidly thinning the ranks, and made our situation by no means either cool or comfortable ... Coote directed his men to take advantage of every means of cover the place afforded; and, encouraging them by his own example, they kept their ground under a galling and destructive fire, from an enemy whom they were unable to answer or even to see.[134]

Only the 95th are specifically mentioned as a regiment that skirmished better than the French: 'They were in fact, as much superior to the French Voltigeurs as the latter were to our skirmishers in general.'[135]

Whereas Rifleman Costello mentioned experience[136] as significant, some other writers refer only to nationality, and seem to imply that aptitude for skirmishing relates to racial origin. One wrote that 'the English do not skirmish so well as the Germans or the French',[137] and another that:

Mohamedan troops ... certainly take their positions and cover their persons ... with a degree of intelligence and alertness that we are perpetually endeavouring to teach and drive into our soldiers' brains, and generally in vain ... our officers would be indifferent whether it was hill or hollow that they were in or on; and our men would stand erect and expose their whole persons in the most useless manner.[138]

Did contemporary officers simply believe that most British troops – both officers and men – were too stupid to learn how to skirmish effectively? Or do their observations reflect some unspoken, or subconscious, belief that there was some noble trait in the national character that made British soldiers unwilling to hide before their enemy, whereas men born in foreign countries infested by *banditti*, or where the *vendetta* and the *stiletto* were admired above the manly art of pugilism, would naturally be more willing to, and adept, at shooting down their enemies from places of concealment?

Having examined how riflemen and light infantrymen skirmished, the tactical significance of such skirmishing must be considered. Oman's statement that the line 'must be screened by a line of skirmishers impenetrable to the enemy's *tirailleurs*'[139] cannot mean that the skirmishers could always prevent the enemy's light troops from driving them back upon their supports, and thus stop the attack columns from closing with the infantry in line, for there are numerous examples of the French doing exactly that! William Green recalled that, at Coruña, 'on the 15th the 52nd regiment was on outlaying picquet. The French had sent out, in front of their army, a number of sharpshooters to attack our position. The 52nd were driven in. The bugle sounded the advance, and double-quick for the rifles, to attack their sharpshooters';[140] whilst at Vimeiro 'about eight or nine o'clock in the morning of the 21st, a cloud of light troops, supported by a heavy column of infantry, entered the wood, and assailing the pickets with great impetuosity, obliged us [the 95th] to fall back for support on the 97th regiment'.[141]

> The piquets extending right and left immediately fell back, under a shower of bullets, from the enemy's light troops, who continued forcing on in spite of all opposition. We gave them in return the full benefit of our small shot, as we occasionally drew up, covered by the vine hedges and olive trees, that lay within our path; and in this manner, alternately firing and retreating, so as to keep the foe aloof, we gained our situation in the line.[142]

Likewise, in the Pyrenees:

> At one point the light troops came running in, their faces begrimed with powder and sweat, quite close to the spot where Sir Rowland Hill and his staff were standing. I distinctly saw him turning back some men and heard his words addressing them: 'Go back my men, you must not let them up. You shall be instantly supported. You must not let them up.' Back they went cheerfully and soon disappeared among the trees and with the aid of a couple of battalion companies, that dashed from the hill at double quick, soon beat down the enemy at this point.[143]

Nor did skirmishers necessarily do much damage to the enemy before retiring. At Vimeiro:

> Some heavy masses of infantry, preceded by a swarm of light troops, were advancing with great resolution, and with loud cries of 'Vive l'Empereur!' 'En avant!' &c. against the hill on which our brigade was posted. In spite of the deadly fire which several hundred riflemen kept up on them, they continued to press forward with great determination, until the old 50th regiment received them with a destructive volley, following it instantly with a most brilliant and decisive charge with the bayonet, which broke and sent back, in utter dismay and confusion, and with great loss, this column, which a short time before was all confidence and exultation.[144]

The writer states clearly that, whatever effect the rifle fire had upon the French *tirailleurs*, it did not halt the progress of the columns of attack. Presumably, therefore, the riflemen had killed or wounded neither sufficient officers nor men to significantly damage the columns' morale. In his opinion, it was the 50th Foot's volley, immediately followed up with a bayonet charge, that threw the

French into confusion and routed them. An account of Vimeiro by an officer of the 50th, however, suggests that this charge was not effected without loss:

> When the latter, in a compact mass, arrived sufficiently up the hill, now bristled with bayonets, the black cuffs[145] poured in a well directed volley upon the dense array. Then, cheering loudly ... the whole regiment rushed forward to the charge, penetrated the formidable columns, and carried all before it. The confusion into which the panic-struck Frenchmen were thrown it would be difficult to express ... the fugitives were running in wild disorder, their white sheep-skin knapsacks discernible among woods far distant. There were, however, many resolute fellows, who, in retiring, took cover behind the hedgerows, saluting us with parting volleys, which did considerable execution among our advancing troops[146] ... The 50th lost a great proportion of rank and file, which chiefly arose from the fire of the French light troops, while covering their column, and during their retreat.[147]

At Bussaco, Leach comments that 'General Loison's division, which led the attack, was allowed by General Crawford [sic] to reach nearly the summit of the ridge, when he ordered a volley from his division, and a charge with the bayonet. The effect was instantaneous and most decisive; and it is impossible to describe the confusion and carnage which instantly ensued in the enemy's ranks.'[148] The use of the word 'allowed' is surely intended to convey the author's belief that Craufurd could, if he had so desired, prevented the column from reaching the crest of the ridge; which could only have been achieved by ordering the Riflemen and *Caçadores* lower down the slope not to fall back before the French advance, and, if necessary, deploying more troops as skirmishers to halt the enemy *tirailleurs* and force the French column to reinforce its own skirmish line.

Why should Craufurd, an experienced and talented officer,[149] wish to allow enemy columns to approach so close to his line? – 'the head of the enemy's column was within a very few yards of him'.[150] Only at close range could a volley of musketry cause a significant number of casualties, disconcert the column, and a decisive bayonet charge be delivered. If the skirmishers resisted the French advance too successfully, and did not 'fire and retire', the enemy would simply deploy more *tirailleurs*, resulting in a prolonged exchange of fire for no appreciable result,

> skirmishing and losing men uselessly. I cannot express how much aversion I have always had for skirmishing. It is difficult to imagine how much it costs in casualties ... Two new attacks against the position, just like the first, would not have been

more deadly ... The skirmishing ended on our side and the enemy started it again. As a matter of fact, it was extremely difficult to stop bickering except by withdrawing our troops, and this was not without inconvenience for either advantageous terrain or the morale of the army.[151]

Only a volley and charge with the bayonet could throw the enemy into confusion, break his morale, and rout him in disorder.

It is the contention of this essay that Wellington and his subordinates did not want their skirmishers to halt advancing French columns completely, but merely to prevent the accompanying *tirailleurs* from harassing their own formed troops, and to cause some casualties and disruption to the columns so that, when they cleared their *tirailleurs* to close with the line, a counter-charge with bayonet would have a good chance of routing them, as described below:

> As soon as we [the 95th] had got clear of the front of the 97th, and passed round its right flank, that regiment poured in such a well-directed fire, that it staggered the resolution of the hostile column, which declined to close and measure its strength with them. About the same time the 2d battalion of the 52d, advancing through the wood, took the French in flank, and drove them before them in confusion.[152]

Skirmishers had, in the words of Colonel David Dundas, 'to vanish before the solid movements of the line.'[153] but it was when withdrawing that they were, perhaps, most at risk:

> We 34th for the last hour had been amusing ourselves in comparative safety, picking off our friends in the distance, when a very large column came down upon us to stop our play. There was but one escape for us now – to run away, or to be riddled to death with French lead. The officer commanding, a brave man, saw how useless it was to contend against such a multitude, gave the word to retire at the double, and away we went down hill at a tearing pace. I never ran so fast in my life! Here the French had another advantage, rather a cowardly one. They kept firing after us for pastime. Every now and then some poor fellow was hit and tumbled over, and many a one carried weight over the course, i.e. a bullet or two in the back of his knapsack.
>
> We were now broken and dispersed. Our bugles sounded, few heard them – some too far away! The old corps was severely handled.[154]

The role of Wellington's skirmishers was to do no more than provide the optimum situation for the line to deliver such a decisive charge: '[Colonel George] Walker now ordered his men to prepare for close attack, and he watched with eagle eye the favorable moment for pouncing on the enemy.'[155] The problem facing British rifle and light infantry officers must have been timing the withdrawal of the skirmishers correctly: retire too soon and the French *tirailleurs* would be able to discomfort the line with their fire; too late, and the infantry in line could not deliver a crashing volley for fear of hitting their own skirmishers, which so concerned Rowland Hill at Talavera that 'it was one of the only two occasions on which he was known to swear':

> So thick was the atmosphere that the defenders heard rather than saw the start of Ruffin's division on its advance, and only realised its near approach when they saw their own skirmishers retiring up the slope towards the main line. The light companies of Hill's division came in so slowly and unwillingly, turning back often to fire, and keeping their order with the regularity of a field-day. The general, wishing to get his front clear, bade the bugles sound to bring them in more quickly, and as they filed to the rear in a leisurely way was heard to shout ... 'D——n their filing, let them come in anyhow.'[156]

One account refers to the line charging through their own skirmishers, who then joined the charge: 'The next minute he [Fane] gave the word to charge, and down came the whole line through a tremendous fire of cannon and musketry. As they came up with us, we sprang to our feet, gave one hearty cheer, and charged along with them'.[157]

To use a sporting metaphor may not be inappropriate – did not Wellington remark that the Battle of Waterloo was 'won on the playing fields of Eton'? – the skirmishers delivered the cross, but the infantry in line had to score the goal. Does Oman's view of Peninsular War skirmishing therefore need serious revision? It has been shown that he was wrong to suggest that the British always deployed more troops as skirmishers at once than the French, and also wrong to suggest that all British Light Infantry had lighter muskets than Line Regiments – although he did not attach any great significance to this difference in weaponry. He may have too readily accepted contemporary accounts of feats of marksmanship at face value, and hence concluded that British skirmishers were able to pick off French soldiers with greater accuracy than was probably the case. Oman cannot, of course, be held responsible for the subsequent depiction of every rifleman as a marksman in the pages of popular fiction.

It is a pity that so much attention has been devoted to Oman's 'Column versus Line' essay, for in the first volume of his *History* will be found the following passage:

His [Wellington's] method was to conceal his main line as long as possible ... To face the *tirailleurs* each battalion sent out its light company, and each brigade had assigned to it several detached companies of riflemen: from 1809 onward some of the 60th Rifles and one or two foreign light corps were broken up and distributed round the various divisions for this special purpose. This gave a line of skirmishers strong enough to hold back the *tirailleurs* for a long time, probably till the supporting columns came up to help them. It was only then that the British skirmishing line gave way and retired behind its main body, leaving the deployed battalions in face of the French column, of which they never failed to give a satisfactory account ... But the combat always went well if the enemy's skirmishers could be kept back, and his supporting columns forced to come to the front, to engage with the regiments in two-deep formation which were waiting for them.[158]

Although Oman's idea that French attacks in column were defeated by fire alone, not expressed in the above extract, has been discredited, his analysis of the role of the skirmish line as a screen to the infantry in line – and therefore not 'a force in itself'[159] but an auxiliary in effecting such defeats – still remains valid today.

Notes

1. Colonel David Dundas, *Principles of Military Movements, Chiefly Applied to Infantry* (London, 1788), p.14.

2. Harry Smith, *The Autobiography of Lieutenant-General Sir Harry Smith GCB* (ed. G.C. Moore Smith, London, 1903; reprinted Bath, 1968), p.174.

3. Benjamin Harris, *A Dorset Rifleman: The Recollections of Rifleman Harris* (ed. Eileen Hathaway, Swanage, 1995), p.133.

4. C.W.C. Oman, *Wellington's Army 1809–1814* (London, 1912), pp.377–83. Of sixty-five memoirs cited in his 'Regimental Bibliography' by officers and men who served in thirty-nine different infantry units (counting the KGL as one formation, and including the Portuguese infantry), twenty-two volumes – 33.8% of the total – were written by nineteen different authors – 31.7% of the total – in rifle or light infantry regiments. The 95th Rifle Brigade contributed 50% of them, with eleven works by nine authors (two each by Kincaid and Leach); the 43rd Light Infantry 18.2%, with four works by three authors; both the 52nd and 71st Light Infantry 9.1%, with two works by two authors; and the 51st, 68th and 85th Light Infantry each contributed 4.5% with one book apiece. The only other infantry regiments for which more than two volumes are cited are the 50th, with four works – 6.2% of the total – by three different authors, and the 42nd and KGL, with three works – 4.6% of the total – again by three different authors.

5. C.S. Forester, *Death to the French*. Rifleman Matthew Dodd of the 95th becomes separated from his battalion and joins a band of *guerrilleros*.

6. Bernard Cornwell, *Sharpe's Rifles, Sharpe's Gold, Sharpe's Eagle, et al*. Sharpe, originally a private soldier serving under Wellesley at Seringapatam and Assaye, is rewarded for saving the future Duke of Wellington's life by a commission in the 95th, and thereafter has numerous adventures in the Peninsular and Waterloo campaigns.

7. In R.F. Delderfield's *Too Few for Drums*, the hero is an inexperienced Ensign in the 51st Foot. In Ronald Welch's *Captain of Foot* (a children's novel), he is a subaltern in the 52nd.

8. Henry Curling, ed., *Recollections of Rifleman Harris* (London, 1848). New editions appeared in 1929, with introduction by J.W. Fortescue; in 1970, edited by Christopher Hibbert; and in 1985, also edited by Hibbert, reprinted in 1997. The most recent, and by far the best edition - replete with biographical notes and cross-references to other memoirs - is Eileen Hathaway's (1995). None of the reprint editions, however, have considered to what extent Curling - listed as the author of several historical novels in the *Dictionary of National Biography* - may have altered, embellished, or even invented some of Harris' anecdotes.

9. Anon, quoted by David Howarth in *Waterloo: A Near Run Thing* (London, 1972), p.9.

10. Thomas Morris (73rd Foot), *The Napoleonic Wars* (ed. John Selby, London, 1967; reprinted 1998).

11. George MacDonald Fraser, *Flashman, Flashman at the Charge, Flashman in the Great Game, et al*.

12. Captain John Kincaid, *Adventures in the Rifle Brigade* (London, 1830; reprinted Staplehurst, Kent, 1998); and *Random Shots from a Rifleman* (London, 1835; reprinted Staplehurst, Kent, 1998). A single-volume (abridged) edition of both was published in 1909 and reprinted 1981. Lieutenant-Colonel J. Leach, *Rough Sketches of the Life of an Old Soldier* (London, 1831; reprinted 1986); Major George Simmons, *A British Rifle Man: Journals and Correspondence during the Peninsular War and the Campaign of Waterloo* (London, 1899; reprinted 1986).

13. David Gates, *The British Light Infantry Arm c.1790–1815: Its Creation, Training and Operational Role* (London, 1987). See also Philip Haythornthwaite's comments in chapter 4, above.

14. George Nafziger, *Imperial Bayonets: Tactics of the Napoleonic Battery, Battalion and Brigade as Found in Contemporary Regulations* (London, 1996), p.111.

15. John Keegan, *The Face of Battle: A Study of Agincourt, Waterloo and The Somme* (London, 1976) p.168.

16. Oman, *Wellington's Army*, p.88.

17. Paddy Griffith, *Forward Into Battle: Fighting Tactics from Waterloo to the Near Future* (Swindon, 1990), chapter 2, pp.12–49.

18. Oman, *op.cit.* chapter IV, pp.61–93.

19. *Ibid* p.79.

20. *Ibid* p.82.

21. *Ibid* pp.88–9.

22. *Ibid* p.85.

23. *To the Right Honourable William Windham on a Partial Reorganization of the British Army* (1799), p.55.

24. *Ibid* pp.38-9.

25. Ian Fletcher, 'Wellington: Architect of Victory' in *The Peninsular War: Aspects of the Struggle for the Iberian Peninsula* (Staplehurst, Kent, 1998), pp.153-4. But contrast contemporary accounts (cited below in footnotes 29, 30 and 31), which show that British skirmishers at Vimeiro thought themselves outnumbered, suggesting that the French were able to drive them back without undue difficulty.

26. Gates, *op.cit.* pp.169-70.

27. *Ibid* p.85.

28. *Ibid* p.174. If Gates is here referring to light infantry in general, including riflemen, as opposed to specifically the light infantry regiments, 'British' may give a false emphasis as, apart from 95th and 5/60th (which, although originally composed of French *émigrés* and Germans, had only nine officers and less than half its rank and file still of German origin by the end of the war), all other rifle-armed troops – the Brunswick *Oels Jagers*, the Portuguese *Caçadores*, and the riflemen of the Calabrian Free Corps – were foreigners.

29. Harris, *op.cit.* p.48.

30. Bugler William Green (95th Foot), *Where Duty Calls Me: The Experiences of William Green of Lutterworth in the Napoleonic Wars* (ed. John and Dorothea Teague, 1975), p.19.

31. Walter Henry (Surgeon 66th Foot), *Surgeon Henry's Trifles: Events of a Military Life* (ed. Pat Hayward, London, 1970), pp.80-1. This, and the other accounts quoted, might, of course, simply be offering a supposed French numerical superiority as an acceptable explanation, or excuse, for the failure of the British light troops to hold their ground.

32. J.J. Pelet, *The French Campaign in Portugal, 1810-1811: An Account by Jean Jacques Pelet* (ed. Donald D. Horward, Minnesota, 1973), p.181.

33. Oman, *Studies in The Napoleonic Wars*, pp.92-3. See also James Arnold's discussion in chapter 3, above, and Brent Nosworthy's in chapter 10.

34. *JRUSI* 1910, pp.1528-9.

35. Moyle Sherer (34th Foot), *Recollections of the Peninsula* (1824; Staplehurst, Kent, 1996), pp.257-8.

36. David Gates, *The Spanish Ulcer: A History of the Peninsular War* (London, 1986), p.24.

37. Griffith, *op.cit.* p.55.

38. Oman, *History*, vol.VI, p.672.

39. *Ibid* p.675.

40. *Ibid* p.678.

41. Harris, *op.cit.* p.47.

42. Oman, *History*, vol.III, appendix XI, p.549.

43. 'Il y arrivera par une ou deux colonnes, en se faisant preceder par des tirailleurs' ('it will arrive there in one or two columns and arrange to be preceded by skirmishers') and 'Il se fera preceder par ses tirailleurs' (it will arrange to be preceded by skirmishers').

44. For biographical details refer to David Chandler, *Dictionary of the Napoleonic Wars* (London, 1979) and *Napoleon's Marshals* (London, 1987).

45. David Gates, *The Spanish Ulcer*, p.24.

46. Pelet, *op.cit.* p.181.

47. *Ibid* p.179.

48. *Ibid* p.181.

49. *cf* Oman, *Wellington's Army*, p.74: 'in each regiment a certain number of men should be selected for good marksmanship, and taught light infantry drill, while still remaining attached to their companies ... certain colonels ... trained fifteen or twenty men per company as skirmishers: they were called "flankers", and were to go out along with the light company.' Surely this is the inspiration/justification for Bernard Cornwell's creation of Sharpe's 'Chosen Men' – a small group of Riflemen attached to a line regiment!

50. Oman, *Wellington's Army*, pp.74–5. Notice Oman's use of the words 'marksman' and 'good shots', emphasising the significance of the fire of line battalions.

51. *JRUSI* 1910, p.1528.

52. Anon, *Vicissitudes in the Life of a Scottish Soldier, written by himself* (London, 1827), p.10.

53. Lieutenant-Colonel G.L. Chambers, *Bussaco* (1910; reprinted 1994), p.203.

54. 2/5th, 1/45th, 1/74th, 2/83rd, 1/88th, three companies 5/60th, two battalions 9th Portuguese Line, and one battalion 21st Portuguese Line.

55. J. Blakiston, *Twelve Years Military Adventure in Three Quarters of the Globe; or, Memoirs of an Officer* (2 vols, London, 1829), vol.II, pp.344–5.

56. George Napier, *The Early Military Life of General Sir George Napier KCB* (London, 1886), pp.123–4.

57. Kincaid, *Random Shots*, p.166.

58. George Hennell, *A Gentleman Volunteer: The Letters of George Hennell from the Peninsular War, 1812-13* (ed. Michael Glover, London, 1979), p.30.

59. Pelet, *op.cit.* p.181.

60. Kincaid, *Adventures in the Rifle Brigade*, pp.8–9.

61. Oman, *Wellington's Army*, p.301. Note that 'Brown Bess' was a nickname used pretty indiscriminately to describe any British Army flintlock smoothbore musket from Queen Anne onwards.

62. Oman, *op.cit.* p.76; *Studies in The Napoleonic Wars*, p.96.

63. See 'Wellington's Infantry Tactics - Line versus Column' in Oman, *Wellington's Army*, chapter IV, pp.61–93; or 'Column and Line in the Peninsula' in his *Studies in The Napoleonic Wars*, chapter V, pp.82–108.

64. For further technical details, and photographs of examples, see De Witt Bailey, *British Military Longarms, 1715-1815* (London, 1971), pp.28–32 and plates 21–28. For its adoption by the Board of Ordnance, see De Witt Bailey and David Harding, 'From India to Waterloo; The "India Pattern" Musket', in *The Road to Waterloo: The British Army and the Struggle Against Revolutionary and Napoleonic France 1793-1815* (ed. Alan J. Guy, London, 1990), pp.48–57.

65. Bailey, *British Military Longarms*, p.15.

66. *Ibid* p.17.

67. For technical details and photographs of both types of 'The Duke of Richmond's Musket', see plates 19 and 20, together with accompanying captions, *ibid* pp.29–32; or see the illustrations in Graeme Rimer, 'The Weapons of Wellington's Army', in *Wellington Commander: The Iron Duke's Generalship* (ed. Paddy Griffith, Chichester, 1983), chapter 8,

p.158. Records show that, although 10,000 were ordered, less than 4000 were delivered, and it is not known to which regiments they were issued.

68. For other technical details of the 'New Land' Pattern musket, see plates 28, 29, and 30, together with accompanying captions, in Bailey, *British Military Longarms*, pp.35-7, and also p.18.

69. Rimer, *op.cit.* p.160.

70. See plate 31 and accompanying caption, Bailey, *British Military Longarms*, pp.36-7.

71. *Ibid* p.37.

72. For 1810, *ibid* p.37; for 1811, Rimer, *op.cit.* p.160.

73. Bailey, *British Military Longarms*, p.37; also Rimer, *op.cit.* p.160.

74. 'Specific references' – not listed – are cited in support of this statement by Bailey and Harding in 'From India to Waterloo', p.56. 'And the Duke of York it also appears to have been who selected for the 52nd regiment the improved light infantry pattern of musket, which it was their good fortune to carry'; Richard Glover, *Peninsular Preparation: The Reform of The British Army 1795-1809* (Cambridge, 1963), p.129.

75. Bryan Fosten, *Wellington's Infantry (1)* (London, 1981), pp.20-1.

76. 'New Land' Pattern (forty-two-inch barrel) 11 lb 6 oz; 'Light Infantry' Pattern (thirty-nine-inch barrel) 11 lb 10 oz. *Ibid* p.22.

77. Bailey and Harding, 'From India to Waterloo', p.57: India Pattern (without bayonet) 9 lb 11 oz; 'New Land' Pattern 10 lb 6 oz. These figures tally with Fosten's for the India Pattern and 'New Land' Pattern, if one assumes that the bayonets for both muskets – which were actually slightly different (see Bailey, *British Military Longarms*, pp.79-80) – weighed 1 lb.

78. Officer of Pack's Brigade at Waterloo, *United Services Journal*, June 1841, p.183.

79. It is, however, the case that a longer barrel allows the explosive gases generated by the detonation of the powder-charge to propel the ball for more time, thereby increasing the maximum range. Brent Nosworthy *Battle Tactics of Napoleon and his Enemies* (London, 1995), p.197.

80. Infantrymen sometimes dispensed with the ramrod altogether, by simply dropping the ball down the muzzle and striking the butt of the musket hard on the ground once or twice to 'seat' the ball on the charge of gunpowder. This was known as 'tap-loading'.

81. Gunther E. Rothenberg, *The Art of Warfare in The Age of Napoleon* (London, 1977), pp.64-5.

82. Bailey, *British Military Longarms*, pp.65-9, 72-4, and plates 81-5 for the history and technical details. Note that Oman's statement that 'the rifleman carried no bayonet, his second weapon being a very short and curved sword' (*Wellington's Army*, p.303) is incorrect in two respects. The 'Pattern of 1801' sword, the standard issue during the Peninsular War, could be fixed to the side of the barrel to serve as a bayonet, and was straight, not curved.

83. Green, *op.cit.* pp.13-14.

84. Harris, *op.cit.* p.33.

85. Costello, *op.cit.* p.32.

86. Green, *op.cit.* p.17.

87. Harris, *op.cit.* p.36.

88. Anon, *Vicissitudes*, p.277.

89. Testimony of French officer, mortally wounded at Vimeiro, to the wife

of an English merchant whilst being nursed by her, and told to George Simmons. Simmons, *op.cit.* p.102.

90. Smith, *op.cit.* p.46.

91. Blakiston, *op.cit.* vol.II, pp.282–3. Blakiston and fellow officers were shocked by this 'disgusting narrative'. The culprit boasted of his action and was sent back to England, 'no longer to disgrace the honourable corps to which he had belonged.'

92. Kincaid, *Random Shots*, p.22.

93. Costello, *op.cit.* p.22.

94. William Surtees, *Twenty-five Years in The Rifle Brigade* (1833; reprinted London, 1973), p.90.

95. Oman, *History*, vol.I, p.569, n.2.

96. G.R. Gleig, *The Subaltern: A Chronicle of the Peninsular War* (1825; reprinted London, n.d.), pp.295–6. It is a pity that Gleig does not state clearly the range at which the *caçadore* first hit his opponents, but only that the final shot which caused the Frenchmen to retire was fired when they were only twenty yards away. Since he mentions earlier in his description of the scene that the French *tirailleurs* were advancing with fixed bayonets, it may not be unreasonable to assume that, having failed to shoot the rifleman, they were attempting to charge his position. Presumably the survivors were not aware that they faced only one man, now with an unloaded weapon, or they would have continued their charge, covering the twenty yards before he could reload.

97. Costello, *op.cit.* p.102. In other words, since the officer probably cannot see his men clearly much of the time anyway, he might as well be occupied loading and firing his own rifle.

98. *Ibid* p.102.

99. Simmons, *op.cit.* p.154.

100. *Ibid* pp.154–5.

101. Anon, *Vicissitudes*, pp.326–7.

102. John Patterson, *The Adventures of Captain John Patterson, with Notices of the Officers &c. of the 50th, or Queen's Own Regiment, from 1807 to 1821* (London, 1837), pp.327–8.

103. Lieutenant-Colonel Charles Cadell, *Narrative of the Campaigns of the Twenty-eighth Regiment, since their Return from Egypt in 1802* (London, 1835), pp.165–6.

104. Patterson, *op.cit.* pp.331–2. But since the range was very short, this was no great achievement, even with common muskets. So why does the author assume the French had rifles?

105. *Ibid* p.19. Presumably casualties from enemy fire caused the writer to believe he was 'within range of their rifles', as well as they being within range of his own weapon, suggesting that the *tirailleurs'* fire was not much less effective than that of the 95th.

106. Green, *op.cit.* pp.12–13.

107. Costello, *op.cit.* p.322. See also Colonel Willoughby Verner, *History and Campaigns of the Rifle Brigade, 1800–1813* (reprinted 1995), pp.116–17.

108. Costello, *op.cit.* p.95.

109. Harris, *op.cit.* pp.46, 49. But perhaps this refers to a 'mad minute' as the French columns advanced through their *tirailleurs* to close with the British line, rather than to less hurried exchanges of fire between

skirmishers.

110. Sherer, *op.cit.* p.238.

111. Anon, *Vicissitudes*, pp.281-2.

112. *Ibid* p.323.

113. *Ibid* pp.313-14.

114. For examples of assisting wounded men, see Costello, *op.cit.* pp.64, 66, and Green, *op.cit.* p.28. Harris, *op.cit.* p.38, describes leaving his post to comfort a dying man.

115. Harris, *op.cit.* pp.47-8.

116. *Ibid* p.39.

117. Kincaid, *Random Shots*, p.92.

118. *Ibid* pp.92-3.

119. For Peninsular War uniforms of all nations involved, in one volume, see either Martin Windrow and Gerry Embleton, *Military Dress of the Peninsular War* (London, 1974), or Philip Haythornthwaite and Michael Chappell, *Uniforms of the Peninsular War 1807-1814* (Poole, 1978). There are numerous studies of the various armies – and, for the British and French armies of the Napoleonic Wars, the individual arms of service – in the Men-at-Arms, Warrior, and Elite series, by Osprey Publishing.

120. Costello, *op.cit.* p.119.

121. Gleig, *op.cit.* quoted above, n.90.

122. Blakiston, *op.cit.*, vol.II, pp.344-5.

123. Harris, *op.cit.* p.46.

124. *Ibid* pp.38-9.

125. Green, *op.cit.* p.19.

126. Harris, *op.cit.* p.36.

127. Green, *op.cit.* p.13.

128. Colonel George Landmann, *Recollections of My Military Life* (London, 1854), vol.II, p.219. If one accepts the author's estimation of the distance, it seems that the *tirailleur* must either have been taking cover from the fire of Wellesley's riflemen, or expected to be able to pick off enemy soldiers from that distance with his musket.

129. Leach, *op.cit.* p.46.

130. Patterson, *op.cit.* p.41.

131. Blakiston, *op.cit.* vol.II, p.312.

132. Patterson, *op.cit.* p.48.

133. Green, *op.cit.* p.18.

134. Patterson, *op.cit.* pp.41-2. Notice the reference to 'French riflemen'.

135. Blakiston, *op.cit.* vol.II, pp.344-5.

136. Costello, *op.cit.* quoted above, n.113.

137. Sherer, *op.cit.* p.238; when memoirists write of 'the Germans' they must be referring to the 5/60th, and possibly to the Brunswick *Oels Jagers* as well.

138. Lieutenant-General Sir W. Stewart, *The Cumloden Papers: The Correspondence of Lieutenant-General Sir William Stewart* (Edinburgh, 1871), p.45.

139. Oman, *Wellington's Army*, p.79.

140. Green, *op.cit.* p.18.

141. Leach, *op.cit.* p.50.

142. Patterson, *op.cit.* pp.40-3.

143. Quoted by Rory Muir, *Tactics and the Experience of Battle in the Age*

of Napoleon (London, 1998), p.164, citing Lieutenant-Colonel Charles Cadell, *Narrative of the Campaigns of the Twenty-eighth Regiment* (London, 1835), as the source, supposedly from *With Wellington in the Pyrenees*, by Brigadier-General F.C. Beatson CB (London 1912), p.212. I cannot find this quotation in Cadell – and reading Beatson carefully suggests that Muir has misunderstood a footnote to a later quotation on the same page, and that Surgeon Walter Henry was the writer of this extract.

144. Leach, *op.cit.* pp.50–1; see also Griffith's account of the action in *Forward Into Battle*.

145. The 50th Foot had black facings – hence their other nickname 'The Dirty Half-Hundred'.

146. Patterson, *op.cit.* pp.45–6. Presumably these Frenchmen were the *tirailleurs* who had screened the columns of attack, which had advanced beyond them to close with the 50th before being repulsed.

147. *Ibid* p.48. According to Patterson, one officer – Major Charles Hill – was wounded and two – Captain A.G. Coote and Lieutenant I.N. Wilson – were killed. Oman gives the rank and file strength of the 1/50th at Vimeiro as 945 (*History*, vol.I, p.256), which gives a total strength of 1063 all ranks, if one adds one-eighth to allow for officers, non-commissioned officers and musicians. The 'table of losses for Vimeiro' referred to in a footnote (*History*, vol.I, p.261) is unfortunately missing from the appendices; but Fortescue states that the 50th had eighty-nine casualties (*History of the British Army*, London, 1910–30, vol.VI, p.234). Therefore, eighty-six other ranks must have been casualties.

148. Leach, *op.cit.* p.165.

149. For biographical details see Michael Barthorp, *Wellington's Generals* (London, 1978); Chandler, *Dictionary of The Napoleonic Wars*; Alexander H. Craufurd, *General Craufurd and his Light Division* (London, 1898; reprinted Cambridge, 1987); Ian Fletcher, *Craufurd's Light Division* (Staplehurst, Kent, 1991). It is surely ironic that the officer most closely associated with the success of the Light Division in the Peninsula should be one whose attitude towards, and treatment of, the soldiers under his command was so contrary to the principles of Sir John Moore!

150. Napier, *op.cit.* p.124.

151. Pelet, *op.cit.* pp.182–3.

152. Leach, *op.cit.* pp.50–1.

153. Dundas, *op.cit.* p.13.

154. George Bell, *Soldier's Glory being 'Rough Notes of an Old Soldier'* (ed. Brian Stuart, London, 1956), p.84.

155. Patterson, *op.cit.* p.45, on the 50th at Vimeiro.

156. Oman, *History*, vol.II, pp.523–4, citing *Military Journal of Leslie of Balquhain*, p.147.

157. Harris, *op.cit.* pp.47–8 (also Vimeiro).

158. Oman, *History*, vol.I, pp.116–17.

159. Fletcher, *op.cit.* p.154.

Chapter 12

Oman's *History* in its Spanish Context

by Dr Charles Esdaile

One of the most remarkable aspects of Sir Charles Oman's *History of the Peninsular War* is that it is just that – a history of the *Peninsular* War. Thus, Sir William Napier may fairly be said to have included the Spaniards in the comparable work that he had published half a century before for little other reason than to belittle them, and had, indeed, gloried in neglecting 'the thousand narrow winding currents of Spanish warfare to follow that mighty stream of battle, which, bearing the glory of England in its course, burst the barriers of the Pyrenees, and left deep traces of its fury in the soil of France'.[1] However, for Oman the struggle was one in which the Spaniards had played a major part. Fascinated though he clearly was by the figures of Sir John Moore and the Duke of Wellington and the campaigns that they waged, Oman therefore overtly took Napier to task, remarking, for example, that 'in his indignation at the arrogance and obstinacy with which they often hampered his hero, Wellington, he refuses to look at the extenuating circumstances which often explain, or even excuse, their conduct'.[2] Particularly damning in Oman's view, meanwhile, was the manner in which Napier had at every turn been uncritical in his acceptance of French versions of events in the Spanish war, whilst at the same time treating their Spanish counterparts with the utmost contempt. Inherent in his own *History*, then, was a fixed determination to encourage British readers in particular to understand that the conflict was much wider and more complex than they were wont to recognise. As he himself put it, in short: 'Every student of the Peninsular War must read Napier, but he must not think that, when the reading is finished, he has mastered the whole meaning and importance of the great struggle.'

Insofar as the purely military side of things is concerned, Oman may be said to have been successful. Whilst there to this day remain large numbers of 'buffs' for whom the Peninsular War is but a recital of such hallowed British battle honours as Vimiero (the correct spelling is Vimeiro), Talavera, and Salamanca, there is no excuse for such ignorance. Recounted in no fewer than 961 pages – not counting, that is, the many hundreds more covering battles and campaigns in which the forces of the Anglo-Portuguese and the Spaniards were conjoined – the efforts of the Spanish guerrillas and regulars alike are discussed in great detail. Indeed, such is Oman's mastery of the subject that subsequent scholars have found it hard to say anything new: setting aside the many British histories of the Peninsular War that turn out to be nothing more than exercises in Wellingtonian narrative, the only two works to have addressed the subject in the grand style since the publication of Oman's masterpiece – David Gates' handy *Spanish Ulcer* and the semi-official multi-volume history of the war that is currently being written under the aegis of the Spanish military archives – add little to the picture which he painted.[3]

To paraphrase Oman himself, however, his readers must not think that, when the reading is finished, they will have mastered the whole meaning and importance of the great struggle. Far from it, alas. Oman was a product of a time when the historical art in essence consisted of the writing of narrative that was, by its very nature, military, naval, high political, or diplomatic in character. Furthermore, a deeply conservative man, he also made it his business to champion the traditional style in the face of the challenge that it was facing from a new generation of historians strongly influenced by fresh approaches to the study of history. Unable to conceive of the importance of social and economic history, it is futile to look to him for a satisfactory explanation of the conflict.[4] Still worse, perhaps, the content of what he has to say even on such matters as high politics is often doubtful. True, Wellington's relations with successive British governments are portrayed in a fairer manner than is the case in Napier, but when it comes to Spanish politics the situation is very different. So damning, indeed, is the picture painted by Oman of successive Spanish régimes, whether they are those of Godoy, the *Junta Suprema Central*, or the regency and the *cortes*, that the reader might be forgiven for thinking that his intentions towards the Spaniards were much less favourable than he professed, his closing words on the subject being that Spain's 'resistance was ill-managed, the politicians who obtained civil power ... narrow and factious'.[5]

To understand this prejudice, we have only to turn to the sources which Oman relied upon as a guide to the political background of the period. Of primary importance here, we have the papers of the various British service and diplomatic personnel who came into direct contact with the Spanish authorities, good examples being Richard and Henry Wellesley, both of whom served as ambassadors to the Spanish government, and, of course, Wellington himself. The documents that have come down to us from these sources being liberally peppered with expressions of frustration, resentment, outrage, and disgust, it was natural enough that Oman should have taken their remarks at face value, and all the more so as he was absolutely secure in his faith in the collective judgement and capacity of the Wellesley family. In this connection, however, it is worth noting that, thanks to a combination of simple ignorance and a variety of historical, religious, and cultural influences, most contemporary British perceptions of early nineteenth-century Spain were fundamentally flawed. The views that were expressed by the sort of observer on whom Oman was relying were therefore more than somewhat unidimensional. That said, of course, even if it is unclear how much archival work he ever undertook in Spain, Oman was much too fine a historian to have relied solely on British sources. On the contrary, he specifically urges his readers to turn to the two main Spanish historians of the Peninsular War in the persons of the Conde de Toreno and General José Gómez de Arteche y Moro, it being in large part their narratives – the one largely high-political and the other largely military – which form the basis of his account of the Spanish side of events. Yet these sources were in their own way just as flawed. Himself a leading figure in the famous *cortes* of Cádiz, Toreno produced a history that was as partisan as it was misleading, whilst, as a general, Gómez de Arteche could not but be moulded by the prejudices and political conceits that characterised the Spanish officer corps right up till the era of General Franco.[6]

To turn to Oman for an understanding of the politics of the war is therefore likely to prove disappointing; but the problem is compounded by the fact that the subject has in large part been neglected by anglophone historians of the epoch. Whilst a few monographs and scholarly articles have dealt with one or other of its aspects, the only general study is Gabriel Lovett's *Napoleon and the Birth of Modern Spain*. Published in New York in 1965, this was a seminal work, which continues to constitute vital reading for any student of the Peninsular War. That said, however, it is based on historical perceptions that are in their own way just as unsatisfactory as those of Oman. Above all, following Toreno, ideology is regarded as paramount, the myth of the heroic Spanish people – the idea that the population of Spain rose up as one man to defend *dios, rey y patria* (God, King and Fatherland) against a foreign aggressor – being accepted at face value. Whilst Lovett certainly added enormously to the detail afforded by Oman, he therefore did little to correct many of the latter's misapprehensions.

Before we go any further, let it be made crystal clear that none of these comments are in any way intended to constitute a 'hatchet job'. Sir Charles Oman, after all, never set out to write a general study of Spain in the Napoleonic era. Convinced that military narrative was at the forefront of the historical art, he rather set out to produce an account (or 'chronicle') of the battles and campaigns of the Peninsular War, and, what is more, did so in the most admirable fashion – at the risk of being patronising, Oman's *Peninsular War* is a joy to read, and a mine of information. A pioneering work in its own day – it is, beyond doubt, a huge improvement on Napier – it remains of considerable importance. As Oman himself tells us, 'History ... starts with the chronicler', the fact being that, without his narrative efforts, it would now be impossible to pursue the other themes of which his work is so deficient.[7]

No violence, then, is intended to the shade of Sir Charles Oman – on the contrary, to think his work sufficiently important to warrant a project of this sort may rather be regarded as a compliment – but the fact remains that in a number of areas his *History* is at the very least open to revision. Not the least of these is the portrait which he affords of the Spanish statesman, Manuel de Godoy. In 1808 officially *generalissimo* – a post specially created for him as a means of giving him supreme control of the armed forces – Godoy had come to the Spanish court in 1788 as a trooper in the royal bodyguard known as the *Guardias de Corps*. By no means as lowly a post as this might imply – troopers in the bodyguard had the rank of sub-lieutenant in terms of the army list as a whole, whilst at the same time being recruited solely from the ranks of the nobility – this position quickly brought the young Extremaduran nobleman to the attention of the then heir to the Spanish throne, Prince Carlos, and his wife, María Luisa. Indeed, no sooner had the couple succeeded to the throne on the death of King Carlos III in December 1788, than the young Godoy (he had been only twenty-one at the time of his arrival in the Spanish court) began to experience an improvement in his fortunes that can only be described as vertiginous. A scion of an obscure family of the petty nobility, by 1792 he had been made a grandee of the first order, promoted to the rank of Captain-General, and appointed to the post of Secretary of State (roughly equivalent to prime minister). Showered with decorations and riches, for good measure he had also married a minor member of the royal family, whilst in 1795 he was awarded the title *Príncipe de la Paz* (Prince of the Peace) following his negotiation of relatively lenient terms with the victorious French Republic. Remaining Secretary of State until March 1798, he then briefly fell from favour, only to be brought back, first to command the forces dispatched against Portugal in the brief 'War of the Oranges' of 1801, and then to take charge of the general programme of military reform sparked off by that conflict.[8]

Following Toreno – and, for that matter, virtually every other Briton, Spaniard, or Frenchman who had ever written on the issue – Oman was in no doubts as to the reasons for all this, nor, still less, as to its implications for the history of Spain. The new king – Carlos IV – we are told, was 'a good-natured and benevolent imbecile', and his wife, María Luisa, 'self-confident, flighty, reckless ... bold, shameless, pleasure-loving, and as corrupt as southern court morality allows'. Oman does not quite say so much, true, but the implication is clear: Godoy became the lover of the queen and owed his elevation to high office entirely to his prowess in her bedchamber, Carlos IV being either fooled or bullied into granting the favourite his reward. What made all this still worse was that Godoy was by no means worthy of the high office to which he had been raised, being 'corrupt and licentious ... profoundly ignorant ... capable of any outburst of pride and ambition ... an upstart charlatan'. In the years of power which he proceeded to enjoy, there were in consequence few redeeming traits. He 'endeavoured to popularise the practice of vaccination, waged a mild and intermittent war with the Inquisition, and ... tried to suppress the custom of bull-fighting', but, for the rest, he simply 'stowed away enormous riches', whilst at the same time disorganising the armed forces, following a ruinous foreign policy based on the most absolute subservience to France, impoverishing the treasury, and filling up the senior ranks of the administration and the high command with 'those who were most ready to do him homage, to wink at his peculations, to condone his jobs, and to refrain from worrying him for the money needed for reforms and repairs'. Last but not least, meanwhile, he was responsible for much of the predicament in which Spain found herself in 1808, the presence of the large army which Napoleon had sent over the frontier from the autumn of 1807 onwards having been largely the result of the favourite's desire to secure a principality for himself in Portugal. 'Fifteen years of power had so turned his head that for a long time he had been taking himself quite seriously, and his ambition had grown so monstrous that, not contented with his alliance by marriage with the royal house, he was dreaming of becoming a sovereign prince.'[9]

The would-be student of the Peninsular War is therefore presented by Oman with a bleak picture of the régime of what its three members jokingly referred to as the 'trinity upon the earth', a picture that is softened only by unflattering reflections to the effect that the fault was not theirs alone but that of the Spanish nation as a whole (if the Spanish army was antiquated, for example, it was due to 'the national temperament, with its eternal relegation of all troublesome reforms to the morrow'[10]). There never being smoke without fire, there is a measure of truth in all of this: Godoy, for example, *was* venal, pleasure-loving, and licentious, just as he did indeed become obsessed with the idea that he was both a great statesman and a military genius. In the same way, with regard to the Spanish army in particular, so far as Oman's remarks go, they are but the literal truth – 'If he had chosen, he possessed the power to change everything; and in some ways he had peddled a good deal with details ... But to make the army efficient he had done very little.'[11] However, if it is a truism that there is no smoke without fire, it is also a truism that history is written by the victors, the picture of Godoy painted in such lurid detail by Oman being very much the picture that was painted of him, first, by the palace clique that was eventually to engineer his overthrow, and, second, by the propagandists of Patriot Spain (*ie* all Spaniards, of whatever political tendency, who could unite to resist the French). Possessed of many faults though he undoubtedly was, there was rather more to the Prince of the Peace than originally seemed to meet the eye, as a number of Spanish historians had already begun to realise by the time that Oman was penning his critique – indeed, even Oman was forced to remark that there was something rather puzzling about certain aspects of Godoy, not least the 'astonishing ... courage' which he displayed in prohibiting *los toros* (bullfighting).[12]

In writing thus, it has to be said that Oman was being all too revealing. Had he known more about either the central pillars of Godoy's rule or the political context in which the favourite was operating, he would have found nothing astonishing at all about Godoy's attack on bullfighting, whilst he would also have been forced to recognise that Godoy's progressive stance on such issues was not a mere pose stemming from the desire 'to be hailed as universal benefactor, and as the introducer of modern civilization into Spain'.[13] Thus, in reality, Godoy was not only very much a genuine reformer himself, but his policies were entirely in line with the general political culture of eighteenth-century Spain. Whereas Oman's assumptions are postulated very much upon the view that Spain was a medieval backwater sunk in archaism and reaction, in fact nothing could have been further from the truth. Since the accession of Carlos III in 1759, she had rather been at the forefront, if not of the Enlightenment, then at least of the movement that has generally been entitled enlightened absolutism. Thus, in common with the monarchies of most of the other states of continental Europe, the Spanish Bourbons had been struggling to erode the power of the Church and the nobility, break down provincial privilege, increase the power of the state, strengthen the armed forces – given Spain's permanent alliance with France, this primarily meant the navy – promote economic development and agricultural reform, and combat ignorance and superstition.[14] Inheriting these policies, Carlos IV and Godoy did not, as is sometimes claimed, abandon them in terror of the French Revolution, but were impelled rather to accelerate them. Thus the period 1798–1808, in particular, witnessed a sustained attempt both to strip the Church of a large part of the immense amount of landed property that it owned in one part of Spain or another in the hope that the estates concerned could be sold off with the aim of raising money for the war effort, and to relieve it of a greater proportion of the revenue that it received from such traditional dues as tithes and first fruits. Meanwhile, if Godoy was not primarily responsible for these measures – they were in fact introduced at the very time that he left the government *per se* – he is certainly innocent of the charge that he neglected the army. Ally Spain with France though he certainly did, he only did so with the gravest reservations, his private papers suggesting that he was above all concerned to win time: believing that a further confrontation with France was inevitable, he made a series of very real attempts to rid the Spanish army of the deficiencies that had become all too apparent in the unsuccessful campaigns that had been waged against France in the course of Spain's two-year participation in the War of the First Coalition. Meanwhile, in addition to abolishing bullfighting – a measure linked to the better use of the land, the preservation of public order, and the 'civilisation' of the populace alike – it was he who faced down the opposition of the Church and forced through the publication of Gaspar Melchor de Jovellanos' noted treatise on agrarian reform known as the *Informe sobre la Ley Agraria* (Report on the Agrarian Law).[15]

Not only was Godoy associated with the continuation of the reformist policies of Carlos III, but it is arguable that he owed his rise to power precisely to a desire on the part of the new monarch to perpetuate those policies. Bright Carlos IV was not, but it did not need much in the way of intelligence to appreciate the advantages that could be derived from the continued application of enlightened absolutism. By the time that he came to power, however, the latter had aroused considerable opposition amongst both the Church and the upper nobility, whilst the ranks of the governing classes were becoming increasingly disrupted by a bitter feud that had developed between two factions known respectively as the 'wigs' and the 'cravats'. The passage of two or three years sufficing to show that all momentum was likely to be lost unless some action was taken to remedy the situation, the king pitched upon the solution of placing the machinery of the state in the hands of a man who was of no party and owed everything to him, whilst yet giving every appearance of being both intelligent and personable. That Godoy had become so prominent as to suggest himself for such an appointment was, to be sure, largely the fruit of the patronage of the queen, but in the context of eighteenth-century Spain even this was not so very scandalous. What few British observers have realised insofar as the tangled affairs of the Spanish court are concerned is that the favourite occupied a position that was entirely consonant with the practices of polite society. Thus, in brief, he was María Luisa's *cortejo*, the latter being the semi-official male companion-cum-champion-cum-lover of a married woman. Interesting though the origins and nature of the custom may be, we cannot, alas, discuss it at any length here. Suffice to say that, by the standards of the day, Godoy's relationship with the queen was not in itself a matter of either scandal or even particular remark.[16]

How, then, did Godoy acquire the reputation which Oman so faithfully retails? In the first place, it has to be said that to be a reformer is not the same as to be a successful reformer. However sincere Godoy may have been in his objectives, it cannot be gainsaid that he in fact presided over a precipitous decline in Spain's fortunes. Still a world power of the first rank in 1788, by 1808 she had been reduced to a state of utter penury, plunged into a major economic crisis, and stripped of the naval power that was the foundation of her whole position. Trapped by unfavourable circumstances as he was, Godoy was in reality but little responsible for these misfortunes, as well as being severely hampered by their consequences, but the fact remains that his many vices rendered matters much worse than they might otherwise have been. Thus, alienating many men of a reformist disposition through his avarice and ostentation, he at the same time lacked the strength of character to push the cause of reform to the limit, the result being that in some areas - a good example is the army - he was indeed reduced to doing little more than tinkering with a few details.[17]

To put it mildly, then, as the years passed Godoy became more and more vulnerable to attack, and it was not long before a faction of grandees were conspiring to bring him down. Outraged by the threat which his policies posed to the status and privileges of the aristocracy, they were soon joined by a variety of figures whom Godoy had for one reason or another denied the patronage which they sought, and, eventually, by the new heir to the throne, Prince Fernando. Grouped in a classic cabal, the conspirators then proceeded to throw themselves into a wholesale campaign to destabilise the favourite's régime.[18] Too complex to go into in any detail here, the events that followed culminated in the overthrow of the 'trinity upon the earth' in a major revolt at the royal palace of Aranjuez in March 1808, the elevation of Fernando to the throne, and the overthrow of the entire Bourbon dynasty by Napoleon in the notorious 'ambuscade of Bayonne'. Needless to say, however, they did not represent just the mere palace intrigue whose picture is painted for us by Oman. As the contemporary examples of Gustav III of Sweden, Paul I of Russia, Joseph I of Austria, and even Louis XVI of France all show, resistance to enlightened absolutism amongst the privileged orders was growing across the length and breadth of the entire continent, the true significance of events in Spain only being fully revealed by their wider context.[19]

Having dealt with the era of Godoy, we now arrive at the uprising of 1808. So far as Oman was concerned, this was again a simple affair. In brief, the Spanish people were disgusted by the failure of the civil and military authorities to resist Napoleon's imposition of his brother, Joseph, in place of *el rey deseado* (literally the 'desired king'; an English equivalent might be 'Prince Charming'), Fernando VII. Led by 'local magnates not actually holding office ... or demagogues of the streets', they therefore rose in revolt and forced their betters to adopt the cause of resistance, on occasion killing those – in large part the creatures of Godoy – who sought to restrain them.[20] According to Oman, then, what motivated the uprising was a mixture of love of Fernando VII, resentment of the French, and hatred of Godoy. However, once again, more recent scholarship has shown that matters were rather more complicated. All of the factors stressed by Oman were present, certainly, but they did not signify exactly what he assumed, whilst the revolt was influenced by a number of other factors of which he was but dimly aware, if at all. Let us take, for example, his remarks with regard to the leadership of the uprising. Who were these 'local magnates not actually holding office'? In what relationship, if any, did they stand to the 'demagogues of the streets'? What goals did they possess? Whilst the answers to these questions are by no means clear in every case, sufficient work has been done to suggest that the rising against the French was a distinctly murky affair that reflected a number of the different tensions that were besetting the body politic. What appears to be the case, in fact, is that the various provincial risings – for there was no concerted uprising as such – were engineered by a variety of 'out' groups who made use of paid agitators to whip up the crowds and instigate a riot.

Motivating the men concerned were a number of different concerns that were sometimes directly at odds with one another. Thus, amongst the leaders of the insurrection were disgruntled office-seekers, radicals eager to make a political revolution, prominent civilians resentful of the privileges of the military estate and jealous of the predominance it had been allowed to assume in Spanish society, discontented subaltern officers who were eager for promotion, conservative clerics horrified by the spoliation of the Church, and members of the aristocracy who were opposed to the creeping advance of royal authority and had in some cases been involved in the plot to overthrow Godoy. As for the crowd, meanwhile, its motivation was once again as much material as it was ideological. There was intense loyalty to the person of Fernando VII, true, but it is clear that this stemmed not so much from who he was as from what he represented. Thus the conspirators who had overthrown Godoy had deliberately represented Fernando as a species of Prince Charming who would right all Spain's ills and usher in a new golden age, this vision being all the more appealing in view of the terrible conditions that by 1808 were being endured by the bulk of the population as a result of epidemic, crop failure, a variety of structural problems, the expropriation of Church lands, and the war against Britain. From the very beginning, the result was that the uprising assumed a strong social dimension.[21]

What, then, of fighting the French? In this respect it is interesting to note that, a few minor affrays aside, wherever the invaders were actually in physical occupation of an area there was no revolt against them (the one major exception is Madrid's famous *Dos de Mayo*). As for the war that proceeded to ensue, the populace were willing enough to spring to arms when they were themselves directly threatened by the invaders, whilst it was not long before traditional forms of violent social protest – above all, banditry – had become subsumed into what was to become the famous *guerrilla* ('little war'). Apart from that, however, there was little enthusiasm for the struggle. Whilst bourgeois town guards that claimed exemption from service in the field were swamped with recruits, recruitment to the regular army did not follow the pattern that might have been expected. Voluntary enlistment was consequently sluggish, whilst attempts to impose conscription met with obstruction and resistance, the fact being that the populace continued to exhibit the marked aversion to military service that had characterised it throughout the eighteenth century. As Oman himself recognised – he points out, for example, that the entire province of New Castile only raised six battalions of infantry and a single regiment of cavalry in the course of 1808 – the picture of a nation united in struggle is therefore very much open to question. However, for explanation he could do no more than blame the inefficiency of the Patriot authorities, or the fact that, lulled by months of irresponsible propaganda, the people were 'living in a sort of fool's paradise', whereas in fact these very real problems explain only a part of the difficulty.[22]

If it is obvious that the answer to such problems requires a knowledge of *mentalités* of a sort that Sir Charles Oman could not conceive; this is even more apparent with regard to the study of the guerrilla struggle to which the war soon gave rise. In Oman's mind an issue that was entirely straightforward – convinced that the efforts of the guerrillas were one of the major keys to Wellington's ability to keep the field in the Peninsula, he was fulsome in his praise of their heroism and efficacy[23] – this has actually proved one of the most complex and contentious aspects in the entire struggle. As many a recent conference debate will testify, it is all but impossible to decide just who the guerrillas were, let alone to arrive at an estimation of their contribution to the struggle. As to the vexed question of whether or not the *guerrilla* was actually a mere *jacquerie*, this was barely addressed by Oman if at all, and virtually defies analysis altogether.

At this point, some words of explanation might be in order. In the impoverished conditions that characterised much of rural Spain right up until the twentieth century, for many peasants and, especially, landless labourers banditry was a vital means of survival – indeed, in many instances the only means of survival. At the same time, too, it was also a means of revenging oneself upon the propertied classes and their representatives, it being the latter who were the most obvious targets for robbery and extortion. One should not go too far in this vein – much banditry consisted of the poor robbing the not quite so poor – but the links with the situation that pertained in 1808 are obvious. Thus conditions were even more desperate than usual, whilst social tensions were increasing, the propertied classes generally being eager to exploit the situation for their own benefit. In the context of French occupation, moreover, banditry acquired a new legitimacy, the fact being that many of the propertied classes had chosen the path of collaboration. As we know that many leading bandits actually became guerrillas, it is therefore impossible not to suspect that at root the 'little war' was in reality but a much accentuated phase in the violence that had characterised social relations in much of rural Spain since time immemorial.[24]

Once again it is important not to go too far. Even at its most inchoate and apolitical, popular violence could be a considerable nuisance to the French, whilst its impact was greatly accentuated by such attempts as were made at militarisation. Moreover, it is but fair to say that, at least insofar as parts of Navarre are concerned, the views expressed by Oman with regard to the guerrillas have in recent years received staunch support from the American historian, John Tone. That said, however, we once again see that the views expressed by Oman need to be placed in the context of the work of later historians (indeed, even Tone notes that the extent of involvement in the struggle in Navarre varied enormously from very high levels that characterised the mountain villages of the north to the relative apathy that typified the much larger 'agro-towns' of the south[25]). Like it or not, in fact, the military history of the war cannot be separated from its political and social counterparts. For further evidence of this we have only to turn to the travails which Wellington experienced during the period from January 1813 to April 1814 in which he exercised the command-in-chief of the Spanish armies, and in the process attempted to bring them up to a standard of discipline and organisation sufficient to allow them to take the field against the French. Insofar as all this is concerned, Oman paints a damning picture of Spanish obstruction and subterfuge. 'No nation,' he admits, 'likes to have ... reforms thrust upon it by a foreigner – more especially by a foreigner whose tone is dictatorial and whose phrases seem almost deliberately worded so as to wound national pride.' At the same time, too, he recognises that 'many Spaniards thought Wellington capable of aiming at a military dictatorship ... and ... that British policy secretly desired the seizure of Cádiz and Minorca and the reduction of Spain to a protectorate'. Some degree of recalcitrance was therefore inevitable, then, but Oman in practice blamed everything on the manoeuvres of powerful vested interests in the temporary Spanish capital of Cádiz, the intrigues of the liberals who had come to dominate the new single-chamber parliament that had been established in that city, and the chronic inefficiency of the Spanish administration, it being above all the last which led to the fact that when Wellington took the field in the campaign of Vitoria in May 1813 less than 25,000 Spanish troops were available for service out of a total force of no fewer than six times that figure.[26]

Once again, all this is very well in its own way – as Oman infers, the Duke was indeed subjected to a sustained campaign of political harassment – but there is much more to all of this than meets the eye. In the first place, Spanish hostility was all the time being inflamed by a matter of which Oman makes no mention, namely the on-going British efforts to mediate between Cádiz and the various rebel administrations that had set themselves up in parts of Spanish America in 1810 on terms that would effectively have placed the whole of the American trade in British hands. In the second, whilst the problem of authority was recognised by Oman – as he rightly points out, one of Wellington's proposals was to place local government entirely in the hands of the military – it can be argued that he does not pay sufficient attention to the conditions that were operative in much of the considerable territory that had now been liberated from the French. We return here, of course, to the question of the guerrillas. Behind the French lines, the 'war of the flea' raged unabated, but elsewhere matters were very different. In many cases little more than bandits, as we have seen, they had never been solely engrossed in the task of fighting the French and their allies, but had rather continued to pursue a traditional agenda to which the presence or absence of the French made little difference. One must except a few of the larger and more disciplined bands which had long since assumed the status of brigades and even Divisions of the regular army and in consequence now came out into the open to join Wellington's forces in their operations. However, for the rest the guerrillas of Andalucia, New Castile, Extremadura, and León did not demobilise but rather lived by pillage, ravaging the countryside, terrorising the propertied classes, and on occasion even raiding British supply trains. Nor, indeed, was banditry the only problem. Stirred up by agrarian policies that in practice perpetuated the burdens of the feudal system which they theoretically abolished, the populace of the liberated territories on more than one occasion turned to riot, attacking the property of their erstwhile lords, tearing down gibbets, and burning the archives that recorded their various obligations.[27] To blame all Wellington's ills on the Spanish authorities is therefore unfair, but, from all that has been said thus far, it will be inferred that Oman's account of the politics of the war is less than flattering.

Often dealt with by popular works in a fashion that is as confused as it is cursory, it might be as well at this point briefly to outline the political developments that were unleashed by the uprising. In brief, power initially lay in the hands of a number of hastily improvised provincial *juntas* and petty military dictatorships (of the latter the only lasting example was that of General Palafox in Saragossa). Prompted both by the urgings of the British and the common sense of many of their leaders, in September 1808 these independent local governments established what amounted to a federal authority known as the *Junta Suprema Central*, or Supreme *Junta*, which sat first at Aranjuez and then at Seville. The political history of the next year was dominated on the one hand by the efforts of the provincial *juntas* to defy the authority of the government they had created, and on the other by the schemes of assorted aristocratic generals to overthrow the Supreme *Junta* and replace it with some sort of regency, their hope being that this would entrench the position of the nobility and establish a firm bulwark against any further encroachment on its rights. Under constant threat of a military coup, faced by a difficult strategic situation – by December 1808 the French had reoccupied Madrid and were consequently in occupation of much of the centre of the country – and wrestling with the difficult problem of the political shape that should be given to Patriot Spain, the Supreme *Junta* threw itself into a desperate search for military victory. Of this, however, there could be but one consequence: ill-supplied, ill-clothed, ill-trained, ill-organised, and ill-commanded, and for the most part operating without direct British support (the one exception is the campaign of Talavera), the Spanish armies were defeated on almost every occasion that they took the field.

The Supreme *Junta's* resources being anything but infinite, by January 1810 the remaining bulwarks of the Patriot cause – most notably Andalucia – were wide open to French conquest, almost the whole of the south, in fact, being immediately overrun by a massive offensive. Forced to evacuate Seville, which was promptly gripped by an uprising against its rule, the Supreme *Junta* fled to the island haven of Cádiz and neatly pre-empted its critics by surrendering power into the hands of a regency of its own making, from which the aristocratic *frondeurs* who had beset it for so long were excluded. In September 1810, meanwhile, the political situation was amended still further. Some time prior to its downfall the Supreme *Junta* had announced that it intended to summon a new parliament, or *cortes*, to oversee the war effort and elaborate the general plan of reform for which most elements of educated opinion were calling. Opening in Cádiz in September 1810, the assembly was for various reasons almost immediately captured by a small faction of ideologues. Known as the *liberales* from their determination to free (*liberar*) Spain, they gave us the modern word 'liberal', whilst at the same time proceeding to force through a radical programme of reform (encompassing such projects as the abolition of the Inquisition) which was encapsulated in the fundamental political text known as the Constitution of 1812. In doing so, however, they split educated opinion down the middle. Thus, whilst the need for reform was agreed by almost everyone, there was no agreement as to what form it should take. For the *liberales* it was, in effect, the creation of a modern capitalist society buttressed by constitutional institutions and the rule of law. Implied in this programme, however, was not just the limitation of the power of the monarchy but also the overthrow of the privileges of the Church and the nobility. Initially attracted by a trend that promised to put an end to the onward march of enlightened absolutism, significant elements of public opinion had therefore soon been propelled into a position of resistance. Hence the emergence of a powerful opposition party known as the *serviles* (so-called because the *liberales* accused them of being unwilling to throw off the chains of despotism). As a result, the period 1812–14 was one of extreme tension, the end product being the military coup that restored Fernando VII - now released by Napoleon - as absolute ruler of Spain in 1814.[28]

What does Oman make of all this? Given the nature of his work, the subject is necessarily dealt with *en passant*. However, the main outline of events is clear enough, and Oman is also far less careless than many later chroniclers of Wellington's campaigns (he does not, for example, make the common mistake of confusing the Supreme *Junta* with the provincial *junta* that also sat at Seville). That said, there are nonetheless few areas of Oman's work where his judgement is more deficient. Misled on the one hand by the reams of complaint and denigration that may be found amongst British correspondence of the period, and on the other by the prejudices of Gómez de Arteche, the professor proceeds from one fixed principle - that 'it was hard to constitute a capable government on the spur of the moment in a country which had suffered twenty years of Godoy's rule'.[29] Whilst prepared to concede that the leaders of the insurrection contained 'many intelligent patriots [and] a certain number of statesmen who had been kept down ... by Godoy', Oman appears to have believed that the majority were 'ambitious windbags and self-seeking intriguers'.[30] On the subject of the provincial *juntas* and the *Junta Suprema Central* alike, he is therefore scathing - the latter, in particular, is repeatedly accused of having been interested in little else but the perpetuation of its own power - whilst the *cortes* of Cádiz is decried as being 'neither satisfactory nor representative', Oman taking particular offence at the fact that Supreme *Junta* and *cortes* alike devoted themselves to elaborating programmes of political reform when they should have been primarily engaged in fomenting the war effort.[31]

All this is bad enough, but still worse is Oman's judgement of such figures as the head of the insurrection in Saragossa, José Palafox, and the erstwhile commander of the Spanish division that had in 1807 been sent at the behest of Napoleon to the Baltic, the Marqués de la Romana. Whilst aware that neither of these figures could be called a military genius, Oman was inclined to regard both of them with considerable favour. Consequently Palafox receives fulsome praise for his 'courage and energy', 'untiring activity', and 'talent for rapid work', whilst La Romana is remembered as 'a general of ... very high and meritorious record' whose death in 1811 was 'a real disaster to the cause of the allies'. In both cases it is true that Oman notes the existence of a rival point of view – in brief, that the two generals were factious and ambitious incompetents, and, in the case of Palafox, a coward to boot – but the dissident voices are dismissed out of hand and put down in large part to 'scurrilous accusations made ... in pamphlets and newspapers published at Cádiz'.[32] What the historian faces here is a classic problem of interpretation, it being impossible to substantiate the argument either way, but the fact remains that such a position is no longer easy to sustain. Whatever conclusions may be reached with regard to their courage and energy, both Palafox and La Romana were all too evidently bitterly at odds with the political situation that developed in the wake of the uprising of 1808, as well as being involved in a series of intrigues that in the case of the former at least had a most serious impact upon the conduct of the war.[33]

To conclude, the seven volumes of Oman's *History* remain a vital first port of call – indeed, *the* vital first port of call – for anyone who wishes to become a serious student of the Spanish War of Independence of 1808–14. Some of Oman's judgements may be criticised, some of his information corrected, and some of his perspectives expanded; but he completed the task that he set himself extremely well. Moreover, being both clear and in many respects reasonably fair, the narrative that he has left us has opened the way for others to explore the different approaches that have been opened up by new developments in the study of history. The latter has moved on – indeed, modern historical methods may even be more revealing on those questions where a combination of military, social, political, and economic factors are at work – but the framework for further study which he established remains unchallenged in its necessity and unequalled in its importance. *A History of the Peninsular War*, in short, will continue to be read with profit and pleasure for many years to come.

Notes

1. W. Napier, *History of the War in the Peninsula and in the South of France from the Year 1807 to the Year 1814* (London, 1828-34), vol.I, p.vii.

2. Oman's strictures on Napier may be found in *A History of the Peninsular War* (Oxford, 1902-30), vol.I, pp.xi-xii.

3. *cf* D. Gates, *The Spanish Ulcer: A History of the Peninsular War* (London, 1986), and J. Priego López, *Guerra de la Independencia, 1808-1814* (Madrid, 1972 on).

4. For some examples of Oman's historical thought, *cf* Oman, *Studies in the Napoleonic Wars* (London, 1929), pp.1-36. Especially revealing is his statement that 'history is not so often the history of the progressive development of a race or an empire, as the story of the working of individual great men on their contemporaries' (p.11).

5. Oman, *History*, vol.VII, p.516. Scathing as this line is, it is all the more surprising in view of the rather more nuanced picture that had been presented in R.W. Southey, *History of the Peninsular War* (London, 1823-32).

6. The two works referred to are Conde de Toreno, *Historia del Levantamiento, Guerra y Revolución de España* (Paris, 1838), and J. Gómez de Arteche y Moro, *Guerra de la Independencia: Historia Militar de España de 1808 a 1814* (14 vols, Madrid, 1868-1903).

7. For Oman's thoughts on the question of narrative, *cf* Oman, *Studies in the Napoleonic Wars*, p.3.

8. For two recent studies of Godoy, *cf* C. Seco Serrano, *Godoy: el hombre y el político* (Madrid, 1978), and L. González Santos, *Godoy: príncipe de la paz, siervo de la guerra* (Madrid, 1985). The Iberian background in the 1790s is covered by Professor Livermore in appendix 3, below.

9. For Oman's views on Carlos IV, María Luisa, and Godoy, *cf* Oman, *History*, vol.I, pp.12-16, 96-8.

10. *Ibid* p.96.

11. *Ibid*.

12. *Ibid* p.15.

13. *Ibid*.

14. For an introduction to the operations of enlightened absolutism in Spain, *cf* C. Noel, 'Charles III of Spain', in H.M. Scott, ed., *Enlightened Absolutism: Reform and Reformers in Eighteenth-Century Europe* (London, 1990), pp.119-44; A. Guimerá, ed., *El Reformismo Borbónico: una Visión Interdisciplinar* (Madrid, 1996); and C.J. Crowley, 'Luces and Hispanidad: Nationalism and Modernisation in Eighteenth-Century Spain', in M. Palumbo and W. Shanahan, *Nationalism: Essays in Honour of Louis L. Snyder* (Westport, Connecticut, 1981), pp.87-102.

15. For the survival of enlightened reform under Godoy and Carlos IV see Hamnett, *La Política Española en una Epoca Revolucionaria* (México, D.F., 1985), pp.43-57; R. Herr, *The Eighteenth-Century Revolution in Spain* (Princeton, 1958), pp.390-433; and W. Callahan, *Church, Politics and Society in Spain, 1750-1874* (Cambridge, Massachusetts, 1984), pp.74-85. Meanwhile, P. Molas Ribalta, ed., *La España de Carlos IV* (Madrid, 1991), is a very helpful collection of essays.

16. For the custom of the *cortejo* see C. Martín Gaite, *Love Customs in Eighteenth-Century Spain* (Berkeley, California, 1991).

17. For a distinctly down-beat modern assessment of Godoy, *cf* J. Lynch,

Bourbon Spain (Oxford, 1989), pp.382–418. The favourite's travails in respect of the army are discussed in C.J. Esdaile, *The Spanish Army in the Peninsular War* (Manchester, 1988), pp.36–68 *passim*.

18. *cf* J. Pérez de Guzmán y Gallo, 'El primer conato de rebelión precursor de la revolución de España', *España Moderna* CCL (1909), pp.109–14, and CCLI (1910), pp.48–68; H. Castro Bonel, 'Manejos de Fernando VII contra sus padres y contra Godoy', *Boletin de la Universidad de Madrid* II (1930), pp.397–408, 493–503; M.E. Martínez Quinteiro, 'Descontento y actitudes políticas de la alta nobleza en los orígenes de la edad contemporánea', *Hispania* XXXVII, no.135 (January, 1977), pp.95–138.

19. For Oman's account of the events of 1808, see his *History*, vol.I, pp.16–24, 33–42. A more recent and comprehensive study is constituted by F. Marti Gilabert, *El Motín de Aranjuez* (Pamplona, 1972).

20. Oman, *History*, vol.I, pp.64–8.

21. For an interesting discussion of the Spanish uprising, *cf* R. Herr, 'Good, evil and Spain's uprising against Napoleon', in R. Herr and H. Parker, eds., *Ideas in History: Essays presented to Louis Gottschalk by his Former Students* (Durham, North Carolina, 1965), pp.157–81. Also of help are Esdaile, *op.cit.* pp.75–90, and Hamnett, *op.cit.* pp.63–8.

22. Oman, *History*, vol.I, pp.363–4, 504–5.

23. *cf* especially *ibid* vol.VI, pp.252–74.

24. For a discussion of the guerrillas, see C.J. Esdaile, 'Heroes or villains? The Spanish guerrillas and the Peninsular War', *History Today* XXXVIII, no.4 (April, 1988), pp.29–35, and C.J. Esdaile, "Heroes or villains" revisited: fresh thoughts on *la guerrilla*', in I. Fletcher, ed., *The Peninsular War: Aspects of the Struggle for the Iberian Peninsula* (Staplehurst, Kent, 1998), pp.93–114. Compare René Chartrand's perspective in chapter 7, above.

25. J. Tone, *The Fatal Knot: the Guerrilla War in Navarre and the Defeat of Napoleon in Spain* (Chapel Hill, North Carolina, 1994), pp.162–9.

26. Oman, *History*, vol.VI, pp.200–6, 524–5.

27. For a general discussion of Wellington's problems with the Spaniards, see C.J. Esdaile, *The Duke of Wellington and the Command of the Spanish Army, 1812–1814* (London, 1990), pp.108–65.

28. An accessible introduction to the politics of Patriot Spain may be found in G. Lovett, *Napoleon and the Birth of Modern Spain* (New York, 1965), pp.285–490.

29. Oman, *History*, vol.I, p.67.

30. *Ibid*.

31. *Ibid* vol.I, pp.359–65; vol.III, pp.5–8, 511–23.

32. *cf ibid* vol.I, pp.143–4; vol.IV, pp.44–6.

33. For a further discussion of these issues, see Esdaile, *Spanish Army*, pp.130–2, and "A petty and ridiculous imitation of Napoleon's 18 Brumaire": the Marqués de la Romana and the Junta of Asturias, 1809', in *Consortium on Revolutionary Europe, Proceedings*, 1993, pp.366–74.

Chapter 13

The Bonaparte Kingdom of Spain

by Ambassador Leopoldo Stampa

The fictitious monarch

The kingdom of Joseph I consisted, to a great extent, only of Joseph himself. The unreality upon which he based his government was comparable to an elaborate theatre set in which rich and realistic perspectives are presented to the audience, whereas only a shoddily-built lash-up of stage scenery is visible from behind the footlights.

King Joseph's character has been analysed from many angles by different authors. Mercader Riba (*La anexión de Cataluña al Imperio francés*, 1947), Claude Martin (*José Napoleon I*, 1969), Juan Antonio Vallejo Nájera (*Yo el Rey*, 1980), and Miguel Artola (*Los Afrancesados*, 1989), to name the best among them, have made distinguished studies of his reign and personality. Their consensus indicates that Joseph was a weak man, well intentioned, vain, naïve in his planning, mild-mannered, with delusions of grandeur and high culture. He was undoubtedly well educated, having graduated in law in Pisa in 1787, practised as an attorney in Bastia in 1788, and served as a judge in Ajaccio in 1791. The war upset his plans, and with the British occupation of Corsica in 1793 he retired to Marseille, where he married the daughter of a rich merchant. His economic independence allowed him to dabble in other activities, and among them he entered politics. Knowing his moderate temperament, his brother Napoleon sent him on various diplomatic missions, among which he was Minister Plenipotentiary to Rome and then, after the coup of Brumaire, 1799, he was a member of the delegation which negotiated the peace treaty with the USA. His diplomatic work continued with his participation in such negotiations as the Treaty of Lunéville with Austria, the Peace of Amiens with Britain, and the Concordat with the Holy See. Nevertheless, Napoleon must have known Joseph's limitations.

Napoleon's elevation to Emperor came as a thunderbolt which poisoned relations between the two. Joseph imagined he had the right to succeed his brother, but the statute of 28 Floreal, year XII, excluded him from the direct succession in favour of Napoleon's eventual natural legitimate offspring, or any heir that he might decide. After no little argument, Joseph eventually had to accept the pompous title of Prince of France, and a generous annual allowance of a million francs, but without, it is thought, abandoning his claim to the throne. Even so, this incident marked the first break in confidence between the two brothers, and it would to some extent influence their relationship forever afterwards. Napoleon pointed to the illogicalities in Joseph's case when he joked that 'My brother thinks I have deprived him of his right, as the first-born, to the legacy of our father the king'. Yet Joseph remained touchy and suspicious, and never accepted the Emperor's manoeuvres. As Marshal Soult would later comment about their relations, 'wounds to pride are often the most difficult to cure.' They were partially cured by the offer of the throne of Naples.

Joseph's experience in Naples, where he was enthusiastically welcomed, doubtless conditioned his future conduct in Spain. Juan José Luna[1] said of this first Napoleonic régime that Joseph 'established his court with splendour, distributed offices, decorated and embellished his palaces, and fostered culture'. He protected the arts and the theatre and raised his own army, manned exclusively by Neapolitans, as well as organising his own royal guard. All of this paraphernalia quickly produced what can only be called a perfect 'comic opera' décor, since it was the French army, and not Joseph's Neapolitan one, which would fight the British and the Calabrian guerrillas when the conflict became serious. Hence Joseph's court in Naples was in effect a mixture of dreams and fictions, just as his one in Spain would later become.

Miguel Artola[2] gave a masterly description of the Bonaparte dynasty in Spain as the history of a régime based 'upon two hostile realities – a people in arms and a foreign invasion'. These two realities left little room for the king to manoeuvre. If Joseph imagined that to be king of Spain in such circumstances consisted essentially in dedicating himself to ceremonial and the pleasures of the courtly life, he was entirely mistaken. His arrival in Spain could not have been more dispiriting. According to Geoffrey de Grandmaison,[3] 'his welcome was disastrous'. Surrounded only by the adulatory ministers who had encouraged him to go to Madrid, the king entered a capital which greeted him with resentful silence. His entry was also overshadowed by a French victory over the Spanish armies, since it was scarcely a week since the forces of Mouton and Sebastiani had routed Cuesta and Blake at Medina de Rio Seco. From that moment onwards Joseph was confronted by the indifference of the Spanish people.

Criticism, satire, and contempt quickly followed. His taste for good food and good wine brought him the nickname *Pepe Botella* (or 'Joe Bottle'); his love for creating his own orders of chivalry – as he had instituted the 'Royal Order of the Two Sicilies' in Naples – led him to set up 'The Royal and Military Order of Spain', in the shape of an enamelled star coloured ruby, worn on a red sash, which was immediately dubbed the 'Order of the Aubergine'. Finally his attempt to raise his own army of Spanish troops, in the way he had done in Naples, meant that he had to fill the ranks largely from prisoners captured in battles against the French, and so it was a catastrophic failure. The units formed were uniformed, armed, and organised ...and unfailingly ended by deserting *en masse* to the Spanish regular armies that were still fighting against Napoleon. Joseph was sarcastically dubbed 'the Spanish army's best recruiting sergeant'. The popular classes also laughingly began to change their manner of invoking the Holy Family when someone sneezed, substituting 'Jesus, Mary, and the father of Our Lord' for the classic 'Jesus, Mary, and Joseph', so they would not have to mention the name of the king. Yet wherever one went, contempt for Joseph predominated over hatred. Oman said that 'it is a great testimony in his favour that the Spanish people despised rather than hated him', and equally that the king was 'perpetually hoodwinked, buffled and bullied, alike by his generals, his ministers and his mistresses. But they never really hated him.'

Oman tells us very little about the details of Joseph's administration; but his desire to make reforms, which was authentically sincere at the beginning, soon turned into opportunism. It was the only way he could survive in a situation that forced him to divide his attention between too many different fronts – the Spanish insurgents, the marshals and generals of the Emperor, the demands of his own brother, and the state finances. They were all problems which became entangled around the throne in such a way that his reign was turned into a nightmare, and his effective exercise of royal government into a fiction. Almost nobody took him seriously, because no-one is scared by fictions.

Miguel Artola, who has made a deep study of the phenomenon of the *afrancesados* and the figure of Joseph himself, has for the sake of clarity distinguished four phases in the history of his reign. The first period is almost symbolic, much more than the subsequent ones could be. This extended from the entry into Madrid in July 1808 to the moment in December of the same year when Napoleon's presence in the capital imposed a temporary suspension of Joseph's authority. The second period began with Napoleon's departure and Joseph's reoccupation of his throne by default; and ended in one of the major crises between the two brothers, in February 1810, when, under the pretext that the expenses of the French army in Spain were excessive, the Emperor seized control over the finances of the four provinces north of the Ebro. He appointed four provincial administrations – Catalonia, Aragón, Navarre, and Vizcaya – and nominated a governor at the head of each, with powers to direct all administrative and military services, and to appropriate the income of each province for the payment and supply of the French soldiers. Thus King Joseph not only saw himself deprived of the financial resources that he needed, but was also forced to suffer the amputation of his kingdom, at least in political terms. In the dramatic letters that he sent to Paris to his wife Queen Julia, his mediator with Napoleon, Joseph expressed his anguish that he was so totally lacking in authority.

The third phase of Joseph's reign unfolded during the period when he made a personal intervention with the Emperor in Paris, attempting to avoid this blatant annexation of a part of his kingdom. When he arrived at his wife's residence in Mortefontaine, during his trip to Paris, she found he had drifted into a different world: 'I talked long with him but I found he had become a stranger; his frivolity was inconceivable, and his self-confidence was equally inexplicable. He was surprised that we did not look at him with admiration, so convinced was he that he had performed great deeds.' The fourth and final phase covers the last two years of this sorry reign, which ended with its rout and extinction. Artola's characterisation of this period could not be more expressive: 'In 1812 Joseph was a spineless individual; totally bankrupt; collapsed over, rather than sitting on, the throne, and lacking the strength to hold his sceptre. During the last fourteen months remaining to him as a monarch, he couldn't raise enough energy to exercise even his nominal power.'

The failed politician

In the summer of 1808 Joseph found it hard to understand that his success depended on the pacification of the country, and he wanted to give up on it. He had arrived on the Spanish throne too quickly and under several delusions, and it became repugnant to him in the aftermath of Bailén. In a letter to Napoleon of 14 August 1808, when he had occupied the throne for less than a month, he revealed a clear intention to abdicate and return to Naples.

His ministers and advisers, however, took an opposite point of view, and urged it as an essential precondition for the establishment of the dynasty and the exercise of government. It required a two-sided policy: on the one hand to keep at bay the pressures exercised by the Emperor, so that the military occupation could gradually be lifted; and on the other hand to reach a settlement with the insurgents through a policy of conciliation, which would be sufficiently generous to allow transformation into a state of normality, and eventually peace. It must be stressed that this policy did not arise from any genuine inclination on Joseph's part.

Knowing that abdication would spell the end, the members of the government and the *afrancesados* who surrounded it tried to open new avenues of hope. An initial plan was hatched among the five government ministers – Cabarrús, Azanza, Urquijo, Mazarredo, and O'Farril – in an attempt to find an accord with the insurgents. The ministers were aware that the military occupation might inflict irreparable damage, but an act of abdication could not be contemplated, regardless of the king's melancholy mood. In a memorandum of 2 August 1808 the ministers explained the need to choose between three possible solutions: 'Renounce, Conquer, or Negotiate'. It was clear from their *reductio ad absurdum* that they discounted the first two, leaving only negotiation. Thus it was a plan which originated not in Bonapartist generosity, but in the opportunist nature of the *afrancesado* nucleus surrounding Joseph, who needed a solid basis for their position in the long term.

French opposition was encountered from the outset, and a mission to Paris by Azanza and Urquijo met no success. Napoleon could not accept their policies while his forces were still retreating from the disaster of Bailén, just as it would prove to be unthinkable for General Castaños and the Supreme *Junta* to enter a dialogue when they had just won a victory over the occupation forces. In view of this situation, Cabarrús took a more determined and realistic step, making the project more acceptable to Paris, when he proposed a mixed system which combined negotiation with conquest: an *afrancesado* version of the tactic of the carrot and the stick.

In Juan Luna's work it is argued that Joseph's government thereafter began to assert its legitimacy, and organise the areas it controlled, as fast as it could. In this it was following a confused and ill-defined – but highly intelligent – theory that the advocates of resistance would appear to be championing anarchy; an unstable and dangerous state that all right-thinking conservatives and decent orderly folk would fear as leading to 'the dissolution of society'. Anarchy would threaten them with a terrible crisis that none would wish to face. According to Luna it was Llorente who expressed this idea most clearly, in justification of his support for King Joseph, when he said 'I am always a realist. I believe I can be of most use to my country by supporting the monarchical system against republicanism.' Thus he neatly identified 'republicanism' with anarchy and 'the dissolution of society' to which it supposedly led. It was this undoubtedly attractive idea which lay at the root of the offer of negotiation which Cabarrús proposed to the *Junta*: that one or other of the monarchic dynasties should be accepted, whether Bourbon or Bonaparte, in order to avoid the anarchy to which 'republicanism' would surely lead if the divisions between the Spanish people persisted.

However, the Cabarrús plan ignored two factors which would destroy the whole basis of his 'negotiate and conquer' initiative. By that time the Franco–Spanish and Spanish–Spanish conflicts had acquired an expanded dimension through the participation of Great Britain, with whom the insurgents had entered into negotiations through Admiral Collingwood in Gibraltar. From that moment British opinion would count in any attempt to make a separate peace, which was not something the new allies had envisaged, and which would in any case be ruled out by article IV of the 'treaty of peace, armistice and alliance' between Spain and Britain.[4] Secondly, the Supreme *Junta*'s measures for confiscating the assets of King Joseph's supporters, upon the entry of Spanish troops into Madrid after Bailén, had further deepened the gulf separating the partisans of the two sides.

To complicate the situation even more, the plan was hatched with a view to the winter campaign of 1808; but that would bring Napoleon himself to Madrid, after defeating Spanish armies at Gamonal, Espinosa de los Monteros, Tudela, and Somosierra. At that time his thinking about 'the affairs of Spain' was crushingly opposed to any attempt at negotiation: 'The fact is that Spain will be French. It is for France that we have conquered Spain.' Frederic Masson[5] has made a lucid analysis of the profound divergence in the assumptions which thereafter divided the two Bonaparte brothers, and led Napoleon to displace Joseph as the head of the government in the occupied country. According to Masson:

> When Napoleon was forced to conquer Spain a second time, he considered himself its sole owner and assumed that all earlier arrangements were dissolved, so that all authority outside his own should be ended ... which accounts for his taking whatever measures in Spain that he thought best for his rule, in his own name. Joseph for his part was convinced that his brother had to give him back the complete possession of his realm, which he had traded for Naples and which he was owed according to what had been agreed.

The French marshals believed they held a position of strength by the end of the winter campaign. But by spring 1809 the military climate had changed. Despite the victories in March, the French offensive was slowing down due to preparations for the war against Austria. The moment was ripe for negotiation, and the Cabarrús initiative was set in motion. On 21 March 1809 he wrote to the Duke of Alburquerque, a restless personality, active and well-connected with the *Junta*, who at this period was the leader of a detachment of forces from the Army of La Mancha. Cabarrús explained the need to win over Joseph, while General Sebastiani sent another letter on the following day, which itemised the desperate military situation of the Spanish armies. It was an inopportune day to send letters of this nature, since it was likely to reach Alburquerque either just before or just after the battle of Medellín (28 March), in which his forces, joined with those of

Cuesta, were routed by Marshal Victor, at a time when the French were also hard on the heels of the Spanish in La Mancha and of the British in Portugal. But maybe the moment was chosen deliberately, and we are entitled to ask what motive the French generals might have had for offering to make peace in the middle of their spring campaign. The initiative certainly did not spring from pure altruism. Indeed, after the much-trumpeted initial triumphs of Ciudad Real, Medellin, and Oporto, which all came on practically the same day (27, 28, and 29 March 1808), the French offensive became paralysed for want of men and supplies, and began to encounter organised resistance. After winning the day at Santa Cruz de Mudela on 28 March, Sebastiani was even forced to retire to cover his communications with Madrid. As Colonel Priego[6] has explained, the resulting circumstances were ripe for a *rapprochement*. The prospect of an imminent Austrian war prevented Napoleon from reinforcing the Peninsula, while Wellesley was about to land in Portugal, and the Spanish Supreme *Junta* was already collecting resources to repair the damage suffered in the recent defeats.

King Joseph was well aware of his economic penury and lack of resources, and was prepared to settle matters with the Supreme *Junta* by means of negotiation, for which the ground had been prepared by the letters from Cabarrús and Sebastiani – or at least he believed it had. With this perspective in mind, on 12 April he sent Don Joaquín Sotelo to General Cuesta with a document for the *Junta*. The text announced that Sotelo was authorised by the king to negotiate remedies for the evils experienced by the occupied provinces, so that they should suffer no more, and invited the *Junta* to nominate one or two persons to negotiate with Joseph's envoy.

The letter that Sotelo took to Cuesta had been drawn up by Urquijo. According to the French ambassador La Forest, who obviously supervised its content, it took a 'noble tone', although it did not win the unanimous approval of Joseph's government. Some thought it was confused and failed to define its objective, which was the opening of negotiations. Others thought it was insufficiently cordial, while the rest found it excessively woolly and vague. However, for want of agreement the original text was adopted without modifications. It covered: the need to bring the war to an end; the suffering of the provinces occupied by the French; the unfortunate results of 27 and 28 March (the battle of Medellin), and the desire of King Joseph to right the wrongs that lay within his power. Finally it asked for a meeting with a representative of the Supreme *Junta*. Sotelo duly took it to Cuesta in Monasterio, who forwarded it to the Supreme *Junta* in Seville, accompanied by his own view of the opportunism behind the initiative, indicating that 'Sotelo's mission and proposition indicate that the French are making preparations to withdraw from Spain, due to the situation they face in Germany, they want to extract the highest possible price.' With these ideas of Cuesta's as its prologue, there can be no doubt that Sotelo's mission was seriously damaged from the start. After considerable delay the Supreme *Junta* replied that if Sotelo had the authority to negotiate the restoration of King Fernando VII to the Spanish throne and the evacuation of the French troops, it would make it public and 'would listen if our allies agreed'. But if not, the *Junta* was not interested even in beginning to negotiate. In summary, what the *Junta* wanted in practical terms amounted to little less than unconditional surrender, which implied a clear intention not to negotiate. Furthermore, the mention of allies highlighted for King Joseph's court not only that the *Junta* was no longer alone in the struggle, but that it could not contemplate making a separate peace. Despite this reply Sotelo repeated his requests, but without any success, until finally – on 3 May – General Cuesta, with the *Junta*'s authority, ended the correspondence 'until the *afrancesados* declared themselves straightly and straightforwardly on the side of the *Junta*.'

Thus was Joseph's political manoeuvre closed down, with a deafening crash. He very possibly returned to it towards the end of the conflict, in the winter of 1812. In his memoirs Marshal Soult mentions 'the relations that had been opened with certain Spanish rebels who were disgusted with the *Cortes* and the Cádiz Regency'; while General Lejeune, in his own memoirs, with perhaps a rather exaggerated view, records that the Spanish military leaders 'were disposed to treat with the French against the English, although not with King Joseph. This includes the famous General Castaños, who started negotiations with General Baron de Lejeune when he was a prisoner, demanding the return of Fernando VII and his marriage to a Napoleonic princess, which would thereby secure the French alliance.' Apart from the dubious credibility of this particular story, it is at least certain that during the final years of the war there was open discontent against the *Junta* among the Spanish generals – the case of General Ballesteros is typical – objecting among other things to the appointment of Wellington as *Generalissimo* of the combined armies. If Joseph had wanted to play this as his final card, it would not have been surprising from a man who was so beset with illusions.

King Joseph's diplomacy

The fiction upon which Joseph based his government also permeated his diplomacy. Among Spanish diplomats this situation encouraged what has been called an 'irresolution of loyalties'.[7] On 2 October 1808 King Joseph's secretary of state, the Duke of Campo-Alange, sent out a requirement for all Spanish diplomats serving abroad to swear an oath of loyalty to the new monarch, and the document had to be sent on to the Duke of Frías, King Joseph's ambassador in Paris. According to Ochoa it was 'a necessary act, to allow an assessment of the salaries and expenses that would be occasioned' by the diplomatic service. Meanwhile the Supreme *Junta*, on behalf of all who rejected the newly-enforced dynasty, took an initiative through its own secretary of state, Cevallos, in the same month, to send another circular to all Spanish representatives in foreign countries, informing them of the rising against the French. As Ochoa accurately sums it up, this created a double diplomacy. The two Spains – 'Patriot' and 'Josefina' – would each have to try to enrol all the embassies and legations which had previously represented the Bourbons in the courts of Europe. The reaction was as variable as anyone could wish. If Spain itself was dramatically divided between *afrancesados* and patriots, the situation was no different among diplomats abroad, for the distances and the gaps in information created massive additional difficulties when the moment came to choose sides.

King Joseph's diplomatic activities were naturally centred mainly in those countries which were most sympathetic to him, or which had an alliance with the French Empire. In Denmark the Conde de Yoldi was a convinced *afrancesado*, and in the first moments of the war he had tried to prevent the return of La Romana's Division to Spain. At the end of the war he abandoned his post to serve as Chamberlain in the Danish court, although the consuls at Helsingoor – Juan Agustin Badin – and in Altona – Joaquín de Aréchaga – remained faithful to Joseph. In Berlin the Legation had been headed since 1800 by Rafael de Urquijo, a nephew of Joseph's minister who had few diplomatic talents and duly achieved little.[8] In Hamburg, Juan José Ranz de Romanillos was *chargé d'affaires* until 1809, when Marshal Bernadotte accused him of laxity over La Romana's escape. However, the vice-consuls in Lübeck – Jorge Guillermo Müller – and in Bremen – Joaquin Estler – did recognise the king. In Berne the mission of the 'timid and torpid' Lieutenant José Caamaño passed without incident until he retired to Spain in 1811; but in Naples the *chargé d'affaires* and Secretary of the Legation was Pio Gómez de Ayala, a confirmed *afrancesado* who had hurried to Bayonne to give early allegiance to Joseph. He carried out numerous missions, including helping in the dissolution of the religious orders in 1809; the monitoring of British shipping to Sicily; and reporting on Murat's disaffection from the Russian campaign onwards. Equally, Antonio López Gonzalo was confirmed in his post as consul in Genoa as soon as he had sworn loyalty in October 1808, although he would switch allegiance to Fernando VII when Anglo-Sicilian troops arrived in 1814. Yet at least he had repatriated some 3000 Spaniards at his own expense during the course of the War of Independence. The other consuls in Italian cities also gambled on the new Bonapartist dynasty, for example Castro Manuel Buedo in San Marcos; José Martinez in Leghorn;

Andrés Nicolini in Bastia; Guillermo Dotto in Palermo; and Luis Cesar Baille in Sardinia.

Some played a double game, such as Juan Ventura Bouligny, Joseph's consul in Leghorn until his intrigues were discovered. He was replaced there by Juan Martinez – but was immediately appointed consul in Florence by the *Junta*. Others preferred to remain loyal to Fernando VII, such as Antonio Vargas Laguna, Minister Plenipotentiary to the Papal States, and his secretary Francisco Eleaxaga, and the attachés Antonio Beramendi and José Pando, although they were imprisoned for omitting to renounce King Joseph. The legation in Dresden remained vacant since the departure of Ignacio López de Ulloa; and the Vienna Legation was also unfilled after Diego de la Quadra absented himself from the post without permission. In view of Austria's favourable attitude towards the uprising, the *Junta* sent a representative to Vienna, Eusebio Bardaxi, but he was later recalled to Seville after Wagram. Relations recovered only from 1812, through the agency of a highly controversial character, Justo Machado.

By no means all the diplomats chose to follow the new dynasty. The minister to the Hague, José de Anduaga, would not accept King Joseph and moved to England, being replaced by Leonardo Gómez de Terán. Equally the minister in Florence, Gómez Labrador, refused the oath but was unable to reach safety in time and was arrested in France, although he eventually managed to escape. The consul in Trieste, José David y Tomasich, did take the oath but later switched to the *Junta* and was dismissed by the King. In Stockholm the *chargé d'affaires* was Pantaleón Moreno y Daoiz, who continued his services in favour of the *Junta*.

In his work on the Spanish diplomats during the war, Jesús Pradells[9] describes the circumstances surrounding the envoys to the court of the Czars. Major General Benito Pardo de Figueroa replaced the Conde de Noroña on 13 September 1807 and swore loyalty to King Joseph, being confirmed in his post on 31 August 1809. He was deeply compromised during the rupture between Napoleon and the Czar in June 1812, and was expelled from the court. The consul general, Antonio Colombi, had evaded the oath of loyalty since 1808, and continued in place, working for the Supreme *Junta* and reporting on Spanish affairs from his direct correspondence with it. By contrast the mission of Joaquín de Anduaga had failed when the Czar had refused to receive an envoy from the *Junta*, and a treaty was concluded only after the French invasion, by Zea Bermúdez on 20 July 1812.

In Constantinople the Marqués de Almenara continued his functions. He was a friend of Godoy; a wealthy banker who had been *chargé d'affaires* in Paris under Carlos IV, where he had risen in favour through his daughter's relations with Duroc, the Grand Marshal of the Empire. In Constantinople he competed with the

Junta's representative, the naval captain Juan Jabat, whom the Vizir would not receive. In Smyrna the consul general, Benito Soler, was loyal to the *Junta* and regarded Almenara as 'French'. The *Junta* had another representative in Malta, Alberto Megino, who had left his post in Venice to avoid swearing loyalty to Joseph. In the USA the double diplomacy was even more complicated, since the government had adopted a posture which Pradells calls 'cautious neutrality', in the face of every effort by both Spanish factions to win recognition. Valentin de Foronda had held the office of *chargé d'affaires* during the confused first few months of the war, and had maintained an ambiguous position until finally declaring for the Supreme *Junta*. However he was accused of Bonapartism by the leader of the patriots resident in the USA, Francisco Caballero Sarmiento, from Caracas. The *Junta* therefore tried to bring order to the legation by giving him a partner, in the shape of José Ignacio Viar, who had always remained loyal to Fernando VII. On 5 October 1809 Luis de Onis arrived and calmed the situation, but still failed to win recognition from the United States, which was moving towards a policy that would be hostile not only towards Britain in the war of 1812, but also towards Spain. Both of these powers were militarily fully committed in the Peninsula, so America was able to seize her chance.

In the case of Spain, American aggression was motivated by the desire to occupy Florida and, if convenient, Texas. These aims had featured in every official declaration she had made since the Louisiana purchase in 1803, although she still resorted to the most diverse subterfuges to conceal the aggressions that would follow.[10] In the spring of 1810 a successful revolt was fomented among the American settlers in Baton Rouge against the Spanish authorities. Then the island of Amalia was occupied in the mouth of the Santa Maria river, which marked the frontier between Georgia and Florida. Another occupation was in the region of Mobile, organised by an old friend of Spain, James Wilkinson, who used the pretext that he was 'protecting' it from a British descent – forgetting that Britain was allied to Spain at the time. Equally the Spanish area of Pensacola was occupied by General Jackson after his victory over the British at New Orleans – this time using an army of government troops, but without the government having declared any war. Finally there was a 'spontaneous' attack on San Antonio, in Texas, by American patriots whom the government could disown. Arthur P. Whitaker, cited by José Manuel Allendesalazar, explained the covert nature of these attacks against Spain by the American desire not to make a formal rupture with Napoleon, and particularly not by openly declaring war against his brother. Luis de Onis and his new consul general, José Bernabeu, could do little to alter this state of affairs, and it was small consolation that the Americans were selling wheat to Wellington's army or that representatives of King

Joseph made no appearance in Washington. The Americans, indeed, had the best of both worlds as they were fighting both Britain and Spain in the Americas and simultaneously profiting by feeding the war in the Peninsula.

It was logical that Joseph's diplomacy should concentrate its efforts upon the embassy in Paris, although it depended on the personal political weight of the successive ambassadors rather than any skill in negotiation, since policy was all dictated by Napoleon. From 1805 the ambassador had been Don Carlos Ferrera y Fiesco, Prince of Masserano, but his new credentials were blocked by Napoleon when Fernando VII succeeded to the throne. He was replaced by Diego de la Porteria Fernández de Velasco, Duke of Frías, who gave way in 1811 to the Marqués de Campo-Alange. These ambassadors achieved little success with the Emperor, who understood the fiction of their home régime only too well. Equally, when real crises arose between the two brothers, and genuine negotiations were attempted by the *afrancesado* ministers Urquijo and Azanza, they achieved no better results than the ambassadors, nor even than Joseph himself, when he visited Paris over the annexation of his northern provinces. As for the Spanish consuls in France, seven out of ten remained loyal to Joseph; two took the oath but later transferred to the *Junta*, and only one – Juan La Hora, consul in Bayonne – went to prison for remaining loyal to Fernando VII.

The scale of Spanish representation abroad was by no means reflected by the very small, and shrinking, number of foreign diplomats who attended King Joseph's court. They were put off by his political weakness, by the war and its many effects, and by the efforts of the Seville *Junta* to win the recognition of other governments. When Joseph evacuated Madrid for the first time, after Bailén, he was accompanied only by the ministers of Denmark and Holland, and the *chargé d'affaires* of Saxony. The papal nuncio stayed in Madrid, with the minister plenipotentiary of Russia and the *chargés d'affaires* of Austria and of the USA. Upon the king's return the court was in a state of confusion and few diplomats decided to stay on, apart from the French ambassador La Forest and the Danish representative, Baron de Bourke. Saxony nominated Count Rechten but did not include him in their mission; while the Neapolitan, Prussian, and Russian representatives all failed to take up their posts. As for the Austrian, he left Madrid for Seville as soon as Napoleon won the battle of Wagram.

The frustrated soldier

The disaster of Bailén spurred Joseph to reconquer his kingdom at the head of his troops, and even to ask for a military command. Napoleon, who rated his brother higher as a diplomat than as a soldier, did not agree. On 16 August he wrote: 'My brother, everything that's happening in Spain is deplorable: the army seems to be commanded not by generals but by post office inspectors. I must come!' On arrival at the frontier he was told about Joseph's deployments, and protested that the formations were too scattered or their locations were unknown. Undeterred, Joseph continued his attempts at command, and planned to assemble a force of 50,000 men under his personal command to recapture Madrid; but the Emperor merely replied that 'any general who attempted such an operation would be a criminal'. The king's first efforts at strategy could not have been more humiliating.

Once Napoleon had entered Spain and begun to direct operations, his successes were dazzling. At the first of them, Gamonal, Joseph travelled in the rear of his brother's forces, completely ignored. After the battle, while Napoleon and Soult entered Burgos, Joseph followed at a distance, lagging behind and insulted. That same day, he wrote a pathetic letter to Napoleon from Briviesca, a few kilometres from Burgos:

> Sire, I have reached this town where I have found no one in command and no *Comissaire de Guerre*; my Guard is still far off. It would have been desirable had the Staff left at least one battalion until I had passed through ... The stores have just been pillaged and the church is just about to be, and I have sent a few soldiers I could muster to protect it. The clergy and the inhabitants are begging me to protect them but, in truth, do I have the right to make use of even a single soldier? The Prince of Neuchatel hasn't informed the Army who I am. I don't know how to exercise the powers manifestly and openly granted to me. The Prince of Neuchatel, and Marshal Jourdan likewise, send me a host of letters to be forwarded and orders to be executed. The fact is that I haven't got a single staff officer now that General Belliard has taken them all off with him.
>
> The few Light Horse from my Guard (fewer than 200) are scattered along the road. I have to witness all this disorder without being able to stamp any of it out.
>
> I have no wish to make a formal entrance into Burgos. I did that the first time. This time I have done no more than appear before the enemy with 400 horsemen. What exactly am I in this country?

Joseph could not recover his crown until Napoleon had left Spain, and he never really recovered his authority.

In mid-1809 the king found in Marshal Soult, his Chief of Staff, the support he needed to assert himself in a more prominent military role. The Talavera Campaign of June–July 1809 is clear proof of the role they played. Equally, in spite of disagreements with Marshal Victor about strategy, Jourdan and Joseph did direct French action in the battle of Talavera. At least in theory, Joseph commanded Victor's army corps as well as the General Reserve.[11] Much more cautious than Victor, who persisted in prolonging the struggle on the second day, Joseph and Jourdan manoeuvred strategically, co-ordinating their planning with Soult, who was coming down from north-east Spain to cut off the Anglo-Spanish army at Plasencia. Joseph's withdrawal to Madrid allowed him to unite later with Sebastiani, for the defeat of General Venegas at Almonacid on 16 August.

However, military intuition was not one of the king's virtues. At the beginning of 1810, once the battle of Ocaña had opened the way south to the French armies, the capture of Seville, seat of the *Junta* and the political capital of the Spanish rebels, became a political priority. For Joseph, the capture of Seville could well have meant the end of the war, and in the event his entrance into the city would be very splendid. The population, tired of the anarchy produced by the war, greeted him in the streets with peals of bells from the churches and the cathedral. Doubtless the Sevillanos were disposed to follow the kind of life they yearned for, if not in peace then at least in calm. For the first time, Joseph must have felt he was King of Spain. Nevertheless, in the judgement of Marshal Soult, 'his triumph in Seville cost us Cádiz.' Even though the French advance along the Guadalquivir had been very rapid, they had first had to secure Jaén and Cordoba, and had to wait for the artillery that could only advance along the La Carolina road. This delay was exploited by the Duke of Alburquerque, who sent one Division to Badajoz, and by forced marching entered Andalucia with the rest of his forces by way of Guadalcanal and Carmona. The Supreme *Junta* took refuge in Cádiz, where the population prepared for its defence. To Joseph, Soult had insisted that V Corps and part of Desolles' reserve was more than enough to appear before Seville, while the I Corps should advance rapidly on Cádiz and cut off Alburquerque's forces. Joseph had had to choose. As king, the entry into Seville was more attractive; as soldier, he should have chosen Cádiz. His royal vanity triumphed, to the great annoyance of Soult: 'The invincible resistance that this place [Cádiz] put up against us immobilised a part of the French armies. In this way the final coup which could have put an end to the war was checked.'

On 16 March 1812 Napoleon, tired of the Spanish problem and, absorbed in preparing the Russian campaign, entrusted command of all the armies in Spain to Joseph, with Jourdan as his Chief of Staff. But once again Joseph's new title would be fictitious. The King sent off dozens of dispatches to gather all the French troops in the Peninsula under his own effective command; but Soult, Masséna, and Suchet all threatened to resign their commands if they were forced to give way to the royal prerogative. As Miot de

Melito[12] soundly points out, 'nothing more was left to him than his title, which was ignored, and responsibility without any means of dodging it.' At Vitoria, where he took no decision and could not turn to Jourdan for advice, Joseph – sick, and prey to a high fever – met a resounding failure in the battle which ended his reign. Once the kingdom was lost, says Artola, he parted with it quite calmly. In the first letter he sent to his wife after the battle, on 23 June 1812, he wrote: 'After placing the armies on the frontier, and once the armies of the North and Aragón are united, I shall retire to Mortefontaine, where I should have withdrawn after Salamanca.'

Joseph's army

Just as he had done in Naples, Joseph tried to raise his own army in Spain. Moreover, this practice was common to all the kingdoms governed by the Bonaparte family. But by contrast to Westphalia, Berg, Holland, and Naples itself, the outcome in Spain was calamitous, because of the refusal of the Spanish to enlist. Nonetheless, although the effective strengths of the new units shows there were few recruits, the number of regiments and territorial units was large. As always happened in the court of King Joseph, fiction prevailed over reality.

The Royal Guard included all arms. The infantry was made up of the 1st Grenadier Regiment, created in 1808, whose strength never exceeded 587 men; and by the 1st Regiment of *Tiradores* (*Tirailleurs*), with a strength of some 800 men. Both were formed entirely of French soldiers. They were complemented by a regiment of Fusiliers, formed in Andalucia in 1810 with a maximum strength of approximately 530 men, according to Juan José Sañudo's research. A company of twenty Halberdiers provided the guard within the precincts of the Palace. The Royal Guard's cavalry was made up of a regiment of *Chasseurs* with 459 horsemen; a squadron of 233 Hussars; a company of Guides with 100 men; the Granada Honour Squadron made up of fifty or so horsemen and another called 'Seville' with ninety-eight men, both units raised in Andalucia during the 1810 campaign. The cavalry was completed by a company of fifty men forming the Queen's Dragoons. The Guard Artillery consisted of a battery with 100 men.

On paper the line infantry totalled eleven regiments, which had numbers but were also named after the cities in which they were raised. The best recruited were the 1st Madrid with 400 men and the 2nd Toledo with 344 men, both raised in 1809, and the 3rd Seville, raised in 1810 with 530 men. The weakest, both created in 1810, were the 4th Soria with no more than sixty men, and the 8th Jaén with eighty-five. Among the light regiments, the 1st Castille Light Infantry stands out, managing to achieve a strength of 932 men. The Royal Foreign Legion of Spain, composed of 800 men, was exceptional, in that it was formed at the start of the war and kept going all through, until disbanded in Valencia in 1814.

The cavalry was supposed to have six line regiments, but they could never be raised. There were four regiments of *Chasseurs*: the 1st was created in August 1809 with fifty men, rising to some 400, although one of its squadrons surrendered at Guadalajara in 1812. When the regiment was disbanded in December 1813 it had 349 effectives out of a theoretical roster of 1000. The 2nd *Chasseurs* was created in Old Castille in 1810, and by December 1813 it numbered 398 men. There is no information about the 3rd regiment until 1810, when it appears in Andalucia with 162 troopers. A little later it was stripped of its horses and by November 1814, shortly before being disbanded, its strength was 148. The 4th *Chasseurs* were also formed in 1810 in Andalucia, and were dissolved in 1812 with 361 men. The Light Cavalry was completed by the 7th Lancers, raised in 1811 in Andalucia with cadres from one of the Vistula Legion regiments.

Part of these puny forces served among the 8000 men who regularly escorted Joseph Bonaparte. Of these, 2000, mostly French, belonged to the Guard. The rest, a little more than 5000 with very little cavalry, were organised in a Division that brought together the sum total of the men he had managed to mobilise. The few battles in which they took part included Albuera (the 4th *Chasseurs* were present, organised by Soult); Ocaña and Talavera (the Guard Cavalry participated, with only 600 sabres); and Vitoria. In the last, Joseph's horsemen played a prominent role in covering the army's retreat. These men belonged to the Guard Cavalry, the 1st *Chasseurs*, and part of the 2nd Hussars, totalling some 425 troopers.

In addition to these units, the French recruited a series of small local corps, territorial units to maintain public order, which were finally used in the anti-guerrilla struggle. They weren't formed by King Joseph's administration, as such; but being Spanish they came under his government. The list of these units is long, and is detailed by Colonel Sañudo.[13] In the whole territory they cannot have exceeded 2000 men, although the number of units was over seventy. The first of these, the Madrid Militia, was created in 1808. Four more sprang up in 1809, including the *Miqueletes* of Navarre (114 men), the King's Volunteers (around seventy) and the Catalan *Cazadores* (around 125). The number of units increased in 1810 in proportion to the expanding conquest of territory, and the great majority appeared between 1811 and 1812. Apart from maintaining order in the towns, their anti-guerrilla activity was significant. They had no uniform name and the units took such disparate titles as Free Companies, *Cazadores*, Civic Militias, Municipal Companies, Riflemen, *Miqueletes*, Mounted Riflemen, Guides, *Miñones*, or Mountain *Chasseurs*. Their manpower rarely exceeded a hundred and in some cases, such as the Riflemen of Motril, their maximum strength was less than thirty-four. With 198 men, the Horse *Chasseurs* of Carmona made up one of the better-manned territorial units.

Neither Joseph's regular army nor the territorials carried out important missions. Furthermore, desertion was almost continuous. Their limited numerical importance only underlines the inability of the king's government to rally the Spanish to its cause. Here, as elsewhere, the failure of the Bonaparte monarchy was emphatic.

Notes

1. Juan J. Luna, *La Alianza de Dos Monarquías* (Madrid, 1989).
2. Miguel Artola, *Los Afrancesados* (Madrid, 1989).
3. Geoffrey de Grandmaison, *L'Espagne et Napoléon* (3 vols, Paris, 1914–32).
4. The treaty was signed 14 January 1809. It is not mentioned by Oman, but is discussed in Juan José Sañudo and Leopoldo Stampa, *La Crisis de una Alianza (la campaña del Tajo de 1809)* (Madrid, 1996), pp.38–41.
5. Fréderic Masson, *Napoléon et sa famille* (Paris, 1911).
6. Juan Priego López, *Guerra de la Independencia, 1808-14* (Madrid, 1972 on).
7. By Miguel Angel Ochoa, the historian and ambassador, in his paper on *Las relaciones internacionales de España, 1808-9* (II Seminario Internacional sobre la Guerra de la Independencia, Madrid, 1996).
8. Marqués de Villarrutia, *El rey José Napoléon* (Madrid, 1929); Jesús Pradells, *La diplomacia y los diplomáticos españoles en la Guerra de la Independencia* (II Seminario Internacional sobre la Guerra de la Independencia, Madrid, 1996).
9. Jesus Pradells, *La diplomacia y los diplomaticos españoles en la Guerra de la Independencia* (II Seminario Internacional sobre la Guerra de la Independencia, Madrid, 1996).
10. José Manuel Allendesalazar, *Apuntes sobre la relación diplomática hispano-norteamericana, 1763-1895* (Madrid, 1996).
11. Composed of the 1st Regiment of Grenadiers and the Regiment of *Chasseurs*, both from the Royal Guard; and the Madrid garrison (51st and 103rd *Ligne*, 12th *Légère*, and 27th *Chasseurs*, together with twelve artillery pieces).
12. Miot de Melito, *Mémoires* (Paris, 1873).
13. J.J. Sañudo, 'Pequeñas unidades Napoleónicas' *Researching & Dragona* no.1 (January 1996).

Chapter 14

Britain and the Peninsular War[1]

by Rory Muir

William Napier's *History of the War in the Peninsula and the South of France* (1828–40) quickly established itself as the standard account of the Peninsular War. It was written with a rare combination of personal experience, extensive research in unpublished papers in Britain and France, and a highly coloured, romantic style which was greatly admired at the time, although it appeals less to modern taste. Writing so soon after the events he described, Napier's work inevitably provoked controversy, and he defended his views with a combination of learning and biting invective which left his critics bloodied if not convinced. Naturally these pamphlet wars provoked discussion, adding to the topicality and interest of the *History*, and ultimately to its authority.

By the late nineteenth century, when Charles Oman began work on his own history of the Peninsular War, Napier's place was firmly established as one of the great works of British history. Indeed, more than one friend asked Oman if it was worthwhile to retell the story of the Peninsular War when Napier's work was so well known and widely available. In the preface of his first volume Oman replies to such queries and justifies his purpose. First he pays tribute to 'Napier's splendid work' and disavows – surely with false modesty – any idea of superseding it. Next he refers to the great quantity of new source material, published and unpublished, British and foreign, which had become available since Napier completed his *History*. Then he goes on to qualify his admiration for Napier and by implication make room for his own enterprise:

> I do not think that it is generally realised that it is ... unsafe to go to Napier for an account of the aims and undertakings of the Spanish *Juntas*, or the Tory governments of 1808–14. As a narrator of the incidents of the war he is unrivalled ...
>
> But when he wanders off into politics, English or Spanish, Napier is a less trustworthy guide. All his views are coloured by the fact that he was a bitter enemy of the Tories of his own day. The kinsman not only of Charles James Fox, but of Lord Edward Fitzgerald, he could never look with unprejudiced eyes on their

political opponents. Canning and Spencer Perceval were in his ideas men capable of any folly, any gratuitous perversity. Castlereagh's splendid services are ignored ... [2]

There is no doubt that Oman's criticism was fully justified, and Napier's fierce partisanship, together with his open admiration for Napoleon's politics, as well as his military skill, had provoked complaints from the first.

The prominence which Oman gives the matter in his preface might suggest that correcting Napier's prejudices and re-evaluating the role of the British government in the Peninsular War would be a central element in his work; but this would be a mistake. Oman conceived his own *History* in almost exactly the same terms as Napier: as a narrative of the military campaigns in the Peninsula between 1807 and 1814. Both writers generally treated the struggle in Spain and Portugal in isolation from the wider war against Napoleon, which is usually discussed only insofar as it directly affects military operations – for example, when the defeat of Austria enabled Napoleon to reinforce his armies in Spain, or the invasion of Russia led him to withdraw certain units. In common with most military history of the time – and much since – they describe events primarily from the perspective of the rival generals, while drawing on the memoirs and letters of junior officers and ordinary soldiers to add colour, and to elucidate doubtful points, especially in the great set-piece descriptions of battles and sieges.

By adopting this traditional form of military history and covering exactly the same subject as Napier in much the same way, Oman – despite his protestations to the contrary – was clearly trying to make his reputation by surpassing one of the acknowledged masterpieces of the genre. In the event, Napier's fame was too firmly established to be easily eclipsed; the First World War naturally lessened interest in earlier conflicts; and historical fashions were changing, so that Oman's work never achieved the popular renown of Napier. But its merits are very great indeed, and have been recognised from the outset by those interested in the subject. The prodigious reading of published and unpublished sources in many languages; the effective organisation of material and graceful literary style; the reasoned judgement of controversial issues unmarked by Napier's extremes of enthusiasm or scorn; and the cool, clear-headed sense of the value of statistics, combined with a dogged search for fresh material on intractable points, all distinguish it as one of the finest works of military history to be written in English this century, and undoubtedly the best account of the Peninsular War which is ever likely to appear.

Of course there are flaws. No work of 4000 pages is likely to be free from lapses, especially when it was written at such speed – the first five volumes took only twelve years to appear. There are occasional errors of fact in the text, and a number of trifling mistakes in the wonderfully rich statistical appendices, but the general standard of accuracy is extremely high. More disturbing to modern readers is the light use of source notes, the absence of a bibliography, and especially the habit of silently 'improving' quotations by deleting extraneous material without ellipses, correcting the grammar, and even re-arranging some of the content.[3] Such practices are completely unacceptable in modern scholarly writing, but standards have changed over the course of the century, and while we may regret that Oman's habits were rather loose in this respect, they do not seriously affect the quality of his work. His tampering with quotations appears to have been quite innocent, intended purely to improve the flow of the writing without distorting its sense; and while the absence of a bibliography deprives us of an invaluable tool, it does not cast the slightest doubt over the depth and range of his learning. Oman wrote in Napier's shadow, and in his desire to undo the effects of the latter's strong views he occasionally over-balances slightly in the opposite direction. For example, Napier's ardent defence of Napoleon and Soult stings Oman into a patient elaboration of their faults and follies, which to a reader whose initial views are not formed by Napier, can seem convincing, but rather heavy-handed.[4] Finally he sometimes shows a partiality for a vivid, colourful memoirist – such as Blakeney, Grattan, or Lemonnier-Delafosse – even when other evidence suggests that they should be treated with caution.

But these faults pale into insignificance compared to Oman's achievement in providing such a clear, comprehensive, full, and attractive history of the Peninsular War. On its own terms, as a narrative of the campaigns in Spain, Portugal, and the south of France, Oman's *History* is both indispensable and secure against serious criticism. Later research has corrected occasional mistakes, questioned a few doubtful judgements, and added greatly to our knowledge of particular aspects or episodes of the war; but by and large it has only served to enhance Oman's reputation.

Inevitably, when Oman chose to adopt one approach to his subject, he had to leave other approaches unexplored. There was no room in a narrative account – even though it ran to seven fat volumes and contained much interwoven analysis – to give a full description of the armies which waged the campaigns, of their tactics, or their logistical services. Nor could the impact of the war on Spanish and Portuguese society and politics be dealt with adequately; nor how it was regarded in France, or its impact on her military and financial resources. There is little room in the subject, as Oman conceived it, to integrate the story of the Peninsular campaigns into that of the wider war against Napoleon, to assess its part in his downfall seriously, or to discuss its place in British grand strategy and politics.

This is not a criticism. No history could successfully combine all these different approaches – and many more could be mentioned. By providing a reliable narrative of the campaigns Oman frees other scholars to explore these alternative approaches, and usually does more, for his brief accounts of such questions, although incidental to his own approach, are generally sensible, balanced, and extremely well-informed. Many writers have taken up the challenge. In *Wellington's Army* Oman himself gave an extended descriptive and analytical account of the British forces in the Peninsula, which has since been supplemented by the works of Michael Glover, Philip Haythornthwaite and others. More specialist works have explored its organisation and training (Richard Glover), its staff and administration (S.G.P. Ward), its logistics (T.M.O. Redgrave), and the life of its soldiers on campaign (Antony Brett-James).[5] The French army has received less attention, and though there is much information on their army as a whole in the works of Elting and Blond, the experience of the French in Spain remains a largely unexplored, and very tempting, subject.[6] Charles Esdaile has written admirably on the Spanish army, skilfully integrating military and political history, but the civilian experience of the war, and the ambiguities of local attitudes to the French, the British, the guerrillas, and the Spanish regular forces, have yet to receive comprehensive treatment, despite the good work of John Tone on the guerrilla war in Navarre and Don Alexander on French counter-insurgency operations in Aragón.[7] And this is just mentioning a handful of the scores of works which, in whole or in part, have extended our knowledge of facets of the war lightly touched upon by Oman. Yet even so, there are as many more approaches which remain unexplored. But it is time to turn to the particular subject of this essay, the British government's role in the Peninsular War.

Oman treats the Peninsular War largely in isolation, only loosely related to the wars which convulsed Europe between 1792 and 1815. He does not deny the obvious connections between the events in Spain and the rest of Europe, but he downplays them in order to add to the coherence and unity of his subject. This is a legitimate, indeed probably a necessary, approach, although as we shall see, it has some unfortunate consequences.

Pursuing this approach, Oman naturally begins his *History* with an extended account of Napoleon's relations with Spain and the intrigues of the Spanish court. Indeed, for much of the first volume the British war effort rightly takes second place to a French and Spanish perspective. More than 200 pages pass before news of the Spanish uprising reaches London, and here Oman makes an unfortunate and rather uncharacteristic slip: he gives two different dates for the arrival of the Asturian deputies (4 and 7 June 1808), both of which are wrong. (The correct date is 8 June, although many sources, including the *Annual Register*, are inaccurate on the point.)[8] After this blemish the account proceeds smoothly, with a brief account of the rapturous reception the Spaniards received in London, although the details of the cabinet's consideration of how to respond to the sudden opportunity falls outside the scope of Oman's approach. Instead he turns to military matters and the state of the British army, and on noting the shortage of staff, transport, and cavalry for the expedition to Portugal, he ventures a careless pleasantry: 'Such little contretemps were common in the days when Frederick Duke of York, with the occasional assistance of Mrs Mary Anne Clarke, managed the British army.' He soon came to regret the line, for it provoked objections from reviewers and a magisterial reproof from Fortescue, while Richard Glover, the Duke's ablest and most trenchant modern defender, attacks the remark not once but twice.[9]

This little skirmish makes for entertaining reading and may have taught Oman to be more careful in future; it is generally agreed that in the first volume he does not show quite such complete mastery of the subject as in its successors, so the warning may have been beneficial, while fortunately it did nothing to deaden his style. But there is a more serious observation which may be made here: the unfolding of the narrative does not give Oman the opportunity to establish the context in which the British government acted when it came to consider the Spanish appeals for assistance. For his purposes this did not matter – readers of the time could be assumed to have a reasonable knowledge of Britain's long struggle with Revolutionary and Napoleonic France, and it would have been otiose to break the narrative flow to recapitulate a familiar story. Yet although the outline was familiar, there was at the time no good history of Britain's part in the war. Within a few years Fortescue's *History of the British Army* vols 4-6 had provided an excellent account of the military campaigns, but Fortescue is opinionated and unreliable on questions of grand strategy. There is still no good single history of Britain's whole war from 1793 to 1815, although much can be found in John Ehrman's monumental life of Pitt, Piers Mackesy's brilliant books on the War of the Second Coalition, and the equally fine specialist studies by John Sherwig and Michael Duffy.[10] The more immediate background is extremely well covered in Christopher Hall's *British Strategy in the Napoleonic War, 1803-1815*,[11] which includes useful analytical chapters on issues such as manpower, as well as a good account of the war from 1803 to 1808. Unfortunately his later chapters are less convincing and Hall does not devote enough space to the Peninsular War to provide an effective supplement to Oman. My own contribution to the subject *Britain and the Defeat of Napoleon, 1807-1815*[12] examines the factors which influenced the British government in the formulation and implementation of its policy, ranging from personal quarrels and political intrigues to finance, diplomacy, and the balancing of the demands of one theatre of war against another. It thus describes much of the broader background to the campaigns in the Peninsula, but it does not attempt to give a detailed account of the military operations themselves.

In June 1808 the Portland ministry had been in office for just fifteen months. It was committed to a vigorous prosecution of the war, but due to the defeat of its Continental allies Prussia and Russia it had been able to achieve little other than some much-needed reforms to the army and militia which created a substantial expeditionary force ready for overseas operations, and the attack on Copenhagen which forestalled any immediate threat to Britain's command of the sea. The ministers were strongly predisposed in favour of striking a blow against Napoleon in Europe, but the apparent hopelessness of making an attempt without allies, and fears that Napoleon would succeed in gaining complete control of Spain without resistance, had led them to consider an attempt to raise Spain's American colonies against her. News of the Spanish uprising, however, led to an immediate decision to do all they could to encourage the spirit of resistance, and to welcome this new and unexpected ally with open arms.

It is no mere figure of speech to refer to 'the ministers' deciding policy, for government in those days was remarkably personal. The total staff of the Foreign Office in 1808 consisted of George Canning, the Foreign Secretary, two under-secretaries, a dozen clerks, and a handful of miscellaneous officials such as a librarian; and the duties of all but the most senior consisted of no more than copying, making précis, and some translations.[13] Policy was the preserve of the Foreign Secretary and sometimes one or both of the under-secretaries. There was, as yet, no tradition of a professional public service, no 'Foreign Office line', and no accumulated special expertise such as that which later in the century gave the permanent under-secretary so much power and influence. The same was true of the War Department, where the Secretary of State for War and the Colonies – Castlereagh in 1807– 9 – was responsible for organising British military expeditions overseas, relations with generals in the field, and many other aspects of war policy. (This was not the War Office, a larger but less important department concerned with the internal administration of the army.) The work of the various departments was co-ordinated, and overall policy decided by the cabinet: literally the cabinet ministers meeting together and discussing the questions of the day, often at and after dinner. There was no cabinet secretariat, not even an official to record the decisions reached, and Portland was a weak Prime Minister. Nor was there any regular procedure by which ministers would receive professional military advice: they might, if they wished, ask for it either from the Horse Guards or from individual officers of their acquaintance. The Duke of York, as Commander-in-Chief, had no right as such to be consulted on questions of strategy, although he did occasionally volunteer an opinion, and he was always influential in deciding which officers should receive commands.[14] Other professional advice was sought and received most informally and distinctions were sometimes blurred: thus Castlereagh's half-brother, Charles Stewart, was both under-secretary for war, and an officer on the active list who did not give up his political appointment when he commanded a cavalry brigade in Spain under Moore. He subsequently served as Wellington's Adjutant-General and – after Castlereagh's move to the Foreign Office – as ambassador to Prussia. Wellington himself retained the important office of Chief Secretary for Ireland while taking part in the Copenhagen Expedition and the Vimeiro campaign. When such men gave advice it was impossible to distinguish between the opinion of a ministerial colleague, a professional soldier, a fellow member of the House of Commons, or a friend or relative, for they were all these at once. Such networks may strike modern readers as slightly shocking or improper with their obvious scope for patronage and nepotism. Certainly they were open to abuse and those without such influential connections naturally complained of favouritism. However, there was no ready alternative, and the very informality of the system was often an advantage.

Later in the Peninsular War, after Wellington had returned to Portugal in 1809 and British strategy had become more settled, the role of the ministers diminished. Their instructions gave Wellington very broad discretion in the conduct of his operations, and as the years passed their confidence in him grew ever greater. But in the first year of the war it was the ministers who decided where British troops were to be sent, what role they were to play, and who was to command them.

Oman cannot pause to provide such background, nor does he really need to do so, because it is peripheral to the story as he tells it. Instead he carries on the narrative, giving little space to Britain's relations with the newly constituted Spanish authorities, or to the vast quantities of arms, ammunition, and money which she sent to their support.[15] However, the romantic story of Romana's escape from Denmark with the aid of the Royal Navy is given a brief chapter of its own. Such issues pale beside the decision to send Sir Arthur Wellesley to Portugal with an army and his subsequent supersession by Dalrymple, Burrard, and Moore. This famous imbroglio, which resulted in the British army having three different commanders in twenty-four hours, produced a characteristic outburst from Napier: 'The secret springs of this proceeding are not so deep as to baffle investigation; but that task scarcely belongs to this history: it is sufficient to show the effects of envy, treachery, and base cunning, without tracing those views home to their possessors.' Oman was far less intemperate, and he gives full credit to Castlereagh for his support for Wellesley. But he attributes the supersession to jealousy from the Duke of York and the War Office, and concludes that the arrangements for the command 'were the most ill-managed part of the business.'[16] In fact, this is less than half the story. In 1970 Michael Glover showed, by carefully reconstructing the sequence of events, that fresh intelligence from Portugal indicated that Junot was much stronger than had been originally thought, and that Wellesley's army had to be reinforced with every available man.[17] The ministers tried to keep Wellesley in command, but the King and the Duke of York insisted that such a large force required a more senior officer. Even Moore was probably too junior to satisfy them, and in any case the cabinet distrusted him as a tactless, difficult general, prone to quarrelling with Britain's allies. Faced with this dilemma the ministers chose Dalrymple, the British commander in Gibraltar, a lieutenant-general of great seniority, and who was well informed about the state of affairs in the Peninsula. They hoped that he would exercise only a supervisory command, and leave the day to day management of the army to fighting soldiers such as Wellesley and Moore, but this proved naïve and Castlereagh's hints were counter-productive.[18] Lying beneath this tangle lay another: the difficult question of the ultimate command of the British army in the Peninsula. Oman virtually ignored this issue, which was first really brought to light by D.W. Davies in 1974; more recent research has further advanced our understanding, but much remains uncertain. Put briefly, Dalrymple was given the command only temporarily; the Duke of York was eager for it, but the cabinet were determined that he should not have it, and instead decided that the army should be commanded by Lord Chatham: the son of the Elder Pitt and brother of the Younger, an officer who had seen little service, but who was a minister in the government and a member of the cabinet, and whose complete incapacity for the position was demonstrated in the following year when he commanded the expedition to Walcheren.[19]

Oman gives a full account of the Vimeiro campaign and the Convention of Cintra – indeed, it is worth pausing to note that one of the great virtues of his *History* is that he has the space to deal with such complex issues at leisure. Thus the negotiations leading to the Convention, its implementation in Portugal, and the outcry it produced in England, are all described, while two valuable appendices print the text of the Convention and Lord Moira's detailed critique of it. As always, the account is readable and substantially accurate, while readers who differ from Oman's judgements can do so while still relying upon his narrative. Like Napier, Fortescue, and most other military historians, Oman defends the substance of the Convention: the repatriation of Junot's army without restrictions on its further service. It is hard to dispute such a weight of authoritative opinion, but it does appear that this conclusion has been unduly influenced by the knowledge that Sir Arthur Wellesley took this view. Certainly Oman is at pains to defend Wellesley's role in the Convention while losing no opportunity to denigrate Dalrymple and Burrard; and some of his arguments supporting the repatriation appear strained – for example, 'the loss of 25,000 soldiers would be nothing to Napoleon'.[20] It is at least arguable that it would have been better to continue the campaign – despite the risk of delay or damage to Lisbon which this entailed – rather than agree to the repatriation of Junot's corps. Oman is more convincing on the damaging political clauses of the Convention which embarrassed Anglo-Portuguese relations, though he underrates the damage it did to the Portland ministry in London. Wellesley's role in the Convention has been re-examined from different perspectives by Michael Glover (generally sympathetic) and Richard Schneer (more hostile, very stimulating, but not always convincing). Their accounts add greatly to Oman, but they do not supersede him.[21]

While the furore over Cintra was at its height the British government was considering how it could best use its army to assist the Spaniards to drive the French from their positions on the Ebro back to the Pyrenees. Various plans were put forward only to be abandoned as circumstances changed, and in the end it was decided simply to assemble the British army in Galicia or on the borders of León – well to the rear of the front line – and allow its commander to make subsequent plans in co-operation with the Spanish forces. That commander was Sir John Moore. The ministers still distrusted him, but there was no obvious alternative and after Cintra they had little inclination to experiment. The King was unhappy at so junior an officer being given such a large command, but agreed that further disruption to its senior ranks should be avoided.[22]

The details of Moore's campaign need not concern us here: it is sufficient to note that Oman, reacting to Napier's great partiality, was more critical of Moore than was then customary, and that this aroused some complaints from reviewers and other contemporaries. In retrospect, Oman does not appear unduly harsh, even though some of his specific criticisms have been successfully rebutted.[23]

After Coruña there remained only a small British army in the Peninsula, some 10–12,000 men under Cradock holding Lisbon. Oman has harsh things to say about Cradock's inactivity and 'desponding mind', and certainly the general did not show much enterprise or enthusiasm. However, Oman only briefly touches on the fact that the instructions Cradock received from Castlereagh were almost equally negative.[24] Neither minister nor general thought that Cradock's force could do much more than simply wait for the French to advance, and then evacuate Lisbon. Given the overwhelming strength of the French armies in the Peninsula it was not unreasonable to be desponding.

Oman's description of the reform of the Portuguese army has been discussed in an earlier essay, but his brief account of Beresford's appointment needs to be noticed here. He states that Sir Arthur Wellesley was offered the command of the Portuguese army but declined it; that the post was widely coveted by British officers; and that it is 'hard to see' why the government selected Beresford, although he knew Portuguese and was a friend of Wellesley. Finally he concludes that 'into the secrets of ministerial patronage it is useless to pry.'[25] Fortunately later historians have pried, and though some details remain obscure, we now know much more about the circumstances of Beresford's appointment. The biographical background has been filled in by Samuel Vichness' unpublished doctoral thesis, which shows that Beresford's command of the Portuguese language was limited.[26] More recent research has revealed that the Portuguese government had asked for the loan of a general before the end of 1808, and had privately indicated a preference for Sir Arthur Wellesley. It appears that Wellesley was willing to accept, but that his appointment was blocked by Castlereagh, who believed that he was too valuable to waste in Portugal. Sir John Doyle was then considered, probably at the suggestion of the Duke of York who believed that 'he was the only British Officer who would undertake' the command (so much for its being widely coveted).[27] Doyle was senior to Wellesley, and if he had accepted the position it would have been difficult, if not impossible, to place Wellesley at the head of the British forces in Portugal. Fortunately Doyle was not appointed, apparently because the letter offering him the command went astray (he was then serving in the Channel Islands), and after some further delay Beresford was selected. Accounts differ whether he was actively soliciting the post (Vichness), or whether he was appointed against his will (Glover), and the evidence appears inconclusive.[28]

Beresford's appointment did not signal a wholesale British commitment to the defence of Portugal. This was the subject of considerable debate within the cabinet in January, February, and March 1809, with Canning impatiently urging that more be done while there was still time, but encountering resistance, from, among others, Castlereagh. Wellesley's famous 'Memorandum on the defence of Portugal' (7 March 1809) was drawn up to help persuade the doubters, but it produced no immediate results, and it was another three weeks before Canning secured his objectives: significant reinforcements and the appointment of Wellesley to command the British forces in Portugal. All this has only been discovered in recent years by an examination of the private papers of the cabinet ministers. Oman, like other historians, naturally assumed that Castlereagh, as Wellesley's friend and patron, must have supported his plans, and that the 'Memorandum' persuaded the government to adopt his policy. But although his account of the issue is mistaken, he at least avoids the folly of Fortescue, who wrote that 'Castlereagh had a desperate struggle to prevail with the cabinet' to achieve Wellesley's appointment.[29]

The British government's commitment was limited to the defence of Portugal, for the public and the ministers were both deeply disillusioned by the collapse of the Spanish armies in 1808, and by stories of Spanish apathy and indifference experienced by Moore's army. Other issues had further soured relations, including an almost accidental British attempt to establish a garrison at Cádiz. Wellesley's instructions therefore explicitly prohibited a campaign in Spain. Yet within a fortnight of Wellesley's arrival in Portugal he had written home, asking that these instructions be altered so that he could advance against Victor, and perhaps even drive the French back to the Ebro or beyond. There was great reluctance in the cabinet and from the King to see another British army venture in Spain, but the ministers already had great faith in Wellesley, and as they were considering his request news came of his triumph at Oporto and the expulsion of Soult from Portugal. This tipped the scale and permission was granted, although it was made plain that if Wellesley took his army into Spain it was on his own responsibility.[30]

In fact the Talavera campaign was a calculated gamble. The French armies in Spain were far stronger than the allies, but poorly distributed (largely as a continuing result of the pursuit of Moore), and there was a real possibility of defeating them in detail. Napoleon was preoccupied with the war with Austria and could not spare reinforcements to remedy a French defeat in Spain. As such, the chance was probably worth taking, even though the army's support services were inadequate and there had not been time to assess the likelihood of effective Spanish co-operation.[31] But it must be remembered that this was Wellesley's campaign, and that when he complains that his advance is delayed by lack of money, or that the Spanish armies are unreliable, he is encountering the very problems which made the ministers reluctant to see him venture into Spain in the first place.

More by ill luck than poor design the Talavera campaign failed to achieve its objectives, and despite the hard-fought victory, the British army wearily limped back to the Portuguese frontier. In England the government did its best to celebrate the battlefield victory, making Wellington a peer and granting him a pension, but there was much criticism from the Opposition Whigs and radicals, while even the King was unenthusiastic.[32] Meanwhile the Portland administration was dissolving amidst much personal acrimony, culminating in the famous duel between Canning and Castlereagh. A new government was formed from the wreckage, with Perceval at its head, Liverpool at the War Department, and Lord Wellesley, Wellington's eldest brother, as Foreign Secretary. However, this new ministry was extremely weak and there was much doubt if it could survive the meeting of Parliament and the inevitable outcry over the Walcheren expedition. Given the Opposition's criticism of Wellington and of the government's strategy in the Peninsula, the political crisis threatened the future of Britain's commitment to Portugal. But this threat should not be overstated: if Perceval's government fell it might well have been replaced by yet another Pittite government, including many of the same men, probably led by Lord Wellesley, and determined to pursue the war actively. Even if the Whigs did come into office, there is no certainty that they would have withdrawn Wellington's army: policies advocated in opposition are often abandoned in government.

In the event, Perceval's ministry survived and continued to support Wellington in the defence of Portugal. However, this did not mean that relations between Wellington and the ministers were uniformly harmonious. The government was facing severe financial problems and its attempts to encourage Wellington to be more economical produced outbursts of mingled astonishment and outrage. Matters were not helped by a recurrence of the shortage of specie (*ie* ready money - gold and silver coin), and by delays in the arrival of reinforcements promised to Wellington, largely due to the need to find British troops to garrison Cádiz when the French overran Andalucia at the beginning of 1810. On all these issues Wellington wrote home letters whose intemperance sometimes verged on hysteria - letters which would have done infinite damage to the government and to the cause if they had become public - and the ministers responded with unvarying courtesy and patience.[33] Occasionally they made mistakes: Liverpool privately hinted to Wellington that if it became necessary to evacuate Portugal the government would rather he acted a little sooner, rather than risk his army by hanging on until the last moment. It was an innocent, rather obvious, remark; but Wellington was correct in objecting that the discretion granted in his official instructions should not be curtailed by private hints.[34] For his part, Wellington showed a proper restraint in seldom writing direct to Lord Wellesley - who was soon at odds with the other ministers - but he gave Liverpool gratuitous and naive political advice on the need to strengthen the ministry, while in many private letters he showed his contempt for the weakness of the government.[35]

Oman's account of these problems is slight and rather disappointing. They receive a mere two pages (pp.168-9) in his third volume, and a much better, but still too brief, discussion in volume IV (pp.65-9), which combines the first three months of

1811 with a retrospect of 1810. This improvement was probably inspired by Fortescue, who brought to Oman's attention suppressed passages in Wellington's letters to William Wellesley-Pole, and whose own account of Wellington's relations with the government, published the following year, is excellent.[36] Neither Fortescue nor Oman was at all eager to tarnish Wellington's reputation, and they were both at pains to excuse his intemperance, but they were unwilling to let Napier's calumnies against the ministers pass unchallenged, and wished to correct the impression formed by readers who accepted Wellington's letters at face value. Subsequent research, including Denis Gray's meticulous life of Perceval, has revealed in much more detail the problems which the government faced. Such writers are not always so sympathetic to Wellington's complaints – Gray calls him 'a prince of grumblers'[37] – and correct some details in Fortescue's account; but in general they show that he, who in his earlier volumes had been a most hot-headed and unreliable guide to British politics, was in this case well-informed, perceptive, and fair.

The long stalemate in front of Lisbon, with Masséna's army encamped at Santarem throughout the winter of 1810–11, coincided with the Regency Crisis in Britain. At the end of October, following the death of his daughter Princess Amelia, George III succumbed to a recurrence of his porphyria, which was misdiagnosed as madness. When he failed to recover quickly it became necessary to establish his son as Regent, and as the Prince had long-established ties with the Opposition, and had the power to dismiss the government, this put the future of Perceval's ministry in jeopardy. There is little doubt that if the King had died or been clearly beyond recovery, the Prince would have requested Lords Grenville and Grey to form an administration. (Whether they would have recalled Wellington's army is much more doubtful.) However, the King appeared well on the road to recovery by the time the Regent was sworn in, and there was little point for the Opposition to be brought into office, only for the King to dismiss them again when he recovered his powers. So the Prince retained Perceval in office, while giving ostentatious signs that his preference remained with the Opposition.[38] The King's condition remained promising for most of the first half of 1811, without ever quite gaining the stability needed for him to resume his duties. In July and August there was a relapse; he became critically ill, and though his body recovered, all hope of his mind clearing was ended. The Prince might then have dismissed the ministry without reproach, but he was lazy and indecisive and preferred to allow the existing state of affairs to drift on until the largely symbolic restrictions on his powers expired early in 1812.[39]

It is natural to assume that the military crisis in Portugal and the political crisis in London were related, but it is difficult to establish any close connection between them. Masséna was obviously encouraged by the possibility that a new government might withdraw the British army and so open his road to Lisbon, but there is little reason to believe that this was his principal motive in maintaining his position for so long. Having driven Wellington back to the ramparts of Torres Vedras it was his duty to give Napoleon as much time as possible to prepare the means to break the impasse, while in any case a retreat through Portugal in the depths of winter was hardly inviting. Conversely the state of the campaign did little to influence events in London. The ministers and their supporters had greeted news of Bussaco with enthusiasm and looked forward eagerly to another, more decisive victory. When this failed to occur they were discouraged but far from despair, while the Opposition was confirmed in its opinion of the futility of the campaign.[40] Wellington might have sought to influence events by attacking Masséna at Sobral, when success would have strengthened the government and failure would probably have led to its fall, but he refused to be influenced by such considerations, and showed his usual wise restraint. There is no reason to believe that the Prince's decision to retain Perceval in office at this time was significantly influenced by the state of the war.

Masséna's retreat in early March 1811 led most of the Opposition to abandon their public criticism of Wellington and the government's strategy, although in private they remained pessimistic. The success also forced the cabinet to reconsider their plans. Officially their policy was still limited to the defence of Portugal, and Liverpool had repeatedly warned Wellington that financial constraints made any expansion of the war effort impossible, and even that some of the reinforcements which were sent to Portugal might have to be withdrawn when the immediate crisis was over. Nonetheless, even before the news of Masséna's retreat reached London, Perceval had managed to find money for a substantial increase in the Portuguese subsidy, while Wellington's success further emboldened the ministers. Additional reinforcements were sent out to Portugal, and after some hesitation Wellington's instructions were altered at the end of May, giving him complete discretion in the conduct of his operations.[41]

Among other factors encouraging the ministers to adopt a forward policy were signs of instability elsewhere in Europe. France and Russia had come close to war at the beginning of the year, and although hostilities had been avoided relations remained tense, leaving Austria and Prussia to consider which side they would take if war broke out. Later in the year, Napoleon's relations with Prussia would reach a crisis which was only resolved after the Prussians had seriously considered a suicidal struggle.[42]

Lord Wellesley watched these events with great interest, and managed to infect the Prince Regent with some of his enthusiasm. But in other respects the Foreign Secretary was discontented. He did not work well with his colleagues, and had already considered resignation. Perceval's financial prudence thwarted Wellesley's favourite plans. The increased subsidy to Portugal was useful, but insignificant compared to his proposal for a massive subsidy to Spain, to be used to regenerate her army, which would be placed under Wellington's command. Wellesley's colleagues baulked at this idea, objecting both to its wild extravagance and to the intimate involvement in Spanish affairs which it would bring. At most they would accept any Spanish offer to give Wellington the command of their forces in the provinces in which he was operating, but they knew that they lacked the resources to reform the Spanish army as Beresford had reformed the Portuguese, even if the Spaniards would agree.[43]

Rather surprisingly, Wellington did not greatly favour Wellesley's plan, although even so, he was irritated by Liverpool's emphasis on the need for economy when announcing its rejection. However, in general his relations with the government greatly improved during the course of the year. His distrust of Liverpool slowly dissipated, a process much helped by the absence of any outcry in England over Beresford's incompetence at Albuera. As a result he was more ready to explain his hopes and plans to the ministers, an openness which gave them confidence in the disappointing second half of the year.

The expiration of the Regency restrictions in early 1812 forced the Prince to commit himself. He had grown used to the ministers and when it came to the point his residual sympathy for the Whigs was too weak to lead him to change the government. He made an empty overture which Grey and Grenville scornfully dismissed, and the bulk of the Whigs reacted with great bitterness to the betrayal of hopes which they had cherished for almost thirty years. Lord Wellesley's ambitions were also disappointed. He was unwilling to continue serving under Perceval, and resigned in the hope that this would break up the government, and that the Prince would place him at the head of a new administration, combining the old ministers with important Tories then out of office such as Castlereagh and Canning. But Wellesley misjudged his support. His colleagues were delighted to see him go, having found him inefficient and impractical, and the Prince confirmed Perceval in office. Castlereagh became Foreign Secretary and a few other changes were made, which consolidated the government's position, although it still rested heavily on Perceval's debating skills in the Commons. Perceval and Liverpool were both anxious how Wellington would react to his brother's resignation, and wrote explaining their view of events and promising that they would continue to support the war. Wellington accepted their assurances, although he wrote sympathetically to Lord Wellesley and continued to believe that the government should take a more enlarged view of the war. His own operations were becoming more successful, with the brilliant capture of Ciudad Rodrigo – a triumph which the Regent honoured by making Wellington an earl.[44]

Having made his choice, the Prince must have hoped that the ministry would last for some years at least, but a few months later, on 11 May 1812, Perceval was assassinated in the lobby of the House of Commons. An attempt to carry on the government without him was defeated, and weeks of intricate political negotiation and intrigue followed. Grey and Grenville, leading the main opposition, held out for government in their own right not as part of a coalition, and the Prince would not agree to this except as a last resort. Several plans were put forward to reconstruct the existing government on a broader basis under Lord Wellesley or Lord Moira, but these failed. In the end Liverpool emerged leading the old ministers, and Parliament – which had rejected this ministry only a month before – now confirmed it in office rather than force the Prince to turn to the Whigs. Underlying this *volte face* it is easy to see a widespread desire for a strong, efficient administration committed to the vigorous prosecution of the war; when personal antagonisms made this impossible, the Commons preferred the old ministers to the Whigs.

Liverpool's government was very weak at first, and he made great efforts to bring Canning into the cabinet, but Canning foolishly declined. Nevertheless, the ministry soon gained strength – partly from the progress of the war – and went on to last for fifteen years. Liverpool twice offered the War Department to William Wellesley-Pole (Wellington's brother) but Pole declined, preferring to throw his lot in with Lord Wellesley, much to Wellington's annoyance. The genial and efficient Lord Bathurst therefore became Secretary of State for War and the Colonies, and took up his position with a determination to do all he could to support Wellington. He acted promptly to solve yet another severe shortage of specie, not only putting pressure on the Bank of England to release some of its reserves of gold, but also arranging for the export of guineas to aid Wellington. This was both politically sensitive and technically illegal, and Bathurst was not entirely joking when he told a colleague: 'For this I shall have my Head off, if we should not succeed.'[45] The money was matched with men, for very large reinforcements were sent out to the Peninsula in the second half of the year, although the full benefit was not felt until 1813 because of the very high level of sickness in Wellington's army.[46] Salamanca was greeted with delight: Wellington was raised another step in the peerage, becoming a marquess, and was granted £100,000 to support the honour, while the government resolutely defended him over the failure at Burgos and the retreat back to the Portuguese frontier. In return Wellington behaved well to the ministers, rejecting the attempts of Canning and Wellesley to blame them for Burgos.[47]

Oman naturally does not devote much space to the political crises of 1812 or preceding years, for although they had important implications for the war in the Peninsula, they lie at the very edge of his subject. However, his coverage of Wellington's relations with the ministers in 1812 is richer and more detailed than for earlier years, particularly over specie.

Two possible factors may have encouraged the more open-handed policy adopted by the British government in the second half of 1812: it may be that Perceval's death removed a powerful advocate of caution; and, much more probably, Napoleon's invasion of Russia may have inspired the cabinet to be more venturesome. Napoleon's success or failure would have far more influence on the war as a whole, and on the Peninsula in 1813, than any triumph of Wellington's. If Russia had been defeated, fresh armies might have crossed the Pyrenees, just as they had done in 1810 following the defeat of Austria, and if they did so, Wellington could well have been forced back to Torres Vedras and Andalucia been reoccupied. But if Napoleon was defeated, his whole Empire would be shaken to its foundations. The British government was determined to concentrate its military efforts in the Peninsula, where they helped to tie down more than 200,000 French troops, but it also did what little it could to help the Russians directly, exerting diplomatic pressure on the Ottoman Empire to remain neutral, and on Sweden to take an active part in the war on Russia's side. The Royal Navy provided some co-operation in the Baltic, arms were sent to Russia, and the cabinet, despite being very short of money, even authorised the British ambassador to give the Russians a small subsidy – £500,000 – although in the event this was not called upon.[48]

At the same time Britain also faced an unwanted war with the United States. At first the government hoped that concessions on the principal American grievances would lead to a rapid settlement, and Bathurst resisted calls to divert reinforcements from the Peninsula to Canada. When it became clear that the Americans were determined to fight, a few regiments had to be sent across the Atlantic, but the direct military impact of the war on Wellington was remarkably slight. The indirect impact was potentially far greater but again proved limited in practice. American privateers were a nuisance rather than a serious threat to Wellington's lines of communication, and despite the war the United States continued to export vast quantities of flour to feed the British army in the Peninsula for as long as the British remained willing buyers.[49]

The last eighteen months of the war were blessedly free of political crises in London, while Wellington's prestige with the ministers had risen to such a point that they not only gave him a free hand in the conduct of his operations and all the material support they could, they also sought his advice on other questions.

Nonetheless, difficulties occasionally arose, for example when Wellington crossed pens with the equally sharp-tongued J.W. Croker at the Admiralty. Oman devotes a lengthy chapter in volume VI to 'Wellington and Whitehall' and further passages in volume VII covering the last months of the war. In general these deal with the issues admirably, although naturally some questions and doubts remain. The most serious problem is that he greatly over-states the significance of some letters from the ministers in the middle of 1813 when they raised the possibility of transferring Wellington's army to Germany once the liberation of Spain was complete. There was never any suggestion that the government would impose this move on Wellington against his will; rather they were asking his advice with considerable deference. Nor does Liverpool's suggestion that the Pyrenean passes be fortified on the same principle as the Lines of Torres Vedras – that is, with relatively modest, self-contained works held by second-line troops, while the field army was kept to the rear – deserve the elaborate sarcasm it receives. But such misjudgements are rare.[50]

While Wellington pursued his campaigns in the Peninsula, the government devoted much attention to the wider war against Napoleon. It sought to consolidate the alliance with the Continental Powers and discourage moves for a premature peace, but at the same time to ensure that Britain's vital interests were protected if negotiations could not be avoided. It was a difficult task for Britain's influence in the Continental courts was limited. She was not widely loved on the Continent, and her success and prosperity aroused resentment, although it is fair to say that this was no greater than the jealousy among the Continental Powers themselves. (For example, Russia and Austria distrusted each other far more than either distrusted Britain.) The vast subsidies which Britain paid in 1813–14 bought little influence. They were essential to the allied war effort, but covered only a part of its cost, so that their receipt was not an argument against making peace. Above all, the Continental Powers could afford to take British support for granted, for there was no danger that she would make a separate peace or fail to support them if they carried on the war. What finally thwarted Metternich's hopes of a compromise peace (on terms which would have left the French in Spain and the Low Countries), was not British diplomacy but Alexander's determination and Napoleon's refusal to negotiate in good faith.[51]

The two fronts of the war – in Spain and southern France, and in Germany and eastern France – were, of course, connected. Despite Wellington's efforts, Napoleon naturally withdrew troops from Spain after the disaster in Russia and again after later reverses. The armistice in Germany and the threat of a separate peace are advanced by Oman and other writers to explain Wellington's refusal to invade France in the second half of 1813. There is some truth in this argument, but it ignores the matching point, that news that Wellington had entered Gascony would have given fresh heart to the allies.[52] Similarly, Wellington's refusal to advance in January and February 1814, citing the heavy rains and mud, did not impress the allies who were pushing into France despite deep snow and the coldest winter for a generation. (Which is not to say that Wellington's decision may not have been the only practical one, but it cannot simply be accepted without considering its wider implications.)[53]

It is for this period – the last ten months of the war, from Vitoria to Toulouse – that Oman suffers most from his decision to follow Napier in treating the war in the Peninsula as a self-contained conflict, rather than as one aspect of the wider struggle against Napoleon. As we follow Wellington's slow advance from the Bidassoa to the Nivelle, from the Nivelle to the Nive, from the Nive to Orthez, and from Orthez to Toulouse, we sense uneasily that these operations mattered less than the Battle of Leipzig, the Frankfort Proposals, the advance through Switzerland, the abortive peace conference at Châtillon, the wrangling among the allies, and the final advance which led to the capture of Paris and Napoleon's abdication. The two sectors of the war were inter-related: Wellington's operations kept busy the troops which might otherwise have enabled Napoleon to exploit his brilliant, but in the end barren, victories; while the open support for the Bourbons in Bordeaux finally closed the door on a negotiated peace with Napoleon. But it is difficult to sense these connections in Oman's account, where the main focus is on Wellington, and other operations receive only the occasional glance. In this context claims of the wider significance of events such as the proclamation of the Bourbons at Bordeaux smack of special pleading, even when – viewed from the perspective of the war as a whole – they are fully justified.

And so the last part of the great *History* trails off into a tame ending. The war is over, and a brief, disappointing final chapter promises to discuss 'The Place of the Peninsular War in History', but in fact does not even seriously ask what part it played in Napoleon's downfall. But we should not be too critical: this final volume was published twenty-eight years after the first, thirty-three years after Oman began his researches, and it sustains all the virtues which the *History* has throughout: the clear, comprehensive scholarly narrative never flags. The task begun is completed, though the world in which it was conceived has been changed out of recognition by the First World War and by the revolution in outlook and attitudes which marked the early decades of the twentieth century. The limitations which are most apparent at the end were integral to the original conception of the work, and while a better conclusion might have made them less obvious, it could not have removed them.

Looking at Oman's achievement as a whole, one is staggered first by its sheer scale: a sustained narrative running to over 4000 pages which begins well and grows in authority as it continues, and which maintains its lively interest throughout. It is based on prodigious learning – half-a-lifetime spent in reading and research – but it is never pedantic or heavy-handed in its scholarship; not for Oman the ill-concealed delight of the narrow-minded specialist pouncing on a colleague's careless phrase. This is confident, mature history in full command of its subject, with no need to lay desperate claims to originality or to promote itself with the cry of a spurious controversy. Oman is never bland, but he supports his opinions with a combination of courtesy, learning and calm reason which is far more convincing than invective or heated 'debate'. His judgements are carefully nuanced; always worth consideration, and usually carry conviction. His characters are rounded, and his description of Wellington's strengths and foibles (vol.II, pp.294-311) remains one of the most intelligent and stimulating assessments of the Duke to have appeared anywhere. And here, as elsewhere, his work provides the sound platform for others to use, even if they disagree with his opinions, or wish to explore other approaches to the subject. But perhaps the best testimony to Oman's achievement is that nearly seventy years after the final volume was published, a century after the work began, it remains the indispensable account of the subject, esteemed and enjoyed by academic and general readers alike. It is a rare triumph.

Notes

1. This essay is based largely on my *Britain and the Defeat of Napoleon, 1807-15* (New Haven and London, 1996), supplemented by further research on other aspects of the Peninsular War, some of which has appeared in my *Tactics and the Experience of Battle in the Age of Napoleon* (New Haven and London, 1998).

2. Oman, *History*, vol.I, pp.ix-x.

3. For example the quotation from Andrew Leith Hay's *Narrative of the Peninsular War* given in vol.V, pp.448-9; and that from Denis Le Marchant's *Memoir of the Late Major-General Le Marchant* on p.451, which exhibit all these practices. Oman's reference to the Le Marchant quote is also inaccurate: it is not p.285, but rather pp.296-7.

4. See *inter alia* Oman, *History*, vol.V, pp.iv-vi, 193-5, 546.

5. Oman, *Wellington's Army, 1809-1814* (London, 1913; reprinted 1986); Michael Glover, *Wellington's Army* (Newton Abbot, 1977); Philip Haythornthwaite, *The Armies of Wellington* (London, 1994); Richard Glover, *Peninsular Preparation: The Reform of the British Army, 1795-1809* (Cambridge, 1963); S.G.P. Ward, *Wellington's Headquarters* (Oxford, 1957); T.M.O. Redgrave, 'Wellington's Logistical Arrangements in the Peninsular War, 1809-1814' (unpublished PhD thesis, University of London, n.d., c.1979); Antony Brett-James, *Life in Wellington's Army* (London, 1972).

6. John R. Elting, *Swords Around a Throne: Napoleon's Grande Armée* (London, 1988); Georges Blond, *La Grande Armée* (London, 1995).

7. Charles J. Esdaile, *The Spanish Army in the Peninsular War* (Manchester, 1988), and *The Duke of Wellington and the Command of the Spanish Army, 1812-1814* (Basingstoke, 1990); John Tone, *The Fatal Knot - The Guerrilla War in Navarre and the Defeat of Napoleon in Spain* (Chapel Hill, 1994); Don W. Alexander, *Rod of Iron: French Counterinsurgency Policy in Aragón during the Peninsular War* (Wilmington, 1985).

8. Oman, *History*, vol.I, pp.66, 220. For the correct date see A. Aspinall, ed., *The Later Correspondence of George III* (5 vols, Cambridge, 1962-70), vol.V, p.84; and *The Times*, 9 June 1808.

9. Oman, *History*, vol.I, p.225; E.M. Lloyd reviewing vol.I in *English Historical Review* XVII, October 1902, p.805; J. Fortescue, *History of the British Army* (19 vols, London, 1899-1930), vol.VI, pp.190n-191n; Richard Glover, *op.cit.* pp.14, 41.

10. John Ehrman, *The Younger Pitt*, vol.II *The Reluctant Transition* (London, 1983), and vol.III *The Consuming Struggle* (London, 1996); Piers Mackesy, *Statesmen at War: The Strategy of Overthrow* (London, 1974), *War Without Victory: The Downfall of Pitt, 1799-1802* (Oxford, 1984), and *The British Victory in Egypt, 1801: The End of Napoleon's Conquest* (London, 1985); see also his *The War in the Mediterranean, 1803-10* (Harvard, 1957); John M. Sherwig, *Guineas and Gunpowder: British Foreign Aid in the Wars with France, 1793-1815* (Harvard, 1969); Michael Duffy, *Soldiers, Sugar and Seapower: The British Expeditions to the West Indies and the War against Revolutionary France* (Oxford, 1985).

11. Manchester, 1992.

12. New Haven and London, 1996.

13. J.M. Collinge, *Foreign Office Officials, 1782-1870* (*Office Holders in Modern Britain* vol.VIII, London, 1979), pp.2-3; C.R. Middleton, *The Administration of British Foreign Policy, 1782-1846* (Durham, North Carolina, 1977), pp.151-78, discusses the composition, duties, and work practices of the staff at the Foreign Office.

14. The administrative background of the war effort is explored in more detail in 'Strategic Planning in a time of Small Government: The Wars against Revolutionary and Napoleonic France, 1793-1815' by Rory Muir and Charles Esdaile, *Wellington Studies* I (1996), pp.1-90, especially pp.1-42.

15. See *History*, vol.I, p.365, for Oman's brief account.

16. Napier, *War in the Peninsula*, vol.I, p.115 (book 2, chapter 3); Oman, *History*, vol.I, pp.225-7 - it is far from clear what he means by the 'War Office' in this context.

17. Michael Glover, *Britannia Sickens: Sir Arthur Wellesley and the Convention of Cintra* (London, 1970) pp.59-60, 56.

18. *Ibid* pp.60-68. For the King's role see Aspinall, *op.cit.* vol.V, pp.103-4.

19. D.W. Davies, *Sir John Moore's Peninsular Campaign, 1808-1809* (The Hague, 1974), pp.33-4; Muir, *Britain and the Defeat of Napoleon*, pp.44-7.

20. Oman, *History*, vol.I, p.268.

21. *Ibid* vol.I, pp.274-8; Glover, *Britannia Sickens*, pp.130-45; Richard M. Schneer 'Arthur Wellesley and the Cintra Convention: A New Look at an Old Puzzle' *Journal of British Studies* 19, no.2, Spring 1980, pp.93-119; for my own view see *Britain and the Defeat of Napoleon*, pp.51-9.

22. *Ibid* pp.65-9; Davies, *op.cit.* pp.30-1, 57-60.

23. For example, Oman's criticism (*History*, vol.I, pp.494-6) of Moore's decision to send his artillery on a circuitous route is refuted by Major-General J.F. Maurice, ed., *The Diary of Sir John Moore* (2 vols, London, 1904), vol.II, pp.287, 315-21. Complaints at Oman's treatment of Moore will be found in E.M. Lloyd's review of Oman's first volume in *English Historical Review* XVII, October 1902, pp.804-5, and in Maurice, *op.cit.* vol.I, p.viii, and vol.II, pp.301, 307-9.

24. Oman, *History*, vol.II, pp.201-7, especially pp.203 and 204.

25. *Ibid* pp.215-17.

26. Samuel E. Vichness, 'Marshal of Portugal: The Military Career of William Carr Beresford, 1785-1814' (doctoral thesis presented to Florida State University, 1977), *passim*, and p.131 for his limited command of the language. See also the character sketch of him in Glover, *Wellington's Army*, pp.120-1.

27. Duke of York to Colonel J.W. Gordon, 27 January 1809, BL Add. Ms. 49,473 f.3.

28. Vichness, *op.cit.* pp.121-3; Glover, *Wellington's Army*, p.121; *cf* Muir, *Britain and the Defeat of Napoleon*, pp.84-5.

29. Fortescue, *op.cit.* vol.VII, p.128; Oman, *History*, vol.II, p.287; Muir, *Britain and the Defeat of Napoleon*, pp.85-7; Wellesley's memorandum is printed in the 8-volume 1844 edition *WD*, vol.III, pp.181-3.

30. Muir, *Britain and the Defeat of Napoleon*, pp.94-5. Wellington's request is printed in *WD*, vol.III, pp.219-20; Castlereagh's reply in the *Correspondence, Despatches, and other Papers of Viscount Castlereagh* (12 vols, London, 1848-53), vol.VII, p.71.

31. The extent of Wellesley's ambitions in the campaign is not always recognised: see his letters to Lieutenant-Colonel Carroll and Lieutenant-Colonel Bourke, 19 and 21 June 1809, in *SD*, vol.VI, pp.289-90; and *WD*, vol.III, pp.310-11 respectively.

32. For more details see Muir, *Britain and the Defeat of Napoleon*, p.101.

33. For example, Wellington's letters of 6 January, 14 March, 23 May, and 19 August, *WD*, vol.III, pp.677-8, 781, and vol.IV, pp.87, 234-5.

34. Liverpool to Wellington, 13 March 1810, *SD*, vol.VI, pp.493-4; Wellington to Liverpool, 2 April 1810, *WD*, vol.III, pp.809-12. For the context see Muir, *Britain and the Defeat of Napoleon*, pp.116-17.

35. Wellington's advice: Wellington to Liverpool, 1 March 1810, *WD*, vol.III, pp.759-62; see also his letter to William Wellesley-Pole, 11 January 1811, Raglan Papers, Wellington A no.39, Gwent County Record Office, passage deleted in the published version. For examples of attacks on the government's weakness see his letter to Admiral Berkeley, 7 April 1810, and to J.C. Villiers, 5 June 1810, *WD*, vol.IV, pp.7-8, 103-4.

36. Oman, *History*, vol.IV, p.69n, acknowledges Fortescue's help. Fortescue, *op.cit.* vol.VII, pp.434-50, and see also vol.VIII, pp.3-6, 117-19.

37. Denis Gray, *Spencer Perceval: The Evangelical Prime Minister, 1762-1812* (Manchester, 1963), p.335.

38. For more on this see Muir, *Britain and the Defeat of Napoleon*, pp.136-43.

39. *Ibid* pp.160-2.

40. *Ibid* pp.135-8.

41. *Ibid* pp.143-7, 152-4, and 399 n.25, for a discussion of the variations in the surviving drafts of these instructions.

42. For more on this see *ibid* pp.176-92.

43. *Ibid* pp.119-24, 145.

44. Wellington to Liverpool, 20 January 1811, *SD*, vol.VII, pp.256-7; Perceval to Wellington, 22 January 1811, Spencer Walpole, *The Life of the Rt. Hon. Spencer Perceval* (2 vols, London, 1874), vol.II, p.261; Wellington to Lord Wellesley, 20 March 1811, *SD*, vol.VII, pp.307-8; Muir, *Britain and the Defeat of Napoleon*, pp.193-5, 207-8.

45. Bathurst to Harrowby, 16 September 1812, Harrowby Mss, vol.XIV, ff.59-60.

46. 'Return of troops embarked for the Peninsula since 1st Jan. 1812' Adjutant General's Office, 27 November 1812, Castlereagh Papers, PRO of Northern Ireland D 3030/3387; Muir, *Britain and the Defeat of Napoleon*, pp.205-6.

47. See Muir, *Britain and the Defeat of Napoleon*, pp.209, 405 n.36 and n.37.

48. *Ibid* pp.220-31.

49. W.F. Galpin, 'The American Grain Trade to the Spanish Peninsula, 1810-1814' *American Historical Review* XXVIII (1922), pp.24-44; for the other effects of the War of 1812 see Muir, *Britain and the Defeat of Napoleon*, pp.232-40, and the sources cited there.

50. Liverpool to Wellington, 7 July 1813, *SD*, vol.VIII, pp.64-5; Oman, *History*, vol.VI, pp.558-61; *cf* Muir, *Britain and the Defeat of Napoleon*, pp.262-3.

51. For much more on this see Muir, *Britain and the Defeat of Napoleon*, chapters 14 and 16.

52. Oman, *History*, vol.VI, pp.523-7, 737-8, vol.VII, pp.110-111; *cf* Muir, *Britain and the Defeat of Napoleon*, pp.267-70.

53. Muir, *Britain and the Defeat of Napoleon*, pp.301, 312-13.

Maps

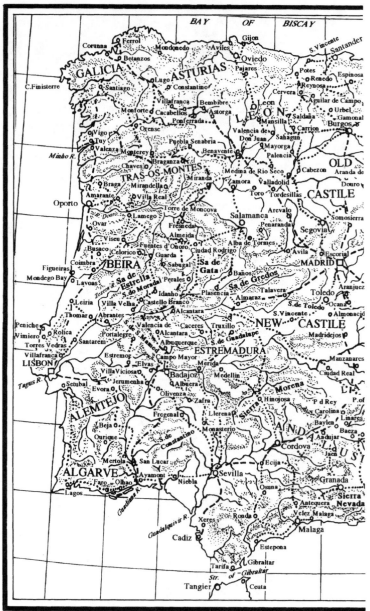

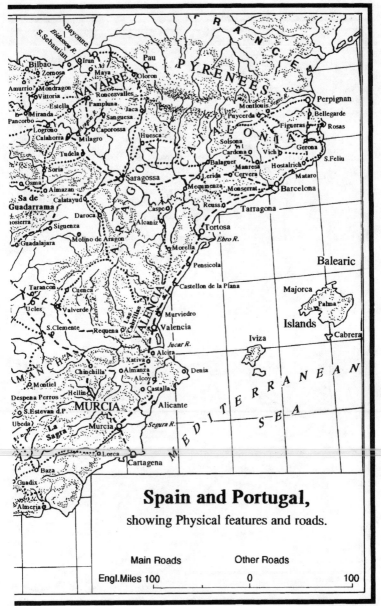

Spain and Portugal,

showing Physical features and roads.

Main Roads   Other Roads

Engl.Miles 100   0   100

The Oxford Geographical Institute

Part of Northern Spain

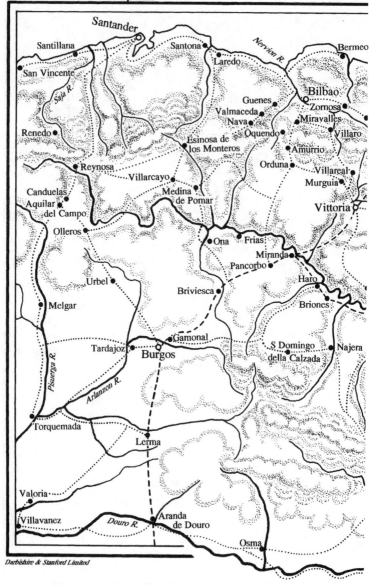

Santander

Santillana

San Vincente

Saja R.

Renedo

Reynosa

Canduelas
Aquilar
del Campo

Olleros

Urbel

Melgar

Pisuerga R.

Tardajoz

Torquemada

Valoria

Villavanez

Douro R.

Santona

Laredo

Nervion R.

Bermeo

Bilbao

Guenes
Valmaceda
Nava

Zornosa

Miravalles

Oquendo

Villaro

Esinosa de
los Monteros

Amurrio

Orduna

Villareal

Villarcayo

Murguia

Medina
de Pomar

Vittoria

Ona

Frias

Miranda

Pancorbo

Haro

Briviesca

Briones

Gamonal

Burgos

S Domingo
della Calzada

Najera

Arlanzon R.

Lerma

Aranda
de Douro

Osma

Darbishire & Stanford Limited

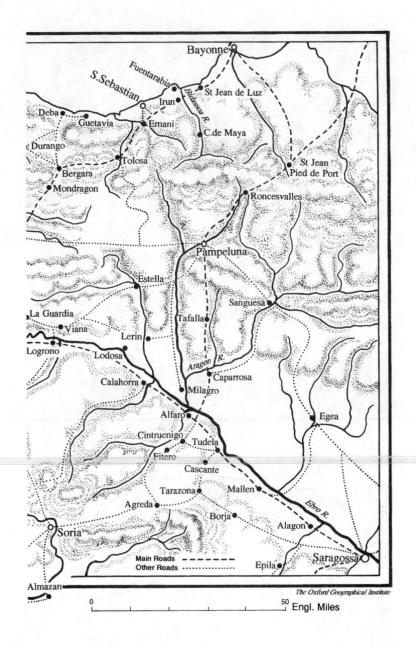

Bayonne

S. Sebastian Fuentarabia
Deba Guetavia Irun St Jean de Luz
Durango Emani Bidassoa R. C. de Maya
Tolosa St Jean Pied de Port
Bergara
Mondragon Roncesvalles

Pampeluna

Estella Sanguesa
La Guardia Tafalla
Viana
Lerin
Logrono Lodosa Aragon R.
Calahorra Caparrosa
Milagro
Alfaro Egea
Cintruenigo Tudela
Fitero
Cascante
Tarazona Mallen
Agreda Borja Ebro R.
Alagon
Soria
Saragossa
Main Roads ---- Epila
Other Roads ......

Almazan
0   50 Engl. Miles

The Oxford Geographical Institute

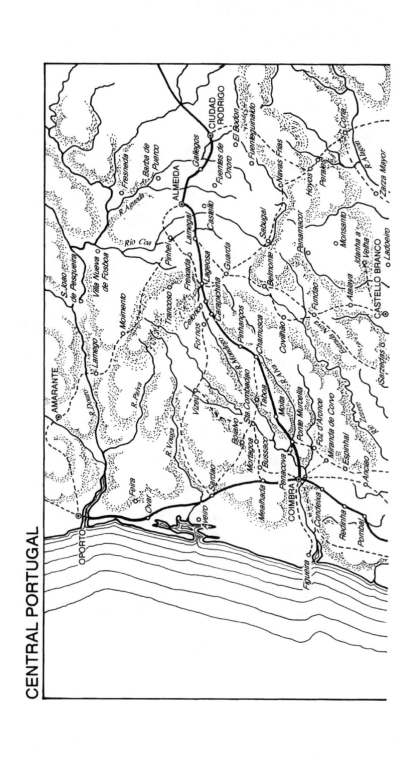

CENTRAL PORTUGAL

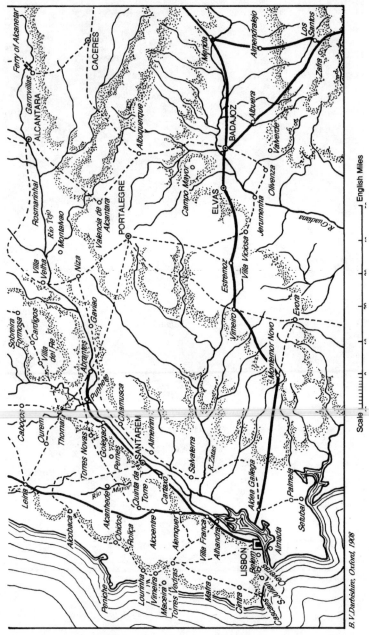

Ferry of Alcanetar
Garrovillas
ALCANTARA
CACERES
Rosmarinhal
Rio Tejo
Montalvao
Villa Velha
Sobreira Formosa
Cardigos
Villa del Re
Niza
Gaviao
Abrantes
Punhete
Chamusca
Caboços
Ourem
Thomar
Torres Novas
Golegao
Pernes
SANTAREM
Almeirim
Salvaterra
R. Zatas
Leiria
Akanhede
Rio Mayor
"Quinta da Torre"
Cartaxo
Obidos
Rolça
Alcoentre
Alenquel
Peniche
Alcobaça
Lourinha
Vimeira
Maceira
Torres Vedras
Mafra
Villa Franca
Alhandra
Aldea Gallega
Cintra
Cascaes
S. Julian
Belem
LISBON
Almada
Palmela
Setubal
Valencia de Alcantara
Albuquerque
PORTALEGRE
Campo Mayor
Estremoz
ELVAS
BADAJOZ
Villa Viçosa
Vimeiro
Jerumenha
Olivenza
R. Guadiana
Evora
Montemor Novo
Merida
Almendralejo
Los Santos
Zafra
Albuera
Valverde

Scale   English Miles

B.V.Darbishire, Oxford, 1908

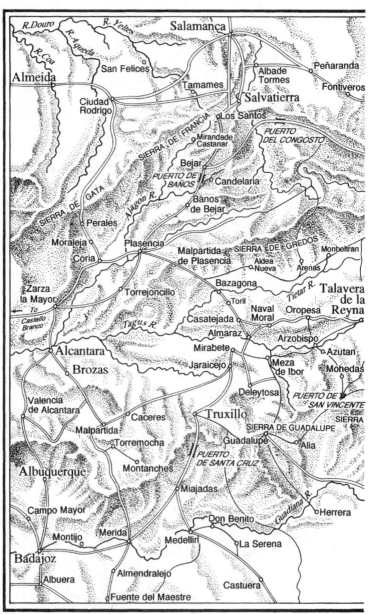

Darbishire & Stanford, Ltd.

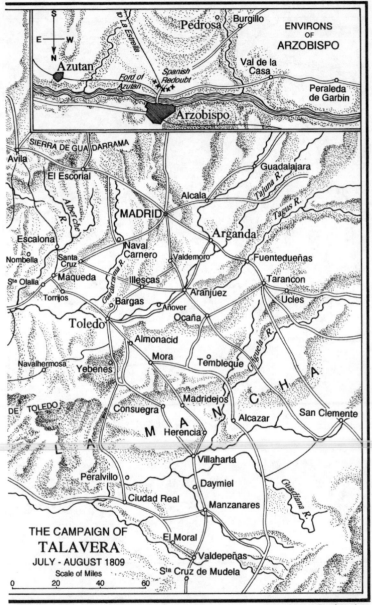

ENVIRONS OF ARZOBISPO

S E W N

Pedrosa

Burgillo

Azutan

Spanish Redoubt

Ford of Azutan

Val de la Casa

Peraleda de Garbin

Arzobispo

SIERRA DE GUADARRAMA

Avila

El Escorial

Guadalajara

Alcala

MADRID

Arganda

Escalona

Naval Carnero

Valdemoro

Fuentedueñas

Nombella

Santa Cruz

Maqueda

Illescas

Aranjuez

Tarancon

Sta Olalla

Torrijos

Bargas

Añover

Ocaña

Ucles

Toledo

Almonacid

Mora

Tembleque

Navalhermosa

Yebenes

L A M A N C H A

Consuegra

Madridejos

Alcazar

San Clemente

DE TOLEDO

Herencia

Villaharta

Peralvillo

Daymiel

Ciudad Real

Manzanares

THE CAMPAIGN OF
TALAVERA
JULY – AUGUST 1809
Scale of Miles

0   20   40   60

El Moral

Valdepeñas

Sta Cruz de Mudela

The Oxford Geog¹ Institute.

ANDALUSIA

B.V.Darbishire, Oxford, 1907

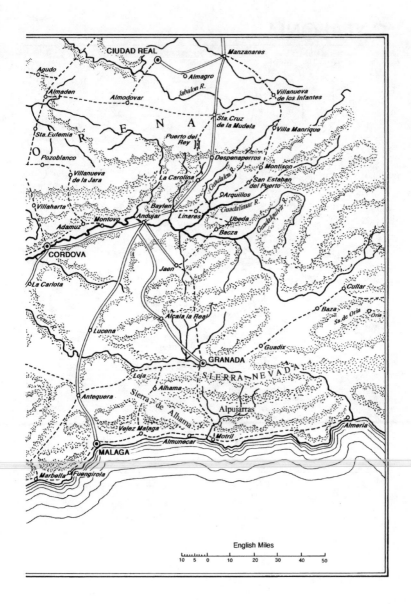

English Miles

10 5 0   10   20   30   40   50

CATALONIA

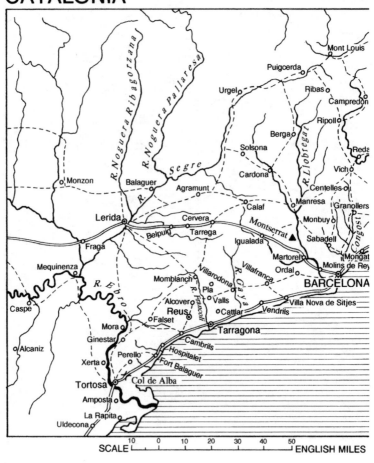

Mont Louis

Puigcerda

Urgel ○   Ribas ○

Camprédon ○

Ripoll ○

Berga ○   Reda

R. Noguera Ribagorzana

R. Noguera Pallaresa

Segre

Solsona ○   Vich ○

Cardona ○   Centelles ○

Monzon ○

Balaguer ○   Agramunt ○   Manresa ○   Granollers ○

R.   Calaf ○   Congost

Lerida ○   Cervera ○   Monbuy ○   Mongat

Belpuig ○   Tarrega ○   Montserrat ▲   Sabadell

Fraga ○   Igualada ○   Martorel ○   Molins de Rey

Mequinenza ○   Villarodona   Villafranca   Ordal ○   BARCELONA

R. Ebro   Momblanch ○   Pla   R. Gaya

Caspe ○   Alcover ○   Valls ○   Vendrils   Villa Nova de Sitjes

Reus ○   R. Francoli   Cattlar ○

Falset ○

Mora ○   Tarragona ○

Alcaniz ○   Ginestar ○   Cambrils

Xerta ○   Perello ○   Hospitalet

Fort Balaguer

Tortosa ○   Col de Alba

Amposta ○

La Rapita ○

Uldecona ○

SCALE |—10—0—10—20—30—40—50—| ENGLISH MILES

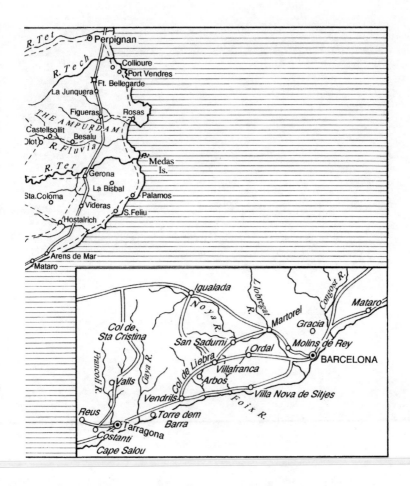

Appendix 1

Family Trees

The Bonaparte Family

Carlo Bonaparte (1746–85) = Marie-Letitzia (*Madame Mère*) 1750–1836

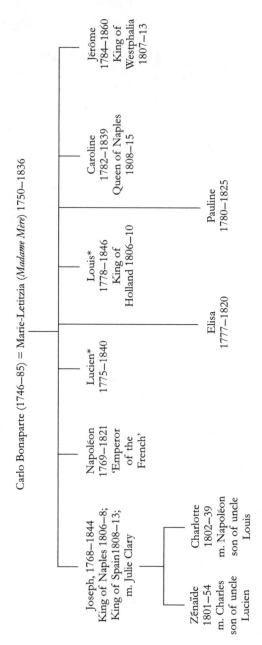

Joseph, 1768–1844
King of Naples 1806–8;
King of Spain 1808–13;
m. Julie Clary

Napoléon
1769–1821
'Emperor
of the
French'

Lucien*
1775–1840

Elisa
1777–1820

Louis*
1778–1846
King of
Holland 1806–10

Pauline
1780–1825

Caroline
1782–1839
Queen of Naples
1808–15

Jérôme
1784–1860
King of
Westphalia
1807–13

Zénaïde
1801–54
m. Charles
son of uncle
Lucien

Charlotte
1802–39
m. Napoléon
son of uncle
Louis

* Both refused Spanish throne, in January and March 1808 respectively.

The Portuguese Royal Family

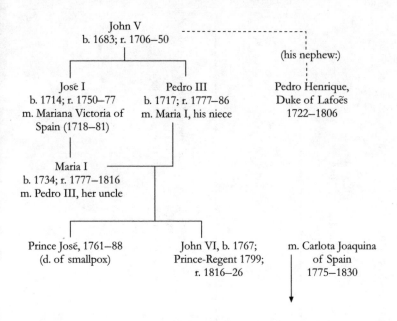

John V
b. 1683; r. 1706–50

(his nephew:)

José I
b. 1714; r. 1750–77
m. Mariana Victoria of
Spain (1718–81)

Pedro III
b. 1717; r. 1777–86
m. Maria I, his niece

Pedro Henrique,
Duke of Lafoẽs
1722–1806

Maria I
b. 1734; r. 1777–1816
m. Pedro III, her uncle

Prince José, 1761–88
(d. of smallpox)

John VI, b. 1767;
Prince-Regent 1799;
r. 1816–26

m. Carlota Joaquina
of Spain
1775–1830

The Spanish Royal Family

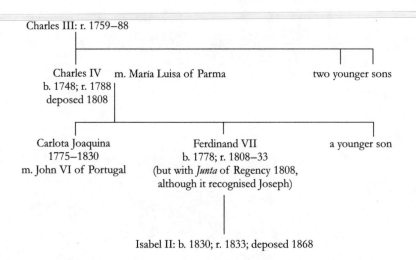

Charles III: r. 1759–88

Charles IV   m. María Luisa of Parma
b. 1748; r. 1788
deposed 1808

two younger sons

Carlota Joaquina
1775–1830
m. John VI of Portugal

Ferdinand VII
b. 1778; r. 1808–33
(but with *Junta* of Regency 1808,
although it recognised Joseph)

a younger son

Isabel II: b. 1830; r. 1833; deposed 1868

The Wellesley Family

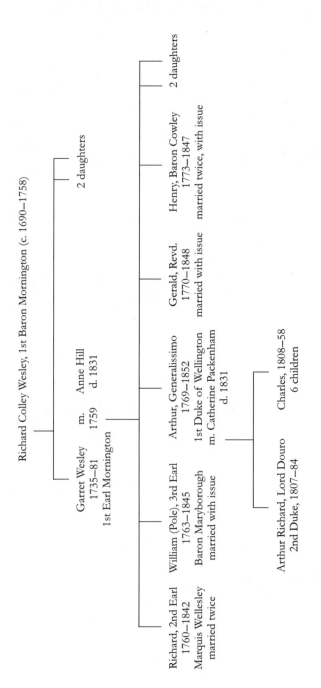

Richard Colley Wesley, 1st Baron Mornington (c. 1690–1758)

Garret Wesley
1735–81
1st Earl Mornington

m.
1759

Anne Hill
d. 1831

2 daughters

Richard, 2nd Earl
1760–1842
Marquis Wellesley
married twice

William (Pole), 3rd Earl
1763–1845
Baron Maryborough
married with issue

Arthur, Generalissimo
1769–1852
1st Duke of Wellington
m. Catherine Packenham
d. 1831

Gerald, Revd.
1770–1848
married with issue

Henry, Baron Cowley
1773–1847
married twice, with issue

2 daughters

Arthur Richard, Lord Douro
2nd Duke, 1807–84

Charles, 1808–58
6 children

Appendix 2

The Battlefields Today

by Paddy Griffith

One of Oman's many services to military history lay in emphasising the value of visiting the battlefields that were being discussed. He personally made an effort to look at many of those in the Peninsula, although his coverage remained extremely patchy both in time – since he did not start his visits until after his first volume had appeared (having already described over fifteen major battles or sieges) – and in space (for example, he never got as far as Castalla, south of Valencia).[1] He acknowledged that some of his contemporaries, such as Fortescue and Beatson,[2] were at least his match in the art of battlefield visiting, and it is true both that their maps (especially Fortescue's) were superior to his, and that Beatson took photography far more seriously than Oman ever did. Oman the numismatist could master all comers when it came to the coinage of the war, with which he liked to emboss the board covers of his books – but he must ultimately be considered as something of a dilettante in battlefield topography.

It is unfortunate that no one in Oman's generation approached the battlefields of the wider war, and especially the Spanish part of it, as thoroughly and systematically as Beatson did for the Pyrenean battles of 1813–14, or as G.M. Trevelyan did for the wars of Garibaldi in Italy.[3] As a result we lack good photographs of many of the Peninsular battlefields as they appeared in the period before 1914, after which the onset of the motor car – and of concrete as a building material – began an ever-accelerating process of deterioration and change. Particularly during the past twenty (not coincidentally post-Franco) years, the advance of progress and prosperity has started to pose a really serious threat to many of the sites, with motorways and city suburbs – not to mention the hypermarket at Coruña (appropriately it is French) – causing massive devastation. The best we have from the era immediately preceding this new wave of building are the photographs in Jac Weller's *Wellington in the Peninsula*,[4] although they nevertheless still constitute a very incomplete record, especially since the author systematically excluded almost every event in which Wellington was not personally involved.

During the past few years there has admittedly been a noticeable upsurge of interest in at least the strictly British battlefields, with the publication of Julian Paget's *Wellington's Peninsular War*; Donald Featherstone's *Campaigning with the Duke of Wellington and Featherstone*; and, especially, Ian Fletcher and Andy Cook in *Fields of Fire: Battlefields of the Peninsular War*.[5] All three of these books include a little advice about visiting the ground today, and the last features some truly sensational photographs of sites which have not yet been desecrated by modernity. Nevertheless, these books all still fall far short of an encyclopaedic guide to the ground, and do not really tell us where the new roads and building developments are cutting into the battlefields. Thus, for example, we are not warned that a reservoir covers the northern part of Talavera, a motorway slices through the centre, the farm buildings on the Paja have doubled in size, and a large private villa now stands on the summit of the Cerro de Medellin, presumably at the spot where Oman was able to sit on a rock making notes. Insult is added to injury on this battlefield by the erection of a gigantic concrete eyesore of a monument, which unconvincingly attempts to demonstrate that the builders of the motorway really cared deeply about the battle and the bones that they were disturbing.[6] Of course the mass graves, or the sites of mass cremations, were not marked on Napoleonic battlefields in the way they have been for wars between about 1870 and 1965,[7] so there was nothing to warn the contractors of what they might be digging into.

Colonel Sañudo and his associates writing for *Researching & Dragona* magazine have recently achieved some remarkable reassessments of many of the battles fought between the Spanish and French; not only in terms of the forces engaged and what they did, but also in terms of analysing and photographing the terrain. For example, at Gamonal they actually succeeded in finding some unspoilt parts of the original battlefield, where the present author could find only an overwhelming succession of high-rise apartment blocks.[8] They have also been in a position to analyse some of the bullet finds, which can provide accurate locations for specific firefights. Their work is admirable but – just as in the case of the writers about the Franco-British battlefields – it still does not amount to a single accessible and systematic guidebook to the state of all the battlefields throughout the Peninsula. Such a book has yet to be written, and it would necessarily have to tackle the whole list of events that Oman mentioned, rather than merely a selection of those that the author happened to find particularly interesting or convenient.

A compact attempt to list the monuments is offered in the 1981 *Guide Napoléonien*, although it is considerably more complete for those inside France than it is for Spain and Portugal.[9] In general the Spanish have erected relatively few monuments to this war, although they yield to none in the extravagance of some of their productions.[10] Nor do they normally seem to make a great mention of their allies – for example, the site of Wellington's breach at Ciudad Rodrigo in 1812 was for many years marked only by a plaque commemorating the Spanish defenders of the same spot in 1810. The Portuguese, by contrast, are more enthusiastic for the alliance, and tend to have a greater interest in monuments, although admittedly a smaller number of battlefields upon which to place them. Their military engineers have also done considerable recent work in reconditioning some of the redoubts in the lines of Torres Vedras, such as Fort Alquedao just south of Sobral. As for the British themselves, their nineteenth-century monuments are mainly funerary, for particular individuals such as Lake at Roliça[11] or Moore at Coruña. However, they do appear to have taken a renewed interest in erecting plaques and monuments during the past twenty years or so, doubtless as a result of the growth not only in tourism, but also in expatriates living within the Peninsula. Stephen Drake-Jones' Wellington Society, based in Madrid, has done some of this work, as have British-based organisations such as the Napoleonic Association.

Worthy though such initiatives may be, however, the present author cannot help feeling that the real need is for effective preservation of the fields themselves. A start has been made with this type of work, albeit mainly inside Britain, by the Battlefields Trust; but there is unfortunately only too little that it can do to extend its operations into the Peninsula. We therefore await the appearance of an equivalent organisation run by native Iberians, since only then can there be any realistic hope of channelling the onward flow of asphalt and cement away from battlefields and into other fields that can boast less direct historical resonances.

Having said all that, it is gratifying to report that all is far from lost, and there are still many battlefields which have not suffered the fate of Talavera and Coruña. For every motorway toll area – such as the one planted in the back garden of the mayor's house at Barouillhet, or the sprawling international frontier post at Hendaye-Irun – there are probably two or three completely unspoilt battlefields nestling in the remoter mountain fastnesses – for example Sabugal, Arroyo dos Molinas, or Maya. For every set of beach houses at Barrossa, hotels at Bussaco, or bourgeois villas (complete with airport) at Toulouse, there is a clear open field at Albuera, Fuentes de Oñoro, and Orthez. A good number of the original fieldworks – a rare and precious thing indeed – may even still be found on and below the Lesser Rhune. Then again, we can also remind ourselves that, although there have been great incursions of building over some parts of the wide field of Vitoria, in other parts – like the curate's proverbial egg – it remains excellent.

A good proportion of the damage to battlefields has been done by the construction of new roads. At the pass of Somosierra, for example, there have been no less than three successive generations of road-building, dating from the 1920s, the 1960s, and the 1990s, each taking out a different slice of the battlefield. The original road used in 1808 may just be detected in places, but it is now no more than a farm path between fields. Indeed, most of the Peninsular roads in Wellington's day were never any better than this standard, as may often still be seen where new roads have followed different routes from their predecessors. Often this has happened either where a town has been bypassed, or where low lying land that was too boggy for traffic in earlier times has been drained during the nineteenth or twentieth centuries. Thus at Medina del Rio Seco the main road leading directly over the hill from that town to Palacios has remained exactly as it was in 1808, while only the more circuitous routes which avoid the high ground have now been metalled. At Linzoain, south-west of Roncesvalles, there is a fascinating stretch of the original road which was hewn from the bare rock, while the more modern motor road goes around the hill on flatter ground. Again, at Roncesvalles itself the old road stuck to the ridge-top of the Altobiscar, which is why the fiercest fighting in 1813 took place at that spot. Yet already in Oman's day the main road had been re-sited to the lowest available ground, passing though the bottom of Val Carlos.[12] Paradoxically, therefore, a battlefield which was eminently accessible to the traveller in 1813 has now become somewhat inaccessible, since the motor car cannot approach it.

Among the fortresses, disappointingly little is left of the most important sites at Badajoz, Saragossa, or Tarragona. Indeed, the sullen mood of Badajoz does not appear to have lifted greatly since the notorious sack of 1812.[13] However, Rodrigo, Fuenterrabia, Tarifa, Elvas, Figueres, Hostalrich, and not a few others are all still in perfectly pristine condition, while almost the only major damage to Almeida was done already in 1810. Apart from these, most of the remaining fortresses, from San Sebastian and Pamplona to Barcelona and Rosas, and from Cádiz and Gibraltar to Tortosa and Saguntum, can still show well over half of their original walls. They all very much repay a visit. Even Burgos, which seems disappointingly slight to the casual visitor, actually still has its enormous hornwork intact, to the north of the citadel.[14]

The main problem with many of these fortress sites is that the towns, which the walls were originally designed to enclose, define, and protect (and tax) have now burst out into the wild, lawless and unsafe glacis areas beyond the walls. Modern buildings have often filled the key ground of tactical importance which lay between an attacker's 'first parallel' and the particular section of wall which he wanted to breach. The case of Ciudad Rodrigo is instructive, since this process had begun even in Wellington's own day, when he had to clear the French from a small suburb and a fortified convent before he was free to shoot at the main wall from his parallels on the greater and lesser Tesons. Yet when the present author visited the site in 1962 he found the original suburb had more than doubled in size, and had spread out to obstruct some of the land over which Wellington attacked. By 1992 the suburbs seemed to have quadrupled, to the extent that we can no longer get a clear view along the lines of sight that were so important to the British engineers and gunners of 1812, and can now reconstruct them only by making a tiresome comparison between Napoleonic maps of the building pattern, and modern maps of the contours.

The many Moorish keeps and other medieval castles in Spain are, of course, justly celebrated for their large number, no less than for their haunting beauty. Many of them played important military roles during the Napoleonic period, alongside a number of seminaries and convents which had originally been built with thick walls to deter ungodly visitors. Few of these buildings had become entirely useless as potential fortifications, and in one way or another they left their mark upon the war. They have usually been well preserved down to the present day, although more for their associations with the distant past than with Napoleonic times. Many of the Moorish keeps have been converted into national hotels, and they usually command extensive views of the surrounding area. Equally, some of the key bridges for the manoeuvres of 1808-14 date as far back as the Roman era, as at Almaraz, while many others are from the middle ages or the Renaissance. They, too, have normally been preserved, even when modern concrete bridges have been erected alongside them. Several of them were the focus of fighting, such as the little stone packhorse bridge at Fuentes de Oñoro (1811) or the fortified medieval bridge at Orthez (1814). Two ancient bridges – one at Barba del Puerco on the Agueda and the other over the Coa behind Almeida – were disputed by Craufurd in 1810 and 1811 respectively.

One very curious case of preservation linked with destruction is the ancient walled town of Belchite, where Marshal Suchet finally administered the *coup de grace* to Blake's attempt to relieve Saragossa on 18 June 1809.[15] This battlefield remained entirely untouched until 1937, when it became the scene of more fierce fighting, this time with the benefit of high explosives. The town was wrecked but, contrary to the normal French and Belgian practice in 1919 and 1945, it was neither patched up nor levelled flat. Instead, it was simply left as it was, as a monument to the heroic fascist garrison, and the population was rehoused in a completely new settlement some 200 yards further down the road. As a result we now enjoy a unique view of the old town as it was in 1937, unspoilt by the many insidious changes seen elsewhere since then – but at the same time it is unfortunate that a big slice of the original Napoleonic battlefield, further to the west, has now been completely covered by the new town!

All in all, it is a sad fact that many of the Peninsular battlefields are gradually being put to new uses which disfigure the terrain. Sometimes the change can be cataclysmic, such as the gigantic cement factory at Molins de Rey – which is presumably manufacturing concrete that can be laid over other battlefields elsewhere. In other places the changes are gradual and relatively small in scale, such as an increase in the farm buildings in the village of Arapiles near Salamanca, and a little quarrying around the top of the French hill of the same name nearby. In many cases the changes have not even begun – yet. Nevertheless, the encroachment of modernity is bound to increase and even accelerate, so the reader is advised to visit these battlefields at an early date, or risk missing a phenomenon that cannot last forever.

Notes

1. Oman, *History*, vol.VI, p.viii. It is doubtless because he did not inspect the ground that it is today difficult to match some parts of his narrative with specific slopes and crests.

2. F.C. Beatson, *With Wellington in the Pyrenees* (London, 1914); *Wellington, the Crossing of the Gaves and the Battle of Orthez* (London, 1925); and *Wellington: The Bidassoa and Nivelle* (London, 1931). Oman acknowledged his debt to the first of these in *History*, vol.VI, pp.viii, xi, since he never personally visited the ground between Roncesvalles and Sorauren. Some of Fortescue's notebooks of his Peninsular travels may be found in the Devon Record Office, 1262M/FD54.

3. G.M. Trevelyan's trilogy – *Garibaldi's Defence of the Roman Republic, 1848-9* (London, 1907); *Garibaldi and the Thousand* (London, 1909), and *Garibaldi and the Making of Italy* (London, 1911) – contained many photographs of the sites.

4. Published London, 1962. The photographs and text actually owed a great deal to Ian Robertson, although this is not acknowledged in the final book.

5. See Bibliography for further details, to which should be added Ian Robertson's forthcoming series of British Peninsular battlefield guides for Pen & Sword's 'Battleground Europe' series. As far as the modern state of Wellington's battlefields is concerned, the present author would dare to suggest that a slightly fuller account is contained in his own 'Notes on the British Peninsular War Battlefields, as at Mid February 1992', published in the *Newsletter* of the Battlefields Trust (issue 2, January 1993), pp.8-13. He would nevertheless hasten to agree that this, too, is extremely incomplete ... and now as dated as it is inaccessible.

6. Colonel Juan José Sañudo was asked to supply a list of units taking part in the battle, to be inscribed on this monument, but he was told that the 23rd Light Dragoons should be left out since they received no battle honour for it! (They have subsequently been added as an afterthought.)

7. The habit since 1965, at least for wealthy nations, has been to repatriate

the bodies of the slain individually, thereby making large scale war graves obsolete. In Napoleonic times this treatment was extended only to a favoured few of the officers.

8. Juan José Sañudo, Miguel Angel Camino, Leopoldo Stampa, and Francisco M. Vela Santiago, 'Gamonal, 10 de Noviembre de 1808' *Researching & Dragona* II, no.4, August 1997, pp.59–111.

9. A. Chappet, R. Martin, A. Pigeard, and A. Robe, *Guide Napoléonien* (Paris, 1981), pp.263–75.

10. The concept of flamboyant gigantism in monuments was by no means initiated at Talavera, as visitors to the Plaza Virgen Blanca in Vitoria will instantly appreciate.

11. See Clive Willis, 'Colonel George Lake and the Battle of Roliça' *Portuguese Studies* 12 (1996), pp.68–77, especially p.76.

12. Oman, *History*, vol.VI, p.609.

13. My former colleague, Dr Christopher Duffy, reports that there were still riots in Badajoz as late as the 1970s, although honour appeared to have been satisfied, in the one that he witnessed, after a single smoke grenade had been thrown. By comparison Oman's report of cavalry charges – albeit without weapons – in the Madrid of 1903, was rather more serious.

14. Oman, *History*, vol.VI, p.viii, 'marvelled at the smallness of the citadel' – so we wonder if he ever progressed to see the hornwork! An excellent companion for visits to Burgos and other fortresses is F. Myatt, *British Sieges of the Peninsular War* (Tunbridge Wells, 1987).

15. Oman, *History*, vol.II, pp.428–31. Alas he offers us no map of Belchite, which makes it difficult to match his narrative to the terrain today.

Appendix 3

Portugal on the Eve of the Peninsular War

by Professor Harold Livermore

The Iberian Wars of 1793 and 1801

Oman's lack of perspective, to use no stronger term, calls for some account of the essential antecedents to the events of 1808, which he does not provide. For Portugal and Spain, the struggle with revolution and aggression was not a 'Peninsular War'. It began, not in 1808, nor with the aggrandisement of Napoleon in 1804, but fourteen years before, in 1793. For both countries the execution of the king of France threatened their own reigning families. For Britain it did not, and regicide attracted little support, belonging to the distant past. If the Hanoverians were not popular, they were at least sound Europeans. But all three countries underestimated the extent to which French royalism had been sapped by decapitation and emigration, and the hold established by the National Convention with its overtones of American supernationalism. Spain had led the opposition. In 1793 France declared war on her and sent a delegate to Lisbon to seek Portuguese neutrality. Britain negotiated an alliance with Spain, and in June Grenville sought a treaty with Portugal. In July Portugal made an offensive and defensive alliance with Spain.

The Portuguese heir Prince John was betrothed to the elder sister of Prince Fernando of Spain, Carlota Joaquina, who, though brought up at the Portuguese court, remained Spanish to the core. She presented John with two sons, of whom the elder, Pedro, was born in 1798, and six daughters, the last born in 1805. Although she was hardly the harridan of liberal caricaturists she was more loyal to Spain than to Portugal, was accessible to the Spanish ambassador, and liked to meddle.[1] Prince John was the reverse of bellicose. The senior member of the Portuguese royal family was the Duke of Lafões, born in 1722, and long resident in Vienna. The founder of the Portuguese Academy of Sciences, he was considered a man of vast culture. He was appointed Marshal-General in 1791 and clung obstinately to his position for a decade, during which Portugal was twice drawn into war with deplorable results. The Anglo-Portuguese alliance covered her security by sea, and as long as Spain remained neutral she could not be attacked by land. She had last been under attack in the closing stages of the Seven Years War, under Pombal, who, faced with the decline of Brazilian gold and the devastation of the great earthquake of 1755, gave the army a low priority. He contracted with the Count of Schaumberg-Lippe, who built the defences at Elvas and drew up reforms in 1764, his instructions being printed in 1789 and 1791. They were for a defensive war in which, as was traditional, each province saw to the raising and supply of its own regiments, fed by local contract, with no central supply system. Although Pombal's College of Nobles was intended to provide a general education for the nobility with modern ideas to revitalise the officer class, his fall deprived it of the favour it had enjoyed under his auspices.

It was recognised that a foreign commander of eminence was required, but Lafões, educated even before the rise of Pombal, resisted further changes that would have eroded his own authority. Some British officers, chief of them Ian Forbes of Skellater, had settled in Portugal. For the first war against the French Republic – the campaign of the Roussillon – he was placed in command of a Portuguese Division sent to supplement the Spanish army on the Catalan front. If at first the combined forces advanced into France, they were totally unprepared for a lengthy war, and particularly for the Pyrenean winter. The Republic, by contrast, expected much of its sons and won their enthusiasm. Godoy could not compete. His army crumbled, and in order to prevent an invasion of Spain concluded the Treaty of Basle, abandoning his allies. Charles IV and María Luisa honoured Godoy, having left themselves with no alternative. Spain became the pawn of the French Republic, and the Portuguese were left to make their way home, while Godoy undertook to mediate between France and Portugal, thus becoming the instrument for demanding a large indemnity and other concessions. The war, though on a limited scale, had plunged the Portuguese finances into confusion. Forbes, out of his depth, had resigned his command, though he remained in Portuguese service and died as governor of Rio de Janeiro. Godoy had changed sides, covering the operation by a cloud of self-justification. The frontier was no longer at the Pyrenees but, potentially at least, on the Portuguese border. Many of the French royalist refugees who had sought shelter in Spain found their way to Portugal. Their sufferings entitled them to every consideration, but their military value was much over-estimated. In 1802, with the short-lived Peace of Amiens, there were many who regarded the war as over and the cause of the Bourbons as doomed. Some former monarchists, among them Talleyrand, placed themselves at the disposal of the rising star, Napoleon. Another was Herman, married to an Englishwoman and now made French consul in Lisbon. It is not surprising that the activities of these turn-coats confused the situation, if only by creating suspicion. In Portugal this confusion did not have much popular effect, but it none the less existed.[2]

After the lamentable end to the war in the Roussillon, a British force was placed in Portugal to strengthen the defence of Lisbon. Its commander was Charles Stuart, who at the end of 1796 had 6828 men, of whom 2504 were British, including the 12th Light Dragoons and the 50th and 51st Foot, returning from the evacuation of Corsica. The remaining 4324 members of the 'British' force included the French *émigré* regiments of Mortemart, Castries, and Chartres, as well as Dillon's Irish, formerly serving France, the Royal *Étrangers*, Rolle's Swiss, and some Corsicans. Stuart found his task full of tribulation. The *émigrés*, though paid by the British government, considered themselves independent of Stuart's orders. Their leader, the Duc de Coigny, had access to the Duke of Portland. Stuart found the Marquis de la Rosière 'impracticable and designing'. Lafões, at seventy-five and infirm, was vigorous 'with a degree of petulance and fire which might make him pose for a much younger man'. He declared that Portugal 'should be neuter', [3] and tried to treat Stuart as a private person. He posed as something of a radical. The Minister for War, Luis Pinto, looked for support to the *émigrés* who flooded Portugal after their expulsion from Spain, confiding in their royalist credentials. Another foreigner, the Prince of Waldeck, arrived in Lisbon to command in May 1797, but Lafões refused to consider changes that would lessen his authority. There were thus four commanders – Lafões, Stuart, Rosière, and Waldeck – but no plan of action. Stuart asked to be relieved, but his request was not granted until 1798, when he was sent to take Minorca. Meanwhile Waldeck made little impact and he died at Sintra in September 1798.

During the diplomatic bargaining in 1796 Lord Malmesbury had made it clear that Portugal must be included in any peace. Luis Pinto played for time, claiming that Portugal had gone to the Roussillon only to aid Spain; but Godoy informed him that France rejected any claim to neutrality. In 1797 Pinto sent his minister at the Hague, António de Araujo, to Paris, with instructions to keep in step with Malmsebury, but to seek a separate negotiation if Malmesbury failed. The French demands were now for an indemnity, admission of their manufactures, and a limit to the use of Portuguese ports by British warships, with a concession of territory in northern Brazil. By insinuating that the Franco-British talks were about to fail, Talleyrand persuaded Araujo to accept. Pinto rebuked him but agreed to the terms, apart from the limitation on British ships. Araujo then signed the treaty on 10 August 1797, accepting neutrality, the indemnity, and the admission of goods, to be ratified in three months. When Napoleon forced the Austrians to make the Peace of Campo Formio, the

Anglo-French negotiations broke down and Pinto asked the British either to accept Araujo's treaty or to promise aid. Failing to obtain that promise, he turned to Spain for support in modifying the articles. The French then accused Araujo of treason and held him in the Temple from December 1797 to March 1798.

The failure of Napoleon's Egyptian campaign (which drew Beresford from India and brought him some fame for the 'Desert March') changed the situation. Pinto declared that Portugal would defend herself if attacked, while Britain sought to detach Spain from France. But despite Pinto's statement little was done to prepare the army. Since 1795 Dom Rodrigo de Sousa Coutinho, as Minister for Marine and Overseas, had rebuilt the Portuguese navy and stimulated the development of Brazil. He was the mainstay of the English alliance. In July 1799 Prince John finally declared himself regent for his mother, and Dom João de Almeida was recalled from London to take over Foreign Affairs and War. He, too, was a strong supporter of the English connection. Another foreign commander was engaged, Count von der Goltz, born at Altona near Hamburg in 1739, and son of a companion of Frederick the Great. He contracted to serve in Portugal for six years (until 1 July 1806) or until peace was made, with the rank of Marshal but subordinate to Marshal-General Lafões. He reached Lisbon in September 1800 and reported in a month that the regiments should be completed, deposits set up, transport of supplies organised, mobile artillery introduced, roads repaired, and 100 pontoons acquired. He also asked to have his own position clarified. Goltz was ready to command, but Lafões remained undecided whether in the event of war he would keep his position or not. Goltz saw the Prince-Regent, and told him that two men at the head of an army were continually in one another's way: one must command and one obey.[4]

In 1801 the struggle was at length brought to Portugal. Napoleon had made an alliance with Tsar Paul, and pressed Godoy to embark on a joint invasion of Portugal, signing a preliminary treaty for the purpose. February saw the resignation of Pitt, and the formation of the Addington-Fox administration. The Portuguese applied for a force of 25,000 men and a subsidy of £1,000,000, but Fox advised negotiations. The Portuguese then sent a negotiator to Paris, but he did not get beyond Madrid. The Spanish ambassador in Lisbon presented an ultimatum, the main object of which was to close Portuguese ports to British ships. The French plan was to induce Spain to invade Portugal in order to place French garrisons in and around Lisbon. On 27 February, Charles IV obediently published a threatening manifesto.

The Spanish King was far from anxious to admit Revolutionary troops onto his soil, so Godoy contrived that the campaign against Portugal should be launched and concluded before the French could appear. On 11 March Goltz informed Pinto – now in charge of

Home Affairs – that the Prince-Regent was disposed to give him the command, but Lafões was not. He played no part in the brief but inglorious 'War of the Oranges', so called when Godoy plucked a branch of Portuguese oranges to send to María Luisa as proof of his triumph. War was declared on 24 May. Lord Hawkesbury had advised the Prince-Regent to negotiate, but now Lafões emerged from his masterly inactivity, and appointed commanders to the frontier: the Marquis of Alorna and Gomes Freire de Andrade. Two weeks after the campaign began, it was ended by the Peace of Badajoz, concluded on 6 June 1801 between Luis Pinto and Godoy. The Spanish forces had taken Juromenha and Olivença; had had the better of the day at Arronches and Flor de Rosa; had received the surrender of Campo Maior; and occupied the city of Portalegre and town of Castelo de Vide. Lafões had lingered at Lisbon, still imagining that, as France tugged at Spain and Britain tugged at Portugal, the two Peninsular states would be able to stay 'neuter'. Finally, on 31 July 1801, the Prince-Regent signed an order for the temporary replacement of Lafões and confirming Goltz as Marshal. From Abrantes the Duke sailed down the Tagus to his Lisbon palace; he was not received at court, and Goltz proceeded with the reform of the army.

The new Marshal was, however, still unable to enforce the drastic reforms that were needed. On 1 December the war minister Almeida set up a committee of himself, Goltz, the French *émigré* Viomesnil, three lieutenant-generals (Forbes, Rosière, and another *émigré*, Dordoz), with Colonel Miguel Pereira Forjaz as secretary. Lafões' protégés, Alorna and Gomes Freire, were invited to submit plans, but not to attend. Alorna composed his *Reflections on the Economic System of the Army*, and Gomes Freire a plan for an enlarged army on the Prussian system, published in 1806. The committee achieved little. Some members were anxious to revise the regulations, and Goltz thought Lippe's provisions good – if they were applied – but by May 1802 he was indignant at the preference given to Viomesnil, and offered to go on leave until needed. His contract was confirmed, but he did not come back, and in a letter of 1803 he noted that he had displeased Almeida and many others. He survived the wars, dying at his native Altona in 1818.

Napoleon rejected the Peace of Badajoz because it did not bring about the expected French garrisons in Lisbon. However, a month later the British and French were again negotiating, and on 1 October 1801 the preliminaries for the future Peace of Amiens were signed in London. The peace itself was concluded on 25 March 1802. In Britain the desire for a respite was such that though few praised the treaty, none opposed it, despite its obvious deficiencies. In Portugal there was a general hope that the peace would be permanent, and much reluctance to contemplate a third war in less than a decade. But if in Britain 'neutrality' meant the continuity of the Ancient Alliance with Portugal, albeit in a state of non-belligerency, in France it meant equality of privilege and access to Portugal, and a demand to share every advantage that Britain was supposed to enjoy. The representative sent to voice these claims was General Lannes, the 'hero of Montebello' – a young veteran who had no use for diplomatic courtesies. By insisting on the right of free entry of French goods, and diplomatic immunity for his personal imports, he was able to secure the removal of the doughty police chief Pina Manique, who combined control of the customs with the suppression of subversive societies and the blocking of revolutionary propaganda. This he achieved in March 1803, having already contrived to build up a faction through the Count of Ega, detailed to look after him.

The Portuguese dilemma from the Peace of Amiens to Junot's invasion

The British representative in Lisbon was Lord Robert Fitzgerald, but the most conspicuous British resident was Prince Augustus, seventh son of George III, who had arrived for a visit in January 1801 and remained a guest of Prince John for four years. An asthmatic, and thought unfit for a military career, he had been educated in Germany, where he was inducted into the Royal York Lodge, and wintered in Italy, where at nineteen he met Lady Augusta Murray, a catholic, and was married to her by a wandering clergyman without the formality of banns or witnesses and in defiance of the Royal Marriage Act. King George was informed and indignant, and the Court of Arches had no difficulty in finding the marriage fictitious. But the Prince persisted in regarding Lady Murray as his wife and mother of his children until he was induced to settle for the title of Duke of Sussex and £12,000 a year, on condition that he never saw her again. Augusta herself arrived in Lisbon and battered in vain at the gate of the duke's apartments at the Necessidades, while he was away visiting his brother, the governor of Gibraltar. In August 1802 her own brother arrived in Lisbon with a brace of pistols, determined to send either the duke or himself to the other world. He got into the Necessidades and departed, not for the other world, but with a deed signed by the duke making over a third of his pension to Augusta and her children. The young duke detested Mr Traill, his bearleader, and devoted himself to the study of religion. He was ardently patriotic, and when the war was resumed asked his father for a military command. His father ignored the request, and he repeated it to the benevolent Prince John, who (he thought) invited him to be a general. He wrote to his father for consent, but seems to have had no reply, the main result of the incident being a vast full-length portrait of himself in full military rig by Pellegrini.

He played a small part in upsetting the Ancient Alliance. An *émigré*, the Comte de Novion, had been appointed commander of the Police Guard, to the dismay of many. When, in July 1803, Freire's Regiment, commanded by Gomes Freire de Andrade, attempted to celebrate a popular festivity in the Campo de Ourique, which had been banned, the Police Guard arrived to quell the riot. Gomes Freire, who like Sussex had been brought up in Germany and was a freemason, arrested Novion and got the duke to drive him to the Prince-Regent, where he tried to force an entry to denounce Novion as a Jacobin. Prince John did not take kindly to this. Nor did his ministers. Gomes Freire was arrested and his regiment sent out of Lisbon. It is likely that he and Alorna had incited the troops against the Police Guard. The Duke of Sussex was sent home and became the head of the combined English freemasons. The incident occurred just as Lieutenant-Colonel James Stewart arrived with a mission to assess the state of the Portuguese army. Almeida had staked his place on British aid and offered every facility. The mission inspected regiments in the capital and in the provinces, as well as supplies and fortifications. The result was discouraging. Apart from the garrison of Lisbon the regiments were below strength, with too many old men and slight boys. There were almost no magazines, and too few horses. Even the diet of Portuguese horses was different from the insular fare of British mounts (although the 12th Dragoons seem to have survived). Stewart's observations pointed to the conclusion that Portugal could not be defended. Almeida was dismissed on 25 August and Dom Rodrigo, the mainstay of the British connection, fell in November.

The result of the mission was a deadlock. The British were reluctant to send troops or weapons, lest Portugal fail to defend herself, while the Portuguese government was well aware that no defence was possible without British aid. With the fall of Dom Rodrigo, the Portuguese government took a new shape. The only alternative to the alliance was negotiation. The Council of State, which had not gathered for eighteen months under Dom Rodrigo, now met frequently. It included Dom Rodrigo as well as nobles and statesmen with differing views. The ministers were less prominent figures. When Luis Pinto died in 1804, the Count of Vila Verde managed internal and foreign affairs. Araujo, who since his abortive negotiations had been relegated to St Petersburg for three years, returned to take the Department of War. He was no more anxious than most Portuguese to see his country overrun, but he had more confidence than most in the chance of negotiating an acceptable neutrality. Since May 1804 Napoleon had been emperor. In Britain, Pitt returned to power and Fox, disillusioned with compromise, joined him. In February Napoleon wrote to Prince John, renewing the demand for the closure of Portuguese ports to British shipping and adding a new condition, the expulsion of all 'English agents', the alternative being war. He had arranged with the Spanish representative in Paris that the two countries should deliver a joint ultimatum, and that 16,000 French troops should accompany 60,000 from Spain. He had recalled the aggressive Lannes, and sent General Andoche Junot, whose methods were supposedly more suave, but whose object was the same. There was as yet no sign of French troops on the frontier and it seemed unlikely that an invasion would be launched so long as the northern powers held out. In October 1805 Nelson effectively cooled Spanish ardour at Trafalgar, but ended his own career.

The Portuguese ports remained open. There was some reason on the French side why this should remain so. French factories depended on Brazilian cotton, all other sources being closed to them. Between 1796 and 1806 cotton imports through Lisbon rose steadily. Usually more than half went to Britain. Before Amiens none went to France, but in 1802 a third went there, and in 1804 and 1806 the French share outgrew the British. Lisbon was also the entrepôt for other colonial goods. Thus the invasion of Portugal would have serious repercussions for France unless swiftly followed by peace with Britain. But if Brazilian goods prevailed at Lisbon, the great trade at Oporto was wine. Most wine consumed in Britain came from Portugal, whilst France consumed none. The total value of Anglo-Portuguese trade was double that with France. If Lisbon might survive on French trade, Oporto could not.

As the threat of war loomed, the strain began to tell on the Prince-Regent. The Spanish ambassador claimed access to Carlota Joaquina as a 'family ambassador'. The birth of the Infanta Ana de Jesus completed the royal family. Carlota Joaquina became more loyal to her younger brother, Fernando, than to her spouse. Vila Verde took Prince John to Mafra and Vila Viçosa, where he was safe from nagging diplomats and his wife. Junot arrived on Good Friday, 12 April 1805, bringing decorations for the Prince, the two dukes, Lafões and Cadaval (his son-in-law), Vila Verde, and Araujo. Napoleon had not troubled to ascertain John's pleasure. Junot reiterated the protest at the presence of the British fleet in the Tagus. Fitzgerald had already put three questions to Araujo: What was Portugal's attitude towards the present war? What forces had she? What generals would she employ? Araujo's answers were that she would observe the actions of France and Spain, and expected that the northern alliance would prevent her from being invaded. It would take time to restore her finances, and the Prince-Regent hoped for neutrality. He wished to reduce the army in size and improve it in discipline: there were 30,000 men and forty-three regiments of militia. In the event of war, it was expected that the command would go to Viomesnil or Goltz (although he had not been seen in Portugal since his withdrawal). With this Fitzgerald departed, leaving his mission in the care of the young Lord Strangford.

Araujo persuaded the Prince-Regent to pay a sum put at 800,000 *cruzados* and sent a messenger to Hope and Co in Amsterdam. The Pope granted the government part of the ecclesiastical revenues in order to redeem the paper money. Strangford saw that the French had designs on Brazil: Alorna was named viceroy there, but he was relieved as he was about to leave and sent to the Alentejo. Payments to France were discontinued, and Talleyrand demanded their resumption. There was already a shortage of coin, and accounts were settled in paper or bonds. In October Nelson's victory at Trafalgar alleviated the pressure and Junot went on leave. At the same time Popham and Baird went to occupy the Cape, avoiding Lisbon but calling at Madeira. Rumours of British designs on Spanish America began to run, arousing fears lest Spain should retaliate at the expense of Portugal. For this reason, the expedition of Popham and Beresford to the River Plate was kept 'unofficial'; but in the middle of 1806, while Beresford was conquering Buenos Aires, Talleyrand in Paris told Lord Yarmouth of the concentration of a large French force at Bayonne. It seemed as if the long-threatened invasion was at hand.

The immediate reaction of the British ministers was to send yet another mission to Lisbon. It was headed by Lord St Vincent and the Earl of Rosslyn, who as Colonel Erskine had commanded the 12th Dragoons. Its secretary was the young Henry Brougham. A token expeditionary force was in St Vincent's fleet to land at Lisbon. The mission reached the Tagus at the end of August, convinced that Napoleon had gathered 30,000 men at Bayonne. For the Portuguese the visit came as a surprise. The Prince-Regent received the famous admiral at Mafra and expressed his gratification at King George's solicitude. But when it came to discussions, Araujo was apprehensive lest the arrival should irritate the Emperor and compromise Portugal's neutrality. His information was that there was no concentration at Bayonne, and no encampment there but a small Italian brigade. He thought that the story had been fabricated by Talleyrand to bring Yarmouth to terms. He pointed out that the policy of neutrality had not been his invention: he had inherited it, but he saw no way to save Portugal except to adhere to it. On 2 September, Rosslyn reported to Fox. He was now convinced that reports of a large French force at Bayonne were false; otherwise merchants and travellers must have seen it. He also reported Araujo's argument that a landing of British troops would be construed as an infraction of neutrality, and recommended that orders be sent not to land the expeditionary force. The chief gain from this comedy was that Britain once again learned the value of the merchant community as a source of information.

St Vincent had instructions to find out if Portugal would take effectual steps to provide for her defence, and to intimate that

Britain would afford substantial assistance. Dom Rodrigo was perhaps the only Portuguese of high standing to have envisaged that Brazil would some day outgrow its parent and that it might become the seat of authority. St Vincent was to suggest that if the Portuguese government considered resistance impracticable, steps should be taken to retire to Brazil. If the court of Lisbon was undecided, he was to ensure that the enemy did not gain possession of the Portuguese navy. Brougham gives details, probably much embroidered, of schemes to get the Prince-Regent aboard in case he proved hesitant. But all this was premature. Rosslyn concluded that, given Araujo's attitude, there was little likelihood of vigorous measures being taken for defence, and little chance that a British contingent, even if reinforced, could repel an invasion. However, when Rosslyn left, Brougham remained until the end of the year to arrange an intelligence service, using Consul Warre and the merchants of Oporto, with their contacts across Spain.

If Araujo had counted on the northern alliance, he was disabused by October 1806, when Napoleon defeated the Prussians at Jena and freed his hands to apply his continental blockade, publishing on November 27 the Berlin Decrees forbidding all commerce with the British Isles. At Madrid, the Tsar was attempting to wean Spain from her subservience to France in the hope of restoring her neutrality and patching up a peace with England. In Portugal there were reports that Prince John was ill, and a group of interested parties proposed that he should appoint his wife regent. Vila Verde stuck close to his master, discovered the plot and banished Alorna and three other nobles from Lisbon. Vila Verde died on 19 November, Lafões having expired the previous day. The effect of the change was to throw greater responsibility on Araujo, who thereafter combined Foreign Affairs with Defence. The country was now divided into half a dozen districts, each to maintain two regiments of foot and one of horse. Recruiting was changed to reduce the power of the *capitães-mores*, local big-wigs who took care, it was said, to ensure that their friends were not deprived of labour. But these reforms alone were unlikely to ensure a vigorous resistance.

The defeat of the Russians and the Peace of Tilsit in July 1807 put an end to any hopes from the northern coalition. Napoleon was back in Paris on 27 July, and two days later summoned Lima, the Portuguese minister, to hear his demands. The news reached Lisbon on 10 August and was at once forwarded to London. The French chargé Rayneval informed Araujo that no people had more reason than the Portuguese to complain of the English, and they must therefore be invaded unless by 1 September they had declared war, recalled their ambassador from London, dismissed the British ambassador from Lisbon, detained British residents, confiscated their goods, closed their ports to British shipping, and placed their own ships at Napoleon's disposal. The Council of State met on 19

August. The Prince-Regent was in no state to resist, and Araujo opted for appeasement. He wrote to Talleyrand welcoming the continental peace, which he hoped would lead to peace at sea; if war continued, the consequences would be disastrous for both Portugal and Spain, whose overseas possessions must pass under British control, depriving France of raw materials. The Prince-Regent would bow to Napoleon's decision; but his honour and his conscience would not allow him to confiscate the goods of the British or arrest them. Araujo knew that the Emperor could take any amount of flattery and laid it on with a trowel: 'the greatest hero who has existed ... infinitely wiser than Turenne in war and politics, sovereign and arbiter of Europe: could he wish for the destruction of the Portuguese monarchy?' It was not a heroic letter.

The British ministers might not be able to stop an invasion of the Iberian Peninsula, but they could at least make sure that France should not reach South America. In 1801 Colonel Clinton had appeared off Madeira with three warships and five transports. The governor was taken by surprise, but acquiesced in the landing of some 3500 men. The Lisbon government had protested, on the ground that the danger had passed. Once the preliminaries of Amiens had been concluded, the evacuation had taken place in January 1802. In the present emergency, however, Madeira was too valuable a pledge to be risked. Castlereagh appointed Beresford, fresh from his Buenos Aires adventure (which had taught him that Spanish Americans would not reject Charles IV in order to submit to George III), to command an expeditionary force to take over the island. As it was unknown what Araujo would do, it had to be assumed that he might be unwilling or unable to reply. Beresford was given ample papers about Clinton's expedition, and was well informed about the governor and his circle. In Lisbon, the Council of State met again on 26 August 1807, approved Araujo's reply and discussed sending John's heir Pedro, now ten, to Brazil. Dom Rodrigo thought Pedro should leave only with his father. The rest thought he should go. Araujo favoured awaiting the result of his last letter. On 2 September the Council returned to the question, and Araujo presented a plan for a council to administer Brazil; but it was agreed that no steps should be taken. On 20 September the French chargé accused Araujo of planning to take the government to Brazil: he replied that there was no desire for this. He hoped that Spain would oppose the passage of French troops and that the Emperor would accept something less than conquest.

These were forlorn hopes. This time there really was a French army at Bayonne. It only awaited Junot and Napoleon's orders. The final act began on 23 September, when the French and Spanish envoys repeated the ultimatum. Two ships of the line and a brig were made ready to sail. Instructions were sent to the minister in London, Dom Rodrigo's brother Dom Domingos António de Sousa

Coutinho, to negotiate a guarantee of the Portuguese possessions. This was not discussed by the Council, meeting at Mafra on 30 September; but it was agreed to close the ports. The Marquis of Belas, as *regedor*, or lord chancellor, ruled that Portugal could not act directly against her ally. Araujo opposed publication of the ruling because the ally, in the person of the young Strangford, was pressing for a decision about Brazil. Publication might cause him to withdraw and declare a blockade. Almeida opposed closure of the ports, since it might justify an English seizure of Brazil. But Araujo clung to the faint hope of a fictitious solution, or a war like that of the Oranges in 1801. The French, however, were now working on Spain to prevent a departure. On 12 October the Council met at Belém and approved plans for departure. At the same time, Napoleon told the Portuguese minister in Paris of his decision, at a reception at Fontainebleau, adding that he had 300,000 Russians at his disposal. Lima at once left, reporting that Napoleon would be satisfied with nothing short of war against Britain. None the less, it was decided to send the Marquis of Marialva to Paris with a quantity of diamonds for use as inducements.

On 22 October Canning concluded a convention with Dom Domingos António guaranteeing transport of the royal family to Brazil. Junot and his vanguard were already trudging across northern Spain. They had been on the go for ten days when, almost as an afterthought, a treaty was signed at Fontainebleau to partition Portugal and her possessions. Its object was to befuddle the management at Madrid while setting up a French garrison at Lisbon. As the Portuguese fleet sailed for Bahia, escorted by Sir Sidney Smith, the first French troops, weary and bedraggled, arrived in Lisbon. The departure had gone according to plan, except that at the last moment many more decided to depart than had been anticipated, influenced by the divergence of official policy. More serious was the confusion arising from the spread of secret societies. The former chief of police, Pina Manique, had attempted to prevent all republican propaganda, and to apply the law forbidding secret societies. By securing his removal, General Lannes had opened the gate to political indoctrination. Among the French there had existed both royalist and republican freemasonry. In France itself the former had been eliminated, but many of the *émigrés* kept it alive and had brought it to Portugal after their expulsion from Spain. This caused some Portuguese to believe that, since the French *émigrés* had been persecuted for their loyalty to God and king, there could be no harm in freemasonry.[5] However, since Amiens many Frenchmen, hitherto royalists, had despaired of the Bourbon cause and welcomed Napoleon.

The Portuguese Council of State ordered the embarkation on 23 November, upon hearing that Junot was at Abrantes and that he had orders to make no concessions. Before going aboard, the Prince-

Regent issued a proclamation explaining why he was going and appointing a Council of Regency: his subjects were not to resist the French and were to avoid provoking reprisals. This left the line between non-provocation and collaboration imprecisely drawn. The regency council was to be presided over by the Marquis of Abrantes, a close kinsman of the Duke of Cadaval who accompanied the royal family to Brazil. The others were the two senior generals, the dean of the Patriarchate (Principal Castro), Pedro de Melo Breyner, and the Count of Sampaio, with his two deputies the Master of the Horse and Dom Miguel Pereira Forjaz. The last had served in the War of Roussillon, had acted as secretary of the committee on military reform, and was to become Beresford's closest colleague.

Junot at once named Herman, the French Consul to Lisbon, as commissioner to the Council of Regency, and installed himself in the mansion of the Count of Ega, the leading collaborator. The commander of the Police Guard, Comte de Novion, became governor of Lisbon. British ships blockaded the Tagus. Foreign trade stopped. The price of food rose. There was much unemployment, with a growing feeling of helplessness as Junot gradually assumed the reins of government. On 1 February 1808 he proclaimed that the House of Braganza had ceased to reign, dissolved the regency council and set up his own ruling council, with Herman in charge of Finance and Home Affairs and other Frenchmen in charge of the Army and security. A war tax of a hundred million francs was ordered, and the church's plate seized. Part of the Portuguese army was disbanded, but a Portuguese Legion was formed to serve Napoleon in central Europe. Its commanders were Alorna and Gomes Freire de Andrade.

On 1 April 1808 Napoleon made Junot 'Duke of Abrantes', a title chosen to supersede the Marquis of Abrantes, president of the regency council, who was bidden to join the Emperor at Bayonne and then detained in France for the duration. The despatch of Junot to Lisbon was followed by that of Murat to Madrid, while Napoleon at Bayonne juggled the Spanish crown from Charles IV and his son Fernando, and presented it, with a French-made constitution, to his own brother Joseph. It was only the decision to carry off the rest of the Spanish royal family that touched off the rising in Madrid on 2 May, the 'Dos de Mayo'.

The French had pursued their design of using Spanish troops to occupy northern Portugal, thus freeing part of Junot's force for service elsewhere. But in the turmoil following the Dos de Mayo the independent Spanish *juntas*, led by that of the Asturias, started to send delegations to Britain to appeal for money and arms. Thus while in Lisbon the French disarmed the Spaniards, in Oporto the Spaniards arrested the French. On 18 June Oporto proclaimed the Prince-Regent and set up a *junta* under the presidency of its bishop.

The neighbouring provinces of the Minho, Trás-os-Montes, and northern Beira – the jurisdiction of the Oporto high court – all freed themselves. Junot responded by sending Loison to protect his communications in the Alentejo and Beira, securing the border fortresses and reinforcing Almeida, which guarded the Beira frontier. But in the countryside the *ordenanças*, of which Oman speaks so slightingly, so harassed the French with armed bands that Junot could not make contact with Oporto.

Notes

1. It was no accident that Pedro was heir to his father and his younger brother Miguel to Carlota Joaquina, who died in 1830 as the civil war known as 'The War of the Two Brothers' was brewing.
2. As it did in the mind of Napier, who was said to have two gods – Sir John Moore and Napoleon, the first of whom failed to defend Portugal and the second to conquer it.
3. Quotations from Beresford's family letters are from copies in my possession.
4. Goltz's letters are in H. de Campos Ferreira Lima, *O Marechal de Goltz* (Famahcão, 1938).
5. The prohibition of secret societies nevertheless remained the law in Portugal, and when British adherents to the cult wished to parade Wellington ruled that the law must be upheld.

Appendix 4

Documents on the Guerrilla Movement

collected by René Chartrand

1: Extracts from the Memoirs of Espoz y Mina

The most successful of the guerrilla chiefs was Francisco Espoz y Mina, a veritable genius at guerrilla warfare who also displayed considerable talents for organisation and management. Although Mina could neither read nor write, save to sign his name, and was truly fluent in Basque rather than Castilian Spanish, he dictated his experiences after the war. A few extracts are given below:

> During this war, not counting the engagements of little importance, I took part in 143 battles or combats, of which the most remarkable are given here in alphabetic order: Aibar, Anizcar, Arlaban, Ayerbe, between Satinas and Arlaban, Erice, Irurozqui, Lerin and the plains of Lodosa, Maneru, Noatin, Peralta de Alcola, and Cabo de Saso, Piedradmillera and Monjardin, Plasencia, Rocafort and Sanguesa, Sanguesa and Valle de Roncal. The engagements which were less successful, although always glorious, were those of Acedo and Arquijas, Alcubierre, Alfaro, Barosoain, Beriain, Buirrun, Boquette de Embic, plaines de Auza, de Maneru, de Muruzabal, Canfran, Carrascal, Castelliscar, Castillo de la Alfageria en Sarragosa, Huesca, Jaca, in the Albaina area, Lumbier, Mendigorria, Mendibil, Monreal, Nazar, Olcoz, Oyarzun, Puente de la Reyna, Puyeo, Sara and Lerga, Santa-Cruz de Campero, Saraza, Segura, Sorlada, Sos, Tafalla, Tarazona, Tebias, Tiermas and Sanguesa, Tudela and Venta de Oyarzun.
>
> Amongst the engagements mentioned above, I would note those of Rocafort and Sangusa, where with just 3000 men, I made 5000 flee, took their artillery and made them lose 2000 men, killed, wounded and prisoners. At the engagements of Salinas and Arlaban, I put the enemy into complete disarray, killing about 700 men, took the whole convoy he escorted, and delivered 6-700 Spanish prisoners being taken to France;

at the engagement of Maneru, I entirely destroyed the Abbé Division, about 5000 strong; I took all his artillery, cut down most of his cavalry, pursued the remainder for most of the night, and for five days, to the gates of Pamplona.

In Navarre, I held up for 53 days a force of 26,000 men which would have taken part in the battle of Salamanca, as they were marching to join Marmont's army; and destroying bridges and blocking roads, I also stopped the conveyance of 80 pieces of artillery which would otherwise have taken part in that battle.

I contributed to the happy success of the battle of Vitoria, as its result would have been doubtful, if the movements that I executed had not prevented the Divisions of Clausel and of Foy, which had about 27 to 28,000 men, to join the French, and if I had not intercepted their dispatches.

Amongst the occasions on which enemy corps were crushed, three times were by myself; viz.: that of Placentia where, in spite of the superiority of the enemy, I made 12,000 infantrymen prisoners and put the whole cavalry to the sword; that of Sanguesa, where I charged the column named the 'Infernal', made it lose 900 men, and pursued the rest up to Sos; and that of Lerin and the plains of Ladosa where, at the head of my cavalry, and although General Barbot had 3000 men at a musket shot's distance from the battlefield and that a force of 6000 men who were only three leagues from us, I broke several times the enemy's infantry square, and destroyed or took prisoner a column of a thousand men: only its commander and two of his men got away.

The French, furious at so many disasters suffered in Navarre as well as being powerless to exterminate our troops, began, in 1811, to wage a total war; they hung or shot all [guerrilla] soldiers or officers who fell into their power. The same fate was reserved for those who helped the volunteers and they carried off to France an infinite number of families. It was at that time that I published, on 14 December, a solemn declaration of 23 articles, of which the first read: 'In Navarre, declaration of war to the death and without quarter, with no distinction for officers or soldiers, including the Emperor of the French.' I put to execution for some time this sort of war; I always kept in the Romal Valley numerous prisoners; if the enemy hung or shot one of my officers, I would do the same by reprisal to four of his officers; for a single soldier, I would sacrifice 20. It was by this way that I managed to horrify the enemy, hoping he would discontinue such an atrocious system, which is indeed what occurred.

Consequent to another article in the cited declaration, I sustained during 22 months, without a break and with the greatest rigour, the blockade of Pamplona, not without fighting a number of battles in its vicinity and up to the city's gates, which reduced this important place to the last extremity, and it surrendered by famine to the national troops, in November 1813. General [Don Carlos de] España had the joy of entering the city, since unexpected orders had called me to another place ...

I was never taken by surprise. Only once, on 23 April 1812 at dawn, was I betrayed by the partisan Malcarado who had made an agreement with [French] General Panetier ... I then found myself in the town of Robles surrounded by 1000 infantry and 200 cavalry; I was attacked by five hussars at the very door of the house I was lodging in. I defended myself against the assailants with the bar of the door, the only available weapon, while my orderly, Luis Gaston, prepared my horse and helped me mount. I then put them to flight, pursued them in the street, cut the arm of one of them with a sabre blow; I quickly gathered several of my brave men, made various attacks on the enemy, delivered many of my soldiers and officers who had been made prisoners, and continued fighting for three quarters of an hour in order to give time for the others to get away. As for Malcarado and his companion, I had them shot the next day while three *alcades* and a parish priest who had taken part in the plot were hung.

In the midst of so many labours and fatigues, which left me with so little time that I could barely find a moment of rest, I never obtained any help from the government, be it in money or any other way ... I did however manage to create, organise, discipline and maintain a Division of infantry and cavalry, composed of nine regiments of infantry and two regiments of cavalry, whose effective numbered, at the end of the war, at 13,500 men.

My Division took from the enemy 13 towns and fortresses, making over 14,000 prisoners, without counting those who were taken during the period we fought without giving quarter; furthermore, an immense quantity of artillery pieces, of clothing, of ammunition and foodstuffs, etc. I furnished official proof of the number of prisoners [taken] ...

There resulted, from the lists of killed, wounded and prisoners, that my losses amounted to 5000 men, and those of the enemy, including the prisoners, were no less than 40,000 men.

The number of Spanish prisoners that I released was over 4000, amongst which were a few generals, many officers of all ranks, and a good number of partisan chiefs ...

I established, for the use of my Division, travelling workshops for clothing, saddlery, weapons and ammunition, which I moved around, put to work, or left hidden in the mountains as magazines.

To keep up these workshops, and to pay my troops, the hospitals, my spies, and other expenses of war, I could only count on the following resources:

The proceeds from the customs I established on the very frontiers of France, since I had even been able to have contributions from the French customs at Irun ... who indeed paid to my commissaries 100 ounces of gold per month;

The proceeds from ... all the branches of national revenue, of convents, etc., which were collected by the French, which I mostly took from their convoys;

The booty otherwise taken from them;

The fines with which I punished a few discontent Spaniards ...

A few donations, either from compatriots or from foreigners ...

Source: We have used an extract of the main highlights of Mina's memoirs as published in A. Hugo, *France Militaire* (Paris, 1837), vol.IV. His complete memoirs, as well as those of his wife, were published in the *Biblioteca de autores espanoles*, vols.147 and 148 (Madrid, 1962).

2: British descriptions of the Guerrillas

In the whole of the northern and midland provinces, those patriot bands were denominated *guerrillas*; in the mountain districts included under the name of Serra de Ronda, in Andalucia, the irregular bands were termed *serranos*. The distinction was, that the guerrillas acted in concert, the serranos on his own responsibility. The dress of the guerrilla was a short jacket of russet brown, and leather leggings of the same dark colour; that of the serrano was velveteen, of an olive green colour, profusely ornamented with silver buttons, and his legs encased in leather *bottinos*. A belt of short leather surrounded the waist of each, stuck full of weapons of the French officers they had slain. When in small parties those predatory bands were called *partidas*.

Source: Lieutenant-Colonel Williams, *The Life and Times of the Late Duke of Wellington* (London & New York, c.1853), vol.I, p.146.

Whenever a volunteer of infantry joins Mina, he is not allowed to bring anything but a pair of sandals, half-stockings, breeches, and jacket ... His arms are all rusty on the outside, but he is particularly careful to have them well cleaned within, and good locks and flints: his bayonets are encrusted with the blood of Frenchmen ... he ordered all his men to put three musket-balls in each of their pieces ... His cavalry, at this time, consisted of 150 intrepid and valiant men, dressed like hussars, with jacket and blue pantaloons; caps like the rest of the army with this difference, that they have about a yard of red cloth hanging down their backs, in a point from the cap, and a gold tassel at the end. All of them wear sandals and spurs; and Mina himself never wears boots, or half-boots, but sandals, in order the more easily to escape, by climbing up the side of mountains, if he gets knocked off his horse ... The French call Mina the King of Navarre ... He never takes either a regular soldier, or a regular bred officer, into his corps. He says, 'They pretend to have too much theory' – and he sees they fail in all their attempts.

Source: 'Account of the celebrated Guerilla, Colonel Don Francis Espoz y Mina, translated from the Spanish of Colonel Don Lorenzo Xeminez', in *Annual Register* 1811, pp.353–5, which is somewhat edited. 'A short Account of the celebrated Guerrilla, Colonel Don Francis Espoz y Mina, and of the brave division of Volunteers of Navarre', in *Gentleman's Magazine*, supplement for 1811, vol.II, pp.619–25, appears to be the complete account.

Don Juan [Sanchez] and Carlos [de España],[1] the great Guerrilla Leaders, joined our Army with their Myrmidons and a more verminous looking set of fellows you never beheld. The infantry [are] in English Clothing and the Cavalry, both Horse and Man, completely armed and equipped in the Spoils of the Enemy, so that it is next to impossible to distinguish Friend from Foe. The Don himself wears a Pelisse like the 16th Dragoons with an immense Hussar Cap and the Eagle of Napoleon reversed. In this dress, accompanied by two aides de camp equally genteel in Appearance, Twelve Lancers, a Trumpeter in scarlet on a grey Horse. [At the Village of Villares, three miles from Salamanca, 28 June 1812.]

Source: S.A.C. Cassels, ed., *Peninsular Portrait 1811–1814: The Letters of Captain William Bragge* (London, 1963), p.57.

[In July 1812, near Madrid] a swarthy, savage-looking Spaniard came up ... The new-comer was armed to the teeth with pistols, daggers and a long gun ... together with his crimson sash and free bearing ... We observed him take rather ostentatiously from his side a long heavy-looking silk purse, the contents of which he emptied ... A general disgust pervaded the minds of my comrades and myself, when we beheld a number of human ears and fingers ... cut off from the bodies of the French whom he himself had slain in battle, each ear and finger having on a golden ring. 'Napoleon' he observed ... 'loves his soldiers, and so do the ravens'.

Source: Anthony Brett-James, ed., *Edward Costello: Military Memoirs, Adventures of a Soldier* (London, 1967), p.112.

3: A French view of the Guerrillas

General J.S. Léopold Hugo was perhaps one of the more successful of the French senior officers to tackle the guerrillas. He certainly did not, could not, solve the problem for the French; but he did pursue relentlessly, using columns made up of French and foreign – especially German – troops with contingents from King Joseph's Spanish troops. He operated mostly in New Castile against El Empecinado's band, which he estimated at 10,000 men in 1811 but who were probably actually less than half that number. His assessment of and opinions on the guerrillas, expressed in his memoirs, are valuable in giving the French point of view. Below are a few extracts:

> The Spanish armies served in the field and in fortresses; their efforts were constantly unhappy. Therefore, the guerrillas compensated for the defeats of their armies ... they obliged young men, *dispersos* [soldiers dispersed after defeats and unable to rejoin their corps], deserters to join them; they forced the French into entrenching themselves everywhere ... They followed and captured convoys from France ... or attacked their escorts when they found favourable occasions or mountain passes. The guerrillas were therefore the only redoubtable part of the Spanish nation for ... resistance ... was not given by massed forces or corps. In the exalted state of the nation, we could, we perhaps had to consider them, in many provinces, as the nation in arms.
>
> The only instance when guerrillas could be joined fruitfully to the Spanish armies was during the concentration of the French forces ... this sort of enemy then became the best of light troops; the army which was concentrating was as if blocked by them, no one could leave it without being killed or captured; they would go ahead of it to paralyse the requisitions for transport and food; they would be on its flanks so that requisitions could only be executed with strong detachments; they would follow it to capture stragglers and idlers, or to catch looters. We found them everywhere when we dreaded to meet them, or found them nowhere when we were strong and looking for them.

On El Empecinado and his guerrillas:

> A perfect knowledge of the area, a Division raised in the country whose every member knows all the byways and

paths; prompt and exact information on the direction taken during our movements; a triple, or quadruple superiority of forces, and always increasing; a numerous cavalry, daring or prudent according to the circumstances, well mounted, and able to exchange its tired horses anywhere; finally, the option of going into a neighbouring government [or province], to recruit there ... such were the advantages of the Empecinado over us ...

To find this skilful partisan, we had to search constantly for him, and to sort out the good information from the false intelligence. When I defeated him, he [and his men] disappeared without a trace; no peasants were to be found anywhere, and information vanished with them; I would often run around for eight days without seeing a single inhabitant; consequently, there was no news nor new directions to pursue. Once our biscuit was eaten, there was no hope of finding bread nor meat. Luck might furnish a few chickens for the famished soldiers; but this was a resource for only a few individuals, and a very slim resource at that. Supplies of all sorts were buried [by the guerrillas], hidden in caves and in the deepest forests in the mountains.

Finally, an obstacle of which all military men appreciate the importance was presented by the bad state of the soldiers' shoes. General Hugo, in a war made up of marches and countermarches, would often be obliged by necessity to save his men's steps:

All marches were so ruinous to soldiers, whose shoes were destroyed in a few hours by the harsh ground, that I did not want to make unnecessary movements. In vain did I grant to corps commanders the hides of slaughtered cattle, to repair the shoes. In vain had the government itself come to their rescue by making extra shoe issues: our movements were so frequent that the soldier had no necessaries left, and made war at his own expense.

On this subject, the enemy had other resources which we did not have, as his soldiers shod themselves, either with the *alpargatas*, made up from Sparto cords, or with the *abarca*, a piece of green leather, attached to the feet and lower legs by thongs. These types of shoes are known to all inhabitants of Spain. I vainly tried to introduce their use in my Division, but the soldiers seemed to be unable to get used to them ...

Source: Joseph Sigibert Léopold Hugo, *Mémoires du Général Hugo* (2 vols, Paris, 1834), vol.I. Extracts can also be found in the military history of the Revolutionary and Napoleonic wars by his son, A. Hugo, *France Militaire* (Paris, 1835), vols.IV–V.

4: List of Spanish Guerrilla bands, early 1811

This long list of guerrilla leaders, where they operated, and, in some cases, the approximate numbers of infantry and cavalry they led, was enclosed in a letter dated at Lisbon on 13 July 1811 from Charles Stuart to the Marquis Wellesley. While incomplete in many respects, it must have taken considerable efforts to compile from various sources of intelligence during the first half of 1811. The way the names of individuals and stations were spelt may not have been always in accurate Spanish; but we have left them as they appeared in the document.

Such as it is, this list must have been extremely valuable to British officials, as it gave them an idea of who the guerrillas were and where they operated within occupied Spain.

Name	Station	Infantry	Cavalry
	Andalucia		
Palmelin	Jerez de la Frontera		
Montegueiro	Fiana		
Juan Fernandez	Parhil		
Juan Totalido Sentinela	Malaga		
Partido de Osuna	Estepo		
Gomez	Do.		
Serrano Valdenetro	Ronda	2000	
Don P. Laldivan	Algeciras		
Don José Aguilar	Do.	100	
Don Juan Buera	Ronda	100	
Frigo	Cartuja		
	Aragón		
El Estudiante	Sanguepa		
Don Manuel Diaz	Terruel		
Don M. Solano	Jaca		
Don Amico Alegre/			
'El Cantenero'	Jaca		
	Asturias		
M. Porlier/			
or 'the Marquisito'	Grado	3000	
Don José Saavedra y			
Pardos	Castropol		
Amovales	Induna	1000	
Don J. de la Vega	Pola		
Escandon			
Mier			
Quiros			
Acebedo			
Collar			
Don Diego			
Fernandez del Barro	Eastern Asturias		
	Catalonia		
Don Juan Claros	Ampurdan		
Don Rovira	Do.		

Don Narcisso Gay	Olivarez	200	
Don Antonio Figuerola	Lerida		
Don Pablo Vives	Pinell somatemes		
Don José Rambla	Do.		
Don Miguel Guillen	Balaguer		
Don Francisco Montardit			
Fevero			
Brigas			
	Old Castile		
Cardino	Villal Pardo	300	
Don Thomas Principe			
or Borbon	Aranda de Duro		500
Cura Marino	Burgos		500
Padilla	Segovia		500
Don Lorenzo Aguilar	Toro		50
Don Juan Japia	Segovia	2000	
Don Antonio Jemprano	Bejar	50	
Don Fernando Saornil	Peafel		380
Echeverria	Do.		
Don Julian Sanchez ⎫			
Oliveria ⎬	Salamanca & ⎫		700
El Frayle ⎭	Ciudad Rodrigo ⎭		
	New Castile		
Don Ger. Thermo	Espega near Siguerza	50	250
Don Juan Martin			
el Empecinado	Huerto Hernado	3000	1000
Garrido	Puertos near Madrid		
	Cordova		
Partido nuevo de Cordova			
Don Francisco Diaz			
el Cojo			
Don Juan Levenzo,			
'Rey de Cerdero'	Velez el Rubio		
	Extremadura		
Don Martin Rodriguez	Badajoz	100	
Don Camilo Gomez	Miajadas		
Clairaco	Do.		
Don Torr. Bustamante,			
'El Caracol'	Puerto de Mirabete		
Don Antonio Bueno	Badajos	200	
	Granada		
Don José Villalobos	Granada y Baja		300
Don Juan Elribe	Abeda		
	Jaen		
Don Hermenegeldo Bielse	Jaen		
Don Jeromino Moreno ⎫			
Don P. Alcade ⎭	Jaen Martes		210
	La Mancha		
Don José Martinez	Alcanez	50	250
Don Juan Palorca			
el Medico	Abolla near Toledo		300
Don F. Sanchez			

Franisiquete	La Mancha		500
Don Juan Avril	Belmonte		
Mir	Guadaloupe		
Medico de Villa Renga	La Mancha		
Arviello ⎫			
Lamarilla ⎭	Valdemoro		
Don Ventura Jimenes	Toledo		
Don Fernando Camizares	Do.		
Don Mateo Viles			
de Guerrera	Do.		
Don Miguel Diaz	Puerto a Puch	200	40
Don Francisco Abad.,			
'el Chaleco'	Almagro		50
Partidos de los Vigote	Ciudad Real		
Don Francisco Avena	Almagro or	200	600
	Valencia el Ventoso		
Don Bernardo Cabeza	La Mancha		
Geraldo	Almonaçid		
Don Casimir Moralega	Aranjuez		
Don Manuel Partrago,			
'Santiago'	Ciudad Real		30
Don Raymondo Hernando	La Mancha		
Viejo de Llerina	Valde Novo		150
Luis Gutierez	Do.		
Don Juan Luis Orobio	La Mancha		
Don Baldemero Torres	Naval Moral		50
Huertas			
Fernandez			
	Montana		
Longa	Valmareda Villacayo	1100	
Campillo	Santander		400
Cura Salazar			
Amor	Escaray		
Don Lorenzo Enero	Villa Laguna Santander		500
Arrana			
Don Juan Marmot			
Don F. Sanchez			
Don F. Garcia	Cape de Gate		
	Navarre		
Mina ⎫			
Pascual Echevarria ⎟			
Chobin ⎟	Estelle	5000	
Lavaleta ⎬			
Malatima d'Ayban ⎟			
Ladron de Limbier ⎟			
Pastor ⎭			
	Rioja		
Don Manuel Ignacio	Soto	300	
Eraso el Mimantino	Rioja	2000	
	Soria		
Esquera	Tudela		
Hernandez	Terruel		

Riverez called
    'el Calhacho'   Villa Vecin
La Fuente
Saviroz

	Valencia	
Don Juan Talon	Arenea	200
Augustin Pardillos	Hijas	

Source: PRO WO 1/400.

5: Report on arms distribution, July–August 1811

This remarkable report on the distribution of arms to guerrillas, and often frustrated attempts to meet with their leaders, was written at Coruña on 6 September 1811 by James Johnston, aide-de-camp to Major-General Walker. The mission had been mooted in London during May 1811 by the Secretary of State for War and Colonies, Lord Liverpool himself. He considered it to be 'of great importance at the present moment that a ship of war should be sent to the northern coast of Spain to communicate with the leaders of the guerrillas in that part of the kingdom; to learn from them the actual state of affairs; to deliver to them a limited supply of arms and ammunition and to consult with them the measures which must be well understood and arranged for the same delivery of a second and more ample supply of arms and stores.' To this end some 500 sabres and 500 pistols would be assigned to Captain Johnson, aide-de-camp to General Walker. From Coruña, in northern Spain, 'confidential persons would be dispatched through the interior to communicate to the guerrillas the exact point of the coast' at which to meet them. The ship from England was also to take on board 2000 muskets at Coruña, with accoutrements and ammunition, for the guerrillas. Once Captain Johnson had received 'communications with the Spanish leaders', it was Lord Liverpool's desire that the ship would return immediately to England and Johnson would report back in person to Lord Liverpool.[2]

It was thus not only a supply trip but a political contact that the British government wished to have with the guerrilla leaders. While there appears to be no record of Captain Johnson's verbal assessment to Lord Liverpool, his long report to Lieutenant-General Walker gives excellent information and insight. It shows the extreme importance of the superior sea power of the British in being able to get the supplies to the coast, and the considerable difficulties of getting them further into the interior. For it is obvious that powerful French columns were criss-crossing the country and trying to prevent contacts between the British and the guerrillas in Navarre and the Asturias (see Oman, *History*, vol.IV, for details). The French had mounted an offensive at the time so the guerrillas were very much on the defensive; but obviously very difficult to catch and probably impossible to destroy, as they could retreat into the mountains of Montana, the northern half of Navarre. Their demands to Johnson were mostly for supplies in clothing, shoes, ammunition, and arms. Here is the report:

Pursuant to the instructions I had received, in addition to the arms &c embarked at Plymouth, viz.: 500 sabres, 500 cutlasses, 500 pistols and 100,000 ball cartridges, I received under my charge at Coruña 2000 muskets & bayonets with their accoutrements & 200,000 musket ball cartridges, & on the 6th of June I sailed from thence; on the 14th in consequence of previous arrangements, Campillo had assembled his whole force at Liendo, a small village in the Montana, in the neighbourhood of Santona, where he proposed receiving a supply of arms and ammunition. After having communicated personally with him, & ascertained his numbers I determined giving him 600 muskets with ammunition, &c. I accordingly in the first instance sent 200, not thinking it advisable to land a larger quantity at a time from the enemy's having passed through Liendo the morning before with a messenger to Castro, & there was a danger of their returning.

Having seen the 200 stands of arms, distributed amongst the soldiers, & the ammunition served out, I was on the point of sending a second 200 when it was reported that the enemy was advancing from Castro and Santona, in consequence of which Campillo retired to the mountains, having arranged to meet me the morning following at Sonabia, the entrance of a small river about a league to the eastward of Liendo, but the enemy being so much on the alert, I determined to endeavour to land a messenger for Mina, more to the eastward, when the vigilance of the enemy had subsided. I accordingly on the 19th landed my messenger at Ondarroa on the coast of Guispozea [*ie* Guipuzcoa], with a letter to Mina, hoping in a few days to receive his answer. I waited until the 4th of July when I received an application for a few arms from Don Gaspar Jameque, better known by the name of El Pastor, commanding the Volunteers of Guipozcoa, to the number of 500, subject to the command of Mina. I therefore appointed to meet him with his force at Mohico on the 10th at the same time forwarding another letter to Mina through him. Accordingly on the 10th Pastor arrived at Mohico with his troops & having ascertained their want I gave them 100 muskets, 50 sabres, 10,000 ball cartridges, 5000 pistol cartridges, 30 pistols & 1000 flints, our pouches not being calculated for the sort of warfare carried on by the Guerrillas, he refused to take any; he complained chiefly of the want of clothing and shoes. Having seen the arms distributed, I forwarded a third letter through him to Mina, but he gave me little hopes of seeing him, from the state of Navarre, & the strength of the enemy in that province; I determined in consequence, to open once more a communication with Campillo and Longa near Santona. On the 14th I had a communication with the shore, when I learned that Mina and Longa were at Villascayo in the province of Burgos, making arrangements for coming to the coast to me. After waiting anxiously until the 20th, I had the mortification to learn that in consequence of the arrangements which Longa had been making for receiving arms, the French under Caffarelli had attacked him at Villascayo, obliging him to retreat upon Mina's troops towards Navarre. On the 25th after many communications with the shore & many disappointments, Campillo assembled a body of troops amounting to about 600 men at Sonabia & in the course of that day & night 400 muskets, 170 pistols, 100 sabres, 21,000 musket cartridges, 10,000 pistol, do. 1000 flints, & 100 cutlasses, were safely landed and distributed. In case of any future supply arriving, he recommends that point (Sonabia) as the best adapted for landing it, & the most secure, there being a high mountain between it and Laredo, the only place from which there is any danger of an attack.

On the 29th, I received an application from General Porlier for a small quantity of arms & ammunition, as it was his intention to dislodge the French from St Andes, and in order that his operation might not be delayed, I sent him by His Majesty's ship Rhine, 200 muskets, 200 sabres, 50,000 musket cartridges & 5000 flints.

On the 30th, a captain of a small party of Guerrillas, bearing a recommendation from Mina, applied for a few muskets, which I gave him, his troop consisted of 50 infantry and 10 cavalry, he received 40 muskets, 24 pistols, 12 sabres, 4000 musket cartridges, 1000 pistol do. I charged him with a letter for Mina at the same time requesting him to bring me all information he could obtain respecting that chief, who I learned had a severe action with the enemy, & was not then in a state to come to the coast. On the 5th of August, I received a letter from Longa, stating that it would be impossible, from the vigilance and strength of the enemy for him to repair to the coast of Guipozcoa, at the same time proposing to meet one at Llanes, a port on the coast of Asturias, where I might disembark his supplies, having made arrangements for meeting him there, & communicated with him personally, I determined to wait the return of one of Mina's officers who had gone to learn the real state of affairs, our information heretofore having been contradictory, & then in the event of there being no hope of seeing Mina to repair to Llanes.

In the meantime, I had received from Mr White [Commissary at Coruña] by the Princess Charlotte, 600 muskets, bayonets & scabbards, 150,000 musket ball cartridges, 400 pistols, 40,500 pistol or carbine cartridges, 20,000 musket flints, 4000 pistol flints, 1 bullet mould & 200 sabres. The above mentioned officer returned on the 7th [August] informing me that Mina had set off on the 5th from Estrella in Navarre, & that I might expect to see him very shortly. That evening he arrived at Motrico where I had the desired communication with him, in consequence of his having been obliged to support Longa who had retired by default towards Navarre, he had inevitably been delayed coming to the coast, & that from the disposition he was obliged to make of his troops, he was able to take but a small quantity of arms &c, that at a future period he would be able to secure a larger supply, & recommended Motrico as the best point for disembarking it. He lost in his late action with the enemy 1500 men. I disembarked that evening 600 muskets, 50,000 musket b. [ball?] cartridges, 10,000 musket flints, 100 pistols, & 50 sabres which, in the course of the night, I saw distributed, for he had brought with him nearly that number of unarmed recruits. I promised that should any arms and ammunition remain after supplying the wants of Longa, that if he would send an officer to take charge of them, they should be delivered to Longa for him; he marched the night following to take his former position in Navarre.

I arrived off Llanes on the 12th but could hear no tidings from Longa. An officer from Gen. Porlier informed Sir George Collier who happened to be off Llanes, that it was the general's intention to attack St Andres, & wished the cooperation of the British squadron. We accordingly, by order of Sir George Collier, made sail for that place but arrived too late, & seeing no prospect of any future exertion on the part of General Porlier, & it appearing necessary to prosecute the original object, we arrived at Llanes on the 18th [August], where Longa's second in command (Don José Abecia) had arrived the day before with 1200 men, chiefly unarmed recruits. Longa on his way to Llanes with a small body of cavalry, having been attacked by the French and obliged to retire, I was disappointed of the desired personal communication with him. I disembarked however the arms & ammunition he required (Viz.: 576 pistols, 300 cutlasses, 288 sabres, 700 muskets, bayonets, scabbards, pouches & belts, 150,000 musket b. cartridges, 80,500 carbine or pistol b.

cartridges, 8000 musket flints, 4000 pistol do.) under his agreement to reserve a small portion for Mina (Viz.: 360 muskets, bayonets and scabbards, 100 pouches & belts, 56,000 musket b. cartridges, 44,000 carbine of pistol b. cartridges & 1 bullet mould).

What these chiefs mostly complain of is the great want of clothing & shoes, their troops being in general, very ragged & barefooted. I do not conceive that, for some time to come, any very considerable quantity of arms (muskets) will be wanted by them, but that it is essential that they should be supplied, as early as possible with ammunition, as it would be dangerous for them to form any sort of depot circumstanced as they are.

Source: PRO WO 1/261.

6: Report on Guerrillas in northern Spain, October 1811

This 'Account of the Guerrillas in the District of the 7th Army' was enclosed with a dispatch from Charles Stuart to the Marquis Wellesley, dated at Lisbon on 9 November 1811. It was a translation of a document obviously compiled in October, designed to give further information on the numbers and condition of the guerrilla bands in northern Spain. While attached on paper to the 7th Spanish Army, the guerrilla bands were at this time quite independent.

Division of Navarre commanded by the colonel Don Francisco Espoz y Mina occupies Navarre, & part of the neighbouring provinces. This corps is well clothed and armed; their clothing and report is principally derived from the funds they raise from the convents, from donations, from the Novenas Cazas excuzadas and the custom houses; particularly from a tax of 4000 reals on every load of wine sold in the Rioja and in Navarre. Infantry 5000. Cavalry 200.

The guerrilla of D. Longa occupies Bureva, the districts of Villarcaio, Losa & part of Alava. They are 2000 recruits, and go on collecting soldiers. Their armed force chiefly cavalry is well clothed; among their trifling funds, their support is derived from the salt mines of Paza; this fund formerly gave the government 200,000 reals but as the enemy frequently passes through this district, it does not give Longa more than 300 reals daily. Infantry 700. Cavalry 350.

The guerrilla of Pastor is in the Guipuzcoa. Infantry 800.

The guerrilla of Sallazar in the neighbourhood of Burgos, Valdesisdans, & Valdeviesso. Infantry 200. Cavalry 150.

The guerrilla of Pinto, in Valle de Mena. Infantry 100. Cavalry 100.

The guerrilla of Amor occupies part of Rioja & the Ascaras.

This cavalry is well clothed, mounted & disciplined. Infantry 150. Cavalry 500.

The guerrilla of the curate of Villaviao, occupies the country from Lerma to Burgos. Infantry 2000. Cavalry 400.

Total: [Infantry] 9000. [Cavalry] 1700.

The last five are supported by the tithes, the public revenues, and the gifts of the districts they inhabit. Other smaller parties are supported by robbery, and injure the respectable character of the greater part of these patriots. If the two first under Mina and Longa are united as is expected under the orders of Gen. Mendizabal, the smaller parties will be destroyed, and several respectable Divisions will be formed in a short time because the whole population ardently desires to take up arms.

Source: PRO WO 1/400.

7: The three types of Spanish forces

In his report of 22 March 1812, Sir Howard Douglas, who was in charge of British supplies coming into Coruña, specifies the three 'perfectly distinct' types of Spanish forces: the army, the guerrillas, and the armed peasantry, which should be armed for the defence of their own district. He also mentions some of the politics between all of them, as well as his own and Mina's clear bias that the guerrillas should not be incorporated into the regular army.

If Mina had arms, he could raise 10,000 men tomorrow – but it would not be advantageous. The corps would ... lose its impetus, and I do not afford him means to increase it. Parties spring up every day, and all these formed I may say by us, are the most attached of our Spanish allies, and excepting some small bands which may be called brigands, are firm patriots.

The guerrilla system has risen upon the ruins of the army, & a great number of their people formerly served in it.

... Now you must observe that for some times past, the Spanish generals have been endeavouring to get the Guerrilla parties in their nominal jurisdiction, put under their orders by the supreme government, and at the same time try to get the arms and stores from me put at their disposal. The latter I refuse. The former I have represented against, & particularly, but secretly, by Mina's desire.

Porlier was formerly an active chief but he is now a regular & inactive general. Since Longa and Campillo were attached to the 7th Army, they have done nothing. These instance are sufficient to shew the prejudicial consequences of putting the guerrillas under regular generals – it destroys their only feature of excellence, and forms very bad regular troops.

... The divisions of peasantry (in Galicia) were formed by an act of the Regency, and are under the orders of the provincial government, and applications to me for arms &c are made by the *Junta* accordingly. Many months ago I was requested to issue a considerable quantity of ammunition to them. Not to do a thing unknown to the general, I informed him of it. He strongly objected to it, saying the peasantry were not organised – that it was dangerous to arm them &c. The *Junta* again pressed me, and seeing in this objection on the part of the general a similar feeling with that borne towards the guerrillas, I told him that I could not object to give ammunition to a description of force sanctioned by the supreme government, and that it was my intention to give it accordingly. He said I might do as I pleased. I have done so, and I am quite certain that I have done right in the present critical state of affairs, not to let my issues of arms or stores, either to the guerrillas, or to the peasantry, depend upon his will.

Source: Sir Howard Douglas to Colonel Torrens, Villagarcia, 22 March 1812, PRO WO 1/262.

8: Ornate sabres and pistols for guerrilla chiefs

In April 1812, Lord Liverpool felt the need to warm relations with guerrilla chiefs by sending them ornate presentation arms. His dispatch of 8 April to the Duke of Wellington on this matter ran as follows:

My Lord,

I acquainted Sir Howard Douglas some time ago with my intention of sending to Coruña some sabres and pistols of the best workmanship and handsomely ornamented to be presented by him, in the name of the British government, to the most distinguished leaders of the Guerrillas, who have cooperated with zeal and efficiency during the late campaign. It has since occurred to me that it may be more advisable to make these presents in your Lordship's name, rather than that of the Prince Regent's government, and instructions will be accordingly sent to Sir Howard Douglas to wait for your Lordship's directions, before he transmits the arms to the different leaders.

The arms are now ready to be shipped, and will be forwarded to Coruña by the first opportunity. They consist of two brace of richly ornamented double barreled pistols of the best manufacture, and six brace of double barreled pistols of less costly workmanship. Also two sabres splendidly mounted with very richly worked scabbards of silver, and six more of a very handsome description, but less expensive. All these arms are of the most useful description for service, as well as magnificent in appearance. When they were first ordered, it had been my intention to present the two richest sabres and the pistols of the most costly pattern to Mina, and the Empecinado and to present the others to Don Julian Sanchez; Don Francisco Longa; Campillo and others of secondary rank and importance. But having now determined to place these arms at your Lordship's disposal, I have to request you will exercise your discretion in the distribution of them, and that you will instruct Sir Howard Douglas accordingly.

Source: PRO WO 6/36.

9: Intelligence report from Porlier, 1812

The British depended on the guerrillas for information on terrain, availability of supplies, and French positions and strength. The document below is a remarkable example of the type of questions asked and of the precision of the answers from the guerrillas. It was enclosed with a dispatch from Home Popham to Admiral Lord Keith, dated 26 July 1812, on HMS *Venables*, off Santander.

Questions to Gen. Porlier with his answers respecting the road from Santander to Valladolid.
1st: How many days will it take to go from Santander to Valladolid?
 Answer – two or three days.
2nd: Is the road good and is it practicable for artillery?
 – Roads very good, artillery may pass every where.
3rd: How many days would it require for five thousand men to march to Valladolid?
 – Spanish troops could perform this march in five days.
4th: Can rations for that number of men be procured on the road?
 – For the first two days march, there will be difficulty in getting rations because the Province of Santander has been much distressed by the enemy.
5th: For what number of horses can rations be procured?
 – Rations can be procured for any number of cavalry one day's march from Santander.
6th: Are there any strong positions that from three to five thousand men can take on the road to defend themselves against any sudden movement of the enemy?
 – From St Andero to Reynosa there are many hills which form very strong positions & the same from thence to Aguilar. From Aguilar to Herrera they will be flanked by a canal on the left, difficult for an army to [illegible] & from

thence to Tromista, they can always fall back on the [illegible] where there are no French, if attacked by a superior force. There are many strong positions between Tromista and Valladolid particularly in the neighbourhood of Terico, between that and Palencia.

7th: Can the troops of Gen. Porlier, Col. Longa or any other Spanish troops act on the flanks of the British in their march till they open a communication with Lord Wellington?

- Most certainly, they can always do so, and form a very powerful army.

8th: As it is very likely that Burgos may be made a central point for the French Army, can it be taken without difficulty. I merely ask this question in case it should be in the contemplation of His Majesty's government to form a depot between Valladolid and St. Andero?

- The French have not lately had many stores at Burgos and they have considerably reduced the garrison. They in general, except a mere guard, sleep in the town; & when it is intended to attack the place, the garrison may be surprised in the town on any settled night, & then the citadel may be taken, but if the troops all get into the garrison it will require six or eight heavy guns to take it.

[Final remarks] The roads the best in this country and plenty of provision and cattle two days march from St Andero.

Source: PRO WO 1/263.

10: Report on effective strength, December 1812

Even as late as December 1812, by which time the British were well into Spain, they were far from certain as to the numbers and nature of the guerrilla forces. Perhaps Mina, who must have perceived Sir Howard Douglas' reticence towards guerrillas as well as towards Spanish forces generally, was rather discreet to his allies. Sir Howard's successor was Colonel Richard Bourke, the author of this report to the Earl of Bathurst, Secretary of State for War. His report was penned at Coruña on 12 December 1812. Below are the extracts from it concerning guerrillas:

I have been able to ascertain with tolerable exactness their strength and state of equipment. The gross numbers, including recruits and convalescents &c, of the corps in Biscay, Navarre and the parts adjacent amount to 20,600 infantry, their effective strength hardly reaches 14,500. Of these 5000 effectives are under the command of Mina in Navarre, and 3500 under Longa near Vitoria. The remaining effectives about 6000 in number under the immediate command of Gen. Mendizabel of the 7th Army, are stationed at and near Bilbao, with the exception of 2200 now drawn near Santona (together with a battalion from Longa) to assist at the siege ...

Of cavalry, there is about 400 effective with Mina, a like number with Longa, and about 120 with Mendizabel. The two former also have some artillery (perhaps as much as they can use) ...

Upon the delivery of two thousand stands of arms and eight thousand sets of accoutrements which I am now sending to Santander, the infantry corps will be armed and equipped. I am still without cavalry equipments ...

In respect to clothing, the whole guerrilla force is represented in a very defective state, and that their hospitals are rapidly filling in this cold season. The corps I saw at Santona are certainly very poorly covered ... The Marques of Wellington by a letter of the 17th October which was not delivered to me by the Spanish officer charged with it until the 22nd of November, has directed clothing and equipments for 2500 men to be sent to Gen. Mina, and 2500 greatcoats to Longa ...

Source: PRO WO 1/263.

Notes

1. Carlos de España was not a guerrilla leader, but was the general commanding a Spanish infantry division of 4000 men formed in 1811. It was supplied with British blue infantry clothing in early 1812 and was attached to Wellington's army.
2. Colonel Bunbury to W. Croken, War Department, 9 May 1811, PRO WO 6/152.

Appendix 5

A List of Peninsular Sieges

by Philip Haythornthwaite

Saragossa
15 June–14 Aug 1808

Defender: Spanish, Captain-General José de Palafox.
Attacker: French, General Baron Verdier.
Result: French withdrew after bombardment and assault failed.

Gerona
24 July–16 Aug 1808

Defender: Spanish, Colonels O'Donovan and La Valeta.
Attacker: French, Generals Philibert Duhesme and Honoré Reille.
Result: siege abandoned upon approach of relief. (An earlier attempt to take the city by Duhesme had failed, having no siege artillery, 20 June 1808).

Rosas
7 Nov–5 Dec 1808

Defender: Spanish, Colonel Peter O'Daly; Trinity Fort garrisoned in part by the British, Lord Cochrane RN.
Attacker: French, General Laurent Gouvion St Cyr, but siege actually undertaken by General Reille.
Result: defenders capitulated after breach was made.

Saragossa
20 Dec 1808–20 Feb 1809

Defender: Spanish, Captain-General José de Palafox.
Attacker: French Marshal Bon-Adrien de Moncey, General Andoche Junot from 29 December (3rd Corps), Marshal Edouard Mortier (5th Corps); Marshal Jean Lannes in command from 22 January.
Result: garrison capitulated after street-fighting of unparalleled savagery.

Gerona 6 June–10 Dec 1809	Defender: Spanish, Mariano Alvarez de Castro. Attacker: French, Marshal Gouvion St Cyr (7th Corps, commanding *armée d'observation*; siege conducted by General Verdier until his retirement in September; St Cyr replaced by Marshal Pierre Augereau. Result: garrison capitulated after great exertions (surrendered by General Juliano Bolivar, Alvarez being ill).
Astorga 21 March–22 April 1810	Defender: Spanish, Colonel José Maria de Santoclides. Attacker: French, General Andoche Junot. Result: garrison surrendered after assault made a lodgement, and defenders almost ran out of ammunition.
Lerida 13 April–14 May 1810	Defender: Spanish, General Jayme Garcia Conde. Attacker: French, General Louis Suchet. Result: garrison surrendered after the civilians were driven into the castle by the French, following the carrying of the breaches, and then bombarded.
Ciudad Rodrigo 26 April–9 July 1810	Defender: Spanish, General Andres de Herrasti. Attacker: French, Marshal Michel Ney. Result: garrison surrendered after defences became untenable.
Mequinenza 15 May–5 June 1810	Defender: Spanish, Colonel Carbon. Attacker: French, General Musnier (from Suchet's 3rd Corps). Result: surrender after castle rendered indefensible by bombardment.
Almeida 25 July–27 Aug 1810	Defender: Portuguese, Brigadier William Cox. Attacker: French, Marshal Michel Ney. Result: garrison capitulated after magazine blew up.

Tortosa
16 Dec 1810–2 Jan
1811

Defender: Spanish, General Conde de
Alacha.
Attacker: French, General Suchet.
Result: garrison surrendered before assault.

Olivenza
11–23 Jan 1811

Defender: Spanish, General Manuel Herck.
Attacker: French, Marshal Jean de Dieu
Soult.
Result: garrison capitulated after defences
breached.

Badajoz
26 Jan–10 March 1811

Defender: Spanish, General Rafael
Menacho, killed 3 March, thereafter José
Imaz.
Attacker: French, Marshal Soult.
Result: garrison capitulated after defences
breached.

Tarragona
5 May–28 June 1811

Defender: Spanish, General Marquis of
Campoverde; after his departure (31 May)
General Juan Senen Contreras.
Attacker: French, General Suchet.
Result: lower city stormed 21 June, upper
city 28 June.

Campo Mayor
15–21 March 1811

Defender: Portuguese, Major José Joaquim
Talaya.
Attacker: French, Marshal Edouard
Mortier.
Result: garrison surrendered after
repelling one assault, when defences
rendered untenable.

Badajoz
6–12 May 1811

Defender: French, General Armand
Philippon.
Attacker: Anglo-Portuguese, Marshal
William Beresford.
Result: siege abandoned upon approach
of relief.

Badajoz
18 May–10 June 1811

Defender: French, General Armand
Philippon.
Attacker: Anglo-Portuguese, Viscount
Wellington.
Result: siege-works commenced 29 May;
siege abandoned after failed assault and
upon approach of relief.

Saguntum   Defender: Spanish, Brigadier Luis Maria
23 Sept-26 Oct 1811   Andriani.
                                Attacker: French, Marshal Suchet.
                                Result: governor surrendered after the
                                defeat of Blake's army.

Tarifa   Defender: Anglo-Spanish, Colonel John
20 Dec 1811-5 Jan   Skerrett and General Francisco Copons.
1812   Attacker: French, Marshal Claude Victor
                                (1st Corps), General Jean François Leval
                                (4th Corps and commanding at the siege).
                                Result: siege abandoned after repulse of
                                assault on 31 December 1811.

Valencia   Defender: Spanish, General Joachim
26 Dec 1811-9 Jan   Blake.
1812   Attacker: French, Marshal Suchet.
                                Result: city surrendered after failed sortie.

Ciudad Rodrigo   Defender: French, General Baron Barrié.
7-20 Jan 1812   Attacker: Anglo-Portuguese, Earl
                                Wellington.
                                Result: city captured by assault.

Pensicola   Defender: Spanish, General Pedro Garcia
20 Jan-2 Feb 1812   Navarro.
                                Attacker: French, Marshal Suchet (siege
                                conducted by General Severoli).
                                Result: position surrendered by
                                treacherous governor.

Badajoz   Defender: French, General Armand
16 March-6 April   Philippon.
1812   Attacker: Anglo-Portuguese, Earl
                                Wellington.
                                Result: city captured by assault.

Salamanca forts (San   Defender: French, *Chef de bataillon*
Vincente, San   Duchemin.
Cayetano, La Merced)   Attacker: Anglo-Portuguese, Earl
17-27 June 1812.   Wellington.
                                Result: forts surrendered after assaults.

Burgos   Defender: French, General Jean Dubreton.
19 Sept-21 Oct 1812   Attacker: Anglo-Portuguese, Earl
                                Wellington.

Result: siege abandoned as relief approached.

Castro-Urdiales
4–12 May 1813

Defender: Spanish, Colonel Pedro Alvarez.
Attacker: French, General Maximilien Foy.
Result: garrison evacuated in British ships as defences stormed.

Pamplona
25 June–31 Oct 1813

Defender: French, General Baron Cassan.
Attacker: Anglo-Portuguese, Marquess Wellington; from 12 July Spanish, Henry O'Donnell; capitulation arranged by Carlos de España.
Result: no proper siege, but a blockade which starved the garrison into submission.

San Sebastian
7–27 July 1813

Defender: French, General Emmanuel Rey.
Attacker: Anglo-Portuguese, Marquess Wellington.
Result: siege suspended after failed assault, then converted into a blockade until siege recommenced fully 24 August.

San Sebastian
24–31 Aug 1813

Defender: French, General Emmanuel Rey.
Attacker: Anglo-Portuguese, Marquess Wellington.
Result: city captured by assault.

Bibliography of Peninsular War Books Since Oman

As early as 1931 Wayne E. Stephens, in his review of the final volume of Oman's *History* (in *Journal of Modern History* III, p.307) was already lamenting its lack of a consolidated bibliography, which is a complaint that we can only echo and amplify today. To make a complete list of the published sources that Oman used, one has to plough through the footnotes to all seven of his volumes - and sometimes the text as well, where sources are often mentioned without being footnoted. When it comes to manuscript sources we are in a very much worse state even than that, since he does not deign to cite the essential reference numbers of the hundreds of cartons of material which he consulted in the archives of four countries. In ordinary language, this means that he simply did not tell us which manuscripts he consulted, and which he did not.

The scholarship that Oman actually delivered in his text was certainly very much deeper than his minimalist scholarly apparatus would seem to suggest, and even his delightful literary musings about his sources (*eg* in *Wellington's Army*, pp.1-38) tease us more by what they leave unsaid than by what they actually reveal. However, it would require a major project of research to reconstruct a full listing of all the material that he used and did not use, and it is to be regretted that no such undertaking can possibly be attempted in our present pages.

Instead, we can offer three small bibliographic services by way of compensation. The first is that the contributors to the present volume have provided references to some of the works that *they* have used, in the 'notes' to their particular chapters.

Secondly, section 'A' of this Bibliography attempts to list the more significant narrative or analytical works on the Peninsular War (mainly those in English) that have been published for the first time in the years since Oman's seventh volume was unveiled in 1930. The aim is to give the reader a general overview of modern work in the field, although, alas, in the interests of space it has been decided not to list more than a very few of the works that were already available before 1930.

As it happens, the majority of all books on the Peninsular War first appeared before the First World War, as is evidenced in the largest recent listing - 'The Peninsular War, 1807-14' by Donald D. Horward, in *Napoleonic Military History, a Bibliography* (ed. Donald D. Horward, Greenhill, London 1986), pp.243-302. Out of some 653 entries, only around 200 (thirty per cent of the total) were first published after Oman's *Wellington's Army* appeared in 1913 (Note that it was completed by Oman in 1912, but published only in 1913). Today we must, of course, add the further new works that have appeared since Professor Horward's list was compiled twelve years ago - but it is unlikely that more than, say, a hundred further titles can be added (*ie* the total from 1913 to 1998 will still be only about 300 out of 753, or some forty per cent of the grand total since 1808).

For the purposes of the present bibliography this imbalance is perhaps fortunate, since it allows us to limit the scale of our undertaking, provided we make a sweeping assumption that Oman himself 'dealt with' everything available in and before his own day. He may have dealt with it well or ill - and sometimes not at all - but in our posture as compilers of the bibliography we may at least concern ourselves mainly with whatever came later, which Oman had no possibility of using. That is mercifully a minority of the whole in terms of quantity, although doubtless it includes much of soaring quality and perceptive modern insight.

During the past twenty years there has certainly been something of an international revolution in the academic study of Napoleonic military history, ranging from Don Horward's vibrant centre in Florida State University to Jean Lochet's less formal but equally interesting grouping centred around the *Empires, Eagles and Lions* magazine; from scholars such as the contributors to the present volume, to others such as Ian Fletcher, John Tone, or Richard Partridge and Michael Oliver. From 1914 to about 1980 it seems that something of a 'halt' was necessarily placed upon Napoleonic studies by the pressing needs of two world wars and a Cold War, although there has subsequently been a great revival. In Spain this happened rather earlier, since, despite the vicious civil war in the 1930s, a certain reawakening of interest in the *Guerra de Independencia* could already be detected under the patriotic Franco state of the 1960s.

Thirdly, in sections 'B' and 'C' we move from narrative and analysis to the rather more specialised field of British memoirs and other biographical material. Our section 'B' offers a list of what has been published for the first time since 1912. That particular date is chosen, rather than 1930, because it is when Oman himself issued a statement of what he believed were the hundred most significant

British memoirs and other biographical materials widely available (*ie* as appendix 3 to his *Wellington's Army*, pp.375–83). Admittedly his listing contains many mistakes, misquotations, and omissions (some of which are cited in section 'C' below); but it is both convenient and appropriate for us to use this list as the starting point for our own additional bibliography of what has been published subsequently.

In compiling this list, considerable agonising took place over whether or not modern reprints and new editions should be included. Of course, the strong recent thrust towards republication is very welcome and healthy, since it gives wide circulation to texts that were formerly hard to find. It opens to democratic scrutiny the secrets that had previously been restricted to a privileged oligarchy, and breathes new life into a subject that had for many years appeared to be all but moribund. Yet against this we are also entitled to wonder whether an obsession with republishing familiar texts is not also in itself a negation of new thinking. In 1912 Oman himself was scarcely very enthusiastic for it, when he said of his 'hundred best memoirs' that 'one or two, above all the little book of "Rifleman Harris", well deserve to be republished, but still await that honour'(*Wellington's Army*, p.3). Even by 1930 no more than a handful had, in fact, been awarded it – although Harris was certainly one of them. For much of the subsequent half-century only 'one or two' of these books were in fact reprinted in any given decade, making a cumulative total of little more than a dozen by 1980. During the 1980s, however, there seems to have been a massive upsurge of interest, as the era of information technology enthusiastically conspired with the post-Vietnam 'Napoleonic manoeuvre warfare hobby' to make the publication of large numbers of short-run reprints both possible and desirable. Today over thirty of Oman's list of memoirs have been reprinted (and sometimes rereprinted), alongside an astonishingly high proportion of his more general bibliography. Even such apparently unlikely pamphlets as the polemics between Napier and Beresford have been reproduced in facsimile, and may now be obtained from discreet specialist dealers. Indeed, it may even be the case that an actual majority of Peninsular War titles currently in print consists of the venerable classics that were already well known to Oman, rather than whatever upstart new arrivals may have come into the field since his time. Within the next decade the wonders of electronic science may credibly allow us to go one step further, so that we can instantly gain internet access to every single item of Oman's pre-1912 (and pre-1930) bibliography, from anywhere in the world. There may not even be any meaningful way in which a 'reprint' can sensibly be defined, except to an emotionally mutilated minority of collectors who are interested in books only for the physical attributes of their pages and covers, rather than for the ideas that they contain.

It has therefore been decided not to make a full list of the convoluted post-1912 reprinting history of the very many books, articles, and documents that Oman used. Such an undertaking would do precisely what we had originally set out not to do – *ie* to repeat the bibliography already laid out by Oman himself. Our listing would also be instantly outdated, so, regrettably, we can offer the reader who seeks this information only a few brief notes and pointers in section 'C' of this bibliography.

Besides, the actual content of a reprinted work is no different from that of the original. Its value lies only in its greater accessibility to the student. 'Perceived added value' is given to a text only when the original is re-packaged into a new edition – even though some editors have an irritating habit of removing portions of the text as often as they restore previously unpublished sections. Admittedly there may be real utility in the various new interpretative essays and 'editorial introductions' that are added with the intention of shining a modern light upon an ancient manuscript – in much the way that this present volume itself hopes to do for Oman's *History*. Yet in many cases such modern introductions are fragmentary, short, platitudinous, and generally of little additional use to the reader. It is for all these reasons that we do not here attempt a full list of new editions any more than reprints, even though in the process we may be losing such gems as Fortescue's 1927 preface to Bunbury; Liddell Hart's to Private Wheeler (1951); Fortescue's to Curling's edition of Rifleman Harris (1929) or, perhaps confusingly, Hibbert's to the same text in 1970. Arthur Harman is particularly enthusiastic about the most recent edition of Harris, which is by Eileen Hathaway (Shinglepicker, Swanage, 1995) and not yet very widely known.

One other question of definition is raised by considerations of nationality and language. Don Horward's 1986 listing of Peninsular books is particularly strong for those produced in Spain and Portugal, of which he finds around eighty published since 1912. This is scarcely less than those he lists as produced since 1912 in Britain (although the latter must be supplemented by regimental histories and periodical literature cited in other chapters of his work). However, the present bibliography will not normally follow Horward's admirable internationalism, but will generally follow the anglocentrism found in appendix 3 to *Wellington's Army*. Although Oman was personally very widely read in the Iberian and, especially, the French literature of the war, he knew that most of his audience was anglophone – as will doubtless also be the case for the present volume. The bulk of our bibliography will therefore be confined to works in the English language. By the same token, most of the memoirs and other biographical materials listed here will tend to be about members of the British Army.

A: Narrative and analytical works which have appeared since the publication of the final volume of Oman's *History* (1930)

This list inlcudes a few 'classics' from before 1930 such as Balagny, Napier, Arteche, and 'WD'. It also includes studies of Wellington and Moore, as well as the Peninsular works of Oman himself.

Anon, *Wellingtonian Studies: Essays on the first Duke of Wellington by five Old Wellingtonian Historians* (Gale & Polden, Aldershot, 1959).

R. Aldington, *Wellington, Being an Account of the Life and Achievements of Arthur Wellesley, First Duke of Wellington* (Heinemann, London, 1946).

Don W. Alexander, 'The Impact of Guerrilla Warfare in Spain on French Combat Strength' in *CREP*, 1975, pp.91-8.

— *Rod of Iron: French Counterinsurgency Policy in Aragón during the Peninsular War* (Wilmington, Delaware, 1985).

José Manuel Allendesalazar, *Apuntes sobre la Relación Diplomática Hispano-Norteamericana, 1763-1895* (Madrid, 1996).

J. Anderson, *The Spanish Campaign of Sir John Moore* (Rees, London, 1906; reprinted R.J. Leach, London, 1990).

James Arnold, 'Column Versus Line in the Napoleonic Wars. A Reappraisal' in *JSAHR* LX (1983), pp.196-208.

J. Gomez de Arteche y Moro, *Guerra de la Independencia: Historia Militar de España de 1808-14* (14 vols, Depósitio de la Guerra, Madrid, 1868-1903).

Miguel Artola, *Los Afrancesados* (Madrid, 1989).

C.T. Atkinson, 'The "Battalions of Detachments" at Talavera' in *JSAHR* XV (1936), pp.32-8.

Carlos de Azeredo, *As populações do norte ... em 1808 e 1809* (Oporto, 1984).

De Witt Bailey, *British Military Longarms, 1715-1815* (Arms & Armour, London, 1971).

D.E.P. Balagny, *Campagne de l'Empereur Napoléon en Espagne, 1808-9* (5 vols, Berger-Levrault, Paris, 1902-6).

R. Barahona, 'The Napoleonic Occupation and its Political Consequences in the Basque Provinces, 1808-13' in *CREP*, 1985, pp.101-16.

M. Barthorp, *Wellington's Generals* (Osprey, London, 1978).

F.C. Beatson, *With Wellington in the Pyrenees* (Goschen, London, 1914).

— *Wellington: The Crossing of the Gaves and the Battle of Orthez* (Heath Cranton, London, 1925).

— *Wellington: The Bidassoa and Nivelle* (Edward Arnold, London, 1931).

D.H. Bell, *Wellington's Officers* (Collins, London, 1938).

Alice Berkeley, ed., *New Light on the Peninsular War* (The British Historical Society of Portugal, Lisbon, 1991).

Howard Blackmore, *British Military Firearms, 1650-1850* (Jenkins, London, 1961).

Peter B. Boyden, 'The Postal Services of Wellington's Army, 1809-18', in J. Guy, ed., *The Road to Waterloo* (qv), pp.149-55.

Antony Brett-James, ed., *Wellington at War, 1794-1815: A Selection of his Wartime Letters* (Macmillan, London, 1961).

— *The British Soldier in the Napoleonic Wars, 1793-1815* (Macmillan, London, 1970).

— *Life in Wellington's Army* (Allen & Unwin, London, 1972).

Michael Broers, *Europe Under Napoleon, 1799-1815* (Edward Arnold, London,1996).

Beatrice Brownrigg, *The Life and Letters of Sir John Moore* (Blackwell, Oxford, 1923).

A. Bryant, *The Years of Victory, 1802-12* (Collins, London, 1944).

— *The Great Duke: or, The Invincible General* (Collins, London, 1971).

J.M. Bueno, *Ejército y Armada en 1808* (privately published, Madrid, 1982).

— *Los Franceses y sus Aliados en España, 1808-14* (vol.I, Falcata, Madrid, 1996).

Alfred Burne, *The Noble Duke of York: The Military Life of Frederick, Duke of York and Albany* (Staples, London, 1949).

W.Y. Carman, 'Infantry Clothing Regulations, 1802' in *JSAHR* XIX (1940), pp.200-35.

Michael Carver, *Wellington and his Brothers* (The Wellington Lecture, University of Southampton, 1989).

David G. Chandler, *The Campaigns of Napoleon* (Weidenfeld & Nicolson, London, and Macmillan, New York, 1967).

— *Dictionary of the Napoleonic Wars* (Greenhill, London, 1993).

— *On The Napoleonic Wars: Collected Essays* (Greenhill, London, 1994), chapters 7-10, pp.130-80.

A. Chappet, R. Martin, A. Pigeard, and A. Robe, *Guide Napoléonien* (Paris, 1981), pp.263-75.

René Chartrand, *Napoleon's Army* (Brassey, London, 1996).

— *The Spanish Army of the Napoleonic Wars* (3 vols, Osprey, London, 1998).

E. Christiansen, *The Origins of Military Power in Spain, 1800-54* (Oxford University Press, London, 1967).

Owen Connelly, *Napoleon's Satellite Kingdoms* (Free Press, New York, 1965).

— *Blundering to Glory: Napoleon's Military Campaigns* (Scholarly Resources, Wilmington Delaware, 1987), chapter 7, 'The Affair of Spain', pp.117-32.

J.E. Cookson, 'The English Volunteer Movement of the French Wars, 1793-1815: Some Contexts' in *The Historical Journal* 32 (1989) pp.867-92.

Leonard Cooper, *The Age of Wellington: The Life and Times of the Duke of Wellington, 1769-1852* (Macmillan, London, 1964).

Rafael Leon Cortada, *The Government of Spain under Joseph Bonaparte, 1808-14* (PhD dissertation, Fordham University, 1968).

C.R.M.F. Cruttwell, *Wellington* (Duckworth, London, 1936).

David W. Davies, *Sir John Moore's Peninsular Campaign, 1808-9* (Nijhof, The Hague, 1974).

G. Davies, *Wellington and his Army* (Blackwell, Oxford, 1954).

G.C. Dempsey jr., 'The Calabrian Free Corps in British Service, 1809-14' in *JSAHR* LXII (1984), pp.28-35.

Michael Duffy, 'British Diplomacy and the French Wars, 1789-1815' in H.T. Dickinson, ed., *Britain and the French Revolution* (London, 1989).

G. Ellis, *The Napoleonic Empire* (Macmillan, London, 1991).

John R. Elting, *Swords Around a Throne* (Free Press, New York, 1988).
— and V.J. Esposito, *A Military History and Atlas of the Napoleonic Wars* (Praeger, New York, 1964; revised edn, Greenhill, London, 1999).
Nina C. Epton, *The Spanish Mousetrap: Napoleon and the Court of Spain* (Macdonald, London, 1973).
Charles Esdaile, *The Spanish Army in the Peninsular War* (Manchester University Press, 1988).
— 'Heroes or Villains? The Spanish Guerrillas and the Peninsular War, 1808-14' in *History Today* XXXVII, no.4 (April 1988), pp.29-35.
— *The Duke of Wellington and the Command of the Spanish Army, 1812-14* (Macmillan, London, 1990).
— 'The Duke of Wellington and the Spanish Army, 1812-14' in Norman Gash, ed., *Wellington: Studies in the Military and Political Career of the First Duke of Wellington* (qv), pp.66-86.
— 'Banditry and Social War in Spain, 1808-14' in Ian Fletcher, ed., *The Peninsular War: Aspects of the Struggle for the Iberian Peninsula* (qv), pp.93-114.
— *The Wars of Napoleon* (Longman, London, 1995).
— and Rory Muir, 'Strategic Planning in a Time of Small Government: The War against Revolutionary and Napoleonic France, 1783-1815' in C. Woolgar, ed., *Wellington Studies* no.1 (qv), pp.1-90.
Donald Featherstone, *Campaigning with the Duke of Wellington and Featherstone* (The Emperor's Press, Chicago, 1990).
Ian Fletcher, *Craufurd's Light Division: The Life of Robert Craufurd and his Command of the Light Division* (Spellmount, Tunbridge Wells, 1991).
— *In Hell Before Daylight: The Siege and Storming of the Fortress of Badajoz, 16 March to 6 April 1812* (Baton, Tunbridge Wells, 1984; reprinted Spellmount, Tunbridge Wells, 1994).
— *Wellington's Foot Guards* (Osprey, London, 1994).
— *Wellington's Regiments: The Men and their Battles from Roliça to Waterloo, 1808-15* (Spellmount, Tunbridge Wells, 1994).
— *The Napoleonic Wars: Wellington's Army* (Brassey, London, 1996).
— *Salamanca* (Osprey, London, 1996).
— *Napoleon's Wars: Wellington's Army* (Brassey, London, 1996).
— *Vittoria 1813* (Osprey, Oxford, 1998).
— ed., *The Peninsular War: Aspects of the Struggle for the Iberian Peninsula* (Spellmount, Staplehurst, 1998).
— and Andy Cook, *Fields of Fire: Battlefields of the Peninsular War* (Spellmount, Staplehurst, 1994).
— and Ron Poulter, *Gentlemen's Sons: The Guards in the Peninsula and at Waterloo, 1808-15* (Spellmount, Tunbridge Wells, 1992).
J.W. Fortescue, *History of the British Army* (13 vols, Macmillan, London, 1899-1930).
— *Following the Drum* (collected essays and edited eyewitness accounts, Blackwwod, Edinburgh, 1931).
— *The Last Post* (collected essays, ed. P. Guadella, Blackwood, Edinburgh, 1934).
Bryan Fosten, *Wellington's Infantry* (2 vols, Osprey, London, 1981).
— *Wellington's Cavalry* (2 vols, Osprey, London, 1982).
M.-S. Foy, *Histoire de la guerre de la Péninsule* (4 vols, Baudouin, Paris,

1827; English trans. as *History of the War in the Peninsula*, Worley, Felling, 1989).

Mildred L. Fryman, *Charles Stuart and the 'Common Cause': The Anglo-Portuguese Alliance, 1810-14* (PhD dissertaition, Florida State University, 1974).

F. de la Fuente, 'The French Revolution and its Impact on Portugal' in *CREP*, 1989, pp.194-200.

J.F.C. Fuller, *Sir John Moore's System of Training* (Hutchinson, London, 1924).

— 'Sir John Moore's Light Infantry Instructions of 1798-99' in *JSAHR* XXX (1952), pp.68-75.

C. Martin Gaite, *Love Customs in Eighteenth-Century Spain* (Berkeley, California, 1991).

Norman Gash, ed., *Wellington: Studies in the Military and Political Career of the First Duke of Wellington* (Manchester University Press with Southampton University, 1990).

— *Wellington Anecdotes: A Critical Survey* (The Wellington Lecture, University of Southampton, 1992).

David Gates, *The Spanish Ulcer: A History of the Peninsular War* (George Allen & Unwin, London, 1986).

— *The British Light Infantry Arm, c 1790-1815: Its Creation, Training and Operational Role* (Batsford, London, 1987).

Michael Glover, *Wellington's Peninsular Victories* (Batsford, London 1963; reprinted Windrush, Gloucestershire, 1996).

— *Wellington as Military Commander* (Batsford, London, 1968).

— *Britannia Sickens: Sir Arthur Wellesley and the Convention of Cintra* (Leo Cooper, London, 1970).

— *Legacy of Glory: The Bonaparte Kingdom of Spain, 1808-13* (Leo Cooper, London, 1971).

— 'Purchase, Patronage and Promotion in the British Army at the time of the Peninsular War' in *Army Quarterly* CIII (1972-3), pp.211-15, 355-62.

— *The Peninsular War, 1807-14: A Concise Military History* (David & Charles, Newton Abbot, 1974).

— *Wellington's Army in the Peninsula, 1808-14* (David & Charles, Newton Abbot, 1977).

— 'The Purchase of Commissions: A Reappraisal' in *JSAHR* LVIII (1980), pp.223-35.

— *That Astonishing Infantry: Three Hundred Years of the History of the Royal Welch Fusiliers, 1689-1989* (history of the 23rd Foot, Leo Cooper, London, 1989).

Richard G. Glover, *Peninsular Preparation: The Reform of the British Army, 1795-1809* (Cambridge University Press, 1963; reprint, Ken Trotman, Cambridge, 1988).

Morton Goldstein, *Great Britain in Spain, 1807-9* (PhD dissertation, University of Chicago, 1969).

— 'The Stuart-Vaughan mission of 1808: The Genesis of the Peninsular Alliance' in *CREP* 1977, pp.99-104.

Donald J. Goodspeed, *The British Campaigns in the Peninsula, 1808-14* (Army Headquarters, Ottawa, 1958).

Geoffrey de Grandmaison, *L'Espagne et Napoléon* (3 vols, Paris, 1914-32).

Daniel S. Gray, *The Services of the King's German Legion in the Army of*

the Duke of Wellington, 1809-15 (PhD dissertation, Florida State University, 1970).
— 'Prisoners, Wanderers and Deserters: Recruiting for the King's German Legion 1803-15' in *JSAHR* LIII (1975), pp.148-58.
John Greham, *Forlorn Hope: The Battles for the Spanish Frontier 1811-12* (London, 1990).
— 'Wellington's Fighting Cocks: The Portuguese Army in the Napoleonic Wars' in Ian Fletcher, ed., *The Peninsular War: Aspects of the Struggle for the Iberian Peninsula* (qv), pp.173-83.
Paddy Griffith, *Forward Into Battle* (Bird, Chichester 1981; 2nd edn, Crowood Press, Swindon, 1990), pp.12-62.
— 'The Peninsular Generals and the Art of the Non Battle' in *EEL* no.74 (September 1983), pp.8-11.
— 'Notes on the British Peninsular War Battlefields, as at Mid February 1992', in the *Newsletter* of the Battlefields Trust, no.2 (January 1993), pp.8-13.
— "Keep step and they cannot hurt us" - the Value of Drill in the Peninsular War', in Ian Fletcher, ed., *The Peninsular War: Aspects of the Struggle for the Iberian Peninsula* (qv), pp.163-72.
— ed., *Wellington - Commander: The Iron Duke's Generalship* (Bird & the Wellington Museum, Chichester, 1985).
P. Guedalla, *The Duke* (Hodder & Stoughton, London and New York, 1931; new edn 1946).
J. Guy, ed., *The Road to Waterloo: The British Army and the Struggle against Revolutionary and Napoleonic France, 1793-1815* (Alan Sutton and the National Army Museum, London, 1990).
Christopher D. Hall, *British Strategy in the Napoleonic War, 1803-15* (Manchester University Press, Manchester, 1992).
John A. Hall, *The Biographical Dictionary of British Officers Killed and Wounded, 1808-14* (published as vol.VIII of Oman's *History*, Greenhill, London, 1998).
B. Hamnett, 'Constitutional Theory and Political Reality: Liberalism, Traditionalism and the Spanish Cortes, 1810-14' in *Journal of Modern History* XL, supplement no.1 (March 1977).
— *La Política Española en una Epoca Revolucionaria* (Mexico, D.F., 1985).
— 'Spanish Constitutionalism and the Impact of the French Revolution, 1808-14' in H.T. Mason and W. Doyle, eds., *The Impact of the French Revolution on European Consciousness* (Alan Sutton, Gloucester, 1989), pp.64-80.
James Harding, *The Duke of Wellington* (Morgan-Grampian, London, 1968).
Jim Harkonnen, 'French Formations at Barrosa' in *EEL* no.111 (October-November 1990), pp.4-7.
Philip Haythornthwaite, *Weapons and Equipment of the Napoleonic Wars* (Blandford, Dorset, 1979).
— *British Infantry of the Napoleonic Wars* (Arms & Armour, London, 1987).
— *Wellington's Specialist Troops* (Osprey, London, 1988).
— *Napoleon's Military Machine* (Spellmount, Tunbridge Wells, 1988).
— *Wellington's Military Machine* (Spellmount, Tunbridge Wells, 1989).

— *Napoleonic Source Book* (Arms & Armour, London, 1990).
— *The Armies of Wellington* (Arms & Armour, London, 1994).
— *The British Cavalryman, 1792-1815* (Osprey, London, 1994).
— and Michael Chappell, *Uniforms of the Peninsular War in Colour* (Blandford, Dorset, 1978).
Charles O. Head, *Napoleon and Wellington* (Hale, London, 1939).
Christopher Hibbert, *Corunna* (Batsford 1961; reprinted Windrush, Gloucestershire, 1996).
— *Wellington: A Personal History* (Harper Collins, London, 1997).
Robin Higham, ed., *A Guide to the Sources of British Military History* (University of California Press, Berkeley, 1971).
Peter Hofschröer, *The Hanoverian Army of the Napoleonic Wars* (Osprey, London, 1989).
Donald D. Horward, *The Battle of Bussaco* (Florida State University Press, Tallahassee, 1965).
— 'The Influence of British Seapower Upon the Peninsular War, 1808-14' in *Naval War College Review* XXXI (1978), pp.54-71.
— *Napoleon and Iberia - The Twin Sieges of Ciudad Rodrigo and Almeida, 1810* (University Presses of Florida, Tallahassee, 1984; reprinted Greenhill, London, 1994).
— 'Wellington and the Defence of Portugal' in *International Historical Review* XI no.1 (1989), pp.39-54.
— ed., *Napoleonic Military History: A Bibliography* (Greenhill, London, 1986).
B.P. Hughes, *British Smoothbore Artillery* (Arms & Armour, London, 1969).
— *Firepower: Weapons Effectiveness on the Battlefield, 1630-1850* (Arms & Armour, London, 1974; reprinted Spellmount, Tunbridge Wells, 1998).
— *Open Fire* (Bird, Chichester, 1983).
J.S. Hyden, 'The Sources, Organisation and Uses of Intelligence in the Anglo-Portuguese Army, 1808-14' in *JSAHR* LXII (1984), pp.92-104, 169-75.
International Congress on the Iberian Peninsula, *New Lights on the Peninsular War: Selected Papers, 1780-1840* (Portugal, 1991).
Gerald Jordan, ed., *British Military History: A Supplement to Robin Higham's Guide to the Sources* (Garland, London, 1988).
H.F.N. Jourdain and E. Fraser, *The Connaught Rangers, 1st Battalion (formerly 88th Foot)* (London, 1924).
George D. Knight, *Lord Liverpool and the Peninsular War, 1809-12* (PhD dissertaion, Florida State University, 1976).
H. Lachouque, *The Anatomy of Glory* (trans. A.S.K. Brown, Brown University, Rhode Island, 1961; reprinted Greenhill, London, 1997).
— *Napoleon's War in Spain* (ed. J. Tranie and J.C. Carmigniani, Arms & Armour, London & Harrisburg, 1982).
J.P. Lawford, *Wellington's Peninsular Army* (Osprey, Reading, 1973).
— *Vitoria 1813* (Knight, London, 1973).
— and P. Young, *Wellington's Masterpiece: The Battle and Campaign of Salamanca* (Allen & Unwin, London, 1972).
James Lawrence, *The Iron Duke: A Military Biography of Wellington* (Weidenfeld & Nicolson, London, 1992).
Nigel de Lee, *French Lancers* (Almark, London, 1976).

Carola Lenanton (*née* Oman), *Sir John Moore* (Hodder & Stoughton, London, 1953).

— *An Oxford Childhood* (Hodder & Stoughton, London, 1976).

Harold V. Livermore, *A History of Portugal* (Cambridge University Press, 1947).

— *A New History of Portugal* (Cambridge University Press, 1966; 2nd edn, 1976).

E.M. Lloyd, reviews of Oman's successive volumes, in *English Historical Review* XVII (1902), pp.302-5; XIX (1904), pp.178-80; XXIII (1908), pp.595-6; XXVII (1912), pp.382-4; and XXX (1915), pp.355-7. 'W.B.W.' (W.B. Wood) reviewed Oman's sixth volume in IXL (1924), pp.472-3.

Marquess of Londonderry, *The Story of the Peninsular War* (Colburn, London, 1829; reissued G.R. Gleig, ed., Blackwood, London, 1857; reprinted R.J. Leach, Aylesford, 1994).

Elizabeth Longford, *Wellington: The Years of the Sword* (Weidenfeld & Nicolson, London, 1969).

Gabriel H. Lovett, *Napoleon and the Birth of Modern Spain* (2 vols, New York University Press, 1965).

— 'The Spanish Guerillas and Napoleon' in *CREP*, 1975, pp.80-90.

Juan Luna, *La Alianza de Dos Monarquías* (Madrid, 1989).

Jay Luvaas, *The Education of an Army* (Cassell, London, 1965).

John Lynch, *The Spanish-American Revolutions, 1808-26* (Weidenfeld & Nicolson, London, 1973).

— *Bourbon Spain, 1700-1808* (Blackwell, Oxford, 1989).

A. Martinien, *Tableaux par corps et par batailles des officiers tués et blessés pendant les guerres de l'Empire* (Paris, 1899; reprinted Editions Militaires Européennes, 1982 and 1994).

J.A. Meyer, *An Annotated Bibliography of the Napoleonic Era: Recent Publications, 1945-75* (Greenwood, Westport, Connecticut, 1987).

Albert Meynier, 'Levées et Pertes d'Hommes sous le Consulat et l'Empire' in *Revue des Etudes* XXX (1930).

J. Mollo, *The Prince's Dolls: Scandals, Skirmishes and Splendours of the 1st British Hussars, 1793-1815* (Pen & Sword, Barnsley, 1997).

Bernard L. Montgomery (of Alamein), *Wellington: A Summary of the Career of the First Duke of Wellington and an Account of Apsley House and its Contents* (English Life, Derby, 1970).

Rory Muir, *Britain and the Defeat of Napoleon, 1807-15* (Yale, London, 1996).

— *Tactics and the Experience of Battle in the Age of Napoleon* (Yale, London, 1998).

— and Charles Esdaile, 'Strategic Planning in a Time of Small Government: The War against Revolutionary and Napoleonic France, 1783-1815' in C. Woolgar, ed., *Wellington Studies* no.1 (qv), pp.1-90.

F. Myatt, *British Sieges of the Peninsular War* (Spellmount, Tunbridge Wells, 1987).

George F. Nafziger, 'French Infantry Drill, Organization and Training' in *EEL* no.39 (October 1979), pp.16-20.

— 'The Thin Red Line: A Tactical Innovation or a Circumstantial Necessity?' in *EEL* no.62 (March 1982), p 4 *ff*.

— *Armies in Spain and Portugal, 1808-15* (Nafziger Napoleonic Guides,

Westchester, Ohio, 1993).

— *Imperial Bayonets* (Greenhill, London, 1996).

— *The French Army - Royal, Republican and Imperial* (5 vols, Westchester, Ohio, 1997).

W.F.P. Napier, *History of the War in the Peninsula and in the South of France, from the year 1807 to the year 1814* (6 vols, Murray, London, 1828-40; new edn, T. & W. Boone, London, 1835-40, and many later reprints).

— *Colonel Napier's justification of his third volume; forming a sequel to his reply to various opponents, and containing some new and curious facts relative to the battle of Albuera* (T. & W. Boone, London, 1833).

Robin Neillands, *Wellington and Napoleon: Clash of Arms 1807-15* (Murray, London, 1994).

A. Nettleship, *That Astonishing Infantry: History of the 7th Foot (Royal Fusiliers) in the Peninsular War, 1809-14* (privately printed, Sheffield, 1989).

A.H. Norris and R.W. Bremner, *The Lines of Torres Vedras: The First Three Lines and Fortifications South of the Tagus* (London, 1972; 2nd edn, British Historical Society of Portugal, Lisbon 1980).

René North, *Soldiers of the Peninsular War, 1808-14* (Almark, London, 1972).

Brent Nosworthy, *Battle Tactics of Napoleon and his Enemies* (Constable, 1995; published in USA as *With Musket, Cannon and Sword*, Sarpedon, New York).

Michael Oliver and Richard Partridge, *Battle Studies in the Peninsula*, vol.I (Constable, London, 1998).

Charles W.C. Oman, *A History of the Art of War in the Middle Ages* (Lothian Prize essay awarded March 1884; first published by Blackwells, Oxford, 1885; new expanded Methuen edition 1898; further expanded Methuen edition, 2 vols, 1924; reprinted Greenhill, London, 1991; new revision edited by John H. Beeler, Ithaca, New York, 1953).

— *A History of the Peninsular War* (7 vols, Oxford, 1902-30; reprinted Greenhill, London, 1995-97).

— 'The Hundred Days' in Acton, Lord J.E.E., ed., *Cambridge Modern History* (1906), vol.IX, pp.616-45.

— 'An Historical Sketch of the Battle of Maida' in *Journal of the Royal Artillery Institution* XXXIV (1908), p.53.

— 'Line and Column in the Peninsular War' in *Proceedings of the British Academy* IV (1910), pp.321-42.

— *Wellington's Army* (Edward Arnold, London, 1912; reprinted Francis Edwards, London, 1968, and Greenhill, London, 1993).

— *Studies in the Napoleonic Wars* (Methuen, London, 1929; reprinted Greenhill, London, 1987).

— *Things I Have Seen* (Methuen, London, 1933).

— 'The Art of War in the Fifteenth Century' in *Cambridge Medieval History*, vol.VIII (Cambridge, 1936).

— *A History of the Art of War in the Sixteenth Century* (Oxford, 1937; reprinted Greenhill, London, 1991).

— *On the Writing of History* (Methuen, London, 1939).

— *Memories of Victorian Oxford and of Some Early Years* (Methuen,

London, 1941).

F.C.G. Page, *Following the Drum: Women in Wellington's Wars* (Deutsch, London 1986).

Julian Paget, *Wellington's Peninsular War* (Leo Cooper, London, 1990).

Peter Paret, ed., *Makers of Modern Strategy* (Princeton University Press, 1986).

S.J. Park and G.F. Nafziger, *The British Military: Its System and Organization 1803-1815* (RAFM, Cambridge, Ontario, 1983).

Roger Parkinson, *The Peninsular War* (Hart-Davis, MacGibbon, London, 1973).

— *Moore of Corunna* (Hart-Davis, MacGibbon, London, 1976).

M.S. Partridge, *The Duke of Wellington, 1769-1852: A Bibliography* (Meckler, London and Westport, 1990).

Charles Petrie, *Wellington: A Reassessment* (Barrie, London, 1956).

John L. Pimlott, *British Light Cavalry* (Almark, London, 1977).

'Otto von Pivka', *The Spanish Armies of the Napoleonic Wars* (Osprey, London, 1975).

— *The Portuguese Army of the Napoleonic Wars* (Osprey, London, 1977). See also some eight other Osprey titles covering troops from many small German states and Italy.

Jesús Pradells, *La Diplomacia y los Diplomáticos Españoles en la Guerra de la Independencia* (II Seminario Internacional sobre la Guerra de la Independencia, Madrid, 1996).

Juan Priego López, *Guerra de la Independencia, 1808-14* (multi-volume work, Madrid, 1972 on).

Julian Rathbone, *Wellington's War (Peninsular Dispatches)* (Michael Joseph, London, 1984).

Jan Read, *War in the Peninsula* (Faber, London, 1977).

T.M.O. Redgrave, *Wellington's Logistical Arrangements in the Peninsular War, 1809-14* (unpublished PhD thesis, University of London, n.d.).

Jean Regnault, 'Une Leçon du Feu et de la Manoeuvre' in *Revue Historique de l'Armée* no.3 (September 1953), pp.35-58.

Donald S. Richards, *The Peninsular Veterans* (Macdonald & Jane's, London, 1975).

R.E.R. Robinson, '*A History of the Peninsular War* by Sir Charles Oman, an assessment', in *JSAHR* LXXV (1997), pp.19-17.

H.C.B. Rogers, *Weapons of the British Soldier* (Seeley Service, London, 1960).

— *Napoleon's Army* (Ian Allan, London, 1974).

— *Wellington's Army* (Ian Allan, London, 1979).

Steven Ross, *From Flintlock to Rifle: Infantry Tactics 1740-1866* (Rutherford, Fairleigh & Dickinson UP, London, 1979).

Georges Roux, *Napoléon et le Guêpier Espagnol* (Flammarion, Paris, 1970).

A.L. Rowse, *Historians I have known* (Duckworth, London, 1995)

Raymond Rudorff, *War to the Death: The Sieges of Saragossa, 1808-9* (Hamilton, London, 1974).

J.H. Rumsby, *The Durhams in the Peninsula* (history of the 68th Foot, English Life, Derby, 1975).

Juan José Sañudo, 'Pequeñas unidades Napoleónicas' in *Researching & Dragona* no.1 (January 1996).

— and Leopoldo Stampa, *Las Crisis de una Alianza (la Campaña del Tajo de 1809)* (Ministry of Defence, Madrid, 1996).

— Miguel Angel Camino, Leopoldo Stampa, and Francisco M. Vela Santiago, 'Gamonal, 10 de Noviembre de 1808' in *Researching & Dragona* II, no.4 (August 1997), pp.59-111.

J. Sarrazin, *History of the War in Spain and Portugal from 1807 to 1814* (London, 1815; reprinted Spellmount, Staplehurst, 1998).

Amoret and Christopher Scott, *Wellington: An Illustrated Life* (Shire, Aylesbury, 1973).

J. Severn, 'Spain, the Wellesleys and the Politics of War: The Anglo-Spanish Alliance, 1808-12' in *CREP* 1995, pp.380-91.

John M. Sherwig, *Guineas and Gunpowder: British Foreign Aid in the Wars with France, 1793-1815* (Harvard University Press, Cambridge, 1969).

Robert W. Southey, LlD, Poet Laureate, *History of the Peninsular War* (3 vols, John Murray, London, 1823-32).

P.H. Stanhope, 5th Earl, *Notes on Conversations with the Duke of Wellington* (John Murray, London, 1888; new edn, Oxford, 1938).

John Strawson, *The Duke and the Emperor: Wellington and Napoleon* (Constable, London, 1994).

Mark Thompson, *'An Officer of Dragoons': The British Cavalry in the Peninsula* (London, 1996).

John L. Tone, *The Fatal Knot - The Guerrilla War in Navarre and the Defeat of Napoleon in Spain* (University of North Carolina Press, Chapel Hill, 1994).

Conde de Toreno, *Historia del Levantamiento, Guerra y Revolución de España* (3 vols, Baudry, Paris, 1838).

W. Verner, *History and Campaigns of the Rifle Brigade, 1800-13* (2 vols, London, 1919; reprinted Buckland & Brown, London, 1995).

S.G.P. Ward, *Wellington's Headquarters* (Oxford University Press, London, 1957).

— *Wellington* (Batsford, London, 1963).

— 'The Portuguese Infantry Brigades, 1809-14' in *JSAHR* LIII (1975), pp.103-12.

Jac Weller: *Wellington in the Peninsula, 1808-14* (Vane, London 1962; reprinted Greenhill, London, 1992).

— 'Wellington's Peninsular War Logistics' in *JSAHR* XLII (1964), pp.197-202.

— *On Wellington: The Duke and his Art of War* (ed. Andrew Uffindell, Greenhill, London, 1998).

Wellington, 1st Duke, *Dispatches of Field Marshal the Duke of Wellington* (13 vols, ed. J. Gurwood, London, 1834-8).

Wellington, 1st Duke, *Supplementary Dispatches and Memoranda of Field Marshal the Duke of Wellington* (15 vols, ed. 2nd Duke of Wellington, London, 1858-72).

Wellington, 7th Duke, ed., *Wellington and his Friends* (London, 1965; new edn, 1993).

Arthur S.A. White, *A Bibliography of Regimental Histories of the British Army* (Naval & Military Press, London, 1992).

Clive Willis, 'Colonel George Lake and the Battle of Roliça' in *Portuguese Studies* 12 (1996), pp.68-77.

Martin Windrow, *Military Dress of the Peninsular War* (Ian Allan, London,

1974).

Terry Wise, *Flags of the Napoleonic Wars* (3 vols, Osprey, London, 1978-81).

C. Woolgar, ed., *Wellington Studies* no.1 (University of Southampton, 1996).

H.R. Wright, *General Moore at Shorncliffe* (Sandgate Society, Sandgate, 1965).

Ned Zuparko, 'Charges, Firefights and Morale' in *EEL* nos.70-3 (March-July 1983), pp.9-13, 35-9, 2-9, 14-20.

B: British Peninsular War memoirs which have appeared since 1912

I have included a few of the many titles that Oman overlooked, but have concentrated mainly on those that were first published after he compiled his list in *Wellington's Army* (1912), pp.376-83. I also exclude Wellington and Moore, who were treated in section 'A', above. I am particularly grateful to Arthur Harman, Richard Partridge and Philip Haythornthwaite for their expert assistance in compiling this and the following section.

Aitchison: W.F.K. Thompson, ed., *An Ensign in the Peninsular War: The Letters of John Aitchison* (Michael Joseph, London, 1981; reprinted 1994). 3rd Foot Guards.

Anderson: Joseph J. Anderson, *Recollections of a Peninsular Veteran* (Edward Arnold, London, 1913). 24th Foot.

Anon: Lord Cannock, ed., 'Cavalry in the Corunna Campaign: The Diary of an Adjutant of the XVth Hussars' in *JSAHR* special publication no.4 (1936).

Badcock: C.T. Atkinson, ed., 'A Light Dragoon in the Peninsula: Extracts from the Letters of Captain Lovell Badcock, 14th Light Dragoons, 1809-14' in *JSAHR* XXXIV (1956), pp.70-9.

Bald: S.G.P. Ward, ed., 'The Letters of Private John Bald, 91st Regiment' in *JSAHR* L (1972), pp.101-6.

Barnard: M. Spurrier, ed., 'Letters of a Peninsular War Commanding Officer: The Letters of Lieutenant-Colonel, later General, Sir Andrew Barnard, GCB' in *JSAHR* XLVII (1969), pp.131-48. 95th Rifles.

Beresford: F.O. Cetre, 'Beresford and the Portuguese Army, 1809-14 ' in Berkeley, *New Lights on the Peninsular War: Selected Papers from the International Congress of the Iberian Peninsula* (British Historical Society of Portugal, Lisbon, 1991), pp.149-55.

— Harold Livermore, *A Biography of Marshal Beresford* (forthcoming, London, 2000).

— Samuel E. Vichness, 'Marshal of Portugal: The Military Career of William Carr Beresford, 1785-1814 (PhD dissertation, Florida State University, 1976).

Blainey: William Blainey, *Bonaparte vs. Blainey* (Tallcot, Union Springs, New York, 1988). 51st Foot.

Bogue: Captain R. Bogue RA, 'Diary of the Corunna Campaign' in J.H. Leslie, *The Services of the Royal Regiment of Artillery in the Peninsular War*

(London, 1908), part II.

Bonaparte: Owen Connelly, *The Gentle Bonaparte: A Biography of Joseph, Napoleon's Elder Brother* (Macmillan, New York, 1968).

— Michael Ross, *The Reluctant King: Joseph Bonaparte, King of the Two Sicilies and Spain* (Sidgwick & Jackson, London, 1976).

Boutflower: Charles Boutflower, *The Journal of an Army Surgeon during the Peninsular War* (Refuge, Manchester, 1912; reprinted Spellmount, Staplehurst, 1998). 40th Foot.

Bragge: S.A.C. Cassels, ed., *Peninsular Portrait, 1811-14: The Letters of Captain William Bragge, Third (King's Own) Dragoons* (Oxford University Press, London and New York, 1963).

Brotherton: Bryan Perrett, ed., *A Hawk at War: The Peninsular War Reminiscences of General Sir Thomas Brotherton* (Chippenham, 1986). 14th Light Dragoons.

Brown: *The Autobiography, or Narrative of a Soldier, by William Brown, late of the 45th Regiment* (J. Paterson, Kilmarnock, 1829; reprinted Maggs, London, n.d., c.1990).

Browne: R.N. Buckley, ed., *The Napoleonic War Journal of Captain Thomas Henry Browne 1807-16* (Army Records Society, London, 1987). HQ staff.

Brumwell: W.M. Egglestone, ed., *Letters of a Weardale Soldier, Lieutenant John Brumwell* (privately published, Stanhope, Co. Durham, 1912). 43rd Foot.

Bunbury: General Henry E. Bunbury, *Narratives of Some Passages in the Great War with France, 1799-1810* (1854; new edn, introduced by Sir John Fortescue, Davies, London, 1927).

Burrows: *A Narrative of the Retreat of the British Army from Burgos, in a series of Letters* (Bristol, 1814). Assistant-Surgeon G.F. Burroughs, 1st Dragoons.

Carss: S.H.F. Johnston, ed., 'The 2nd/53rd in the Peninsular War: Contemporary Letters from an Officer of the Regiment' in *JSAHR* XXVI (1948), pp.2-17, 106-11.

Cochrane: Thomas, 10th Earl of Dundonald (Lord Cochrane), *Autobiography of a Seaman* (London, 1861), vol.I. Royal Navy.

Cocks: Julia V. Page, ed., *Intelligence Officer in the Peninsula: Letters and Diaries of Major the Hon. Edward Charles Cocks, 1786-1812* (Spellmount, Tunbridge Wells, 1986). 16th Light Dragoons.

Cole: Maud Lowry Cole and Stephen Gwynn, eds., *Memoirs of Sir Lowry Cole* (Macmillan, London, 1934).

Colville: John Colville, *The Portrait of a General* (Russell, London, 1980). Sir Charles Colville.

Collett: Barbara Chambers, ed., *John Collett and a Company of Foot Guards, 1803-23* (2 vols, B. Chambers, Droitwich, 1996).

Cradock: Michael D. Bruno, *The Military and Administrative Career of Sir John Cradock, 1762-1814* (MA thesis, Florida State University, 1972).

Crauford: A.A. Craufurd, *General Craufurd and his Light Division* (London, 1898; reprinted Ken Trotman, Cambridge, 1987; *cf* biography by Ian Fletcher cited above).

Daniell: *Journal of an Officer in the Commissariat Department of the Army, comprising a Narrative of Campaigns under Wellington in Portugal, Spain, France and the Netherlands, 1811-15* (London, 1820;

reprinted Ken Trotman, Cambridge, 1996). J.E. Daniell.

Dent: L.W. Woodford, ed., *A Young Surgeon in Wellington's Army: The Letters of William Dent* (Unwin, Old Woking, 1976). 9th Foot.

Douglas: S. Monick, ed., *Douglas's Tale of the Peninsular and Waterloo, 1808-15* (Pen & Sword, Barnsley, 1997). 1st Royal Scots.

Douglas: Antony Brett-James, ed., 'The Diary of Captain Neil Douglas, 79th Foot, 1808-10' in *JSAHR* XLI (1963), pp.101-7.

D'Urban: I.J. Rousseau, ed., *The Peninsular Journal of Major-General Sir Benjamin D'Urban, 1808-17* (Longmans Green, London & New York, 1930; reprinted Greenhill, London, 1988).

Dyneley: F.A. Whinyates, ed., *Letters written by Lt. General Thomas Dyneley CB, RA, while on Active Service between the Years 1806 and 1815* (*Proceedings of the RA Institution*, 1895; reprinted in book form Ken Trotman, Cambridge, 1984).

Eadie: *Recollections of Robert Eadie, Private of His Majesty's 79th Regiment of Infantry ... written by himself* (Kincardine, 1829).

Fenton: C.W. de L. Fforde, ed., 'Peninsular and Waterloo Letters of Captain Thomas Charles Fenton, 4th & 2nd Dragoons, 1809-15' in *JSAHR* LIII (1975), pp.210-31.

Fitzgerald: D.J. Haggard, ed., 'With the 10th Hussars in Spain: Letters of Lt. Edward Fox Fitzgerald' in *JSAHR* XLV (1967), pp.88-113.

Forjaz: Francisco A. De La Fuente, *Dom Miguel Pereira Forjaz: His Early Career and Role in the Mobilization and Defense of Portugal during the Peninsular War, 1807-11* (PhD dissertation, Florida State University, 1980).

Freer: Norman Scarfe, ed., 'Letters from the Peninsula: The Freer Family Correspondence, 1807-14' in *Transactions of the Leicestershire Archaeological Society* XXIX (1953; new edn in book form, Leicester, 1953). 43rd Foot.

Freire: António Pedro Vicente, *Um Soldado da Guerra Peninsular, o General Bernardim Freire de Andrade* (Lisbon, 1970).

Garrett: A.S. White, ed., 'A Subaltern in the Peninsular War: Letters of Lieutenant Robert Garrett, 1811-13' in *JSAHR* XIII (1934), pp.3-22.

Gavin: William Gavin, *The Diary of William Gavin, Ensign and Quarter-Master of 71st Highland Regiment, 1806-15* (Highland Light Infantry Chronicle, 1921).

Gillmor: H.N. Edwards, ed., 'The Diary of Lieutenant C. Gillmor RN, Portugal, 1810' in *JSAHR* XIII (1934), pp.148-61.

Godoy: Jacques Chastenet, *Godoy, Master of Spain, 1792-1808* (trans. J.F. Hunnington, Batchworth, London, 1953).

— L. González Santos, *Godoy: Principe de la Paz, Siervo de la Guerra* (Madrid, 1985).

— C. Seco Serrano, *Godoy: el Hombre y el Politico* (Madrid, 1978)

Goltz: H. de Campos Ferreira Lima, *O Marechal de Goltz* (Famahcão, 1938).

Gordon: H.C. Wylly, ed., *A Cavalry Officer in the Corunna Campaign, 1808-9: The Journal of Captain [Alexander] Gordon of the 15th Hussars* (Murray, London, 1913).

Graham: A. Brett-James, *General Graham, Lord Lynedoch* (St Martins, London & New York, 1959).

Grant: C.J.D. Haswell, *The First Respectable Spy: The Life and Times of Colquhoun Grant, Wellington's Head of Intelligence* (Hamilton,

London, 1968).

Griffith: Norman Tucker, ed., 'Peninsular War Letters written by Major Edwin Griffith, 15th Light Dragoons, and Cornet Frederick Charles Philips' in *The National Library of Wales Journal* XII, no.2 (Aberystwyth, 1961).

Gronow: Rees Howell, *The Reminiscences and Recollections of Captain Gronow, being Anecdotes of the Camp, Court, Clubs, and Society, 1810-60* (London, 1862-6; ed. Christopher Hibbert, Bodley Head, London, 1964; reprinted Kyle Cathie, London, 1991). R.H. Gronow, 1st Foot Guards.

Gunn: R.H. Roy, ed., 'The Memoirs of Private James Gunn, 42nd' in *JSAHR* XLIX (1971), pp.90-120.

Hall: *Fragments of Voyages and Travels* (1831-40; *Selections* pub. University of Exeter, 1975; new edn as *Voyages and Travels of Captain Basil Hall RN*, London, 1895). Royal Navy.

Hall: Francis Hall (Cornet), 'Recollections in Portugal and Spain during 1811 and 1812' in *JRUSI* LVI (July-December 1912). 14th Light Dragoons.

Hamilton: James Colquhoun, ed., *Campaigning with Moore and Wellington* (Troy, New York, 1847; reprinted Spellmount, Staplehurst, 1998). 43rd Foot.

Hardinge: M.E.S. Laws, ed., 'Letters from the Peninsula, 1812-14' in *Journal of the Royal Artillery* LXXXV-LXXXVI (1958-9). Lieutenant Richard Hardinge RA.

Hennell: M. Glover, ed., *A Gentleman Volunteer: The Letters of George Hennell from the Peninsular War, 1812-13* (Heinemann, London, 1979). 43rd Foot.

Hill: C.D. Hall, ed., 'Albuera and Vittoria: Letters from Lt. Colonel J. Hill' in *JSAHR* LXVI (1988), pp.193-8.

Hill: Gordon Teffeteller, *The Surpriser: The Life of Rowland Lord Hill* (University of Delaware Press, Newark, 1983).

— 'Amateur Historian: A Critique of Lord Hill's "Epitome of War"' in *JSAHR* LI (1973), pp.168-76.

Hodenberg: C.W.C. Oman, ed., 'A Dragoon of the Legion' in *Blackwood's Magazine* (March 1913), pp.303-4. C. von Hodenberg.

Hough: J. Leslie, ed., 'Journal kept by Lieutenant Henry Hough from 22 March, 1812, to 13 May, 1813' in *JRUSI* LXI (1916), pp.850-80. Artillery.

Johnson: M. Glover, ed., 'Letters from Headquarters: Peninsular War Letters of H.A. Johnson' in *JSAHR* XLIII (1965), pp.92-104.

Jones: *The Military Autobiography of Maj. Gen. Sir John T. Jones* (privately published, 1853). RE.

Jones: Hon. H.V. Shore, ed., *An Engineer Officer under Wellington in the Peninsula: The Diary and Correspondence of Lieut. Rice Jones, RE, during 1809-10-11-12* (His letters published in *RE Journal* July 1912-March 1913; letters sent to him by RE officers published in *JRUSI* 1916; all reprinted in one volume, Ken Trotman, Cambridge, 1986).

Keep: Ian Fletcher, ed., *In the Service of the King: Letters of William Thornton Keep, from Walcheren, at Home, and in the Peninsula, 1808-14* (Spellmount, Staplehurst, 1997).

Laycock: J.O. Robson, ed., 'Rockets in the Napoleonic Wars: The Diary of Willian Laycock' in *JSAHR* XXVI (1948), p.148*ff*.

Le Marchant: R.H. Thoumine, *Scientific Soldier: A Life of General Le*

Marchant 1766-1812 (Oxford University Press, London, 1968; Le Marchant's memoirs published 1841; reprinted Spellmount, Staplehurst, 1997).

Lewin: *The Life of a Soldier: A Narrative of Twenty Seven Years' Service in Various Parts of the World* (London, 1834). H. Lewin, 32nd Foot (?).

Loison: Donald H. Barry, *The Life and Career of Count Louis-Henri Loison, 1771-1816* (PhD dissertation, Florida State University, 1973).

Long: T.H. McGuffie, ed., *Peninsular Cavalry General, 1811-13: The Correspondence of Lieutenant-General Robert Ballard Long* (Harrap, London, 1951: cf C.E. Long, *The Letters of Long and Beresford, 1832-4*; reprinted Mark Thompson, Sunderland, 1993).

Luard: James Lunt, *Scarlet Lancer* (Hart Davis, London, 1964). John Luard, 16th Light Dragoons.

Ludlam: G.A. Page, *The Soldier-Schoolmaster: A Brief Memoir of Christopher Ludlam* (Louth, 1874). 59th Foot.

Maclean: L. Maclean, ed., *Indomitable Colonel* (Shepheard, Walwyn, 1986). Alan Maclean, 79th Foot.

McGrigor: Richard L. Blanco, *Wellington's Surgeon General: Sir James McGrigor* (Duke University Press, Durham, North Carolina, 1974).

Madden: 'The Diary of Charles Dudley Madden, Lieutenant 4th Dragoons, Peninsular War, 1809-11' in *JRUSI* LVIII (1914).

(Many eye-witnesses): W.H. Maxwell, *Peninsular Sketches by Actors on the Scene* (London, 1844).

— D. Richards, ed., *The Peninsular Veterans* (Macdonald & Jane's, London, 1975).

Marshals: Richard Humble, *Napoleon's Peninsular Marshals* (Macdonald & Jane's, London, 1973).

— David G. Chandler, ed., *Napoleon's Marshals* (Macmillan, New York, 1987).

Mello: S.E. Vichness, 'Lord Wellington and the Francisco de Mello Affair' in *JSAHR* LIII (1975), pp.22-5.

Miller: 'The Adventures of Sergeant Benjamin Miller, whilst serving in the 4th Regiment of the Royal Regiment of Artillery, 1796 to 1815' in *JSAHR* VII (1928; reprinted in book form, Sir W.C. Leng, Sheffield, 1928).

Mills: Ian Fletcher, ed., *For King and Country: The Letters and Diaries of John Mills, Coldstream Guards, 1811-14* (Spellmount, Staplehurst, 1995).

Miranda: W.S. Robertson, *Francisco de Miranda* (2 vols, London, 1929).

Murchison: *The Life of Sir Roderick I. Murchison, Bart ... based on his Journals and Letters* (A. Geikie, London, 1875). 36th Foot.

Napier: Priscilla Napier, *The Sword Dance: Lady Sarah Lennox and the Napiers* (Michael Joseph, London, 1971).

— Rosamund Lawrence (*née* Napier), *Charles Napier, Friend and Fighter, 1782-1853* (Murray, London, 1952).

Neville: J.F. Neville ('A Veteran British Officer'), *Leisure Moments in the Camp and Guard-Room* (York, 1812).

Nightingall: M. Glover, ed., 'The Nightingall Letters: Letters from Major-General Miles Nightingall in Portugal, February-June 1811' in *JSAHR* LI (1973), pp.129-54.

Northcliffe: Charles Dalton, ed., 'A Dragoon's Experiences at Salamanca' in *The Cavalry Journal*, 1912. Lieutenant Northcliffe, 4th Dragoons.

O'Neil: *Military Adventures of Charles O'Neil under Wellington in the*

Peninsula and Waterloo (Worcester, Massachusetts, 1851; new edn, Spellmount, Staplehurst, 1997). 28th Foot.

Paget: Anglesey, Marquess of, *'One Leg': The Life and Letters of Henry William Paget, First Marquess of Anglesey, 1768-1854* (Cape, London, 1961; reprinted Pen & Sword, Barnsley, 1997).

Pearson: A.H. Haley, ed., *The Soldier Who Walked Away: Autobiography of Andrew Pearson, a Peninsular War Veteran* (Edinburgh, 1865; new edn, Bullfinch, Liverpool, n.d., c.1988). 61st Foot.

Pelet: Donald D. Horward, ed., *The French Campaign in Portugal, 1810-11: An Account by Jean Jacques Pelet* (Oxford and Minnesota University Presses, London and Minneapolis, 1973).

Picton: Robert Havard, *Wellington's Welsh General: A Life of Sir Thomas Picton* (Aurum Press, London, 1996).

— F. Myatt, *Peninsular General: Sir Thomas Picton 1758-1815* (David & Charles, Newton Abbott, 1980).

Rice: A.F. Mockler-Ferryman, *The Life of a Regimental Officer during the Great War, 1793-1815, compiled from the Correspondence of Colonel Samuel Rice, 51st Light Infantry, and from Other Sources* (Blackwood, Edinburgh, 1913).

Robinson: C.T. Atkinson, ed., 'A Peninsular Brigadier: Letters of Major General Sir F.P. Robinson, KCB, dealing with the Campaign of 1813' in *JSAHR* XXXIV (1956), pp.153-70.

Romana: Charles Esdaile, "A petty and ridiculous imitation of Napoleon's 18 Brumaire": The Marqués de la Romana and the *Junta* of the Asturias, 1809' in *CREP* 1993 (Tallahassee, 1994), pp.366-74.

— W.C. Goodwin, *The Political and Military Career of Don Pedro Caro y Sureda, Marqués de la Romana* (PhD dissertation, Florida State University, 1973).

— Judith A. Loucks, *The Services of the Marquis de la Romana in the Spanish War for Independence* (MA thesis, Florida State University, 1966).

Rous: Ian Fletcher, ed., *A Guards Officer in the Peninsula: The Peninsular War Letters of John Rous, Coldstream Guards, 1812-14* (Spellmount, Tunbridge Wells, 1992).

Schaumann: A.L.F. Schaumann, *On the Road with Wellington: The Diary of a War Commissary* (first pub. in Germany, 1922; English trans. A.M. Ludovici, Heinemann, London, 1924; reprinted Greenhill, London, 1999). KGL Commissariat.

Slessor: Alethea Hayter, ed., *The Backbone: Diaries of a Military Family in the Napoleonic Wars* (Pentland, Edinburgh, 1993). Mother and daughters of John Henry Slessor, resident in Portugal.

Smith: Joseph Lehman, *Remember you are an Englishman: A Biography of Sir Harry Smith* (Cape, London, 1977). 95th Rifles.

Smith: 'Journal of Captain William Smith of the 11th Light Dragoons during the Peninsular War, May 1811-Nov.1812' in *JRUSI* LX (1915).

Smithies: *The Life and Recollections of a Peninsular Veteran and Waterloo Hero* (Middleton, 1868; reprinted from articles in the *Middleton Albion*). J. Smithies, 1st Dragoons.

Soult: Peter Hayman, *Soult, Napoleon's Maligned Marshal* (Arms & Armour, London, 1990).

Suchet: Marshal L.G. Suchet, *Mémoires &c.* (2 vols, Bossange, Paris, 1828;

English trans. as *Memoirs of the War in Spain*, Worley, Felling, 1986*)*.

Thornton: Elizabeth Longford, ed., *Your Most Obedient Servant: James Thornton, Cook to the Duke of Wellington* (Webb & Bower, Exeter, 1985).

Verner: R.W. Verner, ed., *Reminiscences of William Verner, 1782-1871, 7th Hussars* (Society of Army Historical Research, London, 1965).

Webber: R.H. Wollocombe, ed., *With the Guns in the Peninsula: The Peninsular War Journal of 2nd Captain William Webber, Royal Artillery, 1812-13* (Greenhill, London, 1991).

Wellesley: F. Wellesley, ed., *The Diary and Correspondence of Henry Wellesley, First Lord Cowley, 1790-1846* (London, 1930).

— Iris Butler, *The Eldest Brother: The Marquess Wellesley* (Hodder & Stoughton, London, 1973).

— John K. Severn, *A Wellesley Affair: Richard Marquess Wellesley and the Conduct of Anglo-Spanish Diplomacy, 1809-12* (University Presses of Florida, Tallahassee, 1981).

Wheatley: Christopher Hibbert, ed., *The Wheatley Diary: A Journal and Sketchbook kept during the Peninsular War and the Waterloo Campaign* (Longman, London, 1964; reprinted Windrush, Gloucestershire, 1997). Edmund Wheatley, KGL.

— G.E. Hubbard, ed., 'Letters from the Front, 1812' in *United Services Magazine* LVIII, new series (1919).

Wilson: G. Costigan, *Sir Robert Wilson: A Soldier of Fortune in the Napoleonic Wars* (University of Wisconsin, Madison, 1932).

— Michael Glover, *A Very Slippery Fellow: The Life of Sir Robert Wilson, 1777-1849* (Oxford University Press, Oxford & New York, 1978. Wilson's *Journal* was first published 1861; new edn. by Antony Brett-James, Kimber, London, 1964).

Wooldridge: *Letters from Spain: Being some Correspondence from John Mogg Wooldridge of Cholwell in Somerset, Surgeon in the Army of the Duke of Wellington during the Wars in Spain, 1809-14* (Merchant Venturer's Technical College School of Printing, Bristol, 1941). Royal Horse Artillery.

Woollcombe: S.G.P. Ward, ed., 'Diary of Lt. Robert Woollcombe, RA, 1812-13' in *JSAHR* LII (1974), pp.161-80; reprinted Greenhill, London, 1991.

Younge: 'Some Peninsular Letters' in *United Service Magazine* LXII, new series (1916). Lieutenant K.E. Younge, 38th Foot.

C: Notes updating Oman's 'hundred best biographies' list (1912)

This includes corrections to Oman's entries and attributions, new editions of them, etc. Where merely a name and unit is given, it indicates that Oman's 1912 entry was apparently essentially correct (even if sometimes foreshortened) and remains so far un-reprinted, although it has unfortunately proved impossible to check all details.

Anon, 'A Chelsea Pensioner' (in the cavalry) can now be indentified as Tate of the 15th Light Dragoons; see below.

Anon, *Personal Narrative of Adventures during the War in 1812-13* (cavalry staff corps); was in fact E.W. Buckham. Reprinted (Ken Trotman, Cambridge, 1995).

Anon, *Personal Narrative* 42nd Foot.

Anon, *Memoirs of a Sergeant* 43rd Foot.

Anon, *Vicissitudes in the Life of a Scottish Soldier* (71st Foot) was, in fact, the 1828 reprint of the next entry.

Anon ('TS') = Thomas Howell, *A Soldier of the Seventy First from 1806 to 1815* (Edinburgh, 1819; 2nd edn 1819, reprinted 1822, 1828, and 1835; ed. Christopher Hibbert, Leo Cooper, London, 1975; and Windrush, Gloucestershire, 1998). The 1828 edn was retitled *Vicissitudes in the Life of a Scottish Soldier* (see previous entry).

Anon = 92nd Foot.

Anon = KGL.

J. Anton, *Retrospect of a Military Life* (Edinburgh 1841; reprinted Ken Trotman, Cambridge, 1994) = 42nd Foot.

R. Batty: should be *Campaign of the Left Wing of the Allied Army in the Western Pyrenees and the South of France in the years 1813-14 under Field Marshal the Marquess of Wellington* (London, 1825) = 1st Guards.

G. Bell, *Soldier's Glory, Reminiscences of Sir G. Bell* (2 vols, 1867; reprinted in one volume, Brian Stuart, ed., retitled *Soldier's Glory, being 'Rough Notes of an Old Soldier'* (G. Bell, London, 1956; reprinted Spellmount, Tunbridge Wells, 1991) = 34th Foot.

R. Blakeney, *A Boy in the Peninsular War* (1899; reprinted Greenhill, London, 1989) = 28th Foot.

J. Blakiston = Portuguese Army.

Lord Blayney = Staff.

C. Boothby = RE.

W. Bradford = a Chaplain.

Thomas Bunbury = 3rd Foot and Portuguese army.

Lord Burghersh = Staff.

J.F. Burgoyne = RE.

C. Cadell = 28th Foot.

G.L. Chesterton = Train.

J. Colbourne: should be *The Life of John Colbourne, Field Marshal Lord Seaton ... compiled from his Letters, Records of his Conversations, and Other Sources* (G.C. Moore-Smith ed., London,1903) = 52nd Foot.

J.H. Cooke = 43rd Foot.

J.S. Cooper, *Rough Notes &c.* (Carlisle, 1869; reprinted 1914, and Spellmount, Staplehurst, 1996) = 7th Foot.

Edward Costello, *The Adventures of a Soldier* (London, 1841; Oman cited a longer title from 1857 edn; reprinted as *The Peninsular and Waterloo Campaigns*, ed. A. Brett-James, Longmans, London 1967; and as Eileen Hathaway, ed., *The True Story of a Peninsular War Rifleman*, Shinglepicker, Swanage, 1997) = 95th Rifles.

S. Cotton/Lord Combermere = Staff.

A. Dallas = Train.

A. Dickson: should be *The Dickson Manuscripts* (5 vols; reprinted Ken Trotman, Cambridge, 1987) = Artillery.

J. Donaldson (1825; new edn *Recollections of the Eventful Life of a Soldier*, London, 1856) = 94th Foot .

H. Douglas = Staff.

T. Downman, 'Diary of Major Thomas Downman, Royal Horse Artillery, in the Peninsula, from 30 April 1811 to 17 August 1812' ed. J.H. Leslie, in *JSAHR* V (1927), pp.178–86 (Oman listed it only in passing).

G. Farmer = 11th Light Dragoons.

W. Fernyhough = 95th Rifles.

A. Fitzclarence = Staff.

A.S. Frazer = Artillery.

G.R. Gleig, *The Subaltern* (1823; new edn 1872; reprinted Leo Cooper, London, 1970) = 85th Foot.

W.M. Gomm, his *Letters and Journals* were ed. F. Carr Gomm, London, 1881 = Staff.

Lord Gough = 87th Foot.

Sir T. Graham/Lord Lynedoch (see also the book by Brett-James, cited above) = Staff.

W. Graham = Train.

W. Grattan, *Adventures with the Connaught Rangers from 1808 to 1814* (London, 1847; republished, C.W.C. Oman, ed., London, 1902; reprinted Greenhill, London, 1989) = 88th Foot.

John Green, *The Vicissitudes of a Soldier's Life, or a Series of Occurrences from 1806 to 1815* (Louth, 1827; reprinted EP Publishing, Wakefield, 1973) = 68th Regt.

William Green: now republished as J. and D. Teague, eds., *Where Duty Calls Me: The Experiences of William Green of Lutterworth in the Napoleonic Wars* (Synjon, West Wickham, 1975) = 95th Rifles.

J. Hale = 9th Foot.

J. Harley = 47th Foot.

Benjamin Randall Harris: republished as *The Recollections of Rifleman Harris, as told to Henry Curling* (London, 1929; new edn with introduction by Christopher Hibbert, London, 1970; reprinted by Century, London, 1985, and Windrush, Gloucestershire, 1996; Eileen Hathaway, ed., *A Dorset Rifleman: The Recollections of Benjamin Harris*, Shinglepicker, Swanage, 1995) = 95th Rifles.

J. Hartmann = KGL.

P. Hawker: should be *Journal of a Regimental Officer during the Recent Campaign in Portugal and Spain under Lord Viscount Wellington* = 14th Light Dragoons.

W. Hay (reprinted Ken Trotman, Cambridge, 1992) = 52nd Foot and 16th Light Dragoons.

Head = Train.

R.D. Hennegan: 1846 memoirs (2 vols) = Train.

Walter Henry (London, 1843; republished Chatto & Windus, London, 1970, Pat Hayward, ed., *Surgeon Henry's Trifles: Events of a Military Life*) = 66th Foot and Medical.

J. Hope = 92nd Foot.

John Kincaid, *Adventures in the Rifle Brigade* (1830; reprinted Spellmount, Staplehurst, 1998), and *Random Shots from a Rifleman* (1835; reprinted Spellmount, Staplehurst, 1998; combined in one vol., London, 1908; reprinted Richard Drew, 1981, and Spellmount, Staplehurst, 1998) = 95th Rifles.

R. Knowles: Lees Knowles, ed., *The War in the Peninsula: Some Letters of Lieutenant Robert Knowles of the Seventh, or Royal, Fusiliers, a*

Lancashire Officer (Tillotson, Bolton, 1913, although Oman claimed to have used an edition of 1909) = 7th Fusiliers.

G.T. Landmann = RE.

N. Landsheit = 20th Light Dragoons.

F.S. Larpent = Staff.

W. Lawrence, *The Autobiography of Sergeant William Lawrence, a Hero of the Peninsular and Waterloo Campaigns,* ed. G. Bankes (London, 1886; Oman cited a slightly different title from 1901; reprinted Ken Trotman, Cambridge, 1987) = 40th Foot.

J. Leach, *Rough Sketches &c.* (1831; reprinted Ken Trotman, Cambridge, 1986) = 95th Rifles.

A. Leith-Hay = Staff and 29th Foot.

Charles Leslie: should be *Military Journal of Colonel Leslie, K.H., of Balquhain, whilst serving with the 29th Regt. in the Peninsula, and with the 60th Rifles in Canada* (Aberdeen, 1887) = 29th Foot.

G. L'Estrange = 31st Foot.

J. MacCarthy = 50th Foot.

J. McGrigor (see also the book by Blanco, cited above) = Medical.

H. Mackinnon (Bath, 1812; reprinted Spellmount, Staplehurst, 1998) = Staff.

J. Malcolm = 42nd Foot.

R. Mayne and J.W. Lillie = Portuguese Army.

S. Morley = 5th Foot.

G. Moyle Sherer, *Recollections of the Peninsula* (1823; new edn Spellmount, Staplehurst, 1996) = 34th Foot (not 48th, as Oman had it).

C. Napier = 50th Foot.

G.T. Napier: should be *Passages in the Early Military Life of General Sir George T. Napier, KCB, written by himself* (ed. General W.C.E. Napier, London, 1894) = 43rd and 52nd Foot.

A. Neale = Medical.

C. Ompteda: should be *In the King's German Legion: Memoirs of Baron Ompteda, Colonel in the King's German Legion during the Napoleonic Wars* (Grevel, London, 1894, although apparently there had been a preliminary publication in 1892 as *A Hanoverian-English Officer a Hundred Years Ago: Memoirs of Baron Ompteda, Colonel in the King's German Legion*; reprinted Ken Trotman, Cambridge, 1992) = KGL.

J.W. Ormsby = Chaplain.

J. Patterson = 50th Foot.

T. Picton (see also the books by Havard and Myatt, cited above) = Staff.

R. Ker Porter = Staff.

D. Robertson = 92nd Foot.

H. Ross-Lewin = 32nd Foot.

T. Shaw-Kennedy = Staff.

G. Simmons, *A British Rifle Man, &c.* (ed. W. Verner, London, 1899; reprinted Greenhill, London, 1986) = 95th Rifles

H. Smith, *Autobiography* (1903; reprinted Cedric Chivers, Bath, 1968; see also Lehman's biography, cited above) = 95th Rifles.

T.S. Sorell = Staff.

C. Steevens, should be *Reminiscences of my Military Life from 1795 to 1818* (ed. N. Steevens, Winchester, 1878) = 20th Foot.

S.C. Stepney (Stepney Cowell), *Leaves from the Diary of an Officer in the*

Guards (London, 1854; reprinted Ken Trotman, Cambridge, 1994) = 2nd Foot Guards.

J. Stevenson = 3rd Foot Guards.

C. Stewart = Staff.

W. Stothert: should be *A Narrative of the Principal Events of the Campaigns of 1809, 1810 and 1811, in Spain and Portugal* (London, 1812) = 3rd Foot Guards.

W. Surtees, *25 Years in the Rifle Brigade* (1833; reprinted F. Muller, London, 1973, and with introduction by Ian Fletcher, Greenhill, London, 1996) = 95th Rifles.

W. Swabey: F.A. Whinyates, ed., *Diary of Campaigns in the Peninsula for the years 1811, 12 and 13, by Lieutenant William Swabey, an Officer of 'E' Troop, Royal Horse Artillery* (first appeared in Oman's list under the *Proceedings of the RA Institution*, London, 1984; reprinted Ken Trotman, Cambridge, 1984) = Artillery.

W. Tate (Oman had him 'Anon') = 15th Light Dragoons.

C. Tidy = 24th Foot.

W. Tomkinson (1894; reprinted London 1895, Muller, London, 1971, and Spellmount, Staplehurst, forthcoming 1999) = 16th Light Dragoons.

C.B. Vere = Staff.

R.H. Vivian = 7th Hussars.

Adam Wall: 'Diary of Operations in Spain, under Sir John Moore' in *Proceedings of the Royal Artillery Institution* XIV (1886; included in Oman's 'artillery etceteras', but not named) = Artillery.

W. Warre: should be *Letters from the Peninsula 1808-12, by Lieut. Gen. Sir William Warre* (ed. W.A. Warre, London, 1909; reprinted Spellmount, Staplehurst, 1998) = Portuguese service.

W. Wheeler, *Journal* (1824; reissued as B.H. Liddell Hart, ed., *The Letters of Private Wheeler*, Michael Joseph, London, 1951, New Portway, 1971, and Windrush, Gloucestershire, 1994) = 51st Foot.

S.F. Whittingham: his *Memoir of the Services & c. ed. F. Whittingham* (London, 1868) = Spanish service.

G. Wood, The Subaltern Officer (1825; reprinted Ken Trotman, Cambridge, 1986) = 82nd Foot.

G. Woodberry = 18th Hussars.

Index

For reasons of space this index does not include many of the names that are mentioned only once, or in passing, or which are external either to Oman's life or to the main discussion of his Peninsular War. Nor does it list the most commonly recurring names, such as Oman, the Peninsula, Spain, the Spanish government(s), the various Spanish regions (eg Andalucia, Lèon), Portugal, Britain, Napoleon, Wellington, Tactics, Column vs. Line, or the contributors to the present volume. Some of the notes are referenced, but only if they are more discursive than simple bibliographic references.